Modern Physical Chemistry for Bioscience Students

Friendly and Short Cut Guide for Physical Chemistry

3rd Edition

By

Kazushige Yokoyama

State University of New York Geneseo

Linus Publications, Inc.

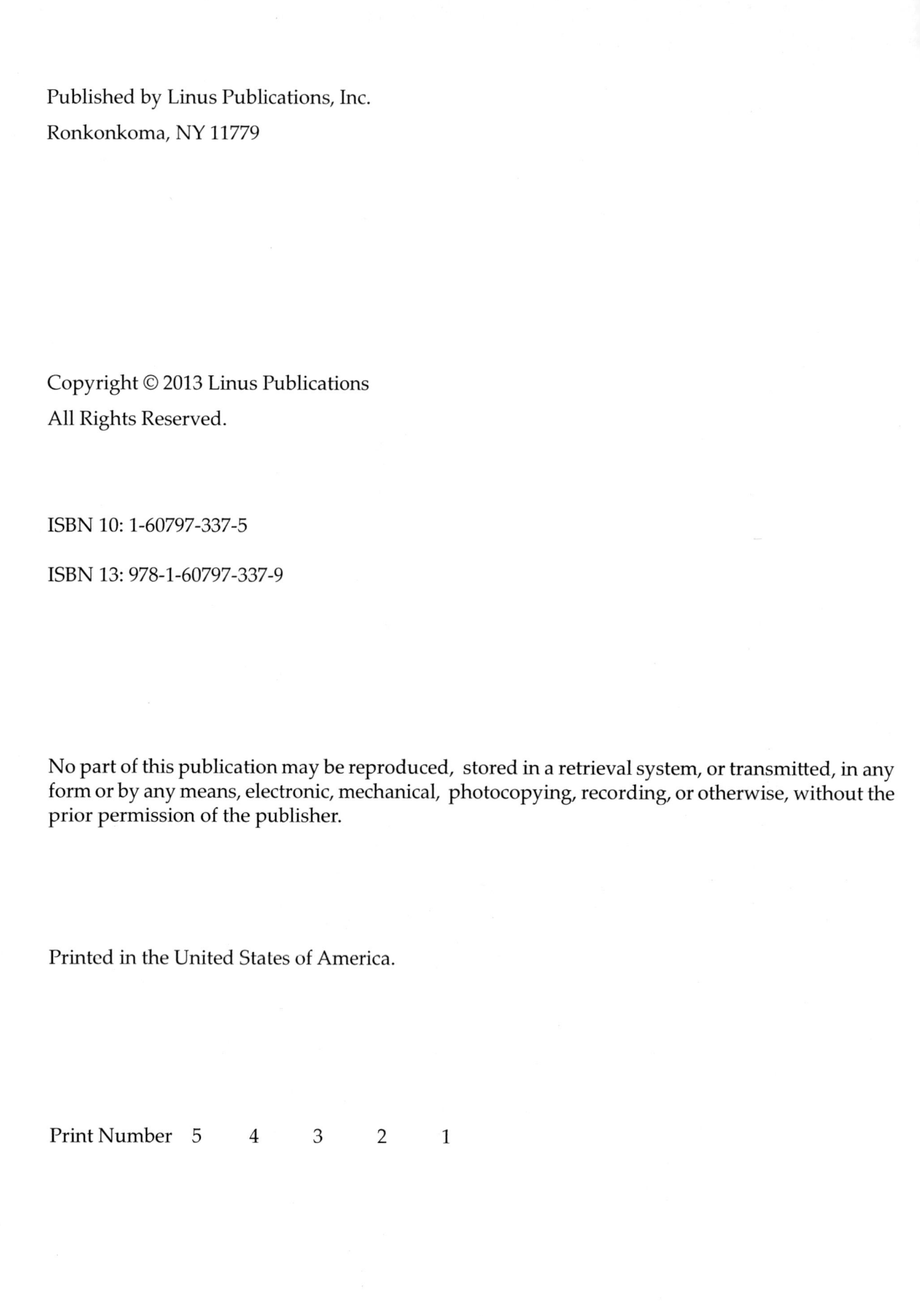

Published by Linus Publications, Inc.
Ronkonkoma, NY 11779

Copyright © 2013 Linus Publications
All Rights Reserved.

ISBN 10: 1-60797-337-5

ISBN 13: 978-1-60797-337-9

No part of this publication may be reproduced, stored in a retrieval system, or transmitted, in any form or by any means, electronic, mechanical, photocopying, recording, or otherwise, without the prior permission of the publisher.

Printed in the United States of America.

Print Number   5   4   3   2   1

Table of Contents

Chapter 1
Thermodynamics

1-1. Systems and Surroundings 4
1-2. The State Functions and Paths Connecting Different States 9
1-3. Energy Transfer in Phase Change 15
1-4. Chemical Reactions and Enthalpy Changes (ΔH) 17
1-5. Temperature Dependence of Enthalpy Change 20
1-6. The Change of Internal Energy of a Reaction 21
1-7. Second Law of Thermodynamics and Entropy 23
1-8. Entropy Change in Chemical Reaction and Its Temperature Dependence ... 25

Chapter 2
Gibbs Energy

2-1. Gibbs Energy 63
2-2. Calculation of Gibbs Energy 64
2-3. Temperature Dependence of Gibbs Energy 68
2-4. Chemical Potential 70
2-5. Chemical Equilibria and Gibbs Energy 71
2-6. Temperature Dependence of an Equilibrium 73

Chapter 3
Chemical Equilibria in Solution

3-1. Equilibrium in Solution 102
3-2. Activity 103
3-3. Chemical Potential and Activity 108
3-4. Thermodynamic Characteristics of the Cell Reaction 110
3-5. Oxidation- and Reduction- Reactions at the Electrode 112

Chapter 4
Inter-Phase Energy Transition

4-1. Energy and Phase Equilibria 133

4-2. Vapor Pressure Lowering -Raoult's Law 136

4-3. The Effect of Pressure on the Solubility of Gases 137

4-4. Energy Transfer between Phases 140

4-5. Equilibrium Dialysis and Measure of Cooperativity 142

4-6. Transfer of Charged Species under the Field 145

Chapter 5
Macromolecular Phase Transitions

5-1. Surface Tension 171

5-2. Langmuir Isotherm 174

5-3. Colligative Properties 178

5-4. Pressure Effect on the Freezing/Melting Points 187

Chapter 6
Molecular Motion and Transport Properties

6-1. Diffusional Motion 221

6-2. Diffusion Coefficient and Molecular Parameters 223

6-3. Shape Factor 226

6-4. Sedimentation 228

6-5. Viscosity 234

6-6. Electrophoresis 236

Chapter 7
Kinetics

7-1 Rates of Chemical Reactions and Rate Law 274

7-2. Half Life 282

7-3. Arrhenius Equation 285

7-4. Transition-State Theory 290

7-5. Very Fast Reactions 293

Chapter 8
Enzyme Kinetics

8-1. Enzyme Kinetics	334
8-2. Michaelis- Kinetics	336
8-3. Kinetic Data Analysis of Michaelis- Equation	338
8-4. Inhibition Processes	343

Chapter 9
A Taste of Quantum Mechanics

9-1. A Bit of Quantum Mechanics	375
9-2. Wave Mechanics and Wave Functions	377
9-3. A Particle in a Square Well Model	381
9-4. A Particle in a Box Model	385
9-5. Transition Energy	387
9-6. Simple Harmonic Oscillator	392

Chapter 10
Intermolecular Interaction and Essences of Spectroscopy

10-1. Charge Distribution and Dipole Moments	429
10-2. Dipole Moment and Transition	435
10-3. Quantum Yield	436
10-4. Intermolecular Forces	438
10-5. Absorption of the Light	441
10-6. Fluorescence Spectroscopy	455

Chapter 11
Scattering

11-1. Scatterings	485
11-2. Railey Scatterings	487
11-3. Mie Scatterings	489
11-4. Brillouin Scatterings	490
11-5. Raman Scatterings	491

11-6. Diffraction 496

11-7. X Ray Diffraction and Determination of Molecular Structure 499

Chapter 12
Statistical Thermodynamics

12-1. Maxwell-Boltzmann Distribution 531

12-2. Partition Function 539

12-3. Canonical Ensemble and Partition Function 544

12-4. Helix-Coil Transition in Polypeptide 547

12-5. Random Walk 551

First,....

As an author of a book, I am hoping to have as many as readers and believe that it is important to establish a trusting relationship between author and reader. Therefore, I should be honest to my readers and confess one thing about myself related with Physical Chemistry. My Physical Chemistry grade at the college was C for Physical Chemistry-I and C+ for Physical Chemistry II. Yes. I am currently teaching college-level physical chemistry and am also conducting undergraduate research related with physical chemistry. While my grade of P-chem is something that I don't want to recall and am not proud of, strangely enough I really loved the subject of Physical Chemistry and was so fascinated with it at the college. I often spent overnight by deriving equations or reading more advanced literature on the topic. How come, I was a bad P-chem student? Even after 25 years, I still have that feeling of thinking why I cannot get a good score in P-Chem no matter how much I study. I was so focusing on advanced or topics which I like and was not studying for the class. (Yes, I was a bad student.)

Getting good score may be thought as a fishing. You have to be at a right bait with right gear to catch fish. Likewise you can solve problems, if you study what will be asked in the exam. Because of my personal experience, I really and truly understand when students complain "I don't understand Physical Chemistry" or "I do not like P-chem". or "I hope P-chem does not exist". The hate probably comes from the fact that students cannot get a good grade in Physical chemistry exam. Especially, I have been feeling pain of those students since I taught One Semester Physical Chemistry to the Biochemistry or Biology students with Chemistry Minor at Geneseo. Whenever I consult with students about P-Chem, they often say, "I don't know how I should study ?" As a result, the exam score becomes low and they start making a vicious circle of don't like P-chem → don't know how to study → low score → ... Ummmmmm.. This is bad, isn't it. The bottom line is that people probably will like P-chem (or at least keep studying) if they get high score in exam.

In any subjects, you need to practice and go through many tricky steps in order to perfect it. It takes time and patience. However, patience will not continue if you think you are not studying right thing. I think there are some topics and problems which are absolutely necessary to be asked. (kind of short cut or the path you really have to walk). I am hoping that I could give those essences to the students who do not know how to start the studying of P-chem. (Basically, the most probable problems and issues which will be asked in the exam.)

I agree and understand that getting high score is not everything in the life. However, if you agree that you use this text book as something to change the way of studying P-chem, please read this. Currently, there are so many excellent Physical chemistry textbooks and no need to have a text book from the one who did not well college P-chem. However, if there is one good advantage or uniqueness of my text book, I may be giving or distributing the aspect or points of physical chemistry textbook from the closest point view of those who do not know how to start studying. Once again, I was there and know how stressful not being able to get a good score in P-chem. (Although some people take it for granted.) Since there are many textbook which brings students P-chem level to the top notch, I thought it may not hurt to produce a textbook who do not like p-chem textbook. I may be the worst in the p-chem score among those whoever wrote p-chem text book, I may the one who understand the feeling of those who are not good at p-chem but want to still learn something from P-chem (and hopefully get a good grade from P-chem). My philosophy of producing this textbook is based on the fact that "P-chem is fun and it is more fun if you can get good score in the P-chem." I wish to reduce the load of the students to prepare for the exam and try to set up the form which should be used as a preparation of the exam. In order not to overfeed the contents, I chose the topic which may be the essence, therefore, I have so many topic that I intentionally did not touch upon. However, if you feel like that something missing and would like to read other advanced "real" P-chem text book or want to search for the web, I really like that. Because I would like you to use my textbook as a starter of P-chem.

Kazushige Yokoyama
Geneseo, NY

How to use this textbook.

In order for you to use this textbook effectively, please note there are some features in this textbook which I want you to note.

①Why do I have to study this chapter?
This paragraph explains the purpose of each chapter for you to study. I highly recommend you to read briefly especially when you are not familiar with particular topic you are studying.

②Expected Hurdles Ahead in this Chapter
This paragraph gives you some warnings on the topics which may cause you some difficulties.

③PREVIEW OF KEY-EQUATIONS
This section lists up the equations showing up in each chapter. I am showing the equations before the chapter begin in order to get you familiar with the core equations which you are studying

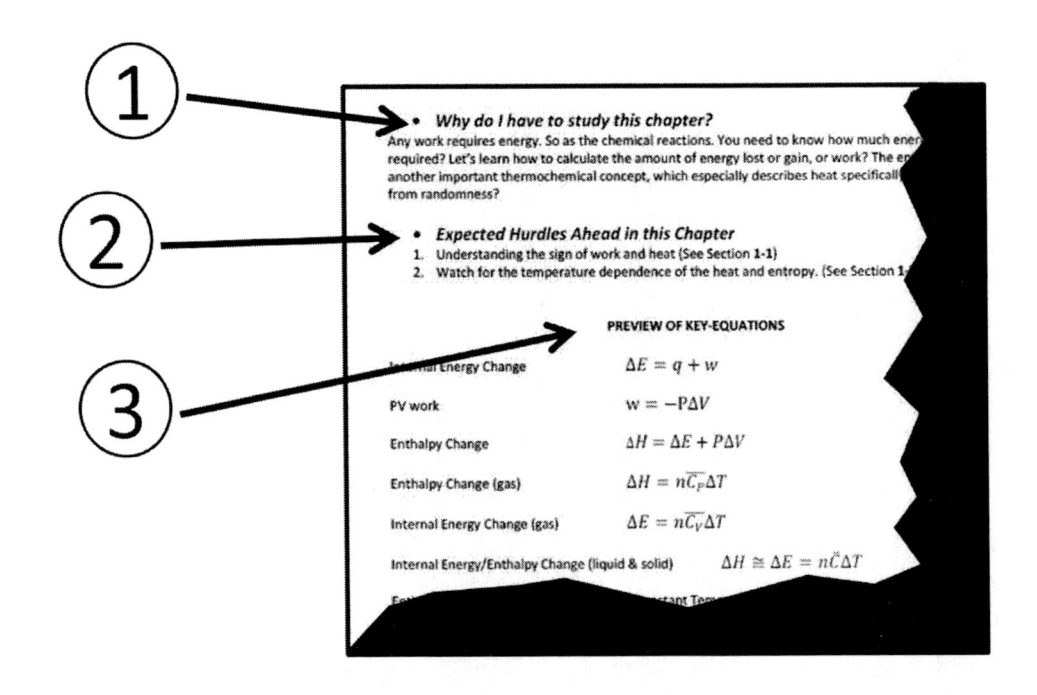

- **Why do I have to study this chapter?**
  Any work requires energy. So as the chemical reactions. You need to know how much energy required? Let's learn how to calculate the amount of energy lost or gain, or work? The e[...] another important thermochemical concept, which especially describes heat specifical[...] from randomness?

- **Expected Hurdles Ahead in this Chapter**
  1. Understanding the sign of work and heat (See Section 1-1)
  2. Watch for the temperature dependence of the heat and entropy. (See Section 1[...])

PREVIEW OF KEY-EQUATIONS

Internal Energy Change	$\Delta E = q + w$
PV work	$w = -P\Delta V$
Enthalpy Change	$\Delta H = \Delta E + P\Delta V$
Enthalpy Change (gas)	$\Delta H = n\overline{C_P}\Delta T$
Internal Energy Change (gas)	$\Delta E = n\overline{C_V}\Delta T$
Internal Energy/Enthalpy Change (liquid & solid)	$\Delta H \cong \Delta E = n\tilde{C}\Delta T$

④PREVIEW OF KEY-TECHNICAL TERMS

New and very important terms used in each chapter are listed for you to preview.

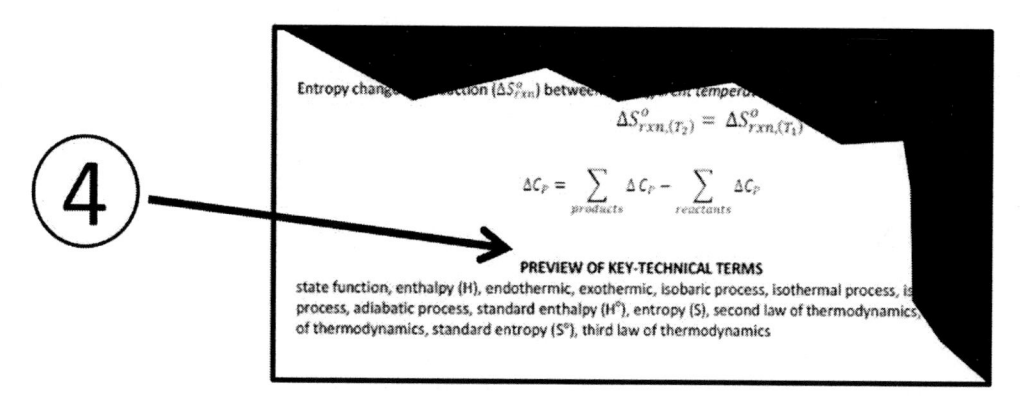

> Entropy change ... ction (ΔS^o_{rxn}) between ... temperat...
>
> $$\Delta S^o_{rxn,(T_2)} = \Delta S^o_{rxn,(T_1)}$$
>
> $$\Delta C_P = \sum_{products} \Delta C_P - \sum_{reactants} \Delta C_P$$
>
> **PREVIEW OF KEY-TECHNICAL TERMS**
> state function, enthalpy (H), endothermic, exothermic, isobaric process, isothermal process, is... process, adiabatic process, standard enthalpy (H°), entropy (S), second law of thermodynamics, ... of thermodynamics, standard entropy (S°), third law of thermodynamics

⑤EXERCISE

Selected exercise problem is listed and explained. It shows the example of how you want to approach it.

❶☞ This sign in **EXERCISE** indicates the tricky part of the problem. It give some help for you to solve the problem correctly.

⑥Most Common Mistake

☹ MCM **Most Common Mistake**

It lists the common mistake which students may commit when they solve the problems. Please review those items before you take the exam.

⑤

> (Eqn. 1-5) with P_{ex} ~1atm. The important unit conversion for calculating the amou[nt]
> from [atm·L] is 1 [atm · L] = 101.3 [J].

EXERCISE 1-1.
Each inhalation to the lungs of an adult involves pushing out about 0[.5 L of]
gas against 1 [atm] of pressure. This occurs about 15,000 times in a [day]. Estimate the amount of work in breathing done by each person [over the] course of 24 [h].

ANSWER

$$w = -\int_{V_1}^{V_2} P_{ex}\,dV = -P_{ex}\Delta V = -P_{ex}(V_2 - V_1)$$

❶☞ 1 [L·atm] = 101.3 [J]
    P = 1 [atm], ΔV = 0.5 [L]
❷☞   P ΔV = − (1 [atm]) (0.5 [L]) (101.3 [J]/ [L·atm]) ~ 50 [J/brea[th]]
    During 24 [h] - 15,000 times
    50 [J /breath] × 15,000 = 750 [kJ]

❶☞ Conversion from [L atm] to [J]
❷☞ It has a negative sign in front of P ΔV!!

⑥

☹ **Most Common Mistake (1)** -Why I cannot calcula[te] the work correctly?
Most common mistake people make in the calcula[tion of] EXERCISE 1-1 can be the unit conversion betwee[n ...]

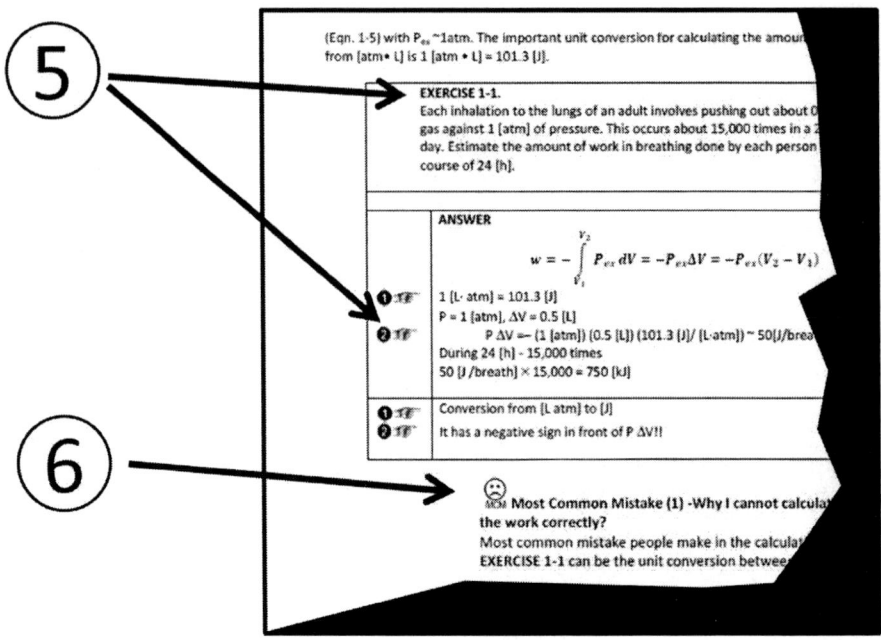

⑦**Derivation of Formulas**

$\overset{\angle}{\Sigma}$ The formula with this mark have derivation at the later section of the chapter. This textbook is intended to give you the short cut of what to know or where to study. In order to focus on the problem solving, the equations or formulas needed for solving problems are given without derivations. Therefore important derivations are given in the later section.

How did you get these equations?-The derivation of selected equations.
This section provides explanations on important formulas need significant steps for derivations.

The formula with $\overset{\angle}{\Sigma}$ sign is treated in this section and the derivations are given.

x

⑦

listed in the above. The following calculations are for the case of gas. Here, we ...
...pacity as $\bar{C}$, and a number of moles, n.

i) **Isobaric process**

$$q_P = n\bar{C}_P(T_2 - T_1) \qquad \text{(Eqn. 1-11)} \; \Sigma$$

$$w_P = -P(V_2 - V_1) = -nR(T_2 - T_1) \qquad \text{(Eqn. 1-12)} \; \Sigma$$

The work at ...

Σ

Chapter 1

How did you get these equations?
-The derivation of selected equations.

(Eqn. 1-11) $\qquad q_P = n\bar{C}_P(T_2 - T_1)$

For any a substance with heat capacity, C_P, at constant ...
heat q_P is given by

$$q_P = \int_{T_1}^{T_2} C_P \, dT = C_P(T_2 - T_1)$$

Since heat capacity is given by

⑧Chapter Summary and Summary Check.

This page shows the table of the summary which can be used for exam review. It shows the item on the left and explanation on the right. This page is meant for you to use quick review for the exam. The summary check is page is for book keeping your summary process. You may want to hold the page to hide the previous page to hide the explanation, and practice for yourself to explain. If you feel comfortable, please check on box. ☐

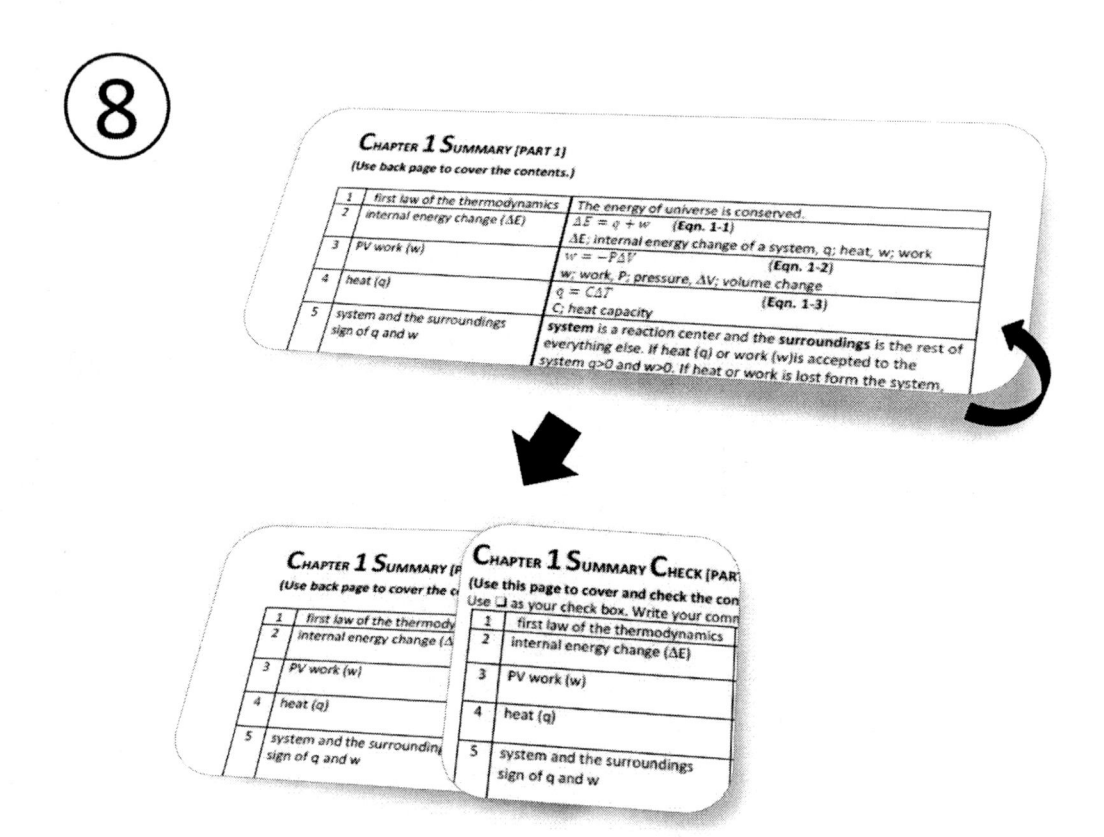

⑨ "Your Teacher May Test You On…"

This section lists up the topics which may be asked in the exam. The recommended EXERCISE and problems are also listed for each item. After you are done with reviewing summary, you may want to go through this section and practice more on your weak spots.

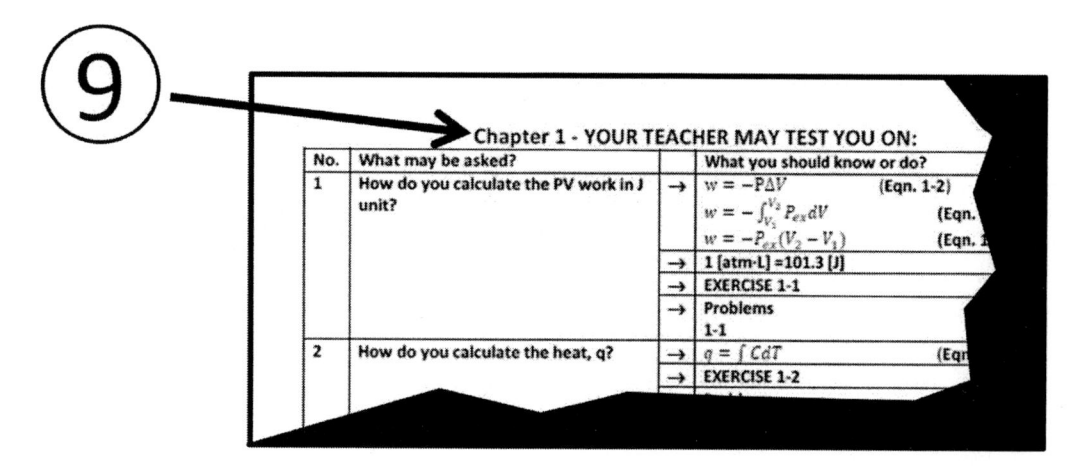

No.	What may be asked?		What you should know or do?	
1	How do you calculate the PV work in J unit?	→	$w = -P\Delta V$	(Eqn. 1-2)
			$w = -\int_{V_1}^{V_2} P_{ex}dV$	(Eqn.
			$w = -P_{ex}(V_2 - V_1)$	(Eqn.
		→	1 [atm·L] =101.3 [J]	
		→	EXERCISE 1-1	
		→	Problems 1-1	
2	How do you calculate the heat, q?	→	$q = \int CdT$	(Eqn
		→	EXERCISE 1-2	

⑩ Unit Check

Many troubles may take place in unit conversion or using wrong unit. This section sums up all terms used in each chapter sometimes with conversion factor or constant values.

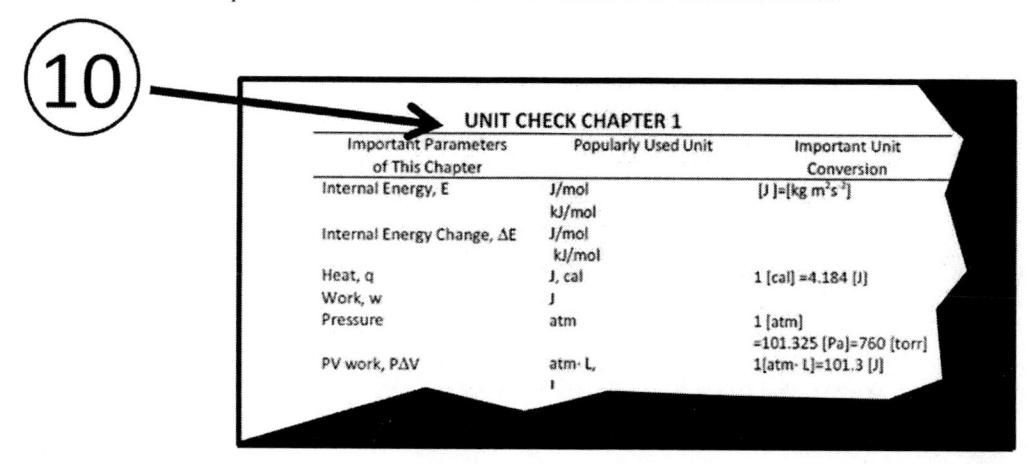

UNIT CHECK CHAPTER 1

Important Parameters of This Chapter	Popularly Used Unit	Important Unit Conversion
Internal Energy, E	J/mol, kJ/mol	[J]=[kg m^{2}s^{-2}]
Internal Energy Change, ΔE	J/mol, kJ/mol	
Heat, q	J, cal	1 [cal] =4.184 [J]
Work, w	J	
Pressure	atm	1 [atm] =101.325 [Pa]=760 [torr]
PV work, PΔV	atm·L	1[atm·L]=101.3 [J]

⑪ Summary of Tricky Traps

This section summarizes briefly on the tricky parts of each section. Use this section before you take exam.

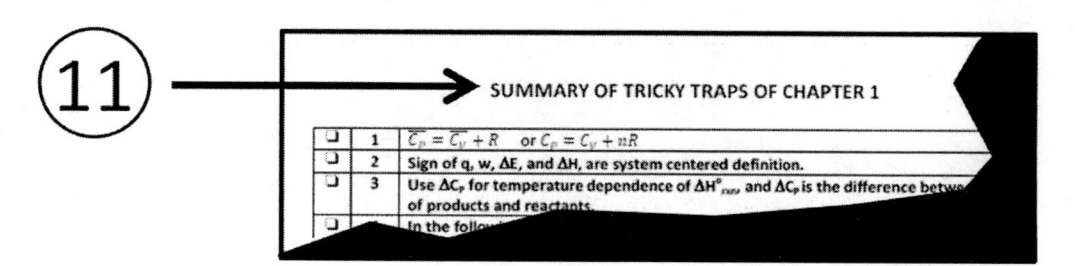

SUMMARY OF TRICKY TRAPS OF CHAPTER 1

☐	1	$\overline{C_p} = \overline{C_v} + R$ or $C_p = C_v + nR$
☐	2	Sign of q, w, ΔE, and ΔH, are system centered definition.
☐	3	Use ΔC$_p$ for temperature dependence of ΔH°$_{rxn}$, and ΔC$_p$ is the difference betwe of products and reactants.
☐		In the follo

⑫ **Last Minute Review of Math**

This section lists up really basic math which you probably do not have to worry about at all. However, I listed them up on purpose, since people seem to get panic before the exam and tend to forget about very simple thing. If you are getting nervous about exam, then take a look at this section at last minute and feel confident and comfortable. Then, take your exam.

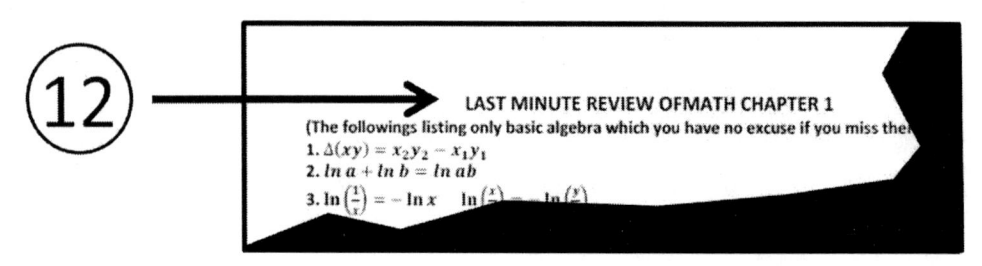

> ⑫ → **LAST MINUTE REVIEW OF MATH CHAPTER 1**
> (The followings listing only basic algebra which you have no excuse if you miss them)
> 1. $\Delta(xy) = x_2 y_2 - x_1 y_1$
> 2. $\ln a + \ln b = \ln ab$
> 3. $\ln\left(\frac{1}{x}\right) = -\ln x$ $\ln\left(\frac{x}{y}\right) = \ln\left(\frac{y}{x}\right)$

Also the following features are added to each chapter:

Nobel Prize and Your Knowledge From Chapter 1

I want you to connect your knowledge of each chapter with scientific achievement recognized by Nobel prize. The contents are focused more to Physical and Biochemical applications.

The focused physical chemistry experimental approach associated with each chapter:

This section adds up advanced experimental technique to what you learned in each chapter. This section can be skipped if you have too much to worry about your study. However, please take a look at one or two sections, you may find them very interesting.

End of Chapter Problems

The related and similar problems with EXERCISE or additional drills on calculations are given. The section "**Your Teacher May Test You On**" suggest you which question you should do for your review. The detail answers for the problem are available separately.

Chapter 1
Thermodynamics

1-1 Systems and Surroundings
1-2 The State Functions and Paths Connecting Different States
1-3 Energy Transfer in Phase Change
1-4 Chemical Reactions and Standard Enthalpies of Formation
1-5 Temperature Dependence of Enthalpy Change
1-6 The Change of Internal Energy of a Reaction
1-7 Second Law of Thermodynamics and Entropy
1-8 Entropy Change in Chemical Reaction and Its Temperature Dependence

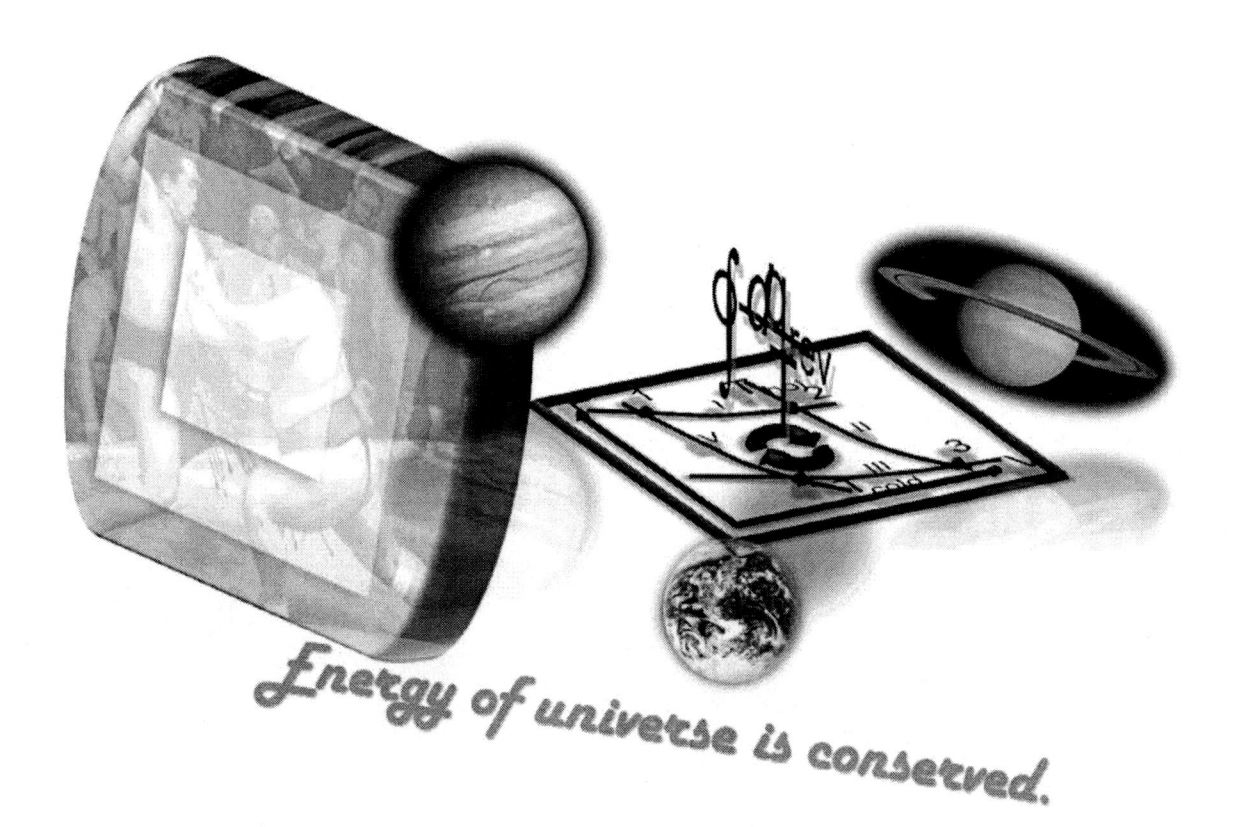

Energy of universe is conserved.

Chapter 1 Thermodynamics

- ### *Why do I have to study this chapter?*

Any work requires energy, and so as the chemical reactions. You need to know how much energy (or heat) is required? Let's learn how to calculate the amount of energy lost or gain, or work? The entropy is another important thermochemical concept, which especially describes heat specifically originating from randomness.

- ### *Expected Hurdles Ahead in this Chapter*
    1. Understanding the sign of work and heat (See Section **1-1**)
    2. Watch for the temperature dependence of the heat and entropy. (See Section **1-7**)

PREVIEW OF KEY-EQUATIONS

Internal Energy Change $\qquad \Delta E = q + w$

PV work $\qquad w = -P\Delta V$

Enthalpy Change $\qquad \Delta H = \Delta E + P\Delta V$

Enthalpy Change (gas) $\qquad \Delta H = n\overline{C_P}\Delta T$

Internal Energy Change (gas) $\qquad \Delta E = n\overline{C_V}\Delta T$

Internal Energy/Enthalpy Change (liquid & solid) $\qquad \Delta H \cong \Delta E = n\bar{C}\Delta T$

Enthalpy Change of Chemical Reaction at Constant Temperature
$$\Delta H^o_{rxn} = \Sigma_{products} \Delta H^o_f - \Sigma_{reactants} \Delta H^o_f$$

Temperature Dependence of Enthalpy Change of a Reaction
$$\Delta H^{T_2}_{rxn} - \Delta H^{T_1}_{rxn} = \Delta C_P (T_2 - T_1)$$

Internal Energy Change of gas involved Chemical Reaction
$$\Delta E_{rxn} = \Delta H_{rxn} - (\Delta n_g)RT$$

Entropy (S) and the number of the state (N) $\qquad S = k \ln N$

Entropy change (*ΔS*) for an Isothermal process $\qquad \Delta S = \dfrac{q_{rev}}{T}$

Entropy change (*ΔS*) between two different temperatures $\qquad \Delta S = C \ln \dfrac{T_2}{T_1}$

(C=C$_P$ or C$_V$)

Chapter 1 Thermodynamics

Second Law of Thermodynamics
$$\Delta S(system) + \Delta S(surroundings) \geq 0$$

Entropy change of a reaction (ΔS^o_{rxn})
$$\Delta S^o_{rxn} = \sum_{products} \Delta S^o_f - \sum_{reactants} \Delta S^o_f$$

Entropy change of a reaction (ΔS^o_{rxn}) between *two different temperatures*
$$\Delta S^o_{rxn,(T_2)} = \Delta S^o_{rxn,(T_1)} + \Delta C_P \ln \frac{T_2}{T_1}$$

$$\Delta C_P = \sum_{products} \Delta C_P - \sum_{reactants} \Delta C_P$$

PREVIEW OF KEY-TECHNICAL TERMS

state function, enthalpy (H), endothermic, exothermic, isobaric process, isothermal process, isochoric process, adiabatic process, standard enthalpy (H°), entropy (S), second law of thermodynamics, first law of thermodynamics, standard entropy (S°), third law of thermodynamics

Chapter 1 Thermodynamics

1-1 Systems and Surroundings

Let's start this first section of this book by stating the most important statement of this chapter. It is "The energy of the universe is conserved." This statement is what is described in the **first law of the thermodynamics**. This law simply shows that no destruction and no creation of energy are caused. Please note again that key word of this chapter is a conservation of energy, and look at the next equation by imaging what parameters will be used to show a conservation of the energy. The first law of the thermodynamics is represented by

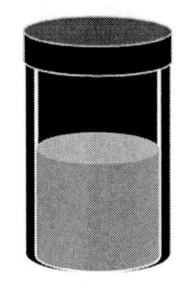

Fig. 1-1 For an isolated system, $\Delta E = 0$.

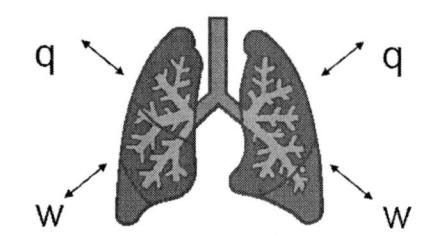

Fig. 1-2 Human lung and the expansion work.

$$\Delta E = q + w \qquad \text{(Eqn. 1-1)}$$

So we use q (heat) and w (work) to represent the energy change, ΔE. The energy change should be none for an isolated system, i.e., $\Delta E = 0$. (This is a very convenient and useful relationship that you should remember and use later on.) **(Fig. 1-1)**

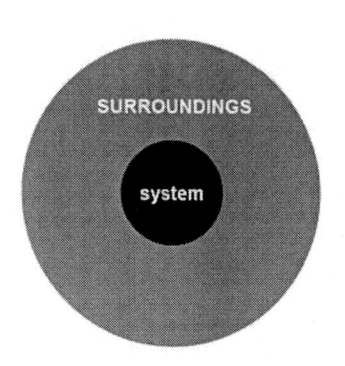

Fig. 1-3 The system and the surroundings.

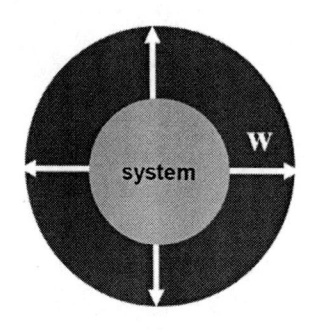

Fig. 1-4 The expansion work done to the surroundings

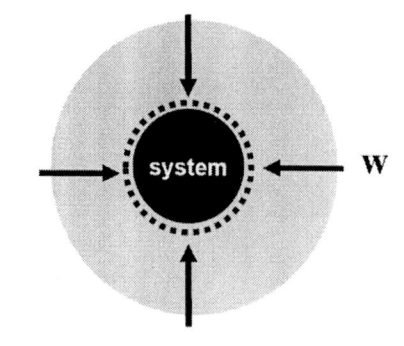

Fig. 1-5 The compression work done to the surroundings.

As an important visualization of a system of thermochemical work, human lung can be used as a container which expand or compress as heat (or energy) is transported.**(Fig. 1-2)** If a system expands or compresses its volume under the constant pressure, P, the work, w, is given by

$$w = -P\Delta V \qquad \text{(Eqn. 1-2)}$$

The work can be given in different expression (kinetic energy or potential energy). However, I promise you that a type of work used in this chapter is only the type given by **(Eqn. 1-2)**. The work is defined as the multiplication between external force and the displacement distance as:

$$\text{work} \equiv \text{external force} \cdot \text{displacement}$$

Chapter 1 Thermodynamics

The heat of a substance with heat capacity C under temperature change ΔT [K or °C] is

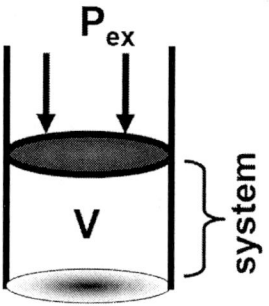

$$q = C\Delta T \qquad \text{(Eqn. 1-3)}$$

Fig. 1-6 The PV type of work under external pressure P_{ex}.

The thermodynamics is an interconversion of heat and other kinds of energy. In order to clarify the direction of energies, I introduce the concept of **system** and the **surroundings**.(**Fig. 1-3**) The most "suitable" and "easier to understand" definition of the system is substance that undergoes a reaction. The surroundings is everything outside this system. By choosing the type of work as expansion or compression of the system, the work and its direction are easily visualized as a function of a volume change. Under the expansion work, the volume is increased toward outside. It is like two chemicals mixed inside a plastic bag producing a gas and expanding the volume of a plastic bag. Thus, the work is done to the surroundings (the system did the work to the surrounding). The sign of work is defined as "positive" when the system receives a work, while it is a negative work if the system does the work to the surroundings. Thus, an expansion of the system is negative work (w < 0) (**Fig. 1-4**), whereas the compression work is carried out as the volume decreases. Since you can picture that as the surrounding squeeze the volume of the system, the system receives work from the surroundings (w > 0) (**Fig. 1-5.**) The direction of the arrows you see in **Figs. 1-4** and **1-5** indicates the flow of direction of the work. (outward → w<0, inward → w>0)

The equation that defines the work is

$$w = -\int_{V_1}^{V_2} P_{ex} dV \qquad \text{(Eqn. 1-4)}$$

$$w = -P_{ex}(V_2 - V_1) \qquad \text{(Eqn. 1-5)}$$

Fig. 1-7 The amount of work given by PV work.

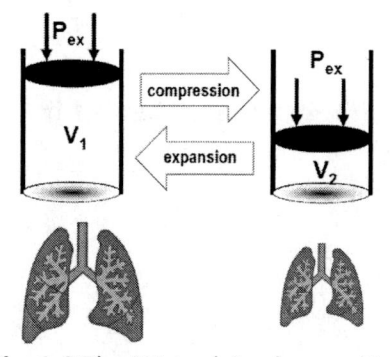

Fig. 1-8 The PV work in observed in a human lung.

Here, w is work [J], P_{ex} is the pressure [atm] acting on the system externally (i.e., external pressure) and the V is the volume [mL or L]. Since an only external pressure is defined, you may wonder what will be the pressure inside. The reversible expansion/compression is defined when the both pressures between internal and external are equilibrated ($P_{system} \approx P_{ex}$). On the other hand, the irreversible expansion/compression takes place when $P_{system} \gg P_{ex}$ or $P_{system} \ll P_{ex}$. The multiplication of the unit in pressure and volume does not give the unit in J. Please see the **Most Common Mistake(1)** for the unit conversion between [atm L] and [J]. The V_1 and V_2 are the initial and the final volume, respectively.(**Fig. 1-6**) If the external pressure P_{ex} takes a constant value during a volume change, work is given by (**Eqn. 1-5**). Please note on the negative sign in front of P_{ex}. A graphical view of the amount of work, w, calculated by (**Eqn. 1-5**) is shown as an area in **Fig. 1-7**. The area in the graph, however, shows the scalar part of the work so that the pressure is taken as a positive value.

Let's confirm the sign of the volume change and work.

Compression: $V_2 < V_1$ and $\Delta V = V_2 - V_1 < 0$ w>0
Expansion: $V_1 < V_2$ and $\Delta V = V_2 - V_1 > 0$ w<0

The crude approximation allows us to imply the above compression/expansion (exhale/inhale) work to the motion and work done by human lung, **(Fig. 1-8)** and the amount involved can be estimated by the **(Eqn. 1-5)** with P_{ex} ~1 [atm]. The important unit conversion for calculating the amount of work in joules from [atm· L] is 1 [atm • L] = 101.3 [J].

EXERCISE 1-1
Each inhalation to the lungs of an adult involves pushing out about 0.5 L of gas against 1 [atm] of pressure. This occurs about 15,000 times in a 24-h day. Estimate the amount of work in breathing done by each person in the course of 24 [h].

ANSWER

$$w = -\int_{V_1}^{V_2} P_{ex}\, dV = -P_{ex}\Delta V = -P_{ex}(V_2 - V_1)$$

❶ 1 [L· atm] = 101.3 [J]
P = 1 [atm], ΔV = 0.5 [L]
❷   P ΔV =– (1 [atm]) (0.5 [L]) (101.3 [J]/ [L·atm]) ~ 50[J/breath]
During 24 [h] - 15,000 times
50 [J /breath] × 15,000 = 750 [kJ]

---

❶ Conversion from [L atm] to [J]
❷ It has a negative sign in front of P ΔV!!

Most Common Mistake (1) -Why I cannot calculate the amount of the work correctly?

Most common mistake people make in the calculation shown in **EXERCISE 1-1** can be the unit conversion between [L·atm] and [J]. If your value is off by 103 from an expected value, I think your unit conversion needs to be revisited. 1 [L· atm] = 101.3 [J]

The heat, q, is understood as the integration of the heat capacity, C, as a function of the temperature, T.

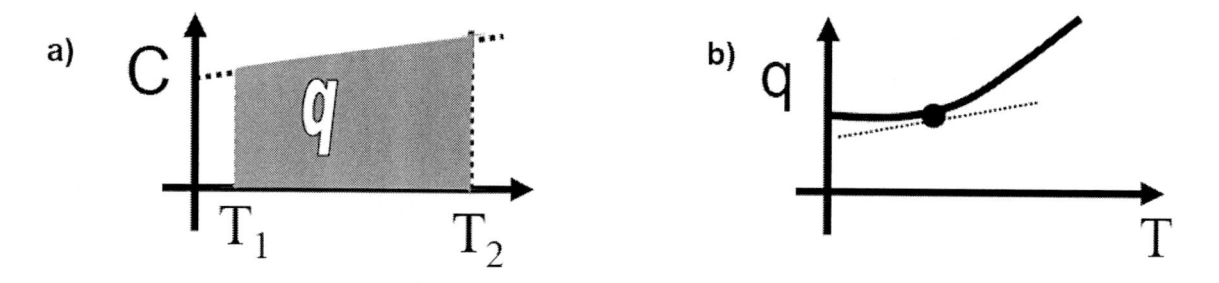

$$q = \int C \, dT \quad \text{(Eqn. 1-6)}$$

Fig. 1-9 a) An integration of heat capacity as a function of temperature. b) A tangential line at a given temperature point endothermic process.

A graphical representation of (**Eqn. 1-6**) is that an entire area integrated between two temperature points corresponds to the amount of the heat q. If the temperature is changed from T_1 to T_2, the area given under the heat capacity between two temperatures are the amount of heat produced. (**Fig 1-9a**). The heat capacity plotted as a function of temperature may not show a linear form (**Fig 1-9b**). The reverse of the relationship given in (**Eqn. 1-6**) states that the differential of the heat q as a function of temperature, T is the heat capacity, C.

$$C = \frac{dq}{dT} \quad \text{(Eqn. 1-7)}$$

When the heat energy can transfers from the surroundings to a system (**endothermic process** (**Fig. 1-10a**) positive value for a system) or transfer from a system to the surroundings (**exothermic process** (**Fig. 1-10b**) negative value for a system).

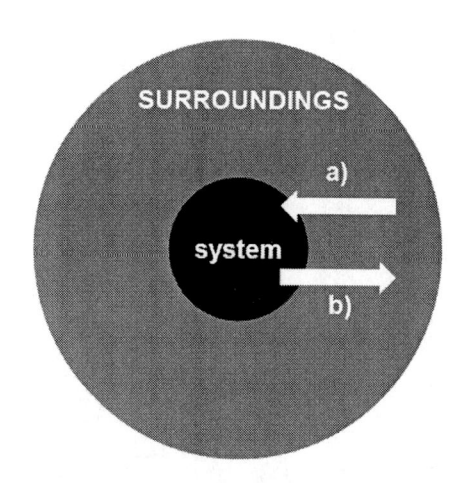

Fig. 1-10 a) endothermic and b) exothermic process.

If heat capacity C is independent of temperature,

$$q = \int_{T_1}^{T_2} C \, dT = C(T_2 - T_1) \quad \text{(Eqn. 1-8)}$$

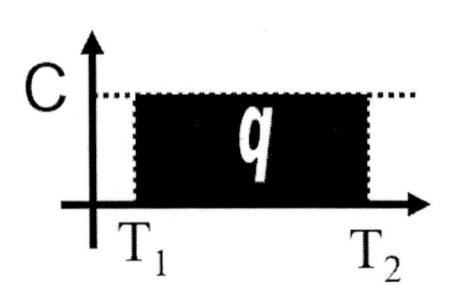

Thus, the heat is corresponds to rectangular area in a graph in (**Fig. 1-11**) under the heat capacity, C, between temperatures T₁ and T₂.

Fig. 1-11 The amount of heat under the temperature independent heat capacity C.

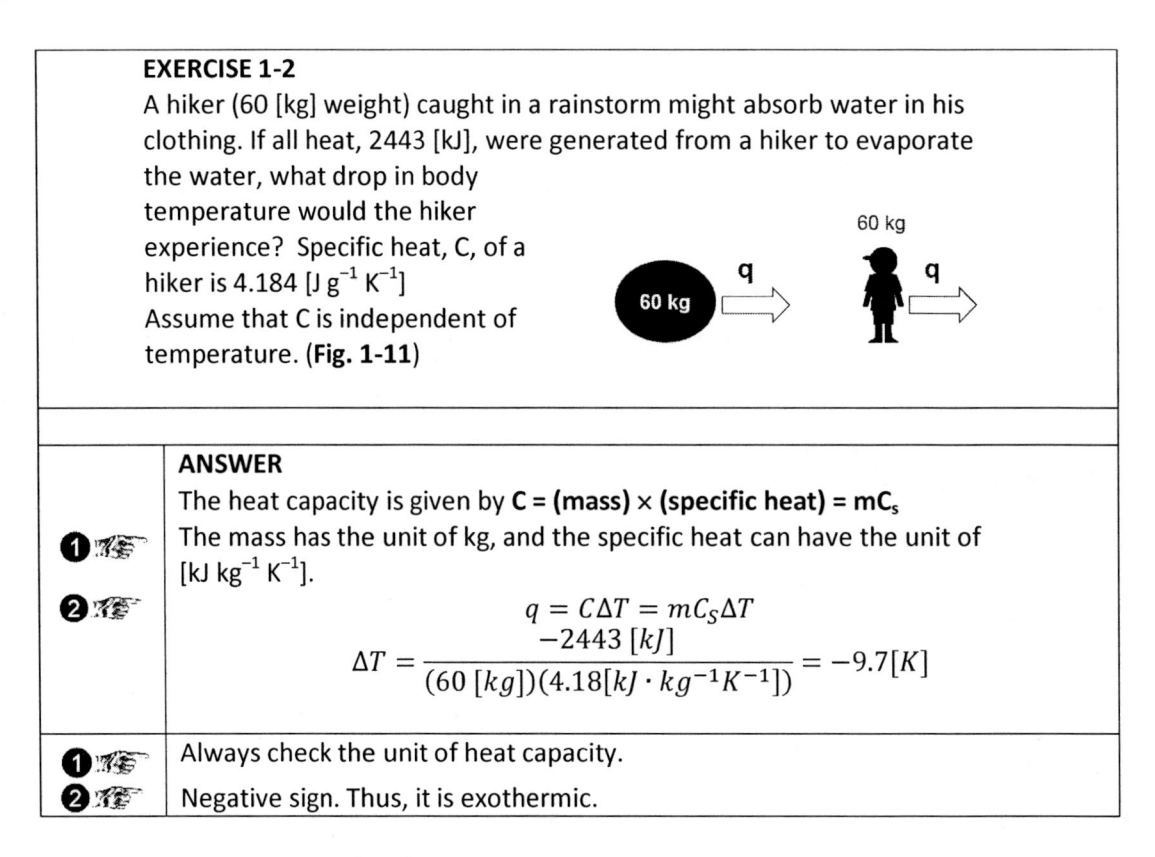

EXERCISE 1-2

A hiker (60 [kg] weight) caught in a rainstorm might absorb water in his clothing. If all heat, 2443 [kJ], were generated from a hiker to evaporate the water, what drop in body temperature would the hiker experience? Specific heat, C, of a hiker is 4.184 [J g⁻¹ K⁻¹]
Assume that C is independent of temperature. (**Fig. 1-11**)

ANSWER
The heat capacity is given by **C = (mass) × (specific heat) = mC_s**
The mass has the unit of kg, and the specific heat can have the unit of [kJ kg⁻¹ K⁻¹].

$$q = C\Delta T = mC_S\Delta T$$
$$\Delta T = \frac{-2443\,[kJ]}{(60\,[kg])(4.18[kJ \cdot kg^{-1}K^{-1}])} = -9.7[K]$$

❶☞ Always check the unit of heat capacity.
❷☞ Negative sign. Thus, it is exothermic.

Let's summarize the direction (sign) of work, w, and heat, q, to or from a system. Remember, the way of a direction is defined as system-centered. If system receives w or q, they are positive. If the system loses w or q, they are negative. (**Fig. 1.12**)

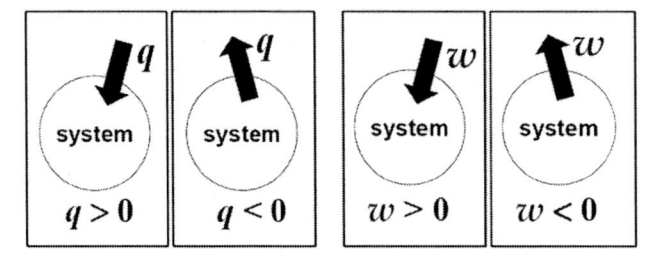

Fig. 1-12 The summary of the sign of q and w for a system.

Chapter 1 Thermodynamics

☹ MCM Most Common Mistake (2) - When w>0 or w<0? I cannot tell.

Don't you think the wording for expressing the positive or negative work are confusing. Here is the list of the way the problem states the work of a system and the corresponding signs.

The system receives the work (w) from the surroundings → w>0
The system does the work (w) against the surroundings → w<0
The surrounding does the work (w) → w>0
The surrounding receives the work (w) → w<0

If you are observing the system, you are part of the surroundings. So that the sign of the work is exactly opposite of your work. (e.g., If you squeeze the container (=system), you (=surroundings) did the work ($w_{surroundings}$<0), therefore, the system receives your work (w_{system}>0)

1-2 The State Functions and Paths Connecting Different States

The height of the mountain does not change no matter what route you take to climb up the mountain. **(Fig. 1-13)** The work or heat required for completing from one state to another state can be varied, whereas the determined amount between two states does not change. The variables of states are often used for describing the state function. The variables of state or State function are the parameters which specify a state sufficiently, and they depend only on the state of system. The examples are P, V, T and E (internal energy of system), which do not depend on the path. On the other hand, heat (q) or work (w) depends on the path.

The state function, H (Enthalpy), is defined as

$$H = E + PV$$

Fig. 1-13 The height of a mountain does not depend on the route.

(Eqn. 1-9)

Generally, the change (Δ) of the value is more convenient or easier for the use. The change of the enthalpy ΔH is

$$\Delta H = \Delta E + \Delta(PV)$$

For the constant pressure P,

$$\Delta H = \Delta E + P\Delta V$$

(Eqn. 1-10)

Chapter 1 Thermodynamics

Let's experience what it really means that state functions do not depend on the path. There are four thermodynamic paths and conditions which I want you to memorize.

> (i)   isobaric Process $\Delta P_{sys} = 0$ where constant pressure is maintained.
> (ii)   isochoric process $\Delta V = 0$ where constant volume is maintained
> (iii)   isothermal process $\Delta T_{sys} = 0$ where constant temperature is maintained
> (iv)   adiabatic process q = 0 where no heat transferred

Then, let's see a bit more in detail for each step by calculating heat, q, and work, w for each process i)-iv) listed in the above. The following calculations are for the case of gas. Here, we adopted the molar heat capacity as $\bar{C}$, and a number of moles, n.

i) Isobaric process

$$q_P = n\overline{C_P}(T_2 - T_1) \qquad \text{(Eqn. 1-11)} \; \Sigma$$

$$w_P = -P(V_2 - V_1) = -nR(T_2 - T_1) \qquad \text{(Eqn. 1-12)} \; \Sigma$$

The work at constant pressure, w_p is graphically demonstrated in (**Fig. 1-14**), where two curves indicate the ideal gas equation (PV =nRT) at a given temperature.

ii) Isochoric process

$$q_V = n\overline{C_V}(T_2 - T_1) \qquad \text{(Eqn. 1-13)} \; \Sigma$$

$$w_V = 0 \qquad \text{(Eqn. 1-14)} \; \Sigma$$

The amount of work (w_p) conducted under constant pressure P between volume change V_1 and V_2 is represented by the rectangular area. The work at constant volume is shown in the plot in (**Fig. 1-15**) where the integration at the same volume provides no area indicating that the work at constant volume is zero.

From now on, whenever you see Σ mark next to the equation number, the derivation is provided at the end of each chapter. See "**How did you get these equations?**"

iii) Isothermal process

$$q_T = -w_T \quad \text{(Eqn. 1-15)}$$

$$w_T = -nRT \ln \frac{V_2}{V_1} \quad \text{(Eqn. 1-16)}$$

The work under the constant temperature, w_T, calculated in the **Eqn. (1-13)** is presented as shaded area in the plot in (**Fig. 1-16**)

iv) adiabatic process

$$q_a = 0 \quad \text{(Eqn. 1-17)}$$

$$w_a = \frac{K(V_2^{1-\gamma} - V_1^{1-\gamma})}{1-\gamma} \quad \text{(Eqn. 1-18)}$$

In this process, the work is conducted without involving any heat. (The work is represented as the shaded area in **Fig. 1-17**). But "No heat" does not mean that "No temperature change". The adiabatic process is described as a jumping from one temperature to the other.

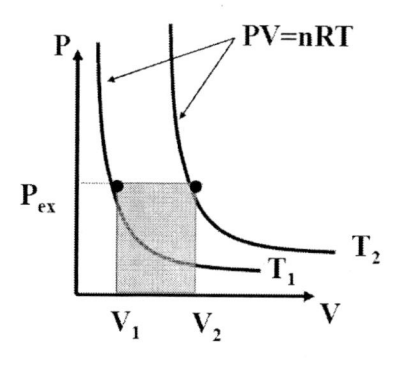

Fig. 1-14 The work conducted under constant pressure. (isobaric process)

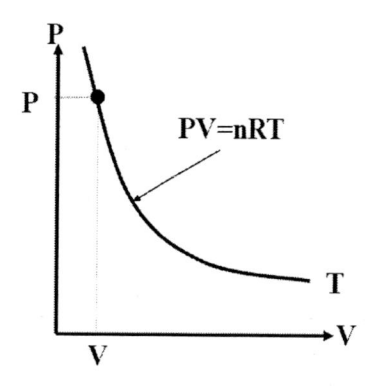

Fig. 1-15 The work conducted under constant volume. (isochoric process)

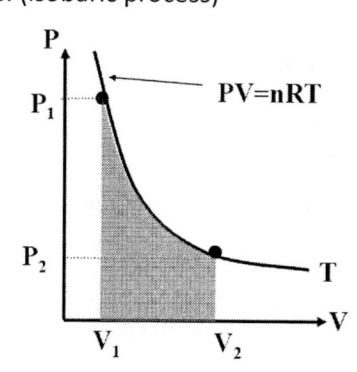

Fig. 1-16 The work conducted under constant temperature. (isothermal process)

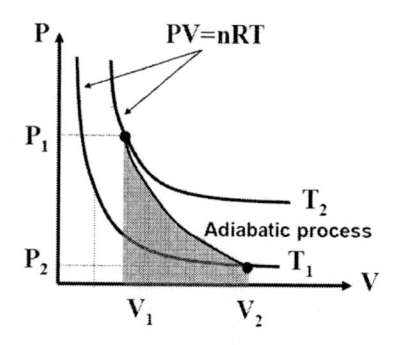

Fig. 1-17 The work conducted under no heat. (adiabatic process)

Now we are ready to make an application to the internal energy change, ΔE, and enthalpy change, ΔH, of a pure substance from one state to the other state, which can be described by using a series of thermodynamic restricted paths given in **Fig. 1-18**. For example, let's take a look at the case when the state is changed from state 1 to state 2.

state 1 (T$_1$, V$_1$, P$_1$) → state 2 (T$_2$, V$_2$, P$_2$)

The change observed from initial state 1 (T$_1$, P$_1$, and V$_1$) to the final state 2 (T$_2$, P$_2$, V$_2$) can be expressed by a series of steps. One way (path A) is to start from isothermal process (ii) ((T$_1$, P$_1$) → (T$_1$, P$_2$)) followed by isobaric process(i) ((T$_1$, P$_2$) → (T$_2$, P$_2$)). The other path (path B) is starting from isothermal process (ii) ((T$_1$, V$_1$) → (T$_1$, V$_2$)) followed by isochoric process(iii) ((T$_1$, V$_2$) → (T$_2$, V$_2$)). These two different paths are shown in **Fig. 1-18**. As we learned about the rule of state function, the value of the state function should be the same no matter which path of **Fig. 1-18** is taken.

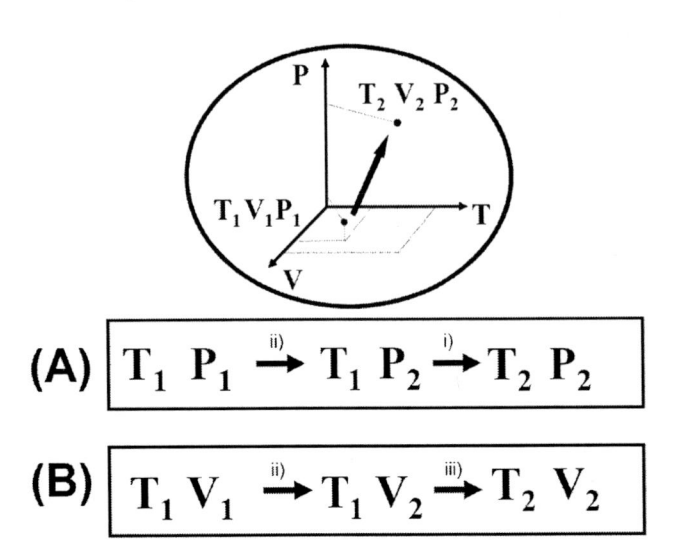

Fig. 1-18 The thermodynamic change can be described by two different series of paths.

The two different paths A and B allows us to calcluate the enthalpy change, ΔH in two different ways. The value calculated by path A is

$$\Delta H = n\overline{C_P}(T_2 - T_1)$$

The same value calculated by path B is

$$\Delta H = n(\overline{C_V} + R)(T_2 - T_1)$$

Since above two paths should give the same values

$$n\overline{C_P}(T_2 - T_1) = n(\overline{C_V} + R)(T_2 - T_1)$$

We can derive new important relationship about heat capacity C$_P$ and C$_V$ as

$$\overline{C_P} = \overline{C_V} + R \qquad \text{(Eqn. 1-19)}$$

or

$$C_P = C_V + nR \qquad \text{(Eqn. 1-20)}$$

Here, $\overline{C_P}$ and $\overline{C_V}$ indicate the heat capacity per mole at constant pressure and constant volume, respectively. Please note that n (number of moles) is multiplied to R in (**Eqn. 1-20**).

Chapter 1 Thermodynamics

You may like the following expressions, since they clearly explain the meaning of internal energy change, ΔE, and an enthalpy change, ΔH for an ideal gas.

$$\Delta E = n\overline{C_V}\Delta T = q_v \quad \text{(for gas)} \quad \text{(Eqn. 1-21)}$$

$$\Delta H = n\overline{C_P}\Delta T = q_P \quad \text{(for gas)} \quad \text{(Eqn. 1-22)}$$

The above two equations should inspire you that internal energy change and enthalpy change correspond to heat under constant volume and constant pressure, respectively. If the heat is measured under constant volume or pressure, ΔE or ΔH is measured.

EXERCISE 1-3
If a breath of air, with a volume of 0.5 [L] at 20 [°C], is drawn into the lungs and comes to 37 [°C] while the pressure remains constant, calculate ΔH of the air (C_P = 30 [J K^{-1} mol^{-1}]).

ANSWER
Assuming that air is an ideal gas at 1 atmospheric pressure,

❶   n = PV /RT

= (1 [atm] × 0.5 [L]) / (0.082 [atm L K^{-1} mol^{-1}] × 293 [K])

= 0.0208 [mol]

$$\Delta H = n\overline{C_P}\Delta T = q_P \quad \text{(Eqn. 1-22)}$$

❷   ΔH = (0.0208 [mol]) × (30 [J K^{-1} mol^{-1}]) × (17 [K])

= 10.608 [J]

---

❶   Many people forget to calculate the number of moles!!
❷   Confirm dimension analysis. [mol] × [J K^{-1} mol^{-1}] × [K] = [J]

😖 **Most Common Mistake (3) Molar or specific? Which one should I use?**

While the relationship between C$_P$ and C$_V$ is clearly shown in (**Eqn. 1-19**) or (**Eqn. 1-20**), there are some confusions about which equation should be used. Simply put, you use (**Eqn. 1-19**) when heat capacities are given by molar heat capacity with units [J mol^{-1} K^{-1}]. Then, you use (**Eqn. 1-20**) if the heat capacities are in [J/K]. You may scream that "I can't memorize all possible situations." If so, the bottom line is you should always watch the unit of the heat capacity and judge what you should do. For example, C$_p$ has the unit of [J/K] and $\overline{C_P}$ has the unit of [J K^{-1} mol^{-1}].

Chapter 1 Thermodynamics

☹ **Most Common Mistake (4) Do I really need to use "Δ" to calculate enthalpy?**

Many complaints I hear are that students feel like there are too many equations in thermochemistry. People feel overwhelmed and cannot tell when to use what equations. One contribution of many equations is due to the definition of the state function and "change" of the state function. For example, enthalpy is defined as

$$H = E + PV \qquad \text{(Eqn. 1-9)}$$

But we also define the enthalpy change ΔH, since the change of the values are always easier to obtain experimentally.

$$\Delta H = \Delta E + P\Delta V \qquad \text{(Eqn. 1-10)}$$

So please note that you end up using Δ of something all the time. Another nightmare is the calculation of heat. There are many equations that deal with heat "q". Only solution to solve this is to "knowing conditions" surrounding the experiment. As a review, I show the list of popularly asked conditions for calculating heat, q.

q, heat	Equation	Parameters
heat of a substance (1)	$q = mC_s\Delta T$	m: sample mass [g] C_s: specific heat capacity [J g^{-1} K^{-1}] ΔT: temperature change [K]
heat of a substance (2)	$q = nC_m\Delta T$	n: number of moles [mol] C_s: molar heat capacity [J mol^{-1} K^{-1}] ΔT: temperature change [K]
heat of a calorimeter	$q_{cal} = C_{cal}\Delta T$	C_{cal}: heat capacity of a calorimeter [J/K] ΔT: temperature change [K]
heat of a reaction	$q_r = n\Delta H_r$	n: number of moles of a targeted substance of a reaction [mol] ΔH_r: enthalpy of a reaction for 1 mol of a targeted substance in a reaction [J/mol]

Chapter 1 Thermodynamics

☹ MCM Most Common Mistake (5) I thought I was using correct heat capacity (C_V), but you are telling me I am not!

A tricky teacher like me may test you if you really understand the definition of ΔH and ΔE for an ideal gas and the relationship between C_P and C_V. The way to do for me is to ask you to calculate the enthalpy change ΔH of a species between T_2 and T_1 with heat capacity C_V. (Did you just notice a tricky part?) The C_V is given to trick you. Since ΔH =q_P, you need to use C_P but not C_V. Thus, you need to calculate C_V from (**Eqn. 1-20**). Also you will see again about an issue of the conversion between C_P and C_V in **Most Common Mistake (9)** in Chapter 2. In there, I talk about the unit of gas constant (R=8.314[J mol^{-1}K^{-1}]). If you want to experience what I am talking about here, please try **Problem 1.11a)** and **1.25** by all means.

1-3 Energy Transfer in Phase Changes

For the solid and liquid substances, the volume change is almost negligible and cause some significant simplification in the thermodynamic values. The enthalpy change, ΔH, shown in (**Eqn. 1.10**)

$$\Delta H = \Delta E + \Delta(PV) \qquad \text{(Eqn. 1-10)}$$

Under the constant pressure and small volume change for the solid/liquid, the Δ(PV) becomes Negligible.

$$\Delta H \cong \Delta E \qquad \text{(for solid/liquid)} \qquad \text{(Eqn. 1-23)}$$

Please note that the (Eqn. **1-23**) does not state that the value of ΔH and ΔE are exactly equivalent. Using the result shown in (Eqn. **1-23**), (Eqn. **1-21**) and (Eqn. **1-22**) give

$$\Delta E = n\overline{C_V}\Delta T = \Delta H = n\overline{C_P}\Delta T \qquad \text{(for solid/liquid)} \qquad \text{(Eqn. 1-24)}$$

Therefore,

$$\overline{C_V} = \overline{C_P} = \overline{C} \qquad \text{(for solid/liquid)} \qquad \text{(Eqn. 1-25)}$$

where $\overline{C}$ indicates the molar heat capacity for solid and liquid substances.

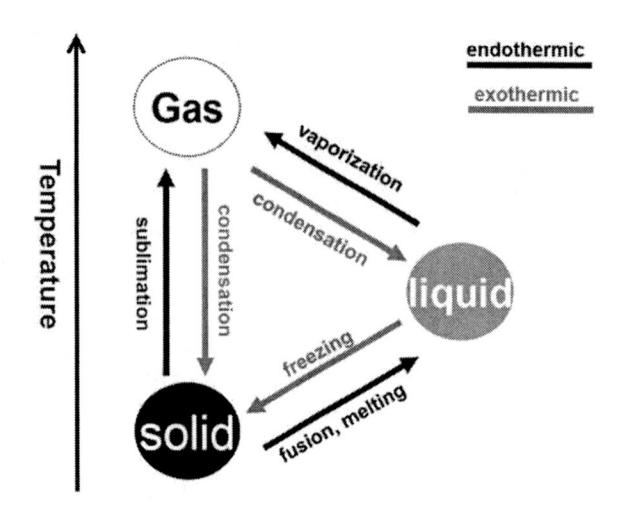

Fig. 1-19 The phase transition and three matters.

In natural phenomena, energy interchange or transfer causes the change in different phases between gas, solid, and liquid. The focus of study now expands to thermochemical processes on substances from one phase to another. Let's learn how to think and describe an energy transfer involving two or more phases. If the phase changes, the heat is always involved (lost or accepted) and resulting in another phase as shown in **Fig. 1-19**. As the heat is accepted to the system (endothermic process), the temperature of the matter (system) is raised. As the heat is removed from the system (exothermic process), it causes the temperature decrease in the system. For example, gas is condensed to become liquid by losing the heat. The gas is formed from liquid by accepting heat (vaporization). With accepting heat, the solid becomes a liquid (melting), while liquid become solid as they lose the heat (fusion). The situation when the solid skips the one phase liquid becomes gas is called sublimation and the reverse situation of this is called condensation. The transition goes toward the gas phase is the direction of an increase of temperature in the system, and the direction of the change into the solid is the direction of and decrease of the temperature in the system.

Let's think about the thermodynamic values work (w), heat (q), change in internal energy (ΔE), and enthalpy change (ΔH).

$$\Delta E_v = \Delta H_v - RT \qquad \textbf{(Eqn. 1-26)}$$

You notice that the difference between ΔE and ΔH is RT ($\Delta H > \Delta E$). A similar relationship shown in (**Eqn. 1-26**) will appear soon for the expression of ca chemical reaction in (**Eqn. 1-31**).

EXERCISE 1-4
A substance changed from a liquid to a gas had an internal energy change of 160 [kJ/mol] at 20 [°C]. Calculate ΔH (in kJ/moL) of this phase change.

ANSWER

❶	$\Delta E_v = \Delta H_v - RT$ (Eqn. 1-29)
	$\Delta H_m \quad = \quad \Delta E_m + RT$
❷	R = 8.3144 [J mol^{-1} K^{-1}]
❸	T= 20 [°C] = 293 [K]
	ΔE_m = 160 [kJ/mol]
❹	ΔH_m = 160 [kJ/mol] + 8.3144 [J mol^{-1} K^{-1}] × 293 [K] = 162 [kJ/mol]

❶	This is for 1 [mol] of gas. (PV =nRT, n=1)
❷	Check the unit and value for gas constant, R.
❸	Temperature unit should be in Kelvins [K].
❹	Confirm $\Delta H > \Delta E$, but they are about the same value.

1-4 Chemical Reactions and Enthalpy Changes (ΔH)

Let's apply our knowledge of thermochemical values to chemical reactions. In chemical reaction, as you may imagine, many parameters will be involved. This is a real test of what you learned in the above section. The chemical reaction involves temperature change, phase change, and volume change as the materials are changed from the reactants to products. General expression of thermochemical equation is

$$n_A A + n_B B \rightarrow n_C C + n_D D \qquad \Delta H \text{ [kJ/mol]}$$

Here, A and B represent are reactants and the C and D represent the products with corresponding number of moles (stoichiometric coefficients) n_A, n_B, n_C, and n_D. At the end, the enthalpy change of the reaction, ΔH in [kJ/mol]. Before we start "real stuff" I point out very basic rules of thermochemical equations. You can, however, skip this paragraph if you are confident on this material. I want to point out only two important rules.

Rule 1. Reversing Eqn. → Reverse sign of ΔH
If the thermochemical equation is reversed, the value of the enthalpy change (ΔH) should be reversed in sign. For example,

Formation of SO_3 (g)
$2SO_2(g) + O_2(g) \rightarrow 2SO_3(g) \quad \Delta H = -198 kJ$

Decomposition of SO_3 (g)
$2SO_3(g) \rightarrow 2SO_2(g) + O_2(g) \quad \Delta H = 198 kJ$

Rule 2. Multiplication (chemical equation) = multiplication (ΔH)
The value multiplied to the thermochemical equation should be equally applied to the thermochemical value (ΔH). For example if the thermochemical equation is

$2SO_2(g) + O_2(g) \rightarrow 2SO_3(g) \quad \Delta H = -198 kJ \qquad \qquad \text{--- (a)}$

Chapter 1 Thermodynamics

2 × (a) $4SO_2(g) + 2O_2(g) \rightarrow 4SO_3(g)$ $\Delta H = -396 kJ$

½ × (a) $SO_2(g) + ½ O_2(g) \rightarrow SO_3(g)$ $\Delta H = -99 kJ$

Please be careful not to forget to complete the operations on the stoichiometric coefficients and the enthalpy change (ΔH).

The Standard Enthalpy is defined as the "Enthalpy change at standard condition" and the standard condition is defined at 1 atmospheric pressure and 25 [°C] (Usually, a circle superscript to a thermochemical symbol is used to notify the standard condition as ΔH°). The enthalpy of formation of A per mole at standard conditions can be expressed in several different ways sometimes noting the temperature 298 [K] (i.e., 273 + 25 = 298 [K]).

$$\bar{H}^o_{298}(A) \equiv \bar{H}^o_{f,298}(A) \equiv \Delta H^o_f(A)$$

Pleased review two popular ways of obtaining the enthalpy change under the standard condition. 1) Direct method and 2) Hess's law.

1) Direct Method
By using the heat of formation for each substance,
enthalpy change of this reaction (ΔH°$_{rxn}$) is represented as

$$\Delta H^o_{rxn} = \Sigma_{products} \Delta H^o_f - \Sigma_{reactants} \Delta H^o_f \quad \text{(Eqn. 1-27)}$$

Please note that Sum of ΔH°$_f$ of <u>products</u> is subtracted by the sum of ΔH°$_f$ of <u>reactants</u>. Here, the ΔH^o_f is the enthalpy change of formation and this is given from the table.
For the general chemical equation,

$n_A A + n_B B \rightarrow n_C C + n_D D$

you should obtain ΔH$_{rxn}$ as

$$\Delta H = n_C \overline{H_C} + n_D \overline{H_D} - [n_A \overline{H_A} + n_B \overline{H_B}]$$

2) Hess's Law (Indirect Method)

The **Hess's law** is a similar concept introduced in the state function, where the final value of the state function does not depend on the path. The Hess's law is also referred to as the "indirect method of obtaining $\Delta H°_{rxn}$". Since we use the information of the enthalpy change of the chemical reactions which are not directly the same as the targeted chemical reaction. **(Fig. 1-26)** If the final value of an enthalpy change ($\Delta H°_{rxn}$) is about the chemical reaction A→ B, this enthalpy change can be also obtained by detouring the calculation path taking A→ C→ D→ E→ F →B. (It looks like a "vector sum", doesn't t?) If the question requests you to use the Hess's law, many thermochemical equations with known enthalpy changes should be given. The trick of the success for this calculation is that you always need to know which substances should stay in reactants or products side and what should be the stoichiometric coefficients. By multiplying or dividing the coefficients of each thermochemical equation, the provided thermochemical equation should construct and match with the coefficients of the targeted chemical reaction and with the wanted enthalpy change.

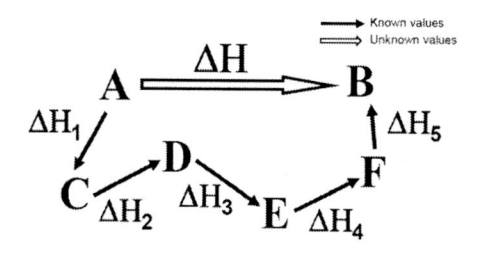

$$\Delta H = \Delta H_1 + \Delta H_2 + \Delta H_3 + \Delta H_4 + \Delta H_5$$

Fig. 1-26 The indirect method for calculating enthalpy change (**Hess's Law**).

Most Common Mistake (6) Why I am not getting a correct ΔH_{rxn}?

The calculation of ΔH_{rxn} is straightforward enough, so that it is very stressful, frustrating, or depressing, if correct value is not obtained. There are small but critical mistakes you should not make (i) People tend to forget the negative sign in front of the summation of the heat of formation of the reactants side. **(Eqn. 1-27)** (ii) The state of the matters, (g), (l), (s), and (aq) should not be overseen. For example, $\Delta H°[H_2O(g)]$, $\Delta H°[H_2O(l)]$, and $\Delta H°[H_2O(s)]$ are all different. Also $\Delta H°[O_2(g)]$ is zero, but $\Delta H°[O_2(l)]$ is not zero. (iii) If you in a hurry, you may forget to multiply the stoichiometric coefficient correctly. (iv) Sometimes, the table lists up the $\Delta H°$ in the unit of kcal/mol instead of kJ/mol, or vice versa. Let's confirm the unit, before you finalize the value. Then, you are ready to go.

> **EXERCISE 1-5**
> The net reaction for sucrose formation in photosynthesis can be written
>
> $$12CO_2(g) + 11H_2O(l) \rightarrow C_{12}H_{22}O_{11}(s) + 12O_2(g)$$
>
> Calculate $\Delta H°$ for the production of 1 [mol] of sucrose at 25 [°C]. Use standard enthalpies of formation.

ANSWER
① $\Delta H°_f[CO_2(g)] = 393.509$ [kJ/mol]
$\Delta H°_f[H_2O(l)] = -285.83$ [kJ/mol]
$\Delta H°_f[C_{12}H_{22}O_{11}(s)] = 2222.1$ [kJ/mol]
② $\Delta H°_f[O_2(g)] = 0$ [kJ/mol]

③ $12CO_2(g) + 11H_2O(l) \rightarrow C_{12}H_{22}O_{11}(s) + 12O_2(g)$
$\Delta H°_f = 2222.1 + 0 \times 12 - [12 \times 393.51 + 11 \times 285.83]$
$= 2222.1 - 1577.99$
$= -644.11$ [kJ/mol]

① Pick the value for "liquid" water but not gas or solid water.
② Yes, it is "0" zero.
③ Check the coefficients and "minus" sign before the term of reactants.

1-5 Temperature Dependence of Enthalpy Change

A bit complicated application of the calculation of ΔH is the temperature dependence. Since reaction can be practically observed at different temperatures, temperature dependence of ΔH_{rxn} is concerning. This dependence indicates that there might be temperatures at which reactions will be suppressed, and those at which they will be enhanced. Especially, some experiments are not easily conducted at the different temperatures and the estimation of the ΔH_{rxn} at different temperature than the standard condition is necessary. The enthalpy change at different of a reaction temperature T_1 and T_2, $\Delta H_{rxn}^{T_1}$ and $\Delta H_{rxn}^{T_2}$ can be given by using the heat capacity of the reaction, ΔC_P

$$\Delta H_{rxn}^{T_2} - \Delta H_{rxn}^{T_1} = \Delta C_P(T_2 - T_1) \qquad \text{(Eqn. 1-28)}$$

$$\Delta C_P = C_{P,C} + C_{P,D} - C_{P,A} - C_{P,B}$$

$$\Delta C_P = n_C \overline{C_{P,C}} + n_D \overline{C_{P,D}} - \left[n_A \overline{C_{P,A}} + n_B \overline{C_{P,B}} \right]$$

Thus, general expression for ΔC_P is

$$\Delta C_P = \sum_{products} \Delta C_P - \sum_{reactants} \Delta C_P \qquad \text{(Eqn. 1-29)}$$

Only concern I have here is if you look carefully at the definition of the ΔC_P, which is a bit complex and some care needs to be taken when you solve for the problems.

EXERCISE 1-6

Estimate the ΔH if the following reaction (oxidation of glucose to ethanol)

$C_6H_{12}O_6(s) \rightarrow 2CH_3CH_2OH(l) + 2CO_2(g)$ $\Delta H° = -66.6$ [kJ]

is carried out by a thermophilic bacterium at 80 [°C] and 1 [atm].
(Calculate ΔH at 80 [°C] for 1 [mol])
[C_p for ethanol(l) = 111.5 [J K^{-1} mol^{-1}], for glucose(s) = 210 [J K^{-1} mol^{-1}], and for CO_2 (g) = 37.1 [J K^{-1} mol^{-1}]

ANSWER

❶ $\Delta H_{rxn}^{T_2} - \Delta H_{rxn}^{T_1} = \Delta C_P(T_2 - T_1)$ (Eqn. 1-28)

Where

$\Delta C_P = n_C \overline{C_{P,C}} + n_D \overline{C_{P,D}} - [n_A \overline{C_{P,A}} + n_B \overline{C_{P,B}}]$ (Eqn. 1-29)

and $\Delta H = n_C \overline{H_C} + n_D \overline{H_D} - [n_A \overline{H_A} + n_B \overline{H_B}]$

C_p for ethanol(l) = 111.5 [J K^{-1} mol^{-1}], for glucose(s) = 210 [J K^{-1} mol^{-1}], and for CO_2 = 37.1 [J K^{-1} mol^{-1}]

$C_6H_{12}O_6(s) \rightarrow 2CH_3CH_2OH(l) + 2CO_2(g)$ $\Delta H° = -66.6$ [kJ]

❷ $\Delta C_P = 2 \times 111.5 + 2 \times 37.1 - 210 = 87.2$ [J K^{-1} mol^{-1}]

❸ and

$\Delta H = -66600$[J] + 1 [mol] $\times 87.2$ [J K^{-1} mol^{-1}] $\times (80 - 25)$[K] = -61.8 [kJ]

❶ Good luck with ΔC_P
❷ Minus sign in front of the term of reactants.
❸ Minus sign in front of the term of reactants.

1-6 The Change of Internal Energy of a Reaction

As you already saw in (**Eqn. 1-26**) internal energy change, ΔE, and enthalpy change of reaction, ΔH_{rxn}, has a certain relationship. Usually ΔH_{rxn} is obtained for a given reaction, and ΔE is derived from ΔH_{rxn}. Especially, the ΔE_{rxn} becomes a bit simpler **if the reaction involves a gas** (note this statement). The (**Eqn. 1-30**) is good for the case only when the gas is involved) in either products or the reactants at a constant pressure. Under the constant pressure, if the reaction involves the gaseous species, we can see more specific part of reaction

$$\Delta E_{rxn} = \Delta H_{rxn} - (\Delta n_g)RT \qquad \text{(Eqn. 1-30)}$$

Chapter 1 Thermodynamics

The definition of the Δn_g is that a number of moles of <u>gaseous</u> products – number of moles of <u>gaseous</u> reactants. Thus, the symbol Δ does not cover over all nRT but only on the n.

☹ MCM Most Common Mistake (7) Am I understanding Δ(PV)?

If you see $\Delta(xy)$ this for the first time, you may wonder about the $\Delta(PV)$. Let's start form the definition of the change Δx, which is
$\Delta x = x_{final} - x_{initial}$,
Thus,
$\Delta(xy) = (xy)_{final} - (xy)_{initial}$,
In a similar way,
$\Delta(PV) = (PV)_{final} - (PV)_{initial} = P_{final} V_{final} - P_{initial} V_{initial}$. The most common mistake may be that $\Delta(PV)$ is interpreted as $P\Delta V$ or $(\Delta P)V$. Of course, $\Delta(PV)$ becomes $P\Delta V$ for a constant P or becomes $(\Delta P)V$ under the constant volume, V.

☹ MCM Most Common Mistake (8)-Why I cannot calculate Δn_g correctly?

If you are chemistry major, you may make a mistake which non-chemistry majors do not. You may think that the definition of Δn_g is (number of moles of products) –(number of moles of reactants), which we teach in chemistry. However, Δn_g is not just the difference in number of moles between products and reactants.

Δn_g = (number of moles of <u>gaseous</u> products) – (number of moles of <u>gaseous</u> reactants).

That is we are only interested in the gaseous molecules or atoms involved in the reactants and the products. Then, what happens if we do not have any gaseous species in both products and reactants. Then, $\Delta n_g = 0$. How about if we have a gaseous reactants but no gaseous products. In this case, $\Delta n_g < 0$, and Δn_g can be negative or positive.(Please try **EXERCISE 1-7**) One more last thing. In (**Eqn. 1-26**), ΔE is always bigger than ΔH. Is this true for the case of reaction? Which is bigger, ΔE_{rxn} or ΔH_{rxn}? Well, it depends on Δn_g.

$$\Delta E_{rxn} - \Delta H_{rxn} = -(\Delta n_g)RT \qquad \text{(Eqn. 1-30)}$$

Thus, $\Delta E_{rxn} < \Delta H_{rxn}$ if $\Delta n_g > 0$. On the other hand, $\Delta E_{rxn} > \Delta H_{rxn}$ if $\Delta n_g < 0$. However, you will see that difference is small as seen in **EXERCISE 1-7**.

Chapter 1 Thermodynamics

EXERCISE 1-7
Calculate the ΔE_{rxn} of the following reaction.

$$C(s) + \tfrac{1}{2}O_2(g) \rightarrow CO(g) \qquad \Delta H_r^\circ = -110.5 \text{ [kJ mol}^{-1}\text{]}$$

ANSWER

❶ $\Delta n_g = 1 - \tfrac{1}{2} = \tfrac{1}{2}$
For 1 [mol] of CO(g) to be produced

❷ $\Delta H_{rxn}^\circ = -110.5$ [kJ/mol]

❸ R = 8.315 [J mol^{-1} K^{-1}]

❹ T = 20 + 273.15 [K]

$\Delta E = \Delta H - RT\Delta n_g$
= −110.5 [kJ] − 8.315 [J mol^{-1} K^{-1}] × (1/2) [mol] × 298[K]
= −110.5 [kJ] − 1.238 [kJ]

❺ = −111.7 [kJ]

You will be surprised or not surprised to see that the difference between ΔE and ΔH is somewhat miniscule. You should note that the change between internal energy and enthalpy change is not that significantly different.

❶ Pick only gaseous substance for calculation.
❷ Pick the value directly from the given equation.
❸ Check the unit [J mol^{-1} K^{-1}] for the gas constant.
❹ Temperature is in kelvins unit.
❺ You see. $\Delta H_{rxn}^\circ \sim \Delta E_{rxn}^\circ$

1-7 Second Law of Thermodynamics and Entropy

Now, we will see unique and important thermochemical value, entropy (S). The "entropy' provides a measure of a disorganization, disorderness, or randomness. So the more the system is disorganized or randomized, the more entropy value increases. A mathematical corresponds to the degree of this randomness must be

$$S = k_B \ln \Omega \qquad \text{(Eqn. 1-31)}$$

Here, Ω is number of the states, and the k_B is the Boltzmann's constant. Using the number of the states is very useful to understand how disorder is increased. If the situation is more disordered, you need to more states to express that condition.(The disordered situation contains the situations which are not present at the ordered situation.) While the above formula in (**Eqn. 1-31**) clearly shows a concept of an entropy, we will not explore this formula any further. You need to wait until Chapter 11 for more details. Instead, we will introduce more thermochemical formula of entropy.

A good example of entropy for biology or biochemistry students can be destruction or construction of a double helix from a base pair. **(Fig. 1-21)** The base-pair formation of DNA is the transformation from an individual nuclear acid to the highly organized helical structure. If a helical structure is more highly organized structure, a direction of entropy increase is the direction of destruction of a helical structure ($\Delta S > 0$). In the case of double strand to single strand transition of DNA under 1 M NaCl solution at near room temperature and pH~7, ΔS is known to be 88 [J K^{-1} mol^{-1}]. A transformation in the RNA from double-strand to single strand possess ΔS as 104 [J K^{-1} mol^{-1}]/ base **(Fig. 1-19)** Knowing that ΔS is a positive value for a transition from double strand to a single strand, we can get a sense that a preferable direction of a transformation is from a helical structure (highly ordered structure) to single strands (more disordered structure) with positive ΔS.

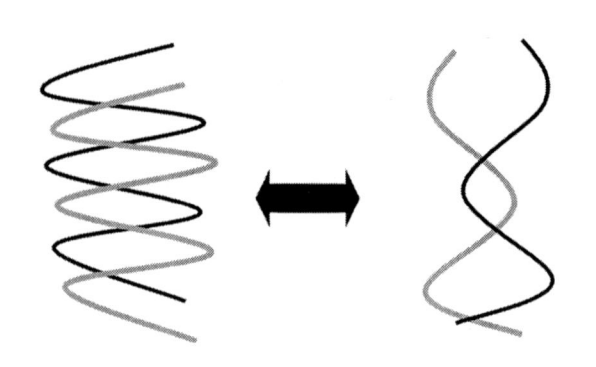

Fig. 1-21 The destruction or construction of a helix.

The concept of "entropy" is not explained by the **First law of the thermodynamics** which states that "Energy is conserved during a reaction".

$$\Delta E = q + w \quad \text{(Eqn. 1-1)}$$

The above formula does not tell which way is a preferable direction of a reaction (i.e., if reaction takes place spontaneously or not). The **Second law of thermodynamics** states that

"The entropy of an isolated system can never decrease".

Thus, it clearly indicates which direction the reaction proceeds. The entropy is one of the thermodynamical indicator of spontaneousness.

The entropy for isothermal process is defined as

$$\Delta S = \int dS = \int \frac{dq_{rev}}{T} = \frac{q_{rev}}{T} \quad \text{(Eqn. 1-32)}$$

Please note that the unit of the entropy is [J/K]. Since entropy is the state function, the entropy change (ΔS) does not depend on the paths. **The Second Law of Thermodynamics** states that

"Entropy is not conserved".

Thus,

$$\Delta S(system) + \Delta S(surroundings) \geq 0$$

$$\Delta S(isolated\ system) \geq 0 \quad \text{(Eqn. 1-33)}$$

Chapter 1 Thermodynamics

The standard molar entropy ($\overline{S^o}$ or S_m^o) is defined under 25 [°C] and 1 [atm] for one mole of substance. The entropy change for a reaction at the standard state is noted as $\overline{\Delta S^o}$ or ΔS_m^o. **The Third Law of Thermodynamics** states

> "The entropy of any pure and perfect crystal is zero at 0 [K]."

1-8 Entropy Change in Chemical Reaction and Its Temperature Dependence

Let's set a general chemical reaction as:

$$n_A A + n_B B \rightarrow n_C C + n_D D$$

For obtaining the entropy change of the reaction, ΔS_{rxn}^o, let's take the same approach of obtaining the enthalpy change of the reaction, ΔH_{rxn}^o. The entropy change of the above reaction is expressed as a difference between the total entropy change of the products and those of the reactants.

$$\Delta S_{rxn}^o = n_C \overline{S_C} + n_D \overline{S_D} - [n_A \overline{S_A} + n_B \overline{S_B}]$$

A general expression of ΔS_{rxn}^o is

$$\Delta S_{rxn}^o = \sum_{products} \Delta S_f^o - \sum_{reactants} \Delta S_f^o \qquad \text{(Eqn. 1-34)}$$

EXERCISE 1-8

$2H_2(g) + O_2(g) \rightarrow 2H_2O(g)$
Calculate $\Delta S^0{}_{298}$

ANSWER

❶ $\Delta S = 2\overline{S_{H_2O(g)}} - \{2\overline{S_{H_2(g)}} + \overline{S_{O_2(g)}}\}$

❷ $\overline{S_{H_2O(g)}} = 188.72 \ [JK^{-1}mol^{-1}]$
$\overline{S_{H_2(g)}} = 130.57 \ [JK^{-1}mol^{-1}]$
$\overline{S_{O_2(g)}} = 205.04 \ [JK^{-1}mol^{-1}]$

❸ $\Delta S = -88.74 \ [J/K]$

---

❶ Don't forget coefficient "2" in front of $S_{H_2(g)}$ and minus sign before the term of reactants
❷ Pick the value of gaseous water not for liquid or solid water.
❸ The unit is [J/K].

The temperature effect of enthalpy change, ΔH^o_{rxn}, exhibited a clear proportionality in temperature increase (if the heat capacity is independent of temperature.) How about the temperature dependence of the entropy? Since entropy change, ΔS^o_{rxn} is a critical indicator of a direction of a reaction, temperature effect to the direction of a reaction can be predicted. The temperature dependence can be examined under constant pressure or under constant volume.

$$\Delta S = \int_{T_1}^{T_2} \frac{C dT}{T} = C \ln \frac{T_2}{T_1}$$

$C = C_p$ (at constant pressure)

$C = C_v$ (at constant volume) **(Eqn. 1-35)**

At constant pressure, the entropy change is given with heat capacity under constant pressure, C_P, and at constant volume, the entropy change is given with the heat capacity under constant volume, C_V. Here, please note that we assume C_P and C_V are independent of temperature while it may not be correct in reality. When checking your calculation, it may be useful to know that $T_2 > T_1$, so the entropy change should be positive.

$$\Delta S = C \ln \frac{T_2}{T_1} > 0 \qquad T_2 > T_1$$

(The heat capacities are always positive.)

EXERCISE 1-9
If a breath of air, with a volume of 250 [mL] at −10 [°C], is drawn into the lungs and comes to 37 [°C] while the pressure remains 1 atm, calculate ΔS of the air. (C_V = 21.7 [J K^{-1} mol^{-1}]). Assume that air is an ideal gas.

ANSWER

❶ $C_P = n\overline{C_P}$

Here, n indicates that number of moles.

❷ The n is calculated by the ideal gas law as

n= PV /RT

❸ =(1 [atm] ×0.25 [L])/(0.082 [atm L mol^{-1} K^{-1}] ×263 [K])

= 0.0116 [mol]

❹ $\Delta S = C_P \ln \frac{T_2}{T_1}$ (Eqn. 1-35)

❺ $\overline{C_P} = \overline{C_V} + R$ (Eqn. 1-19)

❻ R = 8.31 [J mol^{-1} K^{-1}]

Thus, $\overline{C_P}$=21.7+8.3 = 30 [J mol^{-1} K^{-1}]

❸ T_1 = 263 [K] and T_2= 310 [K]

❼ $\Delta S = (0.0116)(30 [J K^{-1} mol^{-1}]) \ln \frac{310\ [K]}{263\ [K]}$

❽ ☞	$\Delta S = 0.0572 \ [J/K]$
❶ ☞	Always check the unit of C_P [J/K] or $\overline{C_P}$ [J mol^{-1} K^{-1}]
❷ ☞	People seem to forget about calculating the number of moles!
❸ ☞	Temperature is in Kelvins unit.
❹ ☞	C = C$_P$
❺ ☞	C$_P$ needs to be calculated from C$_V$.
❻ ☞	The gas constant for this case is R=8.31 [J mol^{-1} K^{-1}]
❼ ☞	Watch for the calculation of natural log
❽ ☞	Unit is [J/K]

MCM Most Common Mistake (9)-Why I am not getting correct ΔS?

Most common mistake people make for calculating the temperature dependence of an entropy is the misusage of the gas constant R. If you need to calculate the $\overline{C_P}$ from $\overline{C_V}$, the R in (**Eqn. 1-19**) is in the unit of [J mol^{-1} K^{-1}]. The chemistry students are so used to the gas constant R= 0.082 [atm·L mol^{-1} K^{-1}], but here you need to use R = 8.314 [J mol^{-1} K^{-1}]. Always "keep an eye on the unit". (If you are wondering, you can derive 8.314 [J mol^{-1} K^{-1}] from 0.082 [atm L mol^{-1} K^{-1}] by multiplying the conversion factor 1 [atm·L] = 101.3 [J].) In physical chemistry, we often use a gas constant in the unit of [atm L mol^{-1} K^{-1}]. Please recall the comment made here when you see a gas constant is used for calculating the energy. The mistake on the value of R is "the most common mistake among most common mistakes"!! Another very minor mistake in calculating the ΔS is that temperature was used in [°C] unit instead of [K] unit. Once again, "keep an eye on the unit".

Now we are ready to apply temperature dependence of entropy "for the reaction" (a bit complicated). As imagined naturally, the reaction can take place at temperatures other than the standard condition 25 [°C], there are so many cases that effect of the temperature on the direction of the reaction is not easily predicted. Let's examine the temperature dependence of the entropy change in the reaction. While the derivation of the formula are preferred to be shown at the end of each chapter under the section of "How did you get these equations?-The derivation of selected equations.", I will go through the process of obtaining the temperature dependence of entropy in this section. The process used below is very important and popular steps taking advantage of the character of the state function (i.e., the value of state function does not depend on the path.)

Let's consider the entropy change of the reaction at new temperature T$_2$, ΔS°(T$_2$), is given by assuming that entropy change of the reaction at temperature T$_1$ (ΔS°(T$_1$)) is known. Usually, T$_1$ is the temperature at the standard condition, T = 25 [°C]. As an example the reaction A➔ B is used. (**Fig. 1-20**). The path shown in **Fig. 1-20** indicates that

Path (iv) = Path (i) + Path (ii) +Path (iii)

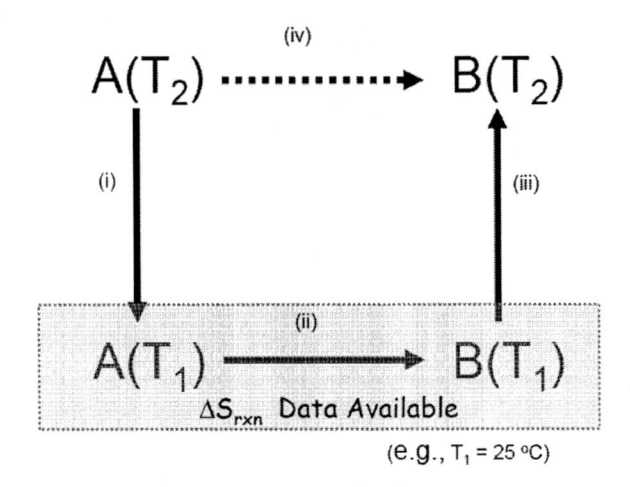

Fig. 1-22 The schematic diagram for obtaining the temperature dependence in entropy change.

The entropy change in Path (iv) is the entropy change of the reaction at T_2, $\Delta S^o_{rxn,(T_2)}$, which is what is wanted in this calculation. Thus, the value of $\Delta S^o_{rxn,(T_2)}$ is obtained by adding the ΔS^o of each spot in the root of $A(T_2) \rightarrow A(T_1) \rightarrow B(T_1) \rightarrow B(T_2)$. The heat capacity of A and B at constant pressure are noted by $\Delta C_P(A)$ and $\Delta C_P(B)$. They are assumed to be independent of temperature.

Path (i): The entropy change in $A(T_2) \rightarrow A(T_1)$

$$\Delta S^o(A) = \int_{T_2}^{T_1} \frac{C_P(A)dT}{T} = \Delta C_P(A) \ln \frac{T_1}{T_2}$$

Path (ii): The entropy change in $A(T_1) \rightarrow B(T_1)$

$$\Delta S^o_{rxn,(T_1)} = \Delta S^o_{T_1}(B) - \Delta S^o_{T_1}(A)$$

Path (iii): The entropy change in $B(T_1) \rightarrow B(T_2)$

$$\Delta S^o(B) = \int_{T_1}^{T_2} \frac{C_P(B)dT}{T} = \Delta C_P(B) \ln \frac{T_2}{T_1}$$

Let's add all up to calculate the $\Delta S^o_{rxn,(T_2)}$

Path (iv): The entropy change in

$A(T_2) \rightarrow B(T_2) = A(T_2) \rightarrow A(T_1) \rightarrow B(T_1) \rightarrow B(T_2)$

$$\Delta S^o_{rxn,(T_2)} = \Delta S^o_{rxn,(T_1)} + \Delta C_P \ln \frac{T_2}{T_1} \qquad \text{(Eqn. 1-36)}$$

Chapter 1 Thermodynamics

Here, please very careful about the definition of ΔC_P,

$$\Delta C_P = \Delta C_P(B) - \Delta C_P(A)$$

The heat capacity in the chemical reaction was defined in (**Eqn. 1-29**).

$$\Delta C_P = \sum_{products} \Delta C_P - \sum_{reactants} \Delta C_P \qquad \text{(Eqn. 1-29)}$$

EXERCISE 1-10
$C_2H_5OH(l) \rightarrow C_2H_6(g) + \frac{1}{2} O_2(g)$
Calculate $\Delta S°_{323}$.

$C_{p,m}$(ethanol) = 111.5 [J mol⁻¹ K⁻¹]
$C_{P,m}$(oxygen) = 29.3 [J mol⁻¹ K⁻¹]
$C_{P,m}$(ethane) = 52.3 [J mol⁻¹ K⁻¹]

ANSWER

❶ From the table,

$\Delta \bar{S}^o_{298}[C_2H_5OH(l)] = 160.67$ [J mol⁻¹ K⁻¹]

$\Delta \bar{S}^o_{298}[C_2H_6(g)] = 229.60$ [J mol⁻¹ K⁻¹]

$\Delta \bar{S}^o_{298}[O_2(g)] = 205.14$ [J mol⁻¹ K⁻¹]

❷ ΔS°₂₉₈ = ½ (205.14 [J/K]) +229.60 [J/K]–160.67 [J/K] = 171.5 [J/K]

❸ $\Delta C_P = \left[\bar{C}_{P,C_2H_6(g)} + \frac{1}{2}\bar{C}_{P,O_2(g)}\right] - \bar{C}_{P,C_2H_5OH(l)}$

❷ = {52.3 [J/K] + (1/2) [mol] (29.3 [J mol⁻¹ K⁻¹])} – 111.5 [J/K]

❹ = – 44.55 [J/K]

$$\Delta S^o_{rxn,(T_2)} = \Delta S^o_{rxn,(T_1)} + \Delta C_P \ln \frac{T_2}{T_1} \qquad \text{(Eqn. 1-36)}$$

❺ $\Delta S^o_{(T_2=323\,K)} = \Delta S^o_{(T_1=298\,K)} + \Delta C_P \ln \frac{323\,[K]}{298\,[K]}$

= 171.5 [J/K] +(-44.55)(0.0805) [J/K]

=171.5 [J/K] – 3.588 [J/K]

❻ =167.9 [J/K]

---

❶ The unit is [J mol⁻¹ K⁻¹]

❷ Don't forget coefficients and the negative sign in front of the term for the reactants.

❸ This is easily forgotten!!

❹ Don't worry for the negative value.

❺ T₁ = 298 [K] and T₂=323 [K] (Kelvins unit)

❻ Since ΔC_P is negative, $\Delta S^o_{(T_2=323\,[K])} > \Delta S^o_{(T_1=298\,[K])}$

Chapter 1 Thermodynamics

In order to emphasize the difference in temperature dependence, here I list up and repeat the temperature dependence of entropy and enthalpy together for a comparison.

$$\Delta H_{rxn}^{T_2} - \Delta H_{rxn}^{T_1} = \Delta C_P(T_2 - T_1) \qquad \text{(Eqn. 1-28)}$$

$$\Delta S_{rxn,(T_2)}^o = \Delta S_{rxn,(T_1)}^o + \Delta C_P \ln \frac{T_2}{T_1} \qquad \text{(Eqn. 1-36)}$$

$$\Delta C_P = \Delta C_P(B) - \Delta C_P(A)$$

Pressure Dependence of Entropy

As a supplementary material, the pressure dependence of entropy change is described.

$$dS = \frac{dq_{rev}}{T} = \frac{dE - dw_{rev}}{T}$$

$$= \frac{-dw_{rev}}{T}$$

$$= \frac{PdV}{T}$$

(dw$_{rev}$ = − PdV)

Since, PV= nRT

$$d(PV) = d(nRT)$$
$$PdV + VdP = nRdT$$
$$PdV + VdP = 0 \text{ (at constant temperature, dT=0)}$$
$$PdV = -VdP.$$

Thus,

$$dS = -\frac{VdP}{T}$$

$$= -\frac{nRdP}{P}$$

(pV =nRT)

Integrating both sides,

$$\int dS = -\int \frac{nR}{P} dP$$

$$\Delta S = -nR \int_{P_1}^{P_2} \frac{dP}{P}$$

$$= -nR \ln \frac{P_2}{P_1}$$

30

Chapter 1

How did you get these equations?
-The derivation of selected equations.

(Eqn. 1-11) $\quad q_P = n\overline{C_P}(T_2 - T_1)$

For any a substance with heat capacity, C_P, at constant pressure, the heat q_P is given by

$$q_P = \int_{T_1}^{T_2} C_P\, dT = C_P(T_2 - T_1) \qquad \text{(Eqn. 1-8)}$$

Since heat capacity is given by

$$C_P = n\bar{C}_P$$

where n is the number of moles and $\bar{C}_P$ is the molar heat capacity at constant pressure.

$$q_P = n\overline{C_P}(T_2 - T_1) \qquad \text{(Eqn. 1-11)}$$

(Eqn. 1-12) $\quad w_P = -P(V_2 - V_1) = -nR(T_2 - T_1)$

If the treated gas is approximated as an ideal gas where the ideal gas law states

$$PV = nRT$$

By substituting V=nRT/P to the V

$$w_P = -nR(T_2 - T_1) \qquad \text{(Eqn. 1-12)}$$

(Eqn. 1-13) $\quad q_V = n\overline{C_V}(T_2 - T_1)$

For any a substance with heat capacity, C_V, at constant volume, the heat produced under constant volume (q_V) is given by

$$q_V = \int_{T_1}^{T_2} C_V\, dT = C_V(T_2 - T_1) \qquad \text{(Eqn. 1-8)}$$

Since heat capacity is given by

$$C_V = n\bar{C}_V$$

where n is the number of moles and $\bar{C}_V$ is the molar heat capacity at constant volume.

$$q_V = n\overline{C_V}(T_2 - T_1) \qquad \text{(Eqn. 1-13)}$$

Chapter 1 Thermodynamics

(Eqn. 1-14) $\quad w_V = 0$

Since the work is between no volume range,

$$w_V = -\int_V^V P_{ex} dV = -\int_V^V \frac{nRT}{V} dV = 0 \quad \text{(Eqn. 1-14)}$$

(Eqn. 1-15) $\quad q_T = -w_T$

Under constant temperature (isothermal process), the change in the internal energy is zero i.e., $\Delta E = 0$. Using $\Delta E = q+w$,

$$w_T = -q_T \quad \text{(Eqn. 1-15)}$$

With the help of the value calculated in (Eqn. 1-16), the value for an isothermal expansion from V_1 to V_2 ($V_2 > V_1$) of an ideal gas is

$$q_T = nRT \ln \frac{V_2}{V_1} = nRT \ln \frac{P_1}{P_2}$$

The last term is derived using an ideal gas law relationship $PV = nRT$.

(Eqn. 1-16) $\quad w_T = -nRT \ln \frac{V_2}{V_1}$

Instead of integrating the pressure as a function of volume, pressure should be represented by the ideal gas law $P=nRT/V$.

$$w_T = -\int_{V_1}^{V_2} P_{ex} \, dV$$
$$= -\int_{V_1}^{V_2} \frac{nRT}{V} dV$$
$$= -nRT \ln \frac{V_2}{V_1} \quad \text{(Eqn. 1-16)}$$

(Eqn. 1-18) $\quad w_a = \frac{K(V_2^{1-\gamma} - V_1^{1-\gamma})}{1-\gamma}$

The work under the adiabatic condition is not easy and straight forward. So the detail derivation process is not introduced here. The adiabatic condition is defined as

$$PV^\gamma = K$$

K is a constant and γ is called as the adiabatic index and defined as

$$\gamma = \frac{C_P}{C_V} = \frac{\alpha + 1}{\alpha}$$

Chapter 1 Thermodynamics

Here, C_P is the specific heat for constant pressure, and C_V is the specific heat for constant volume. In this definition, α represents the number of degrees of freedom divided by 2 (i.e., 3/2 for monatomic gas and it is 5/2 for diatomic gas). The change in internal energy of a system, measured from state 1 to state 2, is equal to

$$\Delta U = \alpha R n_2 T_2 - \alpha R n_1 T_1 = \alpha R (n_2 T_2 - n_1 T_1)$$

The work done by the pressure-volume changes as a result from this process is

$$w = \int_{V_1}^{V_2} P \, dV$$

Under the adiabatic process,

$$\Delta U + W = 0$$

$$PV^\gamma = K = P_1 V_1^\gamma$$

The expression of the above can be arranged as,

$$P = P_1 \left(V_1 / V \right)^\gamma$$

By substituting this pressure to the work, W,

$$w_a = \int_{V_1}^{V_2} P \, dV = -\int_{V_1}^{V_2} P_1 \left(V_1 / V \right)^\gamma dV$$

$$= P_1 V_1^\gamma (1-\gamma) V^{1-\gamma} \Big|_{V_1}^{V_2}$$

$$= P_1 V_1^\gamma \left\{ V_2^{1-\gamma} - V_1^{1-\gamma} \Big/ 1-\gamma \right\}$$

Since $PV^\gamma = K$,

$$P_1 V_1^\gamma = K$$

$$= K \left\{ V_2^{1-\gamma} - V_1^{1-\gamma} \Big/ 1-\gamma \right\}$$

Chapter 1 Thermodynamics

$$w_a = \frac{K(V_2^{1-\gamma} - V_1^{1-\gamma})}{1-\gamma} \quad \text{(Eqn. 1-18)}$$

(Eqn. 1-26) $\quad \Delta E_v = \Delta H_v - RT$

In general, the work involved in a phase change ($w_{a \to b}$) where the phase changes from phase-a to phase-b is represented as

$$w_{a \to b} = P \Delta V_{a \to b}$$

Here the volume change is the involvement of the volume between different phases and

$$\Delta V_{a \to b} = V(Phase\ b) - V(Phase\ a)$$

Then, the thermochemical relationship between enthalpy change ($\Delta H_{a \to b}$) and internal energy change ($\Delta E_{a \to b}$) is shown as

$$\Delta E_{a \to b} = \Delta H_{a \to b} - P \Delta V_{a \to b}$$

The above relationship is from (**Eqn. 1-10**) under a constant pressure P. Please note that the enthalpy change ($\Delta H_{a \to b}$) is given as H(phase b) – H(phase a) and the internal energy change ($\Delta E_{a \to b}$) is given by E(phase b) – E(phase a). If one of the phases involved in the phase change is a gas (i.e., sublimation, condensation, and vaporization), the following simplification will be possible. If the vaporization process takes place under constant pressure P with enthalpy change (ΔH_v) and internal energy change (ΔE_v), they can be related as:

$$\Delta E_v = \Delta H_v - P[V(g) - V(l)]$$

Here, the V(l) and the V(g) are the volumes of liquid phase and the gas phase, respectively. Comparing the gaseous volume, the volume of the liquid is approximated to be negligible. Therefore, the formula given below is approximated as

$$P[V(g) - V(l)] \cong PV(g)$$

Using an ideal gas equation (PV =nRT, n=1) by

$$PV(g) = RT$$

Thus,
$\Delta E_v = \Delta H_v - RT \quad$ **(Eqn. 1-26)**

34

(Eqn. 1-28) $\quad \Delta H_{T_2} - \Delta H_{T_1} = \Delta C_P(T_2 - T_1)$

The general expression for the enthalpy change of a reaction (ΔH_{rxn}) is,

$$\Delta H_{rxn} = n_C \overline{H_C} + n_D \overline{H_D} - [n_A \overline{H_A} + n_B \overline{H_B}]$$

By taking a derivative of the enthalpy change as a function of temperature,

$$\frac{d\Delta H_{rxn}}{dT} = n_C \left[\frac{d\overline{H_C}}{dT}\right] + n_D \left[\frac{d\overline{H_D}}{dT}\right] - \left[n_A \left[\frac{d\overline{H_A}}{dT}\right] + n_B \left[\frac{d\overline{H_B}}{dT}\right]\right]$$

The coefficients n_A, n_B, n_C and n_D are not temperature dependent. Please recall that

$$\frac{dH}{dT} = C_P$$

Thus,

$$\frac{d\Delta H}{dT} = n_C \left[\frac{d\overline{H_C}}{dT}\right] + n_D \left[\frac{d\overline{H_D}}{dT}\right] - \left[n_A \left[\frac{d\overline{H_A}}{dT}\right] + n_B \left[\frac{d\overline{H_B}}{dT}\right]\right]$$
$$= n_C \overline{C_{P,C}} + n_D \overline{C_{P,D}} - [n_A \overline{C_{P,A}} + n_B \overline{C_{P,B}}]$$

Now, let's define a parameter ΔC_P as

$$\frac{d\Delta H}{dT} = n_C \overline{C_{P,C}} + n_D \overline{C_{P,D}} - [n_A \overline{C_{P,A}} + n_B \overline{C_{P,B}}]$$
$$= C_{P,C} + C_{P,D} - C_{P,A} - C_{P,B} = \Delta C_P$$

By integrating both sides of the above formula,

$$\int_{\Delta H_{T_1}}^{\Delta H_{T_2}} d\Delta H = \int_{T_1}^{T_2} \Delta C_P dT$$

If the ΔC_P is assumed not depend on the temperature
$\Delta H_{T_2} - \Delta H_{T_1} = \Delta C_P(T_2 - T_1)$

(Eqn. 1-30) $\quad \Delta E_{rxn} = \Delta H_{rxn} - (\Delta n_g)RT$

Let's recall the relationship between ΔE and ΔH.

$$\Delta H = \Delta E + \Delta(PV)$$

Here, P is not assumed to be a constant and the term of $\Delta(PV)$ needs to be carefully treated. A real meaning of the $\Delta(PV)$ is therefore, $\Delta(PV) =$

$P_{final} V_{final} - P_{initial} V_{initial}$. In the case of the chemical reaction the value $\Delta(PV)$ is defined as: $\Delta(PV)$= PV(products) –PV(reactants), where the final stage is the products and the initial stage is the reactants. However, for most of the cases, the pressure is kept constant during the reaction takes place. Thus, the formula can be re-phrased as:

$\Delta(PV)$= P(V_{final} –$V_{initial}$) = PΔV.

So we may use the formula below in most cases of the reaction undergoes at constant pressure (e.g., P = 1 atm for the most cases.)

$$\Delta E_{rxn} = \Delta H_{rxn} - P\Delta V$$

The volume change for the reaction is $\Delta V = V_{product} - V_{reactant}$. For an ideal gas, PV = nRT is used, and V = nRT/P. Thus,
$\Delta V = n_{g,\,product}$ (RT/P)- $n_{g,\,reactant}$(RT/P)= (RT/P) [$n_{g,\,product} - n_{g,\,reactant}$]

Here, the number of moles of gaseous product or gaseous reactant is given by the symbols of $n_{g,\,product}$ and $n_{g,\,reactant}$, respectively. Let's define

Δn_g= [$n_{g,\,product} - n_{g,\,reactant}$]

Here, the Δn_g is a change in the chemical amount of gases per mole of reaction, since the volume of the gaseous substances are only considered in this calculation and the ideal gas law is applied for only gaseous substances. Therefore, you will see the relation ship

$$P\Delta V = RT\Delta n_g$$
and

$$\Delta E_{rxn} = \Delta H_{rxn} - (\Delta n_g)RT \qquad \text{(Eqn. 1-30)}$$

(Eqn. 1-32) $\qquad \Delta S = \int dS = \int \frac{dq_{rev}}{T} = \frac{q_{rev}}{T}$

Carnot Cycle

In order to further understand how the entropy or concept of the entropy is derived, I have to introduce an important but a bit tedious thermo cycle, Carnot Cycle in this section. Therefore, this section becomes a bit lengthy.(Sorry!) You can skip this section if you only need to know how to use the formula for the entropy change, such as (**Eqn. 1-32**). In this an ideal thermochemical cycle, the energy (work) is conducted as heat transfer takes place between two different temperatures T_{cold} and T_{hot} ($T_{cold} < T_{hot}$). There are four reversible steps (Step I, II, II, and IV) to complete the cycle between four states: state 1 (P_1, V_1), state 2(P_2, V_2), state3 (P_3, V_3) ,and state 4 (P_4, V_4). **(Fig. 1-23)** As a simple picture of this cycle, please imagine a steam driven piston repeats moving up and down.

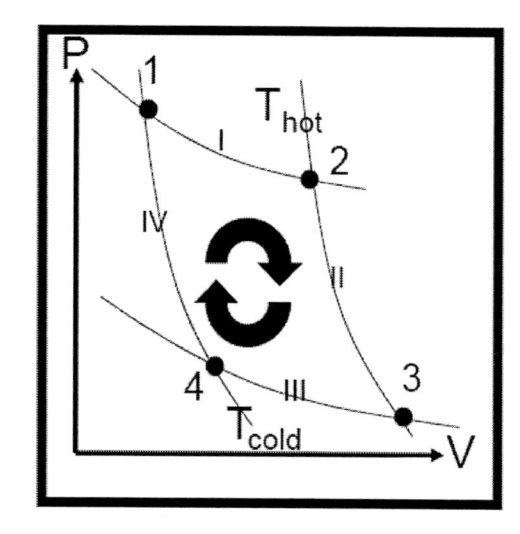

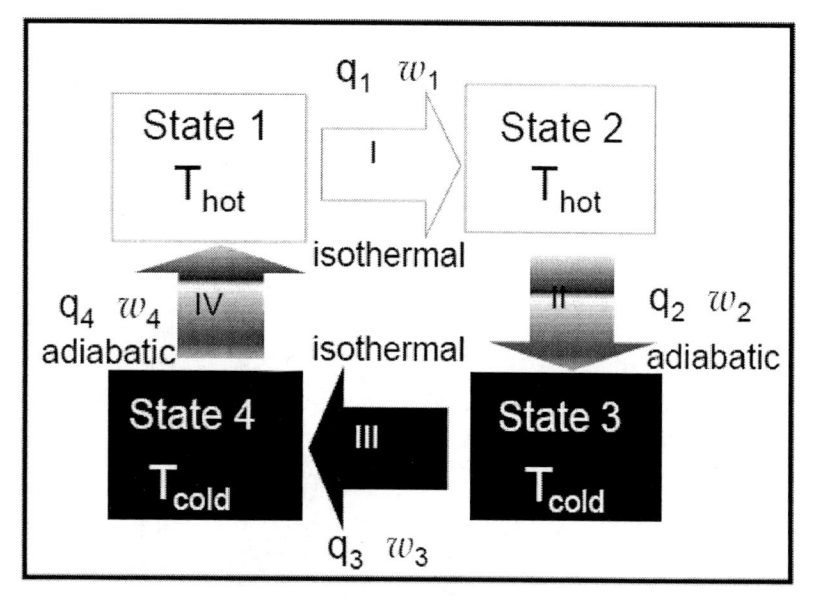

Fig. 1-23 The Carnot cycle in PV diagram (top) and the description of four states/steps.(bottom).

The goal of this section is to derive a thermodynamically relationship on entropy by examining the heat and work involved in this heat cycle.

Step I. Isothermal Reversible Expansion
The first process is an isothermal reversible expansion where the temperature is remained the same as T_{hot} and the volume increases (expands) as the process progresses.**(Fig. 1-24a)** The work of this step I is (w_I) obtained from (**Eqn. 1-16**)

$$w_I = -\int_{V_1}^{V_2} PdV = -nRT_{hot}\ln\frac{V_2}{V_1}$$

An internal energy change (ΔE) for an ideal gas depends on temperature, and ΔE=0 for an isothermal process. According to (**Eqn. 1-1**)

$$\Delta E = q_I + w_I$$

Here, q_I is the heat involved in step I. By replacing ΔE=0,

$$q_1 = -w_1 = nRT_{hot}\ln\frac{V_2}{V_1}$$

Step II. Adiabatic Reversible Expansion
The adiabatic process takes place from state 2 to state 3. (**Fig.1-24b**) under the adiabatic process, no heat is involved

$$q_{II} = 0$$

In adiabatic process, the energy change is equal to the work (ΔE$_{II}$ = w$_{II}$)

$$w_{II} = E_2 - E_1 = C_V dT = C_V(T_{cold} - T_{hot})$$

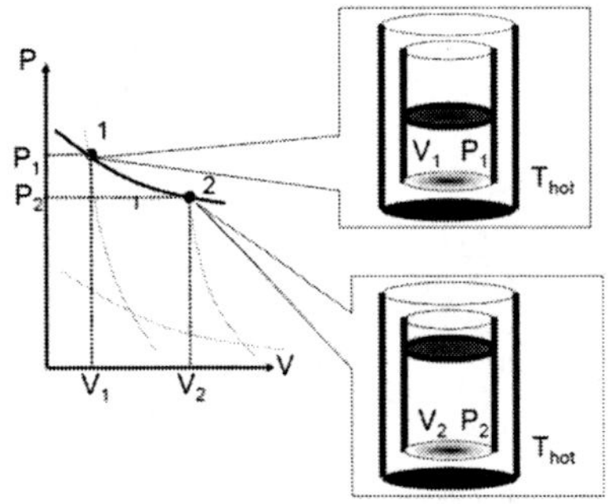

Fig. 1-24a The Carnot cycle-Process I Isothermal expansion

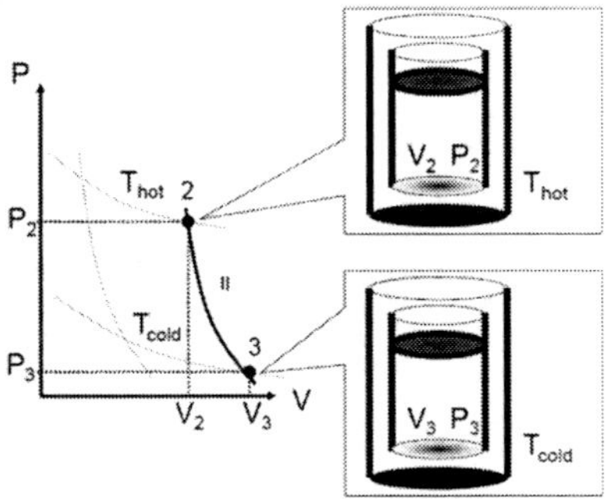

Fig. 1-24b The Carnot cycle-Process II: adiabatic reversible expansion

in step II, an important thermochemical relationship needs to be pointed out. (This relationship is used to derive the entropy expression later.) Next, we use a thermochemical relationship of

$$w_{II} = E_2 - E_1 = C_V dT$$

The work (W$_{II}$) is expressed as "–PdV".

$$C_V dT = -PdV$$

By replacing P=nRT/V (an ideal gas),

$$-PdV = -\frac{nRT}{V}dV$$

Thus,

$$C_V dT = -\frac{nRT}{V}dV$$

Let's integrate the both sides of the above formula for the process II, where temperature changes from T_hot to T_cold and volume changes from V₂ to V₃.

$$C_V \int_{T_{hot}}^{T_{cold}} \frac{dT}{T} = -\frac{nR}{V}\int_{V_2}^{V_3} \frac{dV}{V}$$

$$C_V \ln\frac{T_{cold}}{T_{hot}} = -nR\ln\frac{V_3}{V_2} = nR\ln\frac{V_2}{V_3}$$

OK! Are you still reading this section? We have two more steps to go. But it should be much easier, since we repeat what we did in Step I and II under different condition.

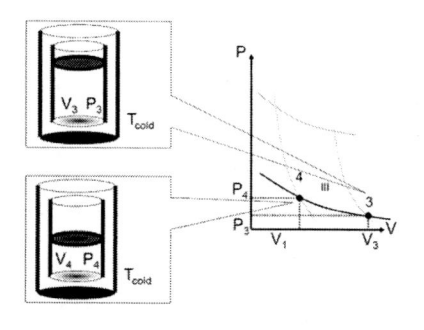

Fig. 1-25a The Carnot cycle- Process I isothermal compression I

Fig. 1-25b The Carnot cycle- Process II: adiabatic reversible compression

III. Isothermal Reversible Compression

The step III is considered in a same way as step I, the work (w_{III}) and heat (q_{III}) are involved under isothermal condition at temperature T= T_cold. (**Fig. 1-25a**) Recalling the procedure made in step I,

$$q_{III} + w_{III} = 0$$
$$q_{III} = -w_{III}$$

And the work at isothermal process (change of volume from V₃ to V₄) is given by

$$w_{III} = -\int_{V_3}^{V_4} PdV = -nRT\ln\frac{V_4}{V_3}$$

Thus, the heat at process III (q_{III}) is

$$q_{III} = -w_{III} = nRT\ln\frac{V_4}{V_3}$$

Step IV. Adiabatic Reversible Compression
The last step IV is considered to be a reverse process of step II. The step IV is an adiabatic reversible compression where the state 4 changes into state 1. (**Fig. 1-25b**) The amount of heat (q_{IV}) in this process is

$$q_{IV} = 0$$

The amount of work (w_{IV}) is

$$w_{IV} = C_V(T_{hot} - T_{cold})$$

Please recall the formula introduced in step II

$$C_V dT = -\frac{nRT}{V} dV$$

By integrating the both sides in the step IV, where temperature changes from T_{cold} to T_{hot} or in volume from V_4 to V_1.

$$C_V \int_{T_{cold}}^{T_{hot}} \frac{dT}{T} = -\frac{nR}{V} \int_{V_4}^{V_1} \frac{dV}{V}$$

$$C_V \ln \frac{T_{hot}}{T_{cold}} = -nR \ln \frac{V_1}{V_4} = nR \ln \frac{V_4}{V_1}$$

Now, we are done in completing the calculation for work and heat of each step I, II, III, and IV. The total heat (q_{total}) involved in one cycle is

$$q_{total} = q_I + q_{II} + q_{III} + q_{IV}$$
$$= nRT_{hot} \ln \frac{V_2}{V_1} + nRT_{cold} \ln \frac{V_4}{V_3}$$

So we are all done with calculating each step. Now, the total amount of work (w_{total}) of one cycle is given by

$$w_{total} = w_1 + w_2 + w_3 + w_4$$

$$= -nRT_{hot} \ln \frac{V_2}{V_1} - nRT_{cold} \ln \frac{V_4}{V_3}$$
$$= -q_{total}$$

The very last term proves that the total change of an internal energy change remained as zero, $\Delta E = 0$ for any closed cyclic system.

$$-w = q$$

We also have two other important relationships.

$$C_V \ln \frac{T_{cold}}{T_{hot}} = nR \ln \frac{V_2}{V_3}$$

Chapter 1 Thermodynamics

$$C_V \ln \frac{T_{hot}}{T_{cold}} = nR \ln \frac{V_4}{V_1}$$

Because somebody tell you to add the above two terms, you will get

$$C_V \ln \frac{T_{cold}}{T_{hot}} + C_V \ln \frac{T_{hot}}{T_{cold}} = nR \ln \frac{V_2}{V_3} + nR \ln \frac{V_4}{V_1}$$

$$C_V \ln \frac{T_{cold}}{T_{hot}} - C_V \ln \frac{T_{cold}}{T_{hot}} = nR \ln \frac{V_2}{V_3} + nR \ln \frac{V_4}{V_1}$$

$$nR \ln \frac{V_2}{V_3} + nR \ln \frac{V_4}{V_1} = 0$$

While I will tell you why, but let's arrange the above to have the term of V_1 and V_2 together as well as the term V_3 and V_4 together. (Recall "ln a +ln b =ln ab".)

$$nR \ln \frac{V_2 V_4}{V_3 V_1} = 0$$
$$nR \ln \frac{V_2 V_4}{V_1 V_3} = 0$$

Therefore,

$$nR \ln \frac{V_2}{V_1} + nR \ln \frac{V_4}{V_3} = 0$$

You may notice that

$$\frac{q_1}{T_{hot}} = nR \ln \frac{V_2}{V_1}$$

$$\frac{q_3}{T_{cold}} = nR \ln \frac{V_4}{V_3}$$

Therefore,

$$\frac{q_1}{T_{hot}} + \frac{q_3}{T_{cold}} = 0$$

We can now state that for any cyclic system

$$\oint \frac{dq_{rev}}{T} = 0$$

Here, $\oint f(x)dx$ indicates that integration of function $f(x)$ as a function of cyclic root of x. Since this indicates that the value dq_{rev}/T does not depend on the path, we know that we have a new state function, and we set it as entropy change, ΔS.

$$\frac{dq_{rev}}{T} = \Delta S \qquad \text{(Eqn. 1-32)}$$

We can end this section right now. However, I want to point out an important measure comes from a Carnot cycle as a bonus for those still reading this section. The critical aim thermodynamical cycle is to obtain an efficiency of a system. The efficiency can be defined as the ration between the amount of the work and the absorbed heat used for this system. For Carnot cycle,

$$\frac{Total\ work\ done\ by\ engine}{Absorbed\ heat} = -\frac{w_{total}}{q_I}$$

Since

$$w_{total} = -q_{total} = -(q_I + q_{III})$$

$$efficiency = -\frac{w_{total}}{q_I} = \frac{q_I + q_{III}}{q_I}$$

We also have the following relationship.
$$\frac{q_I}{T_{hot}} + \frac{q_{III}}{T_{cold}} = 0$$

Therefore,

$$\frac{q_I}{T_{hot}} = -\frac{q_{III}}{T_{cold}}$$

$$\frac{q_{III}}{q_I} = -\frac{T_{cold}}{T_{hot}}$$

Thus, the efficiency (ε) is given as

$$\varepsilon = \frac{q_I + q_{III}}{q_I} = 1 + \frac{q_{III}}{q_I} = 1 - \frac{T_{cold}}{T_{hot}}$$

(Eqn. 1-35)
$$\Delta S = \int_{T_1}^{T_2} \frac{CdT}{T} = C \ln \frac{T_2}{T_1}$$
$$C = C_p \text{(at constant pressure)}$$
$$C = C_v \text{(at constant volume)}$$

The heat capacity C is defined as
$$C = \frac{dq}{dT} \qquad \text{(Eqn. 1-7)}$$

Thus,
$$dq = CdT$$

The entropy change, ΔS, is
$$\Delta S = \int \frac{dq_{rev}}{T} \qquad \text{(Eqn. 1-32)}$$

Thus,
$$\Delta S = \int \frac{dq_{rev}}{T} = \int \frac{CdT}{T}$$

Before calcualting the above integral, let's make a quick review on the basic integration method.

$$\int \frac{dx}{x} = \ln x + \alpha$$

Here, α is a constant. If the heat capacity is assumed not to depend on the temperature,

$$\Delta S = C \int \frac{dT}{T} = C \ln T + \alpha.$$

Under constant pressure, the entropy change between T_1 and T_2 with heat capacity C_P is

$$\Delta S = \int_{T_1}^{T_2} \frac{C_P dT}{T} = C_P \ln \frac{T_2}{T_1} \qquad \text{(Eqn. 1-35)}$$

Under constant volume, the entropy change between T_1 and T_2 with heat capacity C_V is

$$\Delta S = \int_{T_1}^{T_2} \frac{C_V dT}{T} = C_V \ln \frac{T_2}{T_1} \qquad \text{(Eqn. 1-35)}$$

(Eqn. 1-36) $$\Delta S^o_{rxn,(T_2)} = \Delta S^o_{rxn,(T_1)} + \Delta C_P \ln \frac{T_2}{T_1}$$

The value of $\Delta S^o_{rxn,(T_2)}$ is calculated by adding up the three terms given below.

$$\Delta S^o(A) = \int_{T_2}^{T_1} \frac{C_P(A)dT}{T} = \Delta C_P(A) \ln \frac{T_1}{T_2}$$
$$\Delta S^o_{rxn,(T_1)} = \Delta S^o_{T_1}(B) - \Delta S^o_{T_1}(A)$$

$$\Delta S^o(B) = \int_{T_1}^{T_2} \frac{C_P(B)dT}{T} = \Delta C_P(B) \ln \frac{T_2}{T_1}$$

Thus,

$$\Delta S^o_{rxn,(T_2)} = \Delta C_P(A) \ln \frac{T_1}{T_2} + \Delta S^o_{rxn,(T_1)} + \Delta C_P(B) \ln \frac{T_2}{T_1}$$

$$= -\Delta C_P(A) \ln \frac{T_2}{T_1} + \Delta S^o_{rxn,(T_1)} + \Delta C_P(B) \ln \frac{T_2}{T_1}$$

$$= \big(\Delta C_P(B) - \Delta C_P(A)\big) \ln \frac{T_2}{T_1} + \Delta S^o_{rxn,(T_1)}$$

$$= \Delta S^o_{rxn,(T_1)} + \Delta C_P \ln \frac{T_2}{T_1}$$

Here,

$$\Delta C_P = \Delta C_P(B) - \Delta C_P(A)$$

Also, please recall

$$\ln \left[\frac{1}{x}\right] = -\ln x$$

$$\ln \left[\frac{y}{x}\right] = -\ln \left[\frac{x}{y}\right]$$

Thus,

$$\Delta C_P(A) \ln \frac{T_1}{T_2} = -\Delta C_P(A) \ln \frac{T_2}{T_1} \qquad \textbf{(Eqn. 1-36)}$$

Chapter 1 Summary [Part 1]

(Use back page to cover the contents.)

1	first law of the thermodynamics	The energy of universe is conserved.
2	internal energy change (ΔE)	$\Delta E = q + w$ (Eqn. 1-1) ΔE; internal energy change of a system, q; heat, w; work
3	PV work (w)	$w = -P\Delta V$ (Eqn. 1-2) w; work, P; pressure, ΔV; volume change
4	heat (q)	$q = C\Delta T$ (Eqn. 1-3) C: heat capacity
5	system and the surroundings sign of q and w	**system** is a reaction center and the **surroundings** is the rest of everything else. If heat (q) or work (w) is accepted to the system q>0 and w>0. If heat or work is lost form the system, q<0 and w<0.
6	Enthalpy (H)	$H = E + PV$ (Eqn. 1-9) H: enthalpy, E: internal energy, P: pressure, V: volume
7	Four thermodynamic paths	a) isobaric process (ΔP_{sys} = 0) b) isothermal process (ΔT_{sys} = 0) c) isochoric process (ΔV = 0) d) adiabatic process (q = 0)
8	work (w_T) and heat (q_T) under isothermal process	$w_T = -nRT\ln\frac{V_2}{V_1}$ (Eqn. 1-16) $q_T = -w_T$ (Eqn. 1-15)
9	C_P and C_V	$\overline{C_P} = \overline{C_V} + R$ (Eqn. 1-19)
10	ΔE for an ideal gas	$\Delta E = n\overline{C_V}\Delta T = q_v$ (Eqn. 1-21)
11	ΔH for an ideal gas	$\Delta H = n\overline{C_P}\Delta T = q_P$ (Eqn. 1-22)
12	ΔE and ΔH for solid/liquid	$\Delta H \approx \Delta E$ (Eqn. 1-23) $\overline{C_V} = \overline{C_P} = \bar{C}$ (Eqn. 1-25)
13	Enthalpy change of a reaction (ΔH_{rxn})	$\Delta H^o_{rxn} = \sum_{products} \Delta H^o_f - \sum_{reactants} \Delta H^o_f$ (Eqn. 1-30)
14	Temperature dependence of the enthalpy change of a reaction (ΔH_{rxn}) and ΔC_P	$\Delta H^{T_2}_{rxn} - \Delta H^{T_1}_{rxn} = \Delta C_P(T_2 - T_1)$ (Eqn. 1-31) $\Delta C_P = \sum_{products} C_P - \sum_{reactants} C_P$
15	ΔE_{rxn} and ΔH_{rxn} of a reaction involving the gaseous species	$E_{rxn} = \Delta H_{rxn} - (\Delta n_g)RT$ (Eqn. 1-34) Δn_g = (# of moles of <u>gaseous</u> products) − (# of moles of <u>gaseous</u> reactants)

[Fold the page at the double line and cover the right half.]

Chapter 1 Summary Check [Part 1]

(Use this page to cover and check the contents.)

Use ☐ as your check box. Write your comment at far right

1	first law of the thermodynamics	☐ ☐ ☐ ☐ ☐	
2	internal energy change (ΔE)	☐ ☐ ☐ ☐ ☐	
3	PV work (w)	☐ ☐ ☐ ☐ ☐	
4	heat (q)	☐ ☐ ☐ ☐ ☐	
5	system and the surroundings sign of q and w	☐ ☐ ☐ ☐ ☐	
6	Enthalpy (H)	☐ ☐ ☐ ☐ ☐	
7	Four thermodynamic paths	☐ ☐ ☐ ☐ ☐	
8	work (w_T) and heat (q_T) under isothermal process	☐ ☐ ☐ ☐ ☐	
9	C_P and C_V	☐ ☐ ☐ ☐ ☐	
10	ΔE for an ideal gas	☐ ☐ ☐ ☐ ☐	
11	ΔH for an ideal gas	☐ ☐ ☐ ☐ ☐	
12	ΔE and ΔH for solid/liquid	☐ ☐ ☐ ☐ ☐	
13	Enthalpy change of a reaction (ΔH_{rxn})	☐ ☐ ☐ ☐ ☐	
14	Temperature dependence of the enthalpy change of a reaction (ΔH_{rxn}) and ΔC_P	☐ ☐ ☐ ☐ ☐	
15	ΔE_{rxn} and ΔH_{rxn} of a reaction involving the gaseous species	☐ ☐ ☐ ☐ ☐	

Chapter 1 Summary [Part 2]

(Use back page to cover the contents.)

16	entropy (S) and the number of the states (N)	$S = k \ln N$ (Eqn. 1-31)
17	entropy (S) for isothermal process at T with heat (q)	$\Delta S = \frac{q_{rev}}{T}$ (Eqn. 1-32)
18	Second law of thermodynamics	*The entropy of an isolated system can never decrease" or "Entropy is not conserved"* $\Delta S(system) + \Delta S(surroundings) \geq 0$ (Eqn. 1-33)
18	Third law of thermodynamics	*"The entropy of any pure and perfect crystal is zero at 0 [K]."*
19	entropy change of a reaction (ΔS^o_{rxn})	$\Delta S^o_{rxn} = \sum_{products} \Delta S^o_f - \sum_{reactants} \Delta S^o_f$ (Eqn. 1-34)
20	The temperature dependence of an entropy change ($\Delta S(T)$)	$\Delta S = C \ln \frac{T_2}{T_1}$ (Eqn. 1-35) $C = C_p$ (at constant pressure) $C = C_v$ (at constant volume)
21	Temperature dependence of an entropy change of a reaction, $\Delta S^o_{rxn,(T)}$	$\Delta S^o_{rxn,(T_2)} = \Delta S^o_{rxn,(T_1)} + \Delta C_P \ln \frac{T_2}{T_1}$ (Eqn. 1-36) $\Delta C_P = \sum_{products} \Delta C_P - \sum_{reactants} \Delta C_P$ (Eqn. 1-29)

[Fold the page at the double line and cover the right half.]

Chapter 1 Summary Check [Part 2]

(Use this page to cover and check the contents.)

Use ☐ as your check box. Write your comment at far right

16	entropy (S) and the number of the states (N)	☐ ☐ ☐ ☐ ☐	
17	entropy (S) for isothermal process at T with heat (q)	☐ ☐ ☐ ☐ ☐	
18	Second law of thermodynamics	☐ ☐ ☐ ☐ ☐	
18	Third law of thermodynamics	☐ ☐ ☐ ☐ ☐	
19	entropy change of a reaction (ΔS^o_{rxn})	☐ ☐ ☐ ☐ ☐	
20	The temperature dependence of an entropy change ($\Delta S(T)$)	☐ ☐ ☐ ☐ ☐	
21	Temperature dependence of an entropy change of a reaction, $\Delta S^o_{rxn,(T)}$	☐ ☐ ☐ ☐ ☐	

Chapter 1 - YOUR TEACHER MAY TEST YOU ON:

No.	What may be asked?		What you should know or do?
1	How do you calculate the PV work in J unit?	→	$w = -P\Delta V$ (Eqn. 1-2) $w = -\int_{V_1}^{V_2} P_{ex} dV$ (Eqn. 1-4) $w = -P_{ex}(V_2 - V_1)$ (Eqn. 1-5)
		→	1 [atm·L] =101.3 [J]
		→	EXERCISE 1-1
		→	Problem 1-1
2	How do you calculate the heat, q?	→	$q = \int C dT$ (Eqn. 1-6)
		→	EXERCISE 1-2
		→	Problems 1-2, 1-3
3	What are the signs (+ or –) of q or w when heat or work are transferred into a system	→	Fig. 1.10
		→	Problems 1-1, 1-2, 1-3
4	How do you calculate internal energy change (ΔE)?	→	$\Delta E = q + w$ (Eqn. 1-1)
		→	Problems 1-4, 1-5, 1-6, 1-7, 1-8, 1-9
5	What is the definition of enthalpy (or enthalpy change at constant pressure)?	→	$H = E + PV$ (Eqn. 1-9) $\Delta H = \Delta E + P\Delta V$ (Eqn. 1-10) (at constant pressure)
		→	Problems 1-10, 1-11
6	What are the major four thermodynamic paths and work or heat for each process?	→	i). isobaric $\Delta P_{sys} = 0$ ii). isothermal $\Delta T_{sys} = 0$ iii). isochoric $\Delta V = 0$ iv). adiabatic q = 0
		→	i). Isobaric process $q_P = n\overline{C_P}(T_2 - T_1)$ (Eqn. 1-11) $w_P = -P(V_2 - V_1) = -nR(T_2 - T_1)$ (Eqn. 1-12) (Fig. 1-12) ii). Isochoric process $q_V = n\overline{C_V}(T_2 - T_1)$ (Eqn. 1-13) $w_V = 0$ (Eqn. 1-14)(Fig. 1-13) iii). Isothermal process $q_T = -w_T$ (Eqn. 1-15) $w_T = -nRT\ln\frac{V_2}{V_1}$ (Eqn. 1-16)(Fig. 1-14) iv).adiabatic process $q_a = 0$ (Eqn. 1-17) $w_a = \frac{K(V_2^{1-\gamma} - V_1^{1-\gamma})}{1-\gamma}$ (Eqn. 1-18)(Fig. 1-15)
		→	Problems 1-9, 1-11

Chapter 1 Thermodynamics

7	What is the relationship between C_P and C_V? Can you calculate the enthalpy of an ideal gas if only C_V is given?	→	$\overline{C_P} = \overline{C_V} + R$ (Eqn. 1-19) $C_P = C_V + nR$ (Eqn. 1-20)
		→	Problem 1-24
8	How can you calculate ΔE or ΔH from q_P or q_V?	→	$\Delta E = n\overline{C_V}\Delta T = q_v$ (for gas)(Eqn. 1-21) $\Delta H = n\overline{C_P}\Delta T = q_P$ (for gas)(Eqn. 1-22) $\Delta H \cong \Delta E$ (for solid/liquid)(Eqn. 1-23) $\Delta E = n\overline{C_V}\Delta T = \Delta H = n\overline{C_P}\Delta T$ (for solid/liquid)(Eqn. 1-24) $\overline{C_V} = \overline{C_P} = \overline{C}$ (for solid/liquid)(Eqn. 1-25)
		→	EXERCISE 1-3
		→	Problems 1-7, 1-10
9	How can you calculate ΔE or ΔH for the phase change from liquid to gas?	→	$\Delta E_v = \Delta H_v - RT$ (Eqn. 1-26)
		→	EXERCISE 1-4
10	How do you calculate the enthalpy change of the reaction?	→	$\Delta H^o_{rxn} = \sum_{products} \Delta H^o_f - \sum_{reactants} \Delta H^o_f$ (Eqn. 1-27) Hess's law (Fig. 1-18)
		→	EXERCISE 1-5
		→	Problems 1-12, 1-13, 1-14, 1-15, 1-16, 1-17, 1-18, 1-19
11	How do you calculate the enthalpy change at different temperature from the standard condition?	→	$\Delta H^{T_2}_{rxn} - \Delta H^{T_1}_{rxn} = \Delta C_P(T_2 - T_1)$ (Eqn. 1-28) $\Delta C_P = C_{P,C} + C_{P,D} - C_{P,A} - C_{P,B}$ $\Delta C_P = n_C\overline{C_{P,C}} + n_D\overline{C_{P,D}} - [n_A\overline{C_{P,A}} + n_B\overline{C_{P,B}}]$
		→	EXERCISE 1-6
		→	Problems 1-21, 1-22, 1-23, 1-24, 1-25
12	How do you calculate the internal energy change of the reaction? Can you do so for the case the gaseous species are involved or not involved?	→	$\Delta E_{rxn} = \Delta H_{rxn} - (\Delta n_g)RT$ (Eqn. 1-30)
		→	EXERCISE 1-6
		→	Problem 1-26
13	How do you calculate the entropy change, ΔS, at given temperature T with heat (q)?	→	$\Delta S = \int dS = \int \frac{dq_{rev}}{T} = \frac{q_{rev}}{T}$ (Eqn. 1-32)
		→	Problem 1-29
14	What is the second law of thermo dynamics?	→	"Entropy is not conserved" $\Delta S(isolated\ system) \geq 0$ (Eqn. 1-33)
		→	Problem 1-27

Chapter 1 Thermodynamics

15	How do you calculate the entropy change of a reaction, ΔS_{rxn}^o?	→	$\Delta S_{rxn}^o = \sum_{products} \Delta S_f^o - \sum_{reactants} \Delta S_f^o$ (Eqn. 1-34)
		→	EXERCISE 1-8
		→	Problems 1-28, 1-33, 1-34, 1-35, 1-36, 1-37
16	How do you calculate the entropy change, ΔS, at a given temperature?	→	$\Delta S = \int_{T_1}^{T_2} \frac{CdT}{T} = C \ln \frac{T_2}{T_1}$ $C = C_p$ or C_v (Eqn. 1-35)
		→	EXERCISE 1-9
		→	Problems 1-30, 1-31, 1-32
17	How do you calculate the entropy change of a reaction, ΔS_{rxn}^o, at a given temperature	→	$\Delta S_{rxn,(T_2)}^o = \Delta S_{rxn,(T_1)}^o + \Delta C_P \ln \frac{T_2}{T_1}$ (Eqn. 1-36) $\Delta C_P = \sum_{products} \Delta C_P - \sum_{reactants} \Delta C_P$ (Eqn. 1-29)
		→	EXERCISE 1-10
		→	Problems 1-38, 1-39, 1-40

UNIT CHECK CHAPTER 1

Important Parameters of This Chapter	Popularly Used Unit	Important Unit Conversion
Internal Energy, E	J/mol kJ/mol	[J]=[kg m^{2}s^{-2}]
Internal Energy Change, ΔE	J/mol kJ/mol	
Heat, q	J, cal	1 [cal] =4.184 [J]
Work, w	J	
Pressure	atm	1 [atm] =101.325 [Pa]=760 [torr]
PV work, PΔV	atm·L J	1[atm·L]=101.3 [J]
Temperature, T	°C, K	0 [°C] = 273.15 [K]
Temperature difference, ΔT	°C, K	
Enthalpy, H	J/mol kJ/mol	
Enthalpy change, ΔH	J/mol kJ/mol	
Heat capacity, C, C_P, C_V	J/K	
Molar heat capacity, C, $\overline{C_P}$, $\overline{C_V}$	J mol^{-1} K^{-1}	
Difference in number of moles of gaseous species in a reaction, Δn_g	mol	
Gas constant, R	atm L J mol^{-1} K^{-1} J mol^{-1} K^{-1}	8.314472 [J mol^{-1} K^{-1}] 0.082057 [atm L mol^{-1} K^{-1}]
Entropy, S	kJ mol^{-1} K^{-1}	
Entropy change, ΔS	J mol^{-1} K^{-1} kJ mol^{-1} K^{-1}	
Boltzmann constant, k	J/K	1.380 6504(24) × 10^{-23} [J/K]

Chapter 1 Thermodynamics

SUMMARY OF TRICKY TRAPS OF CHAPTER 1

☐	1	$\overline{C_P} = \overline{C_V} + R$ or $C_P = C_V + nR$
☐	2	Sign of q, w, ΔE, and ΔH, are system centered definition.
☐	3	Use ΔC$_P$ for temperature dependence of ΔH°$_{rxn}$, and ΔC$_P$ is the difference between terms of products and reactants.
☐	4	In the following formula, $\Delta E_{rxn} = \Delta H_{rxn} - (\Delta n_g)RT$ Δn$_g$ needs to be handled carefully. The gas constant R is R= 8.314 [J mol^{-1} K^{-1}]
☐	5.	$\Delta S = \int_{T_1}^{T_2} \frac{CdT}{T} = C\ln\frac{T_2}{T_1}$ Temperatures are in Kelvins unit. C has to be either C$_P$ or C$_V$. C$_P$ or C$_V$ are in [J/K] unit. You may have to use $C_P = C_V + nR$ to get one from another. R=8.314 [J mol^{-1} K^{-1}]
☐	6	Use ΔC$_P$ for temperature dependence of ΔS°$_{rxn}$, and ΔC$_P$ is the difference between terms of products and reactants.

LAST MINUTE REVIEW OF MATH CHAPTER 1

(The followings listing only basic algebra which you have no excuse if you miss them.)

1. $\Delta(xy) = x_2 y_2 - x_1 y_1$
2. $\ln a + \ln b = \ln ab$
3. $\ln\left(\frac{1}{x}\right) = -\ln x$ $\ln\left(\frac{x}{y}\right) = -\ln\left(\frac{y}{x}\right)$
4. $\int \frac{dx}{x} = \ln x + C$

Nobel Prize and Your Knowledge From Chapter 1
(*: word appeared in Chapter 1)

The Nobel Prize in Chemistry 1949 was awarded to William F. Giauque "for his contributions in the field of chemical thermodynamics, particularly concerning the behavior of substances at extremely low temperatures". **The third law of thermodynamics***, which developed from the Nernst Heat Theorem, states that all perfect crystalline substances approach zero entropy as the absolute zero of temperature is approached.

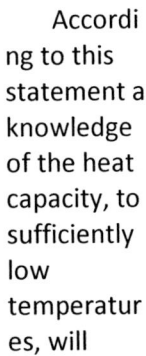

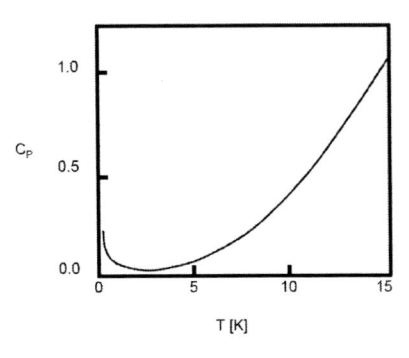

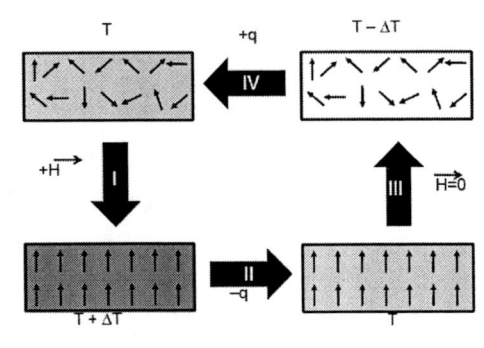

According to this statement a knowledge of the heat capacity, to sufficiently low temperatures, will permit the

Fig. 1-26 Heat capacity of $CoSO_4$ H_2O

Fig. 1-27 Magnetic refrigeration process

calculation of the absolute entropy of a substance. Giauque investigated the relative entropies of glycerine crystals and glass in low temperature. The principal objective of his researches was to demonstrate through range of appropriate tests that the third law of thermodynamics is a basic natural law.

In 1926, he proposed a method for observing temperatures considerably below one kelvin.(**Fig. 1-26**) He developed a magnetic refrigeration device of his own design in order to achieve this outcome, getting closer to absolute zero. The magnetic refrigeration cycle is performed as a refrigeration cycle, analogous to the **Carnot cycle***. (**Fig.1-27**) I. **Adiabatic*** magnetization: A magnetocaloric substance is placed in an insulated environment, and an increase of magnetic field ($+\vec{H}$) causes the magnetic dipoles of the atoms to align, decreasing the material's magnetic **entropy*** and **heat capacity***. Since total entropy is not reduced, the system's temperature is increased to $T + \Delta T_{ad}$. II. Isomagnetic enthalpic transfer: Using a fluid or gas coolant, an extra heat is removed ($-q$) while the magnetic field is held constant to prevent the dipoles from reabsorbing the heat. As temperature is lowered enough, the substance and the coolant are separated. III. Adiabatic demagnetization: Another **adiabatic process*** is conducted keeping total **entropy*** constant, but decreasing the magnetic field. The thermal energy causes the magnetic moments to overcome the field, and thus the sample cools. Energy and **entropy*** transfers from thermal **entropy*** to magnetic **entropy***.($\vec{H} = 0$) IV. Isomagnetic entropic transfer: As constant magnetic field is supplied, the substance is not heated back up. The substance is in contact with the environment being refrigerated. Since the working material is cooler than the refrigerated environment, heat migrates into the working material ($+q$). This cycle begins as the refrigerant and refrigerated environment are in thermal equilibrium,

The low temperature **entropy*** of many substances including condensed gases were determined, and other thermodynamic properties of many gases were also determined from quantum statistics and molecular energy levels available from band spectra as well as other sources. His correlated investigations of the entropy of oxygen with Herrick L. Johnston, led to the discovery of ^{17}O and ^{17}O isotopes in the atmosphere.

THE FOCUSED PHYSICAL CHEMISTRY EXPERIMENTAL APPROACH ASSOCIATED WITH CHAPTER 1

(*: word appeared in Chapter 1)

Differential Scanning Calorimetry

The Differential Scanning Calorimetry (DSC) measures the amount of heat* absorbed or released during phase transitions.[1-2] The difference in the amount of heat required to increase the temperature of a sample and reference is measured as a function of temperature.(**Fig. 1-28**) The reference used in DSC should possess a well-defined **heat capacity*** over the scanning range of temperatures. As the sample undergoes a phase transitions under **isothermal process*** more or less heat flows to it than the reference material placed next to a sample in order to maintain both sample and reference at an equal temperature. The DSC data exhibits a curve of heat flux versus temperature or versus time as shown in **Fig. 1-29**. There are two different conventions: **exothermic reactions*** in the sample shown with a positive or negative peak. By integrating the curve corresponding to a given transition, **enthalpies*** of transitions is calculated.

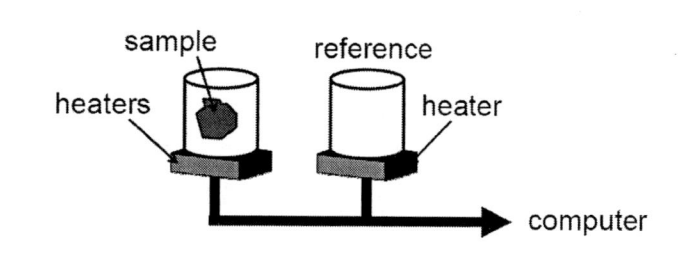

Fig. 1-28 A schematic diagram of DSC set-up.

ΔH = CA

Here, **ΔH is the enthalpy*** of transition, **C is the calorimetric constant**, and A is the area under the curve. At melting temperature (T_m). an endothermic curve can be observed in peak in the DSC and accurate measurement of T_m is conducted and phase diagrams for various chemical systems can be produced.[2] The pharmaceutical industry widely uses DSC for maintaining well-characterized drug compounds.

References

B. Wunderlich Thermal Analysis, Academic Press., New York, 1990.
J.A. Dean The Analytical Chemistry Handbook, McGraw Hill, Inc., New York:, 1995.

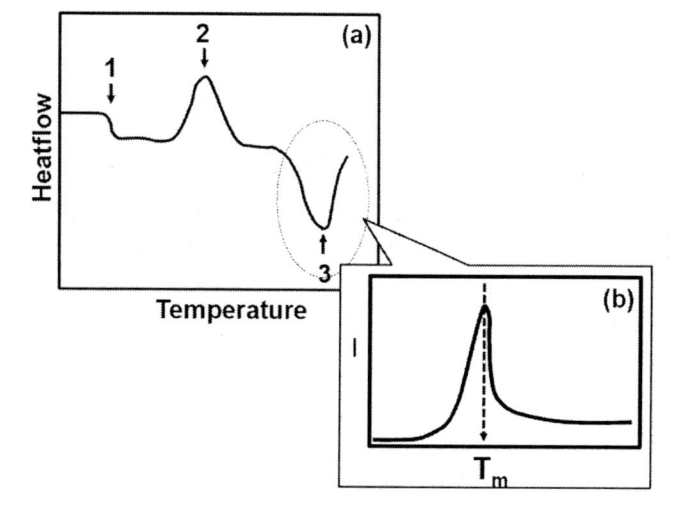

Fig. 1-29 (a)A schematic DSC curve demonstrating the appearance of several features (1: glass transition, 2: crystallization, 3: melting).(b) Normalized DSC peak (I).

Chapter 1 Problems.

1-1 [w calculation] Calculate the PV work done when a system containing a gas expands from 200 [mL] to 1.5 [L] against a constant external pressure of 745 [torr].

1-2 [q calculation] Calculate the heat necessary to change the temperature of 1 [kg] of liquid water by 55 [°C] at constant pressure. Heat capacity of liquid water is 4.184 [cal g^{-1} K^{-1}]

1-3 [C calculation] Hydrogen peroxide, H_2O_2 (g) or H_2O_2(l), decomposes to give water and oxygen:
$$2H_2O_2(aq) \rightarrow 2H_2O(l) + O_2(g)$$
A solution initially 0.3 [M] in H_2O_2 (aq) and at 25.00 [°C] is treated with a small amount of the enzyme. This enzyme efficiently catalyzes the above reaction. If all the heat liberated in the above reaction is retained by the solution and final temperature became 27.15 [°C], what would be the heat capacity of the solution in the unit of [J/g]. Assume that the density of solution is 1 [g/mL].

1-4 [ΔE calculation] Calculate the internal energy change (ΔE) of a system which accepted heat of 90 [J] and did work of 150 [J].

1-5 [ΔE calculation] A chemical reaction is conducted in a container and 50 [kJ] of heat was produced. At the same time this container increased its volume from 1 [L] to 1.55 [L] under 1 [atm] of pressure. Calculate the internal energy change (ΔE) of this system.

1-6 [ΔE calculation] Calculate internal energy change, ΔE, in joules for heating 1 [mol] of **liquid water** from 0 [°C] and 1 [atm] to 95 [°C] and 15 [atm]. The volume per gram of the water is essentially independent of pressure; it can be calculated from the average density of water, 0.98 [g/cm^{-3}].

1-7 [ΔE calculation] Calculate the ΔE on freezing 200 [g] of liquid water at 0 [°C] and 1 [atm].

1-8 [ΔE calculation] One mole of an ideal gas is expanded from an initial state 1 [atm] and 250 [K] to a final state at 0.2 [atm] 200 [K]. Calculate ΔE. (C_v = 12.47 [J K^{-1} mol^{-1}]).

1-9 [w, ΔE calculation] One mole of an ideal gas initially at 27 [°C] and 1 atm pressure is heated and allowed to expand reversibly **at constant pressure** until the final temperature is 327 [°C]. For this gas, C_v = 20.8 [J K^{-1} mol^{-1}] and is constant over the temperature range.
   a) Calculate the work w done on the gas in this expansion.
   b) What is ΔE for the process?

1-10 [ΔH calculation] Calculate the ΔH in joules for heating 1 [mol] of liquid from 25 [°C] and 2 [atm] to 75 [°C] and 5 [atm]. Use the average density of water, 0.98 [g cm^{-3}] to calculate the volume.

1-11 [q, w, ΔE, ΔH calculation] One mole of monoatomic gas initially at 27 [°C] is expanded from an initial pressure of 10 [atm] to a final pressure of 1 [atm]. Calculate q, w, ΔE, ΔH, and the final temperature for this expansion. This expansion was carried out against a constant external pressure of 1 [atm] in a thermally isolated (adiabatic) system. The molar heat capacity at constant volume for a monoatomic gas is C_V = (3/2)R, R is a gas constant.

1-12 [ΔH°$_{rxn}$ -direct method] Calculate the enthalpy of the reaction ΔH°$_{rxn}$ of
$$C_2H_4(g) + 3O_2(g) \rightarrow 2CO_2(g) + 2H_2O(l)$$

1-13 [ΔH°$_{rxn}$ -direct method] The net reaction for sucrose formation in photosynthesis can be written
$$12CO_2(g) + 11H_2O(l) \rightarrow C_{12}H_{22}O_{11}(g) + 12O_2(g)$$
Calculate ΔH° for the production of 1 [mol] of sucrose at 25 [°C]. Use standard enthalpies of formation

1-14 [ΔH°$_{rxn}$-direct method] Estimate the heat of formation, ΔH°$_f$, for gaseous benzene, C_6H_6(g), using any data available in the separate sheet.
[**HINT**: Let's assume that we form benzene from C(graphite) and hydrogen gas, H_2.]

1-15 [ΔH°$_{rxn}$ -direct method] The glucose is oxidized and produce CO_2 and water:
$$C_6H_{12}O_6(s) + 6O_2(g) \rightarrow 6CO_2(g) + 6H_2O(l)$$
Calculate the ΔH°$_{298}$ for the glucose oxidation.

1-16 [ΔH°$_{rxn}$ -direct method] Consider the synthesis of urea according to the equation:

Chapter 1 Thermodynamics

$$CO_2(g) + 2NH_3(g) \rightarrow (NH_2)_2CO(s) + H_2O(l)$$

Calculate the $\Delta H°_{298}$ for the urea synthesis

1-17 [$\Delta H°_{rxn}$-direct method -Energy conversion] A good yield of photosynthesis for agricultural crops in bright sunlight is 20 [kg] of carbohydrate (for example sucrose) per hectare per hour (1 [hectare] = 10^4 [m^2]). The net reaction for sucrose formation in photosynthesis can be written

$$12\ CO_2(g) + 11H_2O(l) \xrightarrow{light} C_{12}H_{22}O_{11}(s) + 12O_2(g)$$

Bright sunlight corresponds to radiation incident on the surface of earth at about 1 [kW m^{-2}]. What percentage of this energy can be stored as carbohydrate in photosynthesis?

1-18 [$\Delta H°_{rxn}$ -Hess's law] Graphite reacts with hydrogen and produces ethylene.

$$2C(graphite) + H_2(g) \rightarrow C_2H_2(g)$$

Calculate the enthalpy of the reaction ΔH^o_{rxn} of the above reaction using the following information.

$2C(graphite) + 2O_2(g) \rightarrow 2\ CO_2(g)$	$\Delta H^o_{rxn}=-787$ [kJ]
$H_2(g) + ½ O_2(g) \rightarrow 2H_2O(l)$	$\Delta H^o_{rxn}=-285.8$ [kJ]
$2CO_2(g) + H_2O(l) \rightarrow C_2H_2O(g) + (5/2)\ O_2(g)$	$\Delta H^o_{rxn}=1299.4$ [kJ]

1-19 [$\Delta H°_{rxn}$ -Hess's law] From the given data, calculate the $\Delta H°$ for the reaction

$$6C(s) + 3H_2(g) \rightarrow C_6H_6(l)$$

$C(s) + O_2(g) \rightarrow CO_2(g)$	$\Delta H° = +393.15$ [kJ]
$H_2(g) + 0.5O_2(g) \rightarrow H_2O(g)$	$\Delta H° = +241.82$ [kJ]
$C_6H_6(l) + 7.5O_2(g) \rightarrow 6CO_2(g) + 3H_2O(g)$	$\Delta H° = 3133.36$ [kJ]

1-20 [ΔH -temperature dependence] Calculate the ΔH in joules for heating 1 [mol] of liquid water from 20 [°C] and 1 [atm] to 50 [°C] and 3 [atm].

1-21 [ΔH temperature dependence] An ideal gas 1 [mol] at 27 [°C] and 1 [atm] is heated and allowed to expand reversibly at constant pressure until the final temperature is 327 [°C]. What is ΔH for the process? (C_v = 20.8 [J K^{-1} mol^{-1}]).

1-22 [ΔH -temperature dependence] If a breath of air, with a volume of 0.5 [L], is drawn into the lungs and comes to thermal equilibrium with the body at 37 [°C] while the pressure remains constant, calculate the increase in enthalpy of the air if the initial air temperature is 20 [°C] and the pressure is 1 [atm]. Heat capacity of the air, C_p, is 30 [J K^{-1} mol^{-1}] between 20 [°C] and 37 [°C].

1-23 [ΔH -temperature dependence] Assume your breath of air with a volume of 450 [mL] is drawn into the lungs at Rochester-New York or at Rochester-Minnesota. The air comes to thermal equilibrium with the body at 37 [°C] while the pressure remains constant. The temperature of the air is 15 [°C] at Rochester-New York and is –15 [°C] at Rochester-Minnesota. Calculate the difference of enthalpy increase of the air between these two cities. The heat capacity of air is about 30 [J K^{-1} mol^{-1}].

1-24 [ΔH -temperature dependence, $C_v \rightarrow C_p$] Assume your breath of air with a volume of 450 [mL] is drawn into the lungs at Rochester, New York or at Miami, Florida. The air comes to thermal equilibrium with the body at 37 [°C] while the pressure remains constant (1 [atm]). The temperature of the air is –5 [°C] at Rochester and is 25 [°C] at Miami. The heat capacity of air at constant volume is about 21.7 [J K^{-1} mol^{-1}]. Consider the air is an ideal gas. Calculate the difference of enthalpy increase of the air between these two cities.

1-25 [$\Delta H°_{rxn}$ temperature dependence] Estimate the change in ΔH if the following reaction (oxidation of glucose to ethanol):

$$C_6H_{12}O_6(s) \rightarrow 2CH_3CH_2OH(l) + 2CO_2(g) \quad \Delta H° = -66.6\ [kJ]$$

is carried out by a thermophilic bacterium at 80 [°C] and 1 [atm]. [C_p for ethanol(l) = 111.5 [J K^{-1} mol^{-1}], for glucose(s) =210 [J K^{-1} mol^{-1}], and for CO_2 = 37.1 [J K^{-1} mol^{-1}].

1-26 [$\Delta H°_{rxn} \rightarrow \Delta E°_{rxn}$] Consider the reaction of carbon dioxide and water at 25 [°C].

$$CO_2(g) + 2H_2O(l) \rightarrow CH_4(g) + 2O_2(g) \quad \Delta H_{rxn}° = 872.5\ [kJ\ mol^{-1}]$$

Calculate $\Delta E_{rxn}°$ for this reaction at 25 [°C].

1-27 [second law of thermodynamics] Express a mathematical equation for the second law of thermodynamics by using $\Delta S_{(sys)}$ and $\Delta S_{(sur)}$. [$\Delta S_{(sys)}$: entropy change in system and $\Delta S_{(sur)}$: entropy change of surroundings]

1-28 [sign of ΔS] Predict the signs of $\Delta S°$ for the reaction

$$CCl_4(l) \rightarrow CCl_4(g)$$

1-29 [ΔS -pressure dependence] 1 [mol] of an ideal gas is compressed from an initial state at P_1, T_1, and V_1 to a final state at P_2, T_2, and V_2. ($P_1 = \frac{1}{2}P_2$, $T_1=T_2$, and $V_1=2V_2$) Calculate ΔS.

1-30 [ΔS -temperature dependence] 1 [mol] of an ideal gas is expanded from an initial state at 2 [atm] and 400 [K] to a final state at 1 [atm] and 300 [K]. Calculate ΔS.

1-31 [ΔS -temperature dependence] Assume your breath of air with a volume of 450 [mL] is drawn into the lungs at Rochester, New York or at Miami, Florida. The air comes to thermal equilibrium with the body at 37 [°C] while the pressure remains constant (1 [atm]). The temperature of the air is −5 [°C] at Rochester and is 25 [°C] at Miami. The heat capacity of air at constant volume is about 21.7 [J K^{-1} mol^{-1}]. Consider the air is an ideal gas. Calculate *the difference* of ΔS of the air between these two cities.

1-32 [ΔS -temperature dependence] If a breath of air, with a volume of 250 [mL] at −10 [°C], is drawn into the lungs and comes to 37 [°C] while the pressure remains 1 [atm], calculate ΔS of the air. (C_V = 21.7 [J K^{-1} mol^{-1}])

1-33 [ΔS°$_{rxn}$] Calculate $\Delta S°_{373}$ for $2H_2(g) + O_2(g) \rightarrow 2H_2O(g)$

1-34 [ΔS°$_{rxn}$] $H_2O(l) \rightarrow H_2(g) + \frac{1}{2}O_2(g)$
Calculate the entropy change, ΔS, at 25 [°C] and 1 [atm] for the decomposition of 1 [mol] of liquid water to H_2 and O_2 gas.

1-35 [ΔS°$_{rxn}$] $C_2H_5OH(l) \rightarrow C_2H_6(g) + \frac{1}{2}O_2(g)$ Calculate $\Delta S°_{298}$

	$\Delta S_{298}°$ [J K^{-1} mol^{-1}]	C_p [J K^{-1} mol^{-1}]
ethanol(l)	175	135
ethane(g)	250	45.7
$O_2(g)$	195	33.7

1-36 [ΔS°$_{rxn}$] Consider the synthesis of urea according to the equation:

$CO_2(g) + 2NH_3(g) \rightarrow (NH_2)_2CO(s) + H_2O(l)$

Calculate the $\Delta S°_{298}$ for the urea synthesis.

1-37 [ΔS°$_{rxn}$] The glycylglycine, $C_4H_8N_2O_3(s)$, was reacted with oxygen gas to form solid urea: $(NH_2)_2CO(s)$, CO_2 gas, and H_2O at 25 [°C] and 1 [atm] according to the equation:

$3O_2(g) + C_4H_8N_2O_3(s) \rightarrow (NH_2)_2CO(s) + 3CO_2(g) + 2H_2O(l)$

Calculate the $\Delta S°_{298}$ for this reaction at 1 [atm] and 25 [°C]

1-38 [ΔS°$_{rxn}$ -temperature dependence] $C_2H_5OH(l) \rightarrow C_2H_6(g) + \frac{1}{2}O_2(g)$
Calculate $\Delta S°_{323}$.

1-39 [ΔS°$_{rxn}$ -temperature dependence] The denaturing transition of a globular protein can be approximated as a phase change. Calculate ΔS for this transition at 40.00 [°C] and 1.00 [atm]. a heat of transition q_m=740.00 [kJ/mol] at T_m=79.0 [°C] at 1.00 [atm]. C_p(initial) = 20 [kJ K^{-1} mol^{-1}] and C_p(final) =27 [kJ K^{-1} mol^{-1}].

1-40 [ΔS°$_{rxn}$ -temperature dependence] $C_2H_5OH(l) \rightarrow C_2H_6(g) + \frac{1}{2}O_2(g)$
Calculate ΔS of the above equation at 317 [K], ΔS_{317}, using the following values given in the table in **1-35**. Your answer should be given with three significant figures.

CHAPTER 1 ANSWERS. For Selected Problems

1-1 129. 1 [J]
1-2 +230.1 [kcal]
1-3 $\Delta H°_{298}$ = –94.66 [kJ/mol] C = 2.989 [kJ/L]
1-4 ΔE = – 60 [J]
1-6 ΔE = 7163 [J]
1-7 –67 [kJ]
1-8 ΔE = – 623.3 [J] q_P = –1039 [J] w_P = 415.7 [J]
1-9 a) w_p = –2.49 [kJ] b) q_p = 8.73 [kJ] ΔE = 6.24 [kJ]
1-10 3780 [J]
1-11 q = 0, ΔE =w =–1.347 [kJ], ΔH = –2.245 [kJ]
1-12 $\Delta H°_{rxn}$ = –1410.9 [kJ]
1-13 $\Delta H°_{298}$ = 5644.138 [kJ]
1-14 241 [kJ]
1-15 $\Delta H°_{298}$ = –2801.6 [kJ]
1-16 $\Delta H°_{298}$ =–133.27 [kJ]
1-17 $\Delta H°$ = 5644.1 [kJ/mol], Stored Energy =14,500 [cal/mol]
1-18 226.6 [kJ]
1-19 –50 [kJ]
1-20 ΔE = 2262 [J]
1-21 8.73 [kJ]
1-22 n = 0.0207 [mol], ΔH = 10.6 [J]
1-23 Rochester, NY $\Delta H°$= 12.61 [J], Rochester, MN $\Delta H°$= 33.07 [J], Difference = 20.46 [J]
1-24 Rochester, NY $\Delta H°$= 25.70 [J], Miami, Florida $\Delta H°$= 6.627 [J], Difference = 19.07 [J]
1-25 approximately –60 [kJ/mol]
1-26 $\Delta E_r°$ = 867.5 [kJ /mol]
1-27 $\Delta S(system) + \Delta S(surroundings) \geq 0$
1-28 $\Delta S°$ >0
1-29 –R ln 2
1-30 –0.217 [J/K]
1-31 Rochester, NY ΔS = 0.0891[J/K], Miami, Florida ΔS = 0.02179[J/K], Difference = 0.0673[J/K]
1-32 0.05 [J/K]
1-33 $\Delta S°$ (T$_1$=298 [K])= – 88.74 [J K^{-1} mol^{-1}]
1-34 $\Delta S°$ =163.34 [J/K]
1-35 171.5 [J K^{-1} mol^{-1}]
1-36 $\Delta S°_{298}$ = –424.13 [J/K]
1-37 $\Delta S°_{298}$ = 80.276 [J K^{-1} mol^{-1}]
1-38 167.9 [J/K]
1-39 $\Delta H(T_2)$= 467 [kJ/mol], $\Delta S(T_2)$= 1.28
1-40 $\Delta S°_{rxn}(T_2)$=168 [J/K]

Chapter 2
Gibbs Energy

2-1　Gibbs Energy
2-2　Calculation of Gibbs Energy
2-3　Temperature Dependence of Gibbs Energy
2-4　Chemical Potential
2-5　Chemical Equilibria and Gibbs Energy
2-6　Temperature Dependence of an Equilibrium

Chapter 2 Gibbs Energy

- **Why do I have to study this chapter?**

Yes, you really have to study this chapter!!! Anybody wish to know which direction reaction goes? (Is a reaction spontaneous or not?) What is Gibbs energy? What does Gibbs energy change (ΔG) tell you? Why Gibbs energy change (ΔG) so important? Is Gibbs energy change (ΔG) related with enthalpy change (ΔH) and entropy change (ΔS)? How are they related? Without knowing this chapter your knowledge of thermochemistry is not complete! By the way, the cover page of this chapter shows a demonstration of three important thermodynamical parameters (ΔG, ΔH, ΔS) emphasized in this textbook.

- **Expected Hurdles Ahead in this Chapter**
1. Watch for the temperature dependence of the Gibbs Energy. (See Section **2-3**)
2. Careful not to confuse Gibbs energy change at equilibrium and at non-equilibrium (See Section **2-4**)
3. Sequential calculation from K, ΔG, ΔH, and ΔS. (See Section **2-6**)

PREVIEW OF KEY-EQUATIONS

Gibbs Energy $\quad G = H - TS$

Gibbs Energy Change $\quad \Delta G = \Delta H - T\Delta S \quad$ (At constant temperature)

$\quad \Delta G = w^*_{rev}$

Gibbs Energy Change of a Reaction $\quad \Delta G^o_{rxn} = \sum_{products} \Delta G^o_f - \sum_{reactants} \Delta G^o_f$

Gibbs Energy Change and Entropy $\quad \dfrac{d\Delta G}{dT} = -\Delta S$

$\quad \Delta G_{T_2} - \Delta G_{T_1} = -\Delta S^o_{rxn}(T_2 - T_1)$

Gibbs-Helmholtz equation $\quad \dfrac{\Delta G_{T_2}}{T_2} - \dfrac{\Delta G_{T_1}}{T_1} = \Delta H^o_{rxn}\left[\dfrac{1}{T_2} - \dfrac{1}{T_1}\right]$

Chemical Potential

$$\mu_A = \left[\frac{\partial G}{\partial n_A}\right]_{T,P,n_j \neq n_A}$$

Equilibrium Constant and ΔG°

$$\Delta G^o = -RT \ln K$$

$$\Delta G = \Delta G^o + RT \ln Q$$

van't Hoff Equation

$$\ln \frac{K_2}{K_1} = -\frac{\Delta H^o_{rxn}}{R}\left[\frac{1}{T_2} - \frac{1}{T_1}\right]$$

PREVIEW OF KEY-TECHNICAL TERMS

Gibbs energy (G), spontaneous process, chemical potential (μ), van't Hoff equation

2-1. Gibbs Energy

In this chapter, we will learn the very important thermo-chemical factor, Gibbs energy change (ΔG). Why is it so important? That is because ΔG shows the direction of a reaction at constant T and P. It means that ΔG will tell you if a reaction proceeds or not. (Is this reaction spontaneous or not?) The Gibbs energy (G) is expressed as a difference between enthalpy and entropy term (Thus, Gibbs energy is a composition of two important thermochemical values given previously)

$$G = H - TS \qquad \text{(Eqn. 2-1)}$$

The Gibbs energy is an extensive variable of state with unit [kJ] or [kJ/mol]. The change of any thermochemical value is important and more meaningful than the absolute value shown in (**Eqn. 2-1**). Thus, let's take the change (Δ) of the Gibbs energy as:

$$\Delta G = \Delta H - \Delta(TS)$$

Most often used form is the formula under the constant temperature

$$\Delta G = \Delta H - T\Delta S \qquad \text{(Eqn. 2-2)}$$

and this is the form of Gibbs energy change to memorize!

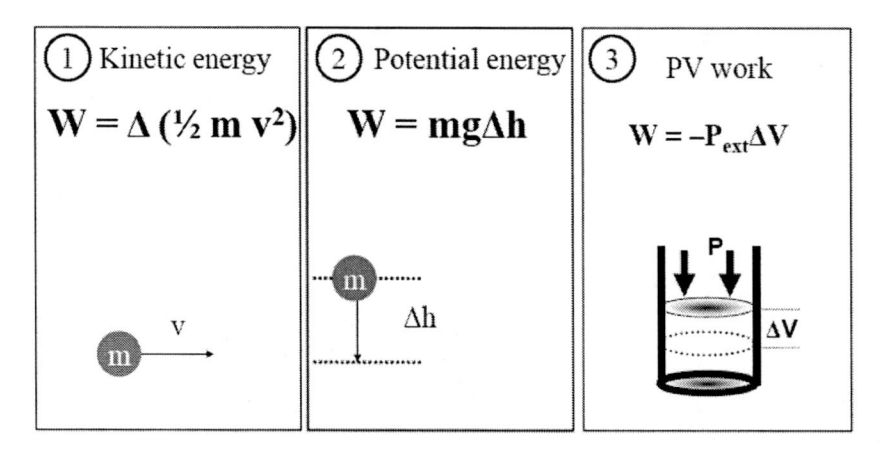

Fig. 2-1 Examples of mechanical works: Three types of energy and the work form.

① Kinetic energy: $W = \Delta(\tfrac{1}{2} m v^2)$

② Potential energy: $W = mg\Delta h$

③ PV work: $W = -P_{ext}\Delta V$

The value given by ΔG represents a system's capacity to do "*non-expansion work*" (i.e., non P-V work). Major types of mechanical work can be categorized in the following three items. **(Fig. 2-1.)** (1) **Kinetic Energy**: A substance with a mass m moves with speed (v) and possesses a kinetic energy of w = $\Delta(1/2\, mv^2)$. (2) **Potential Energy**: The particle with a mass (m) placed at a height (Δh) possesses a potential to do the work, w = mgΔh, where g is a gravitational constant. (3) **PV work**: When an external pressure (P_{ext}) is applied to a constrained space with volume V, the work is proportional to the volume change, w = $-P_{ext}\Delta V$.

An important relationship between the type of work and the Gibbs energy change ΔG is defined as

$$\Delta G = w^*_{rev} \qquad \text{(Eqn. 2-3)}$$

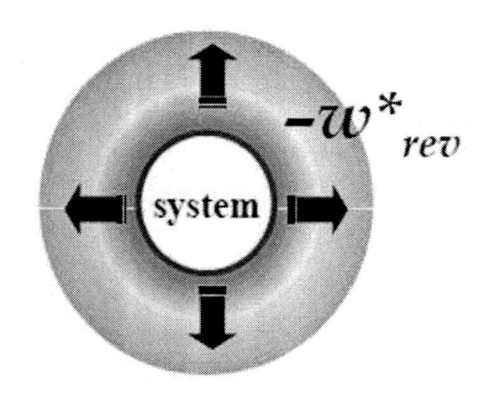

Fig. 2-2 Gibbs energy

The Gibbs energy is the work done under reversible process (w_{rev}) that is equivalent with non-PV work (w^*). The arrow in **Fig.2-2** indicates that system is doing the work toward the surroundings, indicating that the negative sign should be used to indicate that system is losing the work, $-\Delta G$. We can rephrase it as:

$-\Delta G$ = Maximal amount of non-expansion work a system can do on the surroundings

A spontaneous process takes place when "$-\Delta G$" is positive (i.e., $-w^*_{rev} > 0$). Thus, for spontaneous process, $w^*_{rev} < 0$. We now know that Gibbs energy change should be negative ($\Delta G < 0$) for a spontaneous process. We can make an important categorization used for judging the spontaneous process from the sign of ΔG.

Under constant T and P

$\Delta G < 0$ **Spontaneous process**
$\Delta G > 0$ **Non-spontaneous process**
$\Delta G = 0$ **System at equilibrium**

The molar standard Gibbs energy [kJ/mol] is defined under 25 [°C] and 1 [atm], and it is noted by $\overline{G^o}$, or ΔG^o_{298}, and are available from the Tables.

2-2 Calculation of Gibbs Energy

Using ΔG, the Gibbs energy change of a reaction can be calculated. I suggest two ways to calculate ΔG. (1) Using $\Delta G = \Delta H - T\Delta S$ **(Eqn. 2-2)** and (2) using direct method.

(1) Calculating ΔG by using $\Delta G = \Delta H - T\Delta S$
This method (**Eqn. 2-2**) assumes that the situation is kept under constant temperature. For most cases you will be asked to calculate ΔG from known ΔH and ΔS. Here, we review how ΔH and ΔS are obtained.

Chapter 2 Gibbs Energy

$$\Delta H = n\overline{C_P}\Delta T = q_P \quad \text{(Eqn. 1-22)}$$

$$\Delta H^o_{rxn} = \sum_{products} \Delta H^o_f - \sum_{reactants} \Delta H^o_f \quad \text{(Eqn. 1-27)}$$

$$\Delta S = \frac{q_{rev}}{T} \quad \text{(Eqn. 1-32)}$$

$$\Delta S^o_{rxn} = \sum_{products} \Delta S^o_f - \sum_{reactants} \Delta S^o_f \quad \text{(Eqn. 1-34)}$$

$$\Delta S^o_{rxn,(T_2)} = \Delta S^o_{rxn,(T_1)} + \Delta C_P \ln \frac{T_2}{T_1} \quad \text{(Eqn. 1-36)}$$

	EXERCISE 2-1 Calculate ΔG^o when ΔH^o = 285.83 [kJ/mol] and ΔS^o = 163.14 [J K^{-1} mol^{-1}], Is this reaction spontaneous or not?
	ANSWER From $\Delta G = \Delta H - T\Delta S$ **(Eqn. 2-2)** ❶ At 25 [°C] (standard condition) ❷ $\Delta G^o = \Delta H^o - T\Delta S^o$ ❸ If ΔH^o = 285.83 [kJ/mol], ΔS^o = *163.14* [J K^{-1} mol^{-1}], ΔG^o =285.83 [kJ/mol] − (298 [K]) × (0.16314 [kJ K^{-1} mol^{-1}]) =237.19 [kJ/mol] > 0 Therefore, this reaction is not spontaneous reaction.
❶	Convert temperature in Kelvins unit.
❷	Only superscript "o" are attached to (**Eqn. 2-2**)
❸	The unit of ΔH^o is [kJ/mol] and the unit for ΔS^o is [J K^{-1} mol^{-1}]

☹ **Most Common Mistake (10) I can't calculate ΔG by using ΔS.**
Most common mistake people make in this calculation is the unit. In most cases the unit for Gibbs energy change (ΔG) and enthalpy change (ΔH) is [kJ/mol] or [kJ]. However, the unit often used for the entropy change (ΔS) is [J K^{-1} mol^{-1}]. Since ΔG is requested in the unit of [kJ/mol] for most cases, make sure if you have already divided 1000 to the value for ΔS [J K^{-1} mol^{-1}].

☹ **Most Common Mistake (11) - I thought T= 25 [°C].**
This is the story of "unit" again. For the term TΔS in (**Eqn. 2-2**), T should be in the unit of Kelvins [K]. The standard condition is defined at T= 25 [°C], and T in (**Eqn. 2-2**) should be T= 298 [K].

Chapter 2 Gibbs Energy

☹ **MCM Most Common Mistake (12)- I thought T= 25 [°C] = 298 [K].**
The formula given for ΔG at constant temperature can be sometimes very tricky. If ΔH and ΔS are those at 25 [°C] (ΔH° and ΔS°), and the problem is asking for ΔG°, you may use:

$$\Delta G^o = \Delta H^o - T\Delta S^o$$

However, what if you are requested to calculate the ΔG at T= 28 [°C] or T=50 [°C]? If it is T= 28 [°C], you can still assume that ΔH° and ΔS° are close to the values of ΔH and ΔS at 28 [°C]. If the problem states that ΔH and ΔS are assumed to be independent of temperature, you can use ΔH°, ΔS°, and T = 323 [K] in (**Eqn. 2-2**). However, the values at 50 [°C] can be far enough from those at 25 [°C]. Then, you need to consider the temperature dependence of the enthalpy change and entropy change. For ΔH, use (**Eqn. 1-22**) to calculate the enthalpy change of each reactant and product;

$$\Delta H = n\overline{C_P}\Delta T = q_P$$

(The heat capacity should be known.) Then, calculate the ΔH^o_{rxn} from (**Eqn. 1-30**)

$$\Delta H^o_{rxn} = \Sigma_{products} \Delta H^o_f - \Sigma_{reactants} \Delta H^o_f$$

For ΔS, the formula shown in (**Eqn. 1-36**) can be used if ΔC_P is given.

$$\Delta S^o_{rxn,(T_2)} = \Delta S^o_{rxn,(T_1)} + \Delta C_P \ln\frac{T_2}{T_1}$$

(2) Calculating ΔG by direct method
This method is already familiar with you from the calculation of entropy and enthalpy change of a reaction(ΔH^o_{rxn} and ΔS^o_{rxn}). For general chemical reaction,

$$n_A A + n_B B \rightarrow n_C C + n_D D$$

The direct method for obtaining the Gibbs energy change (ΔG^o_{rxn}) is

$$\Delta G^o_{rxn} = n_C \overline{G_C} + n_D \overline{G_D} - [n_A \overline{G_A} + n_B \overline{G_B}]$$

A general expression of the above is given as

$$\Delta G^o_{rxn} = \Sigma_{products} \Delta G^o_f - \Sigma_{reactants} \Delta G^o_f \qquad \text{(Eqn. 2-4)}$$

Always be careful not to forget the negative sign in front of the term of the reactants. Also make sure to multiply the coefficient in front of the Gibbs energy (ΔG^o_f) of each substance.

EXERCISE 2-2

$C_2H_5OH(l) \rightarrow C_2H_6(g) + ½O_2(g)$

Calculate $\Delta G^o{}_{298}$ (Use Table for the values.) by two methods and compare the values.

	ΔH [kJ/mol]	ΔS [J K^{-1} mol^{-1}]
$C_2H_5OH(l)$	-276.98	160.67
$C_2H_6(g)$	-84.68	229.60
$O_2(g)$	0	205.138

ANSWER

As a good way of reviewing we learned, let's solve this problem in two ways (1) Calculating ΔG by using $\Delta G = \Delta H - T\Delta S$ and (2) Calculating ΔG by direct method.

(1) Calculating ΔG by using $\Delta G = \Delta H - T\Delta S$

$\Delta G = \Delta H - T\Delta S$

❶ $\Delta H = (-84.68 \text{ [kJ/mol]}) + ½(0) - (-276.98 \text{ [kJ/mol]}) = 192.3 \text{ [kJ/mol]}$

❶ $\Delta S = (229.60 \text{ [J K}^{-1}\text{ mol}^{-1}\text{]}) + ½ (205.138 \text{ [J K}^{-1}\text{ mol}^{-1}\text{]}) - (160.67 \text{ [J K}^{-1}\text{ mol}^{-1}\text{]})$

  $= 171.499 \text{ [J/mol]}$

❷ T = 298 [K]

❸ $\Delta G = 192.3 \text{ [kJ/mol]} - 298 \text{ [K]} \times 0.1715 \text{ [kJ K}^{-1}\text{ mol}^{-1}\text{]} = 141.19 \text{ [kJ/mol]}$

(2) Calculating ΔG by direct method

From the table

$\Delta G^o_{298}[C_2H_5OH(l)] = -174.14 [kJ/mol]$

$\Delta G^o_{298}[C_2H_6(g)] = -32.82 [kJ/mol]$

$\Delta G^o_{298}[O_2(g)] = 0 [kJ/mol]$

❶ $\Delta G^o_{298} = -32.82 + \frac{1}{2} \times 0 - 174.14 = 141.32 [kJ/mol]$

It is confirmed that both methods provided almost the same answer. So you should feel comfortable to obtain the value from either method.

❶ Don't forget coefficients and watch for the negative sign in front of the term for the reactants.

❷ Convert the temperature in Kelvins.

❸ The unit of ΔS is converted into [kJ K^{-1} mol^{-1}]

2-3 Temperature Dependence of Gibbs Energy

The temperature dependence of Gibbs energy change, ΔG, has a close relationship with entropy change, ΔS. If you plot ΔG as a function of temperature T, you get a straight line and the slope of the graph is –ΔS. **(Fig. 2-3a)**

$$\frac{d\Delta G}{dT} = -\Delta S \qquad \text{(Eqn. 2-5)}$$

The direction of the slope tells if ΔS^o_{rxn} is positive or negative. The negative slope means that $\Delta S^o_{rxn} > 0$, and positive slope means that $\Delta S^o_{rxn} < 0$. The integration of **(Eqn. 2-5)** provides the useful expression of temperature dependence of the Gibbs energy change.

$$\Delta G_{T_2} - \Delta G_{T_1} = -\Delta S^o_{rxn}(T_2 - T_1) \qquad \text{(Eqn. 2-6)}$$

Here, ΔS^o_{rxn} is given by

$$\Delta S^o_{rxn} = \sum_{products} \Delta S^o_f - \sum_{reactants} \Delta S^o_f \qquad \text{(Eqn. 1-34)}$$

For reaction given as

$$n_A A + n_B B \rightarrow n_C C + n_D D$$

the relationship given in **(Eqn. 2-5)** is obtained as:

$$\frac{d\Delta G}{dT} = n_C \left[\frac{d\overline{G_C}}{dT}\right] + n_D \left[\frac{d\overline{G_D}}{dT}\right] - \left[n_A \left[\frac{d\overline{G_A}}{dT}\right] + n_B \left[\frac{d\overline{G_B}}{dT}\right]\right]$$

$$= -n_C \overline{S_C} - n_D \overline{S_D} - [-n_A \overline{S_A} - n_B \overline{S_B}]$$

$$= -\Delta S$$

The Gibbs-Helmholtz equation relates between ΔG and ΔH by

$$\frac{\Delta G_{T_2}}{T_2} - \frac{\Delta G_{T_1}}{T_1} = \Delta H^o_{rxn}\left[\frac{1}{T_2} - \frac{1}{T_1}\right] \qquad \text{(Eqn. 2-7)}$$

Here,

$$\Delta H^o_{rxn} = \sum_{products} \Delta H^o_f - \sum_{reactants} \Delta H^o_f \qquad \text{(Eqn. 1-27)}$$

Following the Gibbs –Helmholtz equation, ΔG/T is plotted as a function of an inverse of temperature(1/T). The slope of this plot corresponds to an enthalpy change of reaction (ΔH^o_{rxn}).**(Fig. 2-3b)** Thus, negative slope and positive slope of **(Fig. 2-3b)** corresponds to exothermic (ΔH<0) and endothermic (ΔH>0)process, respectively.

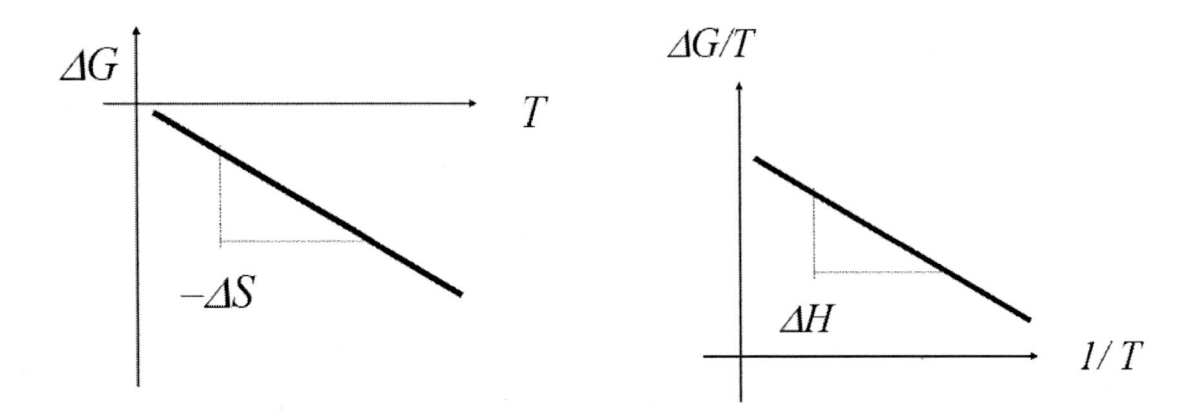

Fig. 2-3 a) Temperature dependence of the Gibbs energy change.

Fig. 2-3b) The plot of ΔG/T vs. 1/T.

If the plot shown in **(Fig. 2-3a)** and **(Fig. 2-3b)** exhibit the linear line, they indicate that the ΔS^o_{rxn} and ΔH^o_{rxn} do not depend on the temperature at least within the temperature region in which the plot is made.

Pressure Dependence of ΔG

dG = VdP − SdT = VdP (at constant T)

$$\int_{G_1}^{G_2} dG = \int_{P_1}^{P_2} V dP = \int_{P_1}^{P_2} \frac{nRT}{P} dP = nRT \ln \frac{P_2}{P_1} = G_2 - G_1$$

For chemical reaction

$$\Delta G(P_2) - \Delta G(P_1) = \Delta nRT \ln \frac{P_2}{P_1}$$

> **EXERCISE 2-3**
> What is the ΔG_{293} of hydrolysis of glycylglycine at 1 [atm].
> $\Delta H°$ (25 [°C]) = – 43.32 [kJ/ mol], $\Delta G°$ (25 [°C]) = – 27.62 [kJ/ mol], and $\Delta S°$ (25 [°C]) = – 52.9 [J K^{-1} mol^{-1}].

ANSWER

☞❶ Here, T_1 = 25 [°C] = 298 [K] and T_2 = 20 [°C] = 293 [K].

Let's solve by both methods and compare the results by **(Eqn. 2-6)** and **(Eqn.2-7)**.

(i) Method by using **(Eqn. 2-6)**

$$\Delta G_{T_2} - \Delta G_{T_1} = -\Delta S^o_{rxn}(T_2 - T_1) \qquad \text{(Eqn.2-6)}$$

☞❷ ΔG_{298} = – 27.6 [kJ/mol] and ΔS_{298} = – 52.9 [J K^{-1} mol^{-1}]

☞❶ ΔG_{293} = –27.6 [kJ/mol] – (– 0.0529 [kJ K^{-1} mol^{-1}]) (293 [K] – 298 [K])

= – 27.62 [kJ/ mol] – 0.26 [kJ/ mol] = – 27.88 [kJ/ mol]

(ii) Method by using **(Eqn. 2-7)**

$$\frac{\Delta G_{T_2}}{T_2} - \frac{\Delta G_{T_1}}{T_1} = \Delta H^o_{rxn}\left[\frac{1}{T_2} - \frac{1}{T_1}\right] \qquad \text{(Eqn.2-7)}$$

ΔH_{298} = – 43.3 [kJ/ mol] and ΔG_{298} = – 27.6 [kJ/ mol]

☞❶ $$\frac{\Delta G_{293}}{293} - \frac{-27.6\,[kJ/mol]}{298\,[K]} = (-43.3\,[kJ/mol])\left[\frac{1}{293[K]} - \frac{1}{298[K]}\right]$$

☞❸ $$\frac{\Delta G_{293}}{293} + 0.0927\,[kJ K^{-1} mol^{-1}]$$

$$= (-43.3\,[kJ/mol]) \times (5.73 \times 10^{-5}\,[K^{-1}])$$

ΔG_{293} = 293 [K] × (-2.48×10^{-3} [kJ K^{-1} mol^{-1}] – 9.27×10^{-2} [kJ K^{-1} mol^{-1}])

= –27.88 [kJ/mol]

Thus, both methods provide the same answer.

☞❶ Temperature unit is in Kelvins.

☞❷ The unit of ΔS is in [J K^{-1} mol^{-1}] not in [kJ K^{-1} mol^{-1}].

☞❸ Calculate at least three significant figures for 1/T.

2-4 Chemical Potential

Gibbs energy is equivalent with the amount of work (capacity) necessary to proceed chemical reaction. Thus, I want you to think that it can be corresponded to a potential energy for a chemical reaction. In a chemical reaction system, you have components (e.g., reactants or products), and each component or species possess a potential energy that contributes positively or negatively to that chemical reaction. For any substances in a system we can define this type of potential energy as a **chemical potential** by using the Gibbs energy (ΔG). A chemical potential of a substance "A" (μ_A) with the number of moles n_A is defined as a partial molar Gibbs energy of substance A.

$$\mu_A = \left[\frac{\partial G}{\partial n_A}\right]_{T,P,n_j \neq n_A} \qquad \text{(Eqn. 2-8)}$$

Chapter 2 Gibbs Energy

In the (**Eqn. 2-8**) the subscripts imply that a chemical potential is defined under constant temperature (T), pressure (P), i.e., isothermal and isobaric process. The indication of " $n_j \neq n_A$" means that the number of moles of substance of all the rest substances except for A are fixed as constant. What happens to a total chemical potential if you have more than one species in a system? As the simplest example, imagine a system made out of two species A and B. (**Fig. 2-4**) Let's think that a system achieved an extreme situation where a chemical reaction completed. So that these two species A and B are like the products of chemical reaction, and no reactants are existent. Then, a total chemical potential of this system is a sum of the chemical potential of the substance A and B, i.e. $\mu_A + \mu_B$. If the number of the moles of the substances A and B are n_A and n_B, respectively, the Gibbs energy for each component is $G_A = n_A\mu_A$ and $G_B = n_B\mu_B$. Thus, the Gibbs energy of this system is

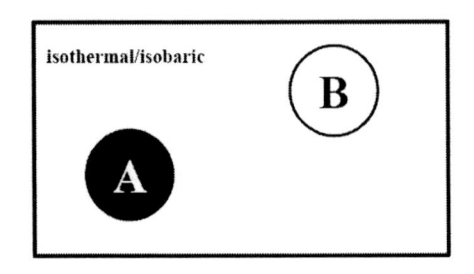

Fig. 2-4 What is a chemical potential of system with A and B?

$$G = n_A\mu_A + n_B\mu_B$$

Then, what happens to the expression of the Gibbs energy when the system has reactants and products coexisting? Let's think a general chemical reaction given by

aA + bB ⇌ cC + dD

From the previous example, you can imagine that Gibbs energy of a system with products only (C and D) is expressed as $G = G_C + G_D = n_C\mu_C + n_D\mu_D$. However, if the reactants are still existent in a system, the contribution of reactants to Gibbs energy should be opposite to that by products. Thus, the total Gibbs energy for this reaction system is given by the difference between products and reactants as

$$\Delta G = \Delta G(T, P, n_A, n_B, n_C, n_D) = [(c\mu_C + d\mu_D) - (a\mu_A + b\mu_B)]$$

The above expression can be more easily understood as a difference of potential energy between final (products) and initial (reactants) states.

2-5 Chemical Equilibria and Gibbs Energy

Gibbs energy change has been mentioned as a way of indicating if a reaction proceeds spontaneously or not. Now, let's relate the concentration of the reactants/products (as a equilibrium constant) with Gibbs energy change of a reaction (ΔG_{rxn}).

At an equilibrium, the system should not have any potential energy to proceed in either way (forward or backward direction), the Gibbs energy change of a reaction should be zero; **ΔG= 0**. The equilibrium constant, K, for a general chemical reaction

aA + bB ⇌ cC + dD

is

Chapter 2 Gibbs Energy

$$K = \left[\frac{[C]_{eq}^c[D]_{eq}^d}{[A]_{eq}^a[B]_{eq}^b}\right]$$ (Eqn. 2-9)

In this expression [x]$_{eq}$ implies that a concentration of x at an equilibrium. At an equilibrium, the change of Gibbs energy of a reaction is

$$\Delta G^o = -RT \ln K$$ (Eqn. 2-10)

Then, what happens if the system is not at an equilibrium? The change of Gibbs energy of a reaction for any general system of chemical reaction which is not at an equilibrium is expressed as

$$\Delta G = \Delta G^o + RT \ln Q$$ (Eqn. 2-11)

Here,

$$Q = \left[\frac{[C]^c[D]^d}{[A]^a[B]^b}\right]$$ (Eqn. 2-12)

[x] is a concentration of x, and the superscripts are the stoichiometric coefficients.
Under an equilibrium, Q becomes K (Q=K) and ΔG=0. Thus, (**Eqn. 2-11**) becomes (**Eqn. 2-10**).

MCM Most Common Mistake (13)- I am not getting correct value of ΔG^o.
Using (**Eqn. 2-10**), ΔG^o should be calculated in the unit of [kJ/mol] with given K and temperature [K].

$$\Delta G^o = -RT \ln K$$ (Eqn. 2-10)

Not only should the unit for temperature be in Kelvins rather than in °C, but the unit and value for the gas constant should be used properly. This issue is a popular one showed up in common mistake (See **Most Common Mistake (9)** in Chapter 1). In (**Eqn. 2-10**), you need to use R = 8.314 [J K^{-1} mol^{-1}] not R= 0.082 [atm L K^{-1} mol^{-1}].

MCM Most Common Mistake (14)- How can I calculate K with given ΔG^o.
The formula in (**Eqn. 2-10**) shows ΔG^o can be calculated with given K at a given temperature.

$$\Delta G^o = -RT \ln K$$ (Eqn. 2-10)

There is, however, another pattern of question from (**Eqn. 2-10**). With given ΔG^o, you can calculate K. Let's review a mathematical relationship for the natural log.

ln X =y

means that
$$x = e^y.$$
Therefore,
$$K = e^{-\frac{\Delta G^o}{RT}}$$

The above formula may not be hard to derive, but students may become unnecessarily stressed if they try to derive it for the first time during an exam. It may make you feel more prepared if you go through this once.

EXERCISE 2-4

In the frog muscle, rectus abdomen is, the concentration of ATP, ADP, and phosphate are 1.25×10^{-3} [M], 0.50×10^{-3} [M], and 2.5×10^{-3} [M], respectively. Calculate Gibbs energy change for the hydrolysis of ATP in muscle. Calculate ΔG at 25 [°C]. Use $\Delta G^o = -31$ [kJ/mol].

ANSWER

Hydrolysis of ATP (adenosine triphosphate) is represented by

ATP → ADP + P

It asks us to use $\Delta G^o = -31$ [kJ].

Since it is not stating it as under an equilibrium, we can use the Q factor as

❶ $Q = \dfrac{[ADP][P]}{[ATP]}$

From $\Delta G = \Delta G^o + RT \ln Q$ (Eqn. 2-11)

[ATP], [ADP], and [phosphate] are

1.25×10^{-3} [M], 0.50×10^{-3} [M], and 2.5×10^{-3} [M].

❷ $\Delta G = -31 [kJ\ mol^{-1}]$
$+ (8.314\ [kJ\ mol^{-1} K^{-1}])(298\ [K]) \ln \dfrac{(0.5 \times 10^{-3}[M])(2.5 \times 10^{-3}[M])}{(1.25 \times 10^{-3}[M])}$

$= -31$ [kJ/mol] -17.1 [kJ/mol] $= -48.1$ [kJ/mol]

❶ Note that problem does not state that it is "at equilibrium".

❷ R=8.314 [J/K mol] and temperature is in Kelvins unit

2-6 Temperature Dependence of an Equilibrium

The equilibrium of the chemical reaction is one of the main focus of chemistry. It is critical to know which way the chemical reaction proceeds and how much of the amount will be shifted under an equilibrium. We now know that an equilibrium constant and the Gibbs energy change of a reaction are closely related. Therefore, as far as the chemical equilibrium constant is available, the Gibbs energy change of a reaction can be calculated for a given temperature. Then, what happens to the equilibrium constant as the temperature is shifted up or down? Do we get more products or less products? The temperature dependence of the Gibbs energy change of a reaction tells exactly what happens and how much. When the reaction is conducted at two different temperatures, T_1 and T_2, and two corresponding equilibrium constants K_1 and K_2 are obtained. If the enthalpy change of this reaction is known (ΔH^o_{rxn}) and ΔH^o_{rxn} is a constant in the given temperature range between T_1 and T_2, the following important relationship, *van't Hoff equation*, is derived.

$$\ln \frac{K_2}{K_1} = -\frac{\Delta H^O_{rxn}}{R}\left[\frac{1}{T_2}-\frac{1}{T_1}\right] \qquad \text{(Eqn. 2-13)}$$

Of course, you may rearrange the temperature term as:

$$\frac{1}{T_2}-\frac{1}{T_1} = \frac{T_1-T_2}{T_2 T_1}$$

EXERCISE 2-5

The enthalpy change of the dissociation reaction of peptide bond under standard condition is: ΔH^o_{rxn} = 225 [kJ/mol]. Calculate that the ratio for the equilibrium constant (K_2/K_1) at different temperatures T_1=35 [°C] and T_2 =60 [°C]. You may assume ΔH^o_{rxn} stays as a constant between 35 [°C] and 60 [°C].

ANSWER

❶ T_1=35 [°C] = 308 [K] and T_2 =60 [°C] = 333 [K]
ΔH^o_{rxn} = 225 [kJ/mol].

$$\ln \frac{K_2}{K_1} = -\frac{\Delta H^o_{rxn}}{R}\left[\frac{1}{T_2}-\frac{1}{T_1}\right] \qquad \text{(Eqn. 2-13)}$$

❷ $$\ln \frac{K_2}{K_1} = -\frac{225\times 10^3\,[J/mol]}{8.314[J/mol]}\left[\frac{1}{333[K]}-\frac{1}{308[K]}\right]$$

❸ K_2/K_1 = 730

---

❶ Temperatures are in Kelvins unit
❷ ΔH^o_{rxn} is converted into J/mol unit.
❸ Ratio is dimensionless. No unit.

Chapter 2 Gibbs Energy

☹ **Most Common Mistake (15): Of course, I used the temperature in Kelvins unit, but why I am not getting a correct answer?**
The van't Hoff equation (**Eqn. 2-13**) requires you to calculate an inverse of the temperature, T [K]. Please do not hurry to calculate 1/T and take less than three significant figures. When T_1 = 20 [°C] = 293.15 [K] and T_2 = 25 [°C] = 298.15 [K], the values of each inverse is the same if you take only one or two significant figures.

e.g., $1/T_1 = 1/293.15 = 0.0034$ and $1/T_2 = 1/298.15 = 0.0034$.
$1/T_2 - 1/T_1 = 0$

So make sure that you take at least three significant figures or more when T_1 and T_2 are very close.
e.g., $1/T_1 = 1/293.15 = 0.003411$ and $1/T_2 = 1/298.15 = 0.003354$
$1/T_2 - 1/T_1 = -5.72 \times 10^{-5}$

A common practice of the van't Hoff equation (**Eqn. 2-13**) is a graphical analysis to derive an enthalpy change of a reaction, (ΔH^o_{rxn}). If you plot the ln K as a function of an inverse of temperature (1/T), the slope of this plot is $-\Delta H^o_{rxn}/R$. Please be careful that you need to multiply negative gas constant (–R) to the slope in order to extract (ΔH^o_{rxn} (You should always be careful which unit is used for R, in this case the unit is kJ/mol K→ see **Most Common Mistake (9)**)
Now you have achieved one big milestone, where you can relate all thermochemical constants introduced in this textbook. You may notice that *van't Hoff* equation plays very critical role to relate the parameters between chemical reaction and thermochemical property.

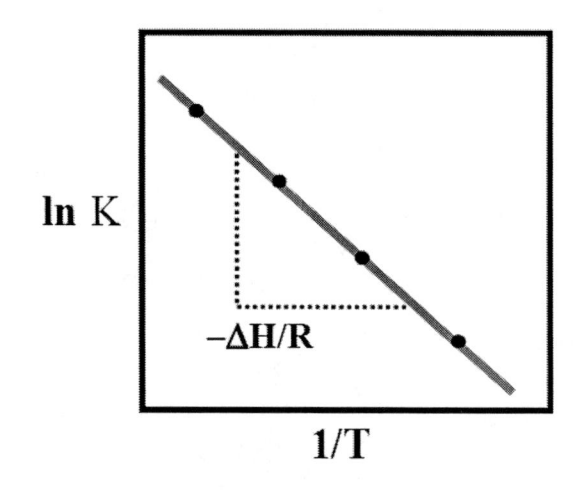

Fig. 2-5 The *van't* Hoff equation and the plot.

Let's make a "strategy" chart for solving a problem to calculate ΔG^o, ΔH^o_{rxn}, and ΔS^o_{rxn} from known equilibrium constant, K, of a reaction. There are four steps and corresponding equations as: **(Fig. 2.5)**

Step a) $\Delta G^o = -RT \ln K$ (**Eqn. 2-10**)

Step b) $\ln \dfrac{K_2}{K_1} = -\dfrac{\Delta H^o_{rxn}}{R}\left[\dfrac{1}{T_2} - \dfrac{1}{T_1}\right]$ (**Eqn. 2-13**)

Step c) $\Delta G_{T_2} - \Delta G_{T_1} = -\Delta S^o_{rxn}(T_2 - T_1)$ (**Eqn. 2-6**)

Step d) $\Delta G = \Delta H^o_{rxn} - T\Delta S^o_{rxn}$ (Eqn. 2-2)

For an alternative to step b, I will list up Gibbs- Helmholtz equation as step e.

Step e) $\dfrac{\Delta G_{T_2}}{T_2} - \dfrac{\Delta G_{T_1}}{T_1} = \Delta H^o_{rxn}\left[\dfrac{1}{T_2} - \dfrac{1}{T_1}\right]$ (Eqn. 2-7)

I thought people usually like to use simpler form of formula than a bit complicated one like Gibbs-Helmholtz equation. Thus, I listed up van't Hoff equation (**Eqn. 2-13**) as a first choice.

$$K \rightarrow \Delta G^o \rightarrow \Delta H^o_{rxn} \text{ or } \Delta S^o_{rxn}$$

a. $\Delta G^0 = -RT \ln K$

b. $\ln \dfrac{K_2}{K_1} = -\dfrac{\Delta H^o_{rxn}}{R}\left(\dfrac{1}{T_2} - \dfrac{1}{T_1}\right)$

c. $\Delta G^o_{T_2} - \Delta G^o_{T_1} = -\Delta S^o_{rxn}(T_2 - T_1)$

d. $\Delta G^o = \Delta H^o_{rxn} - T\Delta S^o_{rxn}$

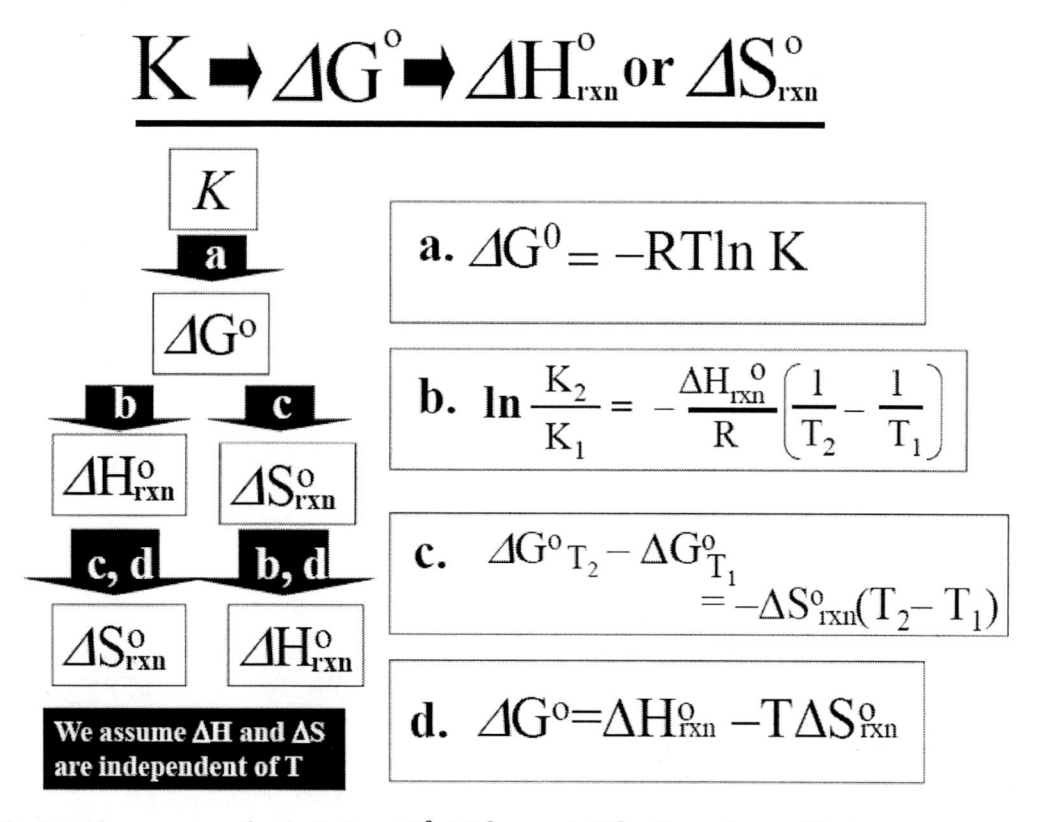

We assume ΔH and ΔS are independent of T

Fig. 2-6 The process of calculating ΔG^o, ΔH^o_{rxn}, and ΔS^o_{rxn} from the equilibrium constant K.

In the beginning, you are able to calculate ΔG^o from K (step a). Then, you have two choices. You may calculate ΔH^o_{rxn} from step b (van't Hoff equation), or ΔS^o_{rxn} is chosen to be calculated from step c. In both step a and b, you usually have the equilibrium constant at two different temperatures (K_1 for T_1 and K_2 for T_2) or Gibbs energy change of a reaction for two different temperatures (ΔG_{T_1} for T_1 and ΔG_{T_2} for T_2). If you have only K_1 and K_2, you may use step b to calculate ΔH^o_{rxn} first, or you can calculate ΔG_{T_1} and ΔG_{T_2} from step a) for T_1 and T_2, respectively. Once you extracted either ΔH^o_{rxn} or ΔS^o_{rxn}, you can calculate the other with known ΔG^o for temperature T by step d. (Of course, you can use step b) or c) for calculations of ΔH^o_{rxn} or ΔS^o_{rxn}, respectively. You will choose any step for each calculation, and the answer should be the same which step you take as far as ΔH^o_{rxn} and ΔS^o_{rxn} are considered to be constants under given temperature range T_1 and T_2.

EXERCISE 2-6
Calculate ΔG^o at 0 [°C] and 50 [°C] and ΔH^o_{rxn} and ΔS^o_{rxn}

T [°C]	K
0	1.35×10^{-10}
50	3.33×10^{-9}

ANSWER

❶ ΔG^o at 0 [°C]

$= -(8.314 \ [J\ K^{-1} mol^{-1}])(273.15\ [K]) \ln(1.35 \times 10^{-10})$

❷ $= 51.61$ [kJ]

❶ ΔG^o at 50 [°C]

$= -(8.314 \ [J\ K^{-1} mol^{-1}])(323.15\ [K]) \ln(3.33 \times 10^{-9})$

❷ $= 52.44$ [kJ]

For ΔH^o_{rxn} (0 [°C] - 50 [°C])

Using van't Hoff Equation

$$\ln \frac{K_2}{K_1} = -\frac{\Delta H^o_{rxn}}{R}\left[\frac{1}{T_2} - \frac{1}{T_1}\right] \quad \text{(Eqn. 2-13)}$$

If we arrange the (**Eqn.2-13**) for the enthalpy change,

❸ $\Delta H^o_{rxn} = -\dfrac{R \ln \frac{K_2}{K_1}}{\left[\frac{1}{T_2} - \frac{1}{T_1}\right]}$

❹ $= -\dfrac{8.314[J \cdot mol^{-1} \cdot K^{-1}] \ln \frac{3.33 \times 10^{-9}}{1.35 \times 10^{-10}}}{\left[\frac{1}{323[K]} - \frac{1}{273[K]}\right]}$

❺ $= -\dfrac{8.314[J \cdot mol^{-1} \cdot K^{-1}](3.205)}{-5.665 \times 10^{-4}}$

❻ $= 47.0$ [kJ/mol]

$\Delta G = \Delta H^o_{rxn} - T\Delta S^o_{rxn} \quad \text{(Eqn. 2-2)}$

$\Delta S^o_{rxn} = \dfrac{(\Delta H^o_{rxn} - \Delta G^o)}{T}$

❼ Using the value at T= 0 [°C] (273.15 [K])

❽ $\Delta S^o_{rxn} = \dfrac{(47000[J/mol] - 51610[J/mol])}{273.15\ K}$

❾ $= -16.767$ [J $K^{-1} mol^{-1}$]

❶ Convert temperature in Kelvins unit.

❷ Here, I am using kJ unit

❸ Carefully derive the equation on ΔH^o_{rxn}

❹ R=8.314 [J $K^{-1} mol^{-1}$]

Chapter 2 Gibbs Energy

❺ ☞	Are you getting correct number for $\frac{1}{T_2} - \frac{1}{T_1}$ term and natural log term?
❻ ☞	Here, I am using [kJ/mol] unit
❼ ☞	ΔS^o_{rxn} is assumed to be constant between 0 [°C] and 50 [°C]
❽ ☞	Did you notice that ΔG^o_{rxn} at 0 [°C] was used.
❾ ☞	Don't worry. ΔS^o_{rxn} can be negative.

☹ Most Common Mistake (16) Which temperature should I use?

Most common mistake people make in the problem like **EXERCISE 2-6** is the last step. You notice that T= 0 [°C] and the Gibbs energy change (ΔG°) at 0 [°C] were used for calculating the entropy change of a reaction for 0 [°C] to 50 [°C]. Each Gibbs energy has different value for each temperature, while entropy change of a reaction (ΔS^o_{rxn}) or enthalpy change of reaction (ΔH^o_{rxn}) are assumed to be a constant for given temperature range. When you use formula

$$\Delta S^o_{rxn} = \frac{(\Delta H^o_{rxn} - \Delta G^o_T)}{T}$$

make sure to use your determined temperature, T, and corresponding ΔG° for temperature T. That is "T" in ΔG^o_T should be the same temperature appearing in the denominator in the above equation.

☹ Most Common Mistake (17) – Gibbs Energy (G) and Helmholtz Energy (A) are the same thing?

If you know or heard about the Helmholtz energy, let's talk about that. But if you have not, you can skip this section. In this textbook, the treatment of Helmholtz energy has been ignored, but it is simple concept and you can understand it easily. The Helmholtz energy (A) and Gibbs energy are both determined as a deviation from (or addition to) internal energy E. They are measures of the amount of energy you need to put in to create a system once the spontaneous energy transfer to the system from the environment is accounted from temperature change (in the case of Helmholtz energy) or temperature and extra amount of work (in the case of Gibbs energy)..The internal energy is regarded as the energy required to create a system without changing temperature or work. When the system can obtain heat transfer from the environment spontaneously by TS, where S is the entropy of the system, the energy of the system is expressed by Helmholtz energy by

A = E − TS

What if not only temperature but an additional amount of work PV is involved in the system? Especially, if volume is altered due to this by this extra amount of work? Then you add another term PV on the top of Helmholtz energy A and define Gibbs energy as

$G = E - TS + PV$

Since $H = E + PV$,

$G = H - TS$

You notice and confirm that the change in Gibbs free energy, ΔG, in a reaction is a very useful parameter, since it can be considered as the maximum amount of work obtainable from a reaction.

Chapter 2

How did you get these equations?
-The derivation of selected equations.

(Eqn. 2-5) $\quad dG/dT = -S$

Starting from a definition of Gibbs energy.

$$G = H - TS \qquad \text{(Eqn. 2-1)}$$

Let's take a difference (Δ) of each term,

$$\Delta G = \Delta H - \Delta(TS)$$

Under constant temperature,

$$\Delta G = \Delta H - T\Delta S$$

By taking a differential of the above formula at *constant pressure*

$$d(\Delta G) = d(\Delta H) - d(T\Delta S)$$

If enthalpy change (ΔH) and entropy change (ΔS) are kept constant under the change of temperature (dT),

$$d(\Delta G) = -\Delta S dT$$

By arranging the above formula,

$$\frac{d(\Delta G)}{dT} = -\Delta S \qquad \text{(Eqn. 2-5)}$$

(Eqn. 2-6) $\quad \Delta G(T_2) - \Delta G(T_1) = -\Delta S(T_2 - T_1)$

By integrating both sides of (**Eqn. 2-5**), the Gibbs energy and the entropy change can be related with an integrated form.

$$\frac{d(\Delta G)}{dT} = -\Delta S \qquad \text{(Eqn. 2-5)}$$

By integrating both sides,

$$\int_{\Delta G(T_1)}^{\Delta G(T_2)} d\Delta G = -\int_{T_1}^{T_2} \Delta S \, dT$$

$$\Delta G(T_2) - \Delta G(T_1) = -\int_{T_1}^{T_2} \Delta S \, dT$$

Therefore,

$$\Delta G(T_2) - \Delta G(T_1) = -\Delta S(T_2 - T_1) \quad \text{(Eqn. 2-6)}$$

Here, ΔS was assumed to be constant within a given temperature range (between T_1 and T_2).

(Eqn. 2-7) $\quad \dfrac{\Delta G_{T_2}}{T_2} - \dfrac{\Delta G_{T_1}}{T_1} = \Delta H_{rxn}^o \left[\dfrac{1}{T_2} - \dfrac{1}{T_1} \right]$

The relationship given in (**Eqn. 2-5**)

$$\frac{d\Delta G}{dT} = -\Delta S \quad \text{(eqn. 2-5)}$$

By rephrasing the above formula as a relationship as the derivative of temperature under constant pressure,

$$\left[\frac{\partial \Delta G}{\partial T}\right]_P = -\Delta S$$

From (**Eqn. 2-2**),

$$\Delta G = \Delta H - T\Delta S \quad \text{(Eqn. 2-2)}$$

The entropy change (ΔS) can be expressed with the enthalpy change (ΔH) and the Gibbs energy change (ΔG).

$$\left[\frac{\partial \Delta G}{\partial T}\right]_P - \frac{\Delta G}{T} = -\frac{\Delta H}{T}$$

We do the following magical or what I call "Ninja" transformation of the term aiming to re-express the relationship with minimum terms.

$$T\left[\frac{\partial}{\partial T}\left[\frac{\Delta G}{T}\right]\right]_P = -\frac{\Delta H}{T}$$

Thus,

$$\left[\frac{\partial}{\partial T}\left[\frac{\Delta G}{T}\right]\right]_P = -\frac{\Delta H}{T^2}$$

Let's make an preparation for an integration by arranging the above as

Chapter 2 Gibbs Energy

$$d\left[\frac{\Delta G}{T}\right]_P = -\frac{\Delta H}{T^2} dT$$

We will integrate the above left term between $\frac{\Delta G_{T_1}}{T_1}$ and $\frac{\Delta G_{T_2}}{T_2}$, right term between T_1 to T_2.

$$\int_{\frac{\Delta G_{T_1}}{T_1}}^{\frac{\Delta G_{T_2}}{T_2}} d\left[\frac{\Delta G}{T}\right]_P = -\int_{T_1}^{T_2} \frac{\Delta H}{T^2} dT$$

Generally, and integration of x^n is

$$\int x^n dx = \frac{1}{n+1} x^{n+1} + constant.$$

$$-\int_{T_1}^{T_2} \frac{\Delta H^o_{rxn}}{T^2} dT = \left.\frac{\Delta H^o_{rxn}}{T}\right|_{T_1}^{T_2}$$

Therefore,

$$\frac{\Delta G_{T_2}}{T_2} - \frac{\Delta G_{T_1}}{T_1} = \Delta H^o_{rxn}\left[\frac{1}{T_2} - \frac{1}{T_1}\right] \quad \textbf{(Eqn. 2-7)}$$

(Eqn. 2-13) $\quad \ln\frac{K_2}{K_1} = -\frac{\Delta H^o}{R}\left[\frac{1}{T_2} - \frac{1}{T_1}\right]$

The Gibbs energy change and the equilibrium constant is related as:

$$\Delta G^o = -RT \ln K \quad \textbf{(Eqn. 2-10)}$$

By taking a derivative of the (**Eqn. 2-10**) against temperature, T,
$\frac{d}{dT}(\Delta G^o) = -\frac{d}{dT}(RT \ln K)$

$$\frac{d(\Delta G^o)}{dT} = -R \ln K - RT\frac{d}{dT}(\ln K)$$

$$\frac{d(\Delta G^o)}{dT} + R \ln K = -RT\frac{d}{dT}(\ln K)$$

$$\frac{d(\Delta G^o)}{dT} - \frac{\Delta G^o}{T} = -RT\frac{d}{dT}(\ln K)$$

The second term used a relationship given in (**Eqn. 2-10**)

The first term of the left side can be replaced by next relationship.

$$\frac{d\Delta G^o}{dT} = -\Delta S^o \quad \textbf{(Eqn. 2-5)}$$

Thus,

$$-\Delta S^o - \frac{\Delta G^o}{T} = -RT\frac{d}{dT}(\ln K)$$

Let's replace ΔG^o with the following relationship

$$\Delta G^o = \Delta H^o - T\Delta S^o \qquad \textbf{(Eqn. 2-2)}$$

$$-\Delta S^o - \left(\frac{\Delta H^o - T\Delta S^o}{T}\right) = -RT\frac{d}{dT}(\ln K)$$

$$-\Delta S^o - \frac{\Delta H^o}{T} + \Delta S^o = -RT\frac{d}{dT}(\ln K)$$

$$-\frac{\Delta H^o}{T} = -RT\frac{d}{dT}(\ln K)$$

$$\Delta H^o = RT^2\frac{d\ln K}{dT}$$

Now, we have a relationship between equilibrium constant K and the enthalpy change, and this term can be arranged as

$$\frac{d\ln K}{d\left[\frac{1}{T}\right]} = -\frac{\Delta H^o}{R}$$

In order to obtain the above formula, we made another magical or "Ninja" arrangement of the following

$$-T^2\frac{1}{dT} = \frac{1}{d\left[\frac{1}{T}\right]}$$

$$T^2\frac{d}{dT} = -\frac{d}{d\left[\frac{1}{T}\right]}$$

We will prepare for an integration process as:

$$\frac{d\ln K}{d\left[\frac{1}{T}\right]} = -\frac{\Delta H^o}{R}$$

$$d\ln K = -\frac{\Delta H^o}{R}d\left[\frac{1}{T}\right]$$

By integrating the above between T_1 and T_2,

$$\int_{T_1}^{T_2} d\ln K = -\frac{\Delta H^o}{R} \int_{T_1}^{T_2} d\left[\frac{1}{T}\right]$$

$$\ln\frac{K_2}{K_1} = -\frac{\Delta H^o}{R}\left[\frac{1}{T_2} - \frac{1}{T_1}\right] \qquad \textbf{(Eqn. 2-13)}$$

Chapter 2 Summary [Part 1]

(Use back page to cover the contents.)

1	Gibbs energy (G)	capacity of doing work $G = H - TS$ (Eqn. 2-1)
2	The Gibbs energy change (ΔG)	$\Delta G = \Delta H - T\Delta S$ (Eqn. 2-2) $\Delta G = w_{rev}^*$ (Eqn. 2-3)
3	ΔG and spontaneous reaction	ΔG < 0 **Spontaneous process** ΔG > 0 **Non-spontaneous process** ΔG = 0 **System at equilibrium**
4	The Gibbs energy of a reaction (ΔG_{rxn}^o)	$\Delta G_{rxn}^o = \sum_{products} \Delta G_f^o - \sum_{reactants} \Delta G_f^o$ (Eqn. 2-4)
5	Temperature dependence of Gibbs energy (graph) with respect to ΔS_{rxn}^o	$\dfrac{d\Delta G}{dT} = -\Delta S$ (Eqn. 2-5) $\Delta G_{T_2} - \Delta G_{T_1} = -\Delta S_{rxn}^o (T_2 - T_1)$ (Eqn. 2-6) *(graph: ΔG vs T, linear decreasing with slope −ΔS)*
6	Gibbs-Helmholtz equation and graph	$\dfrac{\Delta G_{T_2}}{T_2} - \dfrac{\Delta G_{T_1}}{T_1} = \Delta H_{rxn}^o \left[\dfrac{1}{T_2} - \dfrac{1}{T_1}\right]$ (Eqn. 2-7) *(graph: ΔG/T vs 1/T, linear with slope ΔH)*

[Fold the page at the double line and cover the right half.]

Chapter 2 Summary Check [Part 1]

(Use this page to cover and check the contents.)
Use ☐ as your check box. Write your comment at far right

#	Topic	Check	Comment
1	Gibbs energy (G)	☐ ☐ ☐ ☐ ☐	
2	The Gibbs energy change (ΔG)	☐ ☐ ☐ ☐ ☐	
3	ΔG and spontaneous reaction	☐ ☐ ☐ ☐ ☐	
4	The Gibbs energy of a reaction (ΔG^o_{rxn})	☐ ☐ ☐ ☐ ☐	
5	Temperature dependence of Gibbs energy (graph) with respect to ΔS^o_{rxn}	☐ ☐ ☐ ☐ ☐	
6	Gibbs-Helmholtz equation and graph	☐ ☐ ☐ ☐ ☐	

Chapter 2 Summary [Part 2]

(Use back page to cover the contents.)

7	chemical potential (μ)	molar Gibbs energy: $\mu_A = \left[\dfrac{\partial G}{\partial n_A}\right]_{T,P,n_j \neq n_A}$ (Eqn. 2-8)
8	Gibbs energy and reaction and equilibrium constant	$\Delta G^o = -RT \ln K$ (Eqn. 2-10) $$K = \dfrac{[C]_{eq}^c [D]_{eq}^d}{[A]_{eq}^a [B]_{eq}^b}$$
9	Gibbs energy under non-equilibrium condition	$\Delta G = \Delta G^o + RT \ln Q$ (Eqn. 2-11) $$Q = \dfrac{[C]^c [D]^d}{[A]^a [B]^b}$$
10	van't Hoff equation (graph)	$\ln \dfrac{K_2}{K_1} = -\dfrac{\Delta H_{rxn}^o}{R}\left[\dfrac{1}{T_2} - \dfrac{1}{T_1}\right]$ (Eqn. 2-13) Plot of ln K vs 1/T with slope $-\Delta H/R$

[Fold the page at the double line and cover the right half.]

CHAPTER 2 SUMMARY CHECK [PART 1]

(Use this page to cover and check the contents.)
Use ☐ as your check box. Write your comment at far right

7	chemical potential (μ)	☐ ☐ ☐ ☐ ☐	
8	Gibbs energy and reaction and equilibrium constant	☐ ☐ ☐ ☐ ☐	
9	Gibbs energy under non-equilibrium condition	☐ ☐ ☐ ☐ ☐	
10	*van't Hoff equation (graph)*	☐ ☐ ☐ ☐ ☐	

Chapter 2 - YOUR TEACHER MAY TEST YOU ON:

No.	What may be asked?		What you should know or do?
1	How Gibbs energy or Gibbs energy change, ΔG, is defined using other thermodynamical parameters?	→	$\Delta G = \Delta H - T\Delta S$ (Eqn. 2-2)
		→	EXERCISE 2-1
		→	Problems 2-10, 2-11
2	How can you tell a reaction proceeds spontaneously, non-spontaneously, or reaches to an equilibrium?	→	ΔG < 0 Spontaneous process ΔG > 0 Non-spontaneous process ΔG = 0 System at equilibrium
		→	EXERCISE 2-1
		→	Problem 2-1
3	How do you calculate the Gibbs energy change of a reaction?	→	$\Delta G = \Delta H - T\Delta S$ (Eqn. 2-2) $\Delta G^o_{rxn} = \sum_{products} \Delta G^o_f - \sum_{reactants} \Delta G^o_f$ (Eqn. 2-4)
		→	EXERCISE 2-2, 2-3
		→	Problems 2-2, 2-3, 2-4, 2-8, 2-9
4	Can you draw a graph and explain how Gibbs energy change is described as a function of temperature?	→	Fig. 2-3a
		→	Problems 2-6, 2-12, 2-13, 2-14
5	What is Gibbs–Helmholtz relationship? Can you draw a graph displaying Gibbs–Helmholtz equation?	→	$\frac{\Delta G_{T_2}}{T_2} - \frac{\Delta G_{T_1}}{T_1} = \Delta H^o_{rxn}\left[\frac{1}{T_2} - \frac{1}{T_1}\right]$ (Eqn. 2-7)
		→	Fig. 2-3b
		→	Problems 2-5, 2-7
6	What is a chemical potential?	→	$\mu_A = \left[\frac{\partial G}{\partial n_A}\right]_{T,P,n_j \neq n_A}$ (Eqn. 2-8)
		→	Problem 2-15
7	How do you calculate the Gibbs energy change of a reaction with known equilibrium constant of a reaction?	→	$\Delta G^o = -RT \ln K$ (Eqn. 2-10) $K = \left[\frac{[C]^c_{eq}[D]^d_{eq}}{[A]^a_{eq}[B]^b_{eq}}\right]$ (Eqn. 2-9)
		→	Problems 2-16, 2-17
8	How do you calculate the Gibbs energy change of a reaction when it is not at equilibrium?	→	$\Delta G = \Delta G^o + RT \ln Q$ (Eqn. 2-11) $Q = \left[\frac{[C]^c[D]^d}{[A]^a[B]^b}\right]$ (Eqn. 2-12)
		→	EXERCISE 2-4
		→	Problems 2-18, 2-19
9	How do you use van't Hoff equation?	→	$\ln \frac{K_2}{K_1} = -\frac{\Delta H^o_{rxn}}{R}\left[\frac{1}{T_2} - \frac{1}{T_1}\right]$ (Eqn. 2-13)
		→	EXERCISE 2-5
		→	Problems

10	Calculate ΔG, ΔH, and ΔS starting from equilibrium constants, K at given temperature.	→ → →	2-20, 2-21, 2-22, 2-23, 2-24, 2-25 Fig. 2-6 EXERCISE 2-6 Problems 2-26, 2-27

UNIT CHECK CHAPTER 2

Important Parameters of This Chapter	Popularly Used Unit	Important Unit Conversion
Gibbs Energy, G	J/mol kJ/mol	
Gibbs Energy Change, ΔG	J/mol kJ/mol	
Work, w	J	
Temperature, T	°C K	0 [°C] = 273.15 [K]
Enthalpy, H	J/mol kJ/mol	
Enthalpy change, ΔH	J/mol kJ/mol	
Heat capacity, C, C_P, C_V	J/K	
Molar heat capacity, $\bar{C}$, $\overline{C_P}$, $\overline{C_V}$	$J\,K^{-1}mol^{-1}$	
Gas constant, R	$atm\,L\,K^{-1}mol^{-1}$ $J\,K^{-1}mol^{-1}$	$R=8.314472\,[J\,K^{-1}mol^{-1}]$ $=0.08205746$ $[atm\,L\,K^{-1}mol^{-1}]$
Entropy, S	$J\,K^{-1}mol^{-1}$ $kJ\,K^{-1}mol^{-1}$	
Entropy change, ΔS	$J\,K^{-1}mol^{-1}$ $kJ\,K^{-1}mol^{-1}$	
Chemical potential, μ	J/mol kJ/mol	
Equilibrium constant, K	$M^{c+d-(a+b)}$	

SUMMARY OF TRICKY TRAPS OF CHAPTER 2

☐	1	The unit of ΔS is [J/ k mol] whereas the unit of ΔG or ΔH are [kJ/mol]
☐	2	When you use ΔG = ΔH−TΔS or ΔG = −RT ln K, T is in kelvins unit.
☐	3	When you use ΔG = ΔH−TΔS , make sure if ΔH or ΔS are stated as the parameters independent of temperature. (If they do, depended on temperature, you need to calculate the value of the ΔH or ΔS at given temperature. --> See $\Delta H_{rxn}^{T_2} - \Delta H_{rxn}^{T_1} = \Delta C_P(T_2 - T_1)$ (Eqn. 1-28) $\Delta S_{rxn,(T_2)}^o = \Delta S_{rxn,(T_1)}^o + \Delta C_P \ln \frac{T_2}{T_1}$ (Eqn. 1-36)
☐	4	When you use ΔG = −RT ln K, R (gas constant)is R=8.314 [J/K mol]is in kelvins unit.
☐	5	Calculate more than three significant figures for (1/T).
☐	6	You can calculate all ΔG, ΔH,ΔS from equilibrium constants, K.
☐	7	In ΔG = ΔH−TΔS, make sure ΔG, ΔH, and ΔS are all valid at given temperature ,T. (Use ΔG(T), ΔH(T), and ΔS(T)).
☐	8	When you useΔG = −RT ln K, K is the constant at equilibrium only.

LAST MINUTE REVIEW OF MATH CHAPTER 2

(These are basic algebra which you have no excuse if you miss them.)

1. $\ln x = y \quad x = e^y$
2. $\frac{1}{A} + \frac{1}{B} = \frac{B+A}{AB}$
3. $\frac{dy}{dx} = A \quad dy = Adx$
4. $y = mx + b \quad m = \frac{dy}{dx}$

Nobel Prize and Your Knowledge From Chapter 2
(*: word appeared in Chapter 2)

The Nobel Prize in Chemistry 1978 was awarded to **Peter Dennis Mitchell** "for his contribution to the understanding of biological energy transfer through the formulation of the chemiosmotic theory *(discovery of the chemiosmotic mechanism of ATP synthesis)*". In the 1960s, ATP was known to be the energy currency of life, but the mechanism by which ATP was created in the mitochondria was assumed to be by substrate-level phosphorylation. Mitchell's chemiosmotic hypothesis was the basis for understanding the actual process of oxidative phosphorylation. At the time, the biochemical mechanism of ATP synthesis by oxidative phosphorylation was unknown. Mitchell realized that the movement of ions across an **electrochemical membrane potential*** could provide the energy needed to produce ATP. His hypothesis was derived from information that was well known in the 1960s. He knew that living cells had a membrane potential; interior negative to the environment. The movement of charged ions across a membrane is thus affected by the electrical forces (the attraction of plus to minus charges). Their movement is also affected by thermodynamic forces, the tendency of substances to diffuse from regions of higher concentration. He went on to show that ATP synthesis was coupled to this electrochemical gradient. His hypothesis was confirmed by the discovery of ATP synthase, a membrane-bound protein that uses the potential energy of the electrochemical gradient to make ATP.

As a good example of ATP involved reaction and review of what we learned in this chapter, a series of thermodynamic process of metabolism of glucose is shown. The overall chemical reaction and its **Gibbs energy*** is given as:

Glucose + 2NAD$^+$ + 2ADP + 2P$_i$ → 2pyruvate + 2NADH + 2ATP + 2H$^+$ + 2H$_2$O $\Delta G°_{298}$ = –80.6 kJ

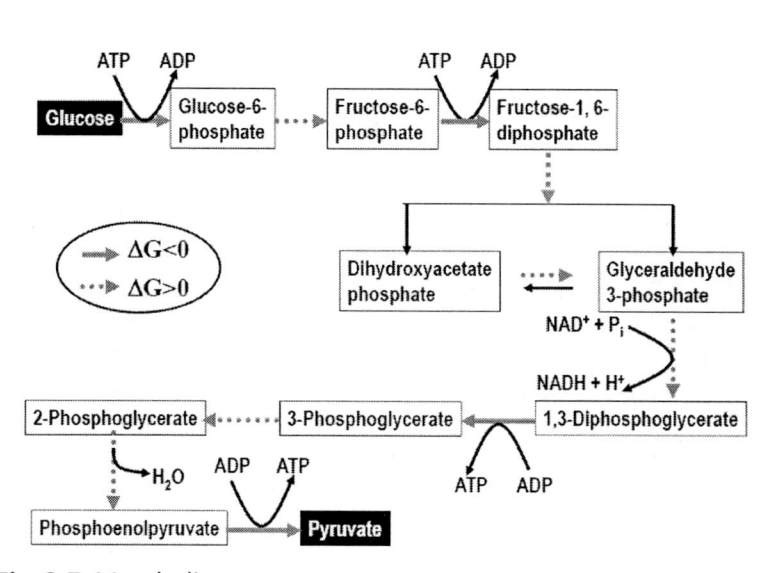

Fig. 2-7 Metabolism process

Please note that this process is picked up from the initial substance Glucose and the last substance pyruvate. The ATP to ADP transformation is marked so many times, and it plays a key role for making an entire metabolic process going. As a overall reaction, it shows that negative Gibbs energy, implying an entire metabolic process is spontaneous. However, a significant amount of intermediate processes are not spontaneous as they are marked as dotted line in **Fig 2-7**. Therefore, it indicates that spontaneous initial and a terminal processes may make an entire process as a spontaneous process.

THE FOCUSED PHYSICAL CHEMISTRY EXPERIMENTAL APPROACH ASSOCIATED WITH CHAPTER 2

(*: word appeared in Chapter 2)

ITC (Isothermal Titration Calorimetry) Method

Isothermal Titration Calorimetry (ITC) determines binding parameters of biomolecular interactions and the involved heat in bindings. Through the measurement of heat, binding constants (K_B), reaction stoichiometry (n), **enthalpy (ΔH)*** and **entropy (ΔS)*** are obtained. (According to (**Eqn.2-2**), **Gibbs energy (ΔG)*** can be obtained as well.) The mechanism of the molecular interaction in binding such as interactions between protein-small molecule, protein-protein, enzyme-inhibitor, antibody-antigen, protein-DNA, protein-lipid, and small molecule-small molecule are identified.

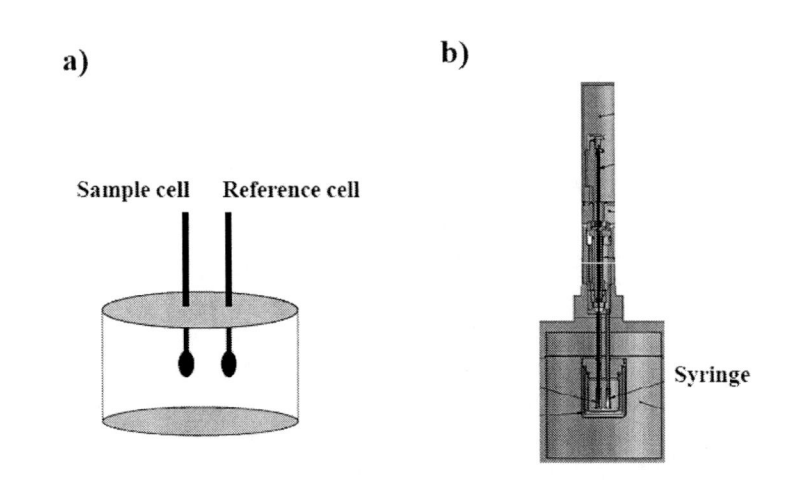

Fig. 2-9 Diagram of ITC cells (a) and syringe (b). The syringe rotates in place to provide continuous mixing in the ITC cell. A computer-controlled plunger injects precise amount of ligand.

Without any labeling or immobilization, ITC can directly measure sub-millimolar to nanomolar binding constants (10^2 to 10^9 [M^{-1}]) and nanomolar to picomolar binding constants. Generally, ITC systems has a cell feedback network to differentially measure and compensate for heat between the sample and reference cell. Twin cells are mounted in a cylindrical chamber which is maintained in an adiabatic environment. Through narrow access tubes (**Fig. 2-9a**), it is connected to outside. The temperature difference between the two cells and the temperature difference between the cells and the jacket are also measured. If chemical reactions occur in the sample cell, heat is released or absorbed while the temperature difference between the sample and reference cells (ΔT) is kept at a constant value (i.e. baseline) by the addition or removal of heat to the sample cell. Thus, total of the power required to maintain ΔT corresponds to a total heat resulting from the reaction process. A schematic drawing of the ITC cells and syringe is shown in **Fig. 2-9b**. A syringe containing a "ligand" solution is titrated into a cell containing a solution of the "macromolecule" at constant temperature.

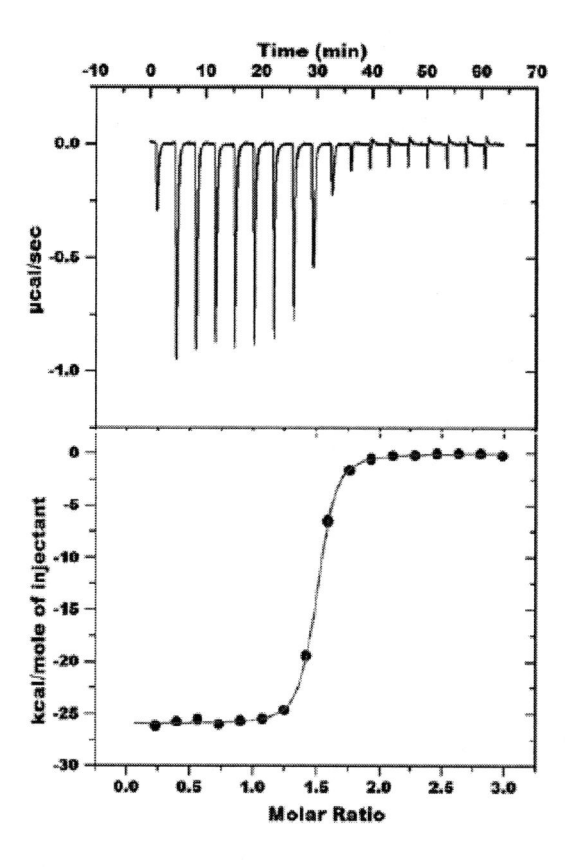

Fig. 2-10 Representative ITC data. The ligand solution is injected 18 times to protein solution in the cell. (Top)Raw data (Bottom) integrated data.

As the ligand is injected into the cell, the interaction takes place, and heat is released or absorbed with proportional amount of binding. When the macromolecule in the cell is saturated with ligand, the heat signal diminishes and only the background heat of dilution is observed (**Fig. 2-10**). The area underneath each peak corresponds to the total heat released for that injection in the top of (**Fig. 2-10**), and an integrated heat is plotted against the molar ratio of ligand added to macromolecule in the cell resulting binding isotherm for the interaction in the bottom of (**Fig. 2-10**). Depending on the model of site (one site model or two sites model) the data is best fitted.

Chapter 2 Problems.

2-1 [ΔG and spontaneous] Choose the correct statement
At constant temperature and pressure, the spontaneous process takes place when:
  a) $\Delta G < 0$ and $\Delta G = 0$.
  b) $\Delta G > 0$ or $\Delta G = 0$.
  c) $\Delta G < 0$ and $\Delta G > 0$.
  d) $\Delta G < 0$ and $\Delta G = 0$.
  e) $\Delta G > 0$.
  f) none of the above.

2-2 [ΔG, direct method] $C_2H_5OH(l) \rightarrow C_2H_6(g) + \tfrac{1}{2}O_2(g)$
  Calculate ΔG^0_{298}

2-3 [ΔG, direct method] The pyruvic acid ($CH_3COCOOH$) coverts into gaseous acetaldehyde (CH_3CHO) and gaseous CO_2. Calculate ΔG^0_{298} (Use CRC Table).

2-4 [ΔG, direct method] Calculate the ΔG_{298} of conversion of pyruvic acid into acetaldehyde and carbon dioxide at 100 [atm].

2-5 [ΔG Temperature dependence] Calculate ΔG^0_{310} when $\Delta G^0_{298} = -26.98$ [kJ/mol] (at the standard condition) and $\Delta H^0 = -43.32$ [kJ/mol]. You can assume ΔH is independent of temperature.

2-6 [ΔG → ΔH → ΔS, temperature dependence]
A single-stranded oligonucleotide can form a base-paired hairpin loop. The equilibrium constant is 0.86 at 25 [°C] and is 0.51 at 37 [°C]. Calculate ΔH and ΔS at 37 [°C].

2-7 [ΔG Temperature dependence] What is the ΔG^0_{293} of hydrolysis of glycilyglycine at 1 [atm].

2-8 [ΔG, direct method] Is the reaction to form solid alanine, and liquid water from $CH_4(g)$, $NH_3(g)$, and $O_2(g)$ spontaneous at 25 [°C] and 1 [atm]? (Use CRC Table).

2-9 [ΔG, direct method] pyruvic acid(l) → acetaldehyde(g) + $CO_2(g)$
Calculate the equilibrium constant at 25 [°C] for the decarboxylation of liquid pyruvic acid to form gaseous acetaldehyde and CO_2.
ΔG(pyruvic acid, (l)) = -463.38 [kJ/mol]
ΔG(acetaldehyde, (g)) = -133.30 [kJ/mol]
$\Delta G(CO_2, (g))$ = -394.36 [kJ/mol]

2-10 [ΔG from ΔH & ΔS]. Consider the synthesis of urea according to the equation:
  $CO_2(g) + 2NH_3(g) \rightarrow (NH_2)_2CO(s) + H_2O(l)$
a) Calculate the ΔH^0_{298} for the urea synthesis
b) Calculate the ΔS^0_{298} for the urea synthesis
c) Answer if this reaction is spontaneous or not.
d) In this reaction, ΔS^0_{298} dependents on the temperature, however ΔH^0_{298} does not. Based on this result, calculate the Gibbs energy for this reaction at 50 [°C] and 1 [atm].

2-11 [ΔG from ΔH & ΔS]
  $C_2H_5OH(l) \rightarrow C_2H_6(g) + \tfrac{1}{2}O_2(g)$

Calculate $\Delta G°_{298}$ (in the unit of kJ/mol) for the above reaction using the values given in the tables below ($\Delta H°_{298}$ (in kJmol^{-1}) and $\Delta S°_{298}$ (in J K^{-1}mol^{-1}). Your answer should be given with three significant figures and in the unit of kJ/mol.

	$\Delta H°_{298}$ [kJmol^{-1}]	$\Delta S°_{298}$ [J K^{-1}mol^{-1}]
$C_2H_5OH(l)$	-270	185
$C_2H_6(g)$	-75.0	255
$O_2(g)$	0	210

2-12 [plot ΔG vs T] The temperature dependence of the Gibbs energy change is equal to the negative value of the entropy change. $\frac{d\Delta G}{dT} = -\Delta S$ Sketch this equation in the plot when $\Delta S > 0$. Make sure to write any necessary parameters in your graph.

2-13 [ΔG from ΔH & ΔS, temperature dependence] Calculate the Gibbs energy change ΔG at 34.9 °C of hydrolysis of glycylglycine at 1 atm. At 19.5 °C, the ΔH, ΔG, and ΔS for this reaction are: ΔH = –44.0 kJ mol^{-1}, ΔG = –30.9 kJ mol^{-1}, ΔS = –54.0 J K^{-1}mol^{-1}. If the temperature range is small, the consistency of ΔH and ΔS is a good approximation. Provide your answer with three significant figures in the unit of kJ mol^{-1}.

2-14 [ΔG from ΔH & ΔS, temperature dependence] The glycylglycine, $C_4H_8N_2O_3(s)$, was reacted with oxygen gas to form solid urea: $(NH_2)_2CO(s)$, CO_2 gas, and H_2O at 25 [°C] and 1 [atm] according to the equation:

$3O_2(g) + C_4H_8N_2O_3(s) \rightarrow (NH_2)_2CO(s) + 3CO_2(g) + 2H_2O(l)$

a) Calculate the enthalpy for this reaction at 1[atm] and 25 [°C].
b) Calculate the $\Delta S°_{298}$ for this reaction at 1 [atm] and 25 [°C].
c) Calculate the Gibbs energy change, $\Delta G°_{298}$, for this reaction at 1 [atm] and 25 [°C].
d) Calculate the Gibbs energy change for this reaction at 65 [°C] and 1 [atm]. Assume $\Delta S°_{298}$ and $\Delta H°_{298}$ do not depend upon the temperature.

2-15 [Chem potential] If a system is consisted of particle A, B and C, what is the expression for the Gibbs energy, G, of this system at constant temperature, T and pressure, P. Express it with the chemical potential of each component μ_A, μ_B, and μ_C, and the number of moles (n_A, n_B, and n_C).

2-16 [K from ΔG] Calculate the equilibrium constant at 30 [°C] for the decarboxylation of liquid pyruvic acid $CH_3COCOOH$?

2-17 [ΔG =–RTlnK] What is the Gibbs-free energy change of forming 1 [mol] of NH_3 at 298 [K] if 5 [atm] of N_2 and 5 [atm] of H_2 are reacted to give 10 [atm] of NH_3 ?

2-18 [ΔG =ΔG° +RTlnQ] In the frog muscle, rectus abdominis, the concentration of ATP, ADP, and phosphate are 1.70×10^{-2} [M], 4.00×10^{-3} [M], and 6.00×10^{-3} [M], respectively. Calculate Gibbs energy change, ΔG, for the hydrolysis of ATP in muscle at 25.0 [°C]. Use $\Delta G°$ (at 25.0 [°C]) is–37.5 [kJ/mol].

2-19 [ΔG =ΔG° +RTlnQ] In the frog muscle, rectus abdominis, the concentration of ATP, ADP, and phosphate are 1.25×10^{-3} [M], 0.50×10^{-3}[M], and 2.5×10^{-3} [M], respectively. Calculate Gibbs energy change for the hydrolysis of ATP in muscle.

2-20 [ΔG , van't Hoff] In general, native proteins are in equilibrium with denatured forms:

Protein x (native) ⇌ Protein x (denatured)

For a protein x, the following concentration data for the two forms were experimentally determined.

Temperature [°C]	Native [mol/L]	Denatured
50	9.97×10^{-4}	2.57×10^{-6}
100	8.6×10^{-4}	1.4×10^{-4}

Determine ΔH° for the denaturing reaction assuming it to be independent of temperature. Then, calculate ΔS° for the denaturing reaction at 50 [°C]. Assume that ΔS° is independent of temperature.

2-21 [ΔG , van't Hoff] In the enzymatic conversion of L-asparate to fumarate and ammonium ion, the equilibrium constant was found to be 0.0160 [M] at 39 [°C] and 0.0074 [M] at 29 [°C]. Calculate ΔS° for the enzymatic reaction at 39 [°C].

2-22 [ΔG , van't Hoff] A single-stranded oligonucleotide can form a base-paired hairpin loop. The equilibrium constant is 0.92 at 25.5 [°C] and is 0.40 at 40.0 [°C]. Calculate ΔH° at 40.0 [°C] and ΔS° at 40.0 [°C].

2-23 [ΔG , van't Hoff] The following statement is about the *van't* Hoff equation. Please *choose the wrong statement*.
a. This equation indicates that you can get a linear line by plotting *ln* K versus 1/T.
b. This equation provides accurate ΔH₀ between given temperature T₁ and T₂ from the slope (−ΔH°/R) of ln K versus 1/T plot.
c. This equation was derived from [∂(*ln* K) / ∂(1/T)]ₚ= −ΔH°/R
d. In this equation, ΔH° needs to be assumed to be a constant.
e. all are correct

2-24 [ΔG , van't Hoff] Calculate pH at body temperature 37 [°C], using the *van't* Hoff equation. The ionization constant of the water is 1.00×10^{-14} at 25 [°C] and ΔH₀ =55.84 [kJ].
a. 6.81
b. 7.00
c. 7.14
d. 8.23
e. none of these

2-25 [ΔG , van't Hoff] The equilibrium constant for ionization of 4-aminopyridine is 1.35×10^{-10} at 0 [°C] and 3.33×10^{-9} at 50 [°C]. Calculate ΔG° at 0 [°C] and 50 [°C] as well as ΔH° and ΔS°.

2-26 [ΔS from K & ΔG] A single-stranded oligonucleotide that has complementary ends can form a base-paired hairpin loop. At 25 [°C], the equilibrium constant K is 0.85. At 34.00 [°C] the equilibrium constant is 0.29. Calculate ΔS at 34.00 [°C].

2-27 [K, ΔG from ΔH & ΔS] $SO_3(g)$ can react with $H_2O(g)$ to form sulfuric acid, $H_2SO_4(g)$. Air that is in equilibrium with water at 25 [°C] has a partial pressure of $H_2O(g)$ of 0.0463 [atm]. Find the equilibrium ratio of partial pressures of $H_2SO_4(g)$ to $SO_3(g)$, [$H_2SO_4(g)$] / [$SO_3(g)$], in air at 25 [°C].

$$\Delta H° (O_2(g)) = 0 \text{ [kJ/mol]}$$
$$\Delta H° (H_2O(g)) = -241.8 \text{ [kJ/mol]}$$
$$\Delta H° (SO_2(g)) = -296.8 \text{ [kJ/mol]}$$
$$\Delta H° (SO_3(g)) = -395.7 \text{ [kJ/mol]}$$
$$\Delta H° (H_2SO_4(g)) = -814.0 \text{ [kJ/mol]}$$

$$\Delta S° (O_2(g)) = 205.1 \text{ [J K}^{-1}\text{mol}^{-1}\text{]}$$
$$\Delta S° (H_2O(g)) = 188.7 \text{ [J K}^{-1}\text{mol}^{-1}\text{]}$$
$$\Delta S° (SO_2(g)) = 248.2 \text{ [J K}^{-1}\text{mol}^{-1}\text{]}$$
$$\Delta S° (SO_3(g)) = 256.8 \text{ [J K}^{-1}\text{mol}^{-1}\text{]}$$
$$\Delta S° (H_2SO_4(g)) = 156.9 \text{ [J K}^{-1}\text{mol}^{-1}\text{]}$$

Chapter 2 Answers. For Selected Problems

2-1 False
2-2 141.3 [kJ/mol]
2-3 −64.3 [kJ/mol]
2-4 11.4 [kJ/mol]
2-6 ΔH= −33.44 [kJ/mol], $\Delta G°_{298}$=373.67 [J/mol], $\Delta G°_{310}$= 1735.4 [J/mol], $\Delta S°_{298}$= 0.1135 [kJ K^{-1}mol^{-1}], $\Delta S°_{310}$ = 0.1135 [kJ K^{-1}mol^{-1}]
2-7 −27.4 [kJ/mol]
2-8 spontaneous
2-9 $\Delta G°$ =−64.28 [kJ], K = 1.85 × 10^{11}
2-10 a) $\Delta H°_{298}$ =−133.27 [kJ/mol] b) $\Delta S°_{298}$ = −424.13 [J/K]
c) $\Delta G°_{298}$ = −7.0[kJ/mol] <0, Spontaneous reaction
d) $\Delta G°_{(50 °C)}$ = 3.55 [kJ/mol]
2-11 $\Delta G°$ =143 [kJ/mol]
2-13 $\Delta G(307.9 [K])$= −30.1 [kJ/mol]
2-14 a) $\Delta H°_{298}$=−1340.11 [kJ/mol] b) $\Delta S°_{298}$ = 80.276 [J K^{-1}mol^{-1}]
c) $\Delta G°$ = − 1364.03 [kJ/mol] d) $\Delta G°$ = −1367.13 [kJ/mol]
2-15 $G = n_A\mu_A + n_B\mu_B + n_C\mu_C$
2-16 1.4 ×10^{11}
2-17 −5.15 [kJ/mol]
2-18 ΔG=−53.8 [kJ/mol]
2-19 −48 [kJ/mol]
2-20 K (T=50 [°C]) = 2.58 × 10^{-3}, K (T=100 [°C]) = 0.1628, ΔH = 83.05 [kJ/mol]
$\Delta G(50 [°C])$ = 16 [kJ/mol], ΔS= 0.207 [kJ K^{-1}mol^{-1}]
2-21 $\Delta H°$ = 14,500 [cal/mol], $\Delta G°$= 2560 [cal/mol], $\Delta S°$= 38.2 [cal K^{-1}mol^{-1}]
2-22 $\Delta H°$= −44.6 [kJ/mol], $\Delta S°$=−149 [J K^{-1}mol^{-1}]
2-24 6.81
2-25 $\Delta H°$= 47 [kJ/mol], $\Delta S°$= −16.78 [J/K]
2-26 $\Delta S°$ = ($\Delta H° - \Delta G°$) / T = −315 [J K^{-1}mol^{-1}]
2-27 ΔH= −176.5 [kJ/mol], ΔS= −288.6 [J K^{-1}mol^{-1}] at T =298 K, [$H_2O(g)$] = 0.00463 [atm]
[$H_2SO_4(g)$] / [$SO_3(g)$] = 3.3×10^{14}

Chapter 3
Chemical Equilibria in Solution

3-1   Equilibrium in Solution
3-2   Activity
3-3   Chemical Potential and Activity
3-4   Thermodynamic Characteristics of the Cell Reaction
3-5   Oxidation- and Reduction- Reactions at the Electrode

Chapter 3 Chemical Equilibria in Solution

- **Why do I have to study this chapter?**

You will realize that the concentration is of the system needs so many corrections. You will learn how to express this dilemma in chemistry for different system. (This is called as an "activity".) By using these corrections, equilibrium constant and Gibbs energy are more accurately obtained. Many important biological reactions can be observed under the electrocell. You will be able to describe how electronic potential is related with the direction of the cell reaction. At the end, you should have a skill to calculate the Gibbs energy change of an electro-chemical reaction from a cell potential.

- **Expected Hurdles Ahead in this Chapter**
  1. Concept of activity (See Section **3-2**)
  2. Relationship between Gibbs energy and reduction potential (See Section **3-4**)
  3. Understanding intensive property and calculating reduction potential of a reaction (See Section **3-5**)

PREVIEW OF KEY-EQUATIONS

Henderson-Hasselbach equation $$pH = PK_a + \log \frac{[A^-]}{[HA]}$$

Chemical potential and activity $$\mu_i = \mu_i^o + RT \ln a_i$$

Activity of solvent $$a_A = \gamma_A X_A$$

Activity of solute $$a_A = \gamma_A C_A$$

Activity of solute $$a_A = \gamma_A m_A$$

Electrode Potential $$\Delta G(eV) = -n\varepsilon = -96.485 n\varepsilon \ [kJ] = -nF\varepsilon \ [J]$$

Chapter 3 Chemical Equilibria in Solution

Nernst equation

$$\varepsilon^o = \frac{RT}{nF} \ln K$$

$$\varepsilon = \varepsilon^o - \frac{RT}{nF} \ln Q$$

$$K = \left[\frac{[C]_{eq}^c [D]_{eq}^d}{[A]_{eq}^a [B]_{eq}^b}\right] \quad \text{and} \quad Q = \left[\frac{[C]^c [D]^d}{[A]^a [B]^b}\right]$$

Entropy change and electropotential

$$\Delta S (J K^{-1}) = 96.485 n \left[\frac{\partial \varepsilon}{\partial T}\right]_P$$

Enthalpy change and electropotential

$$\Delta H (kJ) = 96.485 n \left[-\varepsilon + T \left[\frac{\partial \varepsilon}{\partial T}\right]_P\right]$$

PREVIEW OF KEY-TECHNICAL TERMS

Henderson-Hasselbach equation, activity (a), fugacity (ϕ), solvent standard state, activity coefficient (γ), Faraday constant (F), Nernst equation, intensive or extensive property

Chapter 3 Chemical Equilibria in Solution

3-1 Equilibrium in Solution

Many biologically important reactions take place in solutions. Under the solution environment, ionic species are often involved in reactions. A chemical reaction involving ionic (cationic and anionic species) is given as

$$A^+ + B^- \rightleftharpoons C^+ + D^-$$

Two important physical properties are conserved in the above chemical reaction.

Mass balance: $[A^+] = [C^+] =$ constant
Charge Balance: $[A^+] + [C^+] = [B^-] + [C^-]$

Under an equilibrium, the equilibrium constant K is given as:

$$K_C = \frac{[C^+][D^-]}{[A^+][B^-]}$$

The equilibrium constant for water is given by

$$K_{H_2O} = [H^+][OH^-] = 10^{-14}$$

In solution, pH is a major parameter describing the condition of a reaction. In many biologically important reactions, weak acid or base (buffer) are often used. Thus the calculation of the pH for weak acid is very popular procedure for the students majoring in Biochemistry. While the calculation of pH for strong base and acid is straight forward, the pH for weak acid or base requires to use **Henderson-Hasselbach equation**.

$$pH = pK_a + log\frac{[A^-]}{[HA]} \qquad \text{(Eqn. 3-1)}$$

Here, HA is a weak acid and undergoing a chemical equilibrium of acid dissociation given as

$$HA \rightleftharpoons H^+ + A^-$$

Here, pH$=-log[H^+]$, pK$_a = -logK_a$. The K$_a$ Is defined as

$$K_a = \frac{[H^+][A^-]}{[HA]}$$

It should be noted that an important application of Henderson-Hasselbalch Equation is a preparation for buffer solution. Generally speaking, the buffer solution can be represented as:

$$HA \rightleftharpoons H^+ + A^-$$
$$NaA \rightarrow Na^+ + A^-$$

Here, [OH⁻] and [H⁺] «[Na⁺] and [A⁻]

EXERCISE 3-1
What concentration of sodium acetate solution is needed to prepare a buffer at pH 6.00 from 1 [L] of 0.20 [M] acetic acid ?

ANSWER
From **Henderson-Hasselbach Equation**

$$pH = PK_a + \log \frac{[A^-]}{[HA]} \quad \text{(Eqn. 3-1)}$$

$K_{HOAc} = 1.80 \times 10^{-5}$

pK$_{HOAc}$ = -log K$_{HOAc}$ = 4.75

$$6.00 = 4.75 + \log \frac{[OAc^-]}{[HOAc]}$$

[OAc⁻]: concentration of conjugate OAc⁻ (NaOAc)
[HOAc]: concentration of acid (HOAc)=0.20 [M]

6.00=4.75 + log [OAc⁻] –log0.20

log [OAc⁻]=0.556

[OAc⁻]=$10^{0.556}$ = 3.60 [M]

"pK" means "–logK"
Note that A⁻ is OAc⁻ and HA is HOAc
log x =a → x=10^a

3-2 Activity

Ac**tivity** may appear as a peculiar concept though, this is a modification of the concentration of a component in a mixture in order to explain a real value of the concentration. An activity is defined as an effective concentration that takes into account deviations from ideal behavior. (It is similar to a situation where you use *van der* Waals equation for explaining the property of real gas instead of using an ideal gas equation.) Actually, the necessity of usage of activity is based on thermodynamical phenomena as components are mixed. For an ideal situation, the interactions between each pair of chemical species are considered to be the same. This is equivalent to state that the enthalpy of mixing is zero (ΔH_{mix} = 0), thus total properties of the mixtures are given as summation of each component's concentration. However, for reality, the interactions between each pair of chemical species are not equal and deviations from ideal behavior in a mixture of chemical substances need to be accounted as activity. (The above statement is similar to that corrections by intermolecular attraction or repulsion force is included in *van der* Waals equation while ideal gas equation assumes no interaction between gaseous molecule.) Thus, the activity can be regarded as the real concentration in a solution. Let's learn how this chemical activity is expressed for gas or solutions. At this point, you may feel unsure about what you are heading against, I am hoping that you will feel that it is advantageous and realistic to use activity under chemical reaction. A real contribution of the concentration to the solution should be reflected to the amount of potential work, so that chemical potential, μ, is expressed with activity, a.

$$\mu = \mu^o + RT \ln a$$

However, it is more convenient to define the chemical potential of a component in a mixture.

$$\mu_i = \mu_i^o + RT \ln a_i \qquad \text{(Eqn.3-2)}$$

Here, μ_i is a chemical potential for the i-th component in the system and the μ_i^o is the chemical potential of the i-th component under the standard condition. The a_i is the activity of the i-th component. First, recall that ln x =y gives x=e^y. According to (**Eqn.3-2**), the activity can be obtained with known chemical potential as:

$$a_i = e^{(\mu_i - \mu_i^o)/nRT}$$

Let's look into the way of describing the activity for (i) gas and (ii) solutions.

i) Activity /Fugacity of Gas

Pressure [atm] is used to express the amount of gas in a system, and the gas standard state it is defined at P=1 atm. For an Ideal gas, the activity of gaseous component A, a_A, is defined as:

$$a_A = \frac{P_A}{P} = \frac{P_A}{1\ atm} \qquad \text{(Eqn. 3-3)}$$

Here, P_A is a partial pressure of A. In order to describe a real gas pressure better than the ideal pressure, *fugacity (f) is introduced* with units of pressure.

$$f_A = \phi_A P_A$$

Here, f_A is fugacity, P_A is the ideal gas pressure of A, and is ϕ_A fugacity coefficient of A (dimensionless). The fugacities are either obtained experimentally or estimated under models such as a "*van der* Waals gas" in order to make it closer to reality than an "ideal gas". By adopting that real pressure is given by fugacity in (**Eqn. 3-3**), we can express the activity coefficient as

$$a_A = \frac{f_A}{1\ atm} = \frac{\phi_A P_A}{1\ atm} \qquad \text{(Eqn. 3-4)}$$

where ϕ_A is called fugacity coefficient, P_A *is a partial pressure of A,* and P is the standard pressure (1 [atm]).

After going through (**Eqn. 3-5**), (**Eqn. 3-6**), (**Eqn. 3-7**), and (**Eqn. 3-8**), you may notice that γ is used as the activity coefficient for the solution case and wonder why it is not used for the gas case. The word "fugacity" is derived from the Latin for "fleetness", which is often interpreted as "the tendency to flee or escape". Thus, you may want to think that fugacity coefficient (ϕ) is used like γ. You may consider (**Eqn. 3-4**) as: $a_A = \gamma_A P_A$ under P=1 atm (standard condition). As pressure reaches close to zero, any gas is expressed as an ideal gas. Therefore,

$$\lim_{P \to 0} \frac{f}{P} = 1$$

ii) Activity of Solutions
The activity of the solutions, a, is defined as:

> a = (activity coefficient) (concentration)

Here, the summary of the concentration and the solvent standard state is listed for solvent, solute, and biochemists' standard state.

Table 3-1 Summary of concentration for solution and solvent standard state

		Concentration	Solvent Standard State
a)	Solvent	Mole fraction (X)	1
b)	Solute	Molarity (M)	1 [M]
		Molality (m)	1 [m]
c)	Biochemists' standard state	$\sum_{i}^{species} C_{i,A}$	1 at pH =7 ($C_{I,A}$ is a concentration of i-th component A)

a) Activity of Solvent
The activity of solvent A (a_A) is defined as

$$a_A = \gamma_A X_A \qquad \text{(Eqn. 3-5)}$$

where the mole fraction of solvent A, X_A, is

$$X_A = \frac{n_A}{n_T}$$

The number of moles of A is n_A, and the total number of components in solution is n_T, thus X is unitless and $0 \leq X \leq 1$. The standard state of solvent is determined at mole fraction = 1. Mathematically, this is expressed as

$$\lim_{X_A \to 1} a_A = X_A$$

$$\lim_{X_A \to 1} \gamma_A = 1$$

The activity (a) is equal to X ($a = X$) for the dilute solution or ideal solution, and the activity coefficient (γ) becomes 1 for very dilute solution. As a very important example, please note that the activity of water is approximated to be 1 for an aqueous solution ($a_{H2O} = 1$ or $X_{H2O} = 1$).

b) Activity of Solute
For a real solution, the activity of solute A (a_A) with molarity c_A is given as

$$a_A = \gamma_A c_A \qquad \text{(Eqn. 3-6)}$$

At very dilute condition, the activity coefficient (γ_A) becomes 1 and the activity of solute A is equal to concentration (molarity, c_A)

$$\lim_{c_A \to 0} a_A = c_A$$
$$\lim_{c_A \to 0} \gamma_A = 1$$

Thus, the activity of solute A is expressed as concentration (molarity [M]), i.e., $a_A = c_A$, for dilute solution or an ideal solution.

If we choose to use molality (m_A) for concentration, we can define the activity of solute A (a_A) for a real solution in a similar way as the above.

$$a_A = \gamma_A m_A \qquad \text{(Eqn. 3-7)}$$

For extreme cases,

$$\lim_{m_A \to 0} a_A = m_A$$
$$\lim_{m_A \to 0} \gamma_A = 1$$

Thus, the activity of solute A is equal to the molality for dilute solution or an ideal solution ($a_A = m_A$).

c) Biochemist's Activity
The Biochemist's activity is defined as a summation of concentration of species in the system.

$$a_A = \sum_i^{species} C_{i,A} \qquad \text{(Eqn. 3-8)}$$

The standard state is defined under $a_{H+} = 1$ at pH = 7.

By summarizing the definition of the activity, we can list up the expression of the activity for a real gas, solvent, and solute and for ideal cases. (Here, a_A is an activity of A and γ_A is the activity coefficient of A)

Table 3-2 Summary of ideal and real expression for concentration

	ideal	Real
Gas	P_A	$\gamma_A P_A$
Pure solid/liquid (or very dilute solutions)	1	1
Solvent of solutions	X_A	$\gamma_A X_A$
Solute of solutions	C_A or m_A	$\gamma_A C_A$ or $\gamma_A m_A$
Biochemists'	$\sum_i^{species} C_{i,A}$	$\sum_i^{species} \gamma_{i,A} C_{i,A}$

EXERCISE 3-2

The oxidation of NADH by oxygen is

2 NADH (aq)+ 2H$^+$(aq)+ O$_2$(g) → 2 NAD$^+$ (aq)+ 2 H$_2$O (l)

The above reaction took place in aqueous solution at pH 7.45, and reached to an equilibrium with [NAD$^+$] = 1.00 [mM], [NADH] = 5.00 [mM], and oxygen at a partial pressure of 345.0 [torr]. The equilibrium constant is given by

$$K' = \frac{[H_2O]^2[NAD^+]^2}{[O_2][NADH]^2[H^+]^2}$$

Calculate K'. By the way, the prime on K implies that biochemical standard state is being used. (You will see that again after this exercise.)

ANSWER

❶ For dilute (ideal) solutions, the standard state of the solute is 1.00 [M]. Thus, concentration given in M unit is equivalent with its activity.
[NAD$^+$] = 0.001 [NADH] = 0.005.

The standard state for a gas is a pressure of 1 [atm] or 760 [torr].

❷ Thus, [O$_2$] = 345 [torr]/760 [torr] = 0.454.

❸ The biochemical standard state for hydrogen ion is pH 7, or 10^{-7} [M].

❹ pH =7.45 means that [H$^+$]=10$^{-7.45}$ = 3.55 x 10^{-8} [M]

Thus, [H$^+$] = (3.55 x 10^{-8}[M])/(10^{-7}[M]) = 0.355.

❺ In biochemistry, the activity of water is commonly replaced as 1.00, [H$_2$O] = 1.00

❻ $K' = \dfrac{(1)^2(0.001)^2}{(0.454)(0.005)^2(0.355)^2}$
=0.700

❶ [mM] should be converted to [M]

❷ ☞	Recall that pH 7 means that [H⁺] = 10⁻⁷ [M]
❸ ☞	−log x = a → x = 10⁻ᵃ
❹ ☞	Don't forget to divide it by 10⁻⁷ [M]
❺ ☞	The activity of water is 1.0
❻ ☞	Don't forget "square" on [H₂O], [NAD⁺], [NADH], and [H⁺].

3-3 Chemical Potential and Activity

Chemical potential is expressed as a molar Gibbs energy and is highly associated with the number of species present in a system,

$$\mu_A = \left[\frac{\partial G}{\partial n_A}\right]_{T,P,n_j \neq n_A}$$ (Eqn. 2-8)

Thus, with the use of chemical activity, μ, the chemical potential of a system or a reaction can be more realistically expressed. The Chemical potential and activity is given as:

$$\mu_i = \mu_i^o + nRT \ln a_i$$ (Eqn. 3-9)

For general chemical reaction,

a A + b B → c C + d D

The Gibbs energy change of a reaction is given by

$$\Delta G = [(c\mu_C + d\mu_D) - (a\mu_A + b\mu_B)]$$

By replacing chemical potential with an expression given in (**Eqn. 3-9**),

$$\Delta G = [(c\mu_C + d\mu_D) - (a\mu_A + b\mu_B)] = \Delta G^o + RT \ln Q$$ (Eqn. 3-10)

$$\Delta G^o = -RT \ln K$$ (Eqn. 2-10)

Here, the equilibrium constant is given in terms of the activities (not concentrations).

$$K = \left[\frac{(a_C^{eq})^c (a_D^{eq})^d}{(a_A^{eq})^a (a_B^{eq})^b}\right]$$ (Eqn. 3-11)

and

$$Q = \left[\frac{(a_C)^c (a_D)^d}{(a_A)^a (a_B)^b}\right]$$ (Eqn. 3-12)

In the above representation (**Eqn. 3-11**), the label "eq" indicates an equilibrium. When Biochemical Standard State is used at pH =7 (each product and reactant has a total 1M concentration), we conventionally use the representation with a prime.

$$\Delta G^{o\prime} = -RT \ln K'$$

EXERCISE 3-3
The first metabolic step is

fumarate + H₂O ⇌ malate

Calculate ΔG^o of the reaction at 25 [°C], if the ratio of activity between malate and fumarate at equilibrium is 4.0 ($a_{malate}/a_{fumarate}$ = 4.0). $a(H_2O)$ =1

ANSWER
For a reaction, A+ B ⇌ C

$$K = \left[\frac{(a_C^{eq})}{(a_A^{eq})(a_B^{eq})}\right]$$

$$\Delta G^o = -RT \ln K \qquad \text{(Eqn. 2-10)}$$

Thus,

❶ $\Delta G^o = -RT \ln \frac{a_{malate}}{a_{fumalate} a_{H_2O}}$

$= -RT \ln \frac{a_{malate}}{a_{fumalate}}$

❷ $\Delta G^o = -8.314 [J K^{-1} mol^{-1}] (298 K) \ln 4$

❸ $= -3.43 [kJ/mol]$

---

❶ $a(H_2O)$ =1

❷ R=8.314 [J K⁻¹ mol⁻¹] and T is in Kelvins unit.

❸ Spontaneous process.

☹ **MCM Most Common Mistake (17) – I wish the activity of water is always given in the exam!**

It may not be clear to know when you use activity expression rather than concentration expression. It is more accurate to use activity to reflect the real situation. Thus, it is always recommended to use the activity expression when it is available or mentioned in the problem. When you use the activity for solution, please make sure to use $a(H_2O)$ =1. What if you calculate the concentration of pure water 1[L]? The standard state for a liquid is the pure liquid, so the standard state of water is pure water. Its concentration is 55.5 [M] in 1 [L]. Thus, in reality, the concentration of water in dilute 1 [L] aqueous solutions is approximately 55.5 [M]. If 55.5 [M] is the concentration of the pure water and is regarded as the standard state, [H₂O] =55.5 [M]/55.5 [M] =1.00 should be used for a calculation.

3-4 Thermodynamic Characteristics of the Cell Reaction

Many examples of biologically important reactions are seen where ionic species conduct electricity with a help of electronic potential. Since the Gibbs energy is defined as non-PV work,

$$\Delta G = w^*_{rev} \qquad \text{(Eqn. 2-3)}$$

the electronic potential can be connected to the Gibbs energy change of a reaction, ΔG_{rxn}. Here, w^*_{rev} indicates the reversible electric work. Thus, it is possible to use a chemical potential to predict if a reaction will proceed spontaneously or not. The Gibbs energy(in the unit of [eV]) is related with reversible voltage of cell (ε),

$$\Delta G(eV) = -n\varepsilon \qquad \text{(Eqn. 3-13)}$$

Here, n is a number of electrons in mol, and ε is reversible voltage of cell which is given in the unit of [V].

The formula shown in (**Eqn.3-13**) indicates the sign between Gibbs energy change of a reaction and the cell voltage is <u>opposite</u>.

ΔG	ε	
<0	>0	Spontaneous process
=0	=0	System at equilibrium
>0	<0	Non-spontaneous process

Since cell voltage uses the unit of [V], the clarification between unit of energy [J] or [kJ] and the voltage [V]. An important unit conversion is,

1 [eV] (electron volt) = 96.485 [kJ/mol]

Thus, there are several expressions for ΔG in different units.

$$\Delta G(kJ) = -96.485n\varepsilon \qquad \text{(Eqn. 3-14)}$$

$$\Delta G(J) = -nF\varepsilon \qquad \text{(Eqn. 3-15)}$$

Here, F is the Faraday constant (F = 96,485 [C/mol]) and [V] is [J]= [C V], and n is number of electrons [mol].

In the previous chapter, an important relationship between the chemical equilibrium constant and the Gibbs energy was introduced. It allowed us to predict if the equilibrium is achieved under a certain concentration relationship.

$$\Delta G^o = -RT \ln K \qquad \text{(Eqn. 2-10)}$$

Chapter 3 Chemical Equilibria in Solution

$$K = \left[\frac{[C]_{eq}^c [D]_{eq}^d}{[A]_{eq}^a [B]_{eq}^b}\right] \quad \textbf{(Eqn. 2-9)}$$

$$\Delta G = \Delta G^o + RT \ln Q \quad \textbf{(Eqn. 2-11)}$$

$$Q = \left[\frac{[C]^c [D]^d}{[A]^a [B]^b}\right] \quad \textbf{(Eqn. 2-12)}$$

According to **(Eqn. 3-13)**, **(Eqn. 3-14)**, and **(Eqn. 3-15)**, the Gibbs energy change is directly related to the electronic cell potential (ε). Therefore, electrochemical potential and equilibrium constant in electrochemical reaction must be constructed.
The Nernst equation at equilibrium is

$$\varepsilon^o = \frac{RT}{nF} \ln K \quad \textbf{(Eqn. 3-16)}$$

$$\varepsilon = \varepsilon^o - \frac{RT}{nF} \ln Q \quad \textbf{(Eqn. 3-17)}$$

This formula is called the **Nernst equation**. At an equilibrium, $\Delta G = 0$ and $\varepsilon = 0$. Thus, **(Eqn. 3-17)** becomes **(Eqn.3-16)**. Since this formula is often used with logarithmic form at 25 °C, **(Eqn. 3-17)** is rephrased as

$$\varepsilon = \varepsilon^o - \frac{0.0591}{n} \log Q \quad \text{(at 25 °C) } \textbf{(Eqn. 3-18)}$$

> **MCM** **Most Common Mistake (18) –Am I using the correct Nernst equation?**
> Most common mistake people make is when the formal was chosen with a great care. The formula **(Eqn. 3-17)** is determined with a natural log, while the formula given in **(Eqn. 3-18)** is defined with logarithmic scale (10-base log). Please note that I should mention that the **(Eqn. 3-18)** should be used only for 25 [°C] (T=298 K), not for the other temperatures. Once again, be careful about the unit of the gas constant of R (R= 8.314 [J K^{-1} mol^{-1}]). The Faraday constant is F = 96485 [C/mol], and [J]= [V C] is used to convert the unit into [J].

Please be comfortable with the derivation of K from **(Eqn. 3-17)** and **(Eqn. 3-18)**.

$$K = e^{\frac{nF\varepsilon^o}{RT}}$$

$$K = 10^{\frac{n\varepsilon^o}{0.0591}} \quad \text{(at 25 °C)}$$

3-5 Oxidation- and Reduction- Reactions at the Electrode

The electrode reaction is intrinsically an oxidation and reduction reactions takes place at the electrode. If ε^o is noted as a standard reduction potential, the half-cell reaction is generally represented as

Cathode:　　$A^+ + e^- \rightarrow A$　　　　ε_a^o
(reduction takes place)

Anode: $B \rightarrow B^+ + e^-$　　　　　　$-\varepsilon_b^o$
(oxidation takes place)

$A^+ + B \rightarrow A + B^+$　　　　　　$\varepsilon^o = \varepsilon_a^o - \varepsilon_b^o$

Please note that the reduction potential always lists the value for reduction reaction. Thus, for anode reaction we reversed the direction and sign of the reduction reaction of

$B^+ + e^- \rightarrow B$　　　ε_b^o

Let's take a look at an example for the common case of the galvanic reaction.(**Fig. 3-1**)

$Cu^{2+} + Zn \rightarrow Cu + Zn^{2+}$

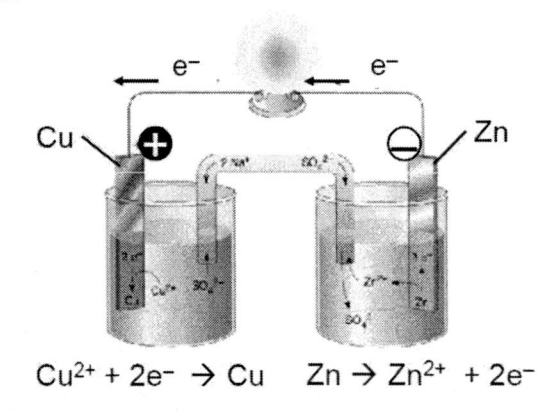

Fig. 3-1 The galvanic reaction:
$Cu^{2+} + Zn \rightarrow Cu + Zn^{2+}$

Cathode: $Cu^{2+} + 2e^- \rightarrow Cu$　　+0.337 [V]
Anode: $Zn \rightarrow Zn^{2+} + 2e^-$　　+0.763 [V]

$Cu^{2+} + Zn \rightarrow Cu + Zn^{2+}$　　　　+1.10 [V]

Once again, please note that we reversed the direction of the formula,

$Zn^{2+} + 2e^- \rightarrow Zn$　　−0.7628 [V]

There are three important reviews on half-cell reaction:

Chapter 3 Chemical Equilibria in Solution

PLEASE DO NOT SKIP THIS PARAGRAPH

1. The more positive ε^o, the greater the tendency to be reduced (strong oxidizing agent).

2. When a reaction is reversed, sign of ε^o changes.

$B^+ + e^- \rightarrow B \qquad \varepsilon_b^o$

$B \rightarrow B^+ + e^- \qquad -\varepsilon_b^o$

3. Changing the stoichiometric coefficients does not affect the value ε^o (since ε^o is intensive property)

$A^+ + e^- \rightarrow A \qquad \varepsilon_a^o$

$2A^+ + 2e^- \rightarrow A \qquad \varepsilon_a^o$

Most Common Mistake (19)-The reduction potential is not changed as n changed?

Most common mistake people make in this calculation is the intensive property introduced in rule 3 for half cell reaction. Truthfully, I don't blame you even if you forget about intensive property. You may remember that the enthalpy change of the reaction needs to be multiplied with the coefficient multiplied to the chemical reaction.

$A + B \rightarrow C \qquad \Delta H_{rxn}^o = x \ [kJ/mol]$
$2A + 2B \rightarrow 2C \qquad \Delta H_{rxn}^o = 2x \ [kJ/mol]$

So you may think that 2 has to be multiplied to the potential (ε^o), when the electron was increase by 2 in rule 3. Intensive variable of state is defined as the one that remains unchanged when a system is subdivided.) The examples are density, energy/mol, temperature, molar heat capacity, and voltage.(Fig.3-2) On the other hand, mass, volume, energy, and heat capacity are called extensive variable of state, where proportionally changes are made when a system is subdivided or multiplied.

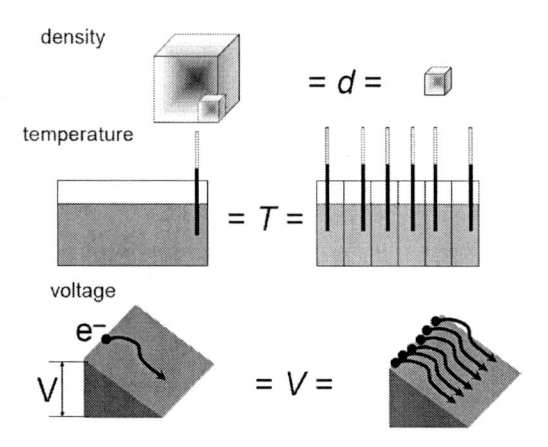

Fig. 3-2 Intensive property.

EXERCISE 3-4
Derive the redox potential for *Cytochrome reductase reaction*
UQH$_2$ + 2Cyt c_{ox} → UQ + 2H$^+$ + 2Cyt c_{red} $\varepsilon^{o'}$ = 0.154 [V] $\Delta G^{o'}$(kJ) = −29.7 [kJ]

Ubiquinone
UQ + 2H$^+$ + 2 e$^-$ → UQH$_2$ $\varepsilon^{o'}$ = 0.10 [V]   at pH =7 ---a)

Cytochrome c
Cyt c_{ox} + e$^-$ → Cyt c_{red} $\varepsilon^{o'}$ = 0.254 [V]   at pH =7 ---b)

ANSWER
The final chemical reaction to construct is:
UQH$_2$ + 2Cyt c_{ox} → UQ + 2H$^+$ + 2Cyt c_{red}

❶ So we will arrange the above reactions as follows: -a) + 2x b)

UQH$_2$ → UQ + 2H$^+$ + 2 e$^-$ $\varepsilon^{o'}$ = −0.10 [V]

❷ 2Cyt c_{ox} + 2e$^-$ → 2Cyt c_{red} $\varepsilon^{o'}$ = 0.254 [V]

Since the voltage of the cell is independent of the number of electrons. Thus, total potential is

$\varepsilon^{o'}$ = (0.254[V] − 0.10 [V]) = 0.154 [V]

$\Delta G(kJ) = -96.485 n\varepsilon$ **(Eqn. 3-14)**

❸ n =2

❹ $\Delta G^{o'}$ = −29.7 [kJ]

---

❶ Don't forget coefficient "2" multiplied to b).

❷ **WARNING!!!** $\varepsilon^{o'}$ = 0.254 [V] remains as it is even as entire chemical equation is multiplied by 2.

❸ The number of moles of electron seen in the half cell reaction.

❹ The unit is [kJ]

> **EXERCISE 3-5**
>
> The standard reduction potential ε^o of ferricyanide/ferrocyanide, $[Fe(CN)_6]^{3-}$ and $[Fe(CN)_6]^{4-}$:
>
> $$[Fe(CN)_6]^{3-} + e^- \rightarrow [Fe(CN)_6]^{4-} \qquad E^o = 0.447 \ [V]$$
>
> The standard reduction potential ε^o of cytochrome-f (Cyt-f) at pH 7 is
>
> $$Cyt\ f_{ox} + e^- \rightarrow Cyt\ f_{red} \qquad \varepsilon^o = 0.387\ [V]$$
>
> At equilibrium 25 [°C] and pH 7, a ratio $[[Fe(CN)_6]^{4-}]/[[Fe(CN)_6]^{3-}] = 1.85$ is found. Calculate a ratio $[Cyt\text{-}f_{red}]/[Cyt\text{-}f_{ox}]$ at an equilibrium.

❶	**ANSWER** The Nernst equation at 25 [°C] and pH=7 is, $\varepsilon = \varepsilon^o - \dfrac{0.0591}{n} \log Q$ (Eqn. 3-18) At equilibrium
❷	$\varepsilon^o(cyt) - 0.0591 \log ([Cyt\text{-}f_{red}]/[Cyt\text{-}f_{ox}])$ $= \varepsilon^o(FeCN) - 0.0591 \log ([Fe(CN)_6^{4-}]/[Fe(CN)_6^{3-}])$
❸	$\varepsilon^o(cyt) - \varepsilon^o(FeCN)$ $= -0.0591 \log ([Fe(CN)_6^{4-}]/[Fe(CN)_6^{3-}]) + 0.0591 \log ([Cyt\text{-}f_{red}]/[Cyt\text{-}f_{ox}])$ By replacing $[Cyt\text{-}f_{red}]/[Cyt\text{-}f_{ox}]$ as x 0.387 V – 0.447 V = –0.0591 log 1.85 + 0.0591 log x log x = –0.0442/0.0591 = –0.748
❹	x = $[Cyt\text{-}f_{red}]/[Cyt\text{-}f_{ox}] = 10^{-0.748} = 0.179$
❶	This equation is only for 25 [°C] and at pH =7
❷	n = 1
❸	Watch for the sign change in log ($[Cyt\text{-}f_{red}]/[Cyt\text{-}f_{ox}]$) term
❹	Log x = –a → x = 10^{-a}

At the end, I will give two more expressions for those wondering about the relationship between ΔS or ΔH and ε. The other thermodynamic properties (ΔS and ΔH) are related with electro potential (ε).

$$\Delta S (JK^{-1}) = 96.485 n \left[\frac{\partial \varepsilon}{\partial T}\right]_P \qquad \text{(Eqn. 3-19)}$$

$$\Delta H (kJ) = 96.485 n \left[-\varepsilon + T \left[\frac{\partial \varepsilon}{\partial T}\right]_P\right] \qquad \text{(Eqn. 3-20)}$$

Here, $\left[\dfrac{\partial \varepsilon}{\partial T}\right]_P$ is a partial derivative of electro potential with respect to temperature (T) under constant pressure. Therefore, two formula (**Eqn. 3-19**) and (**Eqn. 3-20**) indicate that measurements of the reversible voltage of a galvanic cell at several temperatures needs to be observed in order to obtain ΔS and ΔH.

Chapter 3

How did you get these equations?
-The derivation of selected equations.

(Eqn. 3-1) $$pH = PK_a + \log \frac{[A^-]}{[HA]}$$

Here, A^- is a conjugate base and HA is an acid. The condition of the targeted solution (especially Buffer solution) is given as:

$$HA \Leftrightarrow H^+ + A^-$$
$$NaA \rightarrow Na^+ + A^-$$

In this situation, [OH] and [H$^+$] «[Na$^+$] and [A$^-$]

$$K_a = \frac{[H^+][A^-]}{[HA]}$$

If you take the log of both sides,

$$\log K_a = \log \frac{[H^+][A^-]}{[HA]}$$

log ab = log a + log b
log (a/b) = log a − log b
Thus,
$$\log K_a = \log[H^+] + \log[A^-] - \log[HA]$$

Since, $pH = -\log[H^+]$ and $pK_a = -\log K_a$

$$\log K_a = \log[H^+] + \log[A^-] - \log[HA]$$

$$-pK_a = -pH + \log[A^-] - \log[HA]$$

$$pH = pK_a + \log[A^-] - \log[HA]$$
$$pH = PK_a + \log \frac{[A^-]}{[HA]}$$ (Eqn. 3-1)

(Eqn. 3-18) $$\varepsilon = \varepsilon^o - \frac{0.0591}{n} \log Q \qquad \text{(at 25 [°C])}$$

$$\varepsilon = \varepsilon^o - \frac{RT}{nF} \ln Q \qquad \text{(Eqn. 3-17)}$$

Chapter 3 Chemical Equilibria in Solution

First, the conversion between natural log and logarithm on base of 10 is derived as follows. For $x = 10^a$, the log of both sides gives

$\log x = a$.

On the other hand, if we take the natural log of x,
$\ln x = \ln 10^a = a \ln 10 = 2.302\, a$

Since $a = \log x$, $\ln x = 2.302 \log x$
Then, R=8.314472 [J mol^{-1}K^{-1}], F= 96,485 [C/mol], T = 273.15 + 25 [K] = 298.15[K], and [J] = [C V]

$$\frac{RT}{F} = 2.57 \times 10^{-2} [V]$$

So over all,

$$\frac{RT}{F} \ln Q = 2.57 \times 10^{-2} [V] \times 2.302 \log Q = 0.0591 \log Q$$

$$\varepsilon = \varepsilon^o - \frac{0.0591}{n} \log Q \qquad \text{(at 25 [°C])} \textbf{ (Eqn. 3-18)}$$

(Eqn. 3-19) $\qquad \Delta S = 96.485 n \left[\frac{\partial \varepsilon}{\partial T}\right]_P \qquad$ [J/K]

Gibbs energy is related with entropy change as:

$$\frac{d\Delta G}{dT} = -\Delta S \qquad \textbf{(Eqn. 2-5)}$$

By replacing ΔG in **(Eqn. 2-5)** by **(Eqn. 3-14)**

$\Delta G = -96.485 n\varepsilon \qquad$ [kJ] $\qquad$ **(Eqn. 3-14)**

In ΔG, replace ΔG =-96.485 nε [kJ]. Thus,

$$\left[\frac{d\Delta G}{dT}\right]_P = -(96.485n)\left[\frac{\partial \varepsilon}{\partial T}\right]_P$$

By combining the **(Eqn. 3-5)** and the above

$$\Delta S = 96.485 n \left[\frac{\partial \varepsilon}{\partial T}\right]_P \qquad \text{[J/K] } \textbf{(Eqn. 3-19)}$$

Chapter 3 Chemical Equilibria in Solution

(Eqn. 3-20) $\quad \Delta H = 96.485n \left[-\varepsilon + T \left[\frac{\partial \varepsilon}{\partial T} \right]_P \right] \quad$ [kJ]

$$\Delta G = \Delta H - T\Delta S \quad \text{(Eqn. 2-2)}$$

Thus, $\Delta H = \Delta G + \Delta TS$

$\Delta G = -96.485n\varepsilon \quad$ [kJ] **(Eqn. 3-14)**

Let's insert **(Eqn. 3-14)** into ΔG and **(Eqn. 3-19)** into ΔS

$\Delta S = 96.485n \left[\frac{\partial \varepsilon}{\partial T} \right]_P \quad$ [J/K] **(Eqn. 3-19)**

[Please be careful with the unit difference between kJ and J]. Therefore, the expression for enthalpy change is given as:

$\Delta H = 96.485n \left[-\varepsilon + T \left[\frac{\partial \varepsilon}{\partial T} \right]_P \right] \quad$ [kJ] **(Eqn. 3-20)**

Chapter 3 Summary
(Use back page to cover the contents.)

1	chemical reaction involving ionic species	mass balance and charge balance should be conserved.
2	Henderson-Hasselbach equation.	$pH = PK_a + \log \frac{[A^-]}{[HA]}$ (Eqn. 3-1) HA: weak, A– conjugate
3	chemical potential and activity	$\mu_i = \mu_i^o + RT \ln a_i$ (Eqn. 3-2)
4	Activity	a modification of the concentration to a deviation from an ideal value. 		ideal	Real	 |---|---|---| | Gas	P_A	$\phi_A P_A$	 | Pure solid/liquid (or very dilute solutions)	1	1	 | Solvent of solutions	X_A	$\gamma_A X_A$	 | Solute of solutions	C_A or m_A	$\gamma_A C_A$ or $\gamma_A m_A$	 | Biochemists'	$\sum_i C_{i,A}$ species	$\sum_i \gamma_{i,A} C_{i,A}$ species	 ϕ: fugacity γ: activity coefficient
5	Gibbs energy (in the unit of [eV]) and voltage of cell (ε)	$\Delta G = -n\varepsilon$ [eV] (Eqn. 3-13) $\Delta G = -96.485 n\varepsilon$ [kJ] (Eqn. 3-14) $\Delta G = -nF\varepsilon$ [J] (Eqn. 3-15) n: number of moles of electrons
6	Nernst equation	$\varepsilon^o = \frac{RT}{nF} \ln K$ (Eqn. 3-16) $\varepsilon = \varepsilon^o - \frac{RT}{nF} \ln Q$ (Eqn. 3-17) $K = \left[\frac{[C]_{eq}^c [D]_{eq}^d}{[A]_{eq}^a [B]_{eq}^b}\right]$ (Eqn. 2-9) $Q = \left[\frac{[C]^c [D]^d}{[A]^a [B]^b}\right]$ (Eqn. 2-12)
7	ΔS and ΔH and electro potential (ε)	$\Delta S (JK^{-1}) = 96.485 n \left[\frac{\partial \varepsilon}{\partial T}\right]_P$ (Eqn. 3-19) $\Delta H (kJ) = 96.485 n \left[-\varepsilon + T \left[\frac{\partial \varepsilon}{\partial T}\right]_P\right]$ (Eqn. 3-20)

[Fold the page at the double line and cover the right half.]

Chapter 3 Summary Check [Part 1]

(Use this page to cover and check the contents.)
Use ☐ as your check box. Write your comment at far right

1	chemical reaction involving ionic species	☐ ☐ ☐ ☐ ☐	
2	Henderson-Hasselbach equation.	☐ ☐ ☐ ☐ ☐	
3	chemical potential and activity	☐ ☐ ☐ ☐ ☐	
4	Activity	☐ ☐ ☐ ☐ ☐	
5	Gibbs energy (in the unit of [eV]) and voltage of cell (ε)	☐ ☐ ☐ ☐ ☐	
6	Nernst equation	☐ ☐ ☐ ☐ ☐	
7	ΔS and ΔH and electro potential (ε)	☐ ☐ ☐ ☐ ☐	

YOUR TEACHER MAY TEST YOU ON:

No.	What may be asked?		What you should know or do?
1	How you can prepare the buffer solution?	→	Henderson-Hasselbach equation $$pH = PK_a + log\frac{[A^-]}{[HA]} \quad \text{(Eqn. 3-1)}$$
		→	EXERCISE 3-1
		→	Problems 3-1, 3-2, 3-3
2	How activity of gas, solvent, and solute are described?	→	Table 3-2
		→	EXERCISE 3-2
4	How chemical potential is calculated with activities?	→	$\mu_i = \mu_i^o + nRT \ln a_i$ (Eqn. 3-9)
5	How can you calculate the Gibbs energy change of a reaction by using the activities only?	→	$\Delta G^o = -RT \ln K$ (Eqn. 2-10) $$K = \left[\frac{(a_C^{eq})^C (a_D^{eq})^d}{(a_A^{eq})^a (a_B^{eq})^b}\right] \quad \text{(Eqn. 3-11)}$$ $$Q = \left[\frac{(a_C)^C (a_D)^d}{(a_A)^a (a_B)^b}\right] \quad \text{(Eqn. 3-12)}$$
		→	EXERCISE 3-3
		→	Problems 3-4, 3-5, 3-6, 3-7, 3-8, 3-9
6	How can you tell if the electrochemical reaction is spontaneous or not from the electro potential?	→	$\varepsilon > 0$
7	How can you calculate ΔG from ε?	→	$\Delta G(eV) = -n\varepsilon$ (Eqn. 3-13) $\Delta G(kJ) = -96.485 n\varepsilon$ (Eqn. 3-14) $\Delta G(J) = -nF\varepsilon$ (Eqn. 3-15)
		→	EXERCISE 3-4
		→	Problems 3-10, 3-11, 3-12, 3-13, 3-14
8	How can you calculate ε from K?	→	**Nernst Equation** $\varepsilon^o = \frac{RT}{nF} \ln K$ (Eqn. 3-16) $\varepsilon = \varepsilon^o - \frac{RT}{nF} \ln Q$ (Eqn. 3-17) $\varepsilon = \varepsilon^o - \frac{0.0591}{n} \log Q$ (at 25 [°C]) (Eqn. 3-18)
		→	EXERCISE 3-5
		→	Problems 3-15, 3-16, 3-17

UNIT CHECK CHAPTER 3

Important Parameters of This Chapter	Popularly Used Unit	Important Unit Conversion
Concentration	M, mol/L	
	m, mol/kg	
Gibbs Energy, G	J/mol	
	kJ/mol	
Gibbs Energy Change, ΔG	J/mol	
	kJ/mol	
Chemical potential, μ	J/mol	
	kJ/mol	
Temperature, T	°C	0 [°C] = 273.15 [K]
	K	
Activity, a	atm	
	M, mol/L	
	m, mol/kg	
Mole fraction	dimensionless	
Equilibrium constant, K	$M^{c+d-(a+b)}$	
Voltage of cell, ε	V	1 [eV] = 96.485 [kJ/mol]
		[J] = [C V]
Faraday constant, F	C/mol	F = 96,485 [C/mol]
Gas constant, R	atm L mol^{-1} K^{-1}	8.314472 [J mol^{-1} K^{-1}]
	J mol^{-1} K^{-1}	0.08205746 [atm L mol^{-1} K^{-1}]
Entropy, S	J mol^{-1} K^{-1}	
	kJ mol^{-1} K^{-1}	
Entropy change, ΔS	J mol^{-1} K^{-1}	
	kJ mol^{-1} K^{-1}	
Enthalpy, H	J/mol	
	kJ/mol	
Enthalpy change, ΔH	J/mol	
	kJ/mol	

SUMMARY OF TRICKY TRAPS OF CHAPTER 3

☐	1	$a_{H_2O} = 1$
☐	2	$\Delta G \propto -\varepsilon$ spontaneous process when $\Delta G<0$ and $\varepsilon>0$
☐	3	Changing the stoichiometric coefficients does not affect the value ε^o (since ε^o is intensive property) $A^+ + e^- \rightarrow A$ $\quad\quad\quad \varepsilon_a^o$ $2A^+ + 2e^- \rightarrow A$ $\quad\quad \varepsilon_a^o$

LAST MINUTE REVIEW OF MATH CHAPTER 3

(These are basic algebra which you have no excuse if you miss them.)

1. $\ln x = y \quad x = e^y$
2. If x approaches to A as α is changed into β: $\lim_{\alpha \to \beta} x = A$
3. $\log xy = \log x + \log y \quad \log \frac{x}{y} = \log x - \log y$
4. $\ln x = 2.302 \log x$

Nobel Prize and Your Knowledge From Chapter 3

(*: word appeared in Chapter 3)

The Nobel Prize in Chemistry 1997 was awarded to **Paul D. Boyer** and **John E. Walker** "for their elucidation of the enzymatic mechanism underlying the synthesis of ATP (adenosine triphosphate) -ATP synthase" (**Fig. 3-3**) and to **Jens C. Skou** "for the first discovery of an **ion-transporting*** enzyme, Na$^+$/K$^+$ ATPase".(**Fig. 3-4**)

In the binding mechanism for ATP synthesis, energy input was not used primarily to form ATP but to promote the binding of phosphate and mostly the release of tightly bound ATP; that three identical catalytic sites went through compulsory, sequential binding changes; and that the binding changes of the catalytic subunits, circularly arranged on the periphery of the enzyme, were driven by the rotation of a smaller internal subunit. **John Ernest Walker** analyzed the sequences of proteins and then uncovered details of the modified genetic code in mitochondria. In 1978, he decided to apply protein chemical methods to membrane proteins.

Jens Christian Skou had discovered that a substance's anaesthetic action was related to its ability to dissolve in a layer of the lipid part of the plasma membrane, the anaesthetic molecules affected

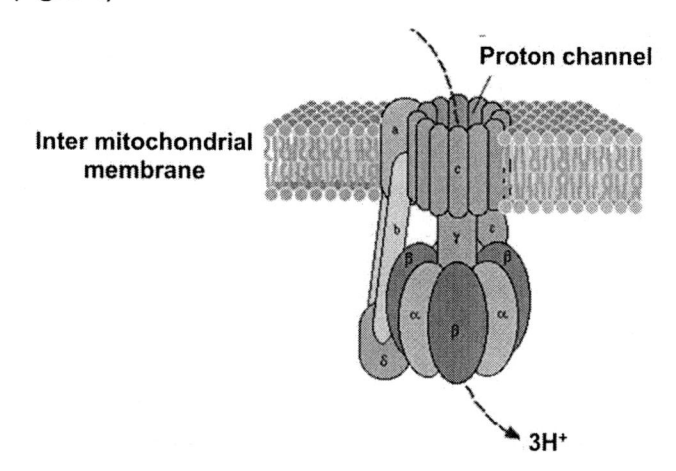

Fig. 3-3 The H$^+$ transporting ATP –synthase (Complex V)

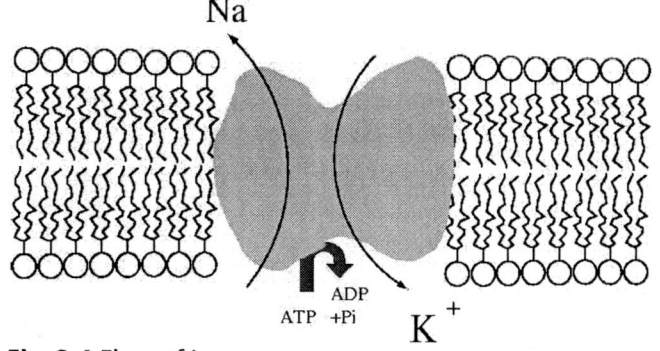

Fig. 3-4 Flow of ions

the opening of sodium channels which he assumed to be protein. This, he argued, would affect the movement of sodium ions and make nerve cells inexcitable, thus causing anaesthesia. Skou thought that other types of membrane protein might also be affected by local anaesthetics dissolving in the lipid part of the membrane. He therefore had the idea of looking at an enzyme which was embedded in the membrane and finding out if its properties were affected by local anaesthetics. He looked at ATPase in crab nerves. Eventually he managed to discover that ATPase was most active when exposed to the right combination of sodium, potassium and magnesium ions. He discovered enzyme called "Ouabain" inhibit the enzyme, thus establishing a link between the enzyme and the sodium-potassium pump.

An important reaction shares the benefit from the above and the learning from Chapter 3 is the hydrolysis of ATP

ATP + H$_2$O → ADP + phosphate $\Delta G' = -31.0$ [kJ/mol]

The prime on ΔG implies that biochemical **standard state*** is used.

THE FOCUSED PHYSICAL CHEMISTRY EXPERIMENTAL APPROACH ASSOCIATED WITH CHAPTER 3

(*: word appeared in Chapter 3)

Enzymatic Biofuel Cells

Before describing Enzymatic Biofuel Cell, a general information of **fuel cell** should be explained. While conventional **electrochemical cell*** batteries store electrical energy chemically in a closed system, fuel cell is an open system and consume reactant from an external source, which must be replenished. A fuel cell converts a source fuel into an electric current generating electricity inside a cell through reactions between a fuel and an oxidant the presence of an **electrolyte***. While this **electrolyte*** remains within the cell, the reactants flow into the cell and the products flow out of the cell. As you may imagine, many combinations of fuels and oxidants are possible and existent. For example, a famous hydrogen fuel cell uses hydrogen as its fuel and oxygen from air as an oxidant.

Fuel cells are made up of the anode (usually made up of Pt powder), the **electrolyte***, and the **cathode*** and sandwiched together.(**Fig. 3-5**) At the anode a catalyst oxidizes the fuel turning into a positively charged ion and electrons. The released electrons travel through and cause electric current, while the ions travel through the **electrolyte***

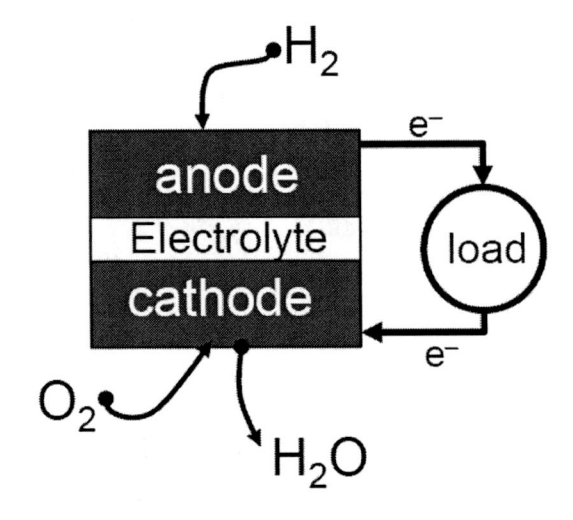

Fig. 3-5 Diagram of fuel cell

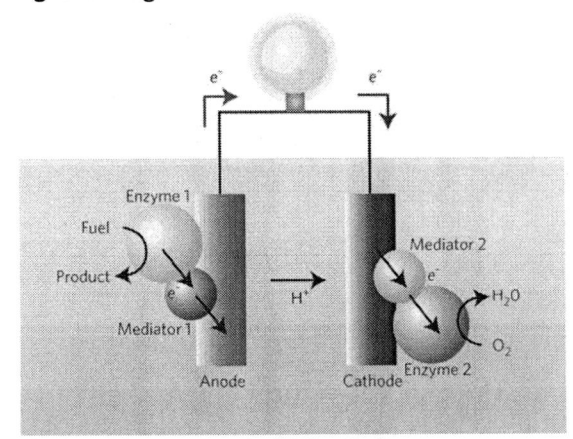

Fig. 3-6 Bioenzymatic fuel cell

to the **cathode*** side (often made up of Ni) and united with the electrons reacting with oxygen to produce water or carbon dioxide. The most common fuel is hydrogen and the type of fuel cell is defined by electrolyte substance. A typical voltage produced from a fuel cell is 0.6 [V] to 0.7 [V]

An **Enzymatic Biofuel Cell** uses enzymes as biocatalysts which catalytically oxidize the fuel at the anode and reduce the ensuing oxidant at the cathode.(**Fig. 3-6**) The specificity of the enzyme reactions at the anode and cathode electrodes of an enzymatic fuel cell eliminates the need for other components required for conventional fuel cells, such as a case and membrane. Unfortunately, Enzymatic Biofuel Cell is very unstable and power gained from this fuel cell is low.

CHAPTER 3 PROBLEMS.

3-1 [Hensderson-Hasselbach] What is the pH in a 0.500 [M] NaOAc solution?

3-2 [Hensderson-Hasselbach] What concentration of sodium acetate solution is needed to prepare a buffer at pH 6.00 from 1 [L] of 0.20 [M] acetic acid?

3-3 [Hensderson-Hasselbach] What amount of solid sodium acetate (CH_3COONa) is needed to prepare a buffer at pH 5.50 from 500 [mL] of 0. 200 [M] acetic acid at 25 [°C]? Assume that the solutions are ideal and that the addition of sodium acetate has a negligible effect on the volume. The equilibrium constant for ionization of acetic acid is 1.8×10^{-5}.

3-4 [activity→ΔG] The enzyme aldolase catalyzes the conversion of fructose-1,6-diphosphate (FDP) to dihydroxyacetone phosphate (DHAP) and glyceraldehyde-3-phosphate (G3P). Under physiological conditions in red blood cells (erythrocytes), the concentrations of these species are [FDP] = 35 [μM], [DHAP] = 130 [μM] and [G3P] = 15 [μM]. Will the conversion occur spontaneously under these conditions?

3-5 [activity→ΔG] The standard free energy for hydrolysis of ATP to ADP (ATP + H_2O → ADP + phosphate) in solution is $\Delta G° = -31.3$ [kJ/mol] at 37 [°C] and 1 [atm].For a ratio of ATP to ADP of 10, what must be the concentration of phosphate to obtain −40 [kJ/mol] for the hydrolysis of ATP? Assume that activity coefficients are 1 for the calculation.

3-6 [activity→ΔG] In the chamber, the reaction given below took place.

$N_2(g) + 3H_2(g) \rightarrow 2NH_3(g)$

a) The Gibbs energy change under standard condition of the above reaction is −32.90 [kJ]. Calculate the equilibrium constant of this reaction at the standard condition.

b) What is the Gibbs energy change if 2 [atm] of N_2 and 2 [atm] of H_2 are reacted to give 1 [atm] of NH_3?

3-7[activity→ΔG] The first metabolic step is

fumarate + H_2O ↔ malate

Calculate $\Delta G°$ of the reaction at 23.5 [°C], if the ratio of activity between malate and fumarate at the equilibrium is 2.90 (that is, $a_{malate}/a_{fumalate}$ = 2.90).

3-8 [activity→ΔG] The following reaction took place in aqueous solution at pH 6.55 and at 25 °C.

Glucose-6-Phosphate(aq) + 2 $NADP^+$ (aq) + $H_2O(l)$
$\rightarrow$ Ribose 5-Phosphate + 2 NADPH + $2H^+$ (aq) + $6CO_2(g)$

It reached to an equilibrium with following activities.

$a_{[Glucose-6-Phosphate]} = a_{[G6P]}$ = 3.50 μM,

$a_{[Ribose-5-Phosphate]} = a_{[R5P]}$ =12.5 μM,

$a_{[NADP+]}$ = 850 nM,

$a_{[NADPH]}$ = 550 nM,

and carbon dioxide at a partial pressure of 29.5 torr. Calculate $\Delta G_o'$ of this reaction at 25 °C by estimating that activity coefficients are approximated to be 1.0.

3-9 [K' →ΔG] Calculate the $\Delta G'$ for the hydrolysis of ATP at 25 [°C] and pH 7.

ATP $\rightarrow$ ADP + phosphate

[ATP] = 1.25×10^{-3}[M], [ADP] = 5.00×10^{-4} [M], and [phospahte]=2.5×10^{-3} M and $\Delta G° = -31.0$ [kJ/mol]

3-10 [ε→ΔG] What is $\Delta G°$ for the following reaction at pH 7 and 25 [°C].

2 cytochrome-c (ferrous) + pyruvate + $2H^+$ $\rightarrow$ 2 cytochrome-c (ferric) + lactate

pyruvate + $2H^+$ + $2e^-$ $\rightarrow$ lactate $\varepsilon^{o'}$= -0.18 [V]

cytochrome-c (ferric, Fe^{III}) + e^- $\rightarrow$ cytochrome-c (ferrous, Fe^{II}) $\varepsilon^{o'}$= +0.25 [V]

3-11 [ε→ΔG] Calculate the equilibrium constant at 25 [°C] and pH 7 for the following reaction.
$$CH_3CH_2OH\ (aq) + \tfrac{1}{2} O_2\ (g) \rightarrow CH_3CHO\ (aq) + H_2O\ (l)$$
Ethanol   acetaldehyde

3-12 [ε→ΔG] $E°$ for the reaction between cytochromes,
$$Fe^{3+}(cyt\ c) + Fe^{2+}(cyt\ b) \rightarrow Fe^{2+}(cyt\ c) + Fe^{3+}(cyt\ b)$$
is found to be 220 [mV] at 25 [°C]. Calculate $\Delta G°$.

3-13 [ε→ΔG] Calculate $\Delta G°$ for the following reaction at pH 7.0 and 25.0 [°C].
2 cytochrome-c (ferrous) + pyruvate + 2H$^+$ → 2 cytochrome-c (ferric) + lactate
when

pyruvate + 2H$^+$ + 2e$^-$ → lactate	$\varepsilon° = -0.16$ [V]
cytochrome-c (ferric) + e$^-$ → cytochrome-c (ferrous)	$\varepsilon° = +0.31$ [V]

3-14 [ε→ΔG] At an equilibrium $\varepsilon°$ is given by $\varepsilon° = (RT/nF)\ \ln K$. At 25 [°C], the above equation can be also expressed with $\varepsilon° = (\alpha/n)\ \ln K$, where α is a number since R, T, and F are all constants. Calculate the α in V.

3-15 [Nernst Equation] Cytochromes are iron-heme proteins that can undergo a one electron oxidation-reduction reaction. Cytochrome f (Cyt f) operates as a redox agent in chloroplast photosynthesis. The standard reduction potential $\varepsilon°$ can be determined by coupling it to an agent of known $\varepsilon°$ for ferricyanide/ferrocyanide:

$$Fe(CN)_6^{3-} + e^- \rightarrow Fe(CN)_6^{4-} \qquad \varepsilon° = 0.440\ [V]$$

In a typical experiment, a solution at 25 [°C] and pH 7 containing a ratio
$\{[Fe(CN)_6^{4-}]/[Fe(CN)_6^{3-}]\} = 2.0$ is found to have ratio [Cyt f_{red}]/ [Cyt f_{ox}] = 0.10 at equilibrium. Calculate the standard reduction potential $\varepsilon°$ (reduction) for cytochrome f by using $\varepsilon°$

3-16 [Nernst Equation] The Cytochrome - c reductase reaction is given by

Reaction-A	UQH$_2$ + 2Cyt-c$_{ox}$ → UQ + 2H$^+$ + 2Cyt-c$_{red}$	
Ubiquinone	½UQ + H$^+$ + e$^-$ → ½UQH$_2$	$\varepsilon°' = 0.100$ [V] at pH =7
Cytochrome-c	Cyt-c$_{ox}$ + e$^-$ → Cyt-c$_{red}$	$\varepsilon°' = 0.254$ [V] at pH =7

a) Calculate the equilibrium constant, K', of Reaction - A at 25 [°C] and pH 7.
b) When the acitivities of Cyt-c$_{red}$ and Cyt-c$_{ox}$ are a(Cyt-c$_{red}$) = 1.25 ×10^{-3} [M] and a(Cyt-c$_{ox}$) = 1.96 × 10^{-3} [M], the reduction potential of the reaction A was found to be 0.278 [V] at 25 [°C] and pH 7. Calculate the fraction of [UQH$_2$] /[UQ].

3-17 [Nernst Equation] The standard reduction potential $\varepsilon°$ of cytochrome-f at pH 7 can be determined by coupling it to an agent known $\varepsilon°$, such as ferricyanide/ferrocyanide, [Fe(CN)$_6$]$^{3-}$ and

$$[Fe(CN)_6]^{4-}: [Fe(CN)_6]^{3-} + e^- \rightarrow [Fe(CN)_6]^{4-} \qquad \varepsilon° = 0.447\ [V]$$

In a typical experiment, a ratio [[Fe(CN)$_6$]$^{4-}$]/[[Fe(CN)$_6$]$^{3-}$] = 2.07 is found to have a ratio [Cyt-f(reduced)]/[Cyt-f (oxidized)] = 0.200 at equilibrium 25 [°C] and pH 7. (Here Cyt-f means cytochrome -f). Calculate E° (reduction) for cytochrome-f.

Chapter 3 Answers. For Selected Problems

- **3-1** ~9
- **3-2** 3.55 [M]
- **3-3** 46.08 [g]
- **3-4** $\Delta G = -500$ [J]
- **3-5** [P] = 0.342 [M]
- **3-6** a) $K = 5.84 \times 10^5$ b) $\Delta G = -3977$ [J/mol]
- **3-7** −2.62 [kJ/mol]
- **3-8** 8.23 [kJ/mol]
- **3-9** −48.1 [kJ/mol]
- **3-10** $\varepsilon^{o\prime} = 82.97$ [kJ]
- **3-11** $K = 1.8 \times 10^{34}$
- **3-12** −5.1 [kcal/mol]
- **3-13** 90.7 [kJ/mol]
- **3-14** 0.0257 [V]
- **3-15** ε^o(cyt) = 0.363 [V]
- **3-16** a) 1.61×10^5 b) 1.61×10^3
- **3-17** ε^o(cyt) = 0.387 [V]

Chapter 4

Inter-Phase Energy Transition

4-1   Energy and Phase Equilibria
4-2   Vapor Pressure Lowering -Raoult's Law
4-3   The Effect of Pressure on the Solubility of Gases
4-4   Energy Transfer between Phases
4-5   Equilibrium Dialysis and Measure of Cooperativity
4-6   Transfer of Charged Species under the Field

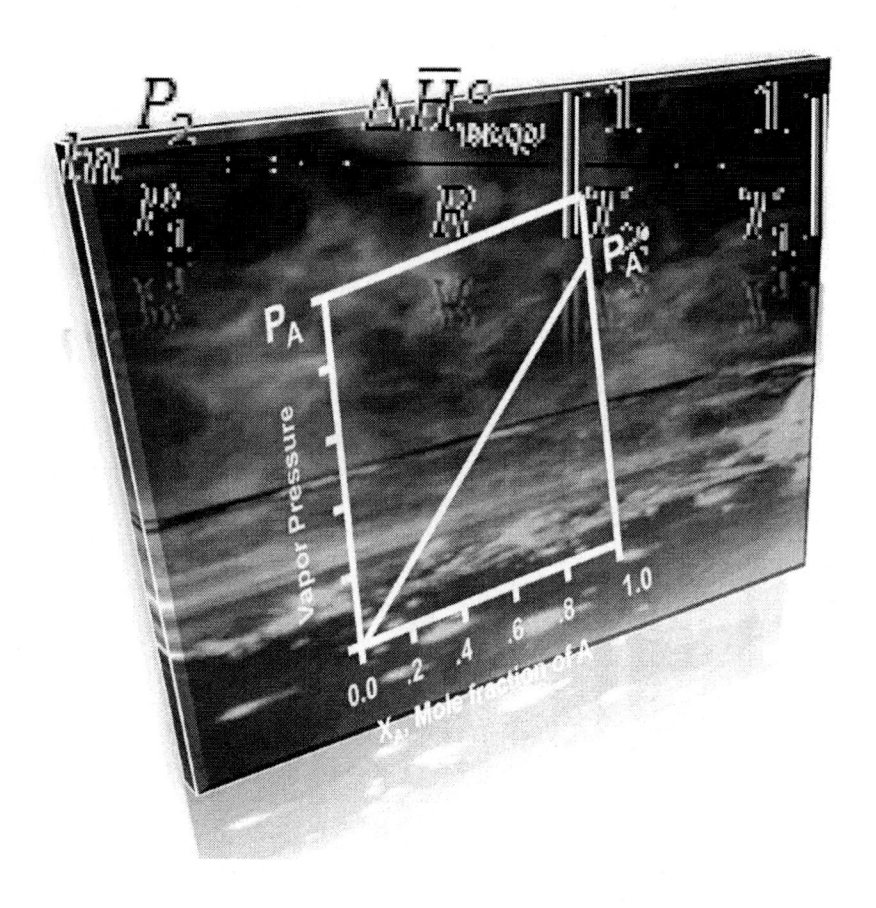

Chapter 4 Inter-Phase Energy Transition

- **Why do I have to study this chapter?**

Many biologically important phenomena take place between different phases (between liquid and gas or gas and liquid). You should be able to learn major phenomena involving different phases and the approaches to deal with phase equilibria. The way of using appropriate energy for each phase transition is prepared.

- **Expected Hurdles Ahead in this Chapter**
    1. Pressure described by Raoult's law (See Section **4-2**)
    2. Assumption made in Dialysis (See Section **4-5**)
    3. Description of cooperativity (See Section **4-5**)

PREVIEW OF KEY-EQUATIONS

Condition of phase equilibrium

$$\mu_A^\bullet(pure\ solvent) = \mu_A^\bullet(gas, P_A^\bullet)$$
$$\mu_A(solutions) = \mu_A(gas, P_A)$$

Clausius-Clapeyron Equation

$$\ln \frac{P_2}{P_1} = -\frac{\Delta \bar{H}_{vap}^o}{R}\left[\frac{1}{T_2} - \frac{1}{T_1}\right]$$

Raoult's Law for ideal solution

$$P_A = X_A P_A^\bullet$$

Henry's law

$$P_B = X_B k_B$$

Energy transfer between two phases

$$\Delta \mu_A = RT \ln \frac{[A]_{phase2}}{[A]_{phase1}}$$

Equilibrium Dialysis- Scatchard equation

$$\frac{\nu}{[A]} = K[N - \nu]$$

Hill Plot (cooperativity in binding)

$$\log \frac{f}{[1-f]} = n \log[A] + \log K$$

Energy transfer under the field

$$\mu_{A,total} = \mu_A + ZF\phi$$

$$\Delta\mu_A = RT\ln \frac{a_{A(phase\ 2)}}{a_{A(phase\ 1)}} + ZFV \qquad (V = \phi_2 - \phi_1)$$

PREVIEW OF KEY-TECHNICAL TERMS

Phase equilibrium, Calusius-Clapeyron equation, Raoult's law, Henry's law, dialysis, Scatchard equation, Hill plot, cooperative binding

4-1 Energy and Phase Equilibria

The transfer of the substances and equilibrium existent in that transformation can be considered as follows. First, let's set up the situation where liquid changes into a gas on substance A.

$$A \text{ (liquid)} \rightarrow A \text{(gas)}$$

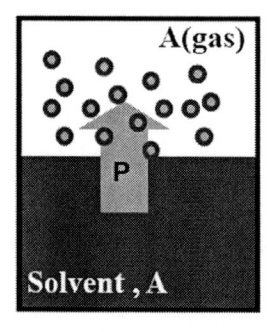

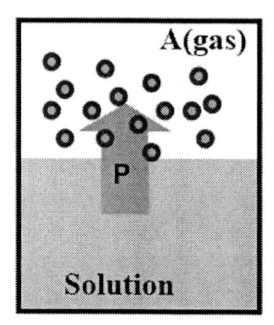

Fig. 4-1 Phase transition of liquid

When a solvent A vaporizes into its gaseous form, it will make an equilibrium where chemical potential of two states become equal as

$$\mu_A^\bullet(pure\ solvent) = \mu_A^\bullet(gas, P_A^\bullet) \quad \text{(Eqn. 4-1)}$$

Here, chemical potential of pure solvent A and vapor from solvent A is given by $\mu_A^\bullet$, where the black circle superscript indicates the pure solvent. $P_A^\bullet$ is a vapor pressure of pure solvent A. (**Fig. 4.1.**) When a component A of a solution (not a solvent) vaporizing into its gaseous form, it will make an equilibrium where chemical potential of two states are equal to be

$$\mu_A(solutions) = \mu_A(gas, P_A) \quad \text{(Eqn. 4-2)}$$

The chemical potential of A is given by μ_A, and P_A is vapor pressure of A for solution. The boiling point is the temperature at which this phase transformation takes place, and the vapor pressure of a liquid is equal to that of an external pressure at this temperature ($P_{ex} = P$). The heat involved for this process is called heat of Vaporization, ΔH_{vap}. (**Fig. 4.2.**) In the vaporization, the gas phase and liquid phase are at an equilibrium and the equilibrium constant K is described as

$$K = \frac{a_{A(g)}}{a_{A(l)}} \quad \text{(Eqn. 4-3)}$$

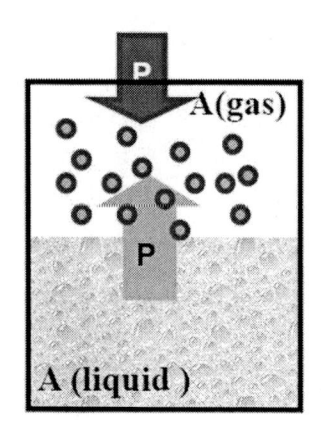

Fig. 4-2 vaporization

where a_A is an activity of substance A, and the (*l*) and (*g*) implies the liquid and gas, respectively. Please note that the activities are used in order to indicate the realistic situation, and the activity of the gaseous species is expressed by the pressures. If the effect of pressure on the activity of the liquid is ignored, $a_A(l) = 1$ and $a_A(g) = P$ [atm].

$$K = P$$

The relationship between equilibrium constant, K, and the enthalpy involved in the reaction is described by **van't Hoff Equation.**

$$\ln\frac{K_2}{K_1} = -\frac{\Delta H^o_{rxn}}{R}\left[\frac{1}{T_2} - \frac{1}{T_1}\right] \quad \text{(Eqn. 2-13)}$$

In this formula, the enthalpy change of a reaction ΔH^o_{rxn} is independent of temperature and regarded as a constant between a given temperature range T_1 and T_2. For a gas vaporizes at two different states 1 and 2 (P_1, T_1) and (P_2, T_2) are existent, the equilibrium constant of the equilibrium (vaporization) is expressed by K=P. In order to relate two different vaporization processes, ΔH^o_{rxn} in (**Eqn. 2-13**) is replaced by $\Delta \bar{H}^o_{vap}$ (molar enthalpy of vaporization), and we can insert $K_1 = P_1$ (P_1: equilibrium vapor pressure of a liquid at temperature T_1) and $K_2 = P_2$ (P_2: equilibrium vapor pressure of a liquid at temperature T_2) in (**Eqn. 2-13**)

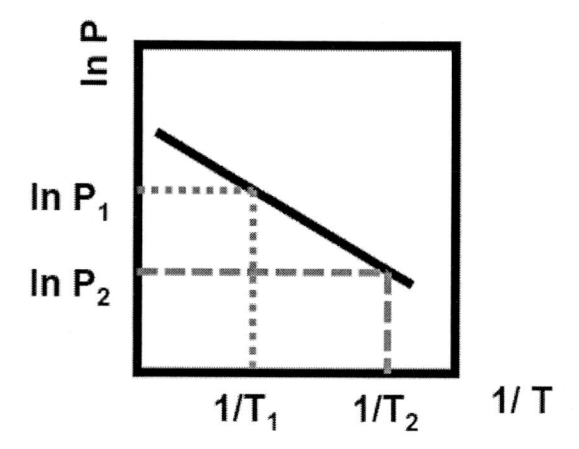

Fig. 4-3 Plot for Clausius-Clapeyron Equation

Clausius-Clapeyron Equation

$$\ln\frac{P_2}{P_1} = -\frac{\Delta \bar{H}^o_{vap}}{R}\left[\frac{1}{T_2} - \frac{1}{T_1}\right] \quad \text{(Eqn. 4-4)}$$

Here, $\Delta \bar{H}^o_{vap}$ is molar enthalpy of vaporization [kJ/mol], and it is assumed to be independent of temperature between T_1 and T_2. (**Fig. 4-3**) The Clausius-Clapeyron equation represents an important relationship between vapor pressure and boiling points under different conditions. While you may often see slightly different expression from (**Eqn. 4-4**), they are all the same.

Chapter 4 Inter-Phase Energy Transition

$$lnP_2 - lnP_1 = -\frac{\Delta H_{vap}}{RT_2} + \frac{\Delta H_{vap}}{RT_1}$$

$$ln\frac{P_2}{P_1} = -\frac{\Delta H^o_{vap}}{R}\left[\frac{T_1-T_2}{T_1 T_2}\right]$$

EXERCISE 4-1

On the imaginary Planet Hollywood, ammonia plays a role similar to that of water on Earth. Ammonia has the following properties: Normal boiling point (1 [atm]) is –33.4 [°C], where its heat of vaporization is 1368 [kJ/kg]. Estimate the temperature at which the vapor pressure of $NH_3(l)$ is 60 [torr].

ANSWER

$$ln\frac{P_2}{P_1} = -\frac{\Delta \bar{H}^o_{vap}}{R}\left[\frac{1}{T_2} - \frac{1}{T_1}\right] \quad \text{(Eqn. 5-4)}$$

$$= -\frac{\Delta H^o_{vap}}{R}\left[\frac{T_2-T_1}{T_1 T_2}\right]$$

❶ P_1 = 1 [atm] = 760 [torr] P_2 = 60 [torr]

❷ T_1 = –33.4 [°C] = 239.6 [K]

❸ From the calculation, ΔH_{vap} =1368 [kJ/kg] =1368 [J/g]

Here, let's think about how it can be converted into [J/mol] unit.

❹ Since 1 [g] NH_3 is 1 [g] ÷ 17 [g/mol] = (1 ÷17) [mol].

Thus,

❺ $\Delta H_{vap} = 1368[J/g] = \frac{1368\,[J]}{1\,[g]} = \frac{1368\,[J]}{(1 \div 17)[mol]}$
$= (1368) \times 17\,[J/mol]$

$$ln\frac{60\,[torr]}{760\,[torr]} = -\frac{(1368)(17)[J/mol]}{8.314[J\,mol^{-1}\,K^{-1}]}\left[\frac{1}{T_2} - \frac{1}{239.6\,[K]}\right]$$

$$= -2797\left[\frac{1}{T_2} - \frac{1}{239.6\,[K]}\right]$$

T_2 =197 [K] = –76 [°C]

❶ Since you will calculate the ratio of pressure, you can keep the unit as in [torr].

❷ Convert the unit of temperature in Kelvins.

❸ Do you know what we are doing here?

❹ Calculating the number of moles of 1 [g] of ammonia.

❺ Converting the unit of [J/g] to [J/mol]

4-2 Vapor Pressure Lowering -Raoult's Law

When a component of a solution vaporizes, there is an intrinsic relationship between the vapor pressure and the amount of the content contained in the solution. (**Fig. 4-4**)

Raoult's Law

$$P_A = X_A P_A^{\bullet} \qquad \text{(Eqn. 4-5)}$$

Here, X_A is a mole fraction of A in solution, $P_A^{\bullet}$ is a vapor pressure of a pure solvent A, and P_A is a partial pressure of A over a solution. (**Fig. 4-4**) Since mole fraction is between 0 and 1 and, X<1 for the case of solution case, P_A is always lower than $P_A^{\bullet}$ ($P_A < P_A^{\bullet}$) The relationship given in Raoult's law indicates that vapor pressure is simply proportional (linear) to a mole fraction in the solution.(**Fig.4-5**)

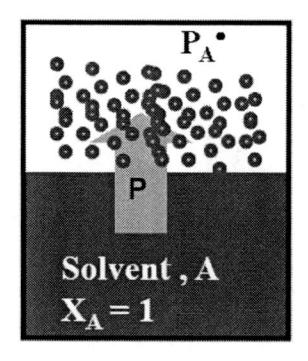

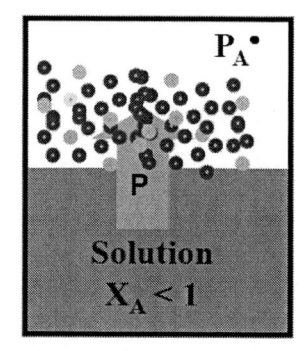

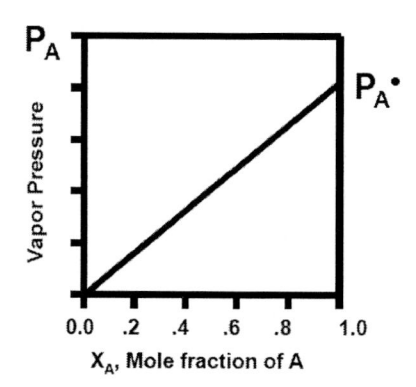

Fig. 4-4 Description of Raoult's law

Fig. 4-5 Plot for Raoult's law

However, when mixture of solution is conducted under "non-ideal solutions", the interactions between molecules of different substances cause a deviation from ideal case of Raoult's law. Please recall the factors introduced in chapter 3 to express "real" situation for gas and solution. The correction for gas non-ideality or deviations from the ideal-gas law is called the fugacity (ϕ). For the correction for interactions in the liquid phase between the different molecules, the activity coefficient (γ) is used. Therefore, modified Raoult's law for component A is given as:

$$P_A \phi_A = P_A^{\bullet} \gamma_A X_A \qquad \text{(Eqn. 4-6)}$$

Chapter 4 Inter-Phase Energy Transition

a. Positive Deviation

b. Negative Deviation

P_A: Partial Pressure of A
P_B: Partial Pressure of B

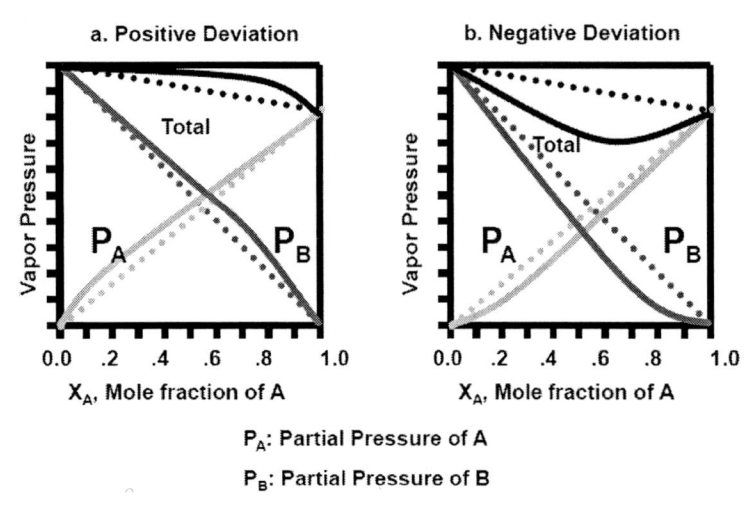

Fig. 4-6 Deviation from Raoult's law

When the adhesive and cohesive forces of attraction are not uniform between the two mixed liquids, deviation from Raoult's law is observed. If the cohesive forces between like molecules overcome the amount of the adhesive forces, the difference in polarity or internal pressure allow both components to vaporize more easily. This makes the vapor pressure greater than the predicted value from the Raoult's law. In this case, the Raoult's law shows positive deviation, and the vapor pressure curve exhibit a maximum at a particular composition (See. **Fig. 4-6a**). (benzene/ethyl alcohol, carbon disulfide/acetone, chloroform/ethanol). On the other hand, if adhesive forces between mixed liquids are more than the cohesive forces within identical molecule, then the vapor pressure of the solution becomes less than the expected vapor pressure showing the negative deviation from Raoult's law. (chloroform / acetone)(See. **Fig. 4.6b**). in which cohesive forces are reduced not only by dilution but also attraction through hydrogen bonds.

> **Most Common Mistake (21)-Am I picking a correct pressure?**
> Most common mistake people make in this concept is the definition of the P_A. It says that is the vapor pressure of A for solution. This means that it is a pressure over the solution caused by a vapor of solution. A common mistake is that people tend to think that the P_A is pressure of solution A (hydrodynamic pressure). The Raoult's law is in a sense tricky law, the terms given by P are dealing with the vapor, while mole fraction X is about the solution.

4-3 The Effect of Pressure on the Solubility of Gases

In the previous condition, Raoult's law, the vapor pressure of a substance is measured under the constant (most likely atmospheric pressure). What if we change the external pressure applied to the solution and if we can control the solubility of the substance in the solution. Let's view the case where gas is dissolved in the solution. In this case, we can make a similar relationship as Raoult's law between the pressure applied to the solution and the amount of the gaseous solute dissolved in a solution by **Henry's law**.

$$P_B = X_B k_H \qquad \text{(Eqn. 4-7)}$$

Here, the P_B is a vapor pressure of solute B (in the unit of [atm]), X_B is the mole fraction of B in liquid solution, and k_H is Henry's Law constant and the unit is [atm]. The familiar environment is a carbonated drink. The Henry's law is valid as the mole fraction is a small value.(**Fig. 4-7**)

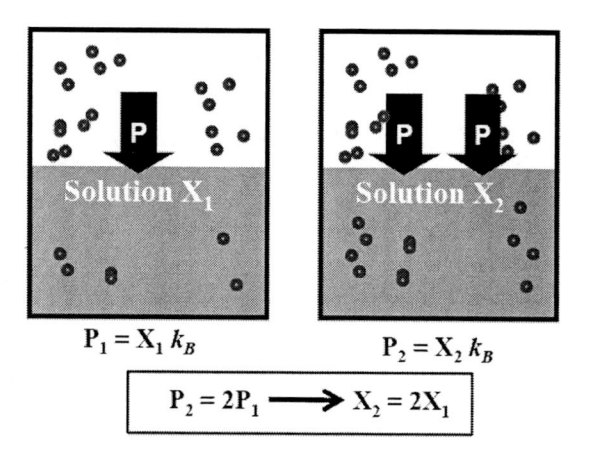

Fig. 4-7 Henry's law

EXERCISE 4-2
The nitrogen gas is placed in a container, and a partial pressure of N_2 is 9.20 [atm] and concentration of N_2 is 5.76 x 10^{-3} [M]. Then, partial pressure of N_2 is changed into 0.79 [atm].
a). Calculate the concentration of N_2.
b). Calculate the mole fraction of water and N_2.

ANSWER
For this problem, let's start from
$$P_B = X_B k_H \quad \text{(Eqn. 4-7)}$$
a) You can think this problem as a "proportionality" problem.
So let's treat the unit of mole fraction as a molarity, [M].

$$\frac{9.20\,[atm]}{5.76 \times 10^{-3}[M]} = \frac{0.79\,[atm]}{x\,[M]}$$

x [M] = 4.95×10^{-4}[M]

b) Moles of water is approximately 1000 [g] ÷ 18 [g/mol] = 55.56 [mol]
Then, let's think about mole fraction of N_2 in the final solution.
The mole fraction of N_2 in solution is given by

$$\frac{moles\ of\ N_2}{moles\ of\ water + moles\ of\ N_2}$$

	$$= \frac{4.95 \times 10^{-4}\ [M]}{55.56[M] + 4.95 \times 10^{-4}\ [M]}$$ =8.90×10⁻⁶ Mole fraction of water is
❸ ☞	1 − 8.90×10⁻⁶ ~1.00
❶ ☞	Of course, you can set up this equation as you like. For example, 9.20 [atm]: 5.76×10⁻³[M] = 0.79 [atm] : x [M]
❷ ☞	1 [L] is approximated as 1000 [g] by using density = 1 [g/mL]
❸ ☞	If a system consists of two components A and B, the mole fraction (X) is $X_A+X_B=1$.

There is another very good application of Henry's law you encounter often as an example in caisson worker's case. This is called as decompression sickness or colloquially known as divers' disease, the bends or caisson disease. It is a condition in which dissolved gases in a solution becomes bubbles inside the body under depressurization process. The bubbles can migrate to any part of the body and it may cause joint pain, rashes, and to paralysis and death.

Here, we will attempt to calculate how much amount of N_2 bubble can be produced when a diver dived into 300 [m] deep and come out of the ocean rapidly. (**Fig. 4-8**) From Henry's Law, we will arrange the equation into the relationship between volume of the nitrogen and the mole fraction of the nitrogen

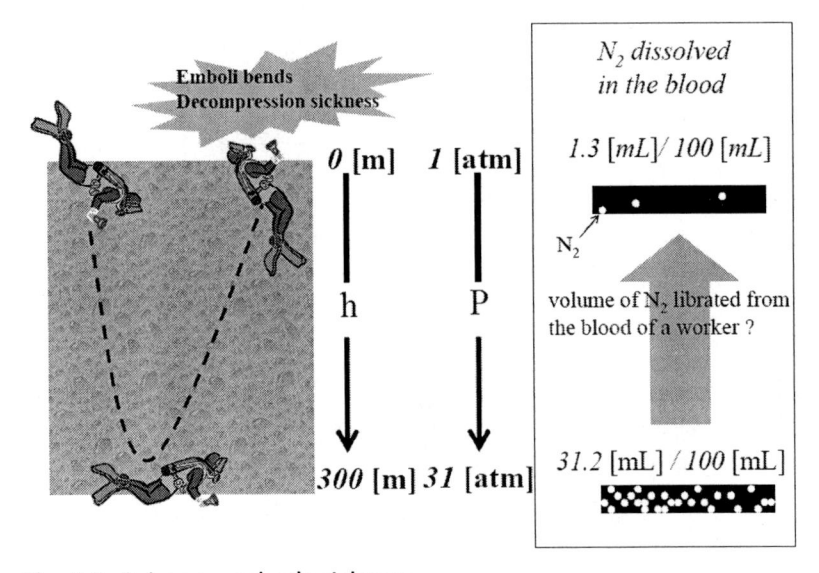

Fig. 4-8 Caisson worker's sickness

$$P_B = X_B\ k_H$$
$$X_{N2} \propto P_{N2}$$
$$V_{N2} \propto X_{N2}$$

Therefore,

$$V_{N2} = k'\ P_{N2}$$

The pressure of air [atm] at a depth of h [mm], use the following equation (**Fig. 4.9**),

$$1\ atm + \frac{\rho_{sea\ water}[g/mL]}{\rho_{Hg}[g/mL]} \frac{h\ [mm]}{760[mm/atm]}$$

At 300 [m] of water, the air pressure in atm is approximately

$$1\ atm + \frac{1.025[g/mL]}{13.6[g/mL]} \frac{3\times10^5\ [mm]}{760[mm/atm]} = 30.8\ [atm]$$

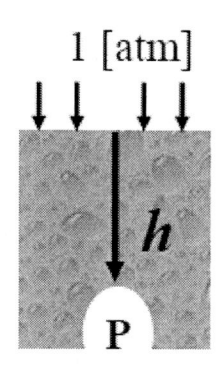

Fig. 4-9 Pressure at depth h [m]

Here, density of Hg is 13.6 [g/mL] and the density of sea water is 1.025 [g/mL].

The air (which diver breathed in) contains 78 volume % N_2

Therefore,

$$P_{N2} = (0.78)(30.8) = 24.0\ [atm]$$

Using the modified Henry's law relationship

$$V_{N2} = k'P_{N2}$$

With k'=1.3 [mL/atm] for 100 [mL] blood.

$$V_{N2} = (1.3)(24.0) = 31.2\ [mL]\ N_2$$

This much (31.2 [mL]) of nitrogen bubble is dissolved for 100 [mL] blood at 300 [m]. Therefore, assuming that a total blood volume of the average adult is 3.2 [L] (3200 [mL]), volume of N_2 liberated at an atmospheric pressure is

$$(31.2\ [mL] - 1.3\ [mL])\ (3200[mL]/100[mL]) = 957\ [mL]$$

The decompression sickness may be observed in scuba diving, caisson working, flying in unpressurised aircraft, and extra-vehicular activity from spacecraft. For preventing it, scuba divers use dive tables or computers to set limits on their exposure to pressure and their ascent speed. Treatment is by hyperbaric oxygen therapy in a recompression chamber.

4-4 Energy Transfer between Phases

The mass transportation between two phases was studied from Raoult's law and Henry's. However, there was no argument on energy involved in the phase transitions. Let's view the energy transferred between two different phases and find out how we can quantitatively investigate the energy change in these phases. Let's think about the two simple cases where two phases (Phase 1 and Phase 2) are existent. If the energy is transferred from Phase 1 to Phase 2, this energy transportation is expressed as a change of the chemical potentials, $\Delta\mu$, of these two phases. (**Fig. 4-10**)

Chapter 4 Inter-Phase Energy Transition

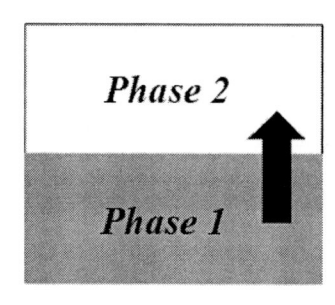

Fig. 4-10a Energy transfer from phase1 to phase2

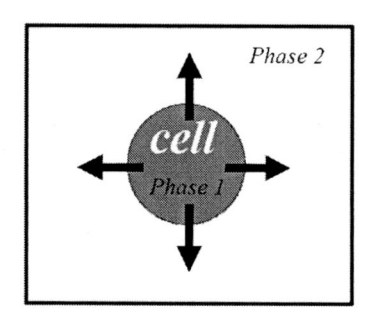

Fig. 4-10b Energy transfer from phase1 (inside of a cell) to phase2 (outside of cell)

$$\Delta\mu_A = \mu_A(phase\ 2) - \mu_A(phase\ 1)$$

$$= RT\ ln\frac{[A]_{phase2}}{[A]_{phase1}} \qquad \textbf{(Eqn. 4-8)}$$

Here, [A]$_{phase\ 1}$ and [A]$_{phase2}$ indicate the concentration of A at phase1 and phase 2, respectively. Please note that the term given by ln{[A]$_{phase2}$ /[A]$_{phase\ 1}$ } exhibit a huge effect as [A]$_{phase\ 1}$ becomes very small value compared to the case when the difference of concentrations, [A]$_{phase2}$ /[A]$_{phase\ 1}$, was taken.

EXERCISE 4-3
Calculate the Δμ for this transport process of a cell at body temperature (37 [°C]) when the phase change take place from inside of the cell to outside. [A]$_{in}$ = 0.02 [M] and [A]$_{out}$ = 0.08 [M]

ANSWER
Energy of transferred between phases 1 and 2

❶ T=273.15 + 37 = 310.15 [K]

❷ $\Delta\mu_A = RT\ ln\frac{[A]_{out}}{[A]_{in}}$

❸ $= (8.314[J\ mol^{-1}K^{-1}])(310.15[K])ln\frac{0.08[M]}{0.02[M]}$

=3573 [J/mol]

---

❶ Temperature is in Kelvins unit.

❷ Don't mix up and down of the fraction. [A]$_{out}$ is the final value and [A]$_{in}$ is the initial value.

❸ R =8.314472[J mol^{-1} K^{-1}]

Chapter 4 Inter-Phase Energy Transition

☹ MCM **Most Common Mistake(22) – Hey which one ? [A]$_{out}$/[A]$_{in}$ or [A]$_{in}$/[A]$_{out}$?**

When you need to calculate the energy transferred between two phases, the order of fraction in natural log term, {[A]$_{phase2}$ /[A]$_{phase 1}$ }, is mistaken. The golden rule is always [(final value) – (initial value)]. Thus,

ln (final value) – ln (initial value)]
= ln (final value) /(initial value)]

If the phase changes from phase1 to phase2 as shown in **Fig. 4.10a**, phase 2 is the final and phase 1 is an initial phase. (There will be the case, of course, phase changes form phase 2 to phase 1. Then, the natural log term becomes ln {[A]$_{phase1}$ /[A]$_{phase 2}$ }. When the phase change takes place from inside of the cell to outside, the final condition is outside of the cell. Thus, you need to use ln {[A]$_{out}$ /[A]$_{in}$} in this case.

4-5 Equilibrium Dialysis and Measure of Cooperativity

As an application of transfer of substances between one phase to the another, dialysis is explained here. (The word Dialysis is originated from Greek "dialusis (dissolution), and is primarily used to provide an artificial replacement for lost kidney function in people with renal failure.)In this section, we will view an equilibrium existent in dialysis. In the dialysis, we will consider the situation where the relatively small substance (ligand) can attach to the macro molecule and can go through the membrane which has the size let the ligand pass but not macromolecules.(**Fig. 4-11**) The equilibrium of the ligand (A) the macromolecule(M) is given as:

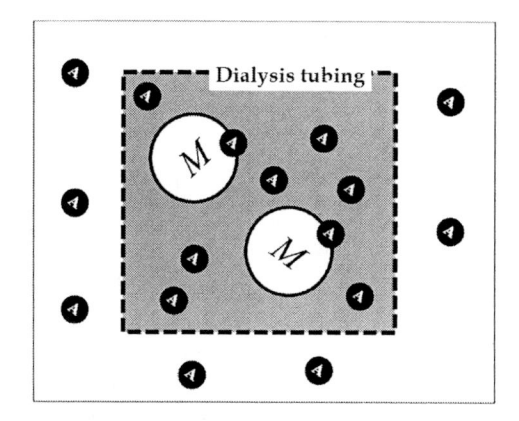

Fig. 4-11 Dialysis: [A]$_{outside}$=[A]$_{inside}$

$$M + A \underset{}{\overset{K}{\rightleftarrows}} M \bullet A$$

Thus, an equilibrium constant is

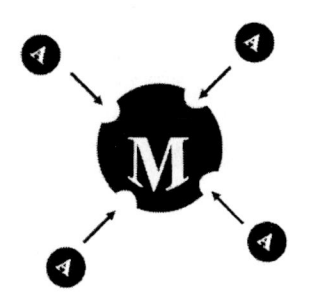

$$K = \frac{[M \bullet A]}{[M][A]} \quad \text{(Eqn. 4-9)}$$

Fig. 4-12 A sketch of binding sites (N=4) of macromolecule (M).

Some ligands are bound to macromolecules and some are not bound (free). If we assume ν ligands (ν is between 0 and N)are bound to one macromolecule and one macro molecule has N independent binding sites, the ratio between total concentration of macromolecule and the concentration of bound ligands [A]$_{bound}$ is expressed as

$$\frac{v}{N} = \frac{[A]_{bound}}{[M]_{total}}$$

The example given in **Fig. 4-12** shows the case when macromolecule (M) has an identical four binding sites (N=4). We also have a very important assumption in this system where the concentration of free (unbound) A inside a membrane, $[A]_{inside}$, is equal to a total concentration of free (unbound) A outside of a membrane, $[A]_{outside}$, under an equilibrium, (i.e., $[A] = [A]_{outside} = [A]_{inside}$) This assumption is very handy when you solve the problem of equilibrium dialysis under given concentration of free A, [A].(**Fig. 4-11**). Under this condition, we can derive **Scatchard equation**

$$\frac{v}{[A]} = K[N - v] \qquad \text{(Eqn. 4-10)}$$

For a graph of (**Eqn. 4-10**), v/A is plotted as a function of v.(**Fig. 4-13**) Then, a graph should show a straight line with a slope of "–K". Also, you can obtain N, from the intercept of x-axis. Furthermore, the K is confirmed form the intercept of the y-axis (NK).

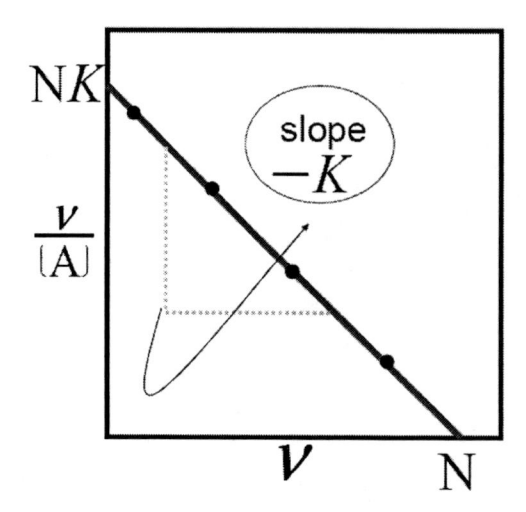

Fig. 4-13 The Scatchrad plot

EXERCISE 4-4
The enzyme tetrahydrofolate has 4 identical binding sites. The concentration of free ATP is 10^{-4} [M] and average number of ligands per one enzyme is 2. Calculate K.

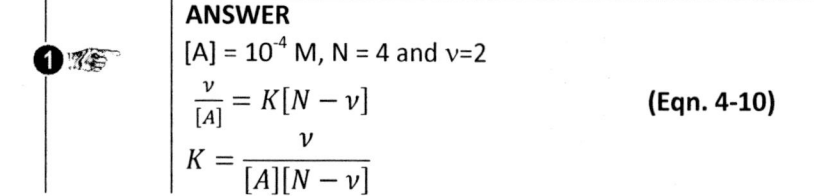

ANSWER
$[A] = 10^{-4}$ M, N = 4 and v=2
$$\frac{v}{[A]} = K[N - v] \qquad \text{(Eqn. 4-10)}$$
$$K = \frac{v}{[A][N - v]}$$

❷	=10⁴ [M⁻¹]
❶	Don't' mix between N and v
❷	The unit of K is [M⁻¹]

Do you think that a binding condition changes as the macromolecule start binding one after another? Yes, there are some cases where binding condition changes as the sites are occupied. If a macromolecule exhibits **cooperativity in a binding**, its affinity for its ligand increases with the amount of ligand already bound.(**Fig. 4-14**) Let's think about a system where a macromolecule (M) binds with more than one ligands (A) as:

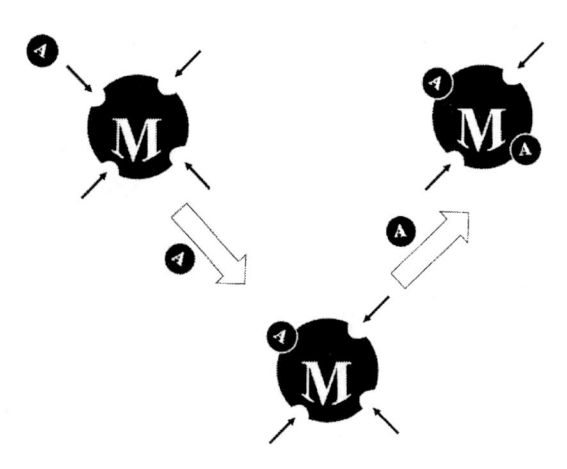

$$M + nA \underset{}{\overset{K}{\rightleftarrows}} M \bullet A^n$$

Fig. 4-14 A sketch of change in the condition of binding sites.

If there are N identical independent binding sites and v ligands are bound to one macromolecule on the average, the fraction of the number of binding ligands per binding sites is

$f = v/N$

Then, we can derive the relationship between equilibrium constant K and fraction, f, as

$$\frac{f}{[1-f]} = K[A]^n \qquad \text{(Eqn. 4-11)}$$

Here, n is called the Hill Constant. By taking the logarithm of both sides of (**Eqn. 4-9**),

Hill Plot

$$\log \frac{f}{[1-f]} = n \log[A] + \log K \qquad \text{(Eqn. 4-12)}$$

Fig. 4-15 The Hill plot

By plotting log [f/(1-f)] as a function of log[A] (**Fig. 4-15**), you will obtain a linear line with slope is n, which is Hill's constant, and log K as y-axis intercept. As a general consensus, n= 1 indicates that there is no cooperativity in binding. If n> 1, it indicates that there are positive cooperativity in binding of the ligands. As a well known examples, n = 1 for Myoglobin binding with O_2 and n = 2.3 for Hemoglobin- O_2 system.

4-6 Transfer of Charged Species under the Field

In the previous section, transportation of neutral species have been studied. However, there are many biological systems where ionic species transfers between two different phases. The transition of ionic species in solution can be controlled by the external field (or the potential) as desired way. Let's take a look at the case where the external voltage is applied using the electrodes in solution.(**Fig. 4-16**) When an external potential ϕ is applied from an electrode, a total chemical potential of a component A, $\mu_{A, total}$ is given as

$$\mu_{A,total} = \mu_A + ZF\phi \quad \textbf{(Eqn. 4-13)}$$

Here, Z is the charge of transferring ions. The difference in a chemical potential ($\Delta\mu_A$) of component A in two different phases is given by

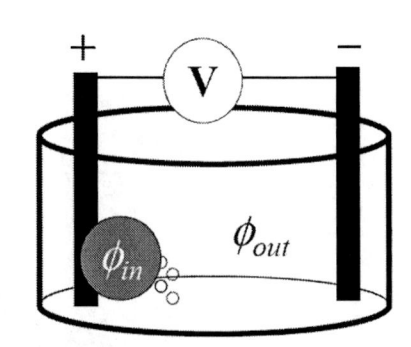

Fig. 4-16 Transfer of charged species in the presence of field

$$\Delta\mu_A = RT\ln\frac{a_{A(phase\ 2)}}{a_{A(phase\ 1)}} + ZFV \quad \textbf{(Eqn. 4-14)}$$

Here, *a* is an activity, *F* is a Faraday Constant, and V is defined as the difference in potential of phase 1 (ϕ_1) and phase 2 (ϕ_2) as

$$V = \phi_2 - \phi_1$$

For example, a charged macromolecule can be attached to one of the electrode and cause a transfer of the charged species inside a macromolecule by applying an external field. (**Fig. 4-16**) If the charged species transfers from inside of the macromolecule (such as cell) to the outside, the potential V is defined as

$$V = \phi_{out} - \phi_{in}$$

When the system reaches to an equilibrium,

$$\mu_{A,tot}(inside) = \mu_{A,tot}(outside)$$

Then, we can approximate (**Eqn. 4-14**) as

$$V \approx -\frac{RT}{ZF}\ln\gamma \qquad \text{(Eqn. 4-15)}$$

where γ is given by acitivity (a) and activity coefficient (γ) of component A as

$$\gamma = \frac{a_A(inside)}{a_A(outside)} = \frac{\gamma_A(inside)}{\gamma_A(outside)}$$

EXERCISE 4-5
A cell membrane at 37 [°C] to be permeable to Ca^{2+} (but not to anions), and inside concentration to be 0.100 [M] and the outside concentration to be 0.001 [M] in Ca^{2+}. Calculate potential difference across the membrane for Ca^{2+}? Assume that activity coefficients(γ) are 1.

ANSWER

$$\Delta\mu_A = RT\ln\frac{a_{A(phase\ 2)}}{a_{A(phase\ 1)}} + ZFV \qquad \text{(Eqn. 4-14)}$$

Now, we can set $\Delta\mu_A = 0$

Thus,

$$ZFV = -RT\ln\frac{a_{A(phase\ 2)}}{a_{A(phase\ 1)}}$$

T = 37 [°C] = 310 [K]

$a_{A(phase\ 2)}$ = 0.001 [M] and $a_{A(phase\ 1)}$ = 0.1 [M]   Z=+2 for Ca^{2+}

$$V = -\frac{8.314 \times 310}{2 \times 96485}\ln\frac{0.001}{0.1}$$

= −0.062 [V]

① At the equilibrium, $\Delta\mu_A = 0$

② Don't forget the minus sign.

③ Temperature is in Kelvins unit.

④ Potential we are looking for is from inside to outside. The inside concentration is initial stage and the outside concentration can be considered as a final stage.

⑤ The negative 0.062 [V] is present on the inside the cell to keep the Ca^{2+} in equilibrium.

When different charged species which are unable to pass through a semi-permeable membrane are placed, uneven electrical charge distribution across the two sides of the membrane is created. This is called **Gibbs–Donnan effect**, and the potential caused by a distribution of ion species between two ionic solutions separated by a semipermeable membrane is called as Donnan potential. Generally, anionic proteins in blood plasma are large enough not to pass through semi-permeable membrane, while small cations are attracted to anionic proteins. However, these cations are not bound to the proteins, so that small anions will cross membrane more than small cations. For example, sickle cells swell with fluid when the sodium pump stops working properly because some ionic species can pass through the membrane while others cannot.

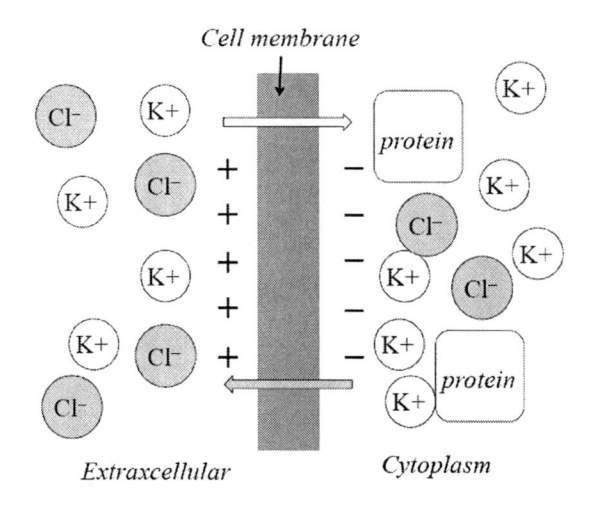

Fig.4-17 Donnan equilibrium across a membrane.

Chapter 4

How did you get these equations?
-The derivation of selected equations.

(Eqn. 4-5) $\quad P_A = X_A P_A^\bullet$

(Eqn. 4-6) $\quad P_A \phi_A = P_A^\bullet \gamma_A X_A$

The chemical potential of component A is:

$$\mu_A = \mu_A^\bullet + RT \ln a_A \quad \text{(Eqn. 3-2)}$$

where μ_A^o is the chemical potential of pure solvent A and a_A is the activity of a solution. Thus the chemical potential of component A in the liquid, $\mu_{A,\,liquid}$, is

$$\mu_{A,liquid} = \mu_{A,liquid}^\bullet + RT \ln a_{A,liquid}$$

At equilibrium, chemical potentials of the component A *in the* solution and the vapor are equal.

$$\mu_{A,liquid} = \mu_{A,vapor}$$

Assuming the liquid is an ideal solution, but using the chemical potential for a real gas:

$$\mu_{A,liquid}^\bullet + RT \ln X_{A,liquid} = \mu_{A,vapor}^\bullet + RT \ln \frac{f_{A,vapor}}{P^o}$$
---a)

where $f_{A,\,vapor}$ is the fugacity of the vapor A and P^o is the standard state (P^o = 1 [atm]). The corresponding equation for pure A in equilibrium with its pure vapor is ($X_{A,\,liquid}$ =1 and ln $X_{A,\,liquid}$ =0),

$$\mu_{A,liquid}^\bullet = \mu_{A,vapor}^\bullet + RT \ln \frac{f_{A,vapor}^\bullet}{P^o} \quad \text{---b)}$$

Subtracting formula b) from formula a)

$$RT \ln a_{A,liquid} = RT \ln \frac{f_{A,vapor}}{f_{A,vapor}^\bullet}$$

Chapter 4 Inter-Phase Energy Transition

If the terms in natural log are extracted

$$a_{A,liquid} = \frac{f_{A,vapor}}{f^{\bullet}_{A,vapor}} = \frac{f_{A,vapor}}{P^{\bullet}_{A,vapor}}$$

At the last term the fugacity of pure solvent is approximated to be the equal to an ideal vapor pressure of solvent. Thus,

$$f_{A,vapor} = a_{A,liquid} P^{\bullet}_{A,vapor}$$

The fugacity and activity are replaced by

$$f_{A,vapor} = \phi_{A,vapor} P_{A,vapor}$$

$$a_{A,liquid} = \gamma_{A,liquid} X_{A,liquid} \quad \text{(Eqn. 3-5)}$$

Thus,
$$\phi_{A,vapor} P_{A,vapor} = P^{\bullet}_{A,vapor} \gamma_{A,liquid} X_{A,liquid} \quad \text{(Eqn. 4-4)}$$

For ideal solution γ_A is 1, and ϕ_A is 1 for an ideal gas. Thus, Raoult's Law for an ideal solution and an ideal gas is

$$P_A = X_{A,liquid} P^{\bullet}_{A,vapor} \quad \text{(Eqn. 4-3)}$$

(Eqn. 4-8) $\quad \Delta\mu_A = RT \ln \frac{[A]_{phase2}}{[A]_{phase1}}$

The chemical potential is given by
$$\mu_A = \mu^{\bullet}_A + RT \ln a_A \quad \text{(Eqn. 3-2)}$$

$$\mu_{A,phase1} = \mu^{\bullet}_{A,phase1} + RT \ln a_{A,phase1}$$
$$\mu_{A,phase2} = \mu^{\bullet}_{A,phase2} + RT \ln a_{A,phase2}$$

The difference of chemical potential between phase 1 and phase 2 is
$$\Delta\mu_A = \mu_A(phase\ 2) - \mu_A(phase\ 1)$$
$$= RT\ln \frac{a_{A,phase2}}{a_{A,phase1}}$$

Here, please note that $\mu^{\bullet}_{A,phase1} = \mu^{\bullet}_{A,phase2}$
For dilute or ideal solution, the activity is shown by a concentration.

$$\Delta\mu_A = RT\ln \frac{[A]_{phase2}}{[A]_{phase1}} \quad \text{(Eqn. 4-6)}$$

(Eqn. 4-10) $\quad \frac{v}{[A]} = K[N - v]$

152

The equilibrium constant K of a reaction is given by

$$K = \frac{[M \bullet A]}{[M][A]}$$

The concentration of the complex [M•A] is equal to the amount of ligands bound to M, [A]$_{bound}$ (i.e., [M•A] =[A]$_{bound}$), and the amount of free macro molecule [M] should be the difference between total concentration of M and the amount used for binding ([M]$_{total}$ − [M•A] = [M]$_{total}$ − [A]$_{bound}$). The concentration of free ligands [A] is equal to the concentration of ligands exist outside of the membrane, i.e., [A] = [A]$_{outside}$) Therefore, the equilibrium constant K i s expressed as:

$$K = \frac{[M \bullet A]}{[M][A]} = \frac{[A]_{bound}}{\{[M]_{total} - [A]_{bound}\}[A]}$$

Let's assume that there are N identical independent binding sites in macromolecule, and v ligands are bound per macromolecule on the average.

$$\frac{v}{N} = \frac{[A]_{bound}}{[M]_{total}}$$

Thus,

$$[A]_{bound} = \frac{v}{N}[M]_{total}$$

By inserting this [A]$_{bound}$ into the expression for K,

$$K = \frac{\frac{v}{N}[M]_{total}}{\left\{[M]_{total} - \frac{v}{N}[M]_{total}\right\}[A]} = \frac{v/N}{\left[1 - \frac{v}{N}\right][A]}$$

By arranging the above,

$$\frac{v/N}{[A]} = K\left[1 - \frac{v}{N}\right]$$

Therefore,

$$\frac{v}{[A]} = K[N - v] \qquad \text{(Eqn. 4-8)}$$

(Eqn. 4-11) $\quad \dfrac{f}{[1-f]} = K[A]^n$

The equilibrium is given as

$$M + nA \underset{\longleftarrow}{\overset{K}{\longrightarrow}} M \bullet A^n$$

Chapter 4 Inter-Phase Energy Transition

Thus, an equilibrium constant is

$$K = \frac{[M\bullet A^n]}{[M][A]^n}$$

If the fraction of bound to the total number of independent binding sites is given by f,

$$f = v/N$$

$$[M\bullet A^n] = f[M]$$

$$[M] = (1-f)[M]$$

Thus,

$$K = \frac{[M\bullet A^n]}{[M][A]^n} = \frac{f[M]}{(1-f)[M][A]^n}$$

Then, we can derive the relationship between equilibrium constant K and fraction, f, as

$$\frac{f}{[1-f]} = K[A]^n \qquad \text{(Eqn. 4-9)}$$

(Eqn. 4-14) $$\Delta \mu_A = RT \ln \frac{a_{A(phase\ 2)}}{a_{A(phase\ 1)}} + ZFV$$

The chemical potential of a substance A under the field, ϕ, is

$$\mu_{A,total} = \mu_A + ZF\phi \qquad \text{(Eqn. 4-10)}$$

The chemical potential expressed for component A is valid for the same component in phase 1 and phase. Thus, the difference in a chemical potential ($\Delta\mu_A$) of component A in two different phases is given by

$$\Delta\mu_A = \mu_{A,total}(phase\ 2) - \mu_{A,total}(phase\ 1)$$
$$= (\mu_{A,phase2} + ZF\phi_2) - (\mu_{A,phase1} + ZF\phi_1)$$
$$\text{(Eqn. 4-21)}$$

Since,
$$\mu_A = \mu_A^\bullet + RT \ln a_A \qquad \text{(Eqn. 3-2)}$$

$$\mu_{A,phase1} = \mu_{A,phase1}^\bullet + RT \ln a_{A,phase\ 1}$$
$$\mu_{A,phase2} = \mu_{A,phase2}^\bullet + RT \ln a_{A,phase\ 2}$$

Thus,

154

Chapter 4 Inter-Phase Energy Transition

$$\Delta\mu_A = (\mu_{A,phase2} + ZF\phi_2) - (\mu_{A,phase1} + ZF\phi_1)$$
$$= \mu^{\bullet}_{A,phase2} + RT \ln a_{A,phase\ 2} + ZF\phi_2 - \mu^{\bullet}_{A,phase1} - RT \ln a_{A,phase\ 1} - ZF\phi_1$$
$$= RT \ln a_{A,phase\ 2} - RT \ln a_{A,phase\ 1} + ZF\phi_2 - ZF\phi_1$$
$$= RT \ln \frac{a_{A,phase\ 2}}{a_{A,phase\ 1}} + ZF(\phi_2 - \phi_1)$$

(This is because $\mu^{\bullet}_{A,phase1} = \mu^{\bullet}_{A,phase2}$.)

Since V is defined as the difference in potential of phase 1 (ϕ_1) and phase 2 (ϕ_2) as

$$V = \phi_2 - \phi_1$$

$$\Delta\mu = RT \ln \frac{a_{A(phase\ 2)}}{a_{A(phase\ 1)}} + ZFV \qquad \textbf{(Eqn. 4-11)}$$

Chapter 4 Summary [Part 1]

(Use back page to cover the contents.)

1	The equilibrium between two phases and chemical potential (μ)	$\mu_A^\bullet(pure\ solvent) = \mu_A^\bullet(gas, P_A^\bullet)$ (Eqn. 4-1) $\mu_A(solutions) = \mu_A(gas, P_A)$ (Eqn. 4-2)
2	equilibrium constant (K) at vaporization	$K = \dfrac{a_{A(g)}}{a_{A(l)}} = P$ (Eqn. 4-3) $a_{A(g)}$: activity of gaseous A, $a_{A(l)}$: activity of liquid A
3	Clausius-Clapeyron Equation	$\ln\dfrac{P_2}{P_1} = -\dfrac{\Delta \bar{H}_{vap}^o}{R}\left[\dfrac{1}{T_2} - \dfrac{1}{T_1}\right]$ (Eqn. 4-4) $\Delta \bar{H}_{vap}^o$: heat of vaporization, P: vapor pressure, T: boiling point
4	Raoult's Law	$P_A = X_A P_A^\bullet$ (Eqn. 4-5) P_A: vapor pressure of solute A of a solution, X_A: the mole fraction of A in solution, $P_A^\bullet$: vapor pressure of solvent A
5	Henry's law	$P_B = X_B k_H$ (Eqn. 4-7) P_B: pressure of solute B, X_B: mole fraction of B, k_H: Henry's law constant
6	chemical potential between two phases (Δμ_A)	$\Delta \mu_A = RT \ln\dfrac{[A]_{phase2}}{[A]_{phase1}}$ (Eqn. 4-8) $[A]_{phase1}$: concentration of A at phase 1 $[A]_{phase2}$: concentration of A at phase 2

[Fold the page at the double line and cover the right half.]

CHAPTER 4 SUMMARY CHECK [PART 1]

(Use this page to cover and check the contents.)

Use ☐ as your check box. Write your comment at far right

1	The equilibrium between two phases and chemical potential (μ)	☐ ☐ ☐ ☐ ☐	
2	equilibrium constant (K) at vaporization	☐ ☐ ☐ ☐ ☐	
3	Clausius-Clapeyron Equation	☐ ☐ ☐ ☐ ☐	
4	Raoult's Law	☐ ☐ ☐ ☐ ☐	
5	Henry's law	☐ ☐ ☐ ☐ ☐	
6	chemical potential between two phases ($\Delta\mu_A$)	☐ ☐ ☐ ☐ ☐	

Chapter 4 Summary [Part 2]

(Use back page to cover the contents.)

7	Scatchard equation	$\dfrac{v}{[A]} = K[N - v]$ (Eqn. 4-10) v: number of bound ligands, [A]: concentration of ligands, K: equilibrium constant of dialysis, N: number of binding sites	Scatchrad plot
8	Hill's plot and cooperativity in a binding	$\log \dfrac{f}{[1-f]} = n \log[A] + \log K$ (Eqn. 4-12) n: cooperativity, f: fraction, n: Hill constant, [A]: concentration of ligands	Hill plot
9	chemical potential (μ) under external field	$\mu_{A,total} = \mu_A + ZF\phi$ (Eqn. 4-13) Z: charge of transferring ions, ϕ: external potential	
10	chemical potential difference ($\Delta\mu_A$) in two different phases	$\Delta\mu_A = RT \ln \dfrac{a_{A(phase\ 2)}}{a_{A(phase\ 1)}} + ZFV$ (Eqn. 4-14) $V = \phi_2 - \phi_1$ ϕ_1: potential of phase 1, ϕ_2: potential of phase 2	

Chapter 4 Summary Check [Part 2]

(Use this page to cover and check the contents.)
Use ☐ as your check box. Write your comment at far right

7	Scatchard equation	☐ ☐ ☐ ☐ ☐	
8	Hill's plot and cooperativity in a binding	☐ ☐ ☐ ☐ ☐	
9	chemical potential (μ) under external field	☐ ☐ ☐ ☐ ☐	
10	chemical potential difference ($\Delta\mu_A$) in two different phases	☐ ☐ ☐ ☐ ☐	

YOUR TEACHER MAY TEST YOU ON:

No.	What may be asked?		What you should know or do?
1	How do you approach to express the equilibrium existent between two different phases?	→ →	$\mu_A(solutions) = \mu_A(gas, P_A)$ (Eqn. 4-2) Problem 4-1
2	What is the expression for the equilibrium constant for the transition between gaseous and liquid phases?	→	$K = \dfrac{a_{A(g)}}{a_{A(l)}}$ (Eqn. 4-3)
3	How do you calculate the vapor pressure at different temperature? How do you calculate the boiling point for a given vapor pressure? How can you calculate the heat of vaporization?	→ → →	**Clausius-Clapeyron Equation** $ln\dfrac{P_2}{P_1} = -\dfrac{\Delta \bar{H}^o_{vap}}{R}\left[\dfrac{1}{T_2} - \dfrac{1}{T_1}\right]$ (Eqn. 4-4) EXERCISE 4-1 Problems 4-6, 4-7, 4-8, 4-9, 4-10, 4-11, 4-12, 4-13, 4-14
4	How vapor pressure of the solution is calculated? How can you calculate the mole fraction of a solution with given vapor pressure?	→ →	**Raoult's Law** $P_A = X_A P_A^\bullet$ (Eqn. 4-5) Problems 4-2, 4-3, 4-4, 4-5
5	How can you calculate the mole fraction of gaseous substance dissolved in a solution under a given pressure? How much pressure do you need to dissolve a gaseous substance (with mole fraction X) in a solution?	→ → →	**Henry's law.** $P_B = X_B k_H$ (Eqn. 4-7) EXERCISE 4-2 Problems 4-15, 4-16
6	How do you calculate the chemical potential difference when energy transfers between two different phases?	→ → →	$\Delta \mu_A = \mu_A(phase\ 2) - \mu_A(phase\ 1)$ $= RT\ ln\dfrac{[A]_{phase2}}{[A]_{phase1}}$ (Eqn. 4-8) EXERCISE 4-3 Problems 4-1a, 4-1b
7	How do you express an equilibrium constant for a dialysis system? What is the approach to obtain the number of independent binding sites of a macromolecule? (Scatchard equation) How do you obtain the equilibrium constant for dialysis system?	→ → →	$\dfrac{\nu}{[A]} = K[N - \nu]$ (Eqn. 4-10) EXERCISE 4-4 Problems 4-17, 4-18, 4-19, 4-20, 4-21, 4-22
8	How do you use the Scatchard plot in order to obtain an equilibrium constant and the number of independent binding sites?	→ → →	Fig. 4-13 $\dfrac{\nu}{[A]} = K[N - \nu]$ (Eqn. 4-10) Problems 4-17, 4-18, 4-19, 4-20, 4-21, 4-22

9	How do you calculate the cooperativity of ligands to a macromolecule?	→	$\log \frac{f}{[1-f]} = n \log[A] + \log K$ (Eqn. 4-12)
10	How do you interpret Hill's plot? What can you extract form the Hill's plot?	→ →	Fig. 4-15 $\log \frac{f}{[1-f]} = n \log[A] + \log K$ (Eqn. 4-12)
11	How do you calculate the chemical potential when the system is placed under a field?		$\mu_{A,total} = \mu_A + ZF\phi$ (Eqn. 4-13)
12	How do you calculate the chemical potential as charged species transfers between two phases when field is applied?	→ → →	$\Delta\mu_A = RT \ln \frac{a_{A(phase\,2)}}{a_{A(phase\,1)}} + ZFV$ (Eqn. 4-14) EXERCISE 4-5 Problems 4-23, 4-24, 4-25

UNIT CHECK CHAPTER 4

Important Parameters of This Chapter	Popularly Used Unit	Important Unit Conversion
Pressure	atm	1 [atm] =101.325 [Pa]=760 [torr]
Molar Enthalpy change of vaporization, $\Delta \bar{H}^o_{vap}$	J/mol kJ/mol	
Mole fraction, X	Dimensionless	
Chemical potential, μ	kJ/mol	
Gas constant, R	atm L mol^{-1}K^{-1} J mol^{-1}K^{-1}	8.314472[J mol^{-1}K^{-1}] 0.08205746 [atm L mol^{-1}K^{-1}]
Temperature, T	°C K	0 [°C] = 273.15 [K]
activity coefficient, γ	Dimensionless	
Henry's law constant, k	atm	
Concentration, [A]	M mol/L	
Number of independent binding sites, N	Dimensionless	
Number of binding ligands, ν	Dimensionless	
Fraction of ν and N (ν/ N), f	Dimensionless	
Charge of ion, Z	Dimensionless	
Faraday constant ,F	C/mol	F= 96,485 [C/mol]
Potential, ϕ	V	[J]= [C V]

Chapter 4 Inter-Phase Energy Transition

SUMMARY OF TRICKY TRAPS OF CHAPTER 4

☐	1	The pressure given by Raoult's law → Pressure of vapor (not liquid) over the solution
☐	2	The mole fraction given by Raoult's law → mole fraction in the solution (not in the vapor)
☐	3	The key assumption of dialysis analysis is $a_{inside} = a_{outside}$ The concentration of ligand between inside and outside of membrane is equal.

LAST MINUTE REVIEW OF MATH CHAPTER 4

(These are basic algebra which you have no excuse if you miss them.)

1. $\ln\left(\frac{x}{y}\right) = -\ln\left(\frac{y}{x}\right)$

2. y = mx + b
X axis Intercept y = b
Y axis intercept x = −(b/m)

Nobel Prize and Your Knowledge From Chapter 4
(*: word appeared in Chapter 4)

The Nobel Prize in Physiology or Medicine 1991 was awarded to **Erwin Neher** and **Bert Sakmann** "for their discoveries concerning the function of single ion channels in cells". In 1976 Neher and Sakmann reported a study using glass recording electrodes (patch clamp electrodes) with microscopic tips pressed against a cell membrane.(**Fig. 4-18**) With this technique, they were able to isolate a tiny patch of the cell membrane and view how the individual proteins permitted certain ions to pass through the cell membrane one at a time but refused others to enter.(inter **phase energy transition***) The patch clamps have an advantage to remove a patch of the membrane and to enter the interior of the cell to observe the intricate mechanism of ion channels. Later on, patch clamping technique was refined to create a better seal between the micropipette and the patch of cell membrane in order to remove outside noise interference. In 1980, the noise level was dropped to

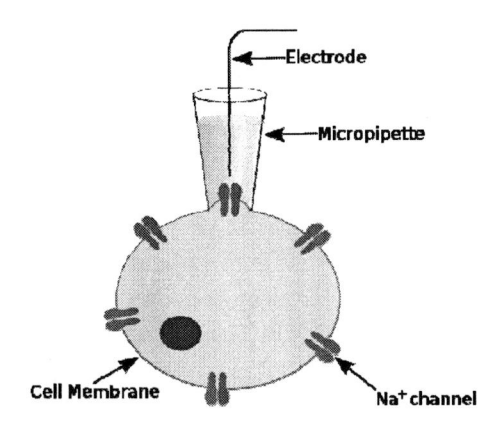

Fig. 4-18 Patch clamp method

almost zero and achieved a tight seal. By using a light suction with a super clean pipette, a high-resistance seal of 10-100 [GΩ]. Under this tight seal, tremendous decrease in background noise was achieved, and numerous methods of controlling cells for patch clamp experimentation can be conducted. Patches from the cell is torn away from the membrane and is used as a membrane coating over the mouth of the pipette. It allows more exact measurement of electrical ion movement. Patch clamping has been fully used for the researches of hormone regulation, cystic fibrosis, and insulin production as well as the development of new drugs for epilepsy, heart disease, and disorders associated with the nervous/muscle systems.

Andrew Fielding Huxley and **Alan Lloyd Hodgkin** developed an action potential theory representing one of the earliest applications of a technique of electrophysiology (voltage clamp). Using the giant axon of Atlantic squid (*Loligo pealei*), they recorded ionic currents. Their work on action potentials of nerve states that the electrical impulses which enable the activity of an organism to be coordinated by a central nervous system. This is a mathematical explanation for nerve impulses with a set of differential equations. This theory provided the basis for the all of the current work on voltage-sensitive membrane channels (or inter **phase energy transition***), which are responsible for the functioning of animal nervous systems. Hodgkin and Huxley's hypothesized ion channels (**Fig. 4-19**), and confirmation of ion channels came with the development of the patch clamp leading to a Nobel prize in 1991 for Erwin Neher and Bert Sakmann. **Hodkin** developed the formulas for the operation of myosin cross-bridges which generates the sliding forces between actin and myosin filaments.(The myosin filaments cause the contraction of skeletal muscles.) **Hodkin** pioneered to clarify the understanding of muscle contraction and it has been extended to provide our understanding of almost all of the movements produced by cells above the level of bacteria.

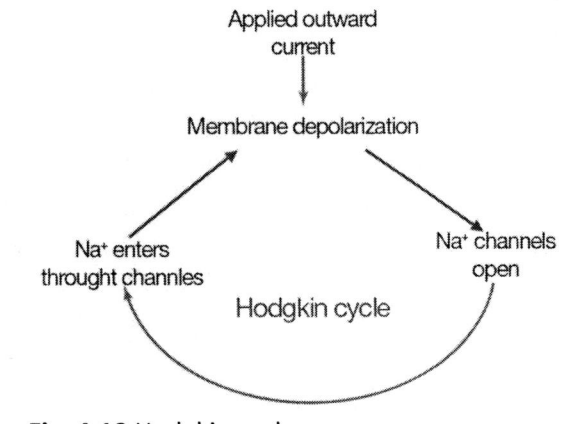

Fig. 4-19 Hodgkin cycle.

THE FOCUSED PHYSICAL CHEMISTRY EXPERIMENTAL APPROACH ASSOCIATED WITH CHAPTER 4
(*: word appeared in Chapter 4)

Measurement of Action Potential

An **action potential** implies the electrical **membrane potential*** of several types of animal cells (neurons, muscle cells, and endocrine cells, and plant cells) which rapidly rises and falls. (See **Fig. 4-20**). The action potential play a key role in inter cellular communication, intracellular activation processes, leading process of to contraction in muscle cell. Action potentials are known to be generated by voltage-gated ion channels embedded in a cell's plasma membrane, and this gate channel is open if the membrane potential reaches over a threshold and causes inward flow of Na⁺ producing an increase of the membrane potential and enhancement of channel opening. The rapid influx of Na+ ions eventually inactivate Na⁺ channels and closes. Then , in turn, K⁺ channels are activated, and there is an outward current of K⁺ ions, returning the electrochemical gradient to the resting state. Two primary types of cause of action potentials in animal cells are:
1. generation by voltage-gated sodium channels (duration of 1 [ms]) and
2. generation by voltage-gated calcium channels.(duration of 100 [msec] or longer)

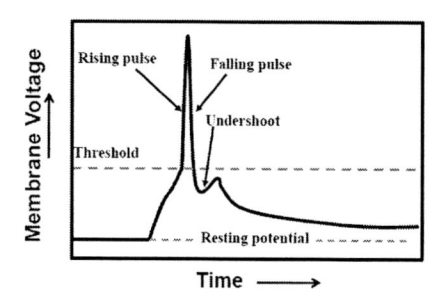

Fig.4-20 Action potential

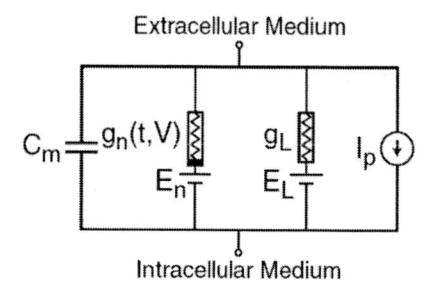

Fig. 4-21 Electrical circuit for the Hodgkin–Huxley model.

As for the method of measuring action potential, voltage clamp method is mainly used (See the previous section). With the crucial development of the voltage clamp, the ionic currents (I_C associated with the capacitance C of the membrane) underlying an action potential was measured. Since the current equals Ck, where k is a rate of change of the transmembrane voltage V_m, a circuit to maintain constant V_m regardless of the currents across the membrane can be designed. Measuring I_C, the current flowing through the membrane is obtained. With usage of the glass micropipette electrode whose electrode tips that are as fine as 100 [Å] (10 [nm]), the sum of the currents passing through many ion channels are measured. The electrical properties of a single ion channel was established by patch clamp method (**Fig. 4-18**). This method verified that ionic channels have discrete states of conductance, such as open, closed and inactivated. Recently, optical imaging is utilized for measuring action potentials using voltage-sensitive dyes.

The most important and accurate mathematical and computational models of an action potential is Hodgkin–Huxley model, and it helped to understand the action potential and testing theories, which describes the action potential by a coupled set of four ordinary differential equations. As shown in **Fig. 4-21,** I_m and V_m represent the current through, and the voltage across, a small patch of membrane, respectively. Here, C_m represents the capacitance of the membrane patch, whereas the four g's represent the conductance of four types of ions. The two conductance on the left represent r potassium (K) and sodium (Na). The arrows indicate that they can vary with the applied voltage, and it shows that they correspond to the voltage-sensitive ion channels. The two conductance on the right are used to determine the resting membrane potential. With larger and more integrated systems of action-potential models and with models of other parts of the nervous system, the application for neural computation is conducted.

CHAPTER 4 PROBLEMS.

4-1 [$\Delta\mu$ between phases] a) True or False: Between phases 1 and 2, the Gibbs energy for the content in phase 2 to transport to phase 1 is negative if the $c_1 > c_2$. (Here, c_1 and c_2 are the original concentrations of substances in phases 1 and 2, respectively.)
b) The concentration of sodium ions inside the living biological cell is 0.02 [M] and its concentration outside the cell is 0.08 [M]. Calculate the $\Delta\mu$ for this transport process at 37 [°C].

4-2 [Raoult's law] Assuming that solution (A) is an ideal solution, calculate the equilibrium vapor pressure at 20 [°C] of a solution of 1.00 [g] of protein x (MW. 69.2 [kDa]) in 100 [g] of water?

4-3 [Raoult's law] How much increase do you expect for molar fraction of N_2 between 1 [atm] to 24.0 [atm] of N_2 partial pressure?

4-4 [Raoult's law] The N_2 gas is dissolved in water (density = 1[g/mL]) with molarity of 3.25×10^{-7} [M]. Over this solution, the partial pressure of N_2 was measured to be 6.50 [atm]. Later, the partial pressure of N_2 was observed as 2.10 [atm]. Calculate the mole fraction of N_2 in water.

4-5 [Raoult's law/Clausis Clapeyron] Substance A is a somewhat volatile solid and soluble substance. Solute A and liquid water allowed to reach equilibrium at 20 [°C] to form an aqueous phase and a gaseous phase. The vapor pressure of pure solid A is 1.0×10^{-2} [torr] at 20 [°C] and 1.0×10^{-1} [torr] at 40 [°C]. The vapor pressure of pure water is 17.535 [torr] at 20 [°C] and 55.324 [torr] at 40 [°C]. What is the mole fraction of A in the gas phase at equilibrium at 20 [°C]?

4-6 [Clausius-Clapeyron Equation] When the sun sets, the air temperature drops to 5 [°C]. Assuming that the excess water vapor is precipitated as rain, calculate the weight of the rain. Please recall that vapor pressure is dependent of the temperature.

4-7 [Clausius-Clapeyron Equation] At 20,320 [ft] altitude, pure water boils at 75 [°C]. What is the atmospheric pressure at this altitude? [Use the heat of vaporization, ΔH_{vap}, given in the CRC Table.]

4-8 [Clausius-Clapeyron Equation] Substance A is a somewhat volatile solid and soluble substance. Solute A and liquid water allowed to reach equilibrium at 20 [°C] to form an aqueous phase and a gaseous phase. The vapor pressure of pure solid A is 1.0×10^{-2} [torr] at 20 [°C] and 1.0×10^{-1} [torr] at 40 [°C]. The vapor pressure of pure water is 17.535 [torr] at 20 [°C] and 55.324 [torr] at 40 [°C]. Calculate the Heat of vaporization of solid A.

4-9 [Clausius-Clapeyron Equation] The protein in aqueous solution is heated at 120 [°C] in a sealed tube. Calculate the internal pressure at this temperature. The normal boiling point and $\Delta H°_{vap}$ are 100 [°C] and 40.66 [kJ/mol], respectively.

4-10 [Clausius-Clapeyron Equation] On the planet Taurus II, ammonia plays a role similar to that of water on Earth. Ammonia has the following properties: Normal boiling point is –33.4 [°C], where its heat of vaporization is 1368 [kJ/kg]. Estimate the temperature at which the vapor pressure of $NH_3(l)$ is 50 [mm Hg].

4-11 [Clausius-Clapeyron Equation] On the planet Taurus II, ammonia plays a role similar to that of water on Earth. Ammonia has the following properties: Normal boiling point (1 [atm]) is –33.4 [°C], where its heat of vaporization is 1368 [kJ/kg]. Estimate the temperature at which the vapor pressure of $NH_3(l)$ is 60 [torr].

4-12 [Clausius-Clapeyron Equation] Protein can be hydrolyzed to amino acids by heating in very dilute aqueous NaOH solution. The protein itself is very dilute. The reaction is carried out at 120 [°C] by heating the solution in a sealed tube that was evacuated prior to sealing. What internal pressure must the tube withstand at this temperature? The normal boiling point and ΔH_{vap} of water may be taken as 100 [°C] and 40.66 [kJ/mol], respectively.

4-13 [Clausius-Clapeyron Equation] True or False: If you add the salt into the solvent, the vapor pressure of this solution decreases.

4-14 [Clausius-Clapeyron Equation] The *Clausius- Clapeyron equation* explains that
a. the vapor pressure decreases as boiling point increases.
b. the heat of freezing can be derived from the plot between pressure and temperature.
c. the vapor pressure increases as the boiling point increases.
d. the boiling point as a function of heat of vaporization
e. *van't* Hoff equation is not true in some cases.

4-15 [Henry's law] A 100 [mL] of blood at 37 [°C] and 1 [atm] dissolves 1.3 [mL] of N_2. Calculate the volume of N_2 likely to be liberated from the blood of a caisson worker returned to 1 [atm] pressure from 300 [m].

4-16 [Henry's law] A 500 [mL] of blood at 37 [°C] and 1 [atm] dissolves 6.5 [mL] of N_2. Calculate the volume of N_2 likely to be liberated from the blood of a caisson worker returned to 1 [atm] pressure from 200 [m]. The total blood volume of this caisson worker is 3.6 [L]. The air contains 78 volume % N_2. (The density of Hg is 13.6 [g/mL] and the density of sea water is 1.025 [g/mL].)

4-17 [Scatchard Equation] Plot v/[A] versus v in a separate graph paper, if the there is a total of ten identical and independent sites per polymer and the intrinsic binding constant is K = 5.0×10^5 [M^{-1}].

4-18 [Scatchard Equation] The enzyme tetrahydrofolate has 4 identical binding sites. The concentration of free ATP is 10^{-4} [M] and average number of ligands per one enzyme is 2. Calculate K.

4-19 [Scatchard Equation] A student made a Scatchard plot for the substrates-polymer binding reaction. Obtain number of binding sites per polymer and the intrinsic binding constant from the graph.

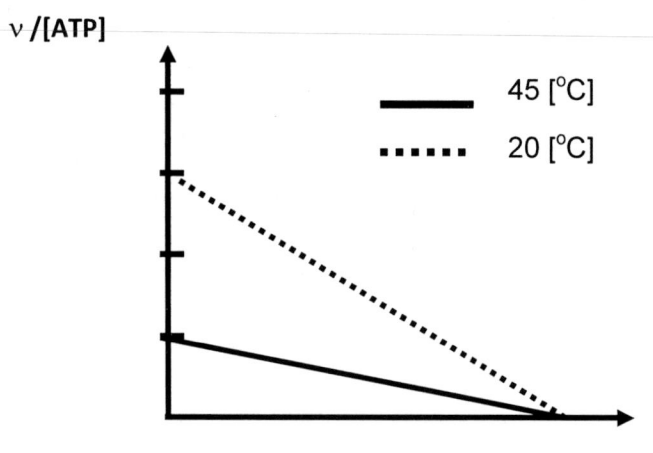

4-20 [Scatchard Equation] The enzyme X has five identical and independent binding sites for its substrate ATP. For an equilibrium dialysis experiment, a solution of the enzyme X was prepared. First, the osmotic pressure of this solution was measured to be 2.0×10^{-3} [atm] at 20 [°C]. Then, the enzyme X solution was placed in a dialysis bag, and the binding of ATP to the enzyme X was measured by equilibrium dialysis at the same temperature. After the binding equilibrium was established, the concentration of free ATP outside the bag was found to be 2.5 $\times 10^{-4}$ [M], and the total ATP concentration inside the bag was found to be 6.5×10^{-4} [M]. The equilibrium dialysis experiment was repeated for a series of outside ATP concentration at 45 [°C], and the Scatchard plots were obtained. Calculate $\Delta H°$ and $\Delta S°$ for the binding of ATP to its site on the enzyme (Assume that $\Delta H°$ and $\Delta S°$ are independent of temperature.)

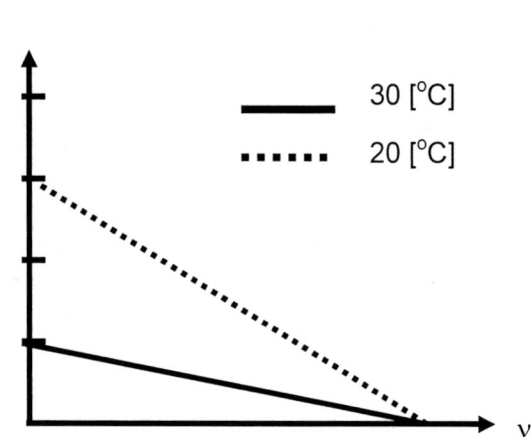

4-21 [Scatchard Equation]
a) In the Scatchard equation, the value shown as an x-axis intercept is
b) For an equilibrium dialysis experiment, a solution of the enzyme X was prepared in solvent "Y". First, enzyme X was dissolved in 750 [mL] solvent Y (Molar mass of Y is 20 [g/mol]). The elevation of boiling point of solution at 1 [atm] was measured to be 0.0015 [°C]. The density of solvent Y is

0.9982 [g/mL] (You may assume that this value does not depend upon temperature). A vapor pressure of pure solvent Y was 1180 [mmHg] at 114 [°C], and the normal boiling point was 101 [°C]. The density of enzyme X solution was the same as density of solvent Y.

Second, this enzyme X solution was placed in a dialysis bag at 20 [°C] in solvent Y, and the binding of ATP to the enzyme X was measured by equilibrium dialysis at the same temperature. After the binding equilibrium was established, the concentration of free ATP outside the bag was found to be 2.0×10^{-3} [M], and the total ATP concentration inside the bag was found to be 6.0×10^{-3} [M]. The enzyme X has three identical and independent binding sites for its substrate ATP. The equilibrium dialysis experiment was repeated for a series of outside ATP concentration at 30 [°C], and the Scatchard plots were obtained as shown above. Calculate $\Delta H°$ and $\Delta S°$ for the binding of ATP to its site on the enzyme (Assume that $\Delta H°$ and $\Delta S°$ are independent of temperature.)

4-22 [Scatchard Equation] In the *Scatchard* equation, the value shown as a y-axis intercept is

4-23 [µ under external field] A cell membrane at 37 [°C] is found to be permeable to Na^+ but not to anions. In this living biological cell, the concentration of sodium ions inside the cell is kept at a lower concentration than the concentration outside the cell. Consider the following process at 37 [°C] and 1 [atm].

1 [mol] NaCl (0.05 [M] inside) → 1 [mol] NaCl (0.20 [M] outside)

If the measured inside potential of process A is +100 [mV] with respect to the outside, what is the minimum (reversible) work required to transfer 1 [mol] of Na^+ from outside to inside? Assume that activity coefficients are equal to 1. Give the sign of the potential inside with respect to that outside.

4-24 [µ under external field] A cell membrane at 37 [°C] is permeable to Ca^{2+} but not to anions. $[Ca^{2+}(inside)] = 0.200$ [M] and $[Ca^{2+}(outside)] = 0.002$ [M]. Calculate the potential difference across the membrane in equilibrium.

4-25 [µ under external field] A cell membrane at 37 [°C] to be permeable to Ca^{2+} (but not to anions), and inside concentration to be 0.100 [M] and the outside concentration to be 0.001 [M] in Ca^{2+}. If the measured inside potential is +100 [mV] with respect to the outside what is the minimum (reversible) work required to transfer 1 [mol] of Ca^{2+} from outside to inside under these conditions?

Chapter 4 Answers. For Selected Problems

4-1	a) False b) 3.6 [kJ]
4-2	P_A = 17.54 [torr]
4-3	factor of 24
4-4	1.89×10^{-9}
4-5	$X_A = 5.70 \times 10^{-4}$
4-6	2.04×10^{11} [g]
4-7	0.38 [atm]
4-8	$\Delta H = +87.8$ [kJ/mol]
4-9	1.95 [atm]
4-10	174 [K]
4-11	197 [K]
4-12	$P_2 = 1.95$ [atm]
4-13	True
4-14	c
4-15	957 [mL]
4-16	714 [mL]
4-18	10^4 [M^{-1}]
4-19	$K = 5.0 \times 10^5$ [M^{-1}]
4-20	$\Delta H = -34.04$ [kJ], $\Delta G°_{293} = -20.8$ [kJ], $\Delta S° = -45.31$ [J/K]
4-21	a) N b) $\Delta H° = -81.09$ [kJ] $\Delta G°_{293} = -15.4$ [kJ] $\Delta S° = -224$ [J/K]
4-22	KN
4-23	$\Delta \mu = -6.08$ [kJ/mol]
4-24	0.06 [kJ]
4-25	$\Delta \mu_A = 31.2$ [kJ]

Chapter 5
Macromolecular Phase Transitions

5-1   Surface Tension
5-2   Langmuir Isotherm
5-3   Colligative Properties
5-4   Pressure Effect on the Freezing/Melting Points

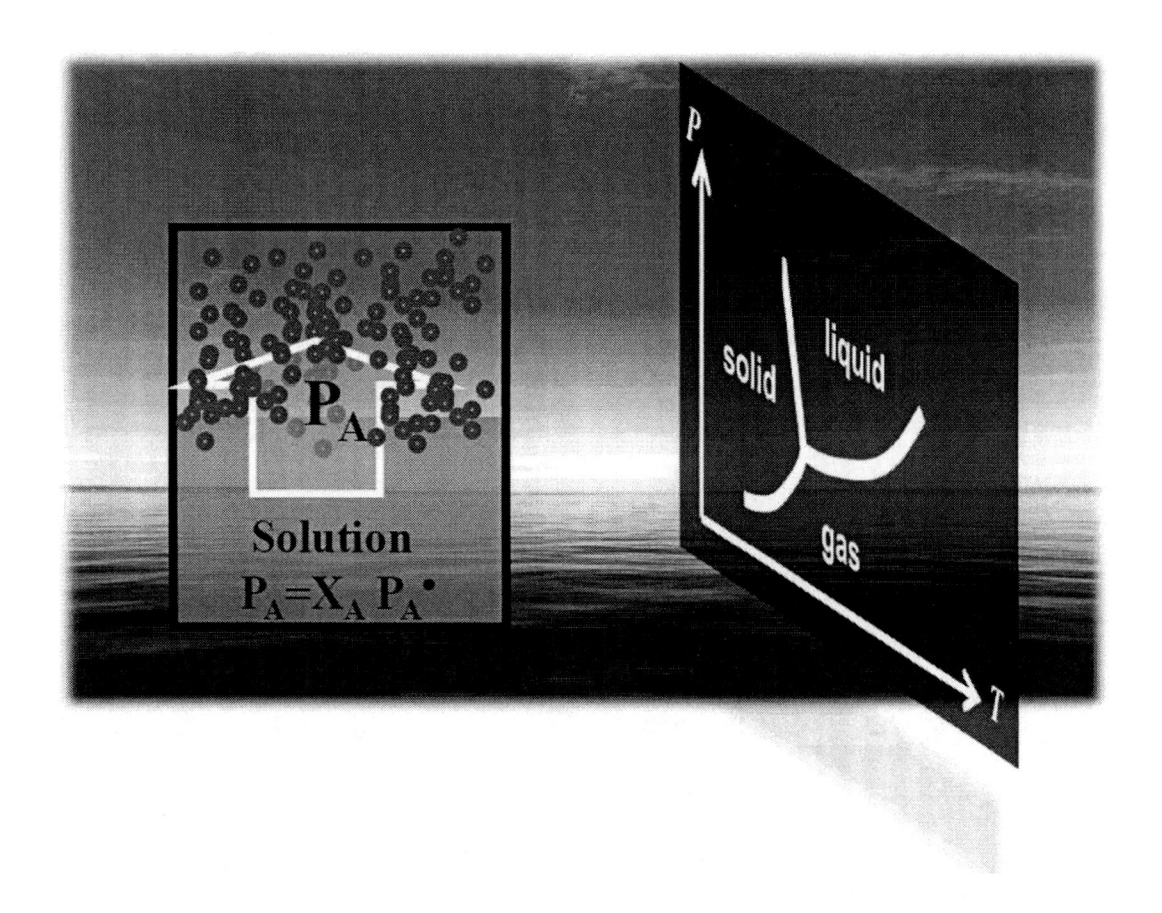

Chapter 5 Macromolecular Phase Transitions

- ## Why do I have to study this chapter?

You will know major important physical properties intrinsic to macromolecules? Can you explain why cell fusion is the direction of spontaneous reaction? You will be able to compare the energy of the macromolecules with different surface areas. You will see the properties of number of molecules to physical property such as melting/boiling points and osmotic pressure. If there is an unknown macromolecule, the molecular weight can be obtained by using one of the methods you are learning in this chapter. If you were wondering how melting point depression constant and boiling elevation constant are expressed, you will see those in this chapter. (The derivations of boiling point elevation, melting point depression, as well as osmotic pressure can be learned as an appendix.)

- ## Expected Hurdles Ahead in this Chapter
1. Calculation of diameter (surface area) change of spherical cells after cell fusion (See Section **5-1**)
2. Calculation of molal boiling point elevation (freezing point depression) constant. (See Section **5-2**)
3. Calculation of activity from heat of vaporization or heat of fusion. (See Section **5-2**)

PREVIEW OF KEY-EQUATIONS

Gibbs energy change by Surface Tension $\quad \Delta G = \gamma \Delta A$

Langmuir Isotherm $\quad \theta = {\alpha P}/{(1 + \alpha P)}$

Colligative Properties

    i. Boiling point elevation $\quad \Delta T_b = K_b m$

$$K_b = \frac{M_A R T_o^2}{1000 \Delta \bar{H}_{vap}}$$

$$\ln a_A = -\frac{\Delta \bar{H}_{vap}}{R}\left[\frac{1}{T_b} - \frac{1}{T_o}\right]$$

    ii. Freezing point elevation $\quad \Delta T_f = K_f m$

$$K_f = \frac{M_A R T_o^2}{1000 \Delta \bar{H}_{fus}}$$

$$\ln a_A = \frac{\Delta \bar{H}_{fus}}{R}\left[\frac{1}{T_f} - \frac{1}{T_o}\right]$$

    iii. Osmtoic Pressure $\quad \Pi = cRT$

Chapter 5 Macromolecular Phase Transitions

iv. Vapor pressure lowering

$$ln\, a_A = \frac{-\overline{V_A}\Pi}{RT}$$

$$\Delta P = \frac{w_B}{M_B}\frac{P'_A}{n_A}$$

Temperature dependence on melting/freezing point

$$\Delta T = \frac{\overline{T}\Delta\overline{V}_{fus}}{\Delta\overline{H}_{fus}}\Delta P$$

PREVIEW OF KEY-TECHNICAL TERMS

Surface tension, Langmuir isotherm, colligative properties, boiling point raising (ΔT_b), freezing point lowering (ΔT_f), osmotic pressure (Π), vapor pressure lowering, phase diagram

5-1 *Surface Tension*

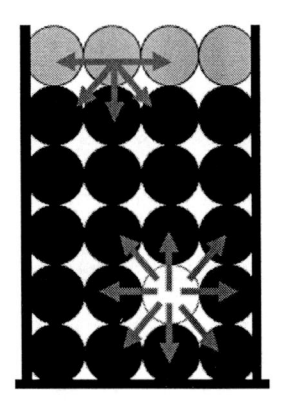

Fig. 5-1. Surface Tension

Surface tension is a unique force which is observed at the surface of a media. For example, water molecules embedded inside the bulk of the solution receive the force from all directions isotropically. On the other hand, the water molecules situated at the surface of the substance will not have any force acting from the direction open to the air.(**Fig.5.1**) The Surface Tension (Γ) is defined by

$$\Gamma = \frac{E_{ST}}{A}$$

Here, E_{ST} is the amount of energy required to stretch the surface and A is the area. In order to minimize the surface area to compensate for the force field, or the force coming from the other directions, surface tension, is induced on the surface to stretch the surface area of the molecules.

A good example of the surface tension for the readers is the case of the cell fusion or cellular differentiation. Cell fusion is an important and clear example in the maturation of cells in order to maintain their specific functions throughout growth. It takes place during differentiation of muscle, bone and trophoblast cells, embryogenesis, and morphogenesis. On the other hand, cellular differentiation is the process of change into a more specialized cell type. It is observed during the development of a multi cellular organism as it changes from a single and simpler cell format to a complex system of tissues/cell types. For example, stem cells divide and create fully-differentiated daughter cells during tissue repair and during normal cell turnover. Both cell fusion and cellular differentiation significantly changes a cell's size, shape, membrane potential, metabolic activity, and responsiveness to signals, so that some amount of energy will be involved.(**Fig. 5-2**) This energy transfer is highly related with the surface area change.

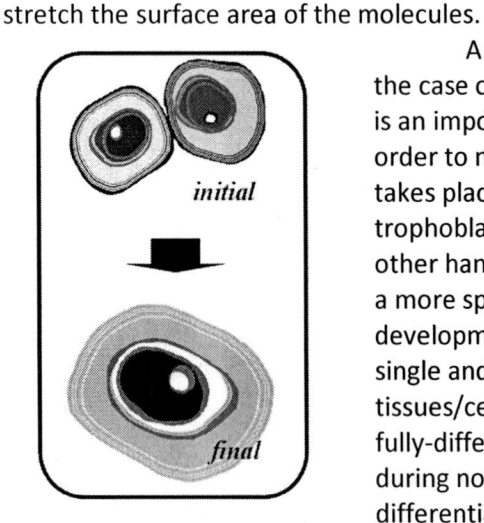

Fig. 5-2. Sketch of cell fusion

Let's set up a stage to understand how we approach the energy of the system related with the change in surface tension. Between Gibbs energy and the surface tension, a straight relationship should be established since Gibbs energy is defined as the "maximal amount of non-expansion work a system can do on the surroundings" in Chapter 2. If the γ is the surface tension with the unit of [N/m], and the dA is a change in surface area [m^2] during a process (**Fig. 5.2**), the Gibbs energy change dG is given by

$$dG = \gamma dA \qquad \text{(Eqn. 5-1)}$$

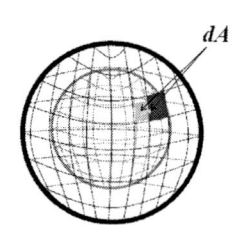

Fig. 5-3 *Surface area change (dA)*

If you take the integration of the both sides of (**Eqn. 5-1**) for an entire surface area,

$$\int dG = \int \gamma dA \qquad \text{(Eqn. 5-2)}$$

Thus, Gibbs energy change (ΔG) caused by the surface area change (ΔA) is

$$\Delta G = \gamma \Delta A \qquad \text{(Eqn. 5-3)}$$

Here, the units used in (**Eqn. 5-3**) may need some cares. The area difference (ΔA), the surface tension (γ), and Gibbs energy change are in the unit of [m^2], [N/m], and [J] = [N m], respectively. The area change ΔA is the difference between final (A $_{initial}$) and initial value of area (A $_{initial}$)

$$\Delta A = A_{final} - A_{initial} \qquad \text{(Eqn. 5-4)}$$

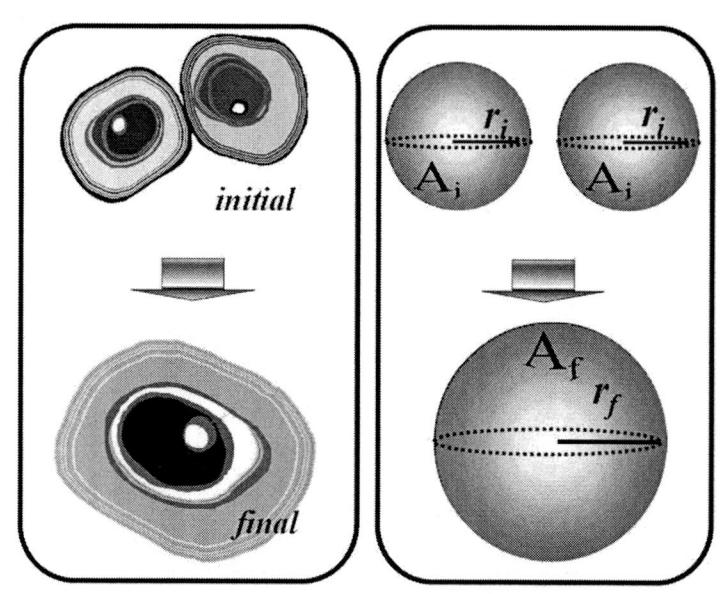

Fig. 5-4 An approach for calculating surface area change in cell fusion

Let's actually calculate the Gibbs energy change (ΔG) due to the cell fusion (**Fig. 5.3**). Let's see how we can calculate the change in surface area (ΔA) for a simple case where two ideally spherical cell with radius r_i merge into a larger one spherical cell with radius r_f. ($r_i < r_f$) If we know the initial smaller cell's radius (r_i), we calculate the radius of a bigger cell (r_f). Knowing the radii (r_i and r_f), the surface areas (A $_{initial}$ and A $_{finial}$) are calculated; A = $4\pi r^2$. By using the relationship in volume, $V_f = 2v_i$, the relationship between the radius of before (r_i) and after (r_f) the fusion is given as

$$r_f = 2^{1/3} r_i$$

The final cell has the surface area of A_f. Thus, the change in surface area, ΔA will be $A_f - 2A_i$. Note that you have two spheres with area A_i at the starting point.

$$\Delta A = \pi \left(2^{1/3} d_1\right)^2 - 2\pi d_1^2 = \left(2^{2/3} - 2\right)\pi d_1^2 < 0 \qquad \text{(Eqn. 5-5)}$$

You will realize that the surface area is decreased by cell fusion (ΔA<0). (The more cells, the more surface area exposed.)

EXERCISE 5-1

Two spherical cell 1 [μm] in radius become into one spherical cell. Calculate the work gained by decreasing the surface area. The surface tension is 1.00×10^{-2} [N/m]. [J]=[N m]

ANSWER

❶ Since $d_1 = 2$ [μm],
$A_1 = \pi d_1^2 = 1.256 \times 10^{-11}$ [m²]

$V_1 = \dfrac{\pi d_1^3}{6}$

❷ $V_2 = 2V_1 = \dfrac{\pi d_1^3}{3}$

$A_2 = [36\pi V_2^2]^{1/3} = 1.9 \times 10^{-11}$ [m²]

❸ $\Delta A = A_2 - 2A_1$
$= 1.9 \times 10^{-11}$ m² $- 2(1.256 \times 10^{-11}$ [m²])
$= -0.4126\, \pi d_1^2$ [m²]

❹ $= -5.18 \times 10^{-11}$ [m²]

$\Delta G = \gamma \Delta A$ (Eqn. 5-3)

❺ $\Delta G = -5.18 \times 10^{-14}$ [N·m]

❶	Radius (r) = 2 diameter (d)
❷	Don't forget $V_2 = 2V_1$
❸	Don't forget to multiply 2 to A_1
❹	Cell fusion is a negative change of the surface area.
❺	ΔG <0. Cell fusion is a spontaneous process.

5-2 Langmuir Isotherm

The **Langmuir isotherm (Langmuir adsorption equation)** describes the coverage of molecules adsorbing on a solid surface to as a function of gas pressure or concentration:

$$\theta = \alpha P / (1 + \alpha P) \qquad \text{(Eqn. 5-6)}$$

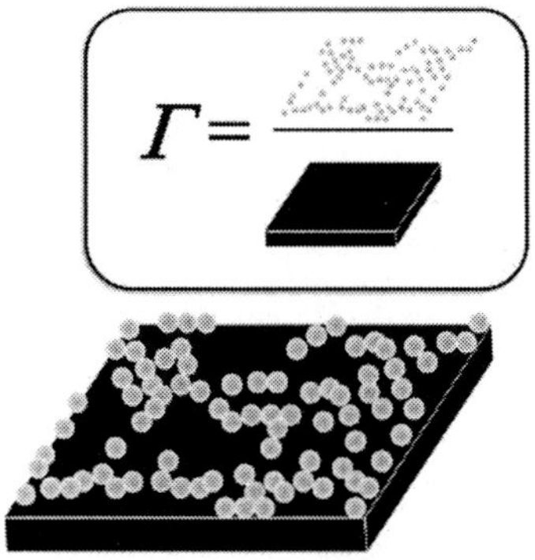

Fig. 5-5a The coverage of molecules adsorbing on a solid surface (Γ).

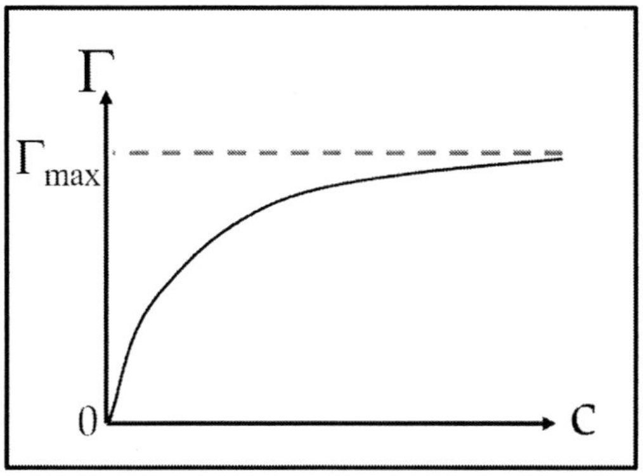

Fig. 5-5b Plot of Langmuir equation

Here, θ is the fractional coverage of the surface, P is the gas pressure or concentration, and α is the **Langmuir adsorption constant** which increases as the binding energy of adsorption increases but as the temperature decreases. The Langmuir equation (**Eqn. 5-5b**) can be also expressed here as:

$$\Gamma = \Gamma_{max} \left[Kc / (1 + Kc) \right] \qquad \text{(Eqn. 5-7)}$$

Here, K is Langmuir equilibrium constant, c is aqueous concentration (or gaseous partial pressure), Γ is amount adsorbed (**Eqn. 5-5a**), and Γ_{max} is a maximum amount adsorbed as c increases. When the concentration is equal to an inverse of K (i.e., c = 1/K):

$$\Gamma = \Gamma_{max} / 2 \qquad \text{(Eqn. 5-8)}$$

For a practical fitting to Langmuir equation one can use **Lineweaver-Burk, Eadie-Hofstee**, and **Scatchard** plot. (Please wait for **Chapter 8** where we used some of the plotting methods in fitting the **Michaelis-Menten equation**)The reciprocal of the terms in Langmuir equation (**Eqn. 5-9**) gives the **Lineweaver-Burk equation**:

$$1/\Gamma = 1/(Kc\Gamma_{max}) + 1/\Gamma_{max} \qquad \text{(Eqn. 5-9)}$$

A plot of $(1/\Gamma)$ versus $(1/c)$ yields a slope of $1/(\Gamma_{max}K)$ and an y-axis intercept of $1/\Gamma_{max}$. This plot is very sensitive to data error and it is governed by the data in the low concentration range since it is plotting an inverse of the concentration. The Langmuir equation in Eadie-Hofstee equation format (**Eadie-Hofstee plot type-I**) is

$$\Gamma = \Gamma_{max} - \Gamma/Kc \qquad \text{(Eqn. 5-10)}$$

A plot of (Γ) versus (Γ/c) yields a slope of $-1/K$ and a y-axis intercept of Γ_{max}. Once again, this plot is governed by the low concentration range since it plots the inverse of the concentration as seen in Lineweaver-Burk plot.

The **Scatchard plotting** form introduced in **Chapter 4** is given by

$$\Gamma/c = K\Gamma_{max} - K\Gamma \qquad \text{(Eqn. 5-11)}$$

A plot of (Γ/c) versus (Γ) yields a slope of $-K$ and a y-axis intercept of $K\Gamma_{max}$. This plot is governed by the values at the higher concentration range. By invert the parameters for x and y axes, (**Eqn. 5-11**) is transformed to the Eadie-Hofstee plot (type-II) (**Eqn. 5-10**). The Langmuir plot is given

$$c/\Gamma = 1/(K\Gamma_{max}) + c/\Gamma_{max} \qquad \text{(Eqn. 5-12)}$$

A plot of (c/Γ) versus (c) yields a slope of $1/\Gamma_{max}$ and y-axis an intercept of $1/(K\Gamma_{max})$. This plot form is almost independent of data error and is governed by middle and high concentration region.

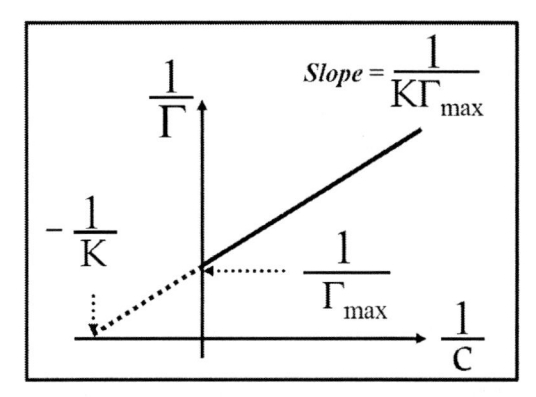

Fig. 5-6 Lineweaver plot of Langmuir equation

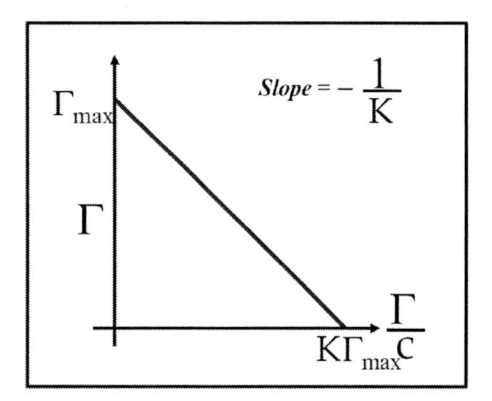

Fig. 5-7 Eadie-Hofstee plot (I) of Langmuir equation

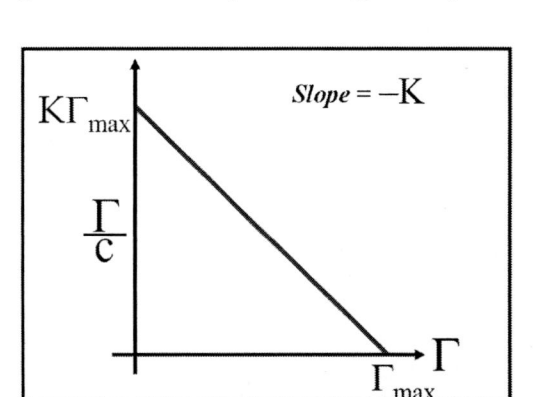

Fig. 5-8 Scatchard plot of Langmuir equation

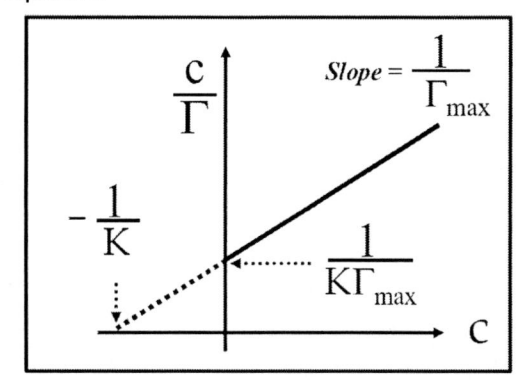

Fig. 5-9 Eadie-Hofstee plot (II) of Langmuir equation

EXERCISE 5-2
The Langmuir isotherm experiment is conducted and Γ is obtained as a function of concentration c.

$c(\times10^2)$	5.23×10^{-2}	3.23×10^{-1}	7.43×10^{-1}	1.22	4.28	7.67
$\Gamma(\times10^2)$	1.16×10^{-2}	7.13×10^{-1}	1.63×10^{-1}	2.65×10^{-1}	8.80×10^{-1}	1.49

Plot the above by Lineweaver-Burke plot and obtain Γ_{max} and K.

ANSWER

$1/c(\times10^2)$	1.91×10^3	3.10×10^2	1.35×10^2	8.20×10^1	2.34×10^1	1.30×10^1
$1/\Gamma(\times10^2)$	8.62×10^3	1.40×10^3	6.15×10^2	3.78×10^2	1.14×10^2	6.71×10^1

According to the "LINEST" in Microsoft Excel, the slope is 4.5045 and intercept 8.333. Linweaber Burke plot,

$$1/\Gamma = 1/(Kc\Gamma_{max}) + 1/\Gamma_{max} \qquad \text{(Eqn. 5-9)}$$

The slope is $1/K\Gamma_{max}$ and y-axis intercept is $1/\Gamma_{max}$.
$1/\Gamma_{max}=8.333$
$\Gamma_{max}=0.12$
$1/K\Gamma_{max}= 4.5045$ and $\Gamma_{max}=0.12$
Thus, K= 1.85

In this textbook, "$c(\times10^2)$" means that the value multiplied by $\times10^2$ is given. Therefore, the real c value needs to be divided by $\times10^2$. The first c value of this table is, therefore, 5.23×10^{-4}

In Lineweaver-Burk plot, you plot $1/\Gamma$ vs. $1/c$.
You may use any least square fitting program.
K is obtained from $1/K\Gamma_{max}$ after Γ_{max} is obtained.

5-3 Colligative Properties

Colligative properties are solution properties which depend on the number of molecules in a given volume of solvent but not on the properties (such as size or mass) of the molecules. The boiling or freezing point of the solutions are raised or lowered, respectively, compared to those of pure solvent. (**boiling point raising** or **freezing point lowering** (**Fig. 5-10**)) Let's take a look at how we can grasp these two phenomena.

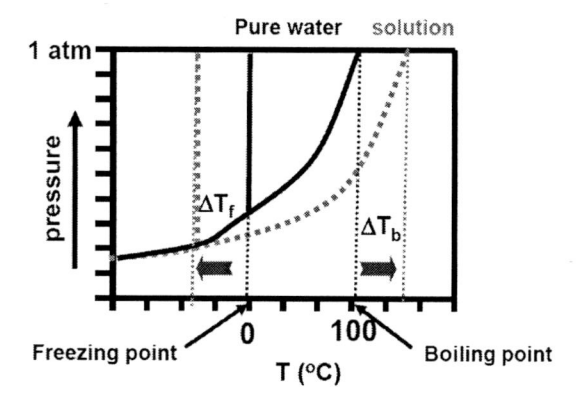

Fig. 5-10 Boiling point elevation (ΔT_b) and freezing point Lowering (ΔT_f).

i. Boiling Point Elevation: For the boiling point, it is at the equilibrium between liquid and gas (please recall Chapter 5),

$$A\,(l) \underset{}{\overset{K}{\rightleftarrows}} A(g)$$

and the Clausis -Clapeyron equation describes the relationship between vapor pressure (P_1 and P_2) at two different boiling points (T_1 and T_2) with molar enthalpy of vaporization $\Delta \bar{H}^o_{vap}$ [kJ/mol] as:

$$ln\frac{P_2}{P_1} = -\frac{\Delta \bar{H}^o_{vap}}{R}\left[\frac{1}{T_2} - \frac{1}{T_1}\right] \qquad \text{(Eqn. 4-4)}$$

Here, $\Delta \bar{H}^o_{vap}$ is assumed to be temperature independent. If we set T_2 to be boiling point of a solution (T_b) and T_1 is boiling point of pure solvent A (T_o), P_1 is set as 1 [atm] and P_2 can be expressed by using an idea of activity introduced in Chapter 3.

$$a_A = \frac{P_A}{P} = \frac{P_A}{1\,atm} \qquad \text{(Eqn. 3-3)}$$

Chapter 5 Macromolecular Phase Transitions

Here, a_A is an activity of A in solution. With $P_1 = 1$[atm] and $P_2 = a_A$ [atm] inserted into (**Eqn. 3-3**),

$$ln a_A = -\frac{\Delta \bar{H}_{vap}}{R}\left[\frac{1}{T_b} - \frac{1}{T_o}\right] \quad \text{(Eqn. 5-13)}$$

Please note that d T_b is boiling point of solution, T_o is boiling point of pure solvent A. The difference of boiling points between solution and solvent (ΔT_b) is given by with molality, m [molality], as

$$\Delta T_b = K_b m \quad \text{(Eqn. 5-14)}$$

Thus, the value given by ΔT_b [°C, K] explains the amount of boiling point elevation by solution. The molal boiling-point elevation constant K_b [°C/molal, K/molal] (molal = molality) is

$$K_b = \frac{M_A R T_o^2}{1000 \Delta \bar{H}_{vap}} \quad \text{(Eqn. 5-15)}$$

Here, M_A is the molar mass of solvent [g/mol], T_o is boiling point of pure solvent [K], and $\Delta \bar{H}_{vap}$ is the molar heat of vaporization [kJ/K], and gas constant R is 8.314472[J/mol·K].
By utilizing the measurement of boiling point elevation of unknown solute with molar mass M_B, you can obtain the molar mass of solute M_B [g/mol] by

$$M_B = \frac{K_b m_B}{\Delta T_b w_A} \quad \text{(Eqn. 5-16)}$$

Here, m_B is the solute sample mass [g] and w_A is the mass of solvent [kg]. (Be careful with the unit of w_A.).

EXERCISE 5-3

On the Planet Taurus II, ammonia plays a role similar to that of water on Earth. Normal boiling point is −33.4 °C, where heat of vaporization is 1368 kJ/kg. When unknown substance is dissolved in 1 kg of liquid ammonia, the boiling point at 1 atm is observed at −32.7 °C. Calculate the molality of this substance

ANSWER

$$K_b = \frac{M_A R T_o^2}{1000 \Delta \bar{H}_{vap}} \quad \text{(Eqn. 5-15)}$$

Here, M_A = 17 [g/mol]

R = 8.3145 [J/ K mol],

T_0 = −33.4 [°C] = 239.75 [K].

$\Delta \bar{H}_{vap}$ = 1368 [kJ/kg] = 1368 [J/g] = 1368 [J/g] / 17 [g/mol]

Please be prepared to convert this value into J/mol.

$$K_b = \frac{M_A R T_o^2}{1000 \Delta \bar{H}_{vap}} = \frac{(17[g/mol])(8.314[JK^{-1}mol^{-1}])(239.75[K])^2}{(1000\,[g/kg])(1368\,[J/g])(17[g/mol])} = 0.3493\,[K/m]$$

$T_b - T_o$ = 33,4[°C] − 32.7 [°C] = 0.7 [K]

m = 0.70/0.349 ~ 2[m]

- M_A is the molar mass of solvent (not solute)
- R = 8.3145 [J/ K mol], not R = 0.082 [atm L mol^{-1} K^{-1}]
- Convert temperature in Kelvins unit
- The unit for the heat of vaporization should be [J/mol]
- Don't forget squaring T_o and dividing it by 1000.
- The difference of temperature can be calculated by Kelvins or °C unit.

ii. Freezing Point Lowering: As for the freezing point, it is understood that an equilibrium between liquid (*l*) and solid (*s*) takes place at this temperature.

$$A\,(l) \xrightleftharpoons{K} A(s)$$

Using the van't Hoff equation introduced in Chapter 2, the relationship of equilibrium constants (K_1 and K_2) between solid and liquid under two different temperatures (T_1 and T_2) is described with enthalpy of reaction $\Delta \bar{H}^o_{rxn}$ [kJ/mol] as:

$$\ln \frac{K_2}{K_1} = -\frac{\Delta H^O_{rxn}}{R}\left[\frac{1}{T_2} - \frac{1}{T_1}\right] \quad \text{(Eqn. 2-13)}$$

From Chapter 3, we learned that the activity of solute A (a_A) with molarity c_A for a real solution is given as

Chapter 5 Macromolecular Phase Transitions

$$a_A = \gamma_A C_A \qquad \text{(Eqn. 3-6)}$$

The modified expression for **van't Hoff equation** is

$$ln a_A = \frac{\Delta \bar{H}_{fus}}{R}\left[\frac{1}{T_f} - \frac{1}{T_o}\right] \qquad \text{(Eqn. 5-17)}$$

The freezing point lowering ΔT_f ($T_o - T_f$) is given as

$$\Delta T_f = K_f m \qquad \text{(Eqn. 5-18)}$$

Here, freezing point depression of solution (ΔT_f) is in the unit of [°C, K], m is molality of the solution [molal], K_f is molal freezing-point elevation in the unit of [°C/molal, K/molal]. The molal freezing point elevation constant is given by

$$K_f = \frac{M_A R T_o^2}{1000 \Delta \bar{H}_{fus}} \qquad \text{(Eqn. 5-19)}$$

Here, M_A is the molar mass of solvent, T_o is freezing point of pure solvent [K] and $\Delta \bar{H}_{fus}$ is the molar heat of fusion [kJ/K], and gas constant R is 8.314472 [J/mol K].

In a similar way seen in the boiling point elevation, by utilizing the measurement of freezing point of elevation of unknown solute with molar mass M_B, you can obtain the molar mass of solute M_B [g/mol] by

$$M_B = \frac{K_f m_B}{\Delta T_f w_A} \qquad \text{(Eqn. 5-20)}$$

Here, m_B is the solute sample mass [g] and w_A is the mass of solvent [kg]. (Be careful with the unit of w_A.).

MCM Most Common Mistake (23) – Am I calculating K_b and K_f with correct molar mass?
The molal boiling point elevation constant (K_b) and the molal freezing point depression constant (K_b) are all about solvent not solute. Therefore, M_A given in **(Eqn. 5-15)** and **(Eqn. 5-19)** are molar mass of solvent (not solute). You do not use **(Eqn. 5-15)** and **(Eqn. 5-19)** to obtain the molar mass of solute, but use **(Eqn. 5-16)** and **(Eqn. 5-20)**. The gas constant, R given in **(Eqn. 5-15)** and **(Eqn. 5-19)** is 8.314472 [J/mol· K] not 0.08205746 [atm ·L/mol· K], since $\Delta \bar{H}_{vap}$ and $\Delta \bar{H}_{fus}$ are in the unit of [kJ/mol].

iii. Osmotic Pressure

Osmotic pressure is the pressure caused by the difference of the amount of particles between two different concentrations of a system. A simple way of thinking about this is that the pressure is raised from the total amount of the force attempting to equilibrate the two different concentrations. (**Fig. 5-5**) If two solutions with different concentrations are placed between a permeable membrane in U-tube, the solution which possess small radius to pass through the membrane can travel into the higher concentration side in order to dilute the concentration. At the equilibrium, the same concentrations are achieved for both sides but it resulting in a height difference due to the transportation of the solvent into one side. (**Fig.5-5.**) As an extra pressure is applied to only one side of a U-tube and if it makes the height of the two sides to be equal, this pressure corresponds to an osmotic pressure, Π. (**Fig. 5-5**) When equilibrium exists between solutions of two sides of the U-tube, the chemical potential of each side should be equal.

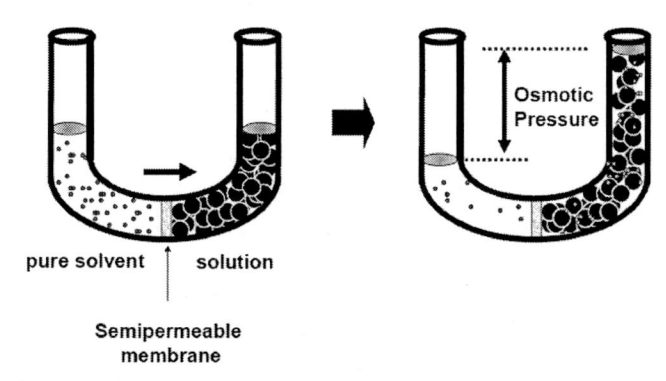

Fig. 5-11. Osmotic Pressure

$$\mu_A(solution, P + \Pi) = \mu_A(solvent, P) \qquad \text{(Eqn.5-21)}$$

If the osmotic pressure was applied under P = 1 [atm],

$$\mu_A(solution, 1 + \Pi) = \mu_A(solvent)$$

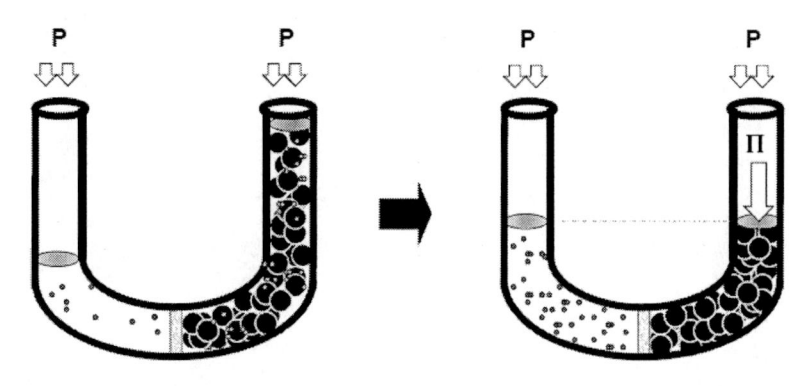

Fig. 5-12. Osmotic Pressure

Under this condition, the activity of solvent A should satisfy the relationship of

$$ln\, a_A = \frac{-\overline{V_A}\Pi}{RT} \qquad \text{(Eqn.5-22)}$$

In (**Eqn. 5-22**), $\overline{V_A}$ is molar volume of solvent and is defined as

$$\overline{V_A} = \frac{volume\ of\ solvent}{Number\ of\ moles\ of\ solvent}$$

The osmotic pressure, Π, is given by

$$\Pi = cRT \qquad \text{(Eqn.5-23)}$$

By utilizing the osmotic pressure measurement of unknown solute with molar mass M_B, you can obtain the molar mass of solute M_B [g/mol] by

$$M_B = \frac{m_B}{\Pi V} RT \qquad \text{(Eqn.5-24)}$$

Here, m_B is the sample mass of solute [g] and V is the volume of solution [L].

MCM Most Common Mistake(24) – Am I using the formula for osmotic pressure?
When a formula of osmotic pressure is used, the concentration can be mistaken as number of moles, n. This can be because the formula for the osmotic pressure was mistaken as an ideal gas law equation (PV =nRT). They are similar, aren't they. You may remember that the osmotic pressure formula is close to an ideal gas law, however, the difference between two equations should be clearly noted. Another mistake is the gas constant, R. (This issue showed up so many times in **"Most Common Mistakes"**. In the case of formula in (**Eqn. 5-23**), the gas constant should be R= 0.08205746 [atm·L/mol·K] but not 8.314472[J/mol·K], since concentration (c)and temperature have the units of [mol/L] and [K], respectively. So that, the unit of osmotic pressure (Π) becomes [atm].

EXERCISE 5-4
Osmotic Pressure of sea water is 25 [atm] at 273 [K]. Molar volume of water is 0.018 [M^{-1}]. Calculate the activity of water in seawater.

ANSWER

$$ln a_A = \frac{-\overline{V_A}\Pi}{RT} \quad \textbf{(Eqn.5-22)}$$

$\overline{V_A}$ is molar volume of solvent

T=273 [K]

R=0.082 [atm L K^{-1} mol^{-1}]

ln a = −(0.018 [M^{-1}])(25 [atm])/ {(0.082 [atm L K^{-1} mol^{-1}])(273 [K])}

= −0.0201

a = 0.980

Don't forget the minus sign in front.

This is molar volume [L/mol], not a volume [L]

Temperature in Kelvins unit.

Gas constant in this case is R=0.082 [atm L K^{-1} mol^{-1}], not R=8.34 [J K^{-1} mol^{-1}]

Use, y =ln x → x=e^y

The activity (a) is almost 1.

EXERCISE 5-5
Calculate an osmotic Pressure of Cytoplasm inside animal cell when the concentration of the solvent is 0.5 [M] at 37 [°C].

ANSWER

Osmotic pressure (Π) [atm] is given as

$$\Pi = cRT \quad \textbf{(Eqn.5-23)}$$

c = 0.5 [M]

R = 0.082 [L·atm K^{-1} mol^{-1}]

T= 37 [°C]=310 [K]

Π = 0.5 [M] × 0.082 [L atm K^{-1} mol^{-1}] × 310 [K]

=12.7 [atm]

Gas constant, R, is 0.082 [L atm K^{-1} mol^{-1}] not R=8.34 [J K^{-1} mol^{-1}]

Temperature in Kelvins unit

It is very high, isn't it!

Up to this point we considered the case of non-dissociating (non-electrolyte solution). If the solute is a strong electrolyte, the solute dissociates into ionic species in the solution. Thus, the number of particles increases accordingly. The colligative properties described above can be enhanced proportionally to the increase of the number. If the number of particles are increased by a factor of "*I*", the resulting boiling point elevation, freezing point depression, and osmotic pressures are given as:

$$\Delta T_b = iK_b m \quad \text{(Eqn. 5-14)'}$$
$$\Delta T_f = iK_f m \quad \text{(Eqn. 5-18)'}$$
$$\Pi = icRT \quad \text{(Eqn. 5-23)'}$$

For example,

i~2 for $\quad AX(s) \rightarrow A^+(aq) + X^-(aq)$
i~3 for $\quad AX_2(s) \rightarrow A^{2+}(aq) + 2X^-(aq)$

iv). Vapor Pressure Lowering

In Chapter 5, we learned the vapor pressure of solvent is reduced if it is made to be solution as Raoults' law state

$$P_A = X_A P_A^{\bullet} \quad \text{(Eqn. 4-3)}$$

Here, X_A is a mole fraction of A in solution, $P_A^{\bullet}$ is a vapor pressure of a pure solvent A, and P_A is a partial pressure of A over a solution.(**Fig. 4-4**) Since $X_A <1$, the vapor pressure P_A should be smaller than $P_A^{\bullet}$ (i.e., the vapor pressure is lowered due to solute added to the solvent.) This means that an effect of solute is reflected to the vapor pressure lowering, and it enables us to calculate the molar mass of solute (M_B) from the amount of the vapor pressure lowered (ΔP).

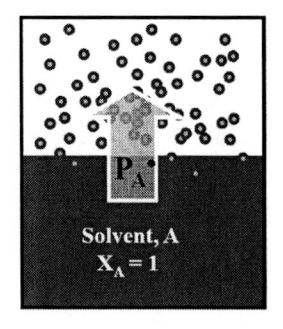

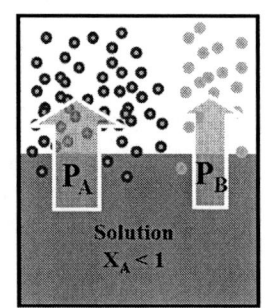

Fig. 5-13 Vapor Pressure Lowering

$$\Delta P = \frac{w_B}{M_B} \frac{P_A^{\bullet}}{n_A} \quad \text{(Eqn. 5-25)}$$

Here, the vapor pressure lowering (ΔP) is defined as

$$\Delta P = P_A^{\bullet} - P_A$$

With known amount of sample mass of solute (w_B) and the observed amount of vapor pressure lowering (ΔP), the unknown molar mass of solute (M_B) can be extracted.

$$M_B = \frac{w_B}{n_A} \frac{P_A^{\bullet}}{\Delta P} \quad \text{(Eqn. 5-26)}$$

Chapter 5 Macromolecular Phase Transitions

Another useful relationship obtained from the vapor pressure lowering is the mole fraction of solute (X_B). If the solution is consisted of two components (e.g., solute B is added to solvent A), mole fraction of solute B is; $X_B = 1 - X_A$. Based on this relationship, the mole fraction of solute B (X_B) is related with the vapor pressure of solvent (P_A and $P_A^\bullet$) as:

$$X_B = \frac{P_A^\bullet - P_A}{P_A^\bullet} \qquad \text{(Eqn. 5-27)}$$

EXERCISE 5-6
A 54.66 g of mannitol (mw. 182.2 [g/mol]) is added to 1 [kg] of water. Calculate vapor-pressure lowering of this solution. $P^\bullet_{water}$ = 17.54 [torr] at 20 [°C]

ANSWER
The mole fraction of solute (X_B) is

$$X_B = \frac{P_A^\bullet - P_A}{P_A^\bullet} \qquad \text{(Eqn. 5-27)}$$

$$X_B = \frac{n_B}{n_A + n_B} = \frac{\left(\frac{54.66\ g}{182.2\ [g/mol]}\right)}{\left(\frac{1000}{18\ [g/mol]}\right) + \left(\frac{54.66\ g}{182.2\ [g/mol]}\right)}$$

= 5.37× 10⁻³

$\Delta P = P_A^\bullet - P_A = X_B P_A^\bullet$

= 5.37× 10⁻³ × 17.54 [torr]

= 0.0942 [torr]

The solute is mannitol (mw =182.2 [g/mol]) is and water (mw 18.0 [g/mol]) is solvent (n_A). Thus, n_B is the number of moles of mannitol, and n_B is the number of moles of water.
Unit of mole fraction is dimensionless.
$\Delta P > 0$ since $P_A^\bullet > P_A$

As one of common practices, people use i) boiling point elevation, ii) freezing point depression, iii) osmotic pressure, iv) vapor pressure lowering for determining the molar mass of unknown sample solute. Here the relationship between molar mass of solute and the measurement of each.

i) From boiling point elevation

$$M_B = \frac{K_b m_B}{\Delta T_b w_A} \qquad \text{(Eqn. 5-16)}$$

ii) From freezing point depression

$$M_B = \frac{K_f m_B}{\Delta T_f w_A} \qquad \text{(Eqn. 5-20)}$$

iii) From osmotic pressure

$$M_B = \frac{m_B}{\Pi V} RT \qquad \text{(Eqn. 5-24)}$$

iv) From vapor pressure lowering

$$M_B = \frac{w_B \, P_A^\bullet}{n_A \, \Delta P} \qquad \text{(Eqn. 5-26)}$$

😖 MCM Most Common Mistake (25) – M_A or M_B?

When it comes to the calculation of colligative properties, you should always ask yourself before starting calculation.

Which one is a solute (B) and which one is solvent (A)?

As represented in (**Eqn. 5-25**), this textbook represents B as solute and A as solvent. Thus, M_A is molar mass of solute and M_B is molar mass of solvent. (In a similar way, n_A is number of moles of solute and n_B is number of moles of solvent.) As a common practice, the molar mass of unknown solute is obtained by using the above mentioned experiments (boiling point elevation, freezing point lowering, osmotic pressure, and vapor pressure lowering.) The summary of equations listed above is for calculating the molar mass of solute (M_B). Usually, solvent is already identified and molar mass of solvent (M_A) should be known.

5-4 Pressure Effect on the Freezing/Melting Points

Up to the above considerations, melting or fusion process are considered to take place under a constant pressure (mostly atmospheric pressure). However, in certain cases with a great amount of time, the water trapped between or inside rocks encounter a great amount of pressure. If enough time passes, on the scale of millions of years, the landscape can change and more rock can overlay and accumulate causing more pressure to be exerted on the trapped water. Under this abnormal pressure condition, the melting or freezing point is expected to be affected. (At higher elevation and lower pressure, the boiling point of water is decreased as predicted from **Clausius-Clapeyron Equation(Eqn. 4-2)**). Let's view the pressure effect or the freezing (or melting) points for the formation of the ice. The transition between liquid to solid is under an equilibrium at freezing point (melting point)

$$A\,(l) \rightleftarrows A(s)$$

If the molar heat of fusion is defined as $\Delta \overline{H}_{fus}$, as solid transforms into liquid the heat amount equal to $\Delta \overline{H}_{fus}$ needs to be supplied to the system (endothermic process), whereas $-\Delta \overline{H}_{fus}$ is produced (i.e., heat amount equal to $\Delta \overline{H}_{fus}$ is released (exothermic process).(**Fig. 5-14**) The difference of freezing point ($\Delta T = T_2 - T_1$) at two different pressure P_1 and P_2 is given by

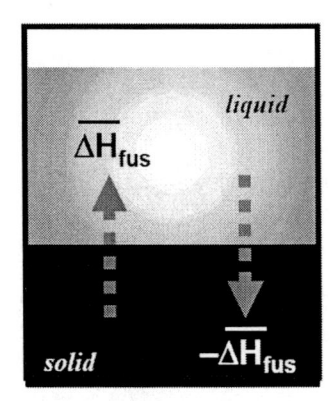

Fig. 5-14 Exchange of *molar* heat of fusion

Chapter 5 Macromolecular Phase Transitions

$$\Delta T = \frac{\bar{T}\Delta \bar{V}_{fus}}{\Delta \bar{H}_{fus}} \Delta P \qquad \text{(Eqn. 5-28)}$$

Here, ΔP is P_2-P_1, the molar volume of fusion is defined as $\Delta \bar{V}_{fus}$, and $\bar{T}$ is the average of T_1 and T_2 (i.e., $\bar{T} = [T_2 + T_1]/2$.)

EXERCISE 5-7

Estimate the maximum pressure that can be developed by water freezing to ice on a cold night (T = −10 [°C]). The densities of ice and water at −10 [°C] may be taken as 0.9 [g/cm³] and 1.0 [g/cm³], respectively.

ANSWER

$\Delta T = \frac{\bar{T}\Delta \bar{V}_{fus}}{\Delta \bar{H}_{fus}} \Delta P \qquad \text{(Eqn. 5-28)}$

$\bar{T} = (273 [K] + 263[K])/2 = 268 [K]$

$\Delta T = T_2 - T_1 = -10 [K]$

$\Delta \bar{V}_{fus} = (1 - 1/0.9) = -0.111 [mL/g]$

$\Delta \bar{H}_{fus} = 333 [J/g]$

$\Delta P = P_2 - P_1$
$= \frac{\Delta T \Delta H_{fus}}{\bar{T} \Delta V_{fus}} \frac{82.05 \,[atm\, mL]}{8.314\, [J]}$
$= 1110 \,[atm]$

$\bar{T} = [T_2 + T_1]/2$, where $T_1 = 0$ [°C] = 273 [K], $T_2 = -10$ [°C] = 263 [K]

Temperature in Kelvins unit.

$\bar{V}$ = volume/mass

Very high!!

We will end this chapter by summarizing the formulas learned in the phase transition by using the P-T (pressure – temperature) phase diagram (**Fig. 5-15**). The borderlines indicated in between the phases represent a). liquid-gas equilibrium, b). liquid-solid equilibrium, and c). solid-gas equilibrium. From Chapter 5, we learned that the liquid –gas equilibrium is represented by Clausius-Clapeyron equation,

$$ln \frac{P_2}{P_1} = -\frac{\Delta \bar{H}^o_{vap}}{R}\left[\frac{1}{T_2} - \frac{1}{T_1}\right] \qquad \text{(Eqn. 5-2)}$$

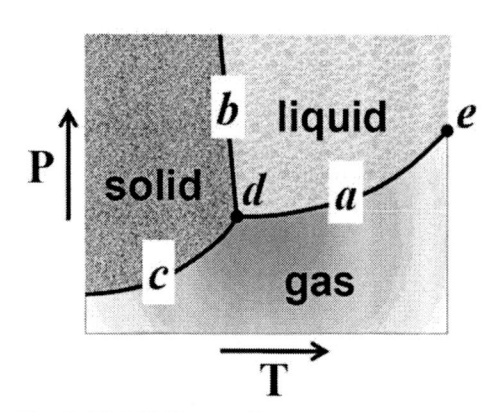

Fig. 5-15 P-T Phase diagram and equilibrium border lines.
a: liquid-gas equilibrium, b: liquid-solid equilibrium, c: solid-gas equilibrium, d: triple point, e: critical point

Here, $\Delta \bar{H}^o_{vap}$ is molar enthalpy of vaporization [kJ/mol]. Therefore, the line labeled as a) in (**Fig. 5-18**) is represented by (**Eqn. 4-2**) while $\Delta \bar{H}^o_{vap}$ may require a consideration of temperature dependence for broad temperature range. From this Chapter 5, the equilibrium between liquid and gas was shown by (**Eqn. 5-28**)

$$\Delta T = \frac{\bar{T} \Delta \bar{V}_{fus}}{\Delta \bar{H}_{fus}} \Delta P \qquad \text{(Eqn. 5-28)}$$

Please note that ΔT and ΔP in (**Eqn. 5-27**) is replaced as $\Delta T = T_2 - T_1$ and $\Delta P = P_2 - P_1$, respectively. The line labeled as b) in (**Fig. 5-15**) is represented by (**Eqn. 4-2**) while $\Delta \bar{H}^o_{fus}$ and $\Delta \bar{V}_{fus}$ may require a considerations of temperature dependence if wider temperature range is taken. As for an equilibrium between solid and gas (sublimation) indicated by line c in (**Fig. 4.9**), the details was not introduced in this book. In a similar manner treated in liquid-gas equilibrium, the equilibrium between solid and gas can be expressed as

$$ln \frac{P_2}{P_1} = -\frac{\Delta \bar{H}^o_{sub}}{R} \left[\frac{1}{T_2} - \frac{1}{T_1} \right] \qquad \text{(Eqn. 5-29)}$$

Here, the $\Delta \bar{H}^o_{sub}$ is the molar enthalpy change for sublimation which may depend on the temperature.

As a summary and a good review, I would like to list up the formulas which can explain the border lines shown in the phase P-T diagram (**Fig. 5-15**), a, b, and c are expressed by the following equations.

a: liquid-gas equilibrium

$$ln \frac{P_2}{P_1} = -\frac{\Delta \bar{H}^o_{vap}}{R} \left[\frac{1}{T_2} - \frac{1}{T_1} \right] \qquad \text{(Eqn. 5-2)}$$

b: liquid-solid equilibrium

$$(T_2 - T_1) = \frac{\bar{T} \Delta \bar{V}_{fus}}{\Delta \bar{H}_{fus}} (P_2 - P_1) \qquad \text{(Eqn. 5-28)}$$

c: solid-gas equilibrium

$$ln \frac{P_2}{P_1} = -\frac{\Delta \bar{H}^o_{sub}}{R} \left[\frac{1}{T_2} - \frac{1}{T_1} \right] \qquad \text{(Eqn. 5-29)}$$

Chapter 5

How did you get these equations?
-The derivation of selected equations.

(Eqn. 5-5) $\Delta A = \pi(2^{1/3}d_1)^2 - 2\pi d_1^2 = (2^{2/3} - 2)\pi d_1^2 < 0$

First, we will establish a formula to obtain an area from a given volume. If a radius of a sphere is r (diameter, d, is d =2r), surface Area (A) and volume (V) are related as follows:

$$A = 4\pi r^2 = 4\pi \left(\frac{d}{2}\right)^2 = \pi d^2$$

On the other hand the volume of a sphere is given by

$$V = \frac{4}{3}\pi r^3 = \frac{4}{3}\pi \left(\frac{d}{2}\right)^3 = \frac{1}{6}\pi d^3$$

If the above formula is solved for diameter (d),

$$d = (6V/\pi)^{1/3}$$

Thus, by inserting the above expression in to spherical area (A),

$$A = \pi d^2 = \pi(6V/\pi)^{2/3} = (36\pi V^2)^{1/3}$$

In the present system, the volume of final cell (V_2) should be the same as twice of that of original cell's volume (V_1)

$$V_2 = 2V_1$$

Thus,

$$V_2 = \frac{\pi d_2^3}{6}$$

$$2V_1 = \frac{\pi d_1^3}{3}$$

and

$$\frac{\pi d_1^3}{3} = \frac{\pi d_2^3}{6}$$

From the above, we have an important relationship between d_1 and d_2 as

Chapter 5 Macromolecular Phase Transitions

$$d_2 = 2^{\frac{1}{3}} d_1$$

The area of the final sphere is given

$$A_2 = \pi d_2^2 = \pi (2^{1/3} d_1)^2$$

and

$$A_1 = \pi d_1^2$$

The area change ΔA is the difference between final (A_{final}) and initial value of area ($A_{initial}$)

$$\Delta A = A_{final} - A_{initial} \quad \text{(Eqn. 5-4)}$$

In the present case,

$$\Delta A = A_2 - 2A_1 = \pi(2^{1/3} d_1)^2 - 2\pi d_1^2$$

$$= (2^{2/3} - 2)\pi d_1^2$$
$$= -0.4126 \pi d_1^2 \quad \text{(Eqn. 5-5)}$$

(Eqn. 5-6) $\quad \theta = \alpha P / (1 + \alpha P)$

If there is an equilibrium between empty surface sites, A, particles (P) and sites filled with particles (AP)

$$A + P \leftrightarrow AP$$

The equilibrium constant K is

$$K = \frac{[AP]}{[A][P]}$$

If the number of filled surface sites [AP] is considered to be proportional to θ, the number of unfilled sites [A] is proportional to $1-\theta$. The number of particles is proportional to the gas pressure or concentration (P), by replacing K to a constant α, the equilibrium condition can be rephrased as:

$$\alpha = \theta / (1 - \theta) P$$

By solving the above for θ,

$\alpha P(1 - \theta) = \theta$
$P\alpha - P\theta\alpha = \theta$

$P\alpha = \theta + P\theta\alpha$
$P\alpha = \theta(1 + P\alpha)$

Thus,

$$\theta = \alpha P/(1 + \alpha P) \qquad \text{(Eqn. 5-6)}$$

(Eqn. 5-13) $\quad ln\, a_A = -\dfrac{\Delta \bar{H}_{vap}}{R}\left[\dfrac{1}{T_b} - \dfrac{1}{T_o}\right]$

(Eqn. 5-14) $\quad \Delta T_b = K_b m$

(Eqn. 5-15) $\quad K_b = \dfrac{M_A R T_o^2}{1000\Delta \bar{H}_{vap}}$

The **Clausius-Clapeyron equation** states,

$$ln\dfrac{P_2}{P_1} = -\dfrac{\Delta \bar{H}_{vap}^o}{R}\left[\dfrac{1}{T_2} - \dfrac{1}{T_1}\right] \qquad \text{(Eqn. 4-4)}$$

P_1 is set as 1 [atm] and P_2 can be expressed by

$$P_2 = a_A = \dfrac{P_A}{1\, atm} \qquad \text{(Eqn. 3-3)}$$

Here, a_A is an activity of A in solution. With $P_1 = 1$ [atm] and $P_2 = a_A$ [atm]. Thus, (**Eqn 4-4**) becomes

$$ln\, a_A = -\dfrac{\Delta \bar{H}_{vap}}{R}\left[\dfrac{1}{T_b} - \dfrac{1}{T_o}\right] \qquad \text{(Eqn. 5-13)}$$

Then, we make an approximation in a temperature term as,

$$\left[\dfrac{1}{T_b} - \dfrac{1}{T_o}\right] \cong \dfrac{T_o - T_b}{T_o^2}$$

Here, $T_b T_o$ is approximated to be T_o^2. Also the natural log term on the right can be approximated as

$$ln\, a_A \cong -\dfrac{n_B}{n_A}$$

Taylor series expansion of natural log term is

$$\ln(x) = (x-1) - \dfrac{(x-1)^2}{2} + \dfrac{(x-1)^3}{3} - \dfrac{(x-1)^4}{4} \ldots$$

Utilizing the first term of Taylor series expansion,

$ln\, a_A = a_A - 1$
For the dilute solution,
$a_A = \gamma_A X_A \qquad \text{(Eqn. 3-5)}$

If γ_A is approximated to be 1, $a_A = X_A$. Also, the total mole fraction is given by $X_A + X_B = 1$, and $X_B = 1 - X_A$.

$$\ln a_A = a_A - 1 = X_A - 1 = -X_B$$

Since the number of moles of solute (n_B) is negligible compared to the number of moles of solvent (n_A), the mole fraction of solute (X_B) is

$$X_B = \frac{n_B}{n_A + n_B} \cong \frac{n_B}{n_A}$$

Thus,

$$\ln a_A \cong -\frac{n_B}{n_A}$$

If the present system contains a kg of solvent (1000 [g]) with molar mass M_A, and n_B moles of solute, the molality of solute B (m) is

$$m = \frac{n_B[mol]}{1\,[kg]}$$

The number of moles of solvent (1000g) is given

$$n_A = \frac{1000\,[g]}{M_A[g/mol]}$$

Therefore,

$$\frac{n_B}{n_A} \cong \frac{M_A m}{1000}$$

In summary, we can derive for $\ln a_A$ as

$$\ln a_A \cong -\frac{n_B}{n_A} \cong -\frac{M_A m}{1000}$$

By inserting the results given in this section into both sides of **(Eqn. 5-13)**

$$-\frac{M_A m}{1000} = -\frac{\Delta \bar{H}_{vap}}{R} \frac{T_o - T_b}{T_o^2}$$

The difference in boiling point (boiling point elevation) ΔT_b is

$$\Delta T_b = T_o - T_b = \frac{M_A R T_o^2}{1000 \Delta \bar{H}_{vap}} m$$

Here the coefficient of molality is molal boiling point elevation constant, K_b

$$K_b = \frac{M_A R T_o^2}{1000 \Delta \bar{H}_{vap}} \qquad \textbf{(Eqn. 5-15)}$$

By using the coefficient, we can express the boiling point Elevation as a simple form as:

$$\Delta T_b = K_b m \quad \text{(Eqn. 5-14)}$$

Here, ΔT_b is boiling point elevation of solution in the unit of either [°C, K], and K_b is molal boiling-point elevation [°C/m, K/m], and m is molality of the solution [m]. Let me re-explain the constant K_b.

$$K_b = \frac{M_A R T_o^2}{1000 \Delta \bar{H}_{vap}} \quad \text{(Eqn. 5-15)}$$

In here 1000 is the unit conversion to g from kg (g/kg). Please be careful about the unit for each parameter as: K_b [K / m], M_A [g/mol], R [J / K mol], T_o[K], $\Delta \bar{H}_{vap}$ [J/mol], and m is molality [mol/kg].

(Eqn. 5-17) $\quad \ln a_A = \frac{\Delta \bar{H}_{fus}}{R}\left[\frac{1}{T_f} - \frac{1}{T_o}\right]$

(Eqn. 5-18) $\quad \Delta T_f = K_f m$

(Eqn. 5-19) $\quad K_f = \frac{M_A R T_o^2}{1000 \Delta \bar{H}_{fus}}$

From **Chapter 3**, we learned that the activity coefficient (γ_A) of very dilute solution becomes 1 and the activity of solute A is equal to concentration (molarity, c_A)

$$\lim_{C_A \to 0} a_A = C_A$$
$$\lim_{C_A \to 0} \gamma_A = 1$$

Thus, the concentration (or activity) of A for a dilute solution can be given as
$$a_A = C_A$$

The equilibirum constant, K, for pure solvent at freezing point (T_o) is

$$K_{T_o} = \frac{a_A^\bullet(solid)}{a_A^\bullet(liquid)}$$

Here, $a_A^\bullet(solid)$ and $a_A^\bullet(liquid)$ are the activity of the pure solvent A at solid and liquid condition, respectively. On the other hand, the equilibrium constant for A in solution at freezing point (T_f) should be given as

Chapter 5 Macromolecular Phase Transitions

$$K_{T_f} = \frac{a_A(solid)}{a_A(liquid)}$$

Comparing activities between those in solution and pure solvent, those in pure solvents can be approximated as 1 (standard condition). Furthermore, the activity of solution A in solid can be negligible in solution and $a_A(solid) = 1$ compared to $a_A(liquid)$. Thus,

$$K_{T_f}/K_{T_o} = \left[\frac{a_A(solid)}{a_A(liquid)}\right] / \left[\frac{a_A^\bullet(solid)}{a_A^\bullet(liquid)}\right] = \frac{1}{a_A(liquid)}$$

Here, we replaced the values in (**Eqn. 2-13**) as follows. The temperatures T_1 and T_2 are replaced as T_o and T_f and ΔH_{rxn}^o is replaced by the enthalpy change in fusion (ΔH_{fus}^o). Then, K_1/K_2 is approximated as $1/a_A(liquid)$.

$$-\ln a_A(liquid) = -\frac{\Delta \bar{H}_{fus}}{R}\left[\frac{1}{T_f} - \frac{1}{T_o}\right]$$

Thus,

$$\ln a_A = \frac{\Delta \bar{H}_{fus}}{R}\left[\frac{1}{T_f} - \frac{1}{T_o}\right] \qquad \text{(Eqn. 5-17)}$$

We use the same approximation made by the previous section.

$$\left[\frac{1}{T_f} - \frac{1}{T_o}\right] \cong \frac{T_o - T_f}{T_o^2}$$

$$\ln a_A \cong -\frac{n_B}{n_A} \cong -\frac{M_A m}{1000}$$

Please note the description given in tehsubscripts as: A as solvent and B as solute. Thus the n_A is Number of moles of solvent and n_B is number of moles of solute. Also, M_A is molecular weight of solvent. And we use *m* as molality of solute. From these relationships, we can derive

$$\frac{M_A m}{1000} = \frac{\Delta \bar{H}_{fus}}{R}\frac{T_o - T_f}{T_o^2}$$

Therefore, we can derive the difference in freezing point (freezing point lowering), ΔT_f, as:

$$\Delta T_f = T_o - T_f = \frac{M_A R T_o^2}{1000 \Delta \bar{H}_{fus}} m$$

Here the coefficient of molality, m is

Chapter 5 Macromolecular Phase Transitions

$$K_f = \frac{M_A R T_o^2}{1000 \Delta \bar{H}_{fus}} \qquad \text{(Eqn. 5-19)}$$

$$T_o - T_f = \frac{M_A R T_o^2}{1000 \Delta \bar{H}_{fus}} m = K_f m$$

Using the previous logic as presented in the boiling point elevation freezing Point Depression is simplified as:

$$\Delta T_f = K_f m \qquad \text{(Eqn. 5-18)}$$

Here, ΔT_f is a freezing point depression of solution [°C, K], and K_f is molal freezing-point elevation in the unit of [°C/m, K/m] and m is molality of the solution [m].

(Eqn. 5-16) $\qquad M_B = \dfrac{K_b m_B}{\Delta T_b w_A}$

(Eqn. 5-20) $\qquad M_B = \dfrac{K_f m_B}{\Delta T_f w_A}$

The molality m (not a mass) is given by

$$m = \frac{n_B}{w_A}$$

Here, n_B is the number of moles of solute and w_A is the mass of solvent [kg]. (Be careful with the unit of w_A.) Also the number of moles of solute, n_B is given by

$$n_B = \frac{m_B}{M_B}$$

Here, m_B is the solute sample mass [g] and M_B is the molar mass of solute B [g/mol].
Thus, molality (m) is

$$m = \frac{m_B}{M_B w_A}$$

By substituting molality into (**Eqn. 5-14**),

$$\Delta T_b = \frac{K_b m_B}{M_B w_A}$$

Thus, the molar mass of solute (M_B [g/mol]) is given by

$$M_B = \frac{K_b m_B}{\Delta T_b w_A} \qquad \text{(Eqn. 5-16)}$$

By replacing K_b with K_f and ΔT_b with ΔT_f,

$$M_B = \frac{K_f m_B}{\Delta T_f w_A} \qquad \text{(Eqn. 5-20)}$$

(Eqn.5-23) $\qquad \Pi = cRT$

The Pressure Dependence of Gibbs Free Energy can be expressed as.

$$dG = VdP - SdT = VdP$$

At constant temperature, T

$$dG = VdP$$

If you integrate the both term of the above

$$G(P_2) - G(P_1) = \int_{P_1}^{P_2} VdP$$

The approximation used in the last term is valid for solid or liquid. Since the chemical potential is the molar Gibbs energy,

$$\Delta \mu = \bar{G}(P_2) - \bar{G}(P_1) = \int_{P_1}^{P_2} \bar{V} dP$$

In Chapter 3, we learned

$$\mu_i = \mu_i^o + nRT \ln a_i \qquad \text{(Eqn. 3-9)}$$

Thus,

$$\Delta \mu = \mu_i - \mu_i^o = RT \ln a_A$$

For the system with osmotic pressure present,

$$\Delta \mu_{osm} = \mu_A(solution, 1 atm) - \mu_A^o(solvent) = RT \ln a_A$$

From Chapter 3, we learned that an activity a_A is equal to concentration at very dilute situation.

$$\lim_{C_A \to 0} a_A = C_A$$

For 1 mole of A per V_A [L] of volume, the concentration is given by

$$a_A = C_A = \frac{1[mol]}{V_A[L]} = 1/\bar{V}_A$$

Here the last tem of volume is called Molar volume of solvent. This is defined as

$$\bar{V}_A = \frac{volume\ of\ water}{Number\ of\ moles\ of\ water}$$

Thus,

$$\Delta\mu = RT\ ln a_A = RT ln\left[1/\bar{V}_A\right] = -\int_1^{1+\Pi} \bar{V}_A dP = -\bar{V}_A \Pi$$

Thus,

$$ln a_A = \frac{-\bar{V}_A \Pi}{RT}$$

Please recall the relationship derived from the previous section for deriving (**Eqn. 5-14**) and (**Eqn. 5-18**)

$$ln a_A = -\frac{n_B}{n_A}$$

The n_A is Number of moles of solvent A and n_B is number of moles of solute B. Then,

$$\Pi = \frac{RT}{n_A \bar{V}_A} n_B$$

Since the total volume of solvent, V, is

$$V = n_A \bar{V}_A$$

$$\Pi = \frac{n_B}{V} RT = cRT \qquad \text{(Eqn. 5-23)}$$

Chapter 5 Macromolecular Phase Transitions

(Eqn.5-24) $$M_B = \frac{m_B}{\Pi V} RT$$

The osmotic pressure, Π, is given by

$$\Pi = cRT \qquad \text{(Eqn. 5-23)}$$

Here, c represents a concentration in molarity unit [M]. Since the concentration, c, is given as,

$$c = n_B/V$$

Here, n_B is the number of moles of solute and V [L] is the volume of solution (not a molar volume, $\overline{V_A}$ [L/mol]). The number of moles of solute is

$$n_B = m_B/M_B$$

Here, m_B is the sample mass of solute [g] and M_B [g/mol] is the molar mass of solute. By substituting n_B into **(Eqn. 5-23)**

$$\Pi = (n_B/V)RT = \frac{m_B}{M_B V} RT$$

Therefore, the molar mass of solute M_B [g/mol] is given by

$$M_B = \frac{m_B}{\Pi V} RT \qquad \text{(Eqn. 5-22)}$$

(Eqn. 5-25) $$\Delta P = \frac{w_B}{M_B} \frac{P_A^\bullet}{n_A}$$

(Eqn. 5-26) $$M_B = \frac{w_B}{n_A} \frac{P_A^\bullet}{\Delta P}$$

(Eqn. 5-27) $$X_B = \frac{P_A^\bullet - P_A}{P_A^\bullet}$$

Raoults' law state that

$$P_A = X_A P_A^\bullet \qquad \text{(Eqn. 4-5)}$$

Here, X_A is a mole fraction of A in solution, $P_A^\bullet$ is a vapor pressure of a pure solvent A, and P_A is a partial pressure of A over a solution. When the amount of the vapor pressure lowered is given by ΔP.

$$\Delta P = P_A^\bullet - P_A$$

Also the mole fraction of solvent (X_A) and the solute (X_B) has the relationship of

Also
$$X_B = 1 - X_A$$

$$X_A = \frac{P_A}{P_A^\bullet}$$

Thus,

$$X_B = 1 - \frac{P_A}{P_A^\bullet} = \frac{P_A^\bullet - P_A}{P_A^\bullet} = \frac{\Delta P}{P_A^\bullet} \qquad \text{(Eqn. 5-27)}$$

The mole fraction of B can be approximated to be

$$X_B = \frac{n_B}{n_A + n_B} \cong \frac{n_B}{n_A}$$

Here, the number of moles of solvent is n_A and number of moles of solute is n_B ($n_A \gg n_B$). If the molar mass of solute is M_B and sample weight of solute is w_B,

$$n_B = \frac{w_B}{M_B}$$

Thus,

$$X_B = \frac{w_B}{M_B n_A}$$

and

$$\frac{\Delta P}{P_A^\blacksquare} = \frac{w_B}{M_B n_A}$$

The vapor pressure lowering is

$$\Delta P = \frac{w_B}{M_B} \frac{P_A^\blacksquare}{n_A} \qquad \text{(Eqn. 5-25)}$$

Solving the above for M_B,

$$M_B = \frac{w_B}{n_A} \frac{P_A^\blacksquare}{\Delta P} \qquad \text{(Eqn. 5-26)}$$

(Eqn. 5-28)
$$\Delta T = \frac{\bar{T} \Delta \bar{V}_{fus}}{\Delta \bar{H}_{fus}} \Delta P$$

At equilibrium under constant temperature (T) and pressure (P). The chemical potential between solid and liquid should be equal.

$$\mu_{solid} = \mu_{liquid}$$

Since chemical potential is a molar Gibbs energy ($\bar{G}$),

Chapter 5 Macromolecular Phase Transitions

$$\bar{G}_S = \bar{G}_l$$

If a new equilibrium is achieved after Gibbs energy is increase by $d\bar{G}$:

$$\bar{G}_S + d\bar{G}_S = \bar{G}_l + d\bar{G}_l$$

Here

$$d\bar{G}_S = d\bar{G}_l$$

The Gibbs energy change is given by

$$d\bar{G} = -\bar{S}dT + \bar{V}d$$

Thus,

$$-\bar{S}_S dT + \bar{V}_S dP = -\bar{S}_l dT + \bar{V}_l dP$$

The above formula is arranged as

$$\bar{V}_S dP - \bar{V}_l dP = \bar{S}_S dT - \bar{S}_l dT$$

$$(\bar{V}_S - \bar{V}_l)dP = (\bar{S}_S - \bar{S}_l)dT$$

Let's define $\Delta\bar{V}_{fus}$ and $\Delta\bar{S}_{fus}$

$$\Delta\bar{V}_{fus} = \bar{V}_S - \bar{V}_l$$

$$\Delta\bar{S}_{fus} = \bar{S}_S - \bar{S}_l$$

Therefore,

$$\Delta\bar{V}_{fus} dP = \Delta\bar{S}_{fus} dT$$

By arranging the above,

$$\frac{dT}{dP} = \frac{T\Delta\bar{V}_{fus}}{\Delta\bar{H}_{fus}}$$

Here, the entropy term is replaced by

$$\Delta\bar{S}_{fus} = \frac{\Delta\bar{H}_{fus}}{T}$$

Integrating two above formula

$$\frac{\Delta T}{\Delta P} = \frac{T \Delta \bar{V}_{fus}}{\Delta \bar{H}_{fus}}$$

Thus,

$$\Delta T = \frac{\bar{T} \Delta \bar{V}_{fus}}{\Delta \bar{H}_{fus}} \Delta P \qquad \text{(Eqn. 5-28)}$$

Chapter 5 Summary [Part 1]

(Use back page to cover the contents.)

1	Surface tension	Gibbs energy change (ΔG) is caused by the surface area change (ΔA) $\Delta G = \gamma \Delta A$ (Eqn. 5-3)
2	Langmuir isotherm	The **Langmuir isotherm** describes the coverage of molecules adsorbing on a solid surface to as a function of concentration. K: Langmuir equilibrium constant Γ_{max}: maximum amount adsorbed Four graphical methods (c: aqueous concentration, Γ: amount adsorbed) i) Lineweaver-Burk equation: $1/\Gamma = 1/(Kc\Gamma_{max}) + 1/\Gamma_{max}$ (Eqn. 5-9) ii) Eadie-Hofstee plot (type-I) $\Gamma = \Gamma_{max} - \Gamma/Kc$ (Eqn. 5-10) iii) Eadie-Hofstee plot (type-II) $c/\Gamma = 1/(K\Gamma_{max}) + c/\Gamma_{max}$ (Eqn. 5-12) iv) Scatchard plotting $\Gamma/c = K\Gamma_{max} - K\Gamma$ (Eqn. 5-11)
3	colligative properties	The solutions' **colligative properties** depend on the number of particles in solvent.
4	boiling point elevation	ΔT_b: boiling point elevation $\Delta T_b = K_b m$ (Eqn. 5-14) (m: molality) molal boiling point elevation coefficient $K_b = \dfrac{M_A R T_o^2}{1000 \Delta \bar{H}_{vap}}$ (Eqn. 5-15) a_A: activity of solution $\ln a_A = -\dfrac{\Delta \bar{H}_{vap}}{R}\left[\dfrac{1}{T_b} - \dfrac{1}{T_o}\right]$ (Eqn. 5-13)
5	freezing point depression	ΔT_f: freezing point depression $\Delta T_f = K_f m$ (Eqn. 5-18) (m: molality) molal freezing point depression coefficient $K_f = \dfrac{M_A R T_o^2}{1000 \Delta \bar{H}_{fus}}$ (Eqn. 5-19) a_A: activity of solution $\ln a_A = \dfrac{\Delta \bar{H}_{fus}}{R}\left[\dfrac{1}{T_f} - \dfrac{1}{T_o}\right]$ (Eqn. 5-17)

[Fold the page at the double line and cover the right half.]

Chapter 5 Summary Check [Part 1]

(Use this page to cover and check the contents.)
Use ☐ as your check box. Write your comment at far right

1	Surface tension	☐ ☐ ☐ ☐ ☐	
2	Langmuir isotherm	☐ ☐ ☐ ☐ ☐	
3	colligative properties	☐ ☐ ☐ ☐ ☐	
4	boiling point elevation	☐ ☐ ☐ ☐ ☐	
5	freezing point depression	☐ ☐ ☐ ☐ ☐	

Chapter 5 Summary [Part 2]

(Use back page to cover the contents.)

6	osmotic pressure	Π: osmotic pressure of solution $\Pi = cRT$ (Eqn.5-23) a_A: activity of solvent $\ln a_A = \dfrac{-\overline{V_A}\Pi}{RT}$ (Eqn.5-22) $\overline{V_A}$: volume of solvent
7	vapor pressure lowering (ΔP)	ΔP: vapor pressure lowering ($\Delta P = P_A^\bullet - P_A$) $\Delta P = \dfrac{w_B}{M_B}\dfrac{P_A^\bullet}{n_A}$ (Eqn. 5-25) M_B: molar mass of solute, w_B: mass of solute
8	Change of freezing point (ΔT) by pressure change (ΔP)	ΔT: difference of freezing point ΔP: pressure change $\Delta T = \dfrac{\overline{T}\Delta \overline{V}_{fus}}{\Delta \overline{H}_{fus}}\Delta P$ (Eqn. 5-28) $\Delta \overline{V}_{fus}$: molar volume of fusion $\overline{T} = [T_2 + T_1]/2$.

[Fold the page at the double line and cover the right half.]

Chapter 5 Summary Check [Part 2]

(Use this page to cover and check the contents.)
Use ☐ as your check box. Write your comment at far right

6	osmotic pressure	☐ ☐ ☐ ☐ ☐	
7	vapor pressure lowering (ΔP)	☐ ☐ ☐ ☐ ☐	
8	Change of freezing point (ΔT) by pressure change (ΔP)	☐ ☐ ☐ ☐ ☐	

Chapter 5 - YOUR TEACHER MAY TEST YOU ON:

No.	What may be asked?		What you should know or do?
1	How you calculate the surface area change in cell fusion (from two cells into one cell) and Gibbs energy change (ΔG)?	→	$\Delta A = \pi(2^{1/3}d_1)^2 - 2\pi d_1^2 = (2^{2/3} - 2)\pi d_1^2 < 0$ (Eqn. 5-5) $\Delta G = \gamma \Delta A$ (Eqn. 5-3)
		→	[Fig. 5-4]
		→	EXERCISE 5-1
		→	Problems 5-1, 5-2, 5-3, 5-4
2	How do you extract the maximum amount of absorption (Γ_{max}) and the Langmuir isotherm constant (K)?	→	i) Lineweaver-Burk equation: $1/\Gamma = 1/(Kc\Gamma_{max}) + 1/\Gamma_{max}$ (Eqn. 5-9) ii) Eadie-Hofstee plot (type-I) $\Gamma = \Gamma_{max} - \Gamma/Kc$ (Eqn. 5-10) iii) Eadie-Hofstee plot (type-II) $c/\Gamma = 1/(K\Gamma_{max}) + c/\Gamma_{max}$ (Eqn. 5-12) iv) Scatchard plotting $\Gamma/c = K\Gamma_{max} - K\Gamma$ (Eqn. 5-11)
		→	EXERCISE 5-2
3	How to calculate the molal boiling point elevation (molal freezing point depression) constant.	→	$K_b = \dfrac{M_A R T_o^2}{1000 \Delta \bar{H}_{vap}}$ (Eqn. 5-15) $K_f = \dfrac{M_A R T_o^2}{1000 \Delta \bar{H}_{fus}}$ (Eqn. 5-19)
4	How to calculate boiling point depression (freezing point depression) from known molality of the solute?	→	$\Delta T_b = K_b m$ (Eqn. 5-14) $\Delta T_f = K_f m$ (Eqn. 5-18)
		→	Problems 5-5, 5-6, 5-7, 5-8, 5-20
5	How to calculate the molar mass of the solute from known boiling point elevation (freezing point depression).	→	$M_B = \dfrac{K_b m_B}{\Delta T_b w_A}$ (Eqn. 5-16) $M_B = \dfrac{K_f m_B}{\Delta T_f w_A}$ (Eqn. 5-20)
		→	Problem 5-9
6	How to calculate the activity of solution from known boiling point elevation (freezing point depression).	→	$\ln a_A = -\dfrac{\Delta \bar{H}_{vap}}{R}\left[\dfrac{1}{T_b} - \dfrac{1}{T_o}\right]$ (Eqn. 5-13) $\ln a_A = \dfrac{\Delta \bar{H}_{fus}}{R}\left[\dfrac{1}{T_f} - \dfrac{1}{T_o}\right]$ (Eqn. 5-17)
		→	Problems 5-10
7	How to calculate the osmotic pressure with known concentration of solution.	→	$\Pi = cRT$ (Eqn.5-23)
		→	EXERCISE 5-5
		→	Problems 5-11, 5-12, 5-13, 5-15

8	How to calculate the activity of solution from known osmotic pressure.	→	$ln a_A = \frac{-\bar{V}_A \Pi}{RT}$ (Eqn.5-22)
		→	EXERCISE 5-5
		→	Problem 5-14
9	How to calculate the molar mass of the solute from known osmotic pressure.	→	$M_B = \frac{m_B}{\Pi V} RT$ (Eqn.5-24)
		→	Problems 5-16, 5-17, 5-18, 5-19
10	How to calculate vapor pressure lowering with known molar mass of solute.	→	$\Delta P = \frac{w_B}{M_B} \frac{P_A^*}{n_A}$ (Eqn. 5-25)
		→	EXERCISE 5-6
		→	Problem 5-20
11	How to calculate unknown molar mass of solute with known vapor pressure lowering.	→	$M_B = \frac{w_B}{n_A} \frac{P_A^*}{\Delta P}$ (Eqn. 5-26)
12	How to calculate the melting point change with known amount of pressure change?	→	$\Delta T = \frac{\bar{T} \Delta \bar{V}_{fus}}{\Delta \bar{H}_{fus}} \Delta P$ (Eqn. 5-28)
		→	EXERCISE 5-7

UNIT CHECK CHAPTER 5

Important Parameters of This Chapter	Popularly Used Unit	Important Unit Conversion
Surface tension, Γ	N/m J/m^2	[J] = [Nm]
Gibbs Energy, G	J/mol kJ/mol	
Gibbs Energy Change, ΔG	J/mol kJ/mol	
Temperature, T	°C K	0 [°C] = 273.15 [K]
Temperature change, ΔT	°C K	
activity, a	atm M, mol/L M, mol/kg	
concentration	M, mol/L M, mol/kg	
Activity coefficient, γ	dimensionless	
Chemical potential, μ	J/mol kJ/mol	
Pressure	Atm	1 [atm] =101.325 [Pa]=760 [torr]
Enthalpy	J/mol kJ/mol	
Enthalpy change, ΔH	J/mol kJ/mol	
Gas constant, R	atm L K^{-1} mol^{-1} J K^{-1} mol^{-1}	8.314472 [J K^{-1} mol^{-1}] 0.08205746 [atm L K^{-1} mol^{-1}]
Molality, m	mol/kg	
Molar mass, M	mol/g	
Equilibrium constant, K	dimensionless or M$^{c+d-(a+b)}$	
molal boiling-point elevation, K$_f$	°C/molal, K/molal	
molal freezing-point elevation, K$_f$	°C/molal, K/molal	
Mole fraction, X	dimension less	
Volume, V	L, mL, cc, cm^3, m^3	1L =1000 mL = 1000 cc 1000 cm^3 = 1×10^{-3} m^3 =1 dm^3
molar volume, $\overline{V_A}$	L/mol	
Osmotic pressure, Π	atm	1 [atm] =101.325 [Pa] =760 [torr]

Chapter 5 Macromolecular Phase Transitions

Mass of sample (solute), w_B	g	
Vapor pressure lowering, ΔP	atm	
Number of moles, n	mol	1 mol = 6.0221415×10^{23} particles
Molar volume change of fusion, $\Delta \bar{V}_{fus}$	L/mol	

SUMMARY OF TRICKY TRAPS OF CHAPTER 5

☐	1	More surface created, $\Delta G > 0$. Less surface created, $\Delta G < 0$. Cell fusion → $\Delta G < 0$
☐	2	Solvent (T_b) → Solution (T_b) ↑ and Solvent (T_m) → Solution (T_m) ↓
☐	3	K_b and K_f depend on solvent property only.
☐	4	i = 1 for nonelctrolyte and I ≥ 1 for electrolytes.
☐	5.	Common practice of colligative properties is to obtain M_B (molar mass of unknown solute)
☐	6	The gas constant used for osmotic pressure calculation is 0.081 [atm·L/mol·K]

LAST MINUTE REVIEW OF MATH CHAPTER 5
(These are basic algebra which you have no excuse if you miss them.)

1. y = mx + b

   y axis Intercept y=b

   x axis intercept x= –(b/m)

2. $\ln\left(\frac{1}{x}\right) = -\ln x$

3. $\ln x = a \to x = e^a$

3. $\frac{1}{x} - \frac{1}{y} = \frac{y-x}{xy}$

4. $(x^a)^b = x^{ab}$ $\left(x^{\frac{1}{a}}\right)^{\frac{1}{b}} = x^{\frac{1}{ab}}$

5. $\ln(x) = (x-1) - \frac{(x-1)^2}{2} + \frac{(x-1)^3}{3} - \frac{(x-1)^4}{4} \ldots$

6. $\frac{x}{x+y} \approx \frac{x}{y}$ if $x \ll y$ $\frac{x}{x+y} \approx \frac{x}{x} = 1$ if $y \ll x$

Chapter 5 Macromolecular Phase Transitions

Nobel Prize and Your Knowledge From Chapter 5
(*: word appeared in Chapter 5)

In 1932, **Irving Langmuir** was awarded for the Nobel Prize in Chemistry for his discoveries and investigations in surface chemistry. He improved of the diffusion pump and it led to the invention of the high-vacuum tube. A year later, he and his colleague invented tungsten filament light bulb with an inert gas and contributed many other important developments in the incandescent light bulb. His work in surface chemistry began when he observed the dissociation of hydrogen molecular as it is introduced into a tungsten-filament and formation of **monoatomic layer (Langmuir-Brodget film or LB film)*** over the surface of the bulb. LB films are constructed as amphiphilic molecules (surfactants) interact with air at an air-water interface. Surfactants consists of hydrophobic tails and hydrophilic (polar) heads. (The hydrophobic tails are exposed to the air over the water, since the hydrophilic head-water interaction is more favorable than air-water interaction.) (See **Fig. 5-16**) The surfactant conducts self-assembly if concentration of surfactant is less than critical micellar concentration (CMC), driven by the act of reducing surface tension of water.

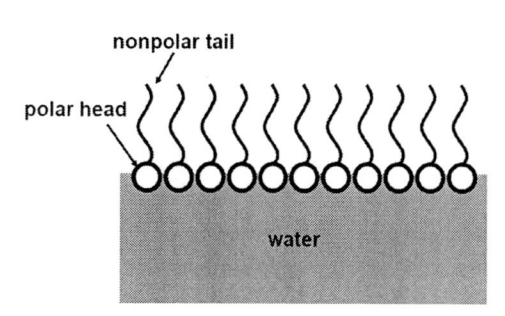

Fig. 5-16 LB film

Adding a monolayer to the surface reduces the surface tension, and the **surface pressure***, Π is given by:

$$\Pi = \gamma_o - \gamma$$

Here, γ_0 is surface tension of the water and γ is the **surface tension*** originated from the monolayer. The concentration-dependence of **surface tension***(**Langmuir isotherm***) is

$$\gamma_o - \gamma = RTK_H C$$
$$= RT\Gamma$$

Therefore,

$$\Pi = RT\Gamma$$

The surface pressure exerted by the monolayer (Π) is measured by so called "Wilhelmy plate". (**Fig.5-17**) A force on the plate due to the surface pressure is described as

$$\Pi = \Delta\gamma = -\left[\frac{\Delta F}{2(d+l)}\right]$$

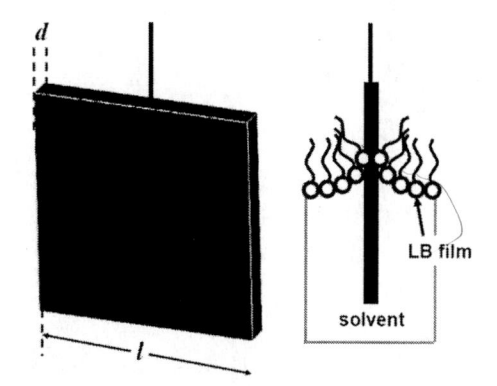

Fig. 5-17. Wilhelmy plate

Here, ΔF indicates the force difference. The thickness of the film was estimated from the volume and area of the oil.

THE FOCUSED PHYSICAL CHEMISTRY EXPERIMENTAL APPROACH ASSOCIATED WITH CHAPTER 5

(*: word appeared in Chapter 5)

Surface Plasmon Resonance Spectroscopy

Surface plasmons are surface electromagnetic waves that propagate in a direction parallel to the metal/dielectric interface, and oscillations of this wave is very sensitive to change of interfacial boundary including adsorption of molecules to the **metal surface***. The **surface plasmon resonance** (SPR) is an event of excitation of these surface plasmons by light.

The excitation of surface plasmons can be conducted by electron or visible or infrared light. Electronic and magnetic surface plasmons obey the following dispersion relation:

$$K(\omega) = \frac{\omega}{c} \sqrt{\frac{\varepsilon_g \varepsilon_m \mu_g \mu_m}{\varepsilon_g \mu_g + \varepsilon_m \mu_m}}$$

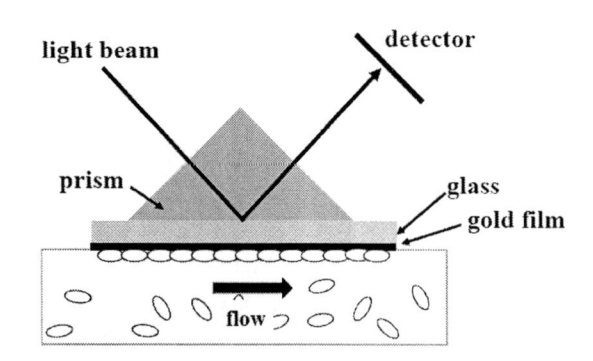

Fig. 5-18 Kretschmann configuration

where ε stands for the dielectric constant, and μ for the magnetic permeability of the materials (g: glass block, m: metal film). Typical metals used are silver and gold, but metals such as copper, titanium or chromium.

In the **Fig. 5-18**, a most practical configuration of surface Plasmon resonance (Kretschmann configuration) is shown. In this configuration, the metal film is evaporated onto the glass block. The light illuminates from the glass, and an **evanescent wave** penetrates through the metal film. Thus, the plasmons are excited at the outer side of the film. A typical SPR curves is shown in **Fig. 5-19**. Here, it shows a curve measured on the adsorption of a polyelectrolyte on a thin gold plate sensor.

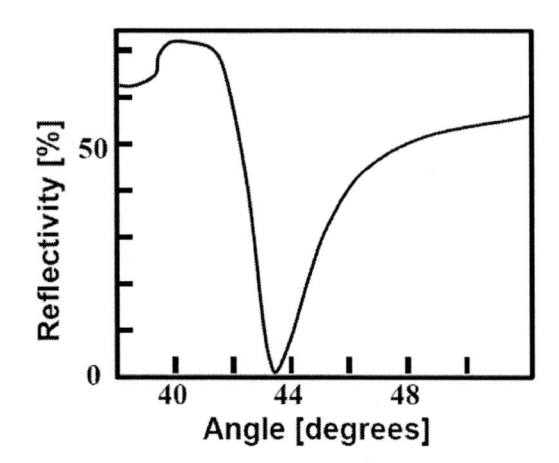

Fig. 5-19 An example of SPR curves measured on gold plate.

Chapter 5 Problems.

5-1 [Cell fusion] Two spherical cell 1 μm in radius become into one spherical cell. Calculate the work gained by decreasing the surface area. The surface tension is 1.00×10^{-2} [N/m].

5-2 [Cell fusion] Two spherical cell become into one spherical cell. Calculate the Gibbs energy change. (Clarify if the sign of Gibbs energy is "+" or "–".) Each spherical cell has a surface area of 1.256×10^{-11} [m^2] The surface tension is 1.00×10^{-2} [N/m].

5-3 [Cell fusion] Four spherical cell become into one spherical cell. Calculate the Gibbs energy change. Each spherical cell has a surface area of 1.256×10^{-11} [m^2]. The surface tension is 1.00×10^{-2} [N/m].

5-4 [Cell fusion] A spherical cell 5 μm in diameter divides into **four** spherical cells. Calculate the work necessary to increase the surface area if its surface tension is 1.23×10^{-3} [N/m]. Assume that the volume of the daughter cells taken together is the same as that of parent.

5-5 [ΔT$_b$] (TRUE or FALSE)
True or false?
If you add the salt into the solvent, the boiling point of this solution increases.

5-6 [ΔT$_f$] What is the freezing point of the above protein solution (A)? Assume that the density of solution (A) is equal to that of water at 0 [°C].

5-7 [ΔT$_f$] Calculate the expected freezing point lowering of the solution containing 6 g of protein α per **10g of solvent** (water). The molal freezing point lowering constant of water K$_f$ is 1.86.

5-8 [ΔT$_f$] A certain non-dissociating solute is subjected to carbon-hydrogen analysis. The empirical formula is shown to be (CH$_2$O)$_x$. A solution of the compound containing 1.00 [g]dissolved in 100.00 [g] of water freezes at –0.103 [°C]. What is the correct molecular formula of this solute?

5-9 [ΔT$_f$, M$_B$] An aqueous protein solution-α containing 1.4 g of protein X per 200 [mL] of solution has an osmotic pressure of 37 [mm] of water at 20 [°C] and at a pH where the protein has no net charge. Calculate the molecular weight of the protein X and the freezing point (give three significant points) of the above protein solution-α at 1 [atm]. The density of water at 20 [°C] is 0.9982 g/ml, and the density of Hg is 13.6 [g/mL] at 20 [°C]. The relationship between molality (m) and molarity (c) is, c = ρm. You may assume that the density of solution-α is equal to that of water at 20 [°C]. The molar freezing point depression coefficient of water is K$_f$=1.86 [K/m].

5-10 [activity-derivation] For small value of x, you can expand the function $f(x)$ with Maclaurin Series as:
$f(x) = f(0) + f'(0)x + \{f''(0)/2!\} x^2$
Here, $f'(x)$ and $f''(x)$ are the first and second derivative of function $f(x)$.
At general condition the activity of the solvent can be given by the mol fraction of solvent as
$\ln a_{solvent} = \ln X_{solvent}$
Using only the first two terms of the Maclaurin Series, choose the correct expression for the natural log of activity of the solvent ($\ln a_{solvent}$) with the number of moles of solvent and the solute ($n_{solvent}$ and n_{solute}).

    a. $-1/n_{solvent}$
    b. $-n_{solute}$
    c. $-n_{solvent}/n_{solute}$
    d. $-n_{solute}/n_{solvent}$
    e. 0

5-11 [osmotic pressure] Calculate the expected osmotic pressure of the solution containing 0.6 [g] of protein α per 100 [mL] of water at 20 [°C] and at a pH where the protein has no net charge.

5-12 [osmotic pressure] Calculate the osmotic pressure (mmHg) of a 1 % solution (10 [mg/mL]) of a protein with molecular weight 10^4 at 25 [°C].

5-13. [osmotic pressure] Calculate the osmotic pressure of *cytoplasm* of 8.7×10^{-4} [mol/mL] at 35.5 [°C].

5-14 [osmotic pressure→activity] Calculate the osmotic pressure and activity of water as a solvent in a solution of 1.00 [g] of glucose in 100 [g] of water at 20 [°C].

5-15 [osmotic pressure] The following data have been obtained in an aqueous buffer for unknown protein α at 20.0 [°C].

$$\text{sedimentation coefficient at 20 [°C]: } s_{20,\,water} = 4.60 \text{ [S]}$$
$$\text{diffusion coefficient at 20 [°C]: } D_{20,\,water} = 6.10 \times 10^{-7} \text{ [cm}^2\text{/sec]}$$
$$\text{partial specific volume: } \overline{v_2} = 0.733 \text{ [cm}^3\text{/g]}$$

The density of the solution at 20.0 [°C] is equivalent to that of water at 20.0 [°C]. d = 0.998 [g/cm³]

Since mercury nanometer was not allowed to use in a laboratory, water manometer was used to measure the osmotic pressure of the solution containing 0.600 [g] of protein α per 100 [mL] of water at 20.0 [°C] and pH where the protein has no net charge. Calculate the height of the water rises inside the manometer tube at 20.0 [°C]. Answer the height in cm unit. (The density of the mercury at 20.0 [°C] is 13.6 [g/cm³] and the density of the water at 20.0 [°C] is 0.998 [g/cm³].)

5-16 [osmotic pressure→ M_B] A protein solution (A) containing 0.6 [g] of protein x per 100 [mL] of solution has an osmotic pressure of 22 [mm] of water at 20 [°C] and at a pH where the protein has no net charge. What is the molecular weight of the protein?

5-17 [osmotic pressure→ M_B] An unknown substance exhibited an osmotic pressure against pure water of 20.44 [torr]. What is the molecular weight of this substance

5-18 [osmotic pressure→ M_B] An unknown substance 100 [mg/L] exhibited an osmotic pressure against pure water of 20.44 [torr] at 25 [°C]. What is the molecular weight of this substance.

5-19 [osmotic pressure→ΔT_f] A protein solution (B) containing 5 [mg] of protein X per 1 [mL] of solution has an osmotic pressure of 0.161 [cm] of mercury at 20 [°C] and at a pH where the protein has no net charge. What is the freezing point of the above protein solution (B)? Assume that the density of solution (B) is equal to that of water at 20 [°C].

5-20 [ΔP] Assuming that solution (A) is an ideal solution, calculate the equilibrium vapor pressure at 20 °C of a solution of 1.00 [g] of protein x in 100 [g] of water?

5-21 [ΔP] Substance A is a somewhat volatile solid and soluble substance. Solute A and liquid water allowed to reach equilibrium at 20 [°C] to form an aqueous phase and a gaseous phase. The vapor pressure of pure solid A is 1.0×10^{-2} [torr] at 20 [°C] and 1.0×10^{-1} [torr] at 40 [°C]. The vapor pressure of pure water is 17.535 [torr] at 20 [°C] and 55.324 torr at 40 [°C].
   a. What is the mole fraction of A in the gas phase at equilibrium at 20 [°C]?
   b. Calculate the Heat of vaporization of solid A.

CHAPTER 5 ANSWERS. For Selected Problems

- **5-3** -1.86×10^{-13} J [Nm]
- **5-4** 5.67×10^{-14} [J]
- **5-5** True
- **5-6** -1.5996×10^{-4} [°C]
- **5-7** -1.63×10^{-2} [°C]
- **5-8** $C_6H_{12}O_6$
- **5-9** -2.76×10^{-4} [°C]
- **5-10** d
- **5-11** $\Pi = 2.108 \times 10^{-3}$ [atm]
- **5-12** 0.0244 [atm] or 18.6 [mmHg]
- **5-13** 22.0 [atm]
- **5-14** $a_A = 0.999001$
- **5-15** M = 68,464 g/mol, $\Pi = 2.108 \times 10^{-3}$ [atm] = 1.602 [mmHg], height = 2.18 cm
- **5-16** $\Pi = 2.12 \times 10^{-3}$ [atm], M = 68039 [g/mol]
- **5-17** 88 [g/mol]
- **5-18** 91 [g/mol]
- **5-19** -1.5996×10^{-4} [°C]
- **5-20** $P_A = 17.54$ [torr]
- **5-21** a) $X_A = 5.70 \times 10^{-4}$ b) $\Delta H = +87.8$ [kJ/mol]

Chapter 6

Molecular Motion and Transport Properties

6-1   Diffusional Motion
6-2   Diffusion Coefficient and Molecular Parameters
6-3   Shape Factor
6-4   Sedimentation
6-5   Viscosity
6-6   Electrophoresis

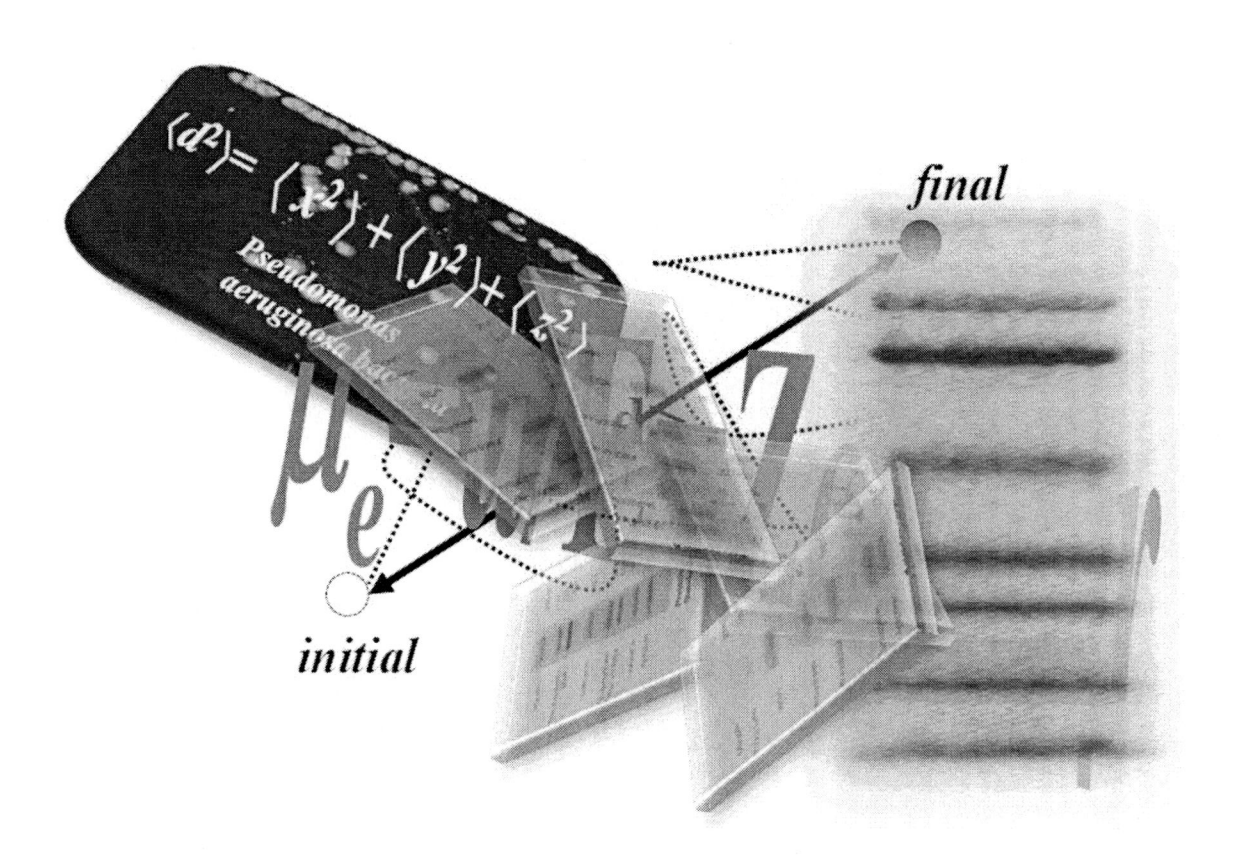

• Why do I have to study this chapter?

If a substance moves, how do you treat them or analyze them? You will learn that there are different approaches depending on the present driving force causing the motion. The way of obtaining speed (velocity) or distance of transportation per unit time will be extracted. Do you think spherical shape of protein and cigar-like shape of protein have different mobility? Yes, they do. The bonus feature of this chapter is that you will encounter many popular experimental approaches which biochemistry students will learn during the college year to describe biologically important macro-molecules (such as proteins, DNA, or RNA). Thus, the methodologies introduced in this chapter are all basic and routinely conducted techniques in research laboratories.

• Expected Hurdles Ahead in this Chapter
1. Understanding the concept of flux (See Section **6-1**)
2. Relating shape of molecule and frictional coefficient (See Section **6-3**)
3. You need to judge which parameters to use among many to choose. (See Section **6-5**)

PREVIEW OF KEY-EQUATIONS

Fick's Law

$$J_x = -D \left(dc/dx \right)$$

Mean square displacement

$$\langle x^2 \rangle = 2Dt$$

Stokes-Einstein equation

$$D = k_B T / f$$

Stokes Law

$$f = 6\pi\eta r$$

$$r = k_B T / 6\pi\eta D$$

Angular velocity

$$\omega = 2\pi v$$

Sedimentation coefficient

$$\sigma = m(1-\bar{v}_2\rho)/f = \left(2.303/\omega^2\right)\left(d\,\log r_{1/2}/dt\right)$$

$$\sigma_{20,w} = \sigma\left(\eta/\eta_{20,w}\right)\left[(1-\bar{v}_2\rho)_{20,w}/(1-\bar{v}_2\rho)\right]$$

Molar mass from sedimentation coefficient

$$M = RT\sigma/[D(1-\bar{v}_2\rho)]$$

Ratio of concentration at sedimentation condition

$$\ln\left(C_1/C_2\right) = M(1-\bar{v}_2\rho)\omega^2(r_2^2 - r_1^2)/2RT$$

Fick's law

$$J = -\eta\left(du_x/dy\right)$$

Viscosity

$$\eta = \left(mg(1-\bar{v}_2\rho)/6\pi r u_t\right)$$

$$\eta_2/\eta_1 = \rho_2 t_2/\rho_1 t_1$$

Specific viscosity

$$\eta_{sp} = (\eta' - \eta)/\eta$$

Intrinsic viscosity

$$[\eta] \equiv \lim_{c \to 0} \eta_{sp}/c$$

$$[\eta] = v(\bar{v}_2 + \delta_1 v_1^o)$$

Electrophoretic mobility

$$\mu_e = u/E = Ze/6\pi\eta r$$

Molar mass and location in gel

$$\log M = \alpha - \beta x$$

PREVIEW OF KEY-TECHNICAL TERMS

Kinetic theory, rms speed (u_{rms}), Maxwell-Boltzmann distribution, most probable speed (u_{mp}), average speed (u_{ave}), diffusion, Fick's law, flux (J), Stokes-Einstein equation, frictional coefficient (f), viscosity (η), shape factor, Sedimentation, angular velocity (ω), centrifugal acceleration, centrifugal force, hydrodynamic volume, velocity gradient, momentum transfer, viscosity, intrinsic viscosity, electrophoretic mobility (μ_e), SDS-PAGE (Sodium Dodecyl Sulfate PolyAcryl amode Gel Electrophoresis), isoelectroc focusing technique, isoelectric point (pI)

6-1 Diffusional Motion

Diffusion is random spreading motion of particles from the higher concentration region to the lower and it is most common transportational phenomena observed in biological systems. Nowadays, advanced microscopic techniques have made it possible to resolve the location of a single molecule (such as a protein) and a motion of each individual molecule can be traced. Therefore, detailed interactions between particles and their surroundings can be studied. We treat the diffusion distance, <d>, as a length between initial and final time, while it does not corresponds to an entire path length of diffusing. However, a diffusion distance gives a measure of the mobility of the substance. **(Fig. 6-1)** In order to describe the relationship between the diffusion distance and diffusional ability, we adopt **Fick's law**. In the Fick's law the flux (J) is described as the derivative of the concentration(C) as a function of the location. For the flux conducts one dimensional flow (J_x), the Fick's law states:

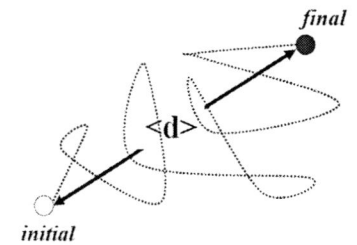

Fig. 6-1 Diffusion distance

$$J_x = -D \left(\frac{dc}{dx} \right) \quad \text{(Eqn. 6-1)}$$

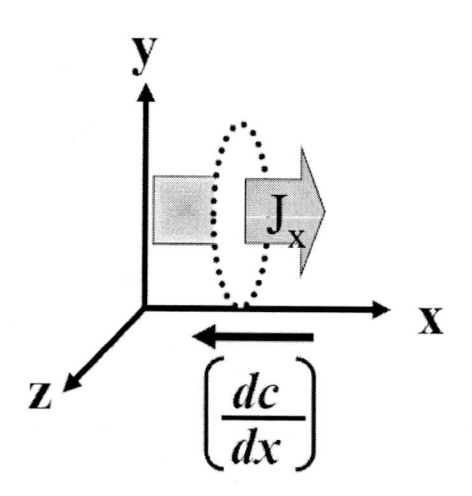

Fig. 6-2 The direction of flux and concentration gradient.

Fig. 6-3 The change in concentration gradient.

Here, D is called as diffusion coefficient in the unit of [cm^2/s]. The flux J_x has the unit of [mol/cm^2 s] and concentration (c) is often described in the unit of [mol/cm^3] for this case. The concentration gradient caused in the direction of x-axis is the negative direction of the flow (J_x). This means that a flux flows into the direction to decrease the difference in the concentrations. This explains that the flux flows into the lower concentration region. At the end (or equilibrium), the concentration gradient diminishes as the flux is properly distributed by following the Fick's law.**(Fig. 6-3)**

😟 MCM Most Common Mistake (26) –Flow to which direction?

Don't you think the **Fig. 6-2** is a bit confusing? The direction of flux and the direction of concentration gradience is facing different direction. According to the Fick's first law, the sign (plus or minus) of flux (of x-direction, J_x) and the sign $\left(\frac{dc}{dx}\right)$ of concentration gradient (on x direction) is opposite. I usually think that flux is the direction when you place a ball on the potential of concentration gradience. For example, if you place a ball on the top of the **Fig. 6-3(a)**, then ball will roll down to slope. The direction to which a ball moves corresponds to the direction of the flow. If you think the ball represents the components of the concentration, the ball stop moving when enough amount shifted to the other side and making a flat surface (no concentration gradience) as shown in **Fig. 6-3'b**, resulting no movement in the boll (no flow).

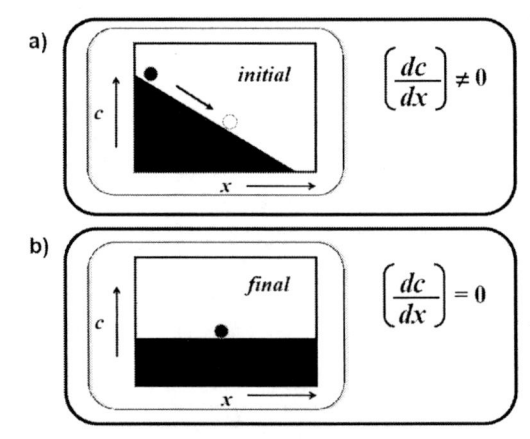

Fig. 6-3' The direction of change in concentration gradient and the flux using an imaginary ball.

The one dimensional mean square displacement $\langle x^2 \rangle$ is defined as

$$\langle x^2 \rangle = 2Dt \qquad \text{(Eqn. 6-2)}$$

Here, x is displacement [cm], t is time [sec], and D is a diffusion coefficient [cm^2/sec]. (The bracket, <>, indicates the average ensemble of the value given inside.) The formula shown in (**Eqn. 6-2**) does not indicate an entire path even a particle is allowed to have two dimensional degrees of freedom (i.e., x-y plane), but shows only the final displacement from the initial location. The mean square displacement provides an index of mobility of the substance at a given time. While it is not described in the formula, the more mobile species may be suspected to possess smaller mass than the particle with lower mobility under the same surrounding environment. (**Fig. 6-4**)

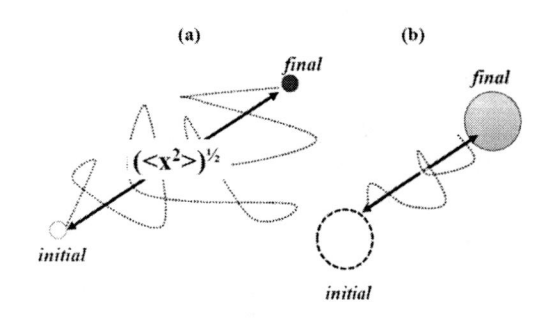

Fig. 6-4 The difference in mean square displacement.

Chapter 6 Molecular Motion and Transport Properties

> **EXERCISE 6-1**
> If the diffusion coefficient of myoglobin (Mb) is 11.3×10^{-7} [cm^2/sec].
> What is $\{<x^2>\}^{1/2}$ achieved by diffusion within 5 [μ sec].

> **ANSWER**
> $\langle x^2 \rangle = 2Dt$ (**Eqn. 6-2**)
> ❶ $\langle x^2 \rangle = 2 \times 11.3 \times 10^{-7}$ [cm^2 sec^{-1}] $\times 5 \times 10^{-6}$ [sec]
> ❷ $= 1.13 \times 10^{-11}$ [cm^2]
> ❸ $\{<x^2>\}^{1/2} = 3.36 \times 10^{-6}$ [cm]
> $= 3.36 \times 10^{-8}$ m = 33 [nm]
>
> ❶ Unit is length squared.
> ❷ Don't forget to take a root mean square.
> ❸ 1 [cm] = 10^{-2} [m] 1 [nm] = 10^{-9} [m]

Using the same idea on the one dimensional diffusional distance, we can develop the mean square displacement, <d^2>, for two (x, y) and three (x, y, z) dimensional cases.

$$\langle d^2 \rangle = \langle x^2 \rangle + \langle y^2 \rangle = 4Dt \qquad \text{(Eqn. 6-3)}$$

$$\langle d^2 \rangle = \langle x^2 \rangle + \langle y^2 \rangle + \langle z^2 \rangle = 8Dt \qquad \text{(Eqn. 6-4)}$$

6-2 Diffusion Coefficient and Molecular Parameters

You may wonder if it is possible to estimate the size (or shape) of a molecule from its mobility represented in the diffusion coefficient, D. We will view that issue in this section. Since diffusional coefficient is a reflection of the mobility, it is natural to imagine that the size of the substance should be reflected on the mobility. There are two important relationships (**Stokes-Einstein equation**) which provide the molecular view in diffusion coefficient.

Stokes-Einstein equation

$$D = {k_B T}/{f} \qquad \text{(Eqn. 6-5)}$$

Stokes' law:
$$f = 6\pi\eta r \qquad \text{(Eqn. 6-6)}$$

Here, f is the frictional coefficient [g /sec], η is viscosity coefficient [P, poise] = [g sec^{-1} cm^{-1}], k_B is a Boltzmann constant ($k_B = 1.3807 \times 10^{-23}$ [J/K]), and r is the radius of the molecule approximated to be a sphere. The viscosity coefficient, η, is defined as a value of a medium but not a value of a substance diffuses. (**Fig. 6-5**). Due to the unit used for viscosity, the unit of the radius of a spherical molecule is in [cm]. While the shape of molecule is approximated or limited to a spherical shape, the description in (**Eqn.6-6**) importantly connect a mobile character of molecule with its size. (Please recall that kinetic theory of gas assumed that a particle is a very small point.) By combining

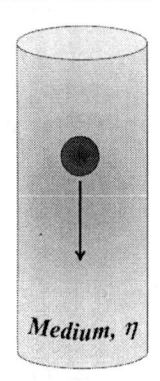

Fig. 6-5 A sketch of viscosity of medium

Chapter 6 Molecular Motion and Transport Properties

the Stoke's and Einstein's law, another useful relationship is derived. The frictional coefficient, f, in (**Eqn. 6-6**) is inserted into f in (**Eqn. 6-5**)

$$D = \frac{k_B T}{6\pi\eta r} \qquad \text{(Eqn. 6-7)}$$

Since diffusion coefficient, D, is inversely proportional to a frictional coefficient, f, and frictional coefficient is proportional to radius, r, the diffusion coefficient decreases as the radius increases. By solving for r,

$$r = \frac{k_B T}{6\pi\eta D} \qquad \text{(Eqn. 6-8)}$$

Using (**Eqn. 6-7**), the radius of spherical molecule is estimated with viscosity of medium, η, and diffusion coefficient of a molecule, D.

EXERCISE 6-2
The diffusion coefficient of a human immunoglobin G (IgG) (mw=156,000) at 20 [°C] in a dilute aqueous buffer is 4.0×10^{-7} [cm^2/sec]. Calculate the friction coefficient of IgG.

ANSWER
From Einstein's law,
$$D = \frac{k_B T}{f} \qquad \text{(Eqn. 6-5)}$$
Thus,

❶ $f = \dfrac{1.3807 \times 10^{-16} [g\, cm^2 s^{-2} K^{-1}] \times 293[K]}{4.0 \times 10^{-7} [cm^2 s^{-1}]}$

❷ $= 1.01 \times 10^{-7} [g/sec]$

❶ Temperature in Kelvins unit
❷ Unit used here is [g/sec]

EXERCISE 6-3
The diffusion constant of the β-lactalbumin (mw=14,000) was measured to be 14.25×10^{-7} [cm^2/sec] at pH 7 and 40 [°C]. The viscosity of the solvent was 0.0101 [P]. Estimate the diameter of this protein, assuming that it is spherical in shape.

ANSWER
$$r = \frac{k_B T}{6\pi\eta D} \qquad \text{(Eqn. 6-7)}$$

❶ $k = 1.3807 \times 10^{-23}$ [J/K] = 1.3807×10^{-16} [erg/K]
❷ T = 313 [K]

Chapter 6 Molecular Motion and Transport Properties

❸ η = 0.0101 [P]

❹ D = 14.25 × 10⁻⁷ [cm²/sec]

Using the (**Eqn. 6-7**),

❺ $$r = \frac{1.3807 \times 10^{-16}[erg/K] \times 313\,[K]}{6\pi \times 0.0101[g cm^{-1} sec^{-1}] \times 14.25 \times 10^{-7}[cm^2 sec^{-1}]}$$

$$= \frac{1.3807 \times 10^{-16}[g cm^2 sec^{-2} K^{-1}] \times 313\,[K]}{6\pi \times 0.0101[g cm^{-1} sec^{-1}] \times 14.25 \times 10^{-7}[cm^2 sec^{-1}]}$$

$$= \frac{4.32159 \times 10^{-14}[g cm^2 sec^{-2}]}{2.7115 \times 10^{-7}[g cm^2 sec^{-2}]}$$

❻ = 1.5938×10⁻⁷ [cm] = 15.938 [Å]

❼ Thus, d = 31.9 [Å]

❶	The cgs version of [J] is [erg]. You will see why we want to do this later. [J] = [kg m² sec⁻²]. and [erg]=[g cm² sec⁻²]
❷	Temperature is in Kelvins unit [K].
❸	Poise = [g cm⁻¹ sec⁻¹]
❹	Use cgs unit system for D as well.
❺	In this calculation, we use cgs unit system [cm] or [g] instead of [m] or [kg].
❻	1 [Å]= 10⁻⁸ [cm]
❼	We are assuming this protein as a spherical shape and diameter (d) = 2 ×radius (r)

MCM Most Common Mistake (27) –Using viscosity? A piece of cake?
In the introduction of Stoke's law (**Eqn. 6-6**), viscosity coefficient, η, is introduced as the value of medium. I want you to take a look at the **Fig. 6-5** one more time and notice that the value of viscosity is indicating that of a medium not a substance flowing. For example, in **Exercise 6-3**, this is the problem to solve the radius of a protein using (**Eqn. 6-8**). However, the viscosity value given in this problem is the value of the solvent not a protein.

6-3 Shape Factor

A big improvement from the kinetic theory to the Einstein-Stoke's law is the involvement of the size factor (r, radius of the sphere). Because of that, we are able to see the size factor and the relationship to the mobility of the substance. It is natural, however, that all the substance cannot be approximated as spherical shape. The frictional coefficient between spherical and oval shapes should cause a drastic effect in the mobility. As a shape deviates from a spherical shape, the frictional coefficient is estimated to increase. Let's see how shape of molecule affect the diffusional motion in this section.

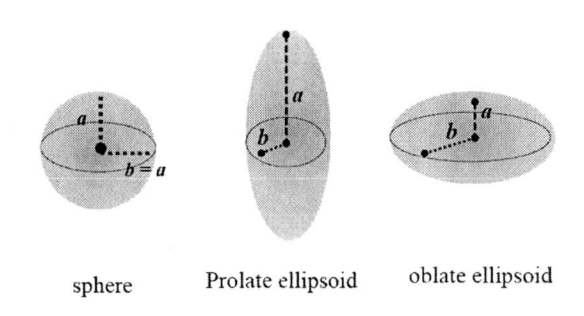

Fig. 6-6 A sphere and prolate/oblate

Table 6-1 Shape factor for frictional coefficient.

	Prolate Ellipsoid			Oblate Ellipsoid		
a/b	1	2	10	1	0.5	0.1
f/f_o	1	1.044	1.543	1	1.042	1.458

For limited cases of shape (spherical, prolate ellipsoid, and oblate ellipsoid) the frictional coefficient against the f_o (frictional coefficient for a sphere), f/f_o as a function a/b Is listed in **Table 6-1**, where a is an equatorial radius and b is a polar radius. A spherical shape is represented at a/b = 1 and $f = f_o$. The prolate shape is like a cigar shape (**Fig.6-6**) and the frictional coefficient is increased as a/b increases. The oblate shape is a pizza-like shape and frictional coefficient increases as a/b decreases. Note that you cannot correctly oblate or prolate shape backwards from f/f_o. For example, f/f_o is about 1.5 for prolate when a/b=10 and oblate when a/b=0.1. Thus, it is at least necessary to know the rough molecular shape where it is prolate or oblate. Based on the frictional

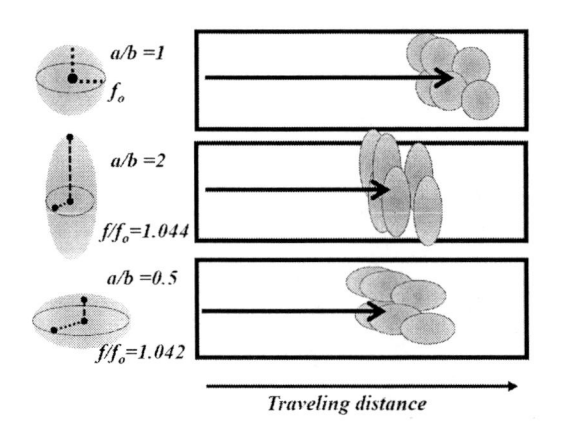

Fig. 6-7 Traveling distance of different shaped molecule.

coefficient estimated from **Table 6-1**, the frictional coefficient of prolate or oblate are larger than that of a sphere. For example, if you let three different shaped molecule (sphere, prolate ellipsoid (a/b = 2), and oblate ellipsoid (a/b = 0.5))to diffuse, you should observe that a sphere shape molecule travel the longest distance, while prolate and oblate ellipsoids equally travel less (**Fig. 6-7**)

Chapter 6 Molecular Motion and Transport Properties

EXERCISE 6-4
The diffusion coefficient of a human immunoglobin G (IgG) (m.w. = 156,000[g/mol]) at 20 [°C] in a dilute aqueous buffer is 4.0×10^{-7} [cm^2/sec]. This protein was found to have a shape of prolate ellipsoid. Estimate the dimensions (a and b) of a prolate ellipsoid of IgG. Assume that unhydrated IgG has a sphere shape, and its radius is 3.629 [nm]. Viscosity for a dilute aqueous buffer at 20 [°C] is 1.00×10^{-2} [g sec^{-1} cm^{-1}]. Assume that they have the same volume.

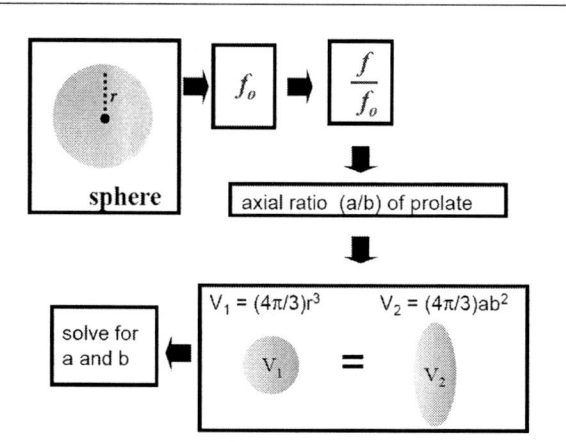

Fig. 6-8 A schematic diagram of approach for Exercise 6-4.

ANSWER
This problem is a bit complicated and needs an organization in the approach. So please use **Fig. 6-8** for a schematic approach.

From Stokes law,

$$f = 6\pi\eta r \quad \text{(Eqn. 6-6)}$$

❶ For sphere
$f_o = 6\pi \times 0.01$ [g cm^{-1} sec^{-1}] $\times 3.629 \times 10^{-7}$ [cm]
$= 6.84 \times 10^{-8}$ [g/sec]

❷ From Einstein's law,

$$D = k_B T / f \quad \text{(Eqn. 6-5)}$$

$D = 4.0 \times 10^{-7}$ [cm^2/sec]

❸ $T = 273 + 20 = 293$ [K]

❹ $k_B = 1.3807 \times 10^{-23}$ [J/K] $= 1.3807 \times 10^{-16}$ [erg/K]

❷ $f = k_B T / D \quad \text{(Eqn. 6-5)}$
$= 1.3807 \times 10^{-16}$ [erg·K^{-1}](293 [K])/ 4.0×10^{-7} [cm^2/sec]
$= 1.01 \times 10^{-7}$ [g/sec]

$f/f_o = 1.01 \times 10^{-7}$ [g/sec] / 6.84×10^{-8} [g/sec] $= 1.48$

❺ According to **Table 6-1**, when f/f_o is around 1.48 axial ratio of prolate, a/b, is 10.

❻ The Volume is $(4\pi/3)r^3 = 2.0 \times 10^{-19}$ [cm^3]

Since $a = 10 \times b$

❼ $(4\pi/3)ab^2 = (4\pi/3)10b^3 = 2.0 \times 10^{-19}$ [cm^3]

❽ $b = 1.68 \times 10^{-7}$ [cm] $= 1.68 \times 10^{-9}$ [m] $= 1.68$ [nm] $= 16.8$ [Å]

❾ $a = 10 \times b = 16.8$ [nm] $= 168$ [Å]

❶ This is a frictional coefficient for a sphere, f_o, and Poise = [g cm^{-1} sec^{-1}]

❷ Next, this is a frictional coefficient for non-sphere or any shape, f.

❸	Temperature is in Kelvins unit [K].
❹	The cgs version of [J] is [erg]. In order to match with other parameter's unit, You may want to use cgs unit system.([cm] or [g] instead of [m] or [kg].) [J] = [kg m²sec⁻²]. and [erg]=[g cm² sec⁻²]
❺	Choose the value from prolate (not from oblate).
❻	This expression is using radius (r), not diameter (d).V= (π/ 6)d³
❼	Don't forget to cube [cm].
❽	1 [Å]= 10⁻⁸ [cm]= 10⁻¹⁰ [m]
❾	a = 10×b and confirm it has a prolate shape.

MCM **Most Common Mistake (28)-"Can I use Stokes' law any time anywhere for anything?"**

No, you can't. (Well, actually, you can use it as you want. But the calculation may not make sense for some cases.) The Stokes' law given in (**Eqn. 6-6**), is appropriate for spherical molecule. Therefore, It may be written as

$$f_o = 6\pi\eta r_o$$

By emphasizing that f_o Is a frictional coefficient of a sphere and r_o is the radius of a sphere. Therefore, in **EXERCISE 6-4**, the frictional coefficient for a prolate ellipsoid should not be calculated from Stokes' law but by Stokes-Einstein equation.

$$D = {k_B T}/{f} \qquad \text{(Eqn. 6-5)}$$

The Stokes-Einstein equation is not limited for a spherical molecule.

6-4.Sedimentation

The sedimentation process utilizes the force attributed from highly spinning stage to extract (or separate) especially macromolecules. If the spinning stage has a rotation frequency of ν [1/sec], an **angular velocity (ω)** is given as

$$\omega = 2\pi\nu \qquad \text{(Eqn. 6-9)}$$

[Example] For example, under the frequency of the rotation of a stage is 24,630 rpm (revolutions per minute), ω is given as:

$$\omega = \{2\pi \times 24{,}630 / 60\} \text{ [sec}^{-1}]$$

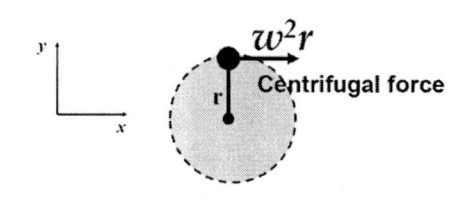

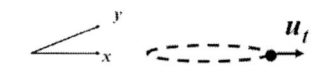

Fig. 6-9 Centrifugal force and terminal velocity.

As a substance is placed at the x from the center of a rotating stage, the "centrifugal acceleration force" works on the material as

$$F_c = \omega^2 r \qquad \text{(Eqn. 6-10)}$$

Please note the direction of arrow shown in (**Fig. 6-9**) that the direction of the centrifugal force is perpendicular to the direction center of the circle and the substance. The velocity achieved in a direction of this centrifugal force is called a terminal velocity (u_t [cm/sec]). (**Fig. 6-9**)

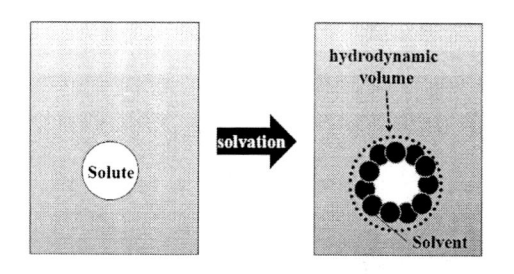

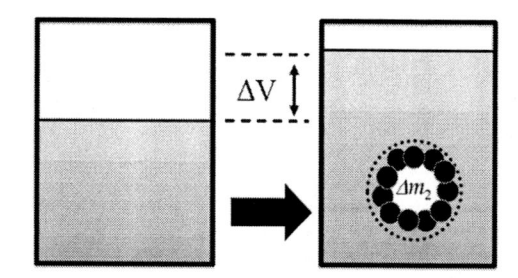

Fig. 6-10 Solvation and hydrodynamic volume

Fig. 6-11 The hydrodynamic volume, $\bar{v}_2$, and mass of solute.

For most of the cases, solute may not exist by itself alone but solvated with water molecules causing more unit volume. (**Fig. 6-11**) This increased volume is called as a hydrodynamic volume, $\bar{v}_2$. This is expressed by

$$\bar{v}_2 = \left(\partial V / \partial m_2\right)_{T,P,w_1} = \Delta V / \Delta m_2 \qquad \text{(Eqn. 6-11)}$$

Here, the mass of solute is Δm_2, and the increase of volume is ΔV. (**Fig. 6-11**) Thus, this hydrodynamic volume, $\bar{v}_2$, can be regarded as a partial specific volume with unit of [cm³/g]. While you may think the volume change due to solvation is negligible, the effect of salvation is significant as molecular mass (of protein or DNA/RNA) becomes relatively high. There is a strong similarity between a particle under a centrifugal force field and a particle under the gravitational force field. Under a centrifugal field, terminal velocity (u_t [cm/sec]) of a particle with mass (m [g]) in a direction of force is (**Fig. 6-9**)

$$u_t = \left(m(1 - \bar{v}_2 \rho)/f\right) \omega^2 r \qquad \text{(Eqn. 6-12)}$$

Here, ρ is density of a substance [g/cm³]. Under this terminal velocity, the sedimentation coefficient (σ) is defined as a ratio between the terminal velocity and centrifugal force as

$$\sigma = u_t / \omega^2 r = m(1 - \bar{v}_2 \rho)/f \qquad \text{(Eqn. 6-13)}$$

Here, ρ [g/cm³] is a density of medium and f [g/sec] is frictional coefficient. The sedimentation coefficient has the unit of Svedberg; [S] and 1 [S] = 10^{-13} [sec].

😟 Most Common Mistake (29) - "Is this [S] or [s] ?":

The unit for the sedimentation coefficient is [S], Svedberg, can be mistaken as [s] or [sec]. The conversion factor is 1 [S] = 10^{-13} [sec]. Thus, choice of using the Svedberg unit is very unfortunate and confusing case. (No offense to Dr. Svedberg though....)In this textbook, an expression for "second" is attempted to use [sec] instead of [s] in order to distinguish from [S]; Svedberg. More confusingly, sedimentation coefficient is abbreviated as "s". Don't confuse it as "second".

As the sample with sedimentation coefficient σ is placed in a rotating container, the location of this substance will shift from the center to the outside because of an applied centrifugal force. Due to a deviation of the location of the substance, the centrifugal force applied to the sample becomes heterogeneous and the final location appears as a band not a point.(**Fig. 6-12**) If the edge of the solvent-solution boundary is located at r from the rotational axis,

$$\sigma = \left(\frac{2.303}{\omega^2}\right)\left(\frac{d\ log r_{1/2}}{dt}\right) \quad \text{(Eqn. 6-14)}$$

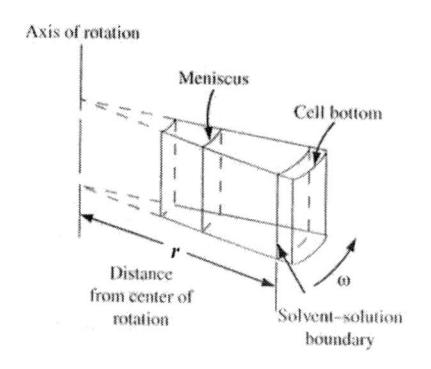

Fig. **6-12** Transformation from a free fall particle into a particle placed under the centrifugal force.

Chapter 6 Molecular Motion and Transport Properties

EXERCISE 6-5
The sedimentation coefficient of a certain DNA in 1M NaCl at 20 [°C] was measured by boundary sedimentation at 24,630 [rpm]. The plot of x (distance of boundary from center of rotation, cm) vs. time (min) showed a slope of 3.32×10^{-4} [min^{-1}]. Calculate the sedimentation coefficient, σ.

ANSWER

$$\sigma = \left(2.303/\omega^2\right)\left(d\,lnr_{1/2}/dt\right) \quad \text{(Eqn. 6-14)}$$

❶ slope = 3.32×10^{-4} [min^{-1}]

❷ = 5.54×10^{-6} [sec^{-1}]

$$\sigma = \frac{2.303}{\omega^2}\frac{d\,\log r}{dt} = \frac{2.303}{\omega^2} \times 5.54 \times 10^{-6}[sec^{-1}]$$

❸ ω = {24,630 × 2π / 60 }[sec^{-1}]

ω² = 6.65×10^{6} [sec^{-2}]

σ = 2.303 × 5.54 × 10^{-6} / 6.65 × 10^{6}

❹ = 1.96×10^{-12} [sec]

= 19.6 [S]

---

❶ The slope corresponds to $\left(d\,lnr_{1/2}/dt\right)$

❷ I think you can do this, but just in case! [min^{-1}]= (1/60) [sec^{-1}]

❸ ω = 2π ν, Here, frequency ν is in the unit of [rpm=revolution per minute]

❹ 1 [S] = 10^{-13} [sec].

Here, $r_{½}$ is the midpoint of boundary and ω is an angular velocity of rotation of the stage. If ln $r_{½}$ is plotted as a function of time (t), it should show a linear line with a slope of the (d ln $r_{1/2}$/dt) **(Fig. 6-13)** The standard condition of the sedimentation coefficient s defined at 20 °C in water as,

$$\sigma_{20,w} = \sigma\left(\eta/\eta_{20,w}\right)\left[(1-\bar{v}_2\rho)_{20,w}/(1-\bar{v}_2\rho)\right]$$

(Eqn. 6-15)

Here, η is viscosity of the sample and $\eta_{20,w}$ is the viscosity at 20 °C in water. The hydrodynamic volume is given by $\bar{v}_2$ and density of the substance is given by ρ.

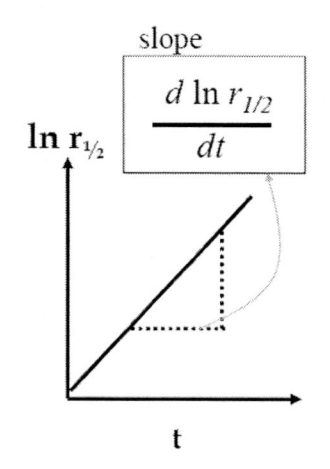

Fig. 6-13 A graph to obtain the sedimentation coefficient.

Chapter 6 Molecular Motion and Transport Properties

EXERCISE 6-6
The σ of the DNA in a given solution 1 [M] NaCl is σ=19.2 [S]. The partial specific volume of the sodium salt of DNA is 0.556 cm^{-3}/g. The viscosity and density of 1 M NaCl and the viscosity of water are 1.104 [cP], 1.04 g cm^{-3}, and 1.005 [cP], respectively. Calculate $\sigma_{20,w}$ for the DNA.

ANSWER

Solution 20 [°C]

η=1.104 [cP], ρ=1.04 [g/cm^3], σ=19.2 [S]

Water 20 [°C]

η=1.005 [cP], ρ=0.998 [g/cm^3], $\bar{v}_2$=0.556 [cm^3/g]

$$\sigma_{20,w} = \sigma \frac{\eta}{\eta_{20,w}} \frac{(1-\bar{v}_2\rho)_{20,w}}{(1-\bar{v}_2\rho)} \qquad \text{(Eqn. 6-15)}$$

$$\sigma_{20,w} = (19.2\ [S]) \frac{(1.104\ [cP])(1-0.556[\ cm^3/g]\times 0.998[g/cm^3])}{(1.005\ [cP])(1-0.556\ [cm^3]/g\times 1.04[g/cm^3])}$$

$$= (19.2)(1.098)(1.055)[S]$$

$$= 22.3\ [S]$$

The subscript of $\sigma_{20,w}$ indicates that temperature is at 20 [°C].

We will take the ratio of two viscosities, so you can keep the unit as it is. (You do not have to convert Poise =[g cm^{-1} sec^{-1}]. [cP] =10^{-2} [P])

1 [S] = 10^{-13} [sec]

As it has been demonstrated in colligative properties (boiling point elevation, freezing point depression, and osmotic pressure), the unknown sample's molar mass can be determined from the measured values. The sedimentation coefficient can be also used to obtain molar mass of unknown sample.

$$M = RT\sigma / [D(1-\bar{v}_2\rho)] \qquad \text{(Eqn. 6-16)}$$

Here, M is the molar mass [g/mol] and D is diffusion coefficient [cm^2/s].

Chapter 6 Molecular Motion and Transport Properties

EXERCISE 6-7
Calculate the molecular weight of human serum albumin using the following data.

$\sigma_{20,w}$ = 4.6 [S]
$D_{20,w}$ = 6.1 × 10^{-7} [cm²/sec]
$[\eta]$ = 4.2 [cm³/g]
$\bar{v}_2$ = 0.733 [cm³/g]
ρ = 0.998 [g/cm³]

ANSWER

$$M = \frac{RT\sigma}{[D(1-\bar{v}_2\rho)]} \quad \text{(Eqn. 6-16)}$$

❶ $\sigma_{20,w}$ = 4.6 [S] = 4.6 × 10^{-13} [sec]
  $D_{20,w}$ = 6.1 × 10^{-7} [cm²/sec]
  $\bar{v}_2$ = 0.733 [cm³/g]
  ρ = 0.998 [g/cm³]
❷ R = 8.3145 × 10^7 [erg K^{-1} mol^{-1}]
❸ T = 20 [°C] = 293.15 [K]

$$M = \frac{8.3145 \times 10^7 [ergK^{-1}mol^{-1}] \times 293.15[K] \times 4.6 \times 10^{-13}[sec]}{6.1 \times 10^{-7}[cm^2 sec^{-1}] \times (1 - 0.733[cm^3 g^{-1}]) \times 0.998[g\, cm^{-3}]}$$
$$= 68,980 \text{ [g/mol]}$$

❶ 1 [S] = 10^{-13} [sec]
❷ R = 8.3145 [J K^{-1} mol^{-1}] = 8.3145 × 10^7 [erg K^{-1} mol^{-1}] 1[J] = 10^7 [erg] = [g cm² s^{-2}]
We are using [erg] in order to match with other parameters using cgs unit system.
❸ The subscript of $\sigma_{20,w}$ indicates that temperature is at 20 °C. temperature should be in Kelvins unit.

MCM Most Common Mistake (30) – Why I cannot obtain correct molar mass from sedimentation coefficient?"

For some reasons, correct molar mass is not calculated in the **EXERCISE 6-6**. If you are getting extremely small (or large values), you may want to think about the following possibilities. First, take a look at is the unit [erg], and it has the relationship of [erg]= [g cm² sec^{-2}]. For example, gas constant (R) commonly uses MKS unit system i.e., [J =kg m² sec^{-2}], and it is not in the same unit system (cgs system) as [erg]. You need to either convert gas constant to cgs system or energy unit to MKS system. Then, be careful with the units for gas constant, R 8.314472[Jmol^{-1} K^{-1}], Svedberg ([S] or 10^{-13}[sec]), and temperature [K].

If the location of the substance is the result of applied centrifugal force, the amount (distribution) of substance can be related with a particular location of corresponding substance. If the concentration of the substance 1 and 2 are given by C_1 and C_2, respectively, the location of those substances X_1 and X_2 are related as

$$\ln\left(C_1/C_2\right) = M(1-\bar{v}_2\rho)\omega^2(r_2^2 - r_1^2)/2RT$$

(Eqn. 6-17)

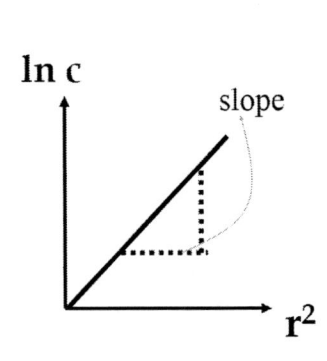

Fig. 6-14 Molar mass and sedimentation coefficient

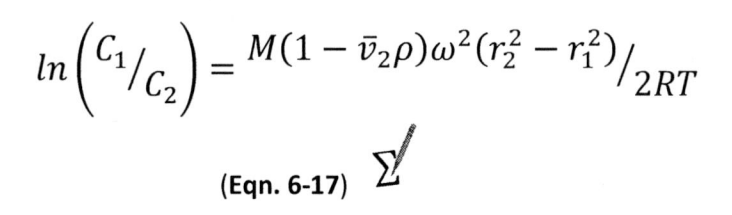

If the natural log of the concentration is plotted against the square of location, r^2, the slope [cm^{-2}] of this linear graph is

$$slope = M(1-\bar{v}_2\rho)\omega^2/2RT \qquad \text{(Eqn. 6-18)}$$

Therefore, as shown in (**Fig.6-14**) you should be able to obtain molar mass, M, by

$$M = (slope) \times 2RT/(1-\bar{v}_2\rho)\omega^2 \qquad \text{(Eqn. 6-19)}$$

6-5. Viscosity

The viscosity is provided as a measure of fluid's resistance to flow. In general, the higher intermolecular forces, the higher the viscosities they have. For example, the hydrogen bonding contributes significantly to the higher viscosity value. By adopting a concept of the flow of flux, J, the viscosity is expressed as

$$J = -\eta\left(du_x/dy\right) \qquad \text{(Eqn. 6-20)}$$

Here, u_x [cm/s] is velocity in x direction and J is the amount of flux of momentum transfer per unit time and area [Poise/s]. Some cares are necessary in the direction implied in (**Eqn. 6-20**).

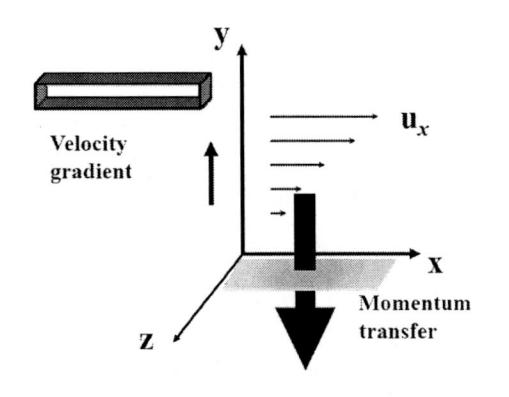

Fig. 6-15 Velocity gradient and momentum transfer in a flux.

The direction of the flux flow is in the direction of increase in x-axis direction. As the flux flowed, the momentum is transferred to the surrounding substances and creates different amount of velocities depending upon the location creating the distribution of the velocities and the gradience of the velocities. The direction of momentum transfer corresponds to the direction of decrease in y-axis (**Fig. 6-15**) You may think as the velocity change is transferred as the momentum transfer, and it is represented as the differential, $\frac{du_x}{dy}$, in the (**Eqn. 6-20**). The negative sign means that the direction of the momentum transfer is an opposite direction of the velocity gradience. Thus, the flux direction is opposite to that of momentum transfer. The momentum transfer takes place in any positions in z-axis in the **Fig. 6-15**, a group of momentum transfer (vectors) can be aligned along z axis and forming a plane (xz plane). Using the previous result on the terminal velocity (u_t [cm sec^{-1}]) observed in sedimentation, the viscosity of medium under the gravitational field can be given as

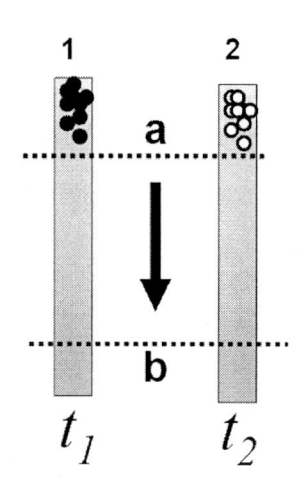

$$\eta = \left(mg(1-\bar{v_2}\rho)\big/6\pi r u_t\right) \quad \text{(Eqn. 6-21)}$$

The unit P(poise) is [g· cm^{-1} s^{-1}] and η [Pa · sec] =[kg m^{-1}sec^{-1}] is viscosity coefficient of fluid, $\bar{v}_2$ [cm^3 g^{-1}] is partial volume of the macromolecule, ρ [g cm^{-3}] is density of medium, m[g] is mass of falling particle, g is standard gravity = 980.66 [cm sec^{-2}], and r is radius of a falling sphere particle in [cm]. Experimentally, it is useful to compare the speed of the substance to reach a unit length (a → b) and measure the time required. For example, if two substances (1 and 2) with densityρ_1 and ρ_2 are placed in the container and the time for reaching from point a to point b is measured **(Fig. 6-16)**, the time required for each substance (t_1 and t_2) are related with

$$\eta_2/\eta_1 = (1-\bar{v}\rho_2)\big/(1-\bar{v}\rho_1) = \rho_2 t_2 / \rho_1 t_1 \quad \text{(Eqn. 6-22)}$$

Fig. 6-16 Flux and viscosity

The relationship between viscosities of solutions and solvent can be described using the specific viscosity, η_{sp} [dimensionless]

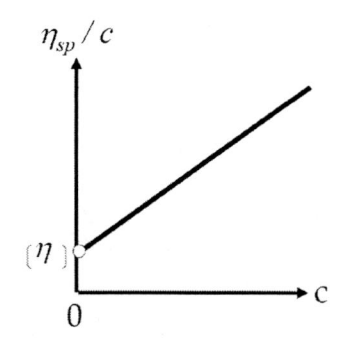

$$\eta_{sp} = (\eta' - \eta)/\eta \quad \text{(Eqn. 6-23)}$$

Here, η' is viscosity of the solution and η is viscosity of the solvent. In order to measure a solute's contribution to the viscosity of a solution, η, the value of specific viscosity (η_{sp}) divided by the concentration of the solution is used

$$[\eta] \equiv \lim_{c \to 0} \eta_{sp}/c \quad \text{(Eqn. 6-24)}$$

Fig. 6-17 Intrinsic viscosity

[η] is called as intrinsic or inherent Viscosity, and the graphical method to obtain [η] is shown in (**Fig. 6-17**). The intrinsic viscosity is also seen with respect to a molecular physical property. By using specific volume of solvent (v_1^o [cm^3 g^{-1}]) and partial volume of the macromolecule, $\bar{v}_2$ [cm^3 g^{-1}].

$$[\eta] = v(\bar{v}_2 + \delta_1 v_1^o) \quad \text{(Eqn. 6-25)}$$

Here, v is called as a shape factor (usually v = 2.5 for a sphere) and δ_1 is hydration factor, which is grams of solvent molecules hydrodynamically associated with each gram of macromolecules . If it is not significantly hydrated $\delta_1 \approx 0$ is a good approximation. For a dilute aqueous solution, v_1^o is 1.0 [cm^3 g^{-1}].

EXERCISE 6-8

A small spherical virus has a molecular weight of 1.25×10^6 [g/mol] and a diameter of 100 [Å]; it is not significantly hydrated. Calculate the intrinsic viscosity in units of [cm^3/g] of an aqueous solution of this virus.

ANSWER

$$[\eta] = \nu(\bar{v}_2 + \delta_1 v_1^o) \qquad \text{(Eqn. 6-25)}$$

$\delta_1 \approx 0$

Thus,

$$[\eta] = \nu(\bar{v}_2 + \delta_1 v_1^o) \approx \nu \bar{v}_2$$

ν is shape factor and δ_1 is hydration factor. v_1^o is specific volume of solvent [cm^3/g].

$$\bar{v}_2 = V/m$$

$$V = (4\pi/3)(50 \times 10^{-8} [cm])^3$$

$$m = \frac{1.25 \times 10^6 [g\ mol^{-1}]}{(6.023 \times 10^{23} [mol^{-1}])}$$

$$[\eta] = \frac{(2.5)(4\pi/3)(50 \times 10^{-8} [cm])^3 (6.023 \times 10^{23} [mol^{-1}])}{1.25 \times 10^6 [g\ mol^{-1}]}$$

= 0.63 [cm^3 g^{-1}]

V is volume of this spherical virus $(4/3)\pi r^3$ (r:radius).
m is the mass of one particle
diameter = 100 [Å]; → radius = 50 [Å];

6-6 Electrophoresis

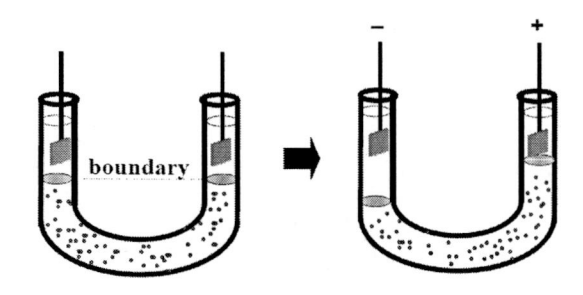

Fig. 6-18. Change in the height of boundary containing negatively charged protein.

The electrophoresis is very common and powerful method to separate macromolecules (proteins or DNA) by molecular weight. This is an electro-kinetic phenomenon where a dispersed particle is moved under a spatially uniform electric field due to the presence of a charged interface between the particle surface and the surrounding fluid. An external electric field exerts an electrostatic Coulomb force an electric surface charge over the dispersed particles' surface.

Imagine, the protein (or DNA) contained solution placed in a U-tube and the electrode with opposite charge cathode and anode are placed at the top of the each end of the tube. If the significant amount of field is applied, the surface of the solution should be biased accordingly. If the charged species in the solution is positive the solution surface at the negative side should rise, and vice versa. **(Fig. 6-18)** Under a moderate electric field strength E [V cm^{-1}], the velocity of a dispersed charged particle u [cm s^{-1}] is proportional to the applied field.

$$u \propto kE$$

Chapter 6 Molecular Motion and Transport Properties

The constant k is called as an electrophoretic mobility μ_e [cm^{2}V^{-1}s^{-1}] and is defined as

$$\mu_e = u/E \qquad \text{(Eqn. 6-26)}$$

This electrophoretic mobility μ_e [cm^{2}V^{-1}s^{-1}] can be related with charged particle size by using Stokes law as

$$\mu_e = Ze/6\pi\eta r \qquad \text{(Eqn. 6-27)}$$

The electrophoretic mobility is considered to be a value of a function of length of polypeptide chain or molecular weight. Therefore, proteins are separated according to their electrophoretic mobility (μ_e) as shown in (**Eqn. 6-26**), and it also means that they are separated by size (molecular weight) as indicated in (**Eqn. 6-27**). Experimentally, SDS-PAGE(Sodium Dodecyl Sulfate - PolyAcrylamide Gel Electrophoresis) is very popularly used to separate proteins. Due to difference in binding between SDS and species with charge per unit mass cause a separation among species with different mass.(**Fig. 6-19**)

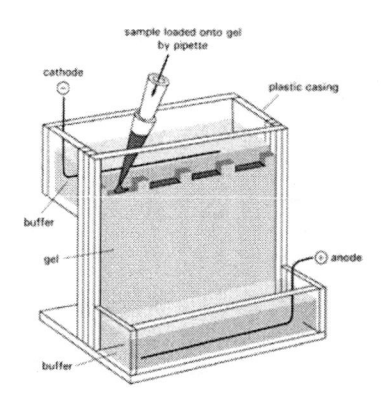

Fig. 6-19 SDS-PAGE

MCM **Most Common Mistake (31) – Mobility is proportional field strength? Oh, No. It is not!**
Please take a look at the (**Eqn. 6-26**). The electrophoretic mobility is inversely proportional to the field strength. This is very confusing isn't it? You may think that things may move more as the field acted from outside gets stronger. However, electrophoretic mobility is defined as "How much speed can be produced per field". So it may make more sense if you use the (**Eqn. 6-26**) as
$$u = \mu_e E \qquad \text{(Eqn. 6-26)'}$$
The speed of the particle is proportional to the electrophoretic mobility and the field strength.

	EXERCISE 6-9
	Estimate μ_e under E = 10 [V/cm] and u= 7[cm/hour].
❶☞	**ANSWER** $\mu_e = u/E$ (Eqn. 6-26) $u = \dfrac{u}{E}$ $= \dfrac{7[\frac{cm}{hour}]}{60 \times 60 [\frac{sec}{hour}] \, 10[\frac{V}{cm}]}$ $= 1.94 \times 10^{-4} [cm^2 sec^{-1} V^{-1}]$
❶☞	Convert [cm/hour] to [cm/sec] (1 [hour] = 60 [min]= 60×60 [sec])

Utilizing that the electrophoretic mobility is proportional to the velocity (u), the location of the sample in the gel (x), can be related empirically with the molar mass of the sample.

$$log\, M = \alpha - \beta x \qquad \text{(Eqn. 6-28)}$$

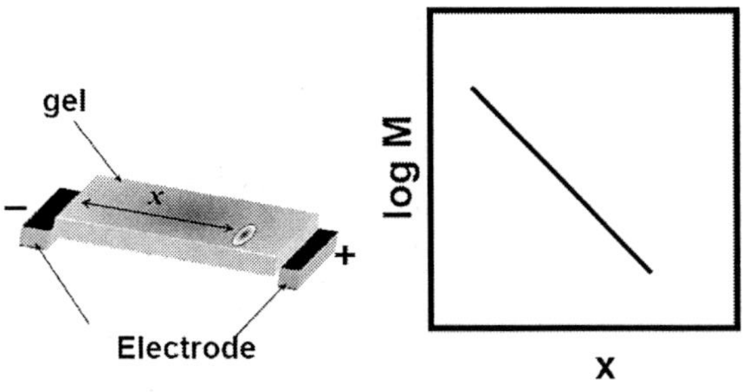

Fig. 6-20 Molar mass and location

Here, M is molar mass of protein [g mol⁻¹], x is distance traveled SDS (sodium dodecyl sulfate) gel [cm], and α or β are parameters obtained from the reference proteins. (**Fig. 6-20**) The constant α is a parameter function of the gel concentration, and the parameter β is proportional to the mobility when the gel concentration is zero. In reality, you can extract the parameters α and β from two standard protein with known molar mass as demonstrated in **EXERCISE 6-10**.

Chapter 6 Molecular Motion and Transport Properties

> **EXERCISE 6-10**
> Protein A and B with molecular weight of 16,500 and 35,400 move 4.60 [cm] and 1.30 [cm], respectively, during electrophoresis. Calculate molecular weight of protein C that moves 2.80 [cm] under the same condition in the same gel.

ANSWER

$$\log M = \alpha - \beta x \qquad \text{(Eqn. 6-28)}$$

$M_1 = 16{,}500$ [g/mol] $x_1 = 4.60$ [cm]
$M_2 = 35{,}400$ [g/mol] $x_2 = 1.30$ [cm]

$\log M_1 = \alpha - \beta x_1$
$\log M_2 = \alpha - \beta x_2$

❶ $\log(16{,}500) = \alpha - \beta \times 4.60$ ---a)
   $\log(35{,}400) = \alpha - \beta \times 1.30$ ---b) $-0.331 = -3.3\beta$

❷ $\alpha = 4.6796$ and $\beta = 0.10046$

❸ $\log M_c = 4.3983$

   $M_c = 10^{4.3983}$

   $M_c = 25021$ [g/mol]

❶ $\log(16{,}500) = 4.217$ and $\log(35{,}400) = 4.549$
❷ First, do a) – b), and cancel α, and obtain β.
❸ $\log x = a \rightarrow x = 10^a$

By using a type of zone electrophoresis technique (Isoelectric focusing (IEF) technique), different molecules are separated by their electric charge differences. It utilizes the fact that a molecule's charge changes with the pH of its surroundings. The IEF method is applied particularly to the study of proteins. In principle, the Isoelectric points (pI) is almost unique to a protein Typical mobility of simple ions~70×10^{-5} [cm^2/V sec] (Fig. 6-21). At low pH, all proteins are positively charged, and carboxyl groups of aspartic and glutamic acid become neutral. Also amino groups of lysine arginine become positive. At high pH, all proteins are negatively charged. Here, all carboxyls are negative and the aminos are neutrals. In IEF method, proteins are introduced into an Immobilized pH gradient gel which is made of polyacrylamide, starch, or agarose. A protein that is in a pH region below its **isoelectric point (pI) is positively charged and migrates towards the cathode (+).** Whereas a net charge of the protein decreases while the protein reaches the pH region that corresponds to its pI as protein migrates the region with an increase of pH gradient. Then, it stops migrating due to not net charge and no electrical attraction resulting a group of proteins construct a stationary band with each

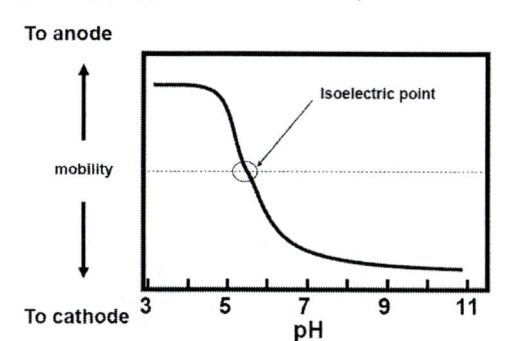

Fig. 6-21 Isoelectric points

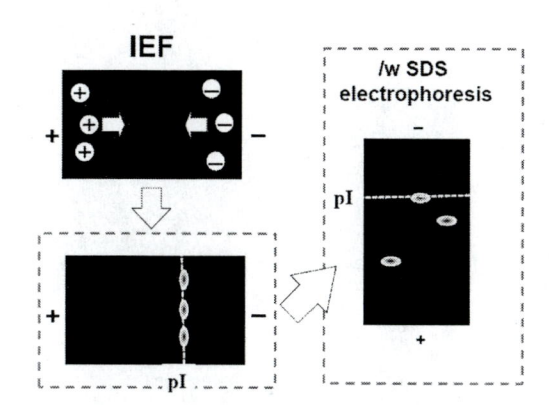

Fig. 6-22 Isoelectric points

protein positioned at a point corresponding pI point. The proteins are separated based on their relative content of acidic and basic residues. The resolution of IEF in terms of difference in pI is approximately 0.01. The proteins are first separated by their pI and then further separated by molecular weight through SDS-PAGE. (**Fig. 6-21**)

Chapter 6

How did you get these equations?
-The derivation of selected equations.

(Eqn. 6-13) $$\sigma = {u_t}/{\omega^2 r} = {m(1-\bar{v}_2\rho)}/{f}$$

Let's consider the situation where a particle with mass m conducts a free fall with velocity, u, and volume, $\bar{v}_2$. In Newtonian mechanics, force is given by

force = mass ×acceleration

Thus, relationship of the forces in act in this system is given as (Fig. 6-23a)

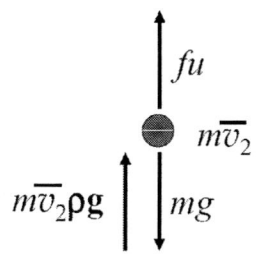

Fig. 6-23a. A free fall particle

$$m\frac{du}{dt} = mg - m\bar{v}_2\rho g - fu$$

When a particle reaches at the terminal velocity of u_t, (Fig. 6-23b)

$$\frac{du}{dt} = 0$$

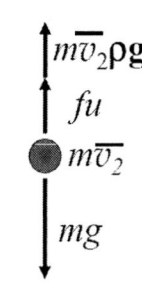

Fig. 6-23b A free fall at the terminal velocity

Thus,

$$m(1-\bar{v}_2\rho)g - fu_t = 0$$

Therefore,

$$u_t = {m(1-\bar{v}_2\rho)g}/{f} \qquad \text{(Eqn. 6-29)}$$

Comparing the situation where a particle reaching at the terminal velocity (u_t) at the free fall with a particle placed on the rotating stage reaching to a terminal velocity under the centrifugal force is applied ($\omega^2 x$), the centrifugal force can be replaced with gravitational constant, g. (Fig. 6-24)

$$u_t = m(1-\bar{v}_2\rho)\omega^2 r / f$$

Here, please note that $\frac{m(1-\bar{v}_2\rho)}{f}$ is a constant for a given particle (mass m, density ρ, frictional coefficient f, and volume $\bar{v}_2$). So we define the sedimentation coefficient σ as:

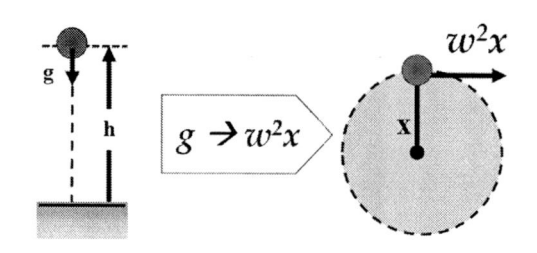

Fig. 6-24 Transformation between free fall and sedimentation.

$$\sigma = u_t / \omega^2 r$$

Thus,

$$\sigma = m(1-\overline{v_2}\rho)/f \qquad \text{(Eqn. 6-13)}$$

(Eqn. 6-14)
$$\sigma = \left(2.303/\omega^2\right)\left(d\, \log r_{1/2}/dt\right)$$

The sedimentation constant (σ) is given as

$$\sigma = u_t/\omega^2 x \qquad \text{(Eqn. 6-13)}$$

The terminal velocity is given as the differential of the terminal spot ($r_{1/2}$) against time, t:

$$u_t = dr_{1/2}/dt$$

Thus,

$$\sigma = \left(1/\omega^2 x_{1/2}\right)\left(dx_{1/2}/dt\right)$$

Let's conduct an arrangement in the differential equation. The differential of the natural log is

$$d\,\ln x/dx = \frac{1}{x}$$

Therefore,

$$\left(d\,\ln r/dr\right)\left(dt/dt\right) = \frac{1}{r}$$

Chapter 6 Molecular Motion and Transport Properties

$$\left(d\ln r/dt\right)\left(dt/dr\right) = \frac{1}{r}$$

$$\left(d\ln r/dt\right)\left(dt/dr\right)\left(dr/dt\right) = \frac{1}{r}\left(dr/dt\right)$$

$$\left(d\ln r/dt\right) = \frac{1}{r}\left(dr/dt\right)$$

You can rephrase this as

$$\left(d\ln r_{\frac{1}{2}}/dt\right) = \frac{1}{r_{\frac{1}{2}}}\left(dr_{\frac{1}{2}}/dt\right)$$

$$\left(dr_{\frac{1}{2}}/dt\right) = r_{\frac{1}{2}}\left(d\ln r_{\frac{1}{2}}/dt\right)$$

$$\sigma = \left(1/\omega^2 r_{1/2}\right)\left(dr_{1/2}/dt\right)$$

$$= \left(1/\omega^2 r_{1/2}\right) r_{\frac{1}{2}} \left(d\ln r_{\frac{1}{2}}/dt\right)$$

$$= \frac{1}{\omega^2}\left(d\ln r_{\frac{1}{2}}/dt\right)$$

Please recall the conversion between ln (natural log) and log (10-base log) introduced in the derivation of (**Eqn. 3-18**). First, the conversion between natural log and logarithm on base of 10 is derived as follows. For $x = 10^a$, the log of both sides gives

$$\log x = a.$$

On the other hand, if we take the natural log of x,

$$\ln x = \ln 10^a = a \ln 10 = 2.302\, a$$

Since $a = \log x$,

$$\ln x = 2.302 \log x$$

$$\sigma = \left(2.303/\omega^2\right)\left(d\log r_{\frac{1}{2}}/dt\right)$$

(Eqn. 6-16) $$M = RT\sigma/[D(1 - \bar{v}_2 \rho)]$$

Stokes-Einstein equation states

$$D = k_B T / f \qquad \text{(Eqn. 6-5)}$$

Thus, the frictional coefficient, f, is given as

$$f = k_B T / D$$

and

$$\sigma = m(1 - \bar{v}_2 \rho) / f \qquad \text{(Eqn. 6-13)}$$

Therefore,

$$\sigma = \frac{m(1 - \bar{v}_2 \rho)}{f} = \frac{m(1 - \bar{v}_2 \rho)}{(k_B T / D)}$$

$$= \frac{mD(1 - \bar{v}_2 \rho)}{k_B T}$$

With the use of Avogadro's number (N_A), the mass of a particle (m) and the molar mass (M) is given by

$$M = m N_A$$

The gas constant (R) and Boltzmann's constant (k_B) is also related as

$$R = k_B N_A$$

Thus, the sedimentation constant is

$$\sigma = \frac{mD(1 - \bar{v}_2 \rho)}{k_B T} = \frac{(M/N_A) D(1 - \bar{v}_2 \rho)}{(R/N_A) T}$$

$$= \frac{MD(1 - \bar{v}_2 \rho)}{RT}$$

By solving the above for molar mass (M),

$$M = \frac{RT\sigma}{D(1 - \bar{v}_2 \rho)} \qquad \text{(Eqn. 6-16)}$$

(Eqn. 6-17) $$\ln(C_1 / C_2) = \frac{M(1 - \bar{v}_2 \rho) \omega^2 (r_2^2 - r_1^2)}{2RT}$$

Chapter 6 Molecular Motion and Transport Properties

The **Boltzmann distribution** provides an important relationship between the number of distribution and energy of the system. For the concept on Boltzmann distribution, I want you to wait or check **Chapter 11**-Statistical Thermodynamics, where a procedure of obtaining (**Eqn. 6-17**) is introduced.

$$P_j/P_i = e^{-E_j/kT}/e^{-E_i/kT} = e^{-(E_j-E_i)/kT}$$

Here, the probability of finding the particles with i-th or j-th (non degenerate) energy level (E_i or E_j) is given by P_i or P_j. The Boltzmann constant is K_B and temperature is T. The concentration of the i-th state (C_i) is proportional to the probability P_i.

$$C_i \propto P_i$$

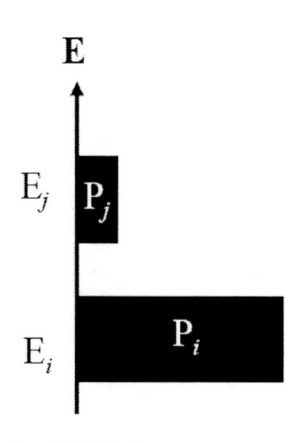

Fig. 6-25 Boltzmann distribution

Using the Boltzmann distribution,

$$C_j/C_i = e^{-(E_j-E_i)/kT}$$

The energy of a particle (ϵ) with mass m with angular velocity (ω) is

$$\epsilon = I\omega^2/2$$

Here, I is the moment of inertia, $I = mr^2$. In the present system,

$$I = (1 - \bar{v}_2\rho)r^2$$

$$\epsilon = (1 - \bar{v}_2\rho)r^2\omega^2/2$$

For 1 mol of particles, $M=N_A m$, the energy E is given as

$$E = (1 - \bar{v}_2\rho)Mr^2\omega^2/2$$

and for the location r_1 and r_2, the energy E_1 and E_2 are given

$$E_1 = (1 - \bar{v}_2\rho)Mr_1^2\omega^2/2$$

$$E_2 = (1-\bar{v}_2\rho)Mr_2^2\omega^2/2$$

Thus, the fraction of concentration between C_1 (located at r_1) and C_2 (located at r_2) is given by

$$C_1/C_2 = e^{-(E_1-E_2)/kT} = e^{(E_2-E_1)/kT}$$

$$= e^{M(1-\bar{v}_2\rho)\omega^2(r_2^2-r_1^2)/2RT}$$

Taking a natural log for both side,

$$\ln(C_1/C_2) = M(1-\bar{v}_2\rho)\omega^2(r_2^2-r_1^2)/2RT \quad \textbf{(Eqn.6-17)}$$

(Eqn. 6-21)
$$\eta = \left(mg(1-\overline{v_2}\rho)/6\pi r u_t\right)$$

The situation in viscosity is compared to a free-fall of a particle with gravitational force g. From the previous derivation for **(Eqn.6-13)**

$$u_t = m(1-\bar{v}_2\rho)g/f \quad \textbf{(Eqn. 6-29)}$$

The Stokes law states

$$f = 6\pi\eta r \quad \textbf{(Eqn. 6-6)}$$

Thus, **(Eqn. 8-21)** becomes

$$u_t = m(1-\bar{v}_2\rho)g/6\pi\eta r$$

Solving for viscosity coefficient (η)

$$\eta = \left(mg(1-\overline{v_2}\rho)/6\pi r u_t\right) \quad \textbf{(Eqn. 6-21)}$$

(Eqn. 6-27)
$$\mu_e = Ze/6\pi\eta r$$

The velocity of charged particle u [m sec^{-1}] with frictional coefficient f [kg/sec] is given as

$$u = ZeE/f$$

Here, Z is the number of charges on particle, E is an electric field [V/m], and electronic charge, $e = 1.6022 \times 10^{-19}$ [C].

From the Stoke's law,

$$f = 6\pi\eta r \qquad \text{(Eqn. 6-6)}$$

Thus, the velocity of charged particle is

$$u = ZeE/f = ZeE/6\pi\eta r$$

The electrophoretic mobility is

$$\mu_e = u/E \qquad \text{(Eqn. 6-26)}$$

Thus,

$$\mu_e = Ze/6\pi\eta r \qquad \text{(Eqn. 6-27)}$$

(Eqn. 6-28) $\qquad \log M = \alpha - \beta x$

In chromatography on various proteins, there is an empirical relationship as

$$\sigma = B - A \log M$$

Here, A and B are empirical constants, and σ is called as a fraction of internal volume available to solute

$$\sigma = V_p/V_i$$

Here, V_p is called as penetrable volume and V_i is called as an accessible volume to particular solute. It is known in solid gel that column cross sectional area available to the solute is proportional to σ. With this respect mobility should be proportional to σ. Therefore, we can replace σ with electrophoretic mobility μ_e,

$$\mu_e = b - a \log M$$

Here, *a* and *b* are considered to be empirical constants. The electrophoretic mobility is also given as

$$\mu_e = u/E \qquad \text{(Eqn. 6-26)}$$

Therefore,

$$u/E = b - a \log M$$

If distance x is achieved with velocity u with time t,

$$u = x/t$$

Therefore,

$$u/E = x/tE = b - a \log M$$

Solving for log M,

$$\log M = -x/btE + b/a$$

By replacing the terms as $\alpha = 1/btE$ and $\beta = b/a$

$$\log M = \alpha - \beta x \qquad \textbf{(Eqn. 6-28)}$$

Chapter 6 Summary [Part 1]

(Use back page to cover the contents.)

1	Fick's law.	$J_x = -D\left(dc/dx\right)$ J: flux, D: diffusion coefficient	(Eqn. 6-1)
2	one dimensional mean square displacement $\langle x^2 \rangle$	$\langle x^2 \rangle = 2Dt$	(Eqn. 6-2)
3	Stokes-Einstein equation	$D = k_B T / f$ D: diffusion coefficient	(Eqn. 6-5)
4	Stokes' law	$f = 6\pi\eta r$ f: friction coefficient	(Eqn. 6-6)
5	Combined the Stokes-Einstein equation and the Stoke's law	$r = k_B T / 6\pi\eta D$	(Eqn. 6-7)
6	Shape factor	The prolate or oblate ellipsoid possess more frictional coefficients (f) than that of sphere (f_o) and the f/f_o can be related with the a/b where a is an equatorial radius and b is a polar radius. (Table 6-1)	
7	angular velocity, ω	$\omega = 2\pi v$	(Eqn. 6-9)
8	terminal velocity reached under the centrifugal force is	$u_t = \left(m(1 - \bar{v_2}\rho)/f\right)\omega^2 r$	(Eqn. 6-12)
9	hydrodynamic volume, $\bar{v}_2$	Due to a solvation, the volume of solute increases with surrounding solvent. $\bar{v}_2 = \Delta V / \Delta \omega_2$ (Eqn. 6-11)	
10	sedimentation coefficient (σ)	$\sigma = u_t / \omega^2 r = m(1 - \bar{v_2}\rho)/f$	(Eqn. 6-13)

[Fold the page at the double line and cover the right half.]

Chapter 6 Summary Check [Part 1]

(Use this page to cover and check the contents.)
Use ☐ as your check box. Write your comment at far right

#	Item	Check	Comment
1	Fick's law.	☐ ☐ ☐ ☐ ☐	
2	one dimensional mean square displacement $\langle x^2 \rangle$	☐ ☐ ☐ ☐ ☐	
3	Stokes-Einstein equation	☐ ☐ ☐ ☐ ☐	
4	Stokes' law	☐ ☐ ☐ ☐ ☐	
5	Combined the Stokes-Einstein equation and the Stoke's law	☐ ☐ ☐ ☐ ☐	
6	Shape factor	☐ ☐ ☐ ☐ ☐	
7	angular velocity, ω	☐ ☐ ☐ ☐ ☐	
8	terminal velocity reached under the centrifugal force is	☐ ☐ ☐ ☐ ☐	
9	hydrodynamic volume, v_2	☐ ☐ ☐ ☐ ☐	
10	sedimentation coefficient (σ)	☐ ☐ ☐ ☐ ☐	

Chapter 6 Summary [Part 2]

(Use back page to cover the contents.)

11	location of the sample is determined as $r_{1/2}$, the sedimentation coefficient	$\sigma = \left(2.303/\omega^2\right)\left(d\,\log r_{1/2}/dt\right)$	(Eqn. 6-14)
12	sedimentation coefficient at the standard condition (20 °C in water)	$\sigma_{20,w} = \sigma\left(\eta/\eta_{20,w}\right)\left[(1-\bar{v}_2\rho)_{20,w}/(1-\bar{v}_2\rho)\right]$	(Eqn. 6-15)
13	molar mass of unknown sample obtained from sedimentation coefficient	$M = RT\sigma/[D(1-\bar{v}_2\rho)]$	(Eqn. 6-16)
14	Concentration ratio at X_1 and X_2	$\ln(C_1/C_2) = M(1-\bar{v}_2\rho)\omega^2(r_2^2 - r_1^2)/2RT$	(Eqn. 6-17)
15	plot of $\ln c$ as a function of r^2	$slope = M(1-\bar{v}_2\rho)\omega^2/2RT$ (Eqn. 6-18) molar mass of unknown sample M $M = (slope) \times 2RT/(1-\bar{v}_2\rho)\omega^2$	(Eqn. 6-19)
16	The viscosity vs. flux.	$J = -\eta\left(du_x/dy\right)$ du_x/dy : gradient of momentum transfer for flux J	(Eqn. 6-20)

[Fold the page at the double line and cover the right half.]

Chapter 6 Summary Check [Part 2]

(Use this page to cover and check the contents.)

Use ☐ as your check box. Write your comment at far right

11	location of the sample is determined as $r_{1/2}$, the sedimentation coefficient	☐ ☐ ☐ ☐ ☐	
12	sedimentation coefficient at the standard condition (20 °C in water)	☐ ☐ ☐ ☐ ☐	
13	molar mass of unknown sample obtained from sedimentation coefficient	☐ ☐ ☐ ☐ ☐	
14	Concentration ratio at X_1 and X_2	☐ ☐ ☐ ☐ ☐	
15	plot of lnc as a function of r^2	☐ ☐ ☐ ☐ ☐	
16	The viscosity vs. flux.	☐ ☐ ☐ ☐ ☐	

Chapter 6 Summary [Part 3]

(Use back page to cover the contents.)

17	The molecular description of the viscosity	$\eta = \left(mg(1-\bar{v}_2\rho) / 6\pi r u_t \right)$ (Eqn. 6-21)
18	relative viscosity	$\eta_2/\eta_1 = (1-\bar{v}\rho_2)/(1-\bar{v}\rho_1) = \rho_2 t_2 / \rho_1 t_1$ (Eqn. 6-22)
19	specific viscosity, η_{sp}	η_{sp} [dimensionless] $\eta_{sp} = (\eta' - \eta)/\eta$ (Eqn. 6-23)
20	intrinsic viscosity	It is a measure of solute's contribution to the viscosity of a solution. $[\eta] \equiv \lim_{c \to 0} \eta_{sp}/c$ (Eqn. 6-24) $[\eta] = \nu(\bar{v}_2 + \delta_1 v_1^o)$ (Eqn. 6-25) ν is a shape factor and δ_1 is hydration factor.
21	electrophoretic mobility μ_e and its molecular view	μ_e [cm^{2}V^{-1}s^{-1}] $\mu_e = u/E$ (Eqn. 6-26) molecular view of μ_e is $\mu_e = Ze/6\pi\eta r$ (Eqn. 6-27)
22	Location of the sample in the gel (x) and the molar mass of the sample(M)	$\log M = \alpha - \beta x$ (Eqn. 6-28)

[Fold the page at the double line and cover the right half.]

Chapter 6 Summary Check [Part 3]

(Use this page to cover and check the contents.)
Use ☐ as your check box. Write your comment at far right

17	The molecular description of the viscosity	☐ ☐ ☐ ☐ ☐	
18	relative viscosity	☐ ☐ ☐ ☐ ☐	
19	specific viscosity, η_{sp}	☐ ☐ ☐ ☐ ☐	
20	intrinsic viscosity	☐ ☐ ☐ ☐ ☐	
21	electrophoretic mobility μ_e and its molecular view	☐ ☐ ☐ ☐ ☐	
22	Location of the sample in the gel (x) and the molar mass of the sample(M)	☐ ☐ ☐ ☐ ☐	

Chapter 6 - YOUR TEACHER MAY TEST YOU ON:

No.	What may be asked?		What you should know or do?
1	How diffusional motion is explained by using the flux and Fick's law? Can you sketch it?	→	$J_x = -D(dc/dx)$ (Eqn. 6-1)
		→	(Fig. 6-2)
2	How do you calculate the diffusional coefficient from the square displacement?	→	$\langle x^2 \rangle = 2Dt$ (Eqn. 6-2)
		→	EXERCISE 6-1
		→	Problems 6-1, 6-2
3	How diffusional coefficient is explained by Stokes-Einstein equation, Stokes' law??	→	Stokes-Einstein equation $D = k_B T / f$ (Eqn. 6-5)
	How frictional coefficient is explained by	→	Stokes' law $f = 6\pi\eta r$ (Eqn. 6-6)
	How radius of a spherical molecule is calculated from known viscosity and diffusional coefficient at a given temperature?	→	Combined the Stokes-Einstein equation and the Stoke's law $D = k_B T / 6\pi\eta r$ (Eqn. 6-7)
		→	$r = k_B T / 6\pi\eta D$ (Eqn. 6-8)
		→	EXERCISE 6-2, 6-3
		→	Problems 6-3, 6-4, 6-5, 6-6
4	How frictional coefficient changes as the molecular shape deviates from a spherical shape?	→	Table 6-1 Fig. 6-8
		→	EXERCISE 6-4
	How can you calculate the equatorial or polar radius of prolate or oblate molecule from known physical parameters (viscosity, frictional coefficient, or diffusional coefficient)?	→	Problems 6-7, 6-8, 6-9, 6-10

Chapter 6 Molecular Motion and Transport Properties

5	How do you calculate the angular velocity?	→	$\omega = 2\pi\nu$ (Eqn. 6-9)
		→	See [Example]
6	How do you calculate the sedimentation coefficient with known mass, hydrodynamic volume, density, and frictional coefficient?	→	$\sigma = \left(2.303/\omega^2\right)\left(d\log r_{1/2}/dt\right)$ (Eqn. 6-14)
		→	Fig. 6-13.
		→	EXERCISE 6-5
		→	Problems 6-12
7	How do you calculate the sedimentation coefficient from the terminal location of sample on the sedimentation plate?	→	$\sigma_{20,w} = \sigma\left(\eta/\eta_{20,w}\right)\left[(1-\bar{v}_2\rho)_{20,w}/(1-\bar{v}_2\rho)\right]$ (Eqn. 6-15) $\sigma_{20,w}$ (sedimentation coefficient at 20 [°C] in water)
		→	EXERCISE 6-6
		→	Problems 6-11
8	How do you calculate the molar mass of unknown sample from the sedimentation experiment with using the sedimentation coefficient, diffusion coefficient, hydrodynamic volume, and density of the substance?	→	$M = RT\sigma/[D(1-\bar{v}_2\rho)]$ (Eqn. 6-16)
		→	EXERCISE 6-7
		→	Problems 6-14, 6-15, 6-16, 6-17, 6-18, 6-19
9	How do you calculate the molar mass of unknown sample from the sedimentation experiment using the concentration of the species at a given location?	→	$M = (slope) \times 2RT/(1-\bar{v}_2\rho)\omega^2$ (Eqn. 6-19)
		→	Fig. 6-14
		→	Problems 6-13

Chapter 6 Molecular Motion and Transport Properties

10	How can you express the viscosity with respect to the flux of flow?	→	$J = -\eta \left(du_x/dy \right)$ (Eqn. 6-20)
		→	Fig. 6-15
		→	Problems 6-20, 6-21
11	How viscosity is related with the location of the sedimentation coefficient, diffusion coefficient, hydrodynamic volume, and density of the substance?	→	$\eta = \left(mg(1-\overline{v_2}\rho)/6\pi r u_t \right)$ (Eqn. 6-21)
12	How the viscosity can be extracted from experimentally?	→	$\eta_2/\eta_1 = \rho_2 t_2/\rho_1 t_1$ (Eqn. 6-22)
13	How specific viscosity is defined?	→	$\eta_{sp} = (\eta' - \eta)/\eta$ (Eqn. 6-23)
14	How do you extract the intrinsic viscosity graphically?	→	Fig. 6-20
15	What is the molecular description of intrinsic viscosity?	→	$[\eta] = v(\bar{v}_2 + \delta_1 v_1^o)$ (Eqn. 6-25)
		→	EXERCISE 6-8
		→	Problems 6-22, 6-23

16	How do you calculate the electrophoretic mobility under a given electric field?	→	$\mu_e = u/E$	(Eqn. 6-26)
17	How do you calculate the electrophoretic mobility from charge, viscosity, and the size of the species?	→	$\mu_e = Ze/6\pi\eta r$	(Eqn. 6-27)
		→	Problems 6-24, 6-25	
18	How do you molar mass of protein sample in SDS gel is related with the location after the electrophoresis.	→	$\log M = \alpha - \beta x$	(Eqn. 6-28)
		→	Fig. 6-10 (log M vs. x, decreasing line)	
		→	EXERCISE 6-10	
		→	Problems 6-26, 6-27	

UNIT CHECK CHAPTER 6

Important Parameters of This Chapter	Popularly Used Unit	Important Unit Conversion
Flux, J or J_x	mol cm^{-2} s^{-1}	
Concentration, c	M mol L^{-1}	
Diffusion coefficient, D	cm^2/s	
Time, t	Sec	
Frictional coefficient, f	g sec^{-1}	
Viscosity coefficient, η	P, poise g sec^{-1} cm^{-1}	
Radius, r	M Cm	
Frequency, ν	1/sec Hz	
Angular velocity, ω	rad/sec	
Centrifugal acceleration force, F_c	rad^2 m /sec^2	
Terminal velocity, u_t	m/sec	
Hydrodynamic volume, $\bar{v}_2$.	cm^3 g^{-1}	
Volume change, ΔV	cm^3	
Weight change, $\Delta \omega_2$	g kg	
Mass, m	g Kg	
Density	g cm^{-3}	
Frictional coefficient, f	g sec^{-1}	
Sedimentation coefficient, σ	S(Svedberg)	1 [S] = 10^{-13} [sec]
Time, t	sec	
Viscosity, η	P, poise g sec^{-1} cm^{-1} kg m^{-1} sec^{-1}	[P]= [g· cm^{-1} sec^{-1}]
Gas constant, R	atm L mol^{-1} K^{-1} J mol^{-1} K^{-1}	8.314472[J mol^{-1} K^{-1}] =8.3145 ×10^7 [erg K^{-1} mol^1] =0.08205746 [atm L mol^{-1} K^{-1}] [erg]= [g cm^2 sec^2] [J]= [kg m^2 sec^{-2}] 1[J] = 10^7 [erg]
Molar mass, M	g/mol	
Temperature, T	°C K	0 [°C] = 273.15 [K]
Diffusion coefficient, D	cm^2/sec	
Concentration	M	

Chapter 6 Molecular Motion and Transport Properties

	mol/L	
Flux, J	cm^3 g^{-1} sec^{-1}	
Gravitational constant, g	cm sec^{-2}	g =980.66 [cm sec^{-2}]
Specific viscosity, η_{sp}	dimensionless	
Intrinsic viscosity, $[\eta]$	cm^3 g^{-1}	
Specific volume of solvent, v_1^o	cm^3 g^{-1}	
Shape factor, ν	dimensionless	
Hydration factor, δ_1	dimensionless	
Partial volume of the Macromolecule, $\bar{v}_2$	cm^3 g^{-1}	
Electric field strength, E	V cm^{-1}	1 [eV] = 96.485 [kJ/mol] [J]= [C V]
Velocity of a dispersed Charged particle u	cm sec^{-1}	
Electrophoretic mobility μ_e	cm^{2}V^{-1}s^{-1}	
Number of charges, Z	dimensionless	
Electric charge, e		e=1.602×10^{-19} [C]
pH	dimensionless	
Isoelectric point, pI	dimensionless	

SUMMARY OF TRICKY TRAPS OF CHAPTER 6

☐	1	In Fick's law, direction of the flux flow is an opposite of the direction of concentration gradience.
☐	2	The viscosity given in Stoke's law is the value of medium not a viscosity of a targeted substance.
☐	3	The shape factor can be the same value but a/b can be different depending on if it is a prolate or oblate.
☐	4	[S]: Svedberg, [sec]: seconds, 1 [S] = 10^{-13} [sec]
☐	5.	Use cgs unit system for D: diffusion coefficient, ρ: density, η: viscosity When you calculate a parameter with D, ρ, and η, the energy unit should be [erg] instead of [J], 1 [J] = 10^7 [erg]
☐	6	In viscosity, flux leaves momentum transfer which is opposite to velocity gradience.
☐	7	Viscosity has several kinds→ intrinsic viscosity, specific viscosity (intrinsic one contains shape factor)
☐	8	Electrophoretcic mobility is inversely proportional to the external electric field.

LAST MINUTE REVIEW OF MATH CHAPTER 6

(These are basic algebra which you have no excuse if you miss them.)

1. $(x^n)^m = x^{nm}$ $\qquad \left(x^{\frac{1}{n}}\right)^m = x^{\frac{m}{n}}$

2. y=mx +b   slope m= $\left(\frac{dy}{dx}\right) = \frac{y_2-y_1}{x_2-x_1}$, $\lim_{x \to 0} y = b$

3. ln x = 2.302 log x

Nobel Prize and Your Knowledge From Chapter 6
(*: word appeared in Chapter 6)

The Nobel Prize in Chemistry 2002 was awarded to **John B. Fenn** and **Koichi Tanaka** for developing methods for identification and structure analyses of biological macromolecules and soft desorption ionization methods. The work by Tanaka and Fenn developing a novel method for mass spectrometric analyses of biological macromolecules. This is associated with the **mobility*** of the charged gaseous macromolecule which is an advanced topic of mobility learned in **Chapter 6**. The Newtonian mechanics states

$$F=ma$$

Here, F is force (field applied to a charged substance), m is mass of sample, and a is a resulting acceleration. Thus,

$$a=F/m$$

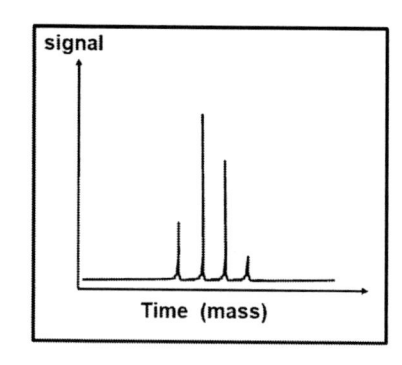

Fig. 6-25 Typical MALDI set up

As the mass gets heavier, the acceleration gets lower and takes more time to reach a given distance. Thus, if you measure the number of particles detected as a function of time, you can analyze the mass of particle. (**Fig. 6-25**)

In order to analyze mass of a macromolecule (e.g., protein), they must be ionized and vaporized by laser irradiation. However, a direct irradiation of an intense laser pulse on a macromolecule break analyte into tiny fragments losing its structure.

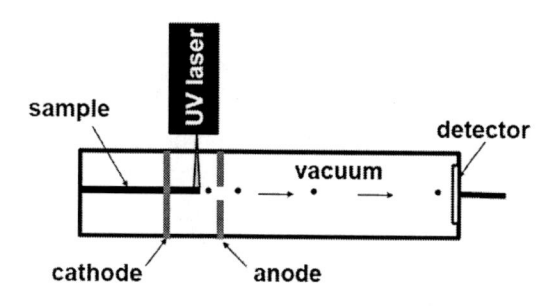

Fig. 6-26 Typical MALDI set up

Tanaka developed soft laser desorption ionization methods or matrix-assisted laser desorption/ionization (MALDI)) for mass spectrometric analyses of biological macromolecules.(**Fig. 6-26**) The MALDI is a laser desorption and ionization process assisted by a matrix compound in order to minimize the fragmentation of macro-molecule. In 1985, Tanaka utilized a mixture of cobalt nanoparticles and glycerol (ultra fine metal plus liquid matrix method), and demonstrated the soft ionization of proteins with nitrogen laser.

John Bennett Fenn developed the electrospray ionization (ESI) technique. In ESI, a sample solution is sprayed from a small tube into a strong electric field in a flow of nitrogen under atmospheric pressure. The droplets are formed and evaporated in a vacuum region, and it causes the charge to increase on the droplets. The multiply charged ions are guided to the detector.

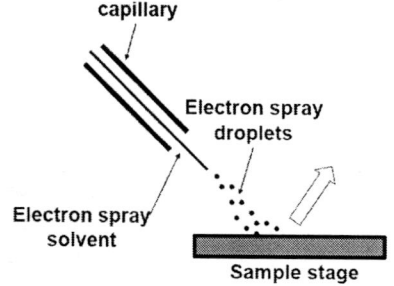

Fig. 6-27 ESI

Chapter 6 Molecular Motion and Transport Properties

Bonus!! Since we have learned sedimentation and electrophoresis in this chapter, two directly related studies are added in (I) **sedimentation*** and in (II) **electrophoresis***.

(I) The Nobel Prize in Chemistry 1926 was awarded to **Theodor Svedberg** for his innovative study on disperse systems. Svedberg's primary focused on colloid chemistry investigated the interaction of colloid suspensions with light as well as their sedimentation processes. He demonstrated that the gas laws were able to be applied to colloidal systems. Svedberg's Ph.D. thesis on the diffusion of platinum colloidal particles supported Einstein's theory concerning the **Brownian motions** of colloidal particles. In 1921, Svedberg invented ultracentrifuge technique and conducted a significant study of the sedimentation of colloidal disperse systems. He demonstrated to separate colloids into sedimentation bands of varying distances from the center of the centrifuge corresponding to particle size. The result was even related to shape and mass of the colloidal particles. (His ultracentrifuge provided centrifugal forces as high as 1,000,000 times of Earth's gravitational force.) These sedimentation bands were able to be photographed as machine was kept running (Schlieren photography). The ultracentrifuge technique is very versatile for identifying shape and molecular mass of macro molecules including carbohydrates, proteins, DNA, and synthetic polymers. Lastly, this is very appropriate to mention to the reader of this textbook that Theodor Svedberg was a physical chemist whereas his work significantly affected the development of biochemistry. It is told that he chose chemistry as his life-work because he believed chemistry to be a tool for greatly understanding of biological systems.

(II) The Nobel Prize in Chemistry 1948 was awarded to **Arne Tiselius** "for study of electrophoresis and adsorption analysis, and for his discoveries of the nature of the serum proteins". Tiselius developed electrophoresis method to be an accurate and useful technique for analyzing chemical compounds. Tiselius studied under **Theodor Svedberg** at University of Uppsala. He focused on chromatography as a possible technique to reduce impurities in the substances. By passing light with a specific frequency through a sample in chromatographic column, Tiselius studied properties of light diffusion through zeolite. Tiselius also created an accurate method to determine the diffusion constant of water molecules through crystals of zeolite. Among his improvements in electrophoretic apparatus, electronic charge was applied through U- tube filled with solution containing the sample. Under external field, the charged elements migrated along the tube. Tiselius was able to identify the migrated species. For example, he showed that different elements are mixed blood plasma by using this technique. By optically tracking the movement of boundaries (the *Schlieren* method) Tiselius resolved the plasma into four distinct elements. For the first time, he isolated α-, β-, *and* γ- globulin (blood protein) *and* discovered antibodies as well. While electrophoretic technique was not able to distinguish the break down products of a polypeptide chain, he developed adsorption methods of analysis by using the column method, where a mixture contains a substance with a specific affinity for absorbing one peptide or another is flushed through a column. Thus, peptides in the original mix was determined by analyzing the eluate which is the wash passed through the column. In 1943 Tiselius invented "displacement analysis which significantly reduced "tailing" (i.e., the corruption of one part of a solution by molecules from the other.)

THE FOCUSED PHYSICAL CHEMISTRY EXPERIMENTAL APPROACH ASSOCIATED WITH CHAPTER 6

(*: word appeared in Chapter 6)

Dynamic Light Scattering (DLS)

In Chapter 6, **Einstein-Stokes equation*** was introduced to describe particle's size by using **diffusion coefficient***, **viscosity***, and **frictional coefficients***. Good application of **Einstein-Stokes equation*** can be found in the Dynamic Light Scattering (DLS) method which determines the particle size. DLS method is a most popular technique which integrate the information of particles sizes and some notion of concentration based on the way in which light scatters off of particles in suspension including bacteria or proteins in suspension. DLS is also known as Photon Correlation Spectroscopy or Quasi-Elastic Light Scattering (See **Chapter 12**). This technique can determine the size distribution profile of particles including nanoparticles in suspension or polymers in solution. The semiclassical light scattering theory states that as light impinges on matter the electric field of the light induces an oscillating polarization of electrons in the molecules. In this case, the molecules then serve as secondary source of light and subsequently scatter light. The size, shape and molecular interactions in the scattering material are considered to cause the frequency shifts, the angular distribution, the polarization, and the intensity of the scatter light.

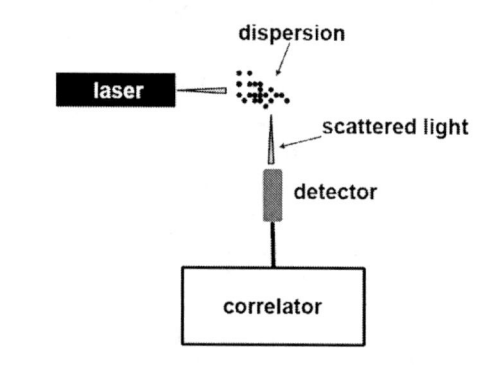

Fig. 6-28 A schematic diagram of DLS measurement.

From the light-scattering spectrum, the autocorrelation function G(t) of the light-scattering intensity is obtained. A characteristic autocorrelation function of the scattered light is shown in (**Fig. 6-29**) where the baseline is proportional to the total intensity *I*. The characteristic decay time of the correlation function is inversely proportional to the linewidth of the spectrum, and the diffusion coefficient (D) can be obtained by fitting the measured correlation function to a single exponential function. With the **Einstein-Stokes equation***, the spherical scattering particle diameter d at temperature T is determined. Let me show you equations what you are familiar with from **Chapter 6**.

Fig. 6-29 Autocorrelation function G(t).

$$r = {k_B T}/{6\pi \eta D} \qquad \text{(Eqn. 6-7)*}$$

The size determined by DLS is the spherical size translates in the same manner as the scatterer. The obtained size may contain molecules bound to the particle or solvent molecules which move with the particle.

CHAPTER 6 PROBLEMS.

6-1 [$<x^2>$] If the diffusion coefficient of Mb is 11.3×10^{-7} [cm²/sec], estimate the diffuse distance $\{<x^2>\}^{\frac{1}{2}}$ achieved by diffusion within 5 [μ sec].

6-2 [$<x^2>$] Calculate the average time (second) required for a protein molecule of diffusion coefficient 10^{-6} [cm²/sec] to move the length of 10^{-4} [cm] of a bacterial cell by diffusion.

6-3 [D, η → r] If the viscosity of a protein (mw=14,000) is 0.0101 [P], estimate radius of this protein. Assume that this protein is spherical shape. The diffusion constant is $D=14.25 \times 10^{-7}$ [cm²/sec] at pH 7 and 40 [°C].

6-4 [D, η → r] The diffusion constant of the β-lactalbumin (mw=14,000) was measured to be 14.25×10^{-7} [cm²/sec] at pH 7 and 40 [°C]. The viscosity of the solvent was 0.0101 [P]. Estimate the diameter of this protein, assuming that it is spherical in shape.

6-5 [D → f] The diffusion coefficient of a human immunoglobin G (IgG) (m.w. = 156,000) at 20 [°C] in a dilute aqueous buffer is $D= 4.0 \times 10^{-7}$ [cm²/sec]. Calculate the friction coefficient of IgG.

6-6 [D, η → r] The diffusion constant of a protein was measured to be $D =28.50 \times 10^{-7}$ [cm²/sec]. The viscosity of the solvent was η=0.0101[P]. Estimate the radius of this protein in [Å], assuming that it is spherical in shape.

6-7 [shape → a/b] The diffusion coefficient of a protein A at 20 [°C] in a dilute aqueous buffer is 3.80×10^{-7} [cm²/sec]. This protein A has a shape of an oblate ellipsoid. Estimate the dimensions (a and b) of an oblate ellipsoid of protein A. Assume that unhydrated form of protein A has a sphere shape, and its diameter is 7.180 [nm], and its viscosity for a dilute aqueous buffer at 20 [°C] is 1.51×10^{-2} [g sec⁻¹ cm⁻¹].

6-8 [shape → D] A hydrated protein X (the density of 0.785 [g/mL]) has a shape of a prolate ellipsoid. but its unhydrated form has a spherical shape. A student measured electrophoretic mobility of this hydrated protein, and the migrated distance of protein X (hydrated), $d_{X\text{-hydrated}}$, was 8.5 [cm]. For known proteins A and B, the distances migrated were d_A = 15 [cm] and d_B = 3 [cm], respectively. The molar mass of protein A is 45 [kDa] and molar mass of protein B is 65 [kDa].

Under surface tension of 5.00×10^{-4} [N/m], a spherical protein X (unhydrated) gave Gibbs energy change, $\Delta G°$, of 5.00×10^{-20} [J], when one spherical protein X (unhydrated) separated into two spherical unhydrated X proteins. The viscosity coefficient, η, of a medium where a protein X (both unhydrated and hydrated) placed was 4.80×10^{-2} [P].

Calculate the time for protein X (hydrated) to travel 5 [μm] of distance, when hydrated protein X is located under the field of 5 [kV/cm].

hydrated protein X

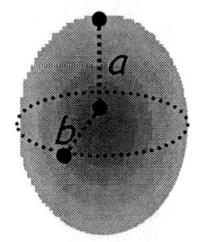

prolate ellipsoid

a×b = 1975.7 [Å²]

unhydrated protein X

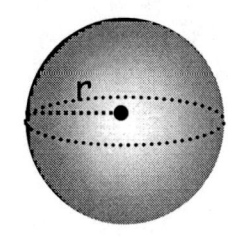

sphere

The protein X (hydrated) has a charge of +1, and the value (a × b) is known to be 1975.7 [Å²] (See the figure).

6-9 [f → a/b] The IgG calculated in **EXERCISE 6-4** was found to have a shape of prolate ellipsoid. Using **Fig. 6.8**, estimate the dimensions (a and b) of a prolate ellipsoid of IgG. Assume that unhydrated IgG has a sphere shape, and its radius is 3.629 [nm]. Viscosity for a dilute aqueous buffer at 20 [°C] is 1.00×10^{-2} [g sec^{-1} cm^{-1}].

6-10 [f/f₀] The diffusion coefficient of a human *immunoglobin G (IgG)* at 23 [°C] in a dilute aqueous buffer is 1×10^{-7} [cm^2 sec^{-1}]. This protein was found to have a shape of an ellipsoid. Assume that unhydrated *IgG* has a sphere shape and its radius is 2.70 [nm]. Viscosity for a dilute aqueous buffer at 23 [°C] is 1.1×10^{-2} [g sec^{-1} cm^{-1}]. Calculate the value of f/f_0. (f: frictional coefficient of hydrated *IgG*, f_0: frictional coefficient of an unhydrated *IgG*)

6-11 [σ₂₀,w] The partial specific volume of the sodium salt of DNA is 0.556 [cm^{-3} g^{-1}]. The viscosity and density of 1 [M] NaCl and the viscosity of water can be found in the International Critical Tables; the values are 1.104 [cP], 1.04 [g cm^3], and 1.005 [cP], respectively. Calculate $\sigma_{20,w}$ for the DNA.

6-12 [ln X₁/₂ vs. t → σ] The sedimentation coefficient of a certain DNA in 1 [M] NaCl at 20 [°C] was measured by boundary sedimentation at 24,630 [rpm]. The plot of x (distance of boundary from center of rotation, cm) vs. time (min) showed a slope of 3.32×10^{-4} [min^{-1}]. Calculate the sedimentation coefficient, σ.

6-13 [ln c vs. x² → M]
a) A sedimentation equilibrium experiment was conducted at 78000 [rpm] (revolutions per minute).

$$\ln\left(C_1/C_2\right) = M(1 - \bar{v}_2\rho)\omega^2(r_2^2 - r_1^2)/2RT \quad \text{(Eqn. 6-17)}$$

We obtained two data points for the above equation:
(a₁, b₁) = (0.0034 [cm^2], –8.23)
(a₂, b₂) = (0.65 [cm^2], –2.31)
Identify what a and b correspond to in the above equation, then obtain slope. Calculate the molecular weight, M (g/mol) of this substance. The conditions of this experiment were: T = 25 [°C], $\bar{v}_2$ = 0.74 [cm^3/g], ρ=0.98 [g/cm^3]

b) The given two points are from a sedimentation equilibrium experiment at 25000 [rpm]. [*ln* c vs. x^2] The value of two points are
(a₁, a₂) = (0.01 [cm^2], –5.5) (b₁, b₂) = (0.09 [cm^2], -4.8)
The conditions of this experiment were:
T = 25 [°C], $\bar{v}_2$ = 0.74 [cm^3/g], ρ=0.98 [cm^3/g]
Using the above information, calculate the molecular weight, M of this substance in the unit of [g/mol].

6-14 [σ, D → M] Calculate the molecular weight of unknown sample using the following data.
$\sigma_{20,w}$ = 23 [S]
$D_{20,w}$ = 3.05 × 10^{-6} [cm^2/sec]
$\bar{v}_2$ = 0.733 [cm^3/g]

6-15 [σ, D → M] The following data have been obtained in an aqueous buffer for unknown protein A at 20 [°C].

sedimentation coefficient at 20 [°C]: $\sigma_{20,w}$ = 4.60 [S]
diffusion coefficient at 20 [°C]: $D_{20,w}$ = 6.10×10^{-7} [cm^2/sec]
partial specific volume: $\bar{v}_2$ = 0.733 [cm^3/g]
[η] = 4.2 [m^3/g]

Calculate the molecular weight of this protein A?

6-16 [D, σ → osmotic pressure] The following data have been obtained in an aqueous buffer for unknown protein α at 20.0 [°C].
sedimentation coefficient at 20 [°C]: $\sigma_{20,\,water}$ = 4.60 [S]

diffusion coefficient at 20 [°C]: $D_{20,water} = 6.10 \times 10^{-7}$ [cm² sec⁻¹]
partial specific volume: $\bar{v_2}$ = 0.733 [cm³/g]

The density of the solution at 20.0 [°C] is equivalent to that of water at 20.0 [°C]. d = 0.998 [g/cm³]. Since mercury nanometer was not allowed to use in a laboratory, water manometer was used to measure the osmotic pressure of the solution containing 0.600 [g] of protein α per 100 [mL] of water at 20.0 [°C] and pH where the protein has no net charge. Calculate the height of the water rises inside the manometer tube at 20.0 [°C]. Answer the height in cm unit. (The density of the mercury at 20.0 [°C] is 13.6 [g/cm³] and the density of the water at 20.0 [°C] is 0.998 [g/cm³].)

6-17 [σ, D → M] The following data have been obtained in an aqueous buffer for unknown protein A at 20 [°C].

$$D_{20,w} = 3.10 \times 10^{-7} \text{ [cm}^2\text{/sec]}$$
$$\bar{v_2} = 0.891 \text{ [cm}^3\text{/g]}$$
$$\sigma_{20,w} = 5.75 \text{ [S]}$$

Calculate the molecular weight of this protein A?

6-18 [σ, D, η → M] The following data have been obtained in an aqueous buffer for unknown protein at 20 [°C].

(Use $\eta_{20,w}$ (aqueous buffer) = 1.00 [cP])

$\sigma_{20,w}$ = 4.85 [S]

$D_{20,w} = 6.24 \times 10^{-7}$ [cm²/sec]

$\bar{v_2}$ = 0.70 [cm³/g]

a) Calculate the molecular weight of this protein ?
b) Assuming that this protein molecule is a sphere, calculate its hydrodynamic radius (in Å) in an aqueous buffer. (Use $\eta_{20,w}$ (aqueous buffer) = 1.00 [cP] = 0.01[P])
c) Another unknown protein B has a molar mass 1.5 times bigger than this protein A. If protein B has the same partial specific volume, obtain the ration of intrinsic viscosity $[\eta]_A / [\eta]_B$.

6-19 [σ, D, η → M] Calculate the molecular weight of human serum albumin using the necessary data from followings.

$$\sigma_{20,w} = 3.8 \text{ [S]}$$
$$D_{20,w} = 5.50 \times 10^{-7} \text{ [cm}^2\text{/sec]}$$
$$\bar{v_2} = 0.780 \text{ [cm}^3\text{/g]}$$
$$[\eta] = 2.2 \text{ [cm}^3\text{/g]}$$
$$\rho = 0.994 \text{ [g/cm}^3\text{]}$$

6-20 [Fick's second law] TRUE or False: The Fick's second law describes the time dependence of the concentration change of the fluid.

6-21 [Fick's law, η sketch]. The equation below is showing a mathematical expression for J_m (rate of momentum transfer) and u_x (speed of flowing substance in x-component). Provide a clear sketch describing the given equation in x, y, z-coordinate. (You are welcome to draw a sketch using any letters and symbols, such as arrow, lines, squares, etc...)

$$J_m = -\eta \left(du_x / dy \right)$$

η : viscosity coefficient

6-22 [η] Viscosity can be conveniently determined by measuring the rate of flow through a cylindrical tube or capillary. The relation between flow rate U (in cm³ per second) and radius (a), pressure drop across the capillary (P), capillary length (l), and viscosity (η) is called Poiseuille's law:

$$U = \frac{\pi P a^4}{8\eta l}$$

The flow of blood through capillaries is controlled in part by constriction of the size of the small vessels called arterioles, which feed the capillaries. Use the above equation to calculate the fractional change in flow rate U produced when the arteriole radius is decreased by a factor 0.8.

6-23 [η$_{intrinsic}$] A small spherical virus has a molecular weight of 1.25×10^6 [g/mol] and a diameter of 100 [Å]; it is not significantly hydrated. Calculate the intrinsic viscosity of an aqueous solution of this virus.

6-24 [μ$_e$] Estimate of μ for Z= 1, r = 10 [Å], η=0.050 [g cm^{-1} sec^{-1}], and E= (eZ/100)[V].

6-25 [μ$_e$] Estimate the order of magnitude of protein mobilities under the following electrophoresis.
Z= 5, r = 20 [Å] η=0.010 [g cm^{-1} sec^{-1}], and V=1/300 [V]

   a. 10×10^{-5} [cm /V]
   b. 20×10^{-5} [cm /V]
   c. 50×10^{-5} [cm /V]
   d. 100×10^{-5} [cm /V]
   e. None of the above

6-26 [log a, log b→ M] Protein A and B with molecular weight of 16,500 and 35,400 move 4.60 [cm] and 1.30 [cm], respectively, during electrophoresis and SDS polyacrylamide gel. Calculate molecular weight of protein C that moves 2.80 [cm] under the same condition in the same gel.

6-27 [log a, log b→ M] A hydrated protein X (density, d_X = 0.785 [g/mL]) has a shape of a prolate ellipsoid, but its unhydrated form has a spherical shape (See Figure in **6-8**). A student measured electrophoretic mobility of this hydrated protein, and the migrated distance of protein X (hydrated) in the gel, $d_{X-hydrated}$, was 8.50 [cm].

For known proteins A and B, the distances migrated in the gel were d_A = 15.0 [cm] and d_B = 3.00 [cm], respectively. The molar mass of protein A is 45[kDa] (M_A = 45,000 [g/mol]) and molar mass of protein B is 65 [kDa] (M_B = 65,000 [g/mol]). The relationship between molecular weight, M, of a protein and the distance d migrate din gel is known to be:

hydrated protein X

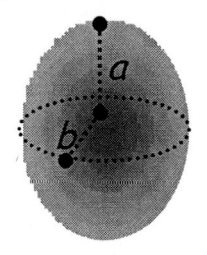

prolate ellipsoid

a×b = 1975.7 [Å²]

unhydrated protein X

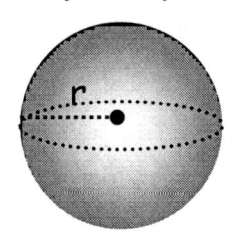

sphere

$$\log M = a - b \times d$$

where *a* and *b* are constants. Under surface tension of 5.00×10^{-4} [N/m], a spherical protein X (unhydrated protein X) gave Gibbs energy change, $\Delta G°$, of $+5.00 \times 10^{-20}$ [J], when one spherical protein X (unhydrated protein X) separated into two spherical unhydrated X proteins. The viscosity coefficient, η, of a medium where a protein X (both unhydrated and hydrated) placed was 4.80×10^{-2} [P]. Calculate the electrophoretic mobility of this hydrated protein and time for this protein to travel 5 [μm] of distance, when hydrated protein X is located under the field of 5 [kV/cm]. The protein X (hydrated protein X) has a charge of +1, and the value (a×b) is known to be 1975.7 [Å^2].

Chapter 6 Answers. For Selected Problems

- **6-1** 33.6 [nm]
- **6-2** a) 5×10^{-3} [sec]
- **6-3** 16 [Å]
- **6-4** 31.94 [Å]
- **6-5** 1.01×10^{-7} [g/sec]
- **6-6** 7.969 [Å]
- **6-7** 22.6 [Å]
- **6-8** 48.2 [sec]
- **6-9** a = 168 [Å] b = 16.8 [Å]
- **6-10** 7.30
- **6-11** 22.3 [S]
- **6-12** 19.6 [S]
- **6-13** a) D   b) 2.304×10^5 [g/mol]
- **6-14** 68500 [g/mol]
- **6-15** 68,400 [g/mol]
- **6-16** M = 68,464 [g/mol], Π = 1.602 [mmHg], height = 2.18 cm
- **6-17** M = 413,647 [g/mol]
- **6-18** b) r = 34.3 [Å] c) t = 7.3×10^{-8} [sec]
- **6-19** M = 7.49×10^4 [g/mol]
- **6-20** True
- **6-22** 0.41
- **6-23** 0.63 [cm^3/g]
- **6-27** u = 1.03837×10^{-4} [m/sec], time = 4.82×10^{-2} [sec]

Chapter 7

Kinetics

7-1 Rates of Chemical Reactions and Rate Law
7-2 Half Life
7-3 Arrhenius Equation
7-4 Transition-State Theory
7-5 Very Fast Reactions

Chapter 7 Kinetics

- **Why do I have to study this Chapter?**

The chemical reaction is one of the core subjects of chemistry. While you are not learning all reaction types, you will be able to characterize the basic type of reaction systematically. You are able to calculate the reaction rate constant for selected types of reactions. You will be able to predict the reaction rate at given temperature and extract the activation energy which governs the reaction process. Then, we see the most popular form of reaction kinetics found in biological applications. Let's explore how to approach very fast reaction with rapid temperature (pressure) changes.

- **Expected Hurdles Ahead in this Chapter**
    1. Categorizing different types of rate expressions (See Section **7-1**)
    2. Obtaining thermodynamical properties from transition state theory (TST) (See Section **7-4**)

PREVIEW OF KEY-EQUATIONS

Speed of reaction
$$v = k[A]^m[B]^n$$

Reaction Rate Law

Order	Reaction Speed	Integrated Form	Half-life
Zero-th	$v = k_0$	$[A] = [A_0] - k_0 t$	$t_{1/2} = [A]_0 / 2k_0$
First	$v = k_1[A]$	$[A] = [A]_0 e^{-k_1 t}$	$t_{1/2} = \dfrac{0.6931}{k_1}$
Second (I)	$v = k_2[A]^2$	$1/[A] = k_2 t + 1/[A]_0$	$t_{1/2} = \dfrac{1}{k_2[A]_0}$
Second (II)	$v = k_2[A][B]$	$\left(\dfrac{1}{[A]_0} - \dfrac{1}{[B]_0}\right) \ln\left(\dfrac{[B]_0[A]}{[A]_0[B]}\right) = k_2 t$	
n-th	$v = k_n[A]^n$	$\dfrac{1}{[A]^{n-1}} = (n-1)k_n t + \dfrac{1}{[A]_0^{n-1}}$	$t_{1/2} = \dfrac{2^{n-1} - 1}{(n-1)k[A]_0^{n-1}}$

k_n is the rate constant for n-th order reaction.
[A] or [B] are the concentration of the reactants A or B.

Arrhenius equation/plot

$$k = Ae^{-(E_a/RT)}$$

$$\ln k = -\left(E_a/RT\right) + \ln A$$

Chapter 7 Kinetics

Transition State Theory

$$k = \frac{k_B T}{h} K^{\neq}$$

Eyring-Polanyi equation

$$k = \left(k_B T/h\right) exp\left[-\Delta G^{\neq}/RT\right]$$

$$k = \left(k_B T/h\right) exp\left[\Delta S^{\neq}/R\right] exp\left[-\Delta H^{\neq}/RT\right]$$

The activated enthalpy change
$$\Delta H^{\neq} \approx E_a$$

The activated entropy change
$$\Delta S^{\neq} \approx R\left[\ln\left(Ah/k_B T\right)\right]$$

Very Fast Reactions

$$A + B \underset{k_{-1}}{\overset{k_1}{\rightleftarrows}} C$$

$$\Delta[C] = \Delta[C]_o e^{-t/\tau} \qquad 1/\tau = k_1([A]_{eq} + [B]_{eq}) + k_{-1}$$

$$A \underset{k_{-1}}{\overset{k_1}{\rightleftarrows}} B$$

$$\Delta[B] = \Delta[B]_o e^{-t/\tau} \qquad 1/\tau = k_1 + k_{-1}$$

PREVIEW OF KEY-TECHNICAL TERMS
Activated state, order of reaction, 0th- 1st- 2nd- 3rd-...nth order reaction, half life, Arrhenius equation, transition state, activation energy (Ea), Arrhenius plot, transition state theory, Eyring-Polanyi equation, steady state approximation

Chapter 7 Kinetics

7-1 Rates of Chemical Reactions and Rate Law

The reaction is a central focus of the chemistry. So far, thermochemical properties or direction of the reaction have been discussed in the previous chapters (Chapters 1 and 2, ΔH, ΔS, ΔG, and K). A key issue dealt with in this chapter is the speed of reaction. "How fast is the product being produced?" and "What kind of reaction mechanism is it?". We also view the thermochemical property between the products and the reactants using the concept of the "**activated state**". The thermochemical values (ΔH, ΔS, and ΔG) do not describe properties of the activated state.

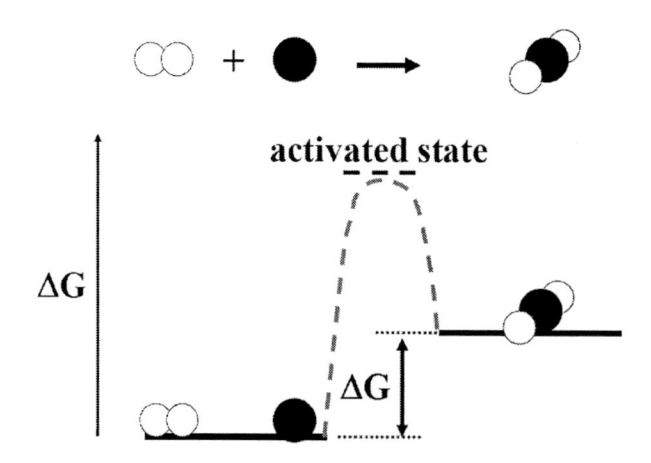

Fig. 7-1. Chemical reaction and enthalpy change of reaction.

As a start, let's define how reaction rate (speed) is described. The speed of the chemical reaction is measured by viewing one of the reactants to be lost or one of the products to be produced. The direction of the change of the reactants is the opposite of that of the products, i.e., when the reactants decreases the products increases. (The sign of the speed is opposite each other.) **(Fig. 7-2)**

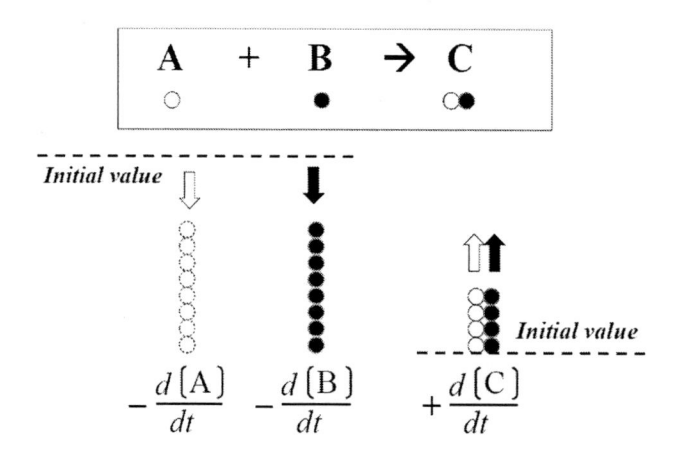

$$-\frac{d[A]}{dt} \quad -\frac{d[B]}{dt} \quad +\frac{d[C]}{dt}$$

Fig. 7-2 Demonstration of reaction rate

Chapter 7 Kinetics

The reaction speed v is considered to be how much reactant A is changed (decreased), ΔA, in a given time change Δt.

$$v = \left(\Delta[A]/\Delta t\right)$$

The rate (or speed) of reaction, v, is commonly expressed by first derivative of concentration of a species against time, t. Using an example shown in (**Fig. 7-2**), the reactants are A and b, and product is C. Then, the reaction speed is

$$v = -\left(d[A]/dt\right) = -\left(d[B]/dt\right) = +\left(d[C]/dt\right) \quad \text{(Eqn. 7-1)}$$

Here, [A], [B], and [C] are the concentrations of A, B, and C, respectively. Since the unit of molarity [M] is popularly used for the concentration, the unit of the reaction speed is [M sec^{-1}].

The rate of reaction describes a basic idea of how chemical reaction proceeds in terms of the concentration of the reactants (or products) – Rate Law. The first step is to identify the reaction process is to know the **order of reaction**. For a general chemical reaction

A + B → C

The reaction speed is defined as:

$$v = k[A]^m[B]^n \quad \text{(Eqn. 7-2)}$$

Here, [A] and [B] are the concentration of A and B, respectively. The k is rate constant, and m or n are the order of reaction with respect to A and B, respectively. (The m and n can be integers or non integers and negative numbers.) **The overall order of Reaction is given by m + n**. There is no straight connection between stoichiometric coefficients of the reactants (products) and the order of the reaction.

> **MCM Most Common Mistake (32) – Can I tell the order of reaction from the chemical equation?**
> The order of chemical reaction is not equal to the stoichiometric coefficients. For example, there is chemical equation given by 2A → B. The reaction speed is not necessary given by
> $$v = k[A]^2$$
> Also you cannot describe as
> $$v = 2k[A]$$
> either. The order of reactions can only be determined experimentally. The amount of stoichiometric coefficients has nothing to do with the reaction order.

EXERCISE 7-1 The stoichiometric equation for a reaction is

$$A + B \rightarrow C + D$$

The initial rate of formation of C is measured with the following results.

	[A]/ [M]	[B]/ [M]	Initial Rate, v [M /sec]
(1)	1.0	1.0	1.0×10^{-3}
(2)	2.0	1.0	5.0×10^{-4}
(3)	1.0	3.0	3.0×10^{-3}

Find the total order of this reaction.

ANSWER

$v = k[A]^m[B]^n$ (Eqn. 7-2)

❶ Comparing 1) and 2), the effect of [A] (increase of factor of (2) can be examined.

❷ $v(2)/v(1) = [A(2)]^m/[A(1)]^m = [2A(1)]^m/[A(1)]^m = (2)^m$

From the table, $v(2)/v(1) = 5.0 \times 10^{-4}/1.0 \times 10^{-3} = 0.5 = (2)^{-1}$

❸ $m = -1$

❹ Comparing (1) and (3), the effect of [B] (increase of factor of (3) can be examined.

❷ $v(3)/v(1) = = [B(3)]^n/[B(1)]^n = [3B]^n/[B]^n = (3)^n$

From the table, $v(3)/v(1) = 3.0 \times 10^{-4}/1.0 \times 10^{-3} = (3)^1$

$n = 1$

The overall order of reaction is m+ n = −1+1 =0

0th order of reaction.

---

❶ Choose this pair since [B] stays the same between (1) and (2)

❷ $(2x)^m/(x)^m = (2x/x)^m = (2)^m$

❸ Recall, m, n can be non integers or negative values.

❹ Choose this pair since [A] stays the same between (1) and (3)

Chapter 7 Kinetics

Now, we will examine the 0-th, first, and second, and n-th order of reactions below.

i. Zero-th Order Reactions

Let's view the reaction given by

$$A \xrightarrow{k_0} C$$

For zero-th order reaction, the first derivative of product against time should be expressed as

$$d[C]/dt = k_0 \qquad \text{(Eqn. 7-3)}$$

Here, the concentration of the product C is [C] and the reaction rate coefficient for the zero-th order is given by k_0. By integrating the (**Eqn. 7-3**), the concentration of product at time t, [C], is given as

$$[C] - [C]_o = k_0 t \qquad \text{(Eqn. 7-4)}$$

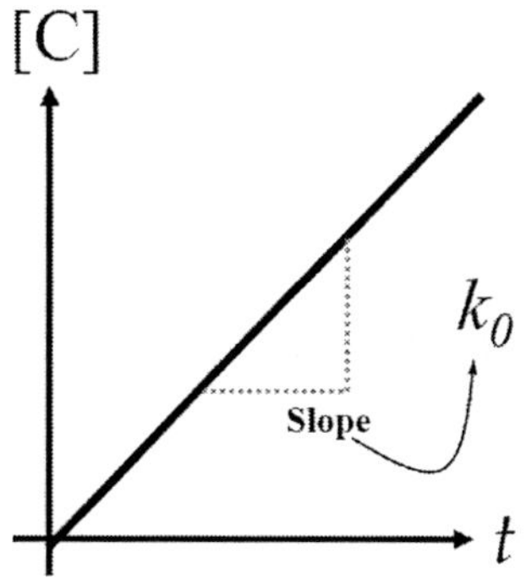

Fig. 7-3a Plot for 0th order reaction on [C].

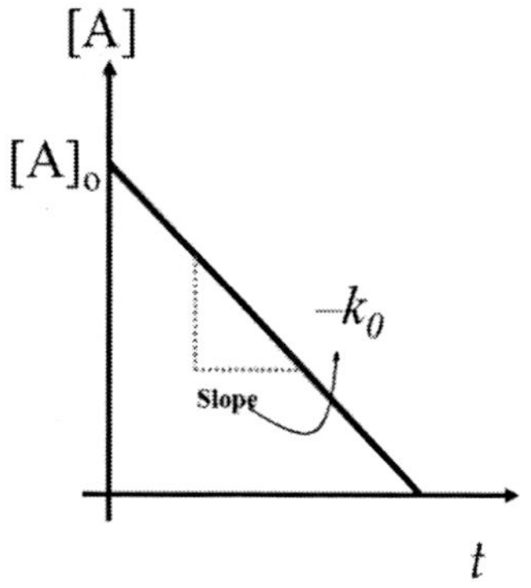

Fig. 7-3b Plot for 0th order reaction on [A].

[C]$_o$ is an initial concentration of product at time, t = 0. (Therefore, it can be zero, i.e., [C]$_o$ =0) . If the reaction follows the zero-th order reaction as shown in (**Eqn. 7-4**), the plot of concentration of C, [C], as a function of time, t, should provide a linear line as shown in (**Fig. 7-3a**) The slope of this linear plot is k_0 (>0). If we derive the concentration of reactant A, [A] following the zero-the order reaction, we will have an expression of

$$[A] = [A_0] - k_0 t \qquad \text{(Eqn. 7-5)}$$

Following the (**Eqn. 7-5**), the concentration of the reactant A, [A] is plotted as a function of time (t) as a linear plot with slope –k_0 (<0).(**Fig. 7-3b**) The concentration of the reactant at time 0 is [A]$_0$, which is an intercept of an x-axis. The negative slope of the plot is consistent with the fact that the concentration of the reactant decreases as time progresses.

ii. First-Order Reactions

Once again, let's view the reaction given by

$$A \xrightarrow{k_1} C$$

If the reaction speed is proportional to the first order of the concentration of the reactant [A], the reaction speed v is given as

$$v = -\frac{d[A]}{dt} = \frac{d[C]}{dt} = k_1[A] \qquad \text{(Eqn. 7-6)}$$

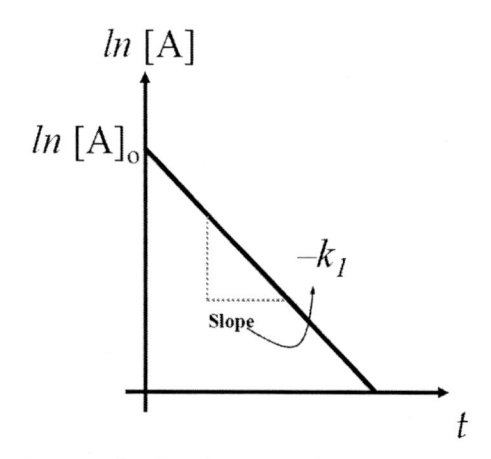

Fig. 7-4 Plot for the 1st order reaction.

Here, k_1 is the rate constant for the first order reaction [sec^{-1}]. The integrated expression of (**Eqn. 7-6**) is

$$\ln\left([A]/[A]_o\right) = -k_1 t \qquad \text{(Eqn. 7-)}$$

or

$$[A] = [A]_o e^{-k_1 t} \qquad \text{(Eqn. 7-)}$$

Based on (**Eqn. 7-7**), the plot of ln [A] as a function time, t, provides a linear plot with slope $-k_1$ (<0). The intercept of y-axis is ln [A]$_0$. (**Fig. 7-4**)

iii. Second-Order Reactions (Type –I)
Let's take a look at the reaction given by

$$A + A \xrightarrow{k_2} C$$

If the reaction follows the second order reaction with respect to the concentration of reactant, [A], the reaction velocity(v) is expressed as

$$v = -\frac{d[A]}{dt} = \frac{d[C]}{dt} = k_2[A]^2 \qquad \text{(Eqn.7-9)}$$

Here, k_2 is the rate constant for the second order(type-I) reaction [$M^{-1}\,sec^{-1}$]. The integrated expression of (Eqn. 7-9) is

$$\frac{1}{[A]} = k_2 t + \frac{1}{[A]_0} \qquad \text{(Eqn. 7-1)}$$

Following the formula shown in (Eqn. 7-10), a linear plot is made for plotting 1/[A] as a function of time, t. The slope of this plot is $k_2(>0)$ and an intercept at x-axis is $1/[A]_0$ as shown in (Fig. 7-5) While slope of this plot is positive, the [A] decreases as time progresses.

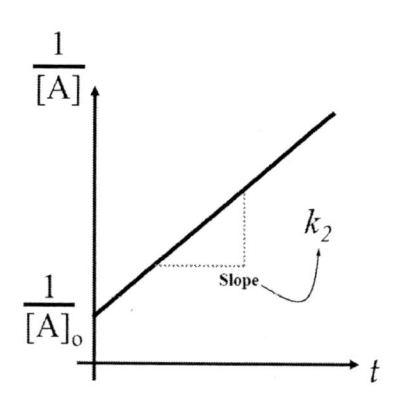

Fig. 7-5 The plot for the second order reaction (type-I).

iv. Second-Order Reactions (Type –II)
When two different reactants are involved in the chemical reaction through second order reaction as

$$A + B \xrightarrow{k_2} C$$

The velocity of the reaction is given as

$$v = -\frac{d[A]}{dt} = -\frac{d[B]}{dt} = \frac{d[C]}{dt} = k_2[A][B] \qquad \text{(Eqn. 7-11)}$$

Here, k_2 is the rate constant for the second order(type-II) reaction [$M^{-1}\,sec^{-1}$]. The integrated expression of (**Eqn. 7-11**) is

$$\left(\frac{1}{[A]_0 - [B]_0}\right) \ln\left(\frac{[B]_0[A]}{[A]_0[B]}\right) = k_2 t \qquad \text{(Eqn. 7-1}\Sigma)$$

Here, $[A]_o$ and $[B]_o$ are the initial concentrations of reactants of A and B at time =0. They should satisfy the relationship of $[A]_o \neq [B]_o$. If the ln [A]/[B] is plotted as a function of time ,t, based on the (**Eqn. 7-12**), the linear line with slope k_2 (>0) with intercept x= ln ($[A]_o/[B]_o$) can be drawn.(**Fig. 7-6**)

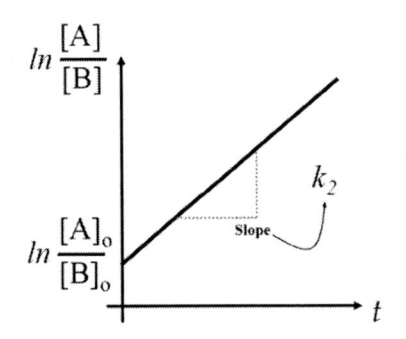

Fig. 7-6 The plot for second order reaction (type -II).

v. nᵗʰ Order Reactions

Let's take a look at the reaction given by

$$nA \xrightarrow{k_n} C$$

If the reaction follows the nᵗʰ order reaction with respect to the concentration of reactant, [A], the reaction velocity(v) is expressed as

$$v = -\frac{d[A]}{dt} = \frac{d[C]}{dt} = k_n[A]^n \quad \text{(Eqn. 7-13)}$$

Here, k_n is the rate constant for the n-th order reaction [M^{-n+1} sec^{-1}]. The integrated expression of (**Eqn. 7-13**) is (n ≠ 1)

$$1/[A]^{n-1} = (n-1)k_n t + 1/[A]_o^{n-1} \quad \text{(Eqn. 7-1)}$$

Following the formula shown in (**Eqn. 7-10**), a linear plot is made for plotting $1/[A]^{n-1}$ as a function of time, t. The slope of this plot is $k_n(>0)$ and an intercept at y-axis is $1/[A]_o^{n-1}$ as shown in (**Fig. 7-7**) The slope of this plot is positive since [A] decreases and $1/[A]^{n-1}$ increases as time progresses.

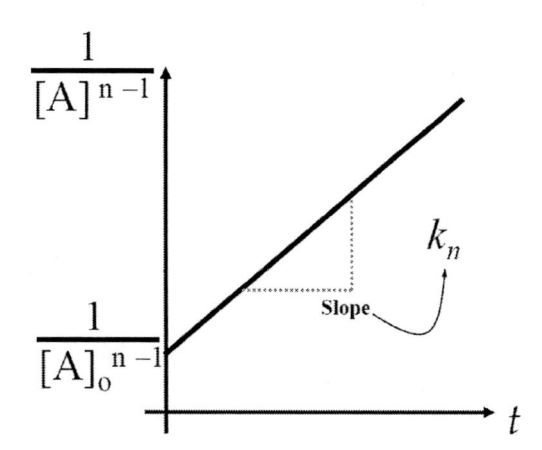

Fig. 7-7 The plot for the n-th order reaction.

7-2 Half-life

There is a very useful index of time to roughly grasp if one reaction has high or low speed. The time required for ½ of [A]₀ to be consumed is called as **half-life** ($t_{1/2}$). For example, the concentration following the first order reaction at half life ($t_{1/2}$) is given as by replacing [A] with [A]₀/ 2.

$$\frac{1}{2}[A]_0 = [A]_0 e^{-k_1 t_{1/2}} \qquad \text{(Eqn. 7-1)}$$

The time corresponds to the half life is indicated in the graph in (**Fig. 7-8**). The half-life is different depending on the order of the reaction.

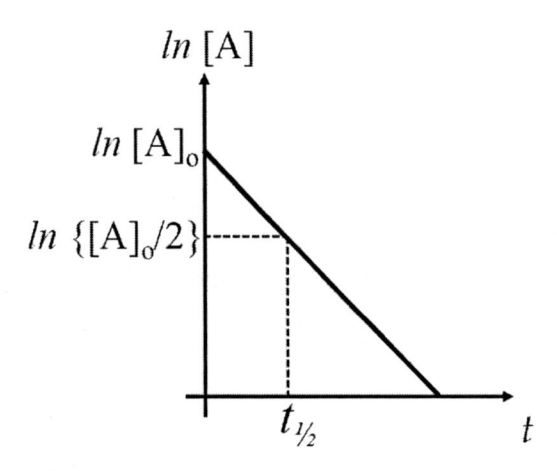

Fig. 7-8 The plot for half-life ($t_{1/2}$) in the 1st order reaction.

The 0th order reaction
$$t_{1/2} = [A]_0 / 2k_0 \qquad \text{(Eqn. 7-1)}$$

The 1st order reaction
$$t_{1/2} = 0.6931/k_1 \qquad \text{(Eqn. 7-1)}$$

The 2nd order reaction (type-I)
$$t_{1/2} = 1/k_2[A]_0 \qquad \text{(Eqn. 7-1)}$$

The nth order reaction (n≠1)
$$t_{1/2} = 2^{n-1} - 1 / (n-1)k[A]_0^{n-1} \qquad \text{(Eqn. 7-1)}$$

In **Table 7-1**, the rate law studied in this chapter is summarized.

Table 7-1 Summary of Reaction Rate Law

Order	Reaction Speed, v	Integrated Form	Half-life	Linear Plot	Unit for k
0th	$v = k_0$	$[A] = [A_0] - k_0 t$	$t_{1/2} = [A]_0 / 2k_0$	[A] vs. t	[M sec^{-1}]
1st	$v = k_1[A]$	$[A] = [A]_0 e^{-k_1 t}$	$t_{1/2} = \dfrac{0.6931}{k_1}$	ln [A] vs. t	[sec^{-1}]
2nd (I)	$v = k_2[A]^2$	$1/[A] = k_2 t + 1/[A]_0$	$t_{1/2} = \dfrac{1}{k_2 [A]_0}$	1/[A] vs. t	[M^{-1} sec^{-1}]
2nd (II)	$v = k_2[A][B]$	$\left(\dfrac{1}{[A]_0} - \dfrac{1}{[B]_0}\right) \ln\left(\dfrac{[B]_0 [A]}{[A]_0 [B]}\right) = k_2 t$		ln ([A]/[B]) vs. t	[M^{-1} sec^{-1}]
n^{th}	$v = k_n[A]^n$	$\dfrac{1}{[A]^{n-1}} = (n-1)k_n t + \dfrac{1}{[A]_0^{n-1}}$	$t_{1/2} = \dfrac{2^{n-1} - 1}{(n-1)k[A]_0^{n-1}}$	$1/[A]^{n-1}$ vs. t	[M^{-n+1} sec^{-1}]

EXERCISE 7-2
The following data were obtained for the concentration [A] vs. time for a certain chemical reaction. Write the reaction rate expression. (Examine the order of reaction up to the second order by linear line plotting.)

Time [sec]	[A] [mM]	Time [sec]	[A] [mM]	Time [sec]	[A][mM]
0	10.00	7	2.50	14	1.36
1	6.91	8	2.22	15	1.23
2	4.98	9	1.91	16	1.20
3	4.32	10	1.80	17	1.13
4	3.55	11	1.65	18	1.09
5	3.21	12	1.52	19	1.00
6	2.61	13	1.42	20	0.92

ANSWER
Here, we use linear line plot approach for 0th, 1st, and 2nd order reaction.

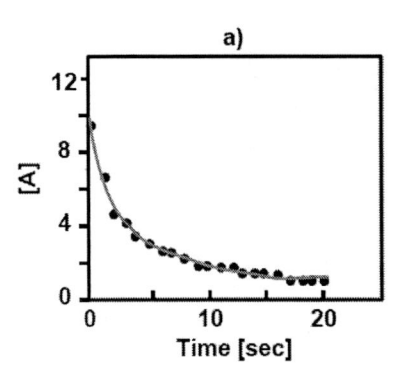

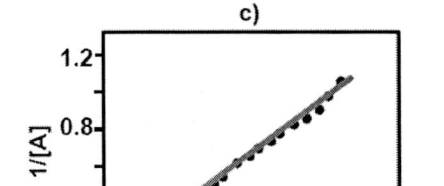

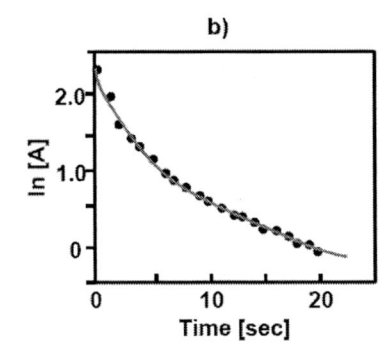

a. 0th order plot
b. 1st order plot
c. 2nd order (type –I) plot

Based on the visual inspection, (up to the 2nd order), the plot of the second order exhibits the linear line. Thus, we can conclude that the observed reaction is the second order reaction.

The LINEST analysis of MS-Excel shows that the slope of the plot c is 0.0474(6).

❹	Thus, the rate constant of this second order reaction is k=0.047 [sec/M]
	The rate expression is v=0.047(sec/M)[A]²
❶	Plot is a)time vs. [A], b)ln {a} vs. time, and c) 1/[A] vs. time.
❷	The correlation (r) for plot c) is 0.997.
❸	The slope is equal to the rate constant of the 2nd order reaction(type –I).
❹	Don't forget this is the second order reaction.

Most Common Mistake (33) –I did not know the order of reaction is guessed from k.

Since the reaction speed(v) has the unit of [M/sec], the reaction rate constant k has the different unit depends on the order of the reaction. (See **Table 7-1**) In some cases, the unit of k can be used to determine the order of reaction. When you need to calculate the reaction rate constant, please make sure to complete correct unit for k.

7-3 Arrhenius Equation

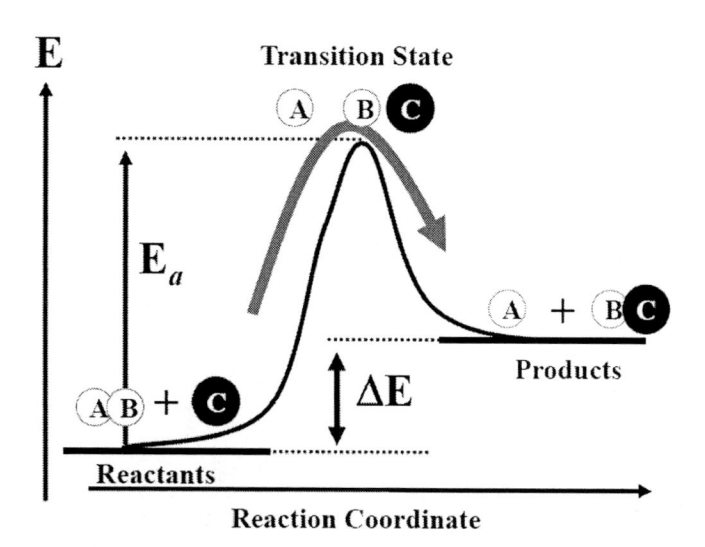

Fig. 7-9 The activated state in a reaction.

As a very important concept on the chemical reaction, the reaction process is considered to go over the "**transition state**" which is a potential barrier with higher energy values than reactants or products. **(See Fig. 7-9)** [Please note that we are limiting single rate-limited thermally activated process.] The reaction coordinate is the coordinate in which molecular structure changes as a reaction takes place. For example,

$$AB + C \rightarrow A + BC$$

the reaction coordinate can be set in the distance between A and B or B and C (r_{A-B} or r_{B-C}). So that the reaction progresses as r_{A-B} increases and r_{B-C} decreases. The reaction has more complicated situation and the reaction coordinate should be chosen wisely. (In some cases, you may have to choose the angles instead of the length.) The reaction rate constant is significantly dependent on the activation energy (E_a) and the temperature given in a system. An empirical equation relates the observed reaction rate and the temperature is described by **Arrhenius equation** as

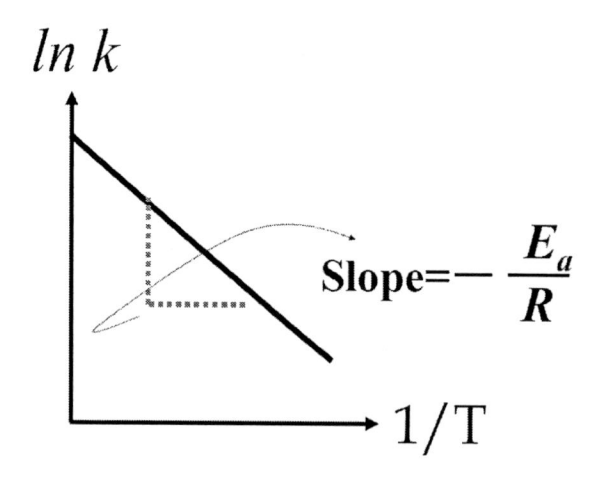

Fig. 7-10 Arrhenius Plot.

$$k = Ae^{-(E_a/RT)} \qquad \text{(Eqn. 7-2)}$$

where E_a is an activation energy [J/mol], T is temperature [K], and k is a reaction rate constant (see **Table 7-1** for the unit of corresponding reaction order) and A is a pre-exponential factor (the unit is the same as that of k). In order to construct a linear plot, we will take a natural log of both sides of (**Eqn. 7-20**).

$$\ln k = -\left(E_a/RT\right) + \ln A \qquad \text{(Eqn. 7-2)}$$

By plotting ln K as a function (1/T), a linear plot with slope $-(E_a/R)$ is obtained.(**Fig.7-10**) The formula given in (**Eqn.7-20**) and (**Eqn. 7-21**) can be said one of the most important formulas introduced in this book!!! !!! As a convenient form of (Eqn. 7-21) for two different temperature T_1 and T_2, the following equation is commonly used.

$$\ln k_1 - \ln k_2 = -\frac{E_a}{R}\left(\frac{1}{T_1} - \frac{1}{T_2}\right) \qquad \text{(Eqn. 7-21)'}$$

Here, k_1 and k_2 are reaction rate constants at temperature T_1 and T_2, respectively.

Chapter 7 Kinetics

☹ **Most Common Mistake (34)** –"Does activation energy depend on the temperature?"

Most common mistake found in Arrhenius plot is a misunderstanding of Ea. Please answer the following question while looking at (**Eqn. 7-20**) or (**Eqn. 7-21**).

>Q. How does the activation energy (E_a) depend on the temperature?
>
>A. We assume NO dependence in temperature.

The activation energy is E_a can be dependent on temperature in some reaction path (or may not be able to be well defined if the reaction possesses more than one transition state.) While you use the Arrhenius plot in this book, Ea is considered to be a constant for a given reaction for an entire temperature range.

☹ **Most Common Mistake (35)** -"I hate Arrhenius plot!"

The Arrhenius plot must be asked in your exam and may be used in your research project. Thus, this is the plot you cannot miss. Let me point out two issues here.

1) 1/T (inverse of the temperature): People tend to rush the calculation and forget to calculate an inverse of the temperature (1/T). The temperature is in Kelvin's unit [K] but not in [°C] unit. Please recall **Most Common Mistake (15)** in **Chapter 2**, where a not on inverse of temperature for *van't Hoff equation*. Make sure to calculate at least three significant figures or more, since one significant figure of (1/T) is all 0.03 for a common temperature range asked (20-100 [°C]). For example, $T_1 = 20$ [°C] = 293.15 [K], $T_2 = 50$ [°C] = 323.15 [K], and $T_3 = 100$ [°C] = 373.15 [K]. The inverses of these temperatures with one significant figure are the same.

$$1/T_1 = 1/293.15 = 0.003411 = 0.003$$
$$1/T_2 = 1/323.15 = 0.003095 = 0.003$$
$$1/T_3 = 1/373.15 = 0.002680 = 0.003$$

2) Another mistake made in the plot is that people forget to take natural log of k but use log (10-based) instead.. What if you used the log (10-based) instead of natural log? Then, please use the conversion factor between ln 10 and log 10, (if you prefer not to recalculate the natural logs.)

Slope 1 (correct)= $-[\ln k_2 - \ln k_1] / [1/T_1 - 1/T_1]$

The conversion between natural log (ln) and log (10-based) is

$$\ln x = 2.303 \log x$$

(If $x = 10^a$, $\log x = a$ and $\ln x = \ln 10^a = a \ln 10 = 2.302 \log x$)

Slope 1 (correct)= $-2.303 [\log k_2 - \log k_1]/[1/T_1 - 1/T_1]$
Slope 2 (wrong) = $-[\log k_2 - \log k_1]/[1/T_1 - 1/T_1]$

If your calculation was doe as shown in "Slope 2", you just need to multiply 2.303 to it in order to get a correct slope value (Slope 1)
Slope 1 (correct) =2.303 × Slope 2

☹ Most Common Mistake (36) –Why I cannot get correct activation energy?"

After you successfully plotted the Arrhenius plot, the activation energy (E_a) is extracted based on (**Eqn. 7-21**). The activation energy (E_a) is extracted from the slope of plot (shown in **Fig. 7-10**) times (−R).

$$E_a = - (slope) \times (R)$$

[I have seen that some people who were in a hurry reported a slope as E_a.] So, a slope itself does not give the value for E_a. Watch for the negative sign. Please see (**Fig. 7-9**) and note that we think the activation energy is postulated to be a positive value. (However, in some special cases, activation energy could be very close to zero.) Lastly, as a popular mistakes listed in many **Most Common Mistakes**, the gas constant R should be properly used. Please note that we commonly express the activation energy in unit of [J/mol], therefore, a gas constant R in [J mol^{-1} K^{-1}] should be used. (R =8.314472[J mol^{-1} K^{-1}] not 0.08205746 [atm L mol^{-1} K^{-1}]).

EXERCISE 7-3

The kinetics of double-strand formation for a DNA oligonucleotide containing a G•T was measured. Determine E_a: 2 (CGTGAATTCGCG) → Duplex

Temperature [°C]	k [M⁻¹ sec⁻¹]
31.8	8.00×10⁴
33.5	1.05×10⁵
36.8	1.77×10⁵
41.8	3.85×10⁵
48.5	9.51×10⁵

ANSWER

T [°C]	T [K]	×10³ 1/T [K⁻¹]	k [M⁻¹ sec⁻¹]	ln k
31.8	304.95	3.28	8.00×10⁴	11.290
33.5	306.65	3.26	1.05×10⁴	11.562
36.8	309.95	3.23	1.77×10⁵	12.084
41.8	314.95	3.18	3.85×10⁵	12.861
48.5	321.65	3.11	9.51×10⁵	13.765

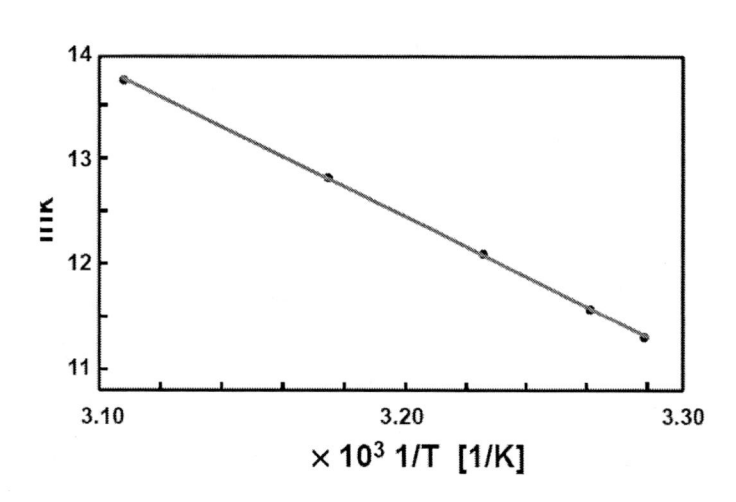

Arrhenius Plot.

Slope is -14603 [K] (The intercept is 59.19)

By multiplying a negative of gas constant (−R): R = 8.31447 [JK⁻¹ mol⁻¹]

E_a = 121400 [J/mol] = 121.4 [kJ/mol]

① Convert temperature in Kelvins unit.

② Calculate 1/T and ln k.
(For 1/t, 10³ is multiplied. For example, 3.28 shown in table was 3.28×10⁻³ before 10³ is multiplied.)

③ Plot ln k vs. 1/T

④ Don't forget that the value "1/T" is multiplied by 10³.

⑤ Don't forget to multiply the slope by −R.

7-4 Transition-State Theory

Let's take a look at an approach called **Transition-State Theory (TST)** (or activated-complex theory) and see how thermochemical values are related with reaction dynamics.

$$AB + C \overset{K^{\neq}}{\leftrightarrow} [ABC]^{\neq} \overset{k^{\neq}}{\rightarrow} A + BC$$

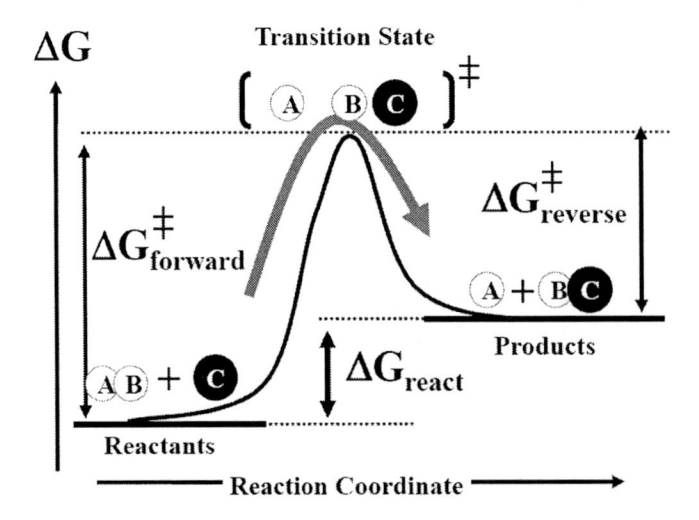

Fig. 7-11 Transition-State Theory

Here, $[ABC]^{\neq}$ is stated as the transition state complex, where is the state the reaction needs to pass through in order to the reaction should be completed. The first step of the reaction is assumed to be quasi-equilibrium between reactants and activated transition state complexes where equilibrium constant is $K^{\neq}$. The second step is non reversible process with the reaction rate constant $k^{\neq}$. The reaction rate in TST is given as

$$k = \frac{k_B T}{h} K^{\neq} \qquad \text{(Eqn. 7-22)}$$

By substituting the equilibrium constant in (**Eqn.7-22**) with an expression with respect to the Gibbs energy change, we have the **Eyring-Polanyi equation**

$$k = \left(k_B T / h \right) exp \left[- \Delta G^{\neq} / RT \right] \qquad \text{(Eqn. 7-23)}$$

The term in exponential, $\Delta G^{\neq}$ corresponds to the Gibbs energy change of forward reaction ($\Delta G^{\neq}_{forward}$) in **Fig. 7-11**.

Chapter 7 Kinetics

$$\Delta G_{react} = \Delta G^{\neq}_{forward} - \Delta G^{\neq}_{reverse}$$

Please be careful with the direction of the reaction and the way the Gibbs energy change (and difference) is defined. The constant $K^{\neq}$ is the equilibrium constant of an equilibrium of the reaction and $k^{\neq}$ Is the reaction rate constant of the second step. The formula given in (**Eqn. 7-22**) indicates "How many particles are passing the TS (transition state) and forming a complex. The pre-exponential factor in (**Eqn. 7-22**) is (k_BT/h), where k_B is the Boltzmann constant and the h is the Planck constant. Therefore, k_BT is a thermal energy at given temperature T and h corresponds to a quantized energy.

"**The unit of the pre exponential factor (k_BT/h) is [sec^{-1}] and implies the number of particles passing the TS per second.**"

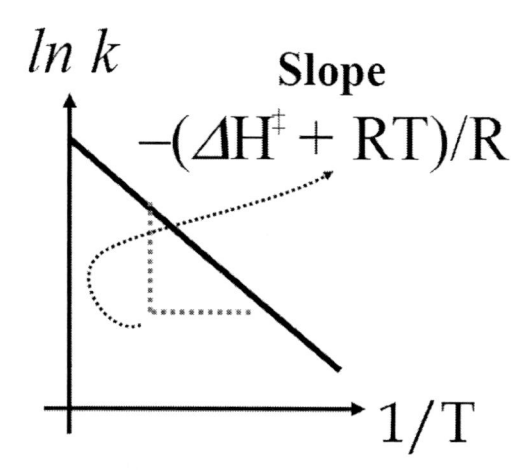

Fig. 7-12 The plot for Eyring's equation.

Unfortunately, TST does not accurately calculate the absolute reaction rate constants since precise information on reaction potential energy surfaces is required for the calculation of the reaction rate. On the other hand, TST can accurately describe the standard enthalpy of activation ($\Delta H^{\ddagger}$), the standard entropy of activation ($\Delta S^{\ddagger}$), and the standard Gibbs energy of activation ($\Delta G^{\ddagger}$) for a particular reaction. Since,

$$\Delta G = \Delta H - T\Delta S \qquad \text{(Eqn. 2-2)}$$

Similarly,

$$\Delta G^{\neq} = \Delta H^{\neq} - T\Delta S^{\neq} \qquad \text{(Eqn. 7-24)}$$

From **Eyring-Polanyi equation (Eqn. 7-23)**

$$k = \left(k_BT/h\right) exp\left[\Delta S^{\neq}/R\right] exp\left[-\Delta H^{\neq}/RT\right] \qquad \text{(Eqn. 7-25)}$$

The natural log of (**Eqn. 7-24**) gives

$$\ln\left(k/T\right) = -\Delta H^{\neq}/RT + \ln\left(k_B/h\right) + \left[\Delta S^{\neq}/R\right] \quad \text{(Eqn. 7-26)}$$

The plot of ln (k/T) as a function of 1/T provides a straight line with slope $-(\Delta H^{\neq}/R)$ and intercept of $\ln(k_B/h) + \Delta S^{\neq}/R$. From the slope, the enthalpy change can be extracted and the entropy change of activvationid obtained from an intercept on y-axis. There are very useful cases and approximations where we can use Eyring-Polanyi equation as a tool to estimate thermochemical values from the reaction rates.

When $\Delta H^{\neq} \gg RT$

$$\Delta H^{\neq} \approx E_a \quad \text{(Eqn. 7-27)}$$

Thus, you may see that (**Eqn. 7-25**) becomes very similar to the Arrhenius equation (**Eqn. 7-21**)

$$k = Ae^{-(E_a/RT)} \quad \text{(Eqn. 7-21)}$$

By comparing (**Eqn. 7-21**) and (**Eqn. 7-25**) under $\Delta H^{\neq} \approx E_a$

$$\Delta S^{\neq} \approx R\left[\ln\left(Ah/k_B T\right)\right] \quad \text{(Eqn. 7-28)}$$

> **EXERCISE 7-4**
> Calculate the entropy of activation energy at 39 °C for the double-strand formation reaction given in the previous example in **EXERCISE 7-3**.

ANSWER
The intercept is ln A = 59.19
A = 5.08×10^{25} [J/K]
T = 39 °C = 312.15 K
h = 6.626×10^{-34} [J s]
k_B = 1.3807×10^{-23} [J/K]
R = 8.3145 [J /K mol]

$$\Delta S^{\neq} \approx R \left[\ln \frac{Ah}{k_B T} \right] \quad \text{(Eqn. 7-28)}$$

$$= 8.3145 [J/K\ mol] \ln \left[\frac{(5.08 \times 10^{25} [J/K])(6.626 \times 10^{-34} [Js])}{(1.3807 \times 10^{-23} [J/K])(312.15 [K])} \right]$$

= (8.3145 [J K mol]) ln (7.811 x 10^{12})

= 8.3145 [J/K mol] (29.68)

= 246.8 [J/ K mol]

ln x = a → x = e^a
Temperature should be in Kelvins unit.
Gas constant R = 8.3145 [J /K mol]

7-5 Very Fast Reactions

As reaction takes place, the molecular structure may alter and atoms or fractions of molecules need to move around. While these molecular movements and formation of the bonds may happen very quickly, they cannot happen in "zero" seconds. In the case of an electron transfer, you can imagine that an electron should transfer much faster than atoms or molecules. There are many chemical reactions (including biological reactions) which occur within short time scale such as micro-, nano-, pico- or even femto second time regime. Recent technology enables us to resolve reactions in this short time scale. Here, let's take a look at an example of fast reactions in a perturbed equilibrium system. When a kind of perturbation is brought into a system which is in equilibrium, this perturbation can be considered as "a trigger" to cause a disturbance to equilibrium. Then, system needs to respond to this trigger in order to reach to a new equilibrium. If a reaction A+B →C is a reversible reaction with forward reaction rate k_1 and inverse reaction rate k_{-1}.

$$A + B \underset{k_{-1}}{\overset{k_1}{\rightleftarrows}} C$$

The production of the C (concentration of c, [C]) is expressed as

$$d[C]/dt = k_1[A][B] - k_{-1}[C] \qquad \text{(Eqn. 7-29)}$$

At the equilibrium,

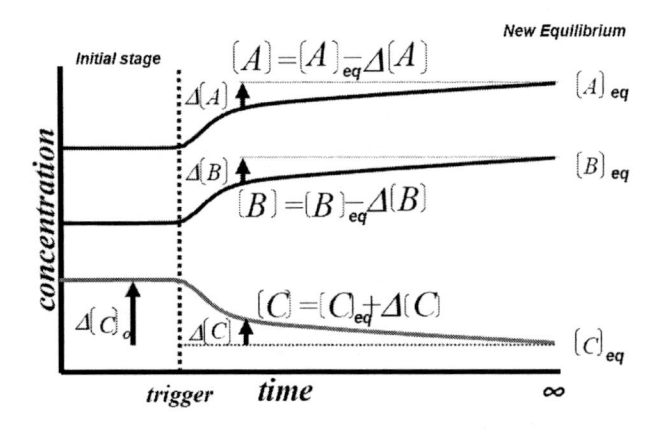

$$K = k_1/k_{-1} = [C]_{eq}/[A]_{eq}[B]_{eq} \qquad \text{(Eqn. 7-30)}$$

Fig. 7-13 Reaching new equilibrium

The concentrations at equilibrium are expressed as $[A]_{eq}$, $[B]_{eq}$, and $[C]_{eq}$. Now, if a perturbation (such as temperature or pressure jump) is caused to reduce a product amount by $\Delta[C]_o$ (**Fig. 7-13**), the change of product at a given time t ($\Delta[C]$) can be expressed as

$$\Delta[C] = \Delta[C]_o e^{-t/\tau} \qquad \text{(Eqn. 7-3)}$$

Here,

$$1/\tau = k_1([A]_{eq} + [B]_{eq}) + k_{-1} \qquad \text{(Eqn. 7-3)}$$

Chapter 7 Kinetics

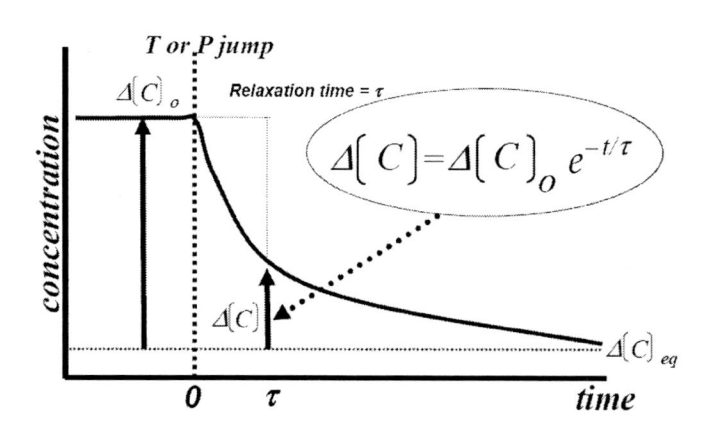

Fig. 7-14. The exponential decay to reach new equilibrium.

$$\Delta[C] = \Delta[C]_0 \, e^{-t/\tau}$$

The change of the product, therefore, indicates the single exponential decay and can be taken as the message of this very fast reaction. In general, the biological very fast reaction can show single exponential change.

The exponential decay constant ($1/\tau$) has the unit of [1/sec], and the τ can be regarded as a decay time [sec].

In the derivation for (**Eqn. 7-31**), a very useful approximation, **steady state approximation**, is used. Let me touch upon this briefly. The **steady state approximation** assumes that the concentration of any intermediate (X) in the reaction is unchanged. This means that the rate of intermediate produced is equal to the rate of consumption. (d[X]/dt=0) While you may be skeptical on this approximation, the benefit of this approximation is great! This approximation will allow to derive the expression for concentration of the intermediate.

EXERCISE 7-5

Transfer RNA can exist in two forms that are in rapid equilibrium with each other; $K=[B]^{eq}/[A]^{eq}=10$ at 28 [°C]. In a temperature-jump experiment, a solution of the t-RNA at a concentration of 10μM is quickly (faster than 10μs) raised in temperature from 25 [°C] to 28 [°C] A relaxation time was measured to be τ=3 [msec]. What are the values of k_1 and k_{-1}, including units? Assume that the mechanism is:

$$A \underset{k_{-1}}{\overset{k}{\rightleftharpoons}} B$$

ANSWER

The formula (**Eqn. 7-33**) and (**Eqn. 7-34**) are derived at the end of this chapter.

$$K = \frac{[B]^{eq}}{[A]^{eq}} = \frac{k_1}{k_{-1}}$$

$$\Delta[B] = [B]_0 e^{-t/\tau} \qquad \textbf{(Eqn. 7-33)}$$

Here,

$$\frac{1}{\tau} = k_1 + k_{-1} \qquad \textbf{(Eqn. 7-34)}$$

$\tau^{-1} = k_1 + k_{-1} = (3 \times 10^{-3} \text{ [sec]})^{-1}$

$K = [B]^{eq}/[A]^{eq} = 10 = k_1 / k_{-1}$

Therefore, $k_1 + k_{-1} = 10\, k_{-1} + k_{-1} = 11\, k_{-1} = (3 \times 10^{-3} \text{ [sec]})^{-1}$

$k_{-1} = 30.3 \text{ [sec}^{-1}\text{]}$

$k_1 = 10 \times 30.3 \text{ [sec}^{-1}\text{]}$

$= 303 \text{ [sec}^{-1}\text{]}$

See the end of chapter page for the derivations.

Use, $K = [B]^{eq}/[A]^{eq} = k_1 / k_{-1}$

Chapter 7

How did you get these equations?
-The derivation of selected equations.

(Eqn. 7-4) $[C] - [C]_o = k_0 t$

The zero-th order reaction is expressed as

$$d[C]/dt = k_0 \qquad \text{(Eqn. 7-3)}$$

Here, the concentration of the product C is [C] and the reaction rate coefficient for the zero-th order is given by k_0. By arranging **(Eqn. 7-3)**

$$d[C] = k_o dt$$

By taking an integral of both sides for [C] from [C]o at time t=0 to [C] at time t,

$$\int_{[C]_o}^{[C]} d[C] = k_0 \int_0^t dt$$

Here, we used $\int dx = x + C$ (C is a constant.)

Thus,
$$[C] - [C]_o = k_0 t \qquad \text{(Eqn. 7-4)}$$

(Eqn. 7-5) $[A] = [A_0] - k_0 t$

The zero-th order reaction with respect to the reactant concentration [A] is expressed as

$$-d[A]/dt = k_0 \qquad \text{(Eqn. 7-3)}$$

The reaction rate constant for the zero-th order is k_0. By arranging **(Eqn. 7-3)**

$$-d[A] = k_o dt$$

By taking an integral of both sides for [A] from [A]o at time t=0 to [A] at time t,

$$-\int_{[A]_o}^{[A]} d[A] = k_0 \int_0^t dt$$

Thus,
$$-[A] + [A]_o = k_0 t$$

$$[A] = [A]_o - k_o t \qquad \text{(Eqn. 7-5)}$$

(Eqn. 7-7) $\qquad \ln\left([A]/[A]_o\right) = -k_1 t$

(Eqn. 7-8) $\qquad [A] = [A]_o e^{-k_1 t}$

In the first order reaction, the reaction speed v is given as

$$v = -\frac{d[A]}{dt} = k_1[A] \qquad \text{(Eqn. 7-6)}$$

By arranging (**Eqn. 7-6**)

$$\frac{d[A]}{[A]} = -k_1 dt$$

By taking an integral of both sides for [A] from [A]$_o$ at time t = 0 to [A] at time t,

$$\int_{[A]_o}^{[A]} \frac{1}{[A]} d[A] = -k_1 \int_0^t dt$$

$$ln[A] - ln[A]_o = -k_1 t$$

$$\ln\left([A]/[A]_o\right) = -k_1 t \qquad \text{(Eqn. 7-7)}$$

Here, we used $\int (1/x) dx = \ln x + C$ (C is a constant)
The (**Eqn. 7-7**) is rephrased in terms of exponential, (ln x=a means that x = e^a)

$$[A]/[A]_o = e^{-k_1 t}$$

Thus,

$$[A] = [A]_o e^{-k_1 t} \qquad \text{(Eqn. 7-8)}$$

(Eqn. 7-10)
$$1/[A] = k_2 t + 1/[A]_0$$

From (**Eqn. 7-9**) the second order reaction (type-I) is given by

$$-d[A]/dt = k_2[A]^2 \qquad \text{(Eqn. 7-9)}$$

By arranging the above, you will get

$$-d[A]/[A]^2 = k_2 dt$$

By taking an integral of both sides for [A] from [A]$_0$ at time t=0 to [A] at time t,

$$-\int_{[A]_o}^{[A]} \left(1/[A]^2\right) d[A] = k_2 \int_0^t dt$$

$$1/[A] - 1/[A]_o = k_2 t$$

Here, we used $\int (1/x^2)\, dx = -1/x + C$ \qquad (C is a constant)

Thus,

$$1/[A] = k_2 t + 1/[A]_0 \qquad \text{(Eqn. 7-10)}$$

(Eqn. 7-12) $$\left(1/([A]_0 - [B]_0)\right) \ln\left([B]_0[A] / [A]_0[B]\right) = k_2 t$$

For the Second-Order Reactions (type –II), the general expression for the reaction speed is

$$v = k_2[A][B]$$

Let's reduce the number of the parameters by expressing the amount of [C] at t as x. Then, [C]=x, [A] = [A]₀ –x , and [B] = [B]₀ –x

Since the reaction speed is also expressed as

$$v = d[C]/dt \quad \textbf{(Eqn. 7-11)}$$

Thus,

$$v = dx/dt = k_2[A][B] = k_2([A]_0 - x)([B]_0 - x)$$

$$dx/dt = k_2([A]_0 - x)([B]_0 - x)$$

By arranging the above,

$$dx/(([A]_0 - x)([B]_0 - x)) = k_2 dt$$

By integrating the above of both sides for x from 0 at time t=0 to x at time t,

$$\int_0^x \left(1/\{([A]_0 - x)([B]_0 - x)\}\right) dx = \int_0^t k_2 \, dt$$

or

$$\int_0^x \left(1/\{(x - [A]_0)(x - [B]_0)\}\right) dx = \int_0^t k_2 \, dt$$

Then,

$$\left(1/([A]_0 - [B]_0)\right) \ln\left([B]_0[A] / [A]_0[B]\right) = k_2 t \qquad \textbf{(Eqn. 7-12)}$$

([A]₀ ≠ [B]₀)

For getting **(Eqn. 7-12)**, we used

$$\int \left(1/[(x + a)(x + b)]\right) dx = \left(1/(b - a)\right) \ln\left\{(a + x)/(b + x)\right\}$$

(a ≠ b)

Chapter 7 Kinetics

(Eqn. 7-14) $\quad 1/[A]^{n-1} = k_n t + 1/[A]_o^{n-1}$

The nth order reaction is given by

$$-d[A]/dt = k_n[A]^n \quad \text{(Eqn. 7-13)}$$

By arranging the above, you will get

$$-d[A]/[A]^n = k_n dt$$

By taking an integral of both sides for [A] from [A]$_o$ at time t=0 to [A] at time t,

$$-\int_{[A]_o}^{[A]} d[A]/[A]^n = k_n \int_0^t dt$$

$$(-1/(1-n))\{1/[A]^{n-1} - 1/[A]_o^{n-1}\} = k_n t$$

Thus,

$$1/[A]^{n-1} = (n-1)k_n t + 1/[A]_o^{n-1} \quad \text{(Eqn. 7-10)}$$

Here, we used

$\int x^n dx = (1/(n+1))x^{n+1} + C$ or $\int x^{-n} dx = (1/(1-n))x^{-n+1} + C$

(C is a constant)

(Eqn. 7-16) $\quad t_{1/2} = [A]_o / 2k_0$

The integrated expression for the zero-th first order reaction is

$$[A] = [A]_o - k_0 t \quad \text{(Eqn. 7-5)}$$

At t$_{1/2}$, [A] =[A]$_o$/2

$$(1/2)[A]_o = [A]_o - k_0 t_{\frac{1}{2}}$$

Thus,

$$t_{1/2} = [A]_0 / 2k_0 \quad \text{(Eqn. 7-16)}$$

Chapter 7 Kinetics

(Eqn. 7-17)
$$t_{1/2} = 0.6931/k_1$$

The integrated expression for the first order reaction is

$$\ln\left([A]/[A]_o\right) = -k_1 t \qquad \text{(Eqn. 7-7)}$$

At $t_{1/2}$, $[A] = [A]_o/2$

$$\ln\left(\frac{([A]_o/2)}{[A]_o}\right) = -k_1 t_{\frac{1}{2}}$$

$$\ln(1/2) = -k_1 t_{1/2}$$

$$\ln 2 = k_1 t_{1/2}$$

Thus, the half life is given as

$$t_{1/2} = \ln 2 / k_1 = 0.6931 / k_1 \qquad \text{(Eqn. 7-16)}$$

(Eqn. 7-18)
$$t_{1/2} = 1/k_2[A]_0$$

The integrated expression for the second order reaction (type-I) is

$$1/[A] = k_2 t + 1/[A]_o \qquad \text{(Eqn. 7-10)}$$

At $t_{1/2}$, $[A] = [A]_o/2$

$$\frac{1}{\frac{1}{2}[A]_o} = k_2 t_{1/2} + \frac{1}{[A]_o}$$

$$1/[A]_0 = k_2 t_{1/2}$$

Therefore, the half life is

$$t_{1/2} = 1/k_2[A]_0 \qquad \text{(Eqn. 7-17)}$$

(Eqn. 7-19)
$$t_{1/2} = \frac{2^{n-1} - 1}{(n-1)k[A]_0^{n-1}}$$

The integrated expression for the nth order reaction is

$$1/[A]^{n-1} = (n-1)k_n t + 1/[A]_0^{n-1} \quad \text{(Eqn. 7-14)}$$

At $t_{1/2}$, $[A] = [A]_0/2$

$$1\bigg/\left([A]_0/2\right)^{n-1} = (n-1)k_n t_{\frac{1}{2}} + 1/[A]_0^{n-1}$$

$$\left(2/[A]_0\right)^{n-1} = (n-1)k_n t_{\frac{1}{2}} + 1/[A]_0^{n-1}$$

$$\frac{2^{n-1} - 1}{[A]_0^{n-1}} = (n-1)k_n t_{\frac{1}{2}}$$

$$t_{1/2} = \frac{(2^{n-1} - 1)}{(n-1)k_n [A]_0^{n-1}} \quad \text{(Eqn. 7-19)}$$

(Eqn. 7-20)
$$\ln k = -\left(E_a/RT\right) + \ln A$$

(Eqn. 7-21)
$$k = A e^{-(E_a/RT)}$$

While the Arrhenius equation is an empirical formula, the format is justified by the **Eyring-Polanyi equation**,

$$k = \left(k_B T/h\right) \exp\left[\Delta S^{\neq}/R\right] \exp\left[-\Delta H^{\neq}/RT\right] \text{(Eqn. 7-25)}$$

The activation energy is expressed as

$$E_a = \Delta H^{\neq} + RT$$

Thus,

$$k = \left(k_B T/h\right) \exp\left[\Delta S^{\neq}/R\right] \exp\left[-\frac{(E_a - RT)}{RT}\right]$$

Chapter 7 Kinetics

$$k = (k_BT/h) \exp[\Delta S^{\ddagger}/R] \exp[-E_a/RT] e$$

$$k = e(k_BT/h) \exp[\Delta S^{\ddagger}/R] \exp[-E_a/RT]$$

If $(e^{k_BT/h}) \exp\left[\dfrac{\Delta S^{\ddagger}}{R}\right]$ is set as a constant, A,

$$k = Ae^{-(E_a/RT)} \qquad \text{(Eqn. 7-21)*}$$

(Eqn. 7-23) $\qquad k = (k_BT/h) \exp[-\Delta G^{\ddagger}/RT]$

From TST,

$$k = \dfrac{k_BT}{h} K^{\ddagger} \qquad \text{(Eqn. 7-22)}$$

Recall very important relationship between Gibbs energy change and the equilibrium constant of a reaction from **Chapter 2** as

$$\Delta G^o = -RT \ln K \qquad \text{(Eqn. 2-10)}$$

Thus,

$$K = e^{-(\Delta G^o/RT)}$$

This can be rephrased as

$$K^{\ddagger} = e^{-(\Delta G^{\ddagger}/RT)}$$

$$k = \dfrac{k_BT}{h} \exp\left[-\dfrac{\Delta G^{\ddagger}}{RT}\right] \quad \text{(Eqn. 7-23)}$$

(Eqn. 7-31) $\Delta[C] = \Delta[C]_o e^{-t/\tau}$

(Eqn. 7-32) $1/\tau = k_1([A]_{eq} + [B]_{eq}) + k_{-1}$

Let's systematically set up the **time dependent concentrations** as:
$[C] = [C]_{eq} + \Delta[C]$
$[A] = [A]_{eq} - \Delta[A] = [A]_{eq} - \Delta[C]$
$[B] = [B]_{eq} - \Delta[B] = [B]_{eq} - \Delta[C]$

From,
$$[C] = [C]_{eq} + \Delta[C]$$
$$d[C]/dt = d\left[[C]_{eq} + \Delta[C]\right]/dt = d[\Delta[C]]/dt$$

This is because
$$d[C]_{eq}/dt = 0$$

$$d[\Delta[C]]/dt = d[C]/dt = k_1[A][B] - k_{-1}[C]$$
$$= k_1\left[[A]_{eq} - \Delta[C]\right]\left[[\bar{B}] - \Delta[C]\right] - k_{-1}\left[[C]_{eq} + \Delta[C]\right]$$

$$= k_1[A]_{eq}[B]_{eq} - k_{-1}[C]_{eq} - k_1\left[[A]_{eq}\Delta[C] + [B]_{eq}\Delta[C] - [\Delta[C]]^2\right] - k_{-1}\Delta[C]$$

By approximating the quadratic term as
$[\Delta[C]]^2 \approx 0$

The steady state approximation makes
$$d[C]_{eq}/dt = k_1[A]_{eq}[B]_{eq} - k_{-1}[C]_{eq} = 0$$

Thus,
$$d[\Delta[C]]/dt = -\{k_1([A]_{eq} + [B]_{eq}) + k_{-1}\}\Delta[C]$$

Please take a close look at the term given by $k_1\{[\bar{A}] + [\bar{B}]\} + k_{-1}$ is independent of time and can be replaced as a one constant expression as:

$1/\tau = k_1([A]_{eq} + [B]_{eq}) + k_{-1}$ \hfill (Eqn. 7-32)

Therefore,

$$d[\Delta[C]]/dt = -\Delta[C]/\tau$$

You may recall and notice this is the form of the first order reaction. We recall how these can be integrated and the integrated form as:

$$\Delta[C] = \Delta[C]_o e^{-t/\tau} \qquad \text{(Eqn. 7-31)}$$

at t=0.

$$\Delta[C] = \Delta[C]_o$$

(Eqn. 7-33) $\quad \Delta[B] = \Delta[B]_o e^{-t/\tau}$
(Eqn. 7-34) $\quad 1/\tau = k_1 + k_{-1}$

Let's systematically set up the time dependent concentrations as:
$[B] = [B]_{eq} + \Delta[B]$

$$[A] = [A]_{eq} - \Delta[A] = [A]_{eq} - \Delta[B]$$

From, $[B] = [B]_{eq} + \Delta[B]$

$$d[B]/dt = d\big[[B]_{eq} + \Delta[B]\big]/dt = d[\Delta[B]]/dt$$

This is because

$$d[B]_{eq}/dt = 0$$

$$d[\Delta[B]]/dt = d[B]/dt = k_1[A] - k_{-1}[B]$$

$$= k_1\big[[A]_{eq} - \Delta[B]\big] - k_{-1}\big[[B]_{eq} + \Delta[B]\big]$$

$$= k_1[A]_{eq} - k_{-1}[B]_{eq} - k_1\Delta[B] - k_{-1}\Delta[B]$$

The steady state approximation makes

$$d[B]_{eq}/dt = k_1[A]_{eq} - k_{-1}[B]_{eq} = 0$$

$$k_1[A]_{eq} = k_{-1}[B]_{eq}$$

Thus,

Chapter 7 Kinetics

$$d[\Delta[B]]/dt = k_{-1}[B]_{eq} - k_{-1}[B]_{eq} - k_1\Delta[B] - k_{-1}\Delta[B]$$

$$d[\Delta[B]]/dt = -\{k_1 + k_{-1}\}\Delta[B]$$

Please take a close look at the term given by $-(k_1 + k_{-1})$ is independent of time and can be replaced as a one constant expression as:

$1/\tau = k_1 + k_{-1}$ (Eqn. 7-34)

Therefore,

$$d[\Delta[B]]/dt = -\Delta[B]/\tau$$

You may recall and notice this is the form of the first order reaction. We recall how these can be integrated and the integrated form as:

$\Delta[B] = \Delta[B]_o e^{-t/\tau}$ (Eqn. 7-33)

at t=0.

$\Delta[B] = \Delta[B]_o$

Chapter 7 Summary [PART 1]

(Use back page to cover the contents.)

1	reaction speed	change of the reactants or products per unit time $$v = \left(\Delta[A]/\Delta t\right)$$ For reaction, A+ B→ C $$v = -\left(d[A]/dt\right) = -\left(d[B]/dt\right) = +\left(d[C]/dt\right) \quad \text{(Eqn. 7-1)}$$
2	Reaction order	reaction of (n+m)-th order $$v = k[A]^m[B]^n \quad \text{(Eqn. 7-2)}$$
3	integrated form for 0th, 1st, 2nd (type-I &II), and n^{th} order reactions	Table 7-1 	Order	Reaction Speed, v	Integrated Form	 |---|---|---| | 0th | $v = k_0$ | $[A] = [A_0] - k_0 t$ | | 1st | $v = k_1[A]$ | $[A] = [A]_o e^{-k_1 t}$ | | 2nd (I) | $v = k_2[A]^2$ | $1/[A] = k_2 t + 1/[A]_0$ | | 2nd (II) | $v = k_2[A][B]$ | $\left(\frac{1}{[A]_0} - \frac{1}{[B]_0}\right) \ln\left(\frac{[B]_0[A]}{[A]_0[B]}\right) = k_2 t$ | | n^{th} | $v = k_n[A]^n$ | $\frac{1}{[A]^{n-1}} = (n-1)k_n t + \frac{1}{[A]_o^{n-1}}$ |

[Fold the page at the double line and cover the right half.]

Chapter 7 Summary Check [Part 1]

(Use this page to cover and check the contents.)
Use ☐ as your check box. Write your comment at far right

1	reaction speed	☐ ☐ ☐ ☐ ☐	
2	Reaction order	☐ ☐ ☐ ☐ ☐	
3	integrated form for 0th, 1st, 2nd (type-I &II), and n^{th} order reactions	☐ ☐ ☐ ☐ ☐	

Chapter 7 Summary [Part 2]

(Use back page to cover the contents.)

4	linear plot for 0ᵗʰ, 1ˢᵗ, 2ⁿᵈ (type-I &II), and nᵗʰ order reactions.		
		[A] vs t plot with slope $-k_0$, intercept $[A]_o$	$\ln[A]$ vs t plot with slope $-k_1$, intercept $\ln[A]_o$
		Plot for 0ᵗʰ order reaction on [A].	Plot for the 1st order reaction.
		$\frac{1}{[A]}$ vs t plot with slope k_2, intercept $\frac{1}{[A]_o}$	$\ln\frac{[A]}{[B]}$ vs t plot with slope k_2, intercept $\ln\frac{[A]_o}{[B]_o}$
		The plot for the second order reaction (type-I).	The plot for the second order reaction (type-II).
		$\frac{1}{[A]^{n-1}}$ vs t plot with slope k_n, intercept $\frac{1}{[A]_o^{n-1}}$	
		The plot for the n-th order reaction.	

[Fold the page at the double line and cover the right half.]

Chapter 7 Summary Check [Part 2]

(Use this page to cover and check the contents.)
Use ☐ as your check box. Write your comment at far right

4	linear plot for 0th, 1st, 2nd (type-I &II), and n^{th} order reactions.	☐ ☐ ☐ ☐ ☐	

Chapter 7 Summary [Part 3]

(Use back page to cover the contents.)

5	half life ($t_{½}$) for 0th, 1st, 2nd (type-I &II), and n^{th} order reactions	<table><tr><th>Order</th><th>Half-life</th></tr><tr><td>0th</td><td>$t_{1/2} = [A]_0 / 2k_0$</td></tr><tr><td>1st</td><td>$t_{1/2} = \dfrac{0.6931}{k_1}$</td></tr><tr><td>$2^{nd}$ (I)</td><td>$t_{1/2} = \dfrac{1}{k_2[A]_0}$</td></tr><tr><td>$n^{th}$</td><td>$t_{1/2} = \dfrac{2^{n-1}-1}{(n-1)k[A]_0^{n-1}}$</td></tr></table>
6	Arrhenius equation and plot	$k = Ae^{-(E_a/RT)}$ (Eqn. 7-20) $\ln k = -(E_a/RT) + \ln A$ (Eqn. 7-21) Arrhenius Plot: $\ln k$ vs $1/T$, Slope $= -\dfrac{E_a}{R}$
7	Transition state theory (TST)	$AB + C \overset{K^{\neq}}{\longleftrightarrow} [ABC]^{\neq} \overset{k^{\neq}}{\longrightarrow} A + BC$ reaction rate constant $k = \dfrac{k_B T}{h} K^{\neq}$ (Eqn. 7-23)

[Fold the page at the double line and cover the right half.]

Chapter 7 Summary Check [Part 3]

(Use this page to cover and check the contents.)
Use □ as your check box. Write your comment at far right

5	half life ($t_{1/2}$) for 0th, 1st, 2nd (type-I &II), and n^{th} order reactions	□ □ □ □ □	
6	**Arrhenius equation and plot**	□ □ □ □ □	
7	Transition state theory (TST)	□ □ □ □ □	

Chapter 7 Summary [Part 4]

(Use back page to cover the contents.)

8	**Eyring-Polanyi equation** and plot	$k = (k_B T/h) \exp[-\Delta G^{\ddagger}/RT]$ (Eqn. 7-25)* $k = (k_B T/h) \exp[\Delta S^{\ddagger}/R] \exp[-\Delta H^{\ddagger}/RT]$ (Eqn. 7-26) *Plot: $\ln k$ vs $1/T$, Slope $= -(\Delta H^{\ddagger} + RT)/R$* The plot for Eyring-Polanyi equation.
9	The activated $\Delta H^{\ddagger}$ and $\Delta S^{\ddagger}$	$\Delta H^{\ddagger} \approx E_a$ (Eqn. 7-27) $\Delta S^{\ddagger} \approx R[\ln(Ah/k_B T)]$ (Eqn. 7-28)
10	The change in product's concentration $\Delta[C]$ of fast reactions $A + B \underset{k_{-1}}{\overset{k_1}{\rightleftarrows}} C$	$\Delta[C] = \Delta[C]_o e^{-t/\tau}$ (Eqn. 7-31) $1/\tau = k_1([A]_{eq} + [B]_{eq}) + k_{-1}$ (Eqn. 7-32)

[Fold the page at the double line and cover the right half.]

Chapter 7 Summary Check [Part 4]

(Use this page to cover and check the contents.)
Use □ as your check box. Write your comment at far right

8	**Eyring-Polanyi equation** and plot	□ □ □ □ □	
9	The activated $\Delta H^{\ddagger}$ and $\Delta S^{\ddagger}$	□ □ □ □ □	
10	The change in product's concentration $\Delta[C]$ of fast reactions $A + B \underset{k_{-1}}{\overset{k_1}{\rightleftarrows}} C$	□ □ □ □ □	

Chapter 7 Kinetics

YOUR TEACHER MAY TEST YOU ON:

No.	What may be asked?		What you should know or do?
1	What is the concept of activated state?	→	Fig. 7-1
2	How do you express the speed of reaction in terms of the reactants or products of the reaction?	→	$v = -\left(d[A]/dt\right) = -\left(d[B]/dt\right) = +\left(d[C]/dt\right)$ (Eqn. 7-1)
		→	EXERCISE 7-1
3	How do you define the order of the reaction?	→	reaction of (n+m)-th order $v = k[A]^m[B]^n$ (Eqn. 7-2)
		→	Problems 7-1, 7-2, 7-3, 7-4
	What is the expression of the reaction speed for the 0-th, first, second (type-I &II), and n-th order of reactions?	→	Table 7-1
	What is the integrated expression of the reaction speed for the 0th, 1st, 2nd (type-I &II), and n^{th} order of reactions?	→	Table 7-1
	How do you make linear plot for the 0th, 1st, 2nd (type-I &II), and n^{th} order of reactions? (How do you extract the reaction rate constant from the linear plot?)	→	Fig. 7-3, 7-4, 7-5, 7-6, 7-7, 7-8
		→	EXERCISE 7-2
		→	Problems 7-5, 7-6, 7-7, 7-8, 7-9, 7-10, 7-11, 7-12
4	What is the half-life of the reaction speed for the 0th, 1st, 2nd (type-I &II), and n^{th} order of reactions?	→	Table 7-1
		→	Problems 7-13, 7-14, 7-15, 7-16, 7-17
5	How do you extract the activation energy from Arrhenius equation? How do you calculate the reaction rate of different temperature (for given temperature change) under given activation energy?	→	$k = Ae^{-(E_a/RT)}$ (Eqn. 7-20) $\ln k = -\left(E_a/RT\right) + \ln A$ (Eqn. 7-21)
		→	Fig. 7-10
		→	EXERCISE 7-3
		→	Problems 7-18, 7-19, 7-20, 7-21, 7-22, 7-23, 7-24, 7-25, 7-26, 7-27
6	What is the reaction path (scheme) of the transition state theory?	→	$AB + C \overset{K^{\neq}}{\leftrightarrow} [ABC]^{\neq} \overset{k^{\neq}}{\to} A + BC$ $k = \frac{k_B T}{h} K^{\neq}$ (Eqn. 7-23) $k = \left(k_B T/h\right) \exp\left[-\Delta G^{\neq}/RT\right]$ (Eqn. 7-25)
		→	Problems 7-28, 7-29
7	How do you calculate the reaction rate from given activated Gibbs energy change?(Eyring –Polanyi equation)	→	$k = \left(k_B T/h\right) \exp\left[\Delta S^{\neq}/R\right] \exp\left[-\Delta H^{\neq}/RT\right]$ (Eqn. 7-26)

		→	Fig. 7-12
		→	EXERCISE 7-4
		→	Problem 7-30
8	How do you extract the activated enthalpy change and activated entropy change?	→	$\Delta H^{\neq} \approx E_a$ (Eqn. 7-27) $\Delta S^{\neq} \approx R \left[\ln \left(Ah / k_B T \right) \right]$ (Eqn. 7-28)
		→	Problem 7-30
9	How do you calculate the exponential decay constant for the product in A+B→ C reactions?	→	$\Delta[C] = \Delta[C]_o e^{-t/\tau}$ (Eqn. 7-31) $1/\tau = k_1([A]_{eq} + [B]_{eq}) + k_{-1}$ (Eqn. 7-32)
		→	EXERCISE 7-5
		→	Problems 7-31

UNIT CHECK CHAPTER 7

Important Parameters of This Chapter	Popularly Used Unit	Important Unit Conversion
Change in concentration, $\Delta[A]$	M mol/L	
Change in time, Δt	sec	
Velocity of reaction, v	M/sec	
Reaction order, n+m	dimensionless	
Reaction rate constant (0th order reaction), k_0	M/sec	
Reaction rate constant (1st order reaction), k_1	sec^{-1}	
Reaction rate constant (2nd order reaction-type-I), k_2	$M^{-1} sec^{-1}$	
Reaction rate constant (2nd order reaction-type-II), k_2	$M^{-1} sec^{-1}$	
Reaction rate constant (n^{th} order reaction), k_n	$M^{n-1} sec^{-1}$	
Half-life, $t_{1/2}$	sec	
Pre-exponential factor for the Arrhenius equation, A	Same as the unit of the n-th order's reaction rate constant	
Temperature, T	°C K	0 [°C] = 273.15 [K]
Gas constant, R	$atm \cdot L \cdot mol^{-1} \cdot K^{-1}$ $J \cdot mol^{-1} \cdot K^{-1}$	R=8.314472 [$J\ mol^{-1}\ K^{-1}$] =0.08205746 [$atm\ L\ mol^{-1}\ K^{-1}$]
Activation energy, E_a	$J \cdot mol^{-1}$ $kJ \cdot mol^{-1}$	
Boltzmann constant, k_B	$J \cdot K^{-1}$	$k_B = 1.3807 \times 10^{-23}$ [$J \cdot K^{-1}$]
Planck constant, h	$J \cdot sec$ $m^2 \cdot kg \cdot sec^{-1}$	6.626068×10^{-34} [$J \cdot sec$]
The activated state Gibbs change, $\Delta G^{\neq}$	$J \cdot mol^{-1}$ $kJ \cdot mol^{-1}$	
The activated state Enthalpy change, $\Delta H^{\neq}$	$J \cdot mol^{-1}$ $kJ \cdot mol^{-1}$	
The activated state entropy change, $\Delta S^{\neq}$	$J \cdot mol^{-1} \cdot K^{-1}$ $kJ \cdot mol^{-1} \cdot K^{-1}$	
Equilibrium constant for the transition state complex formation, $K^{\neq}$	dimensionless or $M^{c+d-(a+b)}$	
Exponential decay time, τ	sec	

SUMMARY OF TRICKY TRAPS OF CHAPTER 7

☐	1	The order of a reaction is NOT given from stoichiometric coefficient of the reaction.
☐	2	For each order of reaction, an integrated rate expression, linear-plot, half-life should be understood. (and memorized.)
☐	3	The rate constant has different unit for corresponding order of reaction.
☐	4	The activation energy does not depend on temperature.
☐	5	For Arrhenius plot, calculate more than three digits for 1/T (inverse of temperature), and don't forget to multiply –R to a slope of line in order to extract E_a.

LAST MINUTE REVIEW OFMATH CHAPTER 7

(These are basic algebra which you have no excuse if you miss them.)

1. $\ln a + \ln b = \ln ab$ $\qquad \ln a - \ln b = \ln \frac{a}{b}$

2. $\ln y = \ln a - x$ $\qquad y = ae^{-x}$

3. $\int x^n dx = \frac{1}{n+1} x^{n+1} + C$ n ≠ 1 and C is a constant

4. $\int \frac{dx}{x} = \ln x + C$

Nobel Prize and Your Knowledge From Chapter 7
(*: word appeared in Chapter 7)

The Nobel Prize in Chemistry 1992 was awarded to **Rudolph A. Marcus** for his contributions to the theory of electron transfer reactions in chemical systems. In 1951 and 1952, Marcus developed RRKM (Rice-Ramsperger-Kassel-Marcus) theory to explain solution **reaction rates***. The RRKM theory utilized the transition state theory (1930s) with statistical ideas of the RRK theory. With his knowledge in electrostatics, Marcus started investigating on electron transfers (the transfer of electrons between molecules in solution) in 1955. While electron transfer takes place, molecular structure of very loosely bonded reacting molecules change without breaking any chemical bonds. In order to make an electron transfer reaction to happen, enough energy to cross over reaction barrier should be supplied. The electron transfer rate is governed by the height of the reaction barrier. Marcus explained that solvent molecules in the immediate vicinity of reacting molecules change their positions and thus increasing the energy in the molecular system. This temporal rise of energy in molecular system causes electron transfer between the molecules. The electron transfer is possible between two states with an equal energy. This condition is achieved by increasing the energy for both reacting molecules. Marcus described the correlation between the electron-transfer reaction and the reaction rate with parabolic (quadratic) function explaining how the energy of the molecular system is affected by structural changes of molecules and calculated the size of the energy barrier (Marcus theory). The basic equation of this theory states the

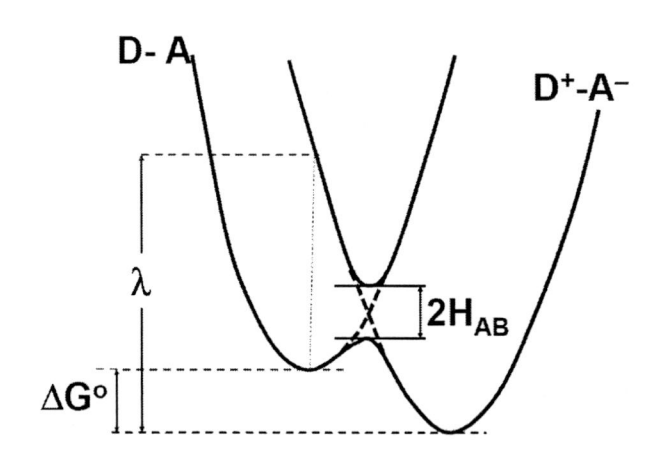

Fig. 7-15 Markus Theory.

rate of electron transfer (k_{et}) as: $k_{et} = (2\pi/\hbar)|H_{AB}|^2 \left(1/\sqrt{4\pi\lambda k_B T}\right) e^{\left(-(\lambda+\Delta G^\circ)^2/4\lambda k_B T\right)}$

Here, $|H_{AB}|$ is the electronic coupling between the initial and final states, λ is the reorganization energy, and ΔG° is the total Gibbs free energy change for the electron transfer reaction (k_B is the Boltzmann constant). This theory can show a connection between electron transfer rate and the Gibbs energy change of the reaction. While it was not well regarded at first, experimental confirmation of Marcus theory was completed in the late 1980s.

The Marcus theory is able to explain electron transfer reactions observed in photosynthesis, corrosion, electrochemical synthesis, the electro-conductivity of conducting polymers, and almost over all areas of chemistry.

Chapter 7 Kinetics

Bonus!!!

I would like to add a bit more to this section with the study related with "fast reaction" explained in this chapter. Especially, the relaxation technique developed by Eigen is exactly explained in this textbook.

The Nobel Prize in Chemistry 1967 was awarded to **Manfred Eigen, Ronald George Wreyford Norrish** and **George Porter** for the research on extremely fast chemical reactions by perturbing the equilibrium with very short pulses.

Manfred Eigen started using the relaxation technique to study extremely **fast ionic reactions*** in solution in 1954. The relaxation method involves a disturbance of an equilibrated system with a pulse of high-frequency sound waves followed by a measurement of the time to relax back to its normal state of equilibrium (ultrasound absorption measurements). This technique was developed to a measuring technique to resolve the reaction takes place at a nanosecond time range. This technique opened a way of calculating the rates of fast reactions including complex biochemical reactions. The theory of relaxation of multi stage processes was developed on various metals' complex reactions. Around 1960, he focused on physical-organic chemistry and individual steps of a series of reaction mechanisms were elucidated, and he experimentally verified a general theory of acid-base catalysis. Eigen also investigated proton reactions. He determined the neutralization rate and discovered the anomalous conduction characteristics of protons in ice crystals. His research emphasis widely covered biochemical system such as hydrogen bridges of nucleic acids, dynamics of code transfer, enzymes and lipid membranes, biological control and regulation processes, and the problem of the storage of information in the central nervous system.

Ronald George Wreyford Norrish and **George Porter** worked together between 1949 and 1965, utilized flash photolysis technique to study the intermediate stages involved in extremely **fast chemical reactions***. In the flash photolysis technique, ultra short burst of light (pump) from a lamp or laser induces photochemical reactions in the gaseous system at equilibrium. The excited molecules start to relax (or moves back to equilibrium). Then, it is followed by a second burst of light (probe) to detect the changes in structures and energy levels before equilibrium is reestablished through relaxation process. In below, the scheme of excitation and relaxation is shown. As molecule M is excited by a photon (hv) to M*, M* returns to its ground state according to the mechanism as shown below (with reaction rates).

Excitation: M + hv → M* (k_1)
Photochemical Reaction: M* → M' (k_2)
Reverse Photochemical Reaction: M' → M (k_3)

During the relaxation process, a number of intermediates and the concentration of these intermediates can be probed by the absorption spectroscopy of any one of these intermediates as function of time. If the excitation process is considered to be instantaneous (i.e., k_1 is very large), the concentration of M' will be determined by rate constants of the following steps (k_2 and k_3). The flash photolysis method has been used as a powerful technique and has been applied for studying light-induced processes in organic molecules, and material science (polymers, nanoparticles, and semiconductors). It is even utilized for biological systems (e.g., photosynthesis in plants, signaling).

THE FOCUSED PHYSICAL CHEMISTRY EXPERIMENTAL APPROACH ASSOCIATED WITH CHAPTER 7

(*: word appeared in Chapter 7)

I. Stopped-Flow Technique

The stopped-flow technique is to rapidly eject small volumes of solutions from syringes into a mixer to initiate a fast reaction. Since the volume injected is limited by the stop syringe, it is called "stopped-flow". When the solution fills the stopping syringe, the plunger hits a block and stops the flow. By combining the stopped flow technique with other spectroscopic techniques, the kinetics of the reaction can be measured. With self-contained computer controlled system, stopped-flow systems enables to collect and analyze **fast reaction**.* Popularly, stopped-flow technique is combined with UV/Vis absorption or fluorescence spectroscopy. Also stopped flow combined with circular dichroism, conductivity and FT-IR measurements can be conducted.

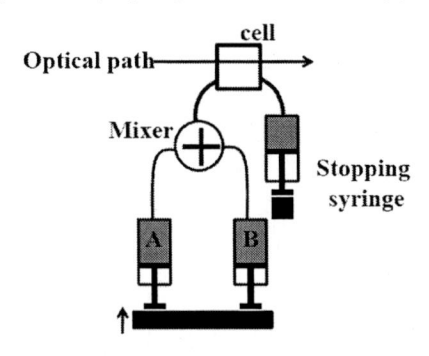

Fig. 7-16a Schematics of single mixing stopped-flow method.

When two solutions (A and B) are mixed, it is called single mixing stopped flow. (**Fig. 7-16a**) When more than two solutions are mixed together, it is called multi-mixing (double mixing or sequential mixing). (For example, four solutions A, B, C, and D are mixed with variable ratio mixing using different size syringes as shown in **Fig. 7-16b**)

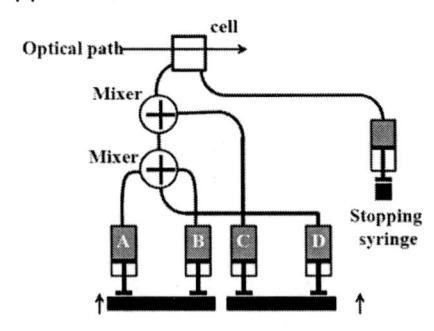

Fig. 7-16b Schematics of double mixing stopped-flow method

For stopped-flow method, the environment for the reagents is very critical. Thus, in some cases, anaerobic condition, low-temperature, or even high pressure stopped-flow applications can be used.

II. Time-Correlated Single Photon Counting

Time-Correlated Single Photon Counting (TCSPC) is very sensitive technique to detect low level of fluorescence signals with typically ~25 picoseconds time resolution. The technique of TCSPC is based on the detection of single photons of a periodical repeated light signal. After enough summations of repeated signal patters as a function of time, the function exhibits the trend (or decay) of the number of photons as a function of time. An important principle of TCSPC is that signal intensity is low enough and has high enough repetition rate to result the probability of detecting one photon in one signal period should be much less than one.

As a photon is detected by the detector, the time of the corresponding detector pulse is recorded, and each one event is collected in a memory box of each corresponding detection time. After repeating many measurements, the histogram of the detection times is constructed. (See **Fig. 7-17**). The time resolution of TCSPC is dominated by the timing accuracy when photon is stored in the detection channel (memory box) but not limited by the width of the detector response. This accuracy of timing is governed by the transit time spread of the single photon pulses in the detector and the electronic triggering timing of an electronics of the detection system.

Typical applications of TCSPC are Fluorescence **lifetime measurements***, fluorescence lifetime Imaging, detection and identification of single molecules, and DNA sequencing.

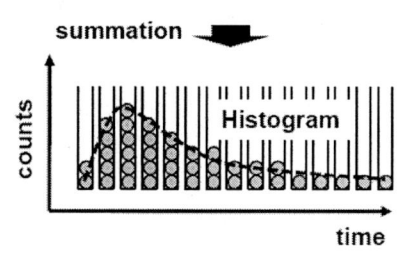

Fig. 7-17 Demonstration of a principle of single photon counting. Each event store only one photon into a memory box corresponding to a specific time. The accumulated signals construct a histogram and wave form (decay signal) as a function of time.

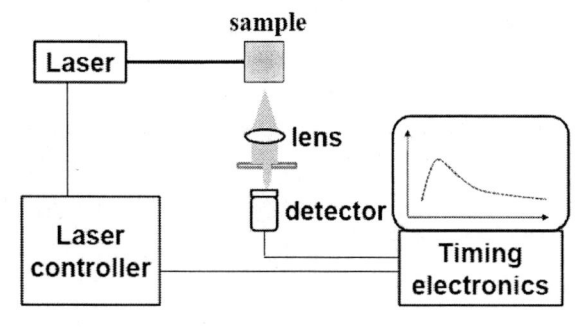

Fig. 7-18 Schematics of TCSPC.

Chapter 7 Problems.

7-1 [initial rate] The rate law can be expressed in the form: $-d[I^-]/dt = k[I^-]^a [OCl^-]^b [OH^-]^c$. Find the values of a, b, and c

$[I^-]_0$	$[OCl^-]_0$	$[OH^-]_0$	Initial rate
4×10^{-3}	3×10^{-3}	1.00	
2×10^{-3}	1.5×10^{-3}	1.00	1.8×10^{-4}
4×10^{-3}	1.5×10^{-3}	1.00	3.6×10^{-4}
2×10^{-3}	3×10^{-3}	2.00	1.8×10^{-4}

7-2 [initial rate] The stoichiometric equation for a reaction is

$$A + B \rightarrow C + D$$

The initial rate of fiormation of C is measured with the following results.

Initial Concentration of A	Initial Concentration of B	Initial Rate
1.0 [M]	1.0 [M]	1.0×10^{-3} [M/sec]
2.0 [M]	1.0 [M]	4.0×10^{-3} [M/sec]
1.0 [M]	2.0 [M]	9.0×10^{-3} [M/sec]

a) What is the order of the reaction with respect to A?
b) What is the order of the reaction with respect to B?
c) Use your conclusion in parts (a) and (b) to write a differential equation for the appearance of C.
d) What is the rate constant k for the reaction? [Do not omit the units of k.]

7-3 [initial rate] The stoichiometric equation for a reaction is

$$A + B \rightarrow C + D$$

The initial rate of formation of C is measured with the following results.

Initial Concentration of A, [A]	Initial Concentration of B, [B]	Initial Rate, v
1.0 [μM]	1.0 [μM]	1.0×10^{-3} [M/sec]
0.2 [mM]	1.0 [μM]	$8.0\times10^{+3}$ [M/sec]
1.0 [μM]	3.0 [μM]	3.0×10^{-3} [M/sec]

Write complete expression of the reaction rate, v, with the reaction rate constant k for the reaction. For example, write it as $v = 2.5\times10^{-3}$ [M^{-2} sec^{-1}] [A]^2[B]. This example shows that $k = 2.5\times10^{-3}$ [M^{-2} sec^{-1}] and this reaction is 2nd order of [A] and 1st order of [B]. <u>This is an example and is not an answer.</u> Please clearly show the unit of the reaction rate constant.

7-4 [rate law] True or false: If the chemical equation is given by A→ P (A is a reactant and P is a product), the rate of reaction (v) should be given by $v = -k[A]$

7-5 [rate law derivation] In the first order reaction, the decay of the concentration of the reactant, A, is given by

$$d[A]/dt = -k\,[A] \qquad (1)$$

where [A] is the concentration of reactant at time t and k is the rate constant.

The integrated form of the first order reaction rate is given by
$$\ln\{[A]_o/[A]\} = k\,t \qquad (2)$$
where $[A]_o$ is initial concentration of reactant. Derive the integrated expression given in the equation (2) from the equation (1)

7-6 [Plotting → Order of reaction] The following data were obtained for the concentration [A] vs. time for a certain chemical reaction. Write the reaction rate expression.

Time [sec]	[A] [mM]	Time [sec]	[A] [mM]	Time [sec]	[A] [mM]
0	10.00	7	2.50	14	1.36
1	6.91	8	2.22	15	1.23
2	4.98	9	1.91	16	1.20
3	4.32	10	1.80	17	1.13
4	3.55	11	1.65	18	1.09
5	3.21	12	1.52	19	1.00
6	2.61	13	1.42	20	0.92

7-7 [Plotting → Order of reaction] A reaction occurs with the following stoichiometry:
$$A + P \rightarrow AP$$
The concentration of A was measured vs. time after mixing; the data are the following:

[A] [nM] (nM = 10^{-9} [M])	Time [sec]
50.0	0
40.0	100
30.0	229
20.0	411
10.0	721

a) There is no dependence of rate on P. What is the order of the reaction? [You may use any methods to determine the order of this reaction. If it is necessary, you can use Calculate the rate constant and give the units.

b) The data given above were measured at 0 [°C]. When the reaction was studied at 10 °C, the rate constant doubled. Calculate the activation energy.

7-8 [1st order reaction] The decomposition of urea in 0.1 M HCl occurs according to the reaction

$$NH_2CONH_2 + 2H_2O \rightarrow 2NH_4^+ + CO_3^{2-}$$

a) This reaction was found out as **the first-order reaction**. There is no dependence of rate on H_2O.
  The following data is the concentration of NH_2CONH_2 measured as a function of time at 35 [°C].
b) Make an appropriate plot of the above data to have a *straight line*.
c) Obtain the reaction rate constant at 35 [°C] from the above graph.

7-9 [1st order reaction] The 2nd order reaction (1st order in each reactant)
  Crystal violet + Hydroxide ⇌ Products
can be approximated as a pseudo- 1st order reaction if
  a. catalyst is used
  b. equilibrium is achieved
  c. hydroxide is present in large excess.
  d. the temperature is sufficiently high

7-10 [2nd order reaction] Which plot will give you a linear plot for the 2nd order reaction (Type I) as a function of time, t. Use the concentration of the reactant A, as [A].

7-11 [2ⁿᵈ order reaction] The following data were obtained for the concentration of reactant A, [A] vs. time for a certain chemical reaction. This reaction is known to be *the second order reaction*. Calculate the rate constant.

time (sec)	[A] (M)
0	1.22×10^3
910	14.5

7-12 [2ⁿᵈ order reaction] See the figure shown on the right. For $2H_2O_2(aq) \rightarrow 2H_2O(l) + O_2(g)$, which plot confirms that the reaction is second order with respect to H_2O_2?

7-13 [half-life] In the first order reaction the *half-life* of a reaction was measured as 10 sec. How much more time do you need to wait until the concentration becomes to be a quarter (1/4) of an initial concentration.

7-14 [half-life] It took 36 seconds to make the concentration to be a half of an initial concentration under the first-order reaction. How much more time do you need to wait until the final concentration becomes 1/8 of an initial concentration?
  a. 18 more seconds
  b. 36 more seconds
  c. 72 more seconds
  d. 108 more seconds
  e. none of these

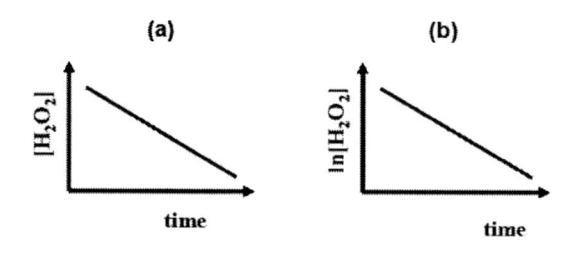

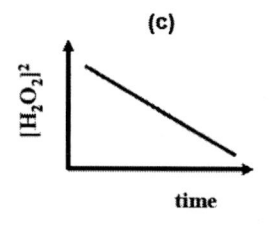

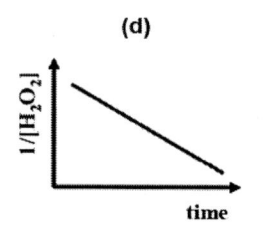

7-15 [half-life → order of reaction] Consider a reaction whose reaction rate depends only on the concentration of reactant A, [A]. When a plot of $[A]^{-1}$ vs. time was made, this plot did not exhibit a linear line. A *half life* of this reaction depended on $[A]^{-2}$. Therefore, this reaction must be the third order reaction.

7-16 [half-life → order of reaction] A reaction is found to have a half-life that is independent of initial concentration. What is the overall order of the reaction?

7-17 [half-life → order of reaction] Calculate a value for the rate constant. ($t_{½}$ is a half-life)

[OH⁻]₀	[ethylacetate]₀	$t_{½}$ [sec]
0.0050	0.0050	2000
0.0100	0.0100	1000

7-18 [activated state] In a chemical reaction involving the formation of an activated complex, which step must always be exothermic?
  a. reactants → products
  b. reactants → activated complex
  c. products → activated complex
  d. activated complex → products
  e. none of these

Chapter 7 Kinetics

7-19 [rate vs. T] If the temperature increased from 10 °C to 20 °C and the rate is found to double, then which property has also doubled?
    a. Average energy
    b. Average velocity
    c. Number of molecular collisions per second
    d. Number of molecular collisions that have at least energy, E_a

7-20 [E_a] A reaction, A→ P, was found out as **the first-order reaction**. The following data is the concentration of product (P) measured as a function of time at 25 [°C].

Time [minutes]	[P] [μM]
0	50
50	30

Then, the first order rate constant k for this reaction was measured as a function of temperature, with following results.

Temperature [°C]	k [min^{-1}]
70.0	2.77×10^{-2}
85.0	9.45×10^{-2}

Calculate numerically the activation energy E_a for this reaction.

7-21 [E_a] The first order tae constant k for this reaction was measured as a function of temperature, with following results.

Experiment	Temperature [°C]	k [min^{-1}]
1	61.0	0.713×10^{-5}
2	71.2	2.77×10^{-5}

Calculate numerically the activation energy E_a for this reaction.

7-22 [E_a] The kinetics of double-strand formation for a DNA oligonucleotide containing a G•T was measured. Determine E_a.

2 CGTGAATTCGCG → DUPLEX

Temperature [°C]	k [M^{-1} sec^{-1}]
31.8	0.8×10^{-5}
36.8	2.3×10^{-5}
41.8	3.5×10^{-5}

7-23 [E_a] Calculate the activation energy for a reaction whose rate constant at room temperature (25 [°C]) is doubled by a 10 [°C] increase in temperature.

7-24 [E_a] A reaction in a human blood is controlled by a diffusional motion of blood. Thus, it is called a "diffusion-controlled reaction".

$$\text{Reactants} \xrightarrow{k_D} \text{Products}$$

The diffusion-controlled rate constant, k_D, in cm^3 molecule^{-1} s^{-1} is given by Eqn. 1

$$k_D = \frac{8RT}{300\eta} \quad \text{(Eqn. 1)}$$

η is a viscosity of human blood, R is a gas constant, and T is a temperature. The viscosity of blood, η, depends on temperature as follows:

$$\eta = Be^{\frac{E'_a}{RT}} \quad \text{(Eqn. 2)}$$

where E_a' is "the activation energy of viscosity" and B is a constant characteristic of the solvent. (Note that η decreases with increasing temperature)

The viscosities of human blood, η, for 10 [°C] and 50 [°C] were measured as shown in the table. Calculate the half life, $t_{1/2}$, of this diffusion controlled reaction, when a reaction took place in human blood with initial concentration of reactant 5×10^{-3} [M] at 25 [°C].

T [°C]	η [Poise]
10	1.375×10^{-3}
50	6.25×10^{-4}

7-25 [Eₐ] The kinetics of a reaction was measured as shown in the table below. Determine the activation energy, Eₐ.

Temperature [°C]	k [sec⁻¹]
24	1.52×10^{-5}
48	6.00×10^{-4}

7-26 [Eₐ] The decomposition of urea in 1 [M] HCl occurs according to the reaction
$$NH_2CONH_2 + 2H_2O \rightarrow 2NH_4^+ + CO_2$$
From the data provided, the activation energy, Eₐ, is

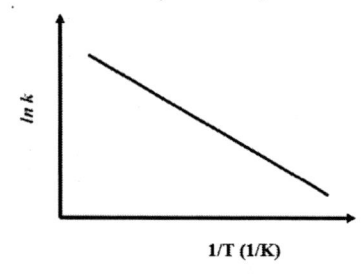

a. −R multiplied by the slope of the line.
b. R multiplied by the slope of the line.
c. the negative of the slope of the line.
d. the slope of the line.

7-27 [Eₐ] The kinetics of a reaction was measured as shown in the table below. Determine the activation energy, Eₐ.

Temperature [°C]	k [sec⁻¹]
15	2.75×10^{5}
75	6.23×10^{6}

7-28 [TST] What is the reaction scheme of the transition state theory? Assume that reactants A and B are making a product C. ([ ]⧧ indicates a transition state.)

7-29 [TST] If the enthalpy change of the transition state, $\Delta H^{\ne}$, is an exothermic process, the Eyring equation will show that the reaction rate will decrease as the temperature increases. (Assume that the entropy change stays constant.)

$$k = \left(\frac{k_B T}{h}\right) e^{\Delta S^{\ne}/R} e^{-\Delta H^{\ne}/RT}$$

7-30 [ΔS⧧] The first order rate constant for a reaction was measured as a function of temperature, with the following results:

Temperature [°C]	k [min⁻¹]

61.0	7.13×10^{-6}
71.2	2.77×10^{-5}

Calculate the entropy change of activation, $\Delta S^{\ddagger}$, at 71.2 [°C] for this reaction. Although you can use any appropriate assumptions or approximations for solving this problem, you need to state them clearly.

7-31 [fast reaction] Transfer RNA can exist in two forms that are in rapid equilibrium with each other; $K=[B]^{eq}/[A]^{eq}=10$ at 28 [°C]. In a temperature-jump experiment, a solution of the t-RNA at a concentration of 10[μM] is quickly (faster than 10 [μsec]) raised in temperature from 25 [°C] to 28 [°C]. A relaxation time was measured to be $\tau=3$ [msec]. What are the values of k_1 and k_{-1}, including units? Assume that the mechanism is:

$$A \underset{k_{-1}}{\overset{k_1}{\rightleftharpoons}} B$$

CHAPTER 7 ANSWERS. For Selected Problems

7-1 $a = 1, b = 1, c = -1$

7-2 a) 2 b) 0 c) $d[C]/dt = k[A]^2$ d) $k = 10^{-3}$ [M^{-1} sec^{-1}]

7-3 $v = 1 \times 10^{21}$ [M^{-3} sec^{-1}] $[A]^3[B]$

7-4 False

7-6 $v = 4.74 \times 10^{-2}$ [$mM^{-1}sec^{-1}$] $[A]^2$

7-7 a) 1st order $k = 1 \times 10^{-3}$ sec^{-1} b) $E_a = 44.6$ [kJ/mol]

7-8 c) -4.02×10^{-6} [sec^{-1}]

7-9 hydroxide is present in large excess.

7-10 plot $[A]_{-1}$ vs. time

7-11 7.49×10^{-5} [M^{-1} sec^{-1}]

7-12 d

7-13 10 more seconds

7-14 72 more seconds

7-15 True

7-16 1

7-17 0.10 [M^{-1} sec^{-1}]

7-18 d. activated complex → products

7-19 d. Number of molecular collisions that have at least energy, E_a

7-21 $E_a = 128.5$ [kJ/mol]

7-22 ~100 [kJ/mol]

7-23 52950

7-24 $t_{½} = 3.03 \times 10^{-7}$ [sec]

7-25 122 [kJ/mol]

7-26 $-R$ multiplied by the slope of the line.

7-27 43 [kJ/mol]

7-28 none of these

7-29 False

7-30 70.707 [J k^{-1} mol^{-1}]

7-31 $k_1 = 303$ [sec^{-1}] $K_{-1} = 30.3$ [sec^{-1}]

Chapter 8

Enzyme Kinetics

8-1 Enzyme Kinetics
8-2 Michaelis-Menten Kinetics
8-3 Kinetic Data Analysis of Michaelis-Menten Equation
8-4 Inhibition Processes

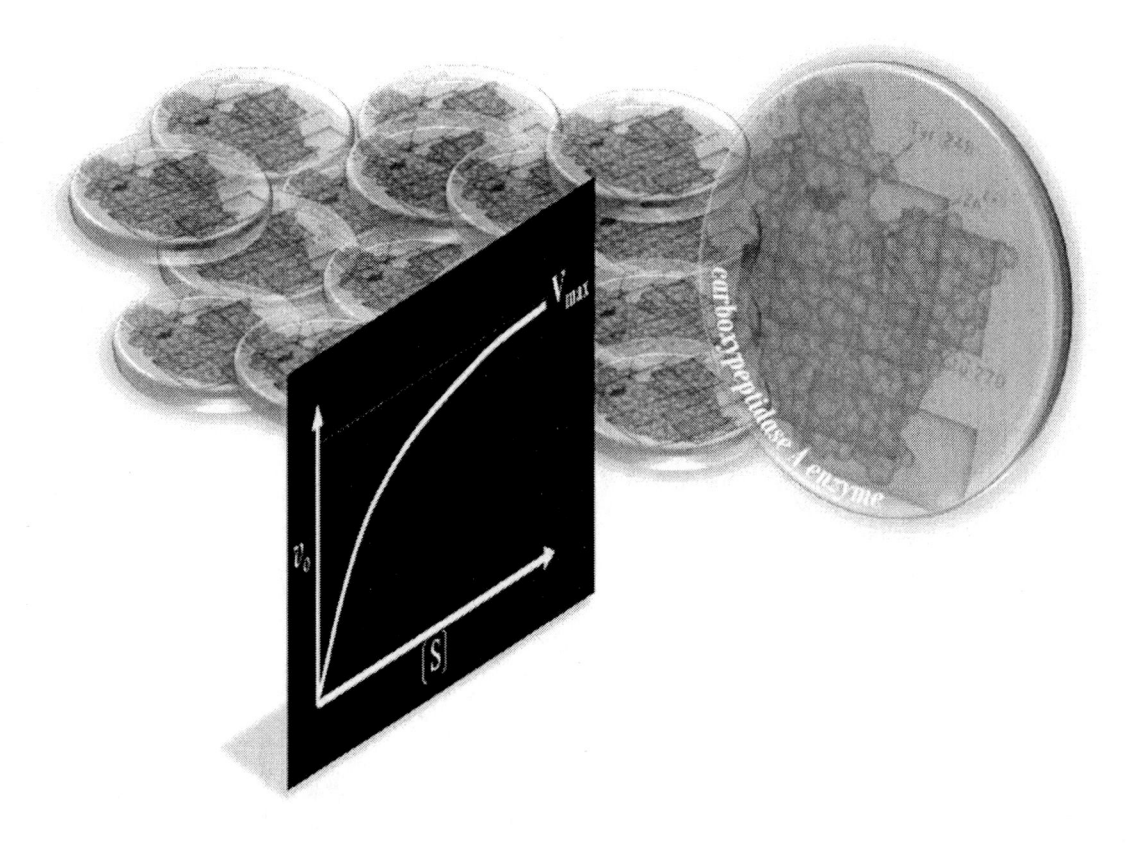

Chapter 8 Enzyme Kinetics

- **Why do I have to study this chapter?**

You will learn how unique (or strange!) the enzyme kinetics is. You can describe the enzyme kinetics systematically. You can simplify the kinetics for some cases. What is the inhibitor? What happens when inhibiter is inserted? Then, you can describe the effect of inhibiter for three cases quantitatively.

- **Expected Hurdles Ahead in this Chapter**
  1. Different rate of reaction at different condition (See Section **8-2**)
  2. Several ways of plotting to extract parameters for enzyme kinetics (See Section **8-3**)
  3. Different mechanism of inhibition process and corresponding effect. (See Section **8-4**)

PREVIEW OF KEY-EQUATIONS

Catalytic Constant
$$k_{cat} = V_{max}/[E]_0$$

Michaelis- Enzyme kinetics

$$E + S \underset{k_{-1}}{\overset{K_1}{\rightleftarrows}} ES \overset{k_2}{\rightarrow} E + P$$

Michaelis- Equation

$$v_0 = V_{max} / \left[1 + K_M/[S]\right]$$

Michaelis-Constant, K_M
$$K_M = [k_{-1} + k_2]/k_1$$

$V_{max} = k_2[E]_0$

At high concentrations of [S] ($K_M \gg$ [S]), $v_0 = V_{max}$

At low concentrations of [S] ($K_M \gg$ [S]), $v_0 = V_{max}[S]/K_M$

When [S] = K_M
$$v_0 = \frac{1}{2} V_{max}$$

Analytical plot

Lineweaver-Burk Plot
$$1/v_0 = 1/V_{max} + \left(K_M/V_{max}\right)\left(1/[S]\right)$$

Chapter 8 Enzyme Kinetics

Dixon Plot
$$[S]/v_0 = [S]/V_{max} + K_M/V_{max}$$

Eadie-Hofstee Plot
$$v_0 = -K_M v_0/[S] + V_{max}$$

Specific constant
$$k_{cat}/K_M$$

$$v_A/v_B = \frac{[k_{cat}/K_M]_A [A]}{[k_{cat}/K_M]_B [B]}$$

Competitive Inhibition
$$K'_M = K_M \left[1 + [I]/K_I\right]$$

PREVIEW OF KEY-TECHNICAL TERMS

Enzyme kinetics, Michaelis- kinetics (equation), substitute, catalytic constant (k_{cat}), turn over number (k_{cat}), specificity constant (k_{cat}/K_M), steady state kinetics (approximation), Michaelis constant (K_M), Lineweaver-Burk plot, Dixon plot, Eadie-Hofstee plot, inhibitor (I), competitive inhibition, uncompetitive inhibition, noncompetitive inhibition

8-1 Enzyme Kinetics

The chemical reaction of the enzyme is a unique reaction which gets help from enzyme to proceed its chemical reaction; otherwise the reaction may not be completed. This is similar to the case for a catalysis reaction. In catalytic reaction, thermochemical property of the system remains the same whereas the reaction barrier for the activated states will be lowered. During the chemical reactions, the process was more enhanced due to the lowering of this potential barrier. (**Fig. 8-1**) A typical enzymatic reaction is shown by

$$E + S \rightarrow ES \rightarrow E + P$$

Here, E is an enzyme, S is substrate, ES is a complex, and P is a product.

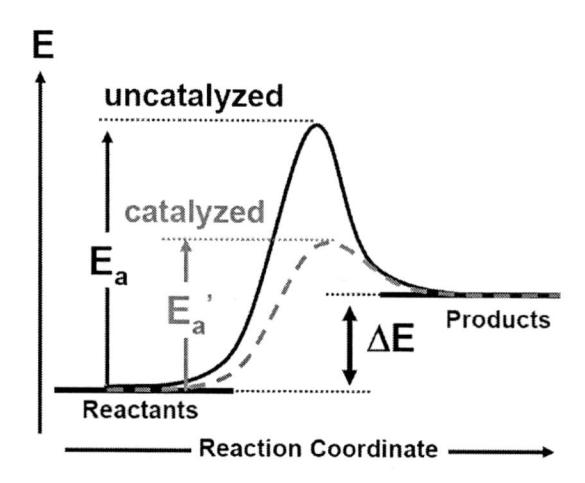

Fig. 8-1 Enzyme Kinetics

The rate of the enzymatic reaction is known to depend on [E] and [S], where [E] is concentration of enzyme, and [S] is concentration of substrate. Generally speaking, the reaction rate is increased as the amount of the enzyme is increased (**Fig. 8-2**). This clearly demonstrates that a mechanism of the enzyme kinetics is significantly enzyme concentration dependent.

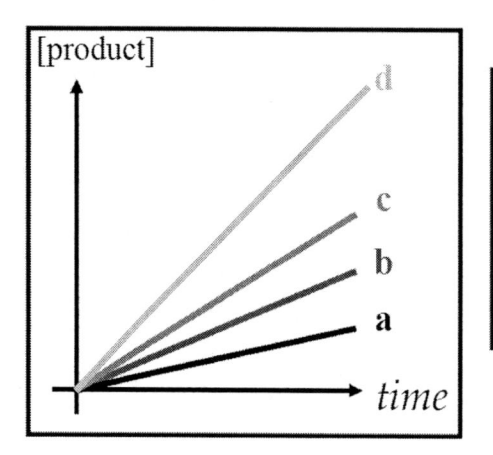

Relative amount of enzyme	
a	×1
b	×2
c	×3
d	×4

Fig. 8-2 Product speed and [E]

Most important concept to understand enzyme kinetics is **Michaelis- Kinetics**, and two situations are considered for a fixed amount of enzyme.

I) When the concentration of substrate, [S], is low enough, the initial rate of the reaction is linearly proportional to the amount of substrate. (**Fig. 8-3**)

$$v_0 = k[S] \qquad \text{(Eqn. 8-1)}$$

ii) At high concentrations of [S] (saturating condition), the initial rate reaches to an asymptote and shows a constant value, V_{max}. (**Fig. 8-3**)

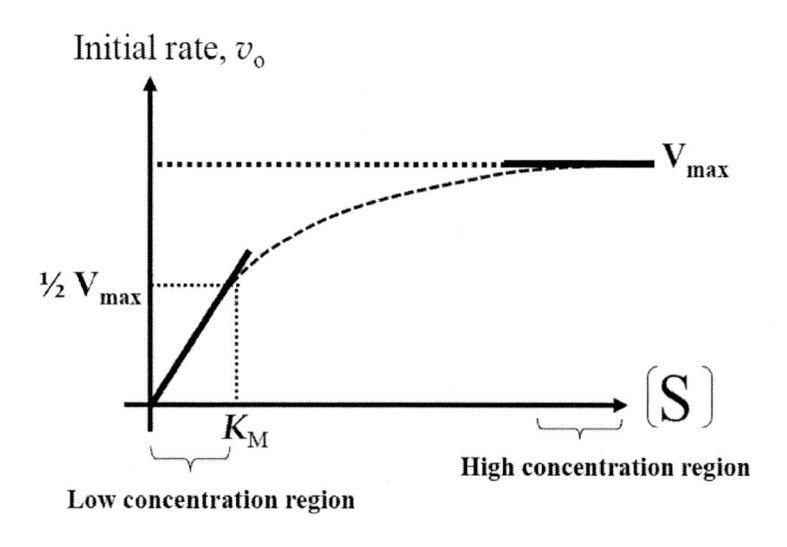

$$v_0 = V_{max} \qquad \text{(Eqn. 8-2)}$$

Fig. 8-3 Two regions of initial velocity for enzyme kinetics

The maximum rate V_{max} [M sec^{-1}] is defined with the catalytic constant, k_{cat}, and total enzyme site concentration $[E]_0$.

$$k_{cat} = V_{max}/[E]_0 \qquad \text{(Eqn. 8-3)}$$

The **catalytic constant**, k_{cat} [sec^{-1}], indicates an overall rate constant observed at high substrate concentration, [S]. The catalytic constant, k_{cat}, is also called as **"turnover number"**, which is the maximum number of substrate molecules converted to product each second by each active site. On the other hand, $1/k_{cat}$ is time [sec] required per molecule, and provides an index of how fast different enzymes catalyze reactions. (**Fig. 8-3**) For example, Catalase has k_{cat} =4×10^7 [sec^{-1}] with substrate of H_2O_2 whereas Rec A protein (an ATPase) has k_{cat} =0.4 [sec^{-1}] with substrate of ATP.

8-2 Michaelis- Kinetics

The Michaelis– equation describes the rates of irreversible enzymatic reactions with respect to the concentration of the substrate, [S]. The mechanism of this kinetics is made of an equilibrium step of a complex between enzyme and substrate (ES) and formation of product by releasing the enzyme. (Take a look at initial and final chemical formula. You have enzyme (E), as if nothing happened to them like a spectator).

$$E + S \underset{k_{-1}}{\overset{k_1}{\rightleftharpoons}} ES$$

$$ES \overset{k_2}{\rightarrow} E + P$$

Reviewing what we learned from **Chapter 7**, the differential equation for the reaction process can be constructed. An important approximation made here is that the process may rely on **steady-state kinetics**, where concentration of the ES complex [ES] is regarded as constant while the processes are taking place. (**Steady-state approximation**)

$$\frac{d[ES]}{dt} \approx 0$$

By using the steady state approximation the initial velocity of reaction is given by **Michaelis- equation**

$$v_0 = \frac{V_{max}}{\left[1 + K_M/[S]\right]} \qquad \text{(Eqn. 8-4)}$$

Here, **Michaelis-Constant**, K_M, is

$$K_M = [k_{-1} + k_2]/k_1 \qquad \text{(Eqn. 8-5)}$$

and

$$V_{max} = k_2[E]_0 \qquad \text{(Eqn. 8-6)}$$

The Michaelis-constant (K_M) is equivalent with the initial concentration of substrate at half-maximum velocity (at half-saturation). The K_M also indicates the affinity of enzyme and substrate when the breakdown of the ES complex is rate-limiting. The lower the value of K_M, the tighter S is bound to E. For example, hexokinase (brain) enzyme with D-glucose substrate gives K_M of 0.05 [mM], while chymotrypsin enzyme with glycyltyrosinylglycine gives K_M of 108 [mM]. Using the Micahelis constant a **specificity constant** k_{cat}/K_M can be defined. The specificity constant is a measure of the specificity of an enzyme for different substrates. For example, it can be approximated as $k_{cat}/K_M = k_2$ at low [S]. For the fastest enzymes, it approaches 10^8 to 10^9 [M^{-1} sec^{-1}] (diffusion-controlled limit). For example, acetylcholineserase enzyme and acetylcholine substrate provides $k_{cat} = 1.4 \times 10^4$ [sec^{-1}] and $K_M = 9 \times 10^{-5}$ [M]. Thus, $k_{cat}/K_M = 1.6 \times 10^8$ [M^{-1} sec^{-1}].

The Michaelis- Equation (**Eqn. 8-4**) can be rephrased as:

$$-d[S]/dt = \frac{V_{max}}{\left(1 + K_M/[S]\right)} \qquad \text{(Eqn. 8-7)}$$

Therefore, by integrating the (**Eqn. 8-7**) an exact solution for the concentration of substrate [S] at time t (integrated expression) can be extracted as

$$k_M \ln\left([S]/[S]_0\right) + [S] - [S]_0 = -V_{max} t \qquad \text{(Eqn. 8-8)}$$

Depending on the concentration of substrate [S], three different expressions for the initial velocity is possible.

<u>I. At low concentration of [S], ($K_M \gg$ [S])</u>

$$v_0 = V_{max}[S]/K_M \qquad \text{(Eqn. 8-9)}$$

In this case, the integrated expression for the concentration of substrate at given time, t is

$$\ln [S]/[S]_0 = -V_{max} t / K_M \qquad \text{(Eqn. 8-10)}$$

<u>ii. At high concentration of [S]</u>

$$v_0 = V_{max} \qquad \text{(Eqn. 8-11)}$$

<u>iii. When [S] = K_M</u>

$$v_0 = \frac{1}{2} V_{max} \qquad \text{(Eqn. 8-12)}$$

341

8-3 Kinetic Data Analysis of Michaelis- Equation

We introduce three plotting methods of kinetic data to analyze Michaelis- equation. (The following three plotting formats are also explained in **Chapter 5** Section **5-2** at **Langmuir isotherm**.) Please always note what are the parameters plotted on x- or y-axes, slope, and x- or y-axes how the intercepts. It is also important to know that we would like to know the K_M and V_{max} always. So that, you should be able to calculate the V_{max} and K_M at any graphs.

1. Lineweaver-Burk Plot

$$1/v_0 = 1/V_{max} + \left(K_M/V_{max}\right)\left(1/[S]\right) \qquad \text{(Eqn. 8-13)}$$

In this analysis, we will plot the $1/v_0$ as a function of $1/[S]$ (**Fig. 8-4**) Since an inverse of [S] and v_0 are plotted, it is very sensitive to small values of [S] and v_0. The slope of this plot is K_M/V_{max} and the x-axis intercept is $-1/K_M$, and the y-axis intercept is $1/V_{max}$. Thus, the V_{max} and K_M can be derived from the inverses of the intercepts independently.

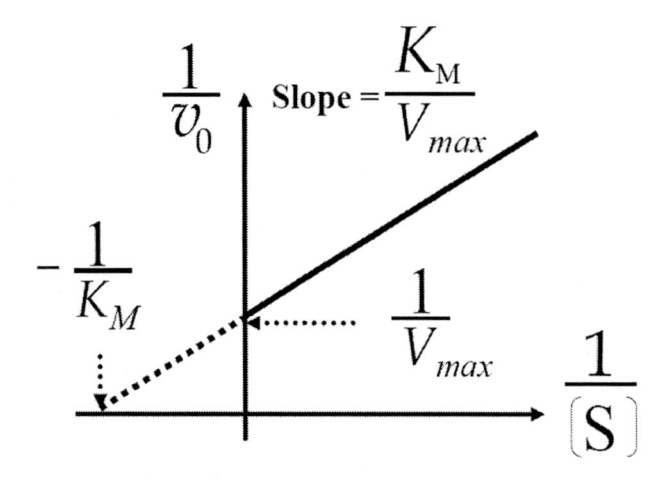

Fig. 8-4 Lineweaver-Burk Plot

2. Dixon Plot

$$[S]/v_0 = [S]/V_{max} + K_M/V_{max} \qquad \text{(Eqn. 8-14)}$$

In Dixon plot, $[S]/v_0$ is plotted as a function of [S], and this plot can be said very straightforward and may avoid making a mistake in the data processing. The slope of this plot is the inverse of $1/V_{max}$. The y-axis intercept is K_M/V_{max}, and the x-axis, and the x-axis intercept is $-K_M$. So that the V_{max} and K_M can be derived from the slope and x-axis intercept, independently.(**Fig. 8-5**) You may, however, need a wide range of the data for substrate, [S] in order to make a reasonable plot.

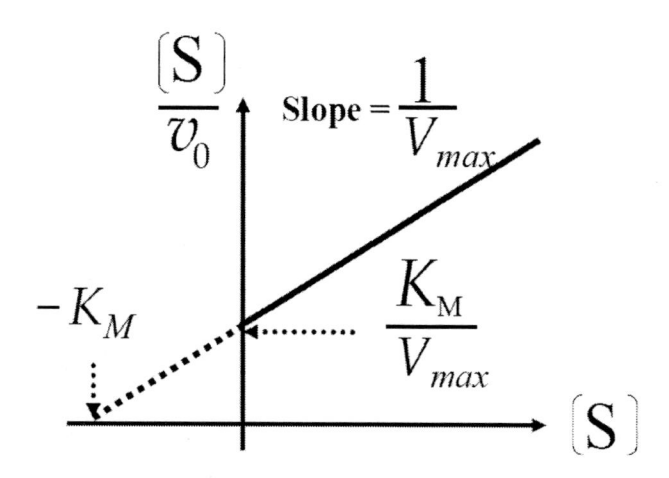

Fig. 8-5 Dixon Plot

3-Eadie-Hofstee Plot

$$v_0 = {-K_M v_0}/{[S]} + V_{max} \qquad \text{(Eqn. 8-15)}$$

The Eadie-Hofstee plot can be regarded also as a straightforward plot which provides the parameters directly from the intercept and the slope. In this plot, you will view the v_0 as a function of $v_0/[S]$ with the slope of $-K_M$. The y-axis intercept is V_{max} and the x-axis intercept is V_{max}/K_M. Since you use the values of v_0 for both x- and y-values, this plot can be very reliable if v_0 is accurate enough. Fig. 8-6)

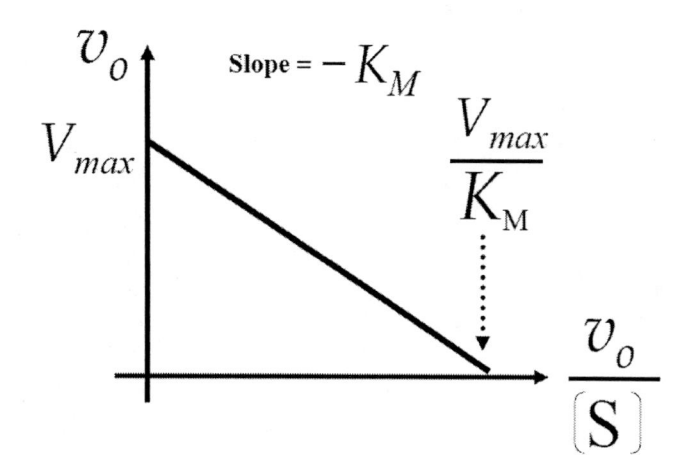

Fig. 8-6 Eadie-Hofstee Plot

EXERCISE 8-1

Make a suitable plot and determine V_{max} and K_M

1/[S] [M^{-1}]	1/v_0 [sec/M]
13×10^4	260
8.5×10^4	175
6.0×10^4	122
3.0×10^4	60
0.50×10^4	10

ANSWER
Lineweaver-Burk Plot

$$1/v_0 = 1/V_{max} + (K_M/V_{max})(1/[S]) \quad \text{(Eqn. 8-13)}$$

❶ Slope (K_M/V_{max})=2.012 ×10^{-3}
  Intercept(1/V_{max}) = 0.6702
❷ Thus, V_{max}=1.492 [M/ sec]
❸ K_M=3.00 ×10^{-3} [M]
❹

❶ MS Excel-LINEST is used.
❷ It is an inverse of intercept. The unit is the one for the velocity.
❸ K_M is (slope)× V_{max}
❹ The unit of K_M is [M].

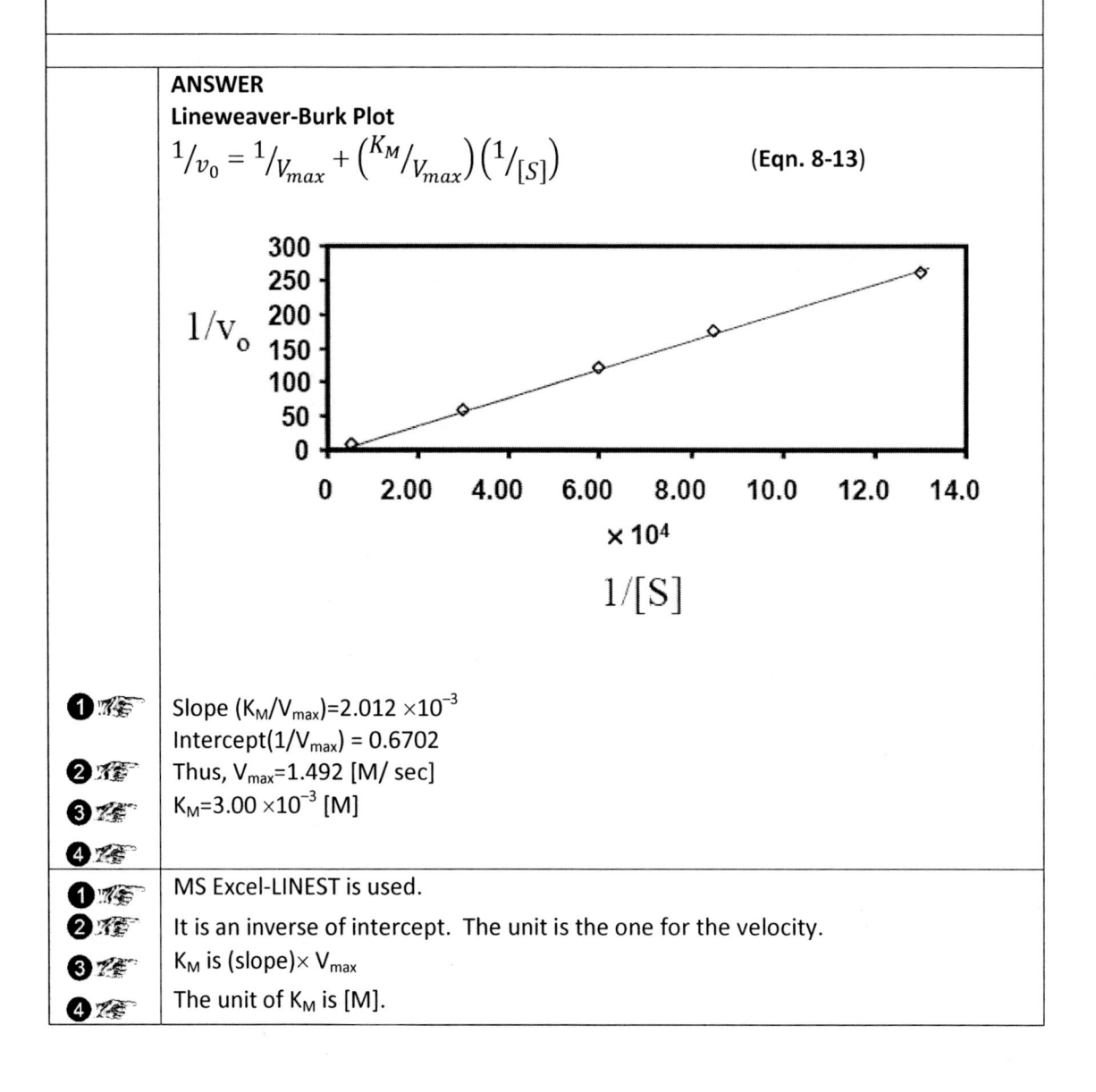

EXERCISE 8-2
Estimate how long it will take for 10^{-5} M substrate to become 10^{-6} [M] in the absence of inhibitor.
Here, $K_M = 10^{-3}$ [M] and $V_{max} = 1$ [M/sec].

ANSWER
At low concentration, $K_M \gg [S]$

❶ ☞ $$\ln {[S]}/{[S]_0} = -{V_{max} t}/{K_M} \quad \text{(Eqn. 8-10)}$$

In the absence of inhibitor: $K_M = 10^{-3}$ [M] and $V_{max} = 1$ [M sec^{-1}]

❷ ☞ $t = -(10^{-3} [M]/1[M\ sec^{-1}])\{\ln(10^{-6}/10^{-5})\}$
$= 2.3 \times 10^{-3}$ [sec]
$= 2.3$ [msec]

❶ ☞ $$k_M \ln\left({[S]}/{[S]_0}\right) + [S] - [S]_0 = -V_{max} t \quad \text{(Eqn. 8-8)}$$

At $K_M \gg [S]$, the second and third term of the left hand side becomes negligible.

❷ ☞ Don't forget to calculate natural log term

Our hypothesis on the Michaelis Menten enzyme kinetics at first was that there is an equilibrium step to form a complex between enzyme and substrate (ES) followed by a formation of product with a release of the enzyme. However, there could be more than single complex formations can be involved in the process of product formation.

$$E + S \underset{k_{-1}}{\overset{k_1}{\rightleftarrows}} ES \underset{k_{-2}}{\overset{k_2}{\rightleftarrows}} ES' \overset{k_3}{\rightarrow} ES'' \overset{k_4}{\rightarrow} E + P$$

Even though there are multiple complex formations involved in the enzyme kinetics, the velocity of reaction is still expressed as:

$$v_0 = \frac{V_{max}}{\left[1 + {K_M}/{[S]}\right]} \quad \text{(Eqn. 8-4)}$$

This is arranged into a different form of expression as:

Chapter 8 Enzyme Kinetics

$$v_0 = \frac{k_{cat}[E]_0[S]}{\{K_M + [S]\}} \approx \frac{k_{cat}}{K_M}[E]_0[S] \qquad \text{(Eqn. 8-16)}$$

The last term is true when $K_M \gg [S]$. Here, k_{cat}/K_M is called **specific constant** which is dependent on the substrate. If there are two different substrates are existent, the ratio of the reaction speed between two competing substrates A and B (concentrations [A] and [B]) is expressed with specific constant of each substrate as:

$$v_A/v_B = \frac{[k_{cat}/K_M]_A[A]}{[k_{cat}/K_M]_B[B]} \qquad \text{(Eqn. 8-17)}$$

Here, v_A and v_B are the speed of reactions on substrate A and B, respectively.

EXERCISE 8-3

A carboxypeptidase was found to have K_M of 2.00 μM and a k_{cat} of 150 [sec^{-1}] for its substrate A. A competing substrate B is added to the solution and its K_M is 10.0 [μM] and k_{cat} is 100 [sec^{-1}]. Calculate the relative rates, v_B/v_A, of substrate reaction for equal concentrations of substrate.

ANSWER

$$v_A/v_B = \frac{[k_{cat}/K_M]_A[A]}{[k_{cat}/K_M]_B[B]} \qquad \text{(Eqn. 8-17)}$$

For substrate A
K_M = 2.00 [μM] k_{cat} = 150 [sec^{-1}]
For substrate B
K_M = 10.0 [μM] k_{cat} = 100 [sec^{-1}]

❶ [A] = [B]

❷ $v_B/v_A = (k_{cat}/K_M)_B / (k_{cat}/K_M)_A$
 =(100/10.00)/(150/2.00)

❸ = 0.133

❶ It is under equal concentration of substrate [A] and [B]
❷ Careful not to mix up the k_{cat} and K_M upside down.
❸ This is the fraction, and dimensionless.

Chapter 8 Enzyme Kinetics

😞 Most Common Mistake (37)-"What is the unit of K_M?"

Most common mistake people make is to the question "What is the unit for K_M?" Since K_M is considered to be a constant, people tend to assume it is dimensionless. This value has the unit of concentration [M]. This can be confirmed from the expression shown in (**Eqn. 8-9**).

$$v_0 = V_{max}[S] / K_M \qquad \text{(Eqn. 8-9)}$$

Since the unit of the velocity (v_o and V_{max}) is [M/sec] and the concentration of the substrate concentration is [M], the unit for K_M has to be the same as that of concentration, [M]. The same type of question although easier is the unit for the V_{max}. The unit of V_{max} is the same as the unit for the reaction speed, [M/sec].

8-4 Inhibition Process

An **inhibitor** is a compound that binds to an enzyme and interferes with its activity by preventing either the formation of the ES complex or it breaks down to enzyme and products. The Inhibition can be either reversible or irreversible. Here, we consider three basic types of reversible inhibition: a) **competitive (Fig 8-7)**, b) **uncompetitive (Fig. 8-8)**, and c) **mixed (noncompetitive) inhibition (Fig. 8-9)** processes.

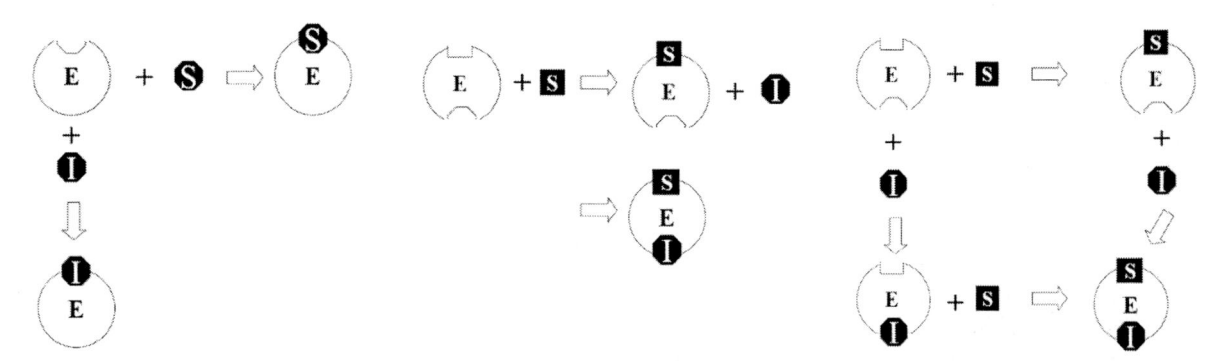

Fig. 8-7 Competitive Inhibition

Fig. 8-8 Uncompetitive Inhibition

Fig. 8-9 Noncompetitive Inhibition

a) Competitive Inhibition

This is a very popular inhibition process. In competitive inhibition, substrate (S) and inhibitor (I) compete for the binding site. (**Fig. 8-7** and **Fig 8-10**) The inhibitor competes with the substrate for a particular binding spot. The process observed in inhibitor and enzyme complex is considered to be under equilibrium with a certain equilibrium constant. The effect of a competitive inhibitor is clearly seen in the velocity of the reaction.(**Fig. 8-11**) In order to reach the same velocity, the concentration of the substrate [S] needs to be increased to compensate the effect of existing inhibitors. The same effect by an inhibitor can be much clearly observed by Lineweaver-Burk Plot. (**Fig. 8-12**) In the

Chapter 8 Enzyme Kinetics

Lineweaver-Burk plot, we plot an inverse of velocity as a function of an inverse of substrate concentration, [S], so that the slope of the line is K_M/V_{max}. As shown in (**Fig. 8-12**), as the inhibitor involved in the reaction, the line shows steeper slope implying an increase in K_M, since $1/V_{max}$ remains the same (i.e., V_{max} is always the same no matter inhibitor is introduced or not.) Since the x-axis intercept shows the negative inverse of the K_M, we can see the effect by the existence of the inhibitor. As the concentration of the inhibitor is increased, the slope of the graph gets steeper and naturally the x-axis intercept goes closer to x=0 axis. What this indicates is that the inverse of the K_M becomes smaller implying that K_M increases as the concentration of inhibitor increases. Since enzyme kinetics is well defined by K_m, it is very useful to express the resulting K_M due to the effect of inhibitor as K_M'.

$$E + S \rightleftharpoons ES$$
$$+$$
$$I \qquad \Updownarrow$$
$$\Updownarrow K_I \qquad E + P$$
$$EI$$

Fig. 8-10 A schematic diagram of competitive Inhibition.

$$K_M' = K_M \left[1 + [I]/K_I\right] \qquad \text{(Eqn. 8-18)}$$

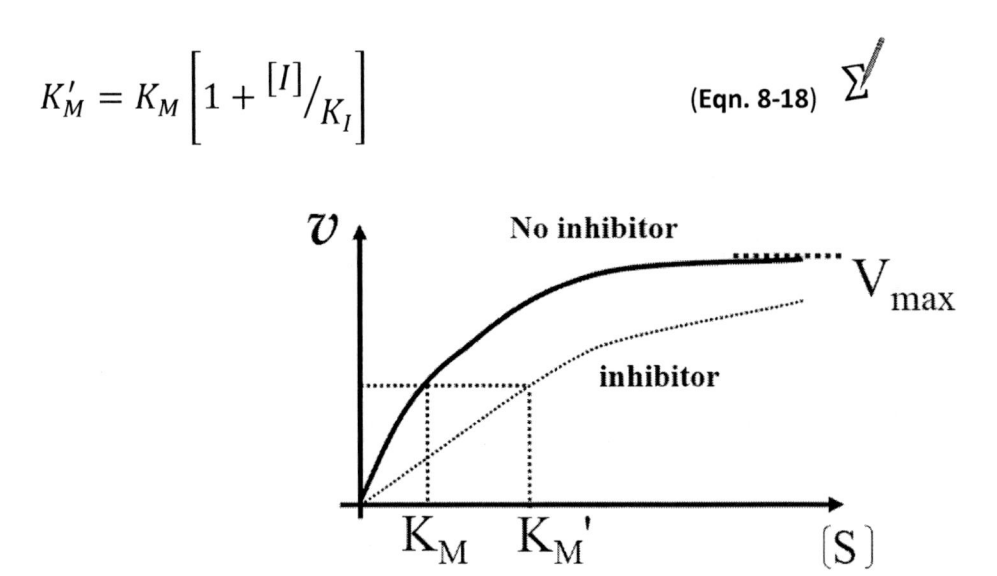

Fig. 8-11 The velocity and concentration relationship with an inhibitor.

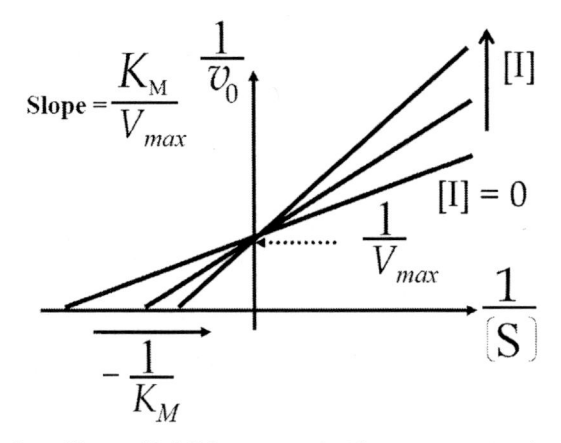

Fig. 8-12 The effect of inhibitor seen in Lineweaver-Burk plot.

Chapter 8 Enzyme Kinetics

EXERCISE 8-4
In **EXERCISE 8-2**, estimate how long it will take for 10^{-5} [M] substrate to become 10^{-6} [M] in the presence of 10^{-4} [M] inhibitor: ($K_I = 10^{-4}$ [M])

ANSWER
From **EXERCISE 8-2**, $K_M = 10^{-3}$ [M] and $V_{max} = 1$ [M sec^{-1}].
Here, inhibitor is [I] = 10^{-4} [M] and $K_I = 10^{-4}$ [M],

❶ $$K'_M = K_M \left[1 + [I]/K_I\right] \quad \text{(Eqn. 8-18)}$$

$= 10^{-3}$ [M]{1+ 10^{-4} [M]/ K_I = 10^{-4} [M]}
❷ $= 2 \times 10^{-3}$ [M].
❸ [S] = 10^{-6} [M] and [S]$_0$ = 10^{-5} [M]}

At low concentration,
❹ $$\ln [S]/[S]_0 = -V_{max}t/K_M \quad \text{(Eqn. 8-10)}$$

Here, K_M is replaced with K_M'
❺ $$\ln \frac{[S]}{[S]_0} = -\frac{V_{max}t}{K'_M}$$
$$\ln 10^{-1} = -\frac{1 \, M/sec}{2 \times 10^{-3} M} \times t$$
t = 4.6 [msec]

---

❶ Since inhibitor is present, K_M' needs to be calculated.
❷ Unit for K_M' is [M].
❸ Initial [S] is = 10^{-5} [M] and final [S] is 10^{-6} [M].
❹ $$k_M \ln \left([S]/[S]_0\right) + [S] - [S]_0 = -V_{max}t \quad \text{(Eqn. 8-8)}$$

At $K_M \gg$ [S], the second and third term of the right hand side becomes negligible.
❺ Be careful not to mix [S] and [S]$_0$ upside down.

b) Uncompetitive Inhibition

In uncompetitive Inhibition, the inhibitor and the substrate owns specific binding site, so that the inhibitor does not have to interfere or compete with the substrate for its binding site with the enzyme as shown in **Fig.8-8** and **Fig. 8-13**. (In a sense, the inhibitor's binding site is reserved.)

The value of V_{max} is lowered to V_{max}' as the inhibitor is introduced, and the K_M value is also sustained due to the inhibitor. Because K_M' is lowered, the $V_{max}/2$ will be decreased to $V_{max}'/2$ as shown in **(Fig. 8-14)**. The effect of inhibitor in the case of

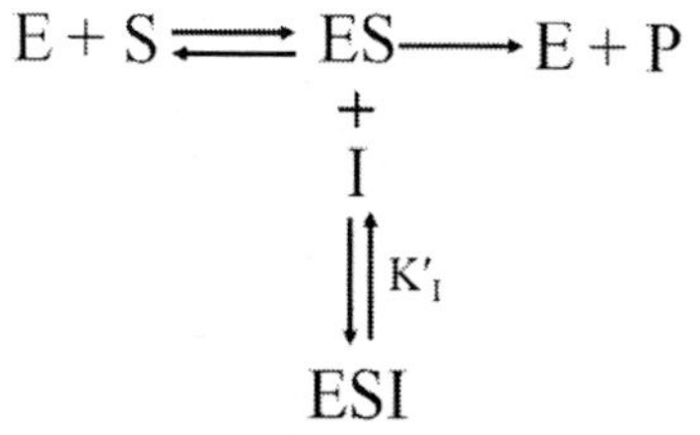

$$E + S \rightleftharpoons ES \longrightarrow E + P$$
$$+$$
$$I$$
$$\updownarrow K'_I$$
$$ESI$$

Fig. 8-13 A schematic diagram of uncompetitive Inhibition.

uncompetitive inhibition can be observed in Lineweaver-Burk Plot as demonstrated in the argument in competitive inhibition. The x-axis intercept ($-1/K'_M$) becomes more negative as an inhibitor concentration increased indicating that the K'_M value reduces. On the other hand, almost no effect is observed on the slope of the line (K'_M / V'_{max}) no matter the inhibitor concentration is increased.

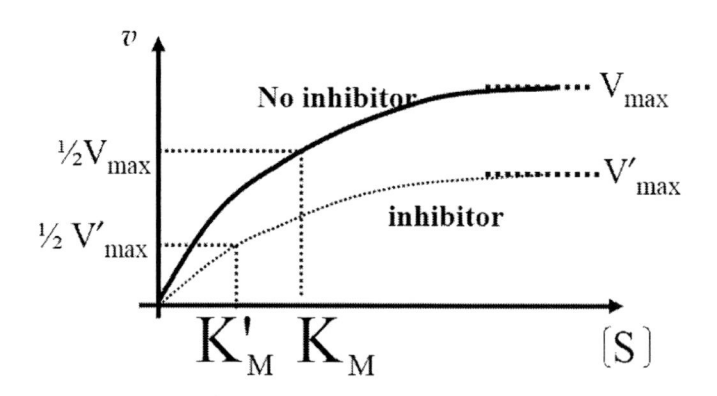

Fig. 8-14 The velocity and concentration relationship with an inhibitor for uncompetitive inhibition.

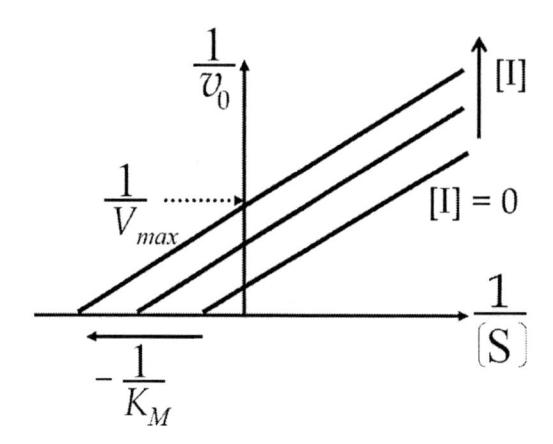

Fig. 8-15 The effect of inhibitor seen in Lineweaver-Burk plot for uncompetitive inhibition.

c) Mixed (noncompetitive) inhibition

In noncompetitive (or mixed) Inhibition process, the binding with a substrate take place almost simultaneously by inhibitor and enzyme. So both ES and EI complexes are produced in a parallel fashion. The inhibitor can bind to either E or ES at a different site from that S is bound. (Please note that the inhibitor binds even with enzyme-substrate complex.) In this case, you can imagine that there is almost no competition between substrate and inhibitor. Thus, the reaction is considered to occur independent of each other. The noncompetitive inhibition is a mixture of competitive and incompetitive inhibitions as

$$E + S \rightleftharpoons ES \longrightarrow E + P$$
$$+ \qquad\qquad +$$
$$I \qquad\qquad I$$
$$\updownarrow K_I \qquad \updownarrow K'_I$$
$$EI + S \rightleftharpoons ESI$$

Fig. 8-16 A schematic diagram of noncompetitive Inhibition.

350

indicated in **Fig.8-9** and **8-16**.

The effect of a non-competitive inhibitor is observed in V_{max}, where the V_{max} is decreased to V'_{max} due to the presence of the inhibitor. On the other hand, K_M does not change even after the inhibitor is inserted (i.e., $K_M = K'_M$). This is confirmed in Lineweaver-Burk plot as shown in **Fig. 8-18**. The slope of the plot (K'_M / V'_{max}) so as y-axis intercept increases as the inhibitor concentration, [I], increases. On the other hand, the x-axis intercepts ($1/K_M$) decrease very slightly or remains the same. Thus, the value of V_{max} must decrease as [I] increases.

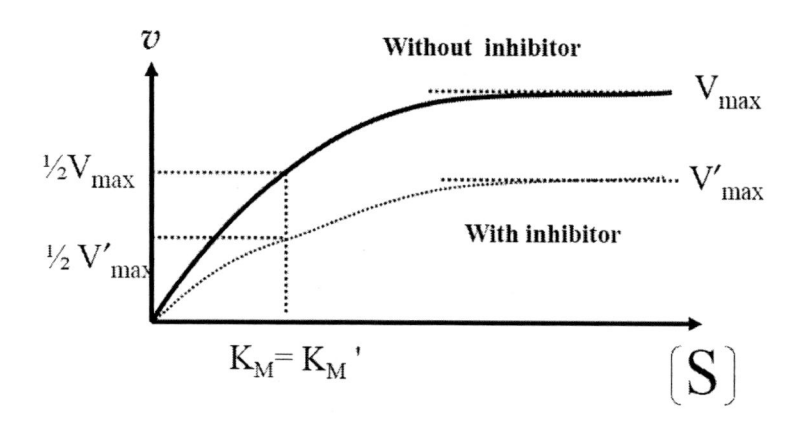

Fig. 8-17 The velocity and concentration relationship with an inhibitor for noncompetitive inhibition.

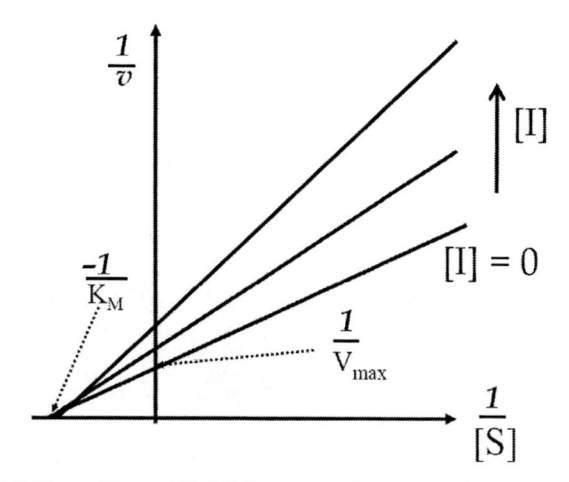

Fig. 8-18 The effect of inhibitor seen in Lineweaver-Burk plot for noncompetitive inhibition.

Chapter 8

How did you get these equations?
-The derivation of selected equations.

(Eqn. 8-4)
$$v_0 = \frac{V_{max}}{\left[1 + \frac{K_M}{[S]}\right]}$$

The rate for formation of ES complex is given as

$$\frac{d[ES]}{dt} = k_1[E][S] - k_{-1}[ES] - k_2[ES]$$

By using a steady state approximation,

$$\frac{d[ES]}{dt} \cong 0$$

Thus,

$$k_1[E][S] - k_{-1}[ES] - k_2[ES] = 0$$

Therefore,

$$[ES] = \frac{k_1[E][S]}{(k_{-1} + k_2)}$$

If we use measurable total enzyme concentration $[E]_o$ and substrate concentration $[S]_o$

$$[E]_o = [E] + [ES]$$

$$[S]_o = [S] + [ES] \cong [S]$$

Because typically

$$[S] \gg [ES]$$

Thus,

$$[E] = [E]_o - [ES]$$

By substituting this expression of [E]

$$[ES] = \frac{k_1[E][S]}{(k_{-1} + k_2)}$$

$$= \frac{k_1([E]_o - [ES])[S]}{(k_{-1} + k_2)}$$

$$= \frac{k_1[E]_o[S]}{(k_{-1} + k_2)} - \frac{k_1[ES][S]}{(k_{-1} + k_2)}$$

Therefore,

$$[ES] + \frac{k_1[ES][S]}{(k_{-1} + k_2)} = \frac{k_1[E]_o[S]}{(k_{-1} + k_2)}$$

$$[ES]\left\{1 + \frac{k_1[S]}{(k_{-1} + k_2)}\right\} = \frac{k_1[E]_o[S]}{(k_{-1} + k_2)}$$

$$[ES] = \frac{\left\{\frac{k_1[E]_o[S]}{(k_{-1} + k_2)}\right\}}{\left\{1 + \frac{k_1[S]}{(k_{-1} + k_2)}\right\}}$$

By dividing the both terms of fraction by $k_1[S]/(k_{-1}+k_2)$

$$[ES] = \frac{[E]_o}{\left\{1 + \frac{(k_{-1} + k_2)}{k_1[S]}\right\}}$$

The velocity of reaction is also given as

$$v_0 = k_2[ES]$$

By inserting the expression of [ES] from the result of the steady state approximation,

$$v_0 = \frac{k_2[E]_o}{\left\{1 + \frac{(k_{-1} + k_2)}{k_1[S]}\right\}}$$

Here we replace two terms as

$$K_M = [k_{-1} + k_2]/k_1$$

$$V_{max} = k_2[E]_o$$

Thus,

$$v_0 = \frac{V_{max}}{[1 + K_M/[S]]} \qquad \text{(Eqn. 8-4)}$$

Chapter 8 Enzyme Kinetics

(Eqn. 8-8) $k_M \ln\left([S]/[S]_0\right) + [S] - [S]_0 = -V_{max} t$

$$-d[S]/dt = V_{max}/\left(1 + K_M/[S]\right) \quad \text{(Eqn. 8-7)}$$

By arranging the (**Eqn. 8-7**),

$$\left(1 + K_M/[S]\right) d[S] = -V_{max} dt$$

By integrating both sides, from time t=0 to t and substrate concentration from $[S]_0$ to $[S]$,

$$\int_{[S]_0}^{[S]} \left(1 + K_M/[S]\right) d[S] = -\int_0^t V_{max} dt$$

$$\int_{[S]_0}^{[S]} d[S] + \int_{[S]_0}^{[S]} \left(K_M/[S]\right) d[S] = -\int_0^t V_{max} dt$$

$$[S] - [S]_0 + k_M \ln\left([S]/[S]_0\right) = -V_{max} t \quad \text{(Eqn. 8-8)}$$

Here, we used $\int (1/x) dx = \ln x + C$ (C is a constant.) for the second term.

(Eqn. 8-10) $\ln [S]/[S]_0 = -V_{max} t / K_M$

The Michaelis- equation states

$$v_0 = V_{max}/\left[1 + K_M/[S]\right] \quad \text{(Eqn. 8-4)}$$

At low concentration of [S], the next approximation is valid.

$$1 + K_M/[S] \approx K_M/[S]$$

Thus, the initial velocity of reaction (decrease rate of substrate concentration) is given as

$$v_0 = -d[S]/dt = V_{max}[S]/K_M$$

Chapter 8 Enzyme Kinetics

This is regarded as the same format solved for the first order reaction introduced in Chapter 9.

$$(1/[S])\,d[S] = -(V_{max}/K_M)\,dt$$

By integrating both sides, from time t=0 to t and substrate concentration from $[S]_0$ to $[S]$,

$$\int_{[S]_0}^{[S]} (1/[S])\,d[S] = -\int_0^t (V_{max}/K_M)\,dt$$

$$\ln [S]/[S]_0 = -V_{max}t/K_M \qquad \text{(Eqn. 8-10)}$$

Here, we used $\int(1/x)dx = \ln x + C$ (C is a constant.)

(Eqn. 8-11) $\quad v_0 = V_{max}$

The Michaelis- equation states

$$v_0 = V_{max}/[1 + K_M/[S]] \qquad \text{(Eqn. 8-4)}$$

At high concentration of [S]

$$1 + K_M/[S] \approx 1$$

Thus,

$$v_0 = V_{max} \qquad \text{(Eqn. 8-11)}$$

Also from **(Eqn. 8-11)**

$$k_{cat} = V_{max}/[E]_0 \qquad \text{(Eqn. 8-3)}$$

and
$$V_{max} = k_{cat}[E]_0$$
$$v_0 = k_{cat}[E]_0$$

(Eqn. 8-12) $\quad v_0 = \frac{1}{2}V_{max}$

The Michaelis- equation states

355

Chapter 8 Enzyme Kinetics

$$v_0 = V_{max} / \left[1 + K_M/[S]\right] \quad \text{(Eqn. 8-4)}$$

If [S] = K_M

$$v_0 = \frac{V_{max}}{1+\frac{[S]}{[S]}} = V_{max}/2 \quad \text{(Eqn. 8-12)}$$

(Eqn. 8-18) $\qquad K'_M = K_M \left[1 + [I]/K_I\right]$

$$[E]_0 = [E] + [ES] + [EI]$$

and

$$K_I = \frac{[E][I]}{[EI]}$$

Then, you can derive,

$$[E]_0 = [E]\left[1 + \frac{[I]}{K_I}\right] + [ES]$$

$$[E]_o = [E]\left[1 + \frac{I}{K_I}\right] + [ES]$$

Rearrange:

$$[E] = \frac{[Eo] - [ES]}{[1 + \frac{I}{K_I}]}$$

$$[ES] = \frac{k_1[E][S]}{k_{-1} + k_2}$$

Substitute in for [E] from above

$$[ES] = \frac{k_1 \left(\frac{[Eo] - [ES]}{[1 + \frac{I}{K_I}]}\right)[S]}{k_{-1} + k_2}$$

$$[ES] = \frac{k_1([Eo] - [ES])[S]}{(k_{-1} + k_2)(1 + \frac{I}{K_I})}$$

Substitute in where: $K_M = \frac{k_{-1}+k_2}{k_1}$

$$[ES] = \{([Eo] - [ES])[S]\} / K_M(1 + \frac{I}{K_I})$$

$$[ES] / ([Eo] - [ES])[S] = 1 / \{K_M(1 + \frac{I}{K_I})\}$$

Chapter 8 Enzyme Kinetics

$$([E]_o - [ES])[S]/[ES] = K_M \left(1 + \frac{I}{K_I}\right) \quad \text{(Eqn. 8-19)}$$

If we use measurable total enzyme concentration $[E]_o$ and substrate concentration $[S]_o$

$$[E]_o = [E] + [ES]$$

$$[S]_o = [S] + [ES] \approx [S]$$

Thus (**Eqn. 8-19**) can be arranged as follows

$$[ES] = \frac{k_1[E][S]}{(k_{-1} + k_2)}$$

$$[ES] = \frac{k_1([E]_o - [ES])[S]}{(k_{-1} + k_2)}$$

$$[ES] = \frac{k_1[E]_o[S]}{(k_{-1} + k_2)} - \frac{k_1[ES][S]}{(k_{-1} + k_2)}$$

$$[ES] + \frac{k_1[ES][S]}{(k_{-1} + k_2)} = \frac{k_1[E]_o[S]}{(k_{-1} + k_2)}$$

$$[ES]\left\{1 + \frac{k_1[S]}{(k_{-1} + k_2)}\right\} = \frac{k_1[E]_o[S]}{(k_{-1} + k_2)}$$

$$[ES] = \frac{\left\{\dfrac{k_1[E]_o[S]}{(k_{-1} + k_2)}\right\}}{\left\{1 + \dfrac{k_1[S]}{(k_{-1} + k_2)}\right\}}$$

By dividing the both terms of fraction by $k_1[S]/(k_{-1}+k_2)$

$$[ES] = \frac{[E]_o}{\left\{1 + \dfrac{(k_{-1} + k_2)}{k_1[S]}\right\}}$$

$$[ES] = [E]_o \Big/ \left\{1 + K_M/[S]\right\}$$

Here,

$$K_M = [k_{-1} + k_2]/k_1$$

Solving the above for K_M,

$$K_M = [S]\left\{[E]_o/[ES] - 1\right\}$$

Thus, we have an expression for K_M as

$$K_M = ([E]_o - [ES])[S]\Big/[ES]$$

If we are solving for the system with inhibitor involved causing the concentration of the substrate and complex as [S] and [ES], the K_M under the inhibitor present is given as K_M'

$$K_M' = ([E]_o - [ES])[S]\Big/[ES] \qquad \text{(Eqn. 8-20)}$$

Now, by comparing (**Eqn. 8-19**) and (**Eqn. 8-20**), we have the relationship as

$$K_M' = K_M\left[1 + [I]/K_I\right] \qquad \text{(Eqn. 8-18)}$$

Chapter 8 Summary [Part 1]

(Use back page to cover the contents.)

1	enzyme kinetics	E + S → ES → E + P E: enzyme, S: substrate, ES: complex, P: product
2	The initial velocity of enzyme reaction (v_o)	I) at small [S] $$v_0 = k[S] \quad \text{(Eqn. 8-1)}$$ ii) at high [S] $$v_0 = V_{max} \quad \text{(Eqn. 8-2)}$$
3	The catalytic constant, k_{cat}	overall rate constant observed at high substrate concentration $$k_{cat} = V_{max}/[E]_0 \quad \text{(Eqn. 8-3)}$$ $1/k_{cat}$: time required per molecule (an index of how fast different enzymes catalyze reactions.)
4	Michaelis- Enzyme kinetics	$$E + S \underset{k_{-1}}{\overset{K_1}{\rightleftharpoons}} ES \overset{k_2}{\rightarrow} E + P$$ initial velocity $$v_0 = \frac{V_{max}}{[1 + K_M/[S]]} \quad \text{(Eqn. 8-4)}$$ **Michaelis-Constant** $$K_M = [k_{-1} + k_2]/k_1 \quad \text{(Eqn. 8-5)}$$ $$V_{max} = k_2[E]_0 \quad \text{(Eqn. 8-6)}$$ integrated expression for the Michaelis- equation $$k_M \ln\left([S]/[S]_0\right) + [S] - [S]_0 = -V_{max}t \quad \text{(Eqn. 8-8)}$$ I. At low [S], ($K_M \gg [S]$) $v_0 = V_{max}[S]/K_M$ (Eqn. 8-9) ii. At high [S] $v_0 = V_{max}$ (Eqn. 8-11) iii. [S] = K_M $v_0 = \frac{1}{2}V_{max}$ (Eqn. 8-12)

[Fold the page at the double line and cover the right half.]

CHAPTER 8 SUMMARY CHECK [PART 1]

(Use this page to cover and check the contents.)

Use ☐ as your check box. Write your comment at far right

1	enzyme kinetics	☐ ☐ ☐ ☐ ☐	
2	The initial velocity of enzyme reaction (v_o)	☐ ☐ ☐ ☐ ☐	
3	The catalytic constant, k_{cat}	☐ ☐ ☐ ☐ ☐	
4	Michaelis- Enzyme kinetics	☐ ☐ ☐ ☐ ☐	

Chapter 8 Summary [Part 2]

(Use back page to cover the contents.)

5	Three analytical plots for Michaelis – equation are suggested	
		Lineweaver-Burk Plot: $$1/v_0 = 1/V_{max} + (K_M/V_{max})(1/[S])$$
		Dixon Plot: $$[S]/v_0 = [S]/V_{max} + K_M/V_{max}$$
		Eadie-Hofstee Plot: $$v_0 = -K_M v_0/[S] + V_{max}$$

[Fold the page at the double line and cover the right half.]

Chapter 8 Summary Check [Part 2]

(Use this page to cover and check the contents.)

Use ☐ as your check box. Write your comment at far right

| 5 | Three analytical plots for Michaelis – equation are suggested | ☐ ☐ ☐ ☐ ☐ | |

CHAPTER 8 SUMMARY [PART 3]
(Use back page to cover the contents.)

6	specific constant	k_{cat}/K_M: an index to compare the speed of reaction of two or more different enzyme reactions. $$v_A/v_B = \frac{[k_{cat}/K_M]_A[A]}{[k_{cat}/K_M]_B[B]} \quad \text{(Eqn. 8-17)}$$
7	three types of inhibition processes and the effect to K_M and V_{max}	<table><tr><th>Type</th><th>Effect on K_M</th><th>Effect on V_{max}</th></tr><tr><td>Competitive</td><td>Increases*</td><td>No change</td></tr><tr><td>Uncompetitive</td><td>Decreases</td><td>Decreases (V_{max}/K_M remains the same)</td></tr><tr><td>Mixed (noncompetitive)</td><td>Increases or no effect</td><td>Decreases</td></tr></table> *K_M for competitive inhibition $$K_M' = K_M\left[1 + [I]/K_I\right] \quad \text{(Eqn. 8-18)}$$

[Fold the page at the double line and cover the right half.]

Chapter 8 Summary Check [Part 3]

(Use this page to cover and check the contents.)
Use ☐ as your check box. Write your comment at far right

6	specific constant	☐ ☐ ☐ ☐ ☐	
7	three types of inhibition processes and the effect to K_M and V_{max}	☐ ☐ ☐ ☐ ☐	

Chapter 8 - YOUR TEACHER MAY TEST YOU ON:

No.	What may be asked?		What you should know or do?
1	What is a schematic of the enzyme reaction?	→	E + S → ES → E + P E: enzyme, S: substrate, ES: complex, P: product
2	What is the general idea for the initial reaction rate for the enzyme reaction at lower or higher substrate concentrations?	→	$v_0 = k[S]$ (at small [S]) (Eqn. 8-1) $v_0 = V_{max}$ (at high [S]) (Eqn. 8-2)
		→	Fig. 8-1
		→	Problems 8-1, 8-2
3	How do you calculate the catalytic constant, k_{cat}?	→	$k_{cat} = V_{max}/[E]_0$ (Eqn. 8-3)
4	How do you describe the reaction scheme for the Michaelis- kinetics?	→	$E + S \underset{k_{-1}}{\overset{k}{\rightleftharpoons}} ES \longrightarrow E + P$
5	How do you calculate the enzyme reaction rate described by the Michaelis- kinetics?	→	$v_0 = V_{max}/[1 + K_M/[S]]$ (Eqn. 8-4)
6	How do you calculate the Michaelis constant, K_M?	→	$K_M = [k_{-1} + k_2]/k_1$ (Eqn. 8-5)
		→	EXERCISE 8-1
		→	Problems 8-3, 8-4, 8-5
7	What is the integrated form to represent the Michaelis- equation?	→	$k_M \ln\left([S]/[S]_0\right) + [S] - [S]_0 = -V_{max}t$ (Eqn. 8-8)
8	How do you calculate the concentration of substrate at given time t for the case of low [S] or high [S]?	→	i. At low [S], $v_0 = V_{max}[S]/K_M$ (Eqn. 8-9) ii. At high [S] $v_0 = V_{max}$ (Eqn. 8-11) iii. [S] = K_M $v_0 = \frac{1}{2}V_{max}$ (Eqn. 8-12)
		→	EXERCISE 8-2

9	What are three analytical plots for Michaelis- kinetics? How do you plot them?		Lineweaver-Burk Plot (Fig. 8-4) $$1/v_0 = 1/V_{max} + (K_M/V_{max})(1/[S]) \text{ (Eqn. 8-13)}$$ Dixon Plot (Fig. 8-5) $$[S]/v_0 = [S]/V_{max} + K_M/V_{max} \text{ (Eqn. 8-14)}$$ Eadie-Hofstee Plot (Fig. 8-6) $$v_0 = -K_M v_0/[S] + V_{max} \text{(Eqn. 8-15)}$$
		→	EXERCISE 8-1
		→	8-6, 8-7, 8-8, 8-9, 8-10
10	How do you calculate specificity constant? How can you compare the velocities of two different enzyme reactions?	→	k_{cat}/K_M $$v_A/v_B = \frac{[k_{cat}/K_M]_A [A]}{[k_{cat}/K_M]_B [B]} \text{(Eqn. 8-17)}$$
		→	EXERCISE 8-3
		→	Problems 8-11, 8-12, 8-13
11	How do you express the Michaelis constant when competitive inhibition is involved in the reaction?	→	Fig. 8-12
		→	$$K'_M = K_M \left[1 + [I]/K_I\right] \text{ (Eqn. 8-18)}$$
		→	Problems 8-14, 8-15, 8-16, 8-17, 8-18, 8-19, 8-20
12	What are major three inhibition processes, and the effect to K_M or V_{max} due to the inhibitors?	→	Competitive inhibition (Fig. 8-7) (Fig 8-11) Uncompetitive inhibition (Fig. 8-8) (Fig. 8-15) noncompetitive inhibition (Fig. 8-9) (Fig. 8-18)

UNIT CHECK CHAPTER 8

Important Parameters of This Chapter	Popularly Used Unit
Concentration of enzyme, substrate, complex, and product [E], [S], [ES], and [P]	M, mol/L
Initial velocity of enzyme reaction, v_0	M/sec
Maximum velocity of enzyme reaction, V_{max}	M/sec
Catalytic constant, k_{cat}	sec^{-1}
Total concentration of enzyme, $[E]_o$	M/sec
Enzyme reaction rate constant, $k_1, k_{-1},$ and k_2	sec^{-1}
Michaelis- constant, K_M	M
Specificity constant, k_{cat}/K_M	$M^{-1} sec^{-1}$
Total concentration of substrate, $[S]_o$	M/sec
Time, t	sec
Michaelis- constant with inhibitant, K'_M	M
Concentration of inhibitant, [I]	M

SUMMARY OF TRICKY TRAPS OF CHAPTER 8

☐	1	Enzyme kinetics is unique and can be described as catalytic reaction (E: enzyme is remained at the end)with a product E + S → ES → E + P
☐	2	**Unit of K_M is a concentration [M]**
☐	3	There are three types of plot for analyzing Michaelis-Menten kinetics(K_M and V_{max}) derived from the same equation.
☐	4	Depending on the inhibition process, the effect to the K_M and V_{max} vary as a function of [I]

LAST MINUTE REVIEW OFMATH CHAPTER 8

(These are basic algebra which you have no excuse if you miss them.)

1. $\int \frac{dx}{x} = \ln x + C$
2. y = mx +b
   x axis Intercept y=b
   y axis intercept x= –(b/m)
3. $\frac{x}{1+y} \approx x \: if \: y \ll 1$ $\qquad \frac{x}{1+y} \approx \frac{x}{y} = 1 \: if \: 1 \ll y$

Nobel Prize and Your Knowledge From Chapter 8
(*: word appeared in Chapter 8)

The Nobel Prize in Chemistry 1989 was awarded jointly to **Sidney Altman** and **Thomas R. Cech** for their discovery of catalytic properties of RNA. The enzymes had been long thought to be catalytic proteins and are the only known biological catalysts. However, The RNA was discovered to form complex secondary structures and was suggested to act as a catalyst by Carl Woese, Francis Crick, and Leslie Orgel in 1967. This discovery completely changed the view of biological catalysis and created new view of **enzymes.*** In the 1980's, **Thomas R. Cech** and **Sidney Altman** discovered ribozymes about the same time. Thomas Cech was studying the excision of introns in a ribosomal RNA gene in *Tetrahymena thermophila* and tried to purify the enzyme responsible for splicing reaction. Cech discovered that intron could be spliced out in the absence of any added cell extract and concluded that no protein associated with the splicing reaction. Cech proposed that the intron sequence portion of the RNA could break and reform phosphodiester bonds. Sidney Altman investigated the procession of tRNA molecules into the cell. They isolated RNase-P which convert a precursor tRNA into the active

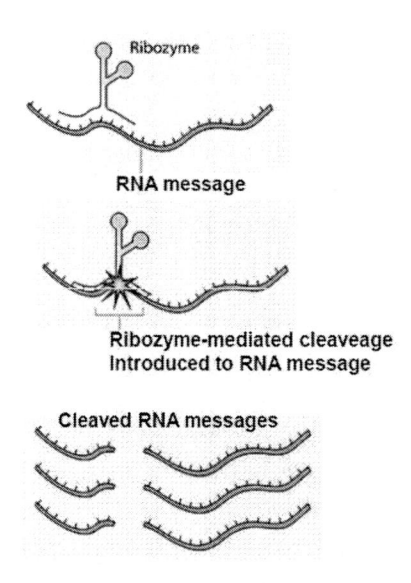

Fig. 8-19 Rybozyme and RNA message

tRNA. The RNase-P was found to contain RNA in addition to protein and that RNA was identified as an active enzyme. Altman also showed that the RNase-P RNA subunit catalyzes the cleavage of precursor tRNA into active tRNA without any protein involved. Altman also demonstrated that Ml RNA and RNase

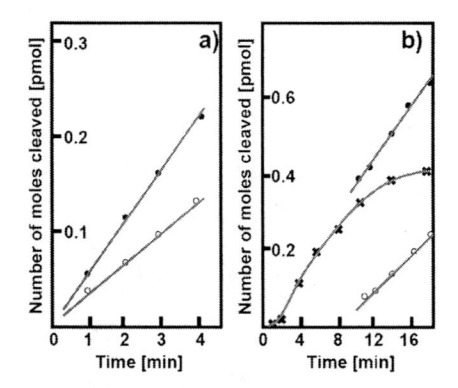

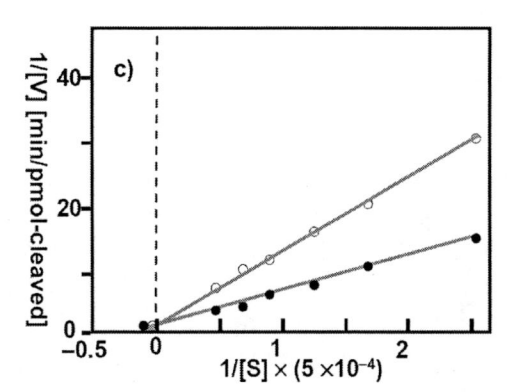

Fig. 8-20 Kinetic analysis of the M1 RNA and RNase P reactions with the precursor to tRNATYR (pTyr) as substrate. (●) RNase P activity: (O) M1 RNA activity. B). (●) pTyr added after 10 min: (X) buffer alone (O) net added pTyr cleaved. c). Lineweaver-Burk plot of a) (●) RNase P in buffer that contained 5 mM $MgCl_2$:(O) M1 RNA in buffer containing MgCl.

P possess a property of enzyme with true **turnover number*** as measured by **Michaelis- analysis*** (See **Fig. 8-20**) Many ribozymes possess either a hairpin – or hammerhead – shaped active center and a unique secondary structure that which cut other RNA molecules at specific sequences. These RNA catalysts will be greatly applied to pharmaceutical field to design a ribozyme which can specifically cleave the RNA associated with diseases.

THE FOCUSED PHYSICAL CHEMISTRY EXPERIMENTAL APPROACH ASSOCIATED WITH CHAPTER 8

(*: word appeared in Chapter 8)

PCR: Polymerase Chain Reaction

The **polymerase chain reaction (PCR)** is a technique to amplify a single or a few copies of a piece of DNA across several orders of magnitude, generating thousands to millions of copies of a particular DNA sequence. This is a thermal cycling (repetition of heating and cooling of the reaction for DNA melting through a series of **enzymatic reaction*** to replicate the DNA). (**Fig. 8-21**)

Major steps of thermal cycling is
1). ***Denaturation step***: heating the reaction at high temperature (e.g., 94–98 °C) causing DNA melting yielding single-stranded DNA molecules.
2).***Annealing step***: At lower temperature (e.g.,50–65 °C)polymerase binds to the primer-template and DNA synthesis is started.
3).***Extension/elongation step***: DNA polymerase aids to selectively amplify the target DNA and synthesizes a new DNA strand

The selectivity of PCR results from the use of primers that are complementary to the DNA region targeted for amplification. Here condition for thermal cycling are very specific. As PCR progresses, the synthesized DNA are used as a template for replication leading a chain reaction. The key components to accomplish selective amplification is the short DNA fragments (primers) containing sequences complementary to the target region along with a DNA polymerase. Taq polymerase is a commonly used heat-stable DNA polymerase.

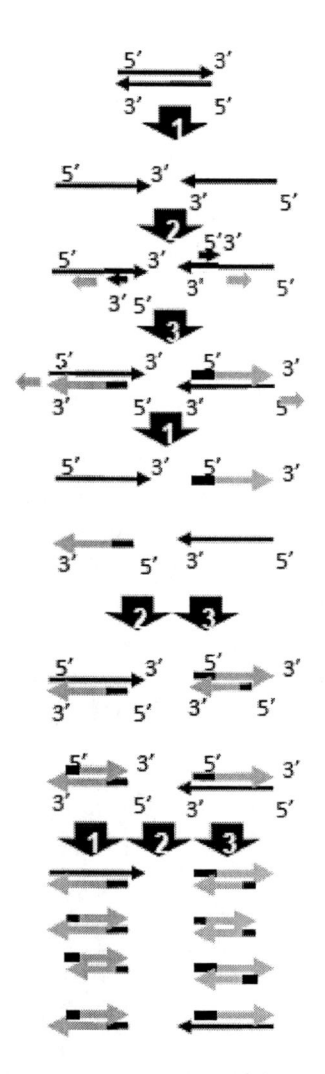

Fig. 8-21 Schematics of the PCR cycle. 1) Denaturing, 2) Annealing, 3) Elongation. DNA template is indicated by black arrow with primers (arrows), DNA polymerase is given by circles. The shorter DNA products are given by lines.

CHAPTER 8 PROBLEMS

8-1[enzyme kinetics] By using enzyme,
    a. the activation energy of the reaction increases.
    b. the activation energy of the reaction decreases.
    c. the activation energy remains the same but the product's enthalpy (or Gibbs energy) decreases.
    d. the activation energy remains the same but the product's enthalpy (or Gibbs energy) increases.
    e. the activation energy and the product's enthalpy (or Gibbs energy) decreases.

8-2 [enzyme kinetics]. At low concentration of the substrate, [S], the rate for the enzyme kinetics is the first order of the concentration, [S]. Thus,
    a. the half life of this reaction is independent of [S].
    b. the rate is almost equal to $V_{max}/2$.
    c. the plot of rate as a function of [S] shows nonlinear behavior (a curve).
    d. the rate is almost equal to V_{max}.
    e. the activation energy is dependent on [S].

8-3 [Michaelis- kinetics] In Michaelis- kinetics, the initial velocity of the reaction under very high concentration of the substrate, [S], can be approximated as:
    a. V_{max}
    b. $V_{max}[S]/K_M$
    c. $V_{max}[S]/\{[S]+K_M\}$
    d. $V_{max}[S]$
    e. none of these

8-4 [$K_M \rightarrow$ Rate] The enzyme-catalyzed hydrolysis of an ester is competitively inhibited by Mg^{2+}. How long it will take for 5.00×10^{-6} [M] substrate to become 4.00×10^{-7} [M] in the presence of 5.00×10^{-4} [M] inhibitor Mg^{2+}. Assume that the affinity of an enzyme for substrate is 10 times of affinity of an inhibitor for substrate. Michaelis constant is $K_M = 1.00 \times 10^{-6}$ [M] and maximum rate is $V_{max} = 0.750$ [M/sec].

8-5 [$K_M \rightarrow$ Rate] Consider the simple Michaelis- mechanism for an enzyme-catalyzed reaction:

$$E + S \underset{k_{-1}}{\overset{k_1}{\rightleftharpoons}} ES \overset{k_2}{\longrightarrow} E + P$$

The following data were obtained: k_1, k_{-1} very fast. $k_2 = 50$ [sec^{-1}] and $K_M = 2.0 \times 10^{-4}$ [M] at 5 [°C]
a) For [S] = 0.05 [M] and $[E]_o = 5.0 \times 10^{-5}$ [M], calculate the rate of formation of product at 5 [°C].
b) What is the value of the equilibrium constant at 5 [°C] for the formation of the enzyme –substrate complex ES from E and S?

8-6 [Lineweaver Burk] Which statement is correct about the Lineweaver-Burk plot?
    a. x-axis intercept increases and slope of the graph decreases as V_{max} increases.
    b. y-axis intercept and slope decreases as V_{max} increases.
    c. x-axis intercept decreases as V_{max} increases.
    d. y-axis intercept remains the same even though V_{max} changes.
    e. none of these

8-7 [Plot] Make a suitable plot and determine K_M

[S] [mM]	10	2.0	1.0	0.50	0.33
V_o [µM sec^{-1}]	1.17	0.99	0.79	0.62	0.50

8-8 [Linewaver-Burk] A person conducted "Lineweaver-Burk plot" for an enzyme kinetics. The following values were obtained. From these results, obtain K_M (Michaelis constant) and V_{max} (maximum rate) of this enzyme reaction.

Slope =75.5 [sec]
Intercept = 11.8 [sec/ mM]

8-9 [Lineweaver Burk] A person analyzed an enzyme reaction with Michaelis- kinetics, and the following values were obtained: V_{max} = 0.0847 [mM/sec], K_M =6.39 [mM].
What is the value for y-axis intercept (sec/mM) if the data were plotted by "Lineweaver-Burk method"?

8-10 [Plot → K_M, V_{max}] Make a suitable plot and determine V_{max} and K_M

1/[S] [M^{-1}]	13×10^4	8.5×10^4	6.0×10^4	3.0×10^4	0.5×10^4
1/V_o [sec M^{-1}]	260	175	122	60	10

8-11 [Relative Rate] The k_{cat}/K_M is called as a *specific constant*, k_S, of a particular enzyme reaction. Here, the specific constant of reaction A, $k_S(A)$, and the specific constant of reaction B, $k_S(B)$ has the relationship as $k_S(A) = 2k_S(B)$. Then, calculate the relationship between reaction speed of A and B (v_A and v_B), when [A] = 4[B].([A] and [B] are the concentrations of A and B, respectively.)

    a. $v_A = 8\ v_B$
    b. $8\ v_A = v_B$
    c. $2\ v_A = v_B$
    d. $v_A = 2\ v_B$
    e. none of these

8-12 [Relative Rate] A carboxypeptidase was found to have K_M of 2.00 [µM] and a k_{cat} of 150 [sec^{-1}] for its substrate A. A competing substrate B is added to the solution and its K_M is 10.0 [µM] and k_{cat} is 100 [sec^{-1}]. Calculate the relative rates of substrate reaction for equal concentrations of substrate.

8-13 [Specific constant] An enzyme was found to have K_M of 1.00 [nM] and a k_{cat} of 10 [msec^{-1}] for its substrate A. Then, competing substrate B is added to the solution, and the relative rates, v_B/v_A, of substrate reaction for equal concentrations of substrate was found to be 0.5. Calculate k_{cat} for competing substrate B when K_M of B is 3.0 [nM].

8-14 [K_I] In a competitive inhibition,
    a. K_I is proportional to the (K_M '– K_M)–1 and [I].
    b. K_I is inversely proportional to [I].
    c. K_I decreases as K_M ' increases.
    d. K_I increases as [I] K_M decreases
    e. none of these

8-15 [K_I] An enzyme X was found to have a Michaelis constant K_M of 4.00 [µM]. The initial concentration of the substrate is 5.00 [µM]. The presence of 5.00 [mM] of a competitive inhibitor decreased the initial rate by a factor of 3. What is the dissociation constant, K_I, for the enzyme inhibitor complex.

8-16 [Rate time for K_M, K_I] The enzyme-catalyzed hydrolysis of an ester is competitively inhibited by Mg^{2+}. Estimate how long it will take for 10^{-5} [M] substrate to become 10^{-6} [M] in the presence of 10^{-4} [M] inhibitor: K_M = 10^{-3} [M], K_I = 10^{-4} [M], and V_{max} = 1 [M/sec].

8-17 [plot→K_M, V_{max}, K_I] The hydrolysis of sucrose by the enzyme invertase was followed by measuring the initial rate of change at various initial concentrations of sucrose. The reaction is inhibited reversibly by the addition of 2 [M] of urea:

The following table gives the initial velocity v_o of this reaction at several sucrose concentrations:

[Sucrose]$_o$ (M)	0.0292	0.0584	0.0876	0.117
v_o [M sec^{-1}]	0.182	0.265	0.311	0.330
v_o + 2M urea [μ M sec^{-1}]	0.083	0.119	0.154	0.167

a. Make **a suitable plot** of the data *in the absence of urea*.
b. From our graph, obtain the Michaelis constant K_M for this reaction in the absence of urea.
c. Obtain the maximum velocity V_{max} in the absence of urea.
d. Urea is **a non competitive inhibitor** of this reaction.
(i) Obtain the value of Michaelis constant K_M' in the presence of this inhibitor.
(ii) Obtain the average value of K_I.

8-18 [plot→K_M, V_{max}, K_I] Sodium succinate is oxidized in the presence of dissolved oxygen to form sodium fumarate in the presence of the enzyme succinoxidase.
The following table gives the initial velocity v_o of this reaction at several succinate concentrations:

[S] (mM)	10	2.0	1.0	0.50	0.33
v_o [μ M sec^{-1}]	1.17	0.99	0.79	0.62	0.50

a) Make a suitable plot of the data
b) Obtain the maximum velocity V_{max}.
c) Obtain the Michaelis constant K_M for this reaction.
d) Malonate is a competitive inhibitor of this reaction. In an experiment with initially 1.0 [mM] succinate, the initial velocity is decreased by 50% in the presence of 30 [mM] of manlonate.
i) Obtain the Michaelis constant K_M' in the presence of this inhibitor.
ii) Obtain K_I, where K_I = [E] [I] /[EI]. [E]: concentration of enzyme, [I]: concentration of inhibitor, and [EI]: concentration of enzyme-inhibitor complex.

8-19 [K_M, K_I→Rate] The enzyme-catalyzed hydrolysis of an ester is competitively inhibited by Mg^{2+}.
a) Estimate how long it will take for 10^{-5} [M] substrate to become 10^{-6} [M]
   ($K_M = 10^{-3}$ [M] and V_{max} =1 [M/sec]).
b) Here, estimate how long it will take for 10^{-5} [M] substrate to become 10^{-6} [M] in the presence of 10^{-4} M inhibitor: ($K_I = 10^{-4}$ [M])

8-20 [K_I] An enzyme X was found to have a Michaelis constant K_M in of 2.00 [μM] and a k_{cat} of 150 [sec^{-1}] for its substrate A. The initial concentration of the substrate is 5.00 [μM] and the enzyme 2 [μg] (a molecular weight of an enzyme X is 20,000 [g/mol]) is prepared as a 0.01 [mL] of solution. The presence of 5.00 [mM] of a competitive inhibitor decreased the initial rate by a factor of 2. What is the dissociation constant for the enzyme inhibitor complex.

Chapter 8 Answers. For Selected Problems

8-1 The activation energy of the reaction decreases.
8-2 The halflife of this reaction is independent of [S].
8-3 Vmax
8-4 16.8 [msec]
8-5 a) 2.49×10^{-3} [Msec^{-1}]   b) $K_{eq} = 3.33 \times 10^{3}$
8-6 The y-axis intercept and slope decreases as Vmax increases.
8-7 $V_{max} = 1.21 \times 10^{-6}$ [M/sec]
8-8 $V_{max} = 0.0847$ [mM/sec], $K_M = 6.39$ [mM]
8-9 11.8 [sec/mM] ~10 [sec/mM]
8-10 $V_{max} = 1.49$ [M/sec] $K_M = 0.022$ [M]
8-11 $v_A = 8 v_B$
8-12 0.133 or 7.5
8-14 K_I is proportional to the $(K_M' - K_M) - 1$ and [I].
8-15 $K_I = 1.11$ [mM]
8-16 ~5 [msec]
8-17 b) 45.5 [mM], c) 0.467 [M/sec], d-I) 44 [mM], d-ii) $K_I = +\infty$
8-18 b) 1.23×10^{-6} [M sec^{-1}] c) 4.85×10^{-4} [M] d-i) $K'_M = 1.97 \times 10^{-3}$ [M], d-ii) $K_I = 9.8 \times 10^{-3}$ [M]
8-19 a) 2.3 [msec],   b) 4.6 [msec]
8-20 $K_M' = 9.00$ [μM], $K_I = 1.43$ [mM]

Chapter 9

A Taste of Quantum Mechanics

9-1   A Bit of Quantum Mechanics
9-2   Wave Mechanics and Wave Functions
9-3   A Particle in a Square Well Model
9-4   A Particle in a Box Model
9-5   Transition Energy
9-6   Simple Harmonic Oscillator

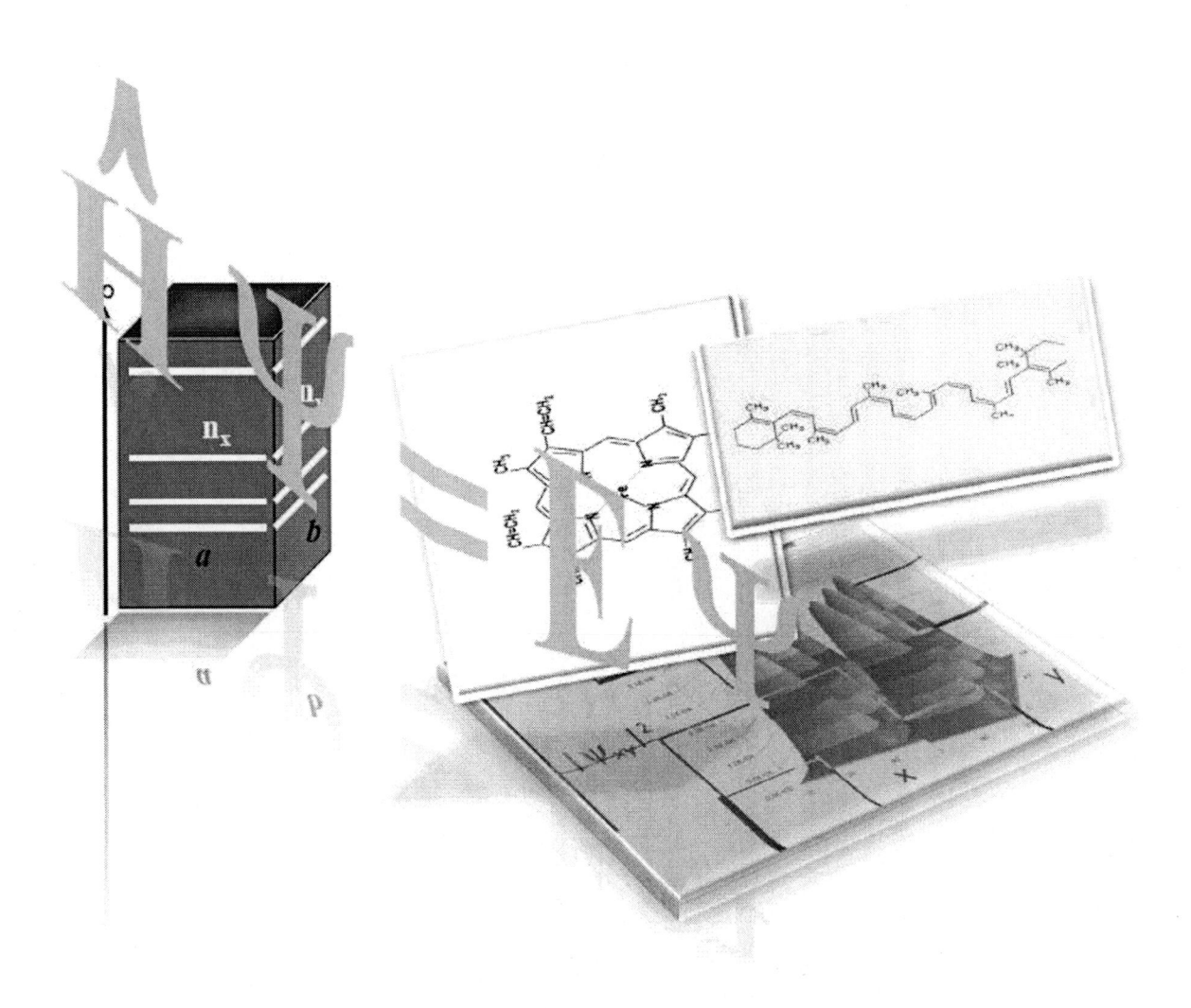

Chapter 9 A Taste of Quantum Mechanics

- ## *Why do I have to study this chapter?*

"When you are in Rome, do as Romans do" When you study about electrons, try to understand how electrons prefer to be treated. The Quantum Mechanics is considered to best explain the properties (energies) of electrons. In this chapter, you will learn the "wavy" idea of describing electrons in a molecular system. The Quantum Mechanics is a different mechanical concept from classical mechanics. The "skill" to calculate energy level and space (distribution) of electrons will be studied, so that you will be able to construct a molecular structure. Since most of you are familiar with the digital world, I am not too worried about your abilities to become familiar with "quantized" energy levels.

- ## *Expected Hurdles Ahead in this Chapter*

There are many hurdles ahead in this chapter. (This chapter itself can be a big hurdle!!!)
1. Dual nature of electron (See Section **9-1**)
2. Wave function and operator (See Section **9-1**)
3. Solving for Schrodinger's equation of particle in a box (See Section **9-3** and **9-4**)
4. Calculation of electron transition energy (See Section **9-5**)
5. Calculation of energy for a harmonic oscillator (See Section **9-6**)

PREVIEW OF KEY-EQUATIONS

Photoelectric effect
$$E = h\nu$$

Dual nature of electron (*de* Broglie wavelength)
$$\lambda = \frac{h}{p}$$

Schrödinger's Equation
$$\hat{H}\Psi = E\Psi$$

Probability density
$$\int_{x_1}^{x_2} \psi_{ns}^* \psi_{ns} d\tau = \int_{x_1}^{x_2} [\psi_{ns}]^2 4\pi r^2 dr$$

Chapter 9 A Taste of Quantum Mechanics

Particle in a square well-wavefunction and eigen values

$$\psi = \left[2/a\right]^{1/2} \sin(n\pi x/a)$$

$$E_n = n^2 h^2 / 8ma^2 \quad n=1, 2, 3......$$

Transition energy of an electron from level n to n+1

$$\Delta E(n \to n+1) = \left(h^2/8ma^2\right)(2n+1)$$

$$\lambda(n \to n+1) = 8mca^2/[h(2n+1)]$$

Potential of harmonic oscillator

$$U = \frac{1}{2}kx^2$$

Energy of harmonic oscillator

$$E_v = h\nu_o\left[v + 1/2\right]$$

Fundamental frequency

$$\nu_o = \left(1/2\pi\right)\sqrt{k/\mu}$$

Reduced mass

$$\mu = m_1 m_2/(m_1 + m_2)$$

Chapter 9 A Taste of Quantum Mechanics

PREVIEW OF KEY-TECHNICAL TERMS

Quantum mechanics, Planck's quantum theory, Planck's constant (h), dual nature of electron, de Broglie equation, wave function (Ψ), Schrödinger's equation, Hamiltonian Operator ($\hat{H}$), electron density, complex conjugate, Bohr radius (a_o), eigen function, eigen value, operator, particle in a box, boundary condition, normalization, transition energy, HOMO, LUMO, harmonic oscillator, vibrational level, Fundamental frequency (ν_o), tunneling effect, zero point energy

Chapter 9 A Taste of Quantum Mechanics

9-1 A Bit of Quantum Mechanics

Many situations in biological sciences commonly require the application of quantum mechanics. This is true in the case of using the approach of physical chemistry. The macro-scale system is nicely understood and described by Newtonian (or classical) mechanics. Naturally, the attempt to use Newtonian mechanics to express physical properties of atomic or molecular system can be conducted. For example, please recall "gas kinetic theory" to be introduced in Chapter 11. (Please note that the assumptions made in that theory lacked interaction between particles.) With several approximations, classical mechanics can describe some properties of systems qualitatively or quantitatively. On the other hand, chemical properties (chemical reactions or chemical interactions) are strongly governed by properties of electrons in systems. For example, we need to know how electrons are distributed in the frame of nuclei in order to characterize the structure (or shape) of atom or molecules.

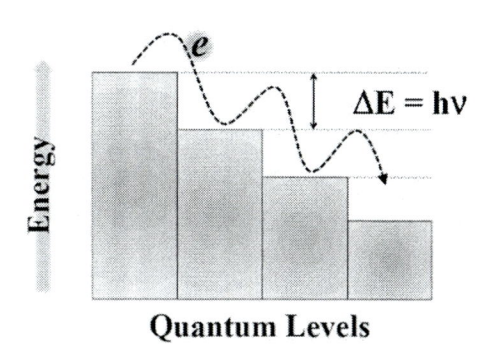

Fig. 9-1 Discrete energy levels in quantum theory.

Classical mechanics fails to describe the energy or location of the electrons. **Quantum mechanics (quantum theory)** is regarded as the best suited mechanics to explain the energetic or special properties of electrons. A key asset to the quantum theory was first established by Planck, where the energy state for the electron possess discrete energy levels, so that the atoms and molecules could emit energy (E) only in discrete quantities. (**Planck's Quantum Theory**). (**Fig. 9-1**) **Albert Einstein** adopted **Planck's** relationship to explain the results of the **photoelectric effect** which showed that the energy (E) of ejected electrons depend on the frequency (ν) of incident light as

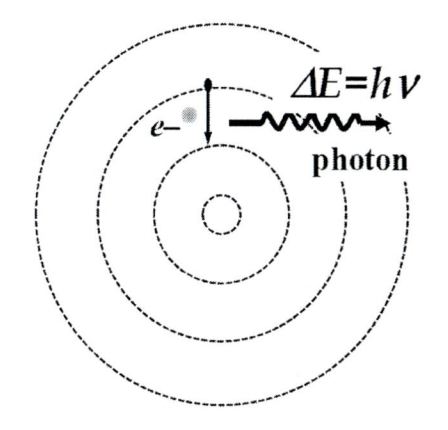

Fig. 9-2 Emission process of in an atomic orbital.

$$E = h\nu \qquad \text{(Eqn. 9-1)}$$

Here, h is Planck's constant (h = 6.62606896(33) ×10^{-34} [J s]). As an electron goes down from the higher energetic level to one lower energetic level, the difference in energy (ΔE) is also described by the above equation (**Eqn. 9-1**). The discrete energy levels and the relation shown in (**Eqn. 9-1**) are reflected in atomic (or molecular) spectrum exhibit as discrete spectral lines. (**Fig. 9-2**)

Chapter 9 A Taste of Quantum Mechanics

Small particles including electrons can possess both the particle and the wave like characters. (**dual nature of electron**) This can be said as the most puzzling and remarkable description explained in quantum mechanics. The mathematical expression indicates this dual character is given by **de Broglie** equation

$$h = p\lambda \qquad \text{(Eqn. 9-2)}$$

where p is a momentum (p= mv, m: mass of a particle [kg], v=velocity [m·sec^{-1}]), and λ is called *de* Broglie wavelength and h is Planck constant. Since the term represented in momentum contains a mass for its expression, the momentum indicates a particle-like character. Also, the *de* Broglie wavelength is the representation of the wave-like character. In (**Eqn. 9-3**), the diffraction interference patterns (fringes) created by electro-magnetic eave (X-ray) and electrons are shown. The fringes (interference patterns) observed in electromagnetic waves can be also observed in electrons implying its wave-like character.

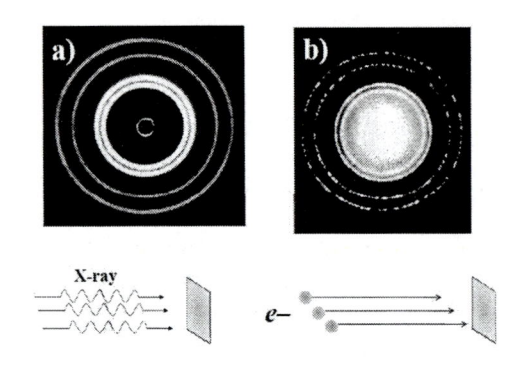

Fig. 9-3 a) X-ray diffraction of aluminum foil
b) electron diffraction of aluminum foil

EXERCISE 9-1
If the velocity of an electron beam of electron microscopy is 1.5×10^8 [m/sec], what is the wavelength of an electron particle?

ANSWER
$$\lambda = h/p \qquad \text{(Eqn. 9-2)}$$
p= m$_e$v

v= 1.5×10^8 [m/sec]

$$\lambda = \frac{6.626 \times 10^{-34} [J \cdot sec]}{9.109 \times 10^{-31}[kg] \times 1.50 \times 10^8 [m/sec]}$$
$$= 4.85 \times 10^{-12} [m] = 4.85 \text{ [pm]}$$

❶ p is momentum
❷ m$_e$ is the mass of an electron m$_e$ = 9.109×10^{-31} [kg]

9-2 Wave Mechanics and Wave Functions

If an electron is interpreted to have a dual nature (particle-like and wave-like characters), you may imagine that you can express the location of the electron like "a wave". You may recall a General Chemistry textbook indicating the atomic structure with electron resides as a cloud around a nucleus. That means that there are some locations that contain more electron density than others. In this case, it is best to use the probability of finding an electron in a given space to locate its electron position instead of counting the number of electrons like particles. (This is similar to mapping the contour of the wave height.) As the undulation of the wave in a given space and time is given mathematically, we can create a mathematical function to express the wave of an electron (Ψ: **wave function**), and this function represents the wave-like property of an electron. Schrödinger formulated mathematical equations to relate the wave function (Ψ) and a given physical property (E: **eigen value**) of the wave. (**Schrödinger's Equation**). When the eigen value is given as E, the Schrödinger's equation is given as

$$\hat{H}\Psi = E\Psi \qquad \text{(Eqn. 9-3)}$$

Here, $\hat{H}$ is called as a **Hamiltonian operator** and the property of eigen values depend on the operator. (**See Table 9-1**)

Table 9-1 The summary of Hamiltonian operators.

Name of operator	Operator (in Cartesian coordinate expression)
Position	X
Momentum (one dimension)	$-i\hbar \left(d/dx \right)$
Momentum (three dimensions)	$-i\hbar \{(\partial/\partial x) + (\partial/\partial y) + (\partial/\partial z)\} = -i\hbar \nabla$
Energy (one dimension)	$-\dfrac{\hbar^2}{2m} \dfrac{\partial^2}{\partial x^2}$
Energy (three dimensions)	$-\dfrac{\hbar^2}{2m} \left\{ \dfrac{\partial^2}{\partial x^2} + \dfrac{\partial^2}{\partial y^2} + \dfrac{\partial^2}{\partial z^2} \right\} + V = -\dfrac{\hbar^2}{2m} \nabla^2 + V$

∇^2: Laplacian operator

A very important concept (or outcome) of the wavefunction is that the square of the wavefunction provides the probability that an electron will be found.

$|\Psi|^2$ is probability of finding electron.

Thus, $|\Psi|^2$ is proportional to the electron density as demonstrated in **Fig. 9-4** for the case of 1s electron, and it clearly shows that electron density decreases drastically as the location is further away from the core. Since electron distribution can be spherically symmetric around the nucleus core center, it is more convenient to express the probability of finding electron in a spherical shell of radius r around the nucleus. This probability is given by

Chapter 9 A Taste of Quantum Mechanics

$$r^2\psi_{ns}^2$$

Here, ψ_{ns} indicate a wave function of ns electron of a hydrogen atom. The probability for 1s, 2s, and 3s electrons is demonstrated in **Fig. 9-5**. The radial part of the wavefunction (ψ_{ns}) for each electron (1s, 2s, and 3s) are listed in **Table 9-2**.

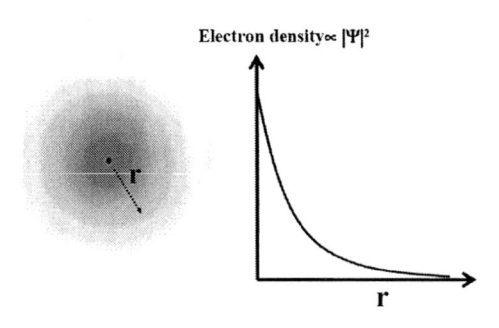

Fig. 9-4 The electron density distribution and probability of finding electron.

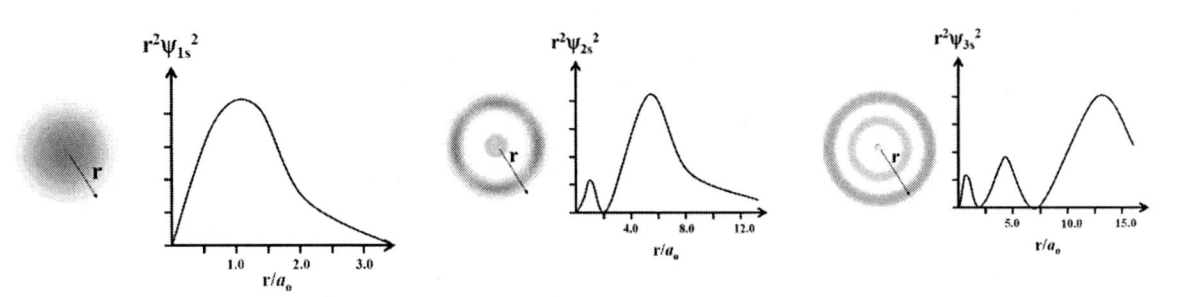

Fig. 9-5 The probability of finding electrons at radius, r for 1s, 2s and 3s electrons.

The **Fig. 9-5** is showing only the slice of the electron density along the radius from 0 to r. Therefore, you may notice that real probability of finding the electron in the entire space should be found by integrating the wavefunction for the entire space (sphere). Thus, a probability of finding the ns electron of H atom between x_1 and x_2 along the radius of sphere in entire space is given by

$$\int_{x_1}^{x_2} \psi_{ns}^* \psi_{ns} d\tau = \int_{x_1}^{x_2} [\psi_{ns}]^2 d\tau \qquad \text{(Eqn. 9-4)}$$

Here, integration for the entire space is given by

$$d\tau = 4\pi r^2 dr \qquad \text{(Eqn. 9-4)'}$$

The meaning of * mark on the first wavefunction in the integral is that you take a complex conjugate of that function if it is available. (For example, a **complex conjugate** of ix is $-ix$, i.e., $(ix)^* = -ix$. The "i" is an imaginary number, i.e., $i^2 = -1$) Please refer to the s electron wavefunction (ψ_{ns}) of H atom in Table 11-2, and note that they do not contain any complex number in it, thus $\psi_{ns}^* = \psi_{ns}$.

Table 9-2 The summary of wave function (ψ_{ns}) for hydrogen atom. Here, a_o is called as Bohr radius and $a_o = 52.9177 \times 10^{-12}$ [m]

n	ψ_{ns}
1s	$\psi_{1s} = \dfrac{1}{\sqrt{\pi}}\left(\dfrac{1}{a_o}\right)^{3/2} e^{-\frac{r}{a_o}}$
2s	$\psi_{2s} = \dfrac{1}{4\sqrt{2\pi}}\left(\dfrac{1}{a_o}\right)^{3/2}\left(2 - \dfrac{r}{a_o}\right) e^{-\frac{r}{2a_o}}$
3s	$\psi_{3s} = \dfrac{1}{81\sqrt{3\pi}}\left(\dfrac{1}{a_o}\right)^{3/2}\left(27 - 18\dfrac{r}{a_o} + 2(r/a_o)^2\right) e^{-\frac{r}{3a_o}}$

EXERCISE 9-2
Calculate the probability of finding the 1s electron of hydrogen between 0 and **Bohr radius**, a_o.

ANSWER
From **Table 9-2**, The wavefunction of 1s electron of H (ψ_{1s}) is

❶ $\psi_{1s} = \dfrac{1}{\sqrt{\pi}}\left(\dfrac{1}{a_o}\right)^{3/2} e^{-\frac{r}{a_o}}$

The probability of finding the 1s electron of H atom between 0 and a_o is

❷ $\int_0^{a_o} \psi_{1s}^* \psi_{1s} d\tau = \int_0^{a_o} [\psi_{1s}]^2 d\tau$ **(Eqn. 9-4)**

Here, the integration for entire space is given by

❸ $d\tau = 4\pi r^2 dr$ Thus,

$$\int_0^{a_o} [\psi_{1s}]^2 d\tau = 4\pi \int_0^{a_o} \left[\dfrac{1}{\sqrt{\pi}}\left(\dfrac{1}{a_o}\right)^{3/2} e^{-\frac{r}{a_o}}\right]^2 r^2 dr$$

In order to make this calculation to be easier,

❹ let's replace r/a_o by ρ ($\rho = r/a_o$) and $dr = a_o d\rho$. Then,

$$4\pi \int_0^{a_o} \left[\dfrac{1}{\sqrt{\pi}}\left(\dfrac{1}{a_o}\right)^{3/2} e^{-\frac{r}{a_o}}\right]^2 r^2 dr = 4 \int_0^1 e^{-2\rho} \rho^2 d\rho$$

Using the following relationship

$$\int x^{-2} e^{ax} dx = \left(\dfrac{x^2}{a} - \dfrac{2x}{a^2} + \dfrac{2}{a^3}\right) e^{ax} + Constant.$$

❺ $\int_0^{a_o}[\psi_{1s}]^2 d\tau = -\left(e^{-2\rho}/2\right)[4\rho^2 + 4\rho + 2]\Big|_0^1 = 0.323$

❶ Choose the right one (1s).
❷ In ψ_{1s}^*, the mark "*" indicates a complex conjugate. Since there is no complex number (i) in ψ_{1s}, $\psi_{1s}^* = \psi_{1s}$.
❸ Don't forget this factor in order to integrate for entire space.
❹ Trust me. This conversion makes your calculation much easier.
❺ Confirm the value is positive and does not exceed 1.

Chapter 9 A Taste of Quantum Mechanics

☹ **MCM Most Common Mistake (38)-"I have no idea about an operator, eigen function, eigen value?**

While the concept of the Schrödinger's equation may not be hard to accept, many people seem to have some difficulty in mathematical expression. Many have difficulties understanding this concept of an operator especially due to unfamiliarity. The operator can be easily omitted and misunderstood, if you have never experienced this type of expression. Literally, the operator operates on something. In this case, operator is a Hamiltonian and Hamiltonian operates on a wavefunction. Most importantly, the operator produces a new value (technically it is called as an eigen value) after it operates. The Hamiltonian operator operates on the wavefunction (eigen function) and produces eigen value as a result.

$$\hat{H}\Psi = E\Psi \qquad \text{(Eqn. 9-3)}$$

Here, the prefix "eigen" came from German word meaning "innate", "idiosyncratic", or "own". Therefore, the function Ψ or physical value E are function and values which belong to a given operator. Without any knowledge about the (**Eqn. 9-3**), you may be tempted to cancel out the wavefunction (Ψ) from both side. However, in this case, you read the above equation in a different way. In (**Eqn. 9-3**), it shows that the operator ($\hat{H}$) operates on the wavefunction (Ψ) on the right hand side. If you look at the right hand side, it shows that the operator will keep (or reproduce) the wavefunction (Ψ), but the operator will disappear by producing eigen value, E. It must make sense when you hear that the typical operator is differential function or multiplication of a variable (See **Table 9-1** for examples of operators.) As for the relation seen in the Schrödinger's equation, I often use an example of buying a snack from a vending machine. In this situation, the machine corresponds to the wave function and the money is the operator. After you insert coin in a vending machine, you push the button to choose a product (operator operated on the wave function), you get a snack as a result, which is similar to that eigen value is given because operator operated on the wavefunction. The vending machine (mechanical part) , however, a vending machine still stays as it was (except for the fact that it lost a snack from the stock, which is similar to that the wave function remains the same even after the operation.

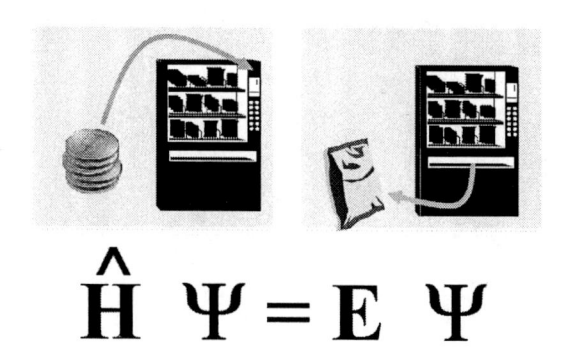

$$\hat{H}\,\Psi = E\,\Psi$$

384

9-3 A Particle in a Square Well Model

The most popular example of solvable Schrodinger's equation is a problem of "particle in a box" model, in which a particle with mass m is trapped inside a box (or square well) where the particle cannot escape. (**Fig. 9-4**) If a particle is very small (like an electron), the energy levels of this particle are discrete (i.e., quantized.) This condition looks a bit far from realistic view dealt in the biological system or molecules studied in chemistry. The examples shown in this chapter is so called one dimensional or two dimensional box traps electron such as conjugated chain molecule or metal porphyrin system. (**Fig. 9-7**)

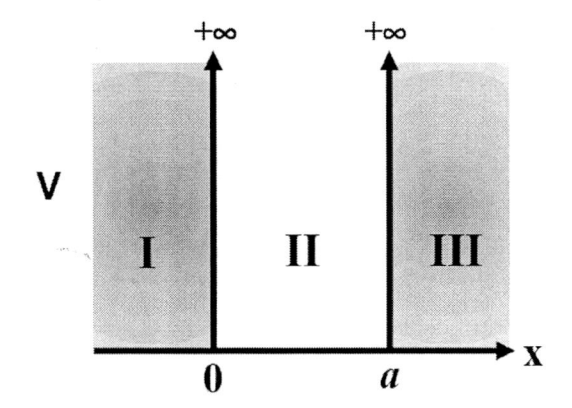

Fig. 9-6 Particle in a square well

Although many restrictions or significant corrections are required, the results derived from this quantum model provides a powerful tool that understands the structure or localization of the electrons. The great benefit is also distributed to the spectroscopic study to quantitatively investigate the energy transition **Particle in a square well.**

Fig. 9-7. Molecular examples for particles in a box model.

Let's imagine a situation where a particle is trapped in a square well (Region II) between two walls (Region I & II) at x=0 and x=a.(**Fig. 9-6**) Let's see how we can describe the energy levels and the wave function of this particle in Region II. How can we solve this? Yes, we can solve this using Schrödinger's equation (**Eqn. 9-3**). If we have an appropriate Hamiltonian (H) for energy (E), the wavefunction (Ψ) and eigen values (E) should be obtained. Besides getting wave function and eigen values, there are always three important issues whenever you start solving the Schrödinger's Equation 1) Hamiltonian and Schrödinger's equation, 2) boundary condition, and 3) normalization condition of the wavefunction as schematically shown in **Fig. 9-8**. (We replace an expression of wavefunction for the particle in a square well as ψ not Ψ.)

1)Hamiltonian and Schrödinger's equation:
The Schrödinger's equation for a particle in a square well is given by

$$-\left(\hbar^2/2m\right) d^2/dx^2 \, \psi = E\psi \qquad \text{(Eqn. 9-5)}$$

Here, $\hbar = h/2\pi$ (h is Planck constant) and V is the potential energy. The wavefunction ψ is time-independent wave function representing the motion takes place in x-axis. Whatever you see in the left hand side except for the wavefunction (ψ) are the operators. It is the kinetic energy operator $(-\hbar^2/2m)[d^2/dx^2]$ and this is the only operator in the case of a particle in a square well, because the potential in a region I is defined as V=0. The "E" on the right hand side is the eigen value, and the eigen value in this case is the kinetic energy since you are using the Hamiltonian of kinetic energy.

2) Boundary condition:
The boundary condition is the situation at the boundary of the wavefunction. For example, in the particle in a box, there is a strict definition of where the wavefunction can exist. The wavefunction should disappear at x=0 and x=a, since the wall has an infinite height at these two points, particle cannot escape over the wall. Thus, wavefunction of the particle does not exist in regions I & III. (You should have zero value in the wave function at x=0 and x=a.) The boundary condition is much more important than you may think, because they will usually define the discrete energy level expression.

3) The Normalization condition:
The wavefunction squared was introduced as the probability density. If you integrate the probability density to an infinite space, a probability of finding an electron is definite (100%). A mathematical expression of this statement is given as an integration of wavefunction square in entire space is a unity.
In the case of particle trapped in a square well with length a, you can take an integration between x=0 and x=a, since a particle cannot exist beyond this region.

$$1 = \int_0^a |\psi^2| dx \qquad \text{(Eqn. 9-6)}$$

After solving the Schrödinger equation, the appropriate wavefunction which satisfies the equation and the normalization condition is

$$\psi = \left[2/a\right]^{1/2} \sin(n\pi x/a) \qquad \text{(Eqn. 9-7)}$$

Here, n =1, 2, 3, .. and this equation is valid for $0 \leq x \leq a$. From the boundary condition you will obtain the energy value as:

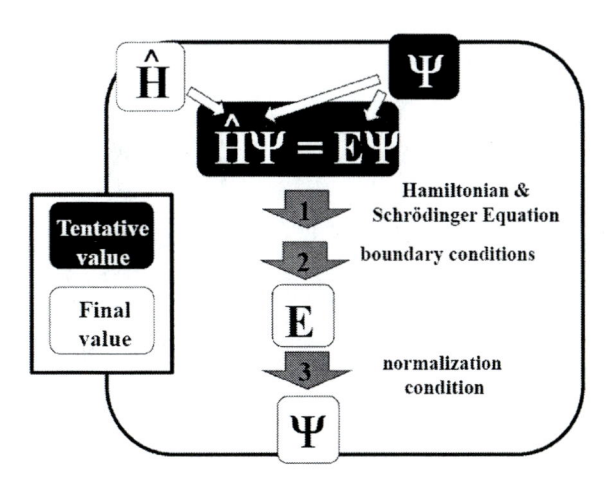

$$E_n = n^2h^2/8ma^2 \qquad \text{(Eqn. 9-8)}$$

Fig. 9-8 Schematics of solving for the Schrödinger's equation.

As you will see from the expression of energy, you are convinced that the energy is quantized as a function of n. Another important message from (**Eqn. 9-9**) is that separation between adjacent levels increases as n increases and that the energy level is inversely proportional to the square of the length, *a,* of the square well. (The energy level decreases quadratically, as the length of the well increases.) Very roughly speaking, you may view that the energy level decreases as the size of a molecule increases. (**Fig. 9-9**)

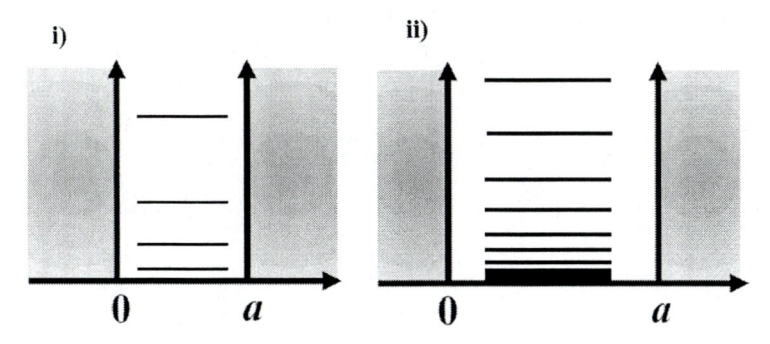

Fig. 9-9 Energy level and width of the well for a particle in a square well, where i) width is narrower and ii) wider.

Chapter 9 A Taste of Quantum Mechanics

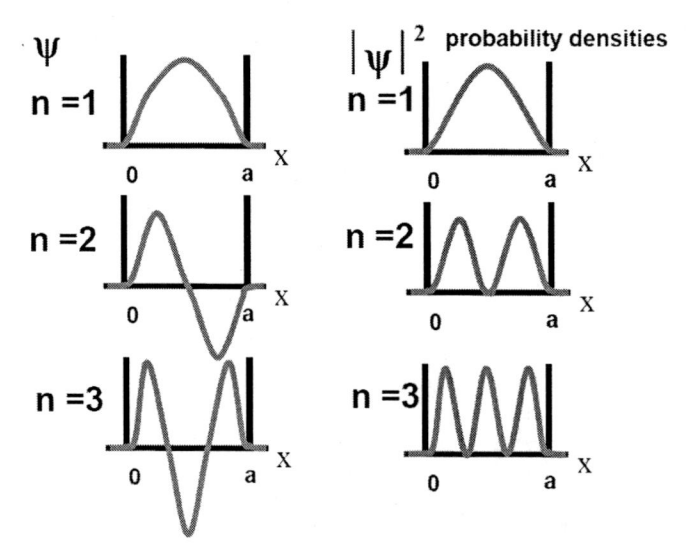

Fig. 9-10 Wavefunction and probability density for a particle in a square well.

As a result of solving the Schrödinger's equation, we have the wavefunction for this particle. In **Fig. 9-10**, the wavefunction for n=1, 2, 3 is plotted on the left, and the probability density of the wavefunction is plotted on the right. The wave function gets more nodes as n increases and the probability density states that the probability of finding the particle is not equal or randomized in a given region. Please note that number of nodes of the wavefunction and the energy level is clearly correlated. For example, the wave function of n=1 has no node. Then, the number of the node increases as one and two n goes n=2, =3. You may think that the number of the peak (band) in the probability density corresponds to n. (The probability density of n=1 has one band, and that of n=2 has two bands, and so on.) You may wonder what happens as n goes close to infinity. Then, you should have almost square shape in the probability density, which is close to the classical mechanics where the probability for finding a particle of a certain energy is equivalent in anywhere within region II.

Let's compare the case in quantum mechanics and the case found in the classical mechanics. (Then, the difference between classical and quantum mechanics will be very clear.)

Table 9-3 Comparison between classical and quantum mechanics

	classically	Quantum mechanically
Minimum energy	0	$h^2/8ma^2$
energy	E≥0	$n^2h^2/8ma^2$ n=1,2,3,......
Probability density	All locations are equally likely	$\|\psi\|^2$

You notice that the classical and quantum mechanics has a distinct difference in the way of taking the energy levels. This corresponds to the probability of finding the particle with a certain energy value.

Chapter 9 A Taste of Quantum Mechanics

😟 **MCM Most Common Mistake (39)-"The quantum number should start from n=0. What! It does not?"**
The lowest energy level of the particle in a square well is n=1, not n=0. The value of n does not take n=0, since wave function becomes zero at n=0.

$$\psi = [2/a]^{1/2} \sin(n\pi x/a) \qquad \text{(Eqn. 9-7)}$$

This means that no wavefunction exists at n=0, thus probability of finding the electron ($|\psi|^2$) becomes zero.

😟 **MCM Most Common Mistake (40) "The expression of the energy for a particle in a square well may upset Mr. Rydberg?"**
You may recall the energy of the electron in H-atom like learned and memorized that the energy level of the Hydrogen-like atom is inversely proportional to n, i.e., $E_n = -R(Z/n)^2$, where n is called as a "principal quantum number", R is the Rydberg constant, and Z is the atomic charge. Since we use the same symbol n for different quantum number, it may cause you confusion. In the case of an H-like atom, electron is trapped in a Coulombic potential ($V = -e^2/r$) created between nucleus and electron. However, there is no potential (V=0) for the case of particle in a square well between x=0 and x=a. To make the long story short, this difference in the potential make the difference in wave function and energy expression.

9-4 A Particle in a Box Model

The idea obtained in a particle in a square well is very useful step to apply it into two or three dimensional cases. For the case of a particle in a box (**Fig. 9-10**), the wave function and the energy level can be given as:

$$\psi(x,y) = \left[4/ab\right]^{1/2} \sin\left(n_x\pi x/a\right) \sin\left(n_y\pi y/b\right) \qquad \text{(Eqn. 9-9)}$$

$$E_{n_x,n_y} = \left(h^2/8m\right)\left[n_x^2/a^2 + n_y^2/b^2\right] \qquad \text{(Eqn. 9-10)}$$

Chapter 9 A Taste of Quantum Mechanics

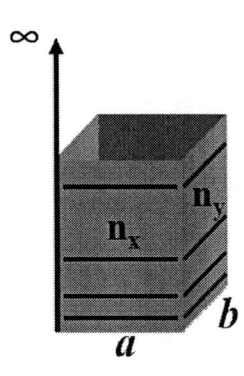

Fig. 9-11 A particle in a box and quantized levels.

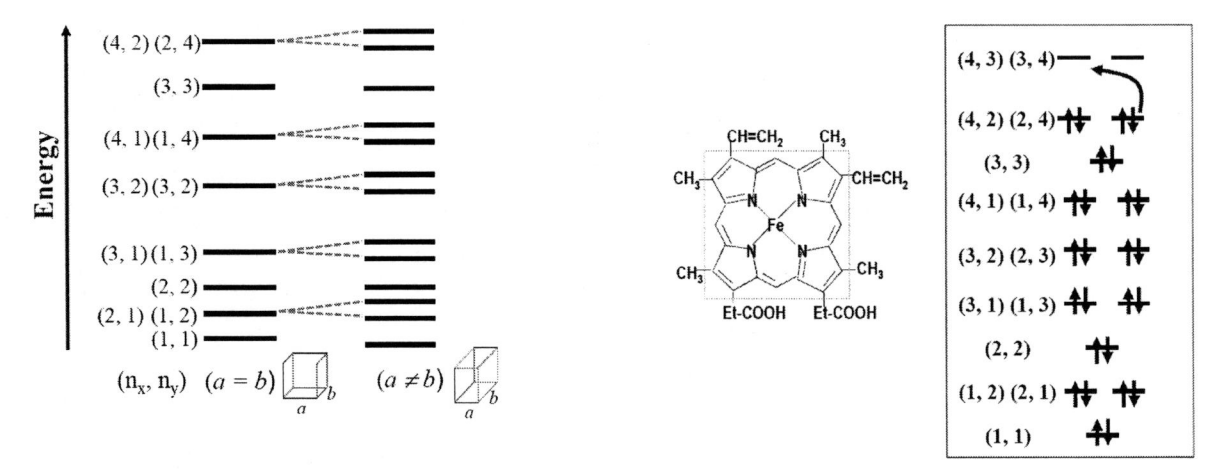

Fig. 9-12 The energy levels in the two dimensional particle in a box

Fig. 9-13 The energy levels in Fe porphyrin, where 26 π electrons are filled.

As you can see the expression for both in wave function and the energy expression is very similar to the case given in one dimensional case. The wave function is the multiplication of the wavefunction of x and y dimensions (with an appropriate normalization factor in front of the wavefunction). However, the energy expression is the constant times the sum of n quantum number in x direction(n_x) and n quantum number in y direction (n_y).(**Fig. 9-11**) The, value a and b are the width of the of the box along x and y axes. If a and b are equal, the energy level for different combination of n_x and n_y are degenerate. (e.g, (n_x, n_y) =(1,3) and (n_x, n_y) =(3,1) will have the same energy level) However, if a and b are different, the energy level for different combination (e.g., $E_{n_x=1, n_y=3}$ ≠ $E_{n_x=3, n_y=1}$) will split into two levels as shown in (**Fig. 9-12**) When a = b, the order of the energy level can be straight forward and depend on the term of n_x and n_y. However, the order of energy levels are not easily predicted when a≠b. A perfect example of a particle in a box is 26 π electrons in Fe-porphyrin are trapped in a box model (**Fig. 9-13**). In this case of iron porphyrin , you can roughly estimate that the a =b. Since each level can take up to two electrons, the electrons are filled up to both (4, 2) and (2,4) levels. (**Fig. 9-13**) Then, let's take a look at a particle in a cube case.(**Fig. 9-14**) The wavefunction for this case is given as:

$$\psi(x,y,z) = \left[8/abc \right]^{1/2} \sin(n_x \pi x / a) \sin\left(n_y \pi y / b \right) \sin(n_z \pi y / c) \quad \textbf{(Eqn. 9-11)}$$

The format is shown in (**Eqn. 9-10**) is a multiplication of wave function obtained in a particle in a square well for x, y, and z-directions. (Please note that the normalization factor is different from other two cases.) Here, a, b, and c indicate the width of the well for each direction. The energy level for this case is given by

$$E_{n_x,n_y,n_z,} = \left(h^2/8m \right)\left[n_x^2/a^2 + n_y^2/b^2 + n_z^2/c^2 \right] \quad \textbf{(Eqn. 9-12)}$$

Fig. 9-14 Particle in a cubical box.

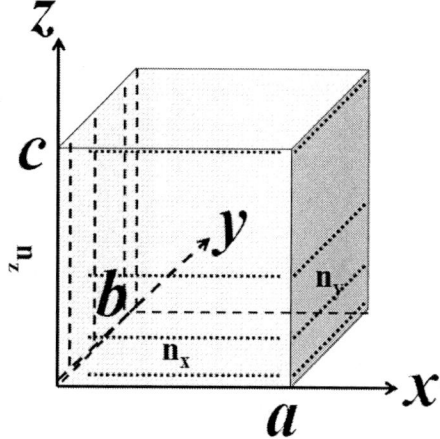

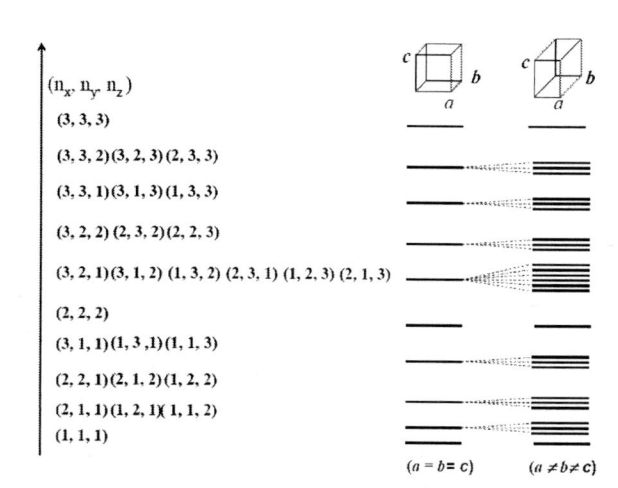

Fig.9-15 The energy level for the case of a particle in a cube.

The energy level diagram provided by the (**Eqn. 9-11**) is demonstrated in (**Fig. 9-15**) for the case of (a=b=c) and (a≠b≠c). The energy level for the case of a =b=c, there are some levels which are degenerate. (For example, the energy levels given by (n_x, n_y, n_z)=(3,2,1), (3,1,2), (1, 3, 2), (2,3,1), (3,1,2), (1,2, 3), (2,1,3) are all degenerate for a =b=c.) The degenerate energy levels split if the length of a, b, and c are different from each other. (The order of the energy level in split energy levels depend on a, b, and c.)

9-5 Transition Energy

You witnessed that energy levels of electrons are discrete. Then, imagine that an electron take one energy level to another as if a ball is dropping from a certain height of one step to the lower step. As different energy is taken up, the amount of transition energy corresponds to the difference, ΔE, of the initial and final steps involved in this transition.(See **Fig. 9-1**) Since we have energy expressions for a particle in a square well or a box as shown in (**Eqns. 9-8, 9-10, and 9-12**), we can calculate the energy difference between two different levels as far as an initial and final energy level is identified. Most clear example of an observation of the transition energy is a detection of sharp line spectra, which corresponds to emission (or absorption) of light as the electron transit from one energy level to another.(**Fig. 9-16**)

After an electron at the ground state is excited by an excitation source (discharged tube or laser light), an excited electron relaxes down to the lower energy state by releasing this energy in a form of light emission. If you detect this light as a function of wavelength, it exhibits a series of spectrum with narrow width in wavelength (or you can say it as a specific color in a visible range), since the energy of the light corresponding to a specific energy difference between two energy levels (transition energy, ΔE).

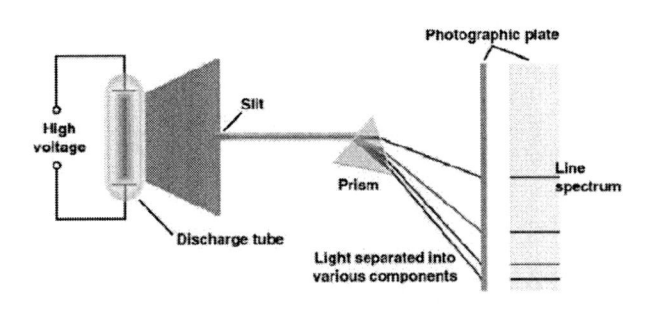

Fig. 9-16 Experimental arrangement used to study emission spectra.

Let's calculate the transition energy for the case of a particle in a square well. If an electron takes a energy level from n to n+1, the transition energy, ΔE, in [J] is

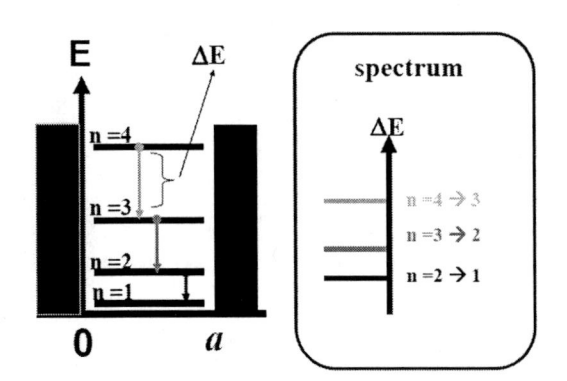

Fig. 9-17 The transition of the electron and the emission spectrum.

$$\Delta E(n \rightarrow n+1) = \left(h^2/8ma^2\right)(2n+1) \qquad \text{(Eqn. 9-13)}$$

It is very convenient if we can get the energy value of the above ΔE in the unit if the wavelength (λ), since the observation of the emission or absorption can be commonly given by the wavelength (A common unit is nm).

$$\lambda(n \rightarrow n+1) = 8mca^2/[h(2n+1)] \qquad \text{(Eqn. 9-14)}$$

Chapter 9 A Taste of Quantum Mechanics

Because the energy level increases as a function of n^2, the energy of spectrum position increases (or wavelength of spectrum decreases) as the energy transition involves the higher n values. (**Fig. 9-17**) (Please note that we used the selection rule of transition as n →n-1.)

EXERCISE 9-3
For a well of length 1 nm (a = 1 nm), the longest wavelength transition is 200 nm. What is the wavelength if the mass of the particle is doubled?

ANSWER

❶ The transition energy in wavelength (λ) expression between n and n+1 can be given by

❷ $$\lambda(n \to n+1) = \frac{8mca^2}{[h(2n+1)]} \quad \text{(Eqn. 9-14)}$$

❸ In this problem, m changes to 2m.

By using (**Eqn. 9-14**), you will see that λ (=200 [nm]) changes to 2λ
Thus, wavelength becomes to 400 [nm]

---

❶ Let's use (**Eqn. 9-14**) in [m] unit instead of (**Eqn. 9-13**) which is in [J] unit.
❷ n is the initial and n+1 is the final state.
❸ You do not have to know an exact value of m in this problem.

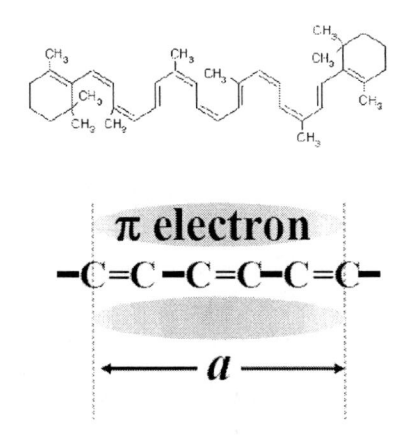

Fig. 9-18 The β-carotene and the conjugated carbon chain.

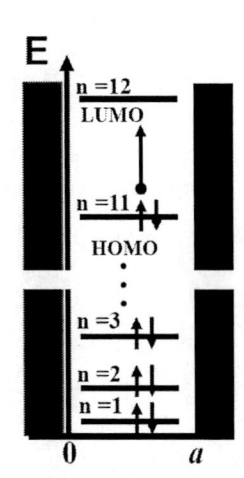

Fig. 9-19 The filling up of the electrons for the case of 22 π electrons.

The Particle in a square well model is a crude but very useful model for dealing with π electrons in molecule with a conjugated carbon chain (such as β-carotin), in where the π electrons can delocalize within the carbon chain creating a condition similar to that of a particle trapped in a square well. (**Fig. 9-18**) By ignoring the fact of the zigzagging of the chain structure, we can estimate the transition energy of this type of molecule by using (**Eqn. 9-13**). Typically, a conjugated chain contains multiple double bonds, thus multiple π electrons. For example, carbon chain contained in β-carotin possess 22π electrons, and these electrons are filled up the levels from n= 1 to 11, since each level can contain up to two electrons with opposite spin by following the **Pauli's exclusion principle**.(**Fig. 9-19**) While a real structure of the β-carotin is not a straight chain (see **Fig 9-18**), a simple the sum of the 10 single (~1.46 Å) and 11 double bonds (~1.35 Å) length involved in the chain of β-carotin, the total chain length becomes about 29 Å.

EXERCISE 9-4

β-Carotene has 11 conjugated double bonds (22 π electrons). By using particle in a square well model, calculate the length of chain. The longest wavelength maximum of β-carotene is about 480 nm.

ANSWER

The transition energy in wavelength expression between n and n+1 is given by (**Eqn. 9-14**)

❶ $$\lambda(n \to n+1) = 8mca^2 / [h(2n+1)] \qquad \text{(Eqn. 9-14)}$$

Since β-carotene contains 22 π electrons, the highest n value is 11.

❷ Here, the transition energy is observed at 480 nm for n = 11 → 12. If the chain length is given by a [m].

❸ $$480 \times 10^{-9}[m] = \frac{8 \times (9.1019 \times 10^{-31}[kg] \times 2.998 \times 10^8[m/s] \times (a[m])^2)}{6.626 \times 10^{-34}[Js] \times (2 \times 11 + 1)}$$

❹ By solving the above for a,

❺ a= 18 [Å]

---

❶ Use the formula of ΔE in [m] wavelength unit.

❷ "The longest wavelength "corresponds to the smallest transition energy considered in this system, and it must be the transition between HOMO (Highest Occupied Molecular Orbital, n=11) and LUMO (Lowest Unoccupied Molecular Orbital n=12) as indicated by arrow in **Fig. 9-19** in order to make an excitation with smallest energy.

❸ M is the mass of electron m_e= 9.109 × 10^{-31} [kg]

❹ Don't forget making root mean square.

❺ 1× 10^{-10} [m]=1 [Å]

☹ **MCM Most Common Mistake (41)** "What!? I can't use a molecular mass?"
Most common mistake seen in the usage of the equation of particle in a box (**Eqns. 11-7, 11-9, 11-11, 11-12, and 11-13**) is the mass which is given as m in these equations. Especially, the case when you use the π electrons of a large molecule, people tend to think that the mass used in the equation is the molecular mass. However, a particle treated in a given example is an electron. Please use the mass of an electron, m_e, which is 9.10938188 × 10^{-31} [kg].

	EXERCISE 9-5 The porphyrin structure measures about 1 [nm] on a side. Estimate the longest – wavelength absorption band of this molecule.
❶ ❷ ❸ ❹ ❺	**ANSWER** The longest wavelength transition is from HOMO to LUMO and it is shown as an arrow from (n_x, n_y) =(4,2) or (2,4) to (4,3) or (3,4) in (**Fig. 9-13**). The energy for a particle in a box is for the energy level of n_x and n_y is given by (**Eqn. 9-10**) $$E_{n_x,n_y} = (h^2/8m)\left[n_x^2/a^2 + n_y^2/b^2\right] \quad \text{(Eqn. 9-10)}$$ The transition energy, $\Delta E(n_x, n_y \to n'_x, n'_y)$, in wavelength from n_x n_y to n_x' and n_y' is given as: $$\lambda(n_x, n_y \to n'_x, n'_y) = 8mcl^2/\{h[(n_x'^2 + n_y'^2) - (n_x^2 + n_y^2)]\} \quad \text{(Eqn. 9-12)'}$$ In the above problem, n_x = 4, n_y =2, n_x'=4, and n_y' =3, respectrively. Since l =1 nm, the wavelength this transition is $\lambda(n_x, n_y \to n'_x, n'_y)$ $= \dfrac{8(9.1019 \times 10^{-31}[kg] \times 2.998 \times 10^8 [m/sec] \times (1 \times 10^{-9}[m])^2)}{6.626 \times 10^{-34}[Js] \times [4^2 + 3^2 - (4^2 + 2^2)]}$ =6.59 ×10^{-7} [m] Thus, the wavelength is 659 [nm].
❶ ❷ ❸ ❹ ❺	This is a two-dimensional problem. In this case, n_x, n_y are initial quantum numbers and n'_x and n'_y are final quantum numbers. m is the mass of electron m_e= 9.109 × 10^{-31} [kg] c is the speed of the light c= 2.998 × 10^8 [m/sec] *a = b= l* 1× 10^{-9} [m]=1 [nm]

9-6 Simple Harmonic Oscillator

We will look into the quantum mechanical treatment of a molecular vibration. The molecular vibration is simply modeled by like a spring possessing a harmonic potential of

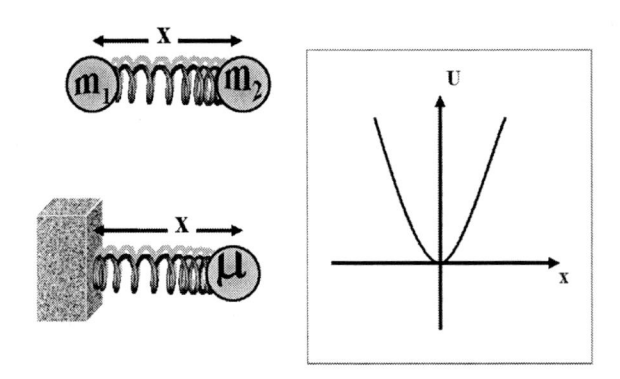

Fig. 9-20 The parabolic potential of the harmonic oscillator.

$$U = \frac{1}{2}kx^2 \qquad \text{(Eqn. 9-15)}$$

Here, k is the force constant and x is the displacement between two oscillating particles. (**Fig.9-20**) This formula shows that the square of the distance from an equilibrium position acts on the particle to pull back to the original position. The distance between two particles can be considered as a bond distance between two atoms. So that a bond is treated like a spring with spring constant k. The best and simplest approach to describe the vibration of diatomic molecules is to reduce the system into an atom with **reduced mass** (μ) oscillating back and forth from the fixed point. When two atoms of a diatomic molecule system have the mass of m_1 and m_2, the reduced mass (μ) is given by

$$\mu = m_1 m_2 / (m_1 + m_2) \qquad \text{(Eqn.9-16)}$$

(You can think of it like a spring attached to a particle with a mass of μ one side, and to the wall on the other side distance x. Since this is a one body problem, it is much simpler to view and solve a problem. The Schrödinger's Equation for the problem of the harmonic oscillator is given with the Hamiltonian with potential U(x) as:

$$\left[-\left(\hbar^2/2\mu\right) d^2/dx^2 + U(x) \right] \psi_v = E_v \psi_v \qquad \text{(Eqn. 9-17)}$$

Here, the wavefunction for the harmonic oscillator is ψ_v, eigen value is E_v, and the potential U(x) is given by (**Eqn. 9-15**). The energy level, E_v, is quantized, and the oscillator also has a discrete energy level in molecular scale as shown in **Fig. 9-21**. The classical harmonic potential (parabolic potential) is given along with the energy level and the wave functions. There are a couple of notes about the potential well for a classical oscillator. The wavefunction of the harmonic oscillator is plotted as a function of the vibrational level v. Also the square of the wavefunction is plotted as a function of the vibrational quantum number. Vibrational level starts from the vibrational quantum number of v=0, and it goes up by integers (1, 2, 3... and so on). The number of nodes observed in the wavefunction corresponds to the vibrational quantum number. For example, the node in the wavefunction of v=0 is zero and the number of node for the v=1 is one. (See **Fig. 9-21**) The energy level increases as a function of v, as is also seen in the case of the particle in a square well (or box). If you take close look at the edge region of wavefunction, you may

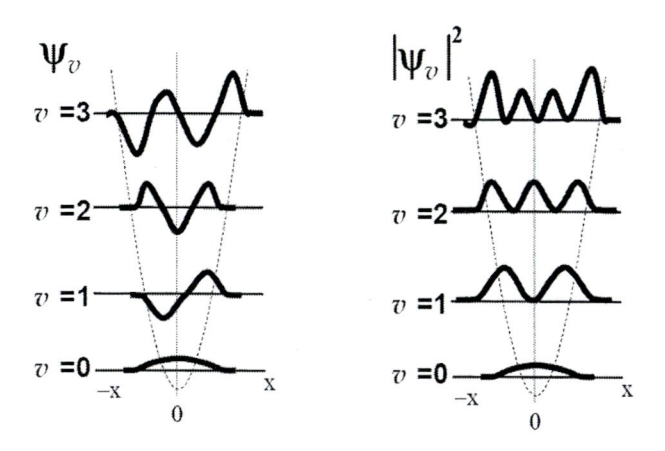

Fig. 9-21 The parabolic potential of the harmonic oscillator.

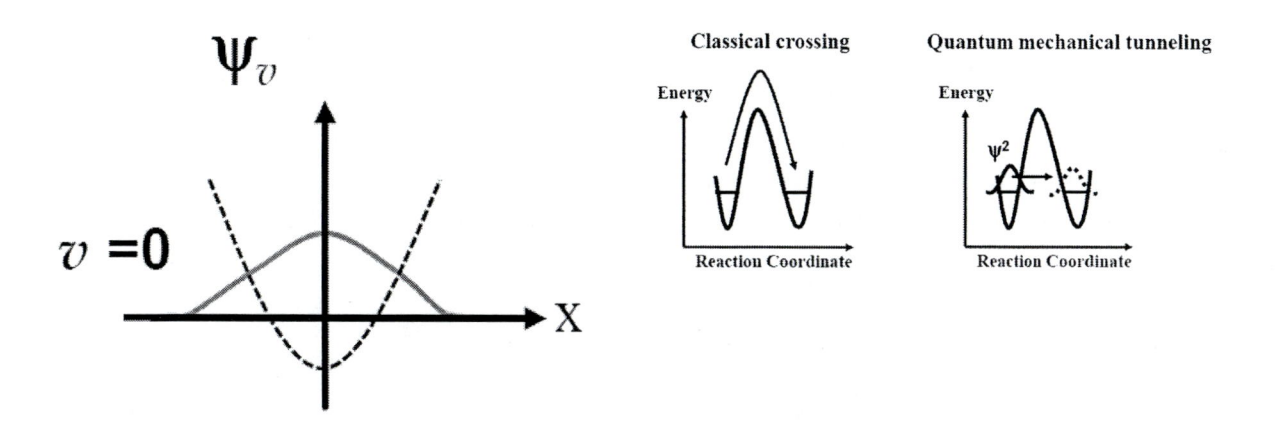

Fig. 9-22 The wave function of harmonic oscillator.

Fig. 9-23 The mechanism of tunneling effect.

see leakage of a portion of the wavefunction out of classical harmonic potential. The wavefunction shown in the **Fig 9-22** is reproduced and magnified for v=0 in **Fig. 9-21**. This leakage is demonstrating a **"tunneling effect"** observed in quantum mechanics, where wavefunction can tunnel through the potential barrier and can exist outside of the potential wall. This effect is more enhanced as the mass of the particle gets smaller (such as electron, H atom or H$^+$ ion) and the potential is height lower. (**Fig. 9-23**) The Energy of harmonic oscillator E_v [J] is given by

$$E_v = h\nu_o \left[v + 1/2\right] \quad \text{(Eqn. 9-18)}$$

Here, ν_o is a fundamental vibrational frequency [Hz] of an oscillator and it is given by

$$\nu_o = \left(1/2\pi\right)\sqrt{k/\mu} \quad \text{(Eqn. 9-19)}$$

Here, k is force constant [N/m] and μ is reduced mass [kg]. With an expression for E_v (**Eqn. 9-18**) in our mind, let's go back to the **Fig.9-21**, and go through important factors seen in the energy level. The first thing you may want to note is that spacing (energy amount) between adjacent levels is almost equal. As mentioned in the above, the vibrational quantum number starts from v= 0, which does not mean that the E_v is zero. The harmonic oscillator possesses an energy value at v=0 (**zero-point energy**), which is

$$E_{v=0} = h\nu_o/2 \quad \text{(Eqn. 9-20)}$$

Here, ν_o is a fundamental vibrational frequency [Hz] of an oscillator and h is the Planck constant [J/s]. Even, the above energy level is noted as "zero-point), the energy level is not at the bottom of the potential (**Fig. 9-21**). The transition energy (ΔE) between the adjacent levels of the harmonic oscillator is given by,

$$\Delta E = h\nu_o \quad \text{(Eqn. 9-21)}$$

However, the above expression in (**Eqn.9-21**) is valid when the vibrational levels are low enough where the potential given in (**Eqn. 9-15**) well represents the potential for a harmonic oscillator.

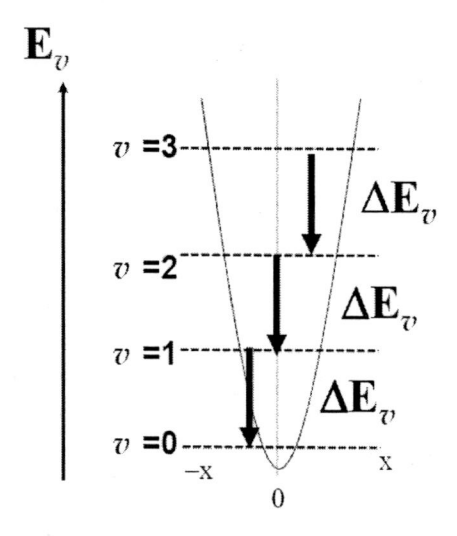

Fig. 9-24 The transition in harmonic oscillator.

Chapter 9 A Taste of Quantum Mechanics

While it will not be mentioned in detail, please note there is a selection rule for the transition in any energy transition in quantum mechanics. For the harmonic oscillator, the vibrational level between adjacent levels is allowed (v → v+1 or v → v −1).

EXERCISE 9-6

The fundamental vibration frequency of gaseous $^{14}N^{16}O$ is 1904 [cm^{-1}]. When $^{14}N^{16}O$ is bound to hemoglobin A, an absorption band at 1615 [cm^{-1}] was observed. Calculate the change in the force constant of $^{14}N^{16}O$ vibrator. Assume that the binding of $^{14}N^{16}O$ does not change the reduced mass.

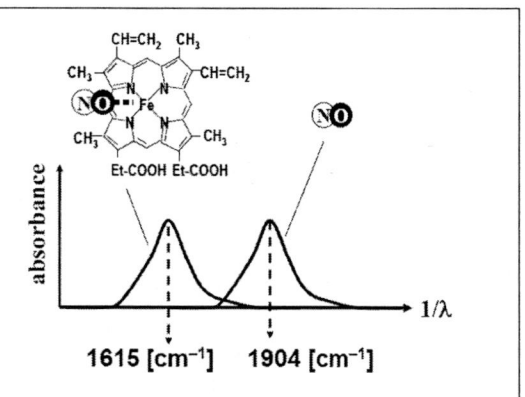

Fig. 9-25 The vibrational frequency of NO and NO attached to iron porphyrin (representing hemoglobin).

ANSWER

First, let's define force constants as
$k_1 = k(^{14}N^{16}O)$..
$k_2 = k(^{14}N^{16}O$ bound to *hemo*)
Let's calculate k_2/k_1
Here, k is force constant [N/m] and fundamental vibrational frequency ν_o (Hz) is given by

❶

$$\nu_o = (1/2\pi)\sqrt{k/\mu} \qquad \text{(Eqn. 9-19)}$$

The relationship between 1/λ and ν is

❷

$$\nu = \frac{c}{\lambda} \propto \frac{1}{\lambda}$$

$$\frac{\nu_o(^{14}N^{16}O-bound\ to\ hemo)}{\nu_o(^{14}N^{16}O)}$$

$$= \frac{\frac{1}{\lambda(^{14}N^{16}O - bound\ to\ hemo)}}{\frac{1}{\lambda(^{14}N^{16}O)}}$$

$$= \frac{1615\ [cm^{-1}]}{1904\ [cm^{-1}]}$$

❸

$$= \frac{\frac{1}{2\pi}\left[\frac{k_2}{\mu}\right]^{\frac{1}{2}}}{\frac{1}{2\pi}\left[\frac{k_1}{\mu}\right]^{\frac{1}{2}}}$$

Chapter 9 A Taste of Quantum Mechanics

❸	$= \left[\dfrac{k_2}{k_1}\right]^{\frac{1}{2}}$ =0.8482
❹	$k_2/k_1 = (0.8482)^2$
❺	=0.71947
❻	

❶ Here, μ implies the reduced mass of NO. However, you do not have to calculate this in this problem as you see later. You may be wondering if the reduced mass will change as NO bond to a porphyrin. However, here the effect of binding of NO to the porphyrin is all accounted in the force constant change (but not reduced mass change).

❷ The most vibrational spectra display the absorbance as a function **wavenumbers** (1/ λ), which has typically uses the unit of [1/cm]. (e.g., 1904 [cm^{-1}] means that there are 1904 waves within 1 [cm].)

❸ Don't forget the root mean square on force constant.

❹ Don't forget to square the result.

❺ This is the ratio and dimensionless.

❻ It shows that the force constant weakened as NO bound to porphyrin. This also makes sense because the wavenumbers decreased as NO is bound to porphyrin.

Will you read this?

Please allow me to make a special remark on the topic of this EXERCISE. The NO (nitric oxide) is an important substance involved as neurotransmitter, cellular toxin, and regulating blood pressure. As the iron porphyrin is used to represent the *hemo*-group of the blood, the attachment of NO to iron porphyrin can be understood as one of the simplest models of the NO conjugation that takes place in the blood. The problem we saw above is that the vibrational frequency of the NO changes as the attachment takes place. (**Fig. 9-25**) In this problem, ^{14}N^{16}O is 1904 [cm^{-1}] and ^{14}N^{16}O bound to hemoglobin 1615 [cm^{-1}]. Thus, by binding the NO with a large molecule, the frequency is reduced. This can be seen because of the reduced mass increase. The fundamental frequency is inversely proportional to the square root of the reduced mass.

Chapter 9

How did you get these equations?
-The derivation of selected equations.

(Eqn. 9-7) $\quad \psi = [2/a]^{1/2} \sin(n\pi x/a)$

(Eqn. 9-8) $\quad E = n^2h^2/8ma^2$

The condition of potential (V) is V=0 for a ≥ x ≥0 and V=∞ for x<0 and for a<x. By setting the time independent wavefunction, ψ, the

$$c - \left\{(\hbar^2/2m) d^2/dx^2 + V\right\}\psi = E\psi \qquad \text{(Eqn. 9-5)}$$

At region I and III (for x<0 and for x>a), V=∞. In these regions, ψ=0, since particle cannot have infinite energy. At region II, the potential energy is set as zero. (V=0) Therefore, the Schrödinger equation (with V=0)

$$-(\hbar^2/2m) d^2/dx^2 \psi = E\psi \qquad \text{(Eqn. 9-5)}$$

As a general answer of ψ to satisfy (Eqn. 11-4), the wavefunction is given as

$$\psi = A \sin rx + B \cos sx \qquad \text{(Eqn. 9-22)}$$

Here, A, B, r, and s are constants. By inserting the above wavefunction into **(Eqn. 9-5)**,

$$-Ar^2 \sin rx - Bs^2 \cos sx = -2mE\hbar^{-2}A \sin rx - 2mE\hbar^{-2}B \cos sx$$

With respect to the term of sin rx,

$$-Ar^2 = -2mE\hbar^{-2}A$$

$$r^2 = 2mE\hbar^{-2}$$
$$r = \sqrt{2mE\hbar^{-2}}$$

With respect to the term of cos sx,

$$-Bs^2 = -2mE\hbar^{-2}B$$

$$s^2 = 2mE\hbar^{-2}$$

Chapter 9 A Taste of Quantum Mechanics

Therefore,
$$s = \sqrt{2mE\hbar^{-2}}$$

$$r = s = \sqrt{2mE\hbar^{-2}}$$

For 0≤x≤a,
$$\psi = A\sin\left(\sqrt{2mE\hbar^{-2}}x\right) + B\cos\left(\sqrt{2mE\hbar^{-2}}x\right)$$

There is a boundary condition stating that ψ=0 at x=0. Thus,

$$A\sin 0 + B\cos 0 = 0$$

Since sin 0 =0 and cos 0 = 1,
$$B = 0$$
Therefore, the wavefunction becomes as

$$\psi = A\sin\left(\sqrt{2mE\hbar^{-2}}x\right) \qquad \text{(Eqn. 9-23)}$$

There is another boundary condition stating that ψ=0 at x=a. Thus,
$$A\sin\left(\sqrt{2mE\hbar^{-2}}a\right) = 0$$

Sine sin function vanishes at 0, ±π, ±2π, ±3π,...., ±nπ, (n=1,2,3,...) In order to make sin function to be zero,
$$\sqrt{2mE\hbar^{-2}}a = \pm n\pi$$
Solving the above for E,
$$2mE\hbar^{-2} = (n\pi/a)^2$$
$$E = {(n\pi/a)^2}/{2m\hbar^{-2}}$$

Since ℏ is h/2π

$$E = {n^2h^2}/{8ma^2} \qquad \text{(Eqn. 9-8)}$$

Here, n is an integer starting from 1 as n=1, 2, 3,...(Please note that the there is no wave function exist when n=0) . By replacing the value for E given in (Eqn. 9-8) to (Eqn. 9-23)

$$\psi = A\sin\left(\sqrt{{2mn^2h^2}/{(8\hbar^2ma^2)}}\,x\right)$$

Since ℏ = h/2π,

$$\psi = A\sin\left(\sqrt{{2mn^2h^2}/{(8\hbar^2ma^2)}}\,x\right)$$

Chapter 9 A Taste of Quantum Mechanics

$$\psi = A\sin\left(\sqrt{8h^2\pi^2 mn^2 / (8h^2 ma^2)}\, x\right)$$

$$\psi = A\sin\left(\sqrt{\pi^2 n^2 / a^2}\, x\right)$$

$\psi = A\sin(n\pi x/a)$ (Eqn. 9-24)

From the normalization condition,

$\int_0^a |\psi^2|\, dx = 1$ (Eqn. 9-6)

$\int_0^a |A|^2 \sin^2(n\pi x/a)\, dx = 1$ (Eqn. 9-25)

From the integration table,

$$\int \sin^2 \alpha x\, dx = (x/2) - (1/4\alpha)\sin \alpha x + c$$

Here, c is a constant. Thus, (**Eqn. 9-25**) becomes,

$|A|^2 \int_0^a \sin^2(n\pi x/a)\, dx = 1$

$$\left. |A|^2(x/2) - \left(\frac{1}{4\left(\frac{n\pi}{a}\right)}\right)\sin\left(\frac{n\pi}{a}\right)x \right|_0^a = 1$$

$$|A|^2(a/2) - \left(\frac{1}{4\left(\frac{n\pi}{a}\right)}\right)\sin\left(\frac{n\pi}{a}\right)a$$

$$-\left\{|A|^2(0/2) - \left(\frac{1}{4\left(\frac{n\pi}{a}\right)}\right)\sin\left(\frac{n\pi}{a}\right)\cdot 0\right\} = 1$$

$$|A|^2(a/2) = 1$$

Here, we used $\sin(n\pi) = 0$.

$$A = \pm\sqrt{2/a}$$

Choosing the positive side of the value.

$$A = \sqrt{2/a}$$

Therefore, final form of the wavefunction is

Chapter 9 A Taste of Quantum Mechanics

$$\psi = \sqrt{2/a}\sin(n\pi x/a)$$

Please note that $a \geq x \geq 0$ and $n=1,2,3,...$

$$\psi = [2/a]^{1/2}\sin(n\pi x/a) \qquad \text{(Eqn. 9-7)}$$

(Eqn. 9-13) $\quad \Delta E(n \to n+1) = \left(h^2/8ma^2\right)(2n+1)$

The energy level for n is given by
$$E_n = n^2h^2/8ma^2 \qquad \text{(Eqn. 9-8)}$$

$$\Delta E(n \to n+1) = E_{n+1} - E_n$$
$$= \frac{h^2}{8ma^2}(n+1)^2 - \frac{h^2}{8ma^2}n^2$$
$$= \frac{h^2}{8ma^2}(n^2 + 2n + 1) - \frac{h^2}{8ma^2}n^2$$
$$= \frac{h^2}{8ma^2}(2n+1)$$

Thus,
$$\Delta E(n \to n+1) = \left(h^2/8ma^2\right)(2n+1) \qquad \text{(Eqn. 9-13)}$$

(Eqn. 9-14) $\quad \lambda = 8mca^2/[h(2n+1)]$

The transition energy, ΔE for n to n+1 level is given by

$$\Delta E(n \to n+1) = \left(h^2/8ma^2\right)(2n+1) \qquad \text{(Eqn. 9-13)}$$

Since the transition energy corresponds to the frequency or wavelength of the light emitted (or absorbed), ΔE is replaced by
$$\Delta E = h\nu = \frac{hc}{\lambda}$$

Thus,
$$\frac{hc}{\lambda} = \left(h^2/8ma^2\right)(2n+1)$$

Therefore, solving for wavelength,
$$\lambda(n \to n+1) = 8mca^2/[h(2n+1)] \qquad \text{(Eqn. 9-14)}$$

(Eqn. 9-9) $$\psi(x,y) = \left[4/ab\right]^{1/2} \sin(n_x\pi x/a)\sin(n_y\pi y/b)$$

The Schrödinger's equation for particle in a box model is

$$-(\hbar^2/2m)\{d^2/dx^2 + d^2/dy^2\}\psi = E\psi \qquad \text{(Eqn. 9-5)}$$

We assume that the new wavefunction is given by a form of multiplication of wavefunction of x- and y-dimensions as

$$\psi = \psi_x \psi_y$$

Here, we utilize the result from a particle in a square well case.

$$\psi_x = A\sin(n\pi x/a)$$

$$\psi_y = B\sin(n\pi y/b)$$

$$\int_0^b \int_0^a |\psi^2| dx dy = 1 \qquad \text{(Eqn. 9-6)}$$

$$\int_0^b \int_0^a |\psi_x^2 \psi_y^2| dx dy = 1$$

$$\int_0^a \psi_x^2 dx \int_0^b \psi_y^2 dy = 1$$

$$\int_0^a A^2 \sin^2(n\pi x/a) dx \int_0^b B^2 \sin^2(n\pi y/b) dy = 1$$

From the integration table,

$$\int \sin^2 \alpha x \, dx = (x/2) - (1/4\alpha)\sin \alpha x + c$$

$$\int_0^a A^2 \sin^2(n\pi x/a) dx$$

$$= |A|^2(a/2) - \left(\frac{1}{4\left(\frac{n\pi}{a}\right)}\right)\sin\left(\frac{n\pi}{a}\right)a$$

$$- \left\{|A|^2(0/2) - \left(\frac{1}{4\left(\frac{n\pi}{a}\right)}\right)\sin\left(\frac{n\pi}{a}\right)\cdot 0\right\}$$

$$= |A|^2(a/2)$$

Thus,

$$\int_0^a A^2 \sin^2(n\pi x/a)\, dx = |A|^2 (a/2)$$

In a similar way, you will get

$$\int_0^b B^2 \sin^2(n\pi y/b)\, dy = |B|^2 (b/2)$$

$$\int_0^a \psi_x^2 dx \int_0^b \psi_y^2 dy = |A|^2(a/2)|B|^2(b/2) = 1$$

$$|A|^2|B|^2 = |AB|^2 = (4/ab)$$

$$AB = \pm 2/\sqrt{ab}$$

By taking a positive side,

$$AB = 2/\sqrt{ab}$$

Since eigen function is expressed as

$$\psi = \psi_x \psi_y = AB \sin(n\pi x/a) \sin(n\pi y/b)$$

The normalization factor is regarded as AB. The final wavefunction is given as

$$\psi = \sqrt{4/ab} \sin(n\pi x/a) \sin(n\pi y/b) \quad \text{(Eqn. 9-9)}$$

(Eqn. 9-10)
$$E_{n_x,n_y} = (h^2/8m)\left[\frac{n_x^2}{a^2} + \frac{n_y^2}{b^2}\right]$$

The Schrödinger's equation for particle in a box model is

$$-(\hbar^2/2m)\{d^2/dx^2 + d^2/dy^2\}\psi = E\psi \quad \text{(Eqn. 9-5)}$$

Inserting the wavefunction given by (Eqn. 9-9)

$$\psi = \sqrt{4/ab} \sin(n_x \pi x/a) \sin(n_y \pi y/b) \quad \text{(Eqn. 9-9)}$$

$$d^2/dx^2 \psi = d/dx\left(\frac{d}{dx}\sqrt{4/ab}\sin(n_x\pi x/a)\sin(n_y\pi y/b)\right)$$

$$= \sqrt{4/ab}\left(\frac{n_x\pi}{a}\right) d/dx \left(\cos(n_x\pi x/a)\sin(n_y\pi y/b)\right)$$

$$= -\sqrt{4/ab}\left(\frac{n_x\pi}{a}\right)^2 \left(\sin(n_x\pi x/a)\sin(n_y\pi y/b)\right) = -\left(\frac{n_x\pi}{a}\right)^2 \psi$$

$$d^2/dy^2 \psi = d/dy\left(\sqrt{4/ab}\sin(n_x\pi x/a)\frac{d}{dy}\sin(n_y\pi y/b)\right)$$

$$= \sqrt{4/ab}\left(\frac{n_y\pi}{b}\right)d/dy\left(\sin(n_x\pi x/a)\cos(n_y\pi y/b)\right)$$

$$= -\sqrt{4/ab}\left(\frac{n_y\pi}{b}\right)^2\left(\sin(n_x\pi x/a)\sin(n_y\pi y/b)\right) = -\left(\frac{n_y\pi}{b}\right)^2\psi$$

Therefore, the (**Eqn. 9-15**) becomes as

$$(\hbar^2/2m)\left\{\left(\frac{n_x\pi}{a}\right)^2 + \left(\frac{n_y\pi}{b}\right)^2\right\}\psi = E\psi$$

Comparing the left and right terms, eigen value E is given as

$$E = (\hbar^2/2m)\left\{\left(\frac{n_x\pi}{a}\right)^2 + \left(\frac{n_y\pi}{b}\right)^2\right\}$$

$$= (h^2/\{2m(2\pi)^2\})\left\{\left(\frac{n_x\pi}{a}\right)^2 + \left(\frac{n_y\pi}{b}\right)^2\right\}$$

Thus,

$$E_{n_x,n_y} = (h^2/8m)\left[n_x^2/a^2 + n_y^2/b^2\right] \qquad \text{(Eqn. 9-10)}$$

(Eqn. 9-11) $\quad \psi(x,y) = [8/abc]^{1/2}\sin(n_x\pi x/a)\sin(n_y\pi y/b)\sin(n_z\pi y/c)$

We take the same approach as shown in the above for a particle in a cube model. The Schrödinger's equation for particle in a cube is

$$-(\hbar^2/2m)\{d^2/dx^2 + d^2/dy^2 + d^2/dz^2\}\psi = E\psi$$

We assume that the new wavefunction is given by a form of multiplication of wavefunction of x- and y-dimensions as

$$\psi = \psi_x\psi_y\psi_z$$

Here, we utilize the result from a particle in a square well case.

$$\psi_x = A\sin(n_x\pi x/a)$$

Chapter 9 A Taste of Quantum Mechanics

$$\psi_y = B\sin(n_y\pi y/b)$$

$$\psi_z = C\sin(n_z\pi z/c)$$

From normalization condition,

$$\int_0^c \int_0^b \int_0^a |\psi^2| dx\, dy\, dz = 1$$

$$\int_0^c \int_0^b \int_0^a |\psi_x^2 \psi_y^2 \psi_z^2| dx\, dy\, dz = 1$$

$$\int_0^a \psi_x^2 dx \int_0^b \psi_y^2 dy \int_0^c \psi_z^2 dz = 1$$

$$\int_0^a A^2 \sin^2(n_x\pi x/a)\, dx \int_0^b B^2 \sin^2(n_y\pi y/b)\, dy \int_0^a C^2 \sin^2(n_z\pi z/c)\, dz = 1$$

From the integration table,

$$\int \sin^2 \alpha x\, dx = (x/2) - (1/4\alpha)\sin \alpha x + c$$

$$\int_0^a A^2 \sin^2(n_x\pi x/a)\, dx$$

$$= |A|^2(a/2) - \left(\frac{1}{4\left(\frac{n_x\pi}{a}\right)}\right)\sin\left(\frac{n_x\pi}{a}\right)a$$

$$- \left\{|A|^2(0/2) - \left(\frac{1}{4\left(\frac{n_x\pi}{a}\right)}\right)\sin\left(\frac{n_x\pi}{a}\right)\cdot 0\right\}$$

$$= |A|^2(a/2)$$

Thus,

$$\int_0^a A^2 \sin^2(n_x\pi x/a)\, dx = |A|^2(a/2)$$

In a similar way, you will get

$$\int_0^b B^2 \sin^2(n_y\pi y/b)\, dy = |B|^2(b/2)$$

$$\int_0^c C^2 \sin^2(n_z\pi y/c)\, dz = |C|^2(c/2)$$

$$\int_0^a \psi_x^2 dx \int_0^b \psi_y^2 dy \int_0^c \psi_z^2 dz = |A|^2(a/2)|B|^2(b/2)|C|^2(c/2) = 1$$

Chapter 9 A Taste of Quantum Mechanics

$$|A|^2|B|^2|C|^2 = |ABC|^2 = \left(8/abc\right)$$

$$ABC = \pm\sqrt{8/abc}$$

By taking a positive side,

$$ABC = \sqrt{8/abc}$$

Since eigen function is expressed as

$$\psi = \psi_x\psi_y\psi_z = ABC \sin(n_x\pi x/a) \sin(n_y\pi y/b) \sin(n_z\pi z/c)$$

The normalization factor is regarded as ABC. The final wavefunction is given as

$$\psi = \sqrt{8/abc} \sin(n\pi x/a) \sin(n\pi y/b) \sin(n_z\pi z/c) \quad \text{(Eqn. 9-11)}$$

(Eqn. 9-12)
$$E_{n_x,n_y,n_z} = \left(h^2/8m\right)\left[n_x^2/a^2 + n_y^2/b^2 + n_z^2/c^2\right]$$

$$\psi = \sqrt{8/abc} \sin(n_x\pi x/a) \sin(n_y\pi y/b) \sin(n_z\pi z/c) \quad \text{(Eqn. 9-11)}$$

The Schrödinger's equation for particle in a cube is

$$-\left(\hbar^2/2m\right)\left\{d^2/dx^2 + d^2/dy^2 + d^2/dz^2\right\}\psi = E\psi$$

Inserting the wavefunction given by (Eqn. 9-11)

$$d^2/dx^2 \psi$$
$$= d/dx\left(\frac{d}{dx}\sqrt{8/abc}\sin(n_x\pi x/a)\sin(n_y\pi y/b)\sin(n_z\pi z/c)\right)$$

$$= \sqrt{8/abc}\left(\frac{n_x\pi}{a}\right) d/dx\left(\cos(n_x\pi x/a)\sin(n_y\pi y/b)\sin(n_z\pi z/c)\right)$$

$$= -\sqrt{8/abc}\left(\frac{n_x\pi}{a}\right)^2 \left(\sin(n_x\pi x/a)\sin(n_y\pi y/b)\sin(n_z\pi z/c)\right)$$

$$= -\left(\frac{n_x\pi}{a}\right)^2 \psi$$

$$d^2/dy^2 \psi$$
$$= d/dy\left(\sqrt{8/abc}\sin(n_x\pi x/a)\frac{d}{dy}\sin(n_y\pi y/b)\sin(n_z\pi z/c)\right)$$

Chapter 9 A Taste of Quantum Mechanics

$$= \sqrt{8/abc} \left(\frac{n_y\pi}{b}\right) d/dy \left(\sin(n_x\pi x/a) \cos(n_y\pi y/b) \sin(n_z\pi z/c)\right)$$

$$= -\sqrt{8/abc} \left(\frac{n_y\pi}{b}\right)^2 \left(\sin(n_x\pi x/a) \sin(n_y\pi y/b) \sin(n_z\pi z/c)\right)$$

$$= -\left(\frac{n_y\pi}{b}\right)^2 \psi$$

$$d^2/dz^2 \psi$$

$$= d/dz \left(\sqrt{8/abc} \sin(n_x\pi x/a) \sin(n_y\pi y/b) \frac{d}{dz} \sin(n_z\pi z/c)\right)$$

$$= \sqrt{8/abc} \left(\frac{n_y\pi}{b}\right) d/dy \left(\sin(n_x\pi x/a) \sin(n_y\pi y/b) \cos(n_z\pi z/c)\right)$$

$$= -\sqrt{8/abc} \left(\frac{n_y\pi}{b}\right)^2 \left(\sin(n_x\pi x/a) \sin(n_y\pi y/b) \sin(n_z\pi z/c)\right)$$

$$= -\left(\frac{n_z\pi}{c}\right)^2 \psi$$

Therefore, the (**Eqn. 9-15**) becomes as

$$(\hbar^2/2m)\left\{\left(\frac{n_x\pi}{a}\right)^2 + \left(\frac{n_y\pi}{b}\right)^2 + \left(\frac{n_z\pi}{c}\right)^2\right\}\psi = E\psi$$

Comparing the left and right terms, eigen value E is given as

$$E = (\hbar^2/2m)\left\{\left(\frac{n_x\pi}{a}\right)^2 + \left(\frac{n_y\pi}{b}\right)^2 + \left(\frac{n_z\pi}{c}\right)^2\right\}$$

$$= (h^2/\{2m(2\pi)^2\})\left\{\left(\frac{n_x\pi}{a}\right)^2 + \left(\frac{n_y\pi}{b}\right)^2 + \left(\frac{n_z\pi}{c}\right)^2\right\}$$

Thus,

$$E_{n_x,n_y,n_z} = (h^2/8m)\left[n_x^2/a^2 + n_y^2/b^2 + n_z^2/c^2\right] \qquad \text{(Eqn. 9-12)}$$

(Eqn. 9-12)' $$\lambda(n_x, n_y \to n'_x, n'_y) = 8mcl^2 \Big/ \{h[(n'^2_x + n'^2_y) - (n^2_x + n^2_y)]\}$$

The energy level of particle in a box at n_x and n_y is given by

$$E_{n_x,n_y} = (h^2/8m)\left[n^2_x/a^2 + n^2_y/b^2\right] \qquad \text{(Eqn. 9-10)}$$

For the case of $a = b = l$,

$$E_{n_x,n_y} = (h^2/8ml^2)(n^2_x + n^2_y) \qquad \text{(Eqn. 9-10)}$$

The transition energy between $(n_x, n_y) \to (n'_x, n'_y)$ is

$$\Delta E(n_x, n_y \to n'_x, n'_y) = (h^2/8ml^2)\{(n'^2_x + n'^2_y) - (n^2_x + n^2_y)\}$$

Since the transition energy corresponds to the frequency or wavelength of the light emitted (or absorbed), ΔE is replaced by

$$\Delta E(n_x, n_y \to n'_x, n'_y) = h\nu = \frac{hc}{\lambda}$$

Thus,

$$\frac{hc}{\lambda} = (h^2/8ml^2)\{(n'^2_x + n'^2_y) - (n^2_x + n^2_y)\}$$

Therefore, solving for wavelength,

$$\lambda = hc \Big/ \{(h^2/8ml^2)\{(n'^2_x + n'^2_y) - (n^2_x + n^2_y)\}\}$$

Thus.

$$\lambda(n_x, n_y \to n'_x, n'_y) = 8mcl^2 \Big/ \{h[(n'^2_x + n'^2_y) - (n^2_x + n^2_y)]\} \qquad \text{(Eqn. 9-15)}$$

Chapter 9 Summary [Part 1]

(Use back page to cover the contents.)

1	Planck's Quantum Theory	An electron possesses discrete and quantized energy levels.
2	Energy and frequency of the light	$E = h\nu$ **(Eqn. 9-1)**
3	*de* Broglie wavelength (dual nature of electron)	$h = p\lambda$ **(Eqn. 9-2)** λ: *de* Broglie wavelength, p: momentum p (p = mv, m: mass of a particle [kg], v=velocity [m·sec^{-1}])
4	Schrödinger's Equation	$\hat{H}\Psi = E\Psi$ **(Eqn. 9-3)** Ψ: wave function, E: eigen value, $\hat{H}$: Hamiltonian operator
5	probability of finding the ns electron of H atom	a probability of finding the ns electron of H atom between from x_1 to x_2 along the radius of sphere in entire space is $\int_{x_1}^{x_2} \psi_{ns}^* \psi_{ns} d\tau = \int_{x_1}^{x_2} [\psi_{ns}]^2 d\tau$ **(Eqn. 9-4)** $d\tau = 4\pi r^2 dr$ ψ_{ns}: wavefunction of an s-electron

[Fold the page at the double line and cover the right half.]

Chapter 9 Summary Check [Part 1]

(Use this page to cover and check the contents.)
Use ☐ as your check box. Write your comment at far right

1	Planck's Quantum Theory	☐ ☐ ☐ ☐ ☐	
2	Energy and frequency of the light	☐ ☐ ☐ ☐ ☐	
3	*de* Broglie wavelength (dual nature of electron)	☐ ☐ ☐ ☐ ☐	
4	Schrödinger's Equation	☐ ☐ ☐ ☐ ☐	
5	probability of finding the ns electron of H atom	☐ ☐ ☐ ☐ ☐	

Chapter 9 Summary [Part 2]

(Use back page to cover the contents.)

6	wave functions(ψ) and the eigen values (E) of particle in a box model	**Particle in a square well** $\psi = [2/a]^{1/2} \sin(n\pi x/a)$ (Eqn. 9-7) $E_n = n^2 h^2/8ma^2$ (n=1,2,3,....) (Eqn. 9-8) **Particle in a box** $\psi(x,y) = [4/ab]^{1/2} \sin(n_x \pi x/a) \sin(n_y \pi y/b)$ (Eqn. 9-9) $E_{n_x,n_y} = (h^2/8m)\left[n_x^2/a^2 + n_y^2/b^2\right]$ (Eqn. 9-10) (n_x, n_y =1,2,3,....) **Particle in a cube** $\psi(x,y,z) = [8/abc]^{1/2} \sin\left(\frac{n_x \pi x}{a}\right) \sin\left(\frac{n_y \pi y}{b}\right) \sin\left(\frac{n_z \pi z}{c}\right)$ (Eqn. 9-11) $E_{n_x,n_y,n_z} = (h^2/8m)\left[n_x^2/a^2 + n_y^2/b^2 + n_z^2/c^2\right]$ (Eqn. 9-12) (n_x, n_y, n_z =1,2,3,....)
7	The sketch of wave function and probability density (Particle in a square well)	Sketches of ψ for n=1, n=2, n=3 and $|\psi|^2$ probability densities for n=1, n=2, n=3 over the interval 0 to a.
8	Comparison of energy levels between classical mechanics and particle in a square well.	(see table below)

	classically	Quantum mechanically
$E_{min.}$	0	$h^2/8ma^2$
E	E ≥	$n^2 h^2/8ma^2$ (n=1,2,3,....).
$|\psi|^2$	All locations are equally likely	$|\psi|^2$

E_{min}: minimum energy
$|\psi|^2$: probability density

[Fold the page at the double line and cover the right half.]

Chapter 9 Summary Check [Part 2]

(Use this page to cover and check the contents.)
Use ☐ as your check box. Write your comment at far right

6	wave functions(ψ) and the eigen values (E) of particle in a box model	☐ ☐ ☐ ☐ ☐	
7	The sketch of wave function and probability density(Particle in a square well)	☐ ☐ ☐ ☐ ☐	
8	Comparison of energy levels between classical mechanics and particle in a square well.	☐ ☐ ☐ ☐ ☐	

Chapter 9 Summary [Part 3]

(Use back page to cover the contents.)

9	A transition energy (ΔE, in [J]) of electron from n to n+1 in a particle in a square well mode	$\Delta E(n \to n+1) = \left(h^2/8ma^2\right)(2n+1)$ $\lambda(n \to n+1) = 8mca^2/[h(2n+1)]$	(Eqn. 9-13) (Eqn. 9-14)
10	Harmonic oscillator: potential, reduced mass, vibrational energy level, fundamental frequency	potential $U = \frac{1}{2}kx^2$ reduced mass $\mu = m_1 m_2/(m_1 + m_2)$ vibrtaional quantum number v is given by $E_v = h\nu_o[v + 1/2]$ (v: vibrtaional quantum number) fundamental harmonic frequency $\nu_o = (1/2\pi)\sqrt{k/\mu}$	(Eqn. 9-15) (Eqn. 9-16) (Eqn. 9-18) (Eqn. 9-19)
11	Sketch of wavefunction of the harmonic oscillator and the probability densities		
12	The transition energy (ΔE) between adjacent vibrational quantum number	$\Delta E = h\nu_o$	(Eqn. 9-21)

[Fold the page at the double line and cover the right half.]

CHAPTER 9 SUMMARY CHECK [PART 3]

(Use this page to cover and check the contents.)
Use ☐ as your check box. Write your comment at far right

9	A transition energy (ΔE, in [J]) of electron from n to n+1 in a particle in a square well mode	☐ ☐ ☐ ☐ ☐	
10	Harmonic oscillator: potential, reduced mass, vibrational energy level, fundamental frequency	☐ ☐ ☐ ☐ ☐	
11	Sketch of wavefunction of the harmonic oscillator and the probability densities	☐ ☐ ☐ ☐ ☐	
12	The transition energy (ΔE) between adjacent vibrational quantum number	☐ ☐ ☐ ☐ ☐	

Chapter 9 A Taste of Quantum Mechanics

Chapter 9 - YOUR TEACHER MAY TEST YOU ON:

No.	What may be asked?		What you should know or do?
1	What does the Planck's Quantum theory state?	→	The energy level is discrete (quantized)
2	How can you calculate the energy of photon with frequency ν?	→	$E = h\nu$ (Eqn. 9-1)
3	How do you calculate the de Broglie wavelength?	→	$\lambda = h/p$ (Eqn. 9-2)
		→	EXERCISE 9-1
		→	Problems 9-1, 9-2, 9-3
4	What is a basic format for Schrödinger's equation?	→	$\hat{H}\Psi = E\Psi$ (Eqn. 9-3)
5	What is the momentum operator (for one dimensional case)?	→	$-i\hbar(d/dx)$ in Table 9-1
6	What is the kinetic energy operator?	→	$-\frac{\hbar^2}{2m}\frac{\partial^2}{\partial x^2}$ in Table 9-1
		→	Problems 9-6, 9-7
7	What is the expression for the probability density of an electron?	→	$|\Psi|^2$
8	How can you calculate the probability of finding an electron in a given region?	→	Use $\int_{x_1}^{x_2} \psi_{ns}^* \psi_{ns} d\tau = \int_{x_1}^{x_2} [\psi_{ns}]^2 d\tau$ (Eqn. 9-4)
		→	The wavefunctions are given in **Table 9-2**.
		→	EXERCISE 9-2
		→	Problem 9-4
9	What is a wavefunction for a particle in a square well?	→	$\psi = [2/a]^{1/2} \sin(n\pi x/a)$ (Eqn. 9-7)
10	What are the possible energy levels of a particle in a square well?	→	n=1,2,3,... (n ≠0)
11	How do you calculate the energy level for a particle in a square well? How the energy level increases as a function of n? How does the energy level changes as a function of well width *a*?	→	$E_n = n^2 h^2 / 8ma^2$ (Eqn. 9-8)
		→	It increases as a function of n^2.
		→	It inversely proportional to a^2.
12	Plot (or sketch) the wavefunction and probability density of the wavefunction for n=1, 2, and 3 for a particle in a square well system.	→	Fig. 9-10
13	Calculate the transition energy with the longest wavelength for the case of β-carotin with 22π electrons by using the particle in a square well model.	→	Use **Fig. 9-19** to identify the quantum numbers involved in this transition.

Chapter 9 A Taste of Quantum Mechanics

		→	**Problems** 9-8, 9-9, 9-10, 9-11, 9-12, 9-13, 9-14, 9-15, 9-16, 9-17, 9-18, 9-19, 9-20
14	How do you calculate the energy levels for the particle in a box or a cube?	→	a particle in a box, $E_{n_x,n_y} = (h^2/8m)\left[n_x^2/a^2 + n_y^2/b^2\right]$ (Eqn. 9-10)
		→	a particle in a cube, $E_{n_x,n_y,n_z} = (h^2/8m)\left[n_x^2/a^2 + n_y^2/b^2 + n_z^2/c^2\right]$ (Eqn. 9-12)
15	Plot the energy level for a particle in a box and cube for the degenerate cases (i.e., a=b or a=b=c).	→	a particle in a box → **Fig. 9-12**
		→	a particle in a cube → **Fig. 9-15**
		→	$\lambda(n \to n+1) = \dfrac{8mca^2}{[h(2n+1)]}$ (Eqn. 9-14)
		→	**EXERCISE 9-4**
16	Estimating the longest wavelength transition for the iron porphyrin by using the particle in a box model.	→	Use energy level diagram shown in **Fig. 9-13** to identify the quantum numbers
		→	$\lambda(n_x, n_y \to n_x', n_y') = \dfrac{8mcl^2}{\{h[(n_x'^2+n_y'^2)-(n_x^2+n_y^2)]\}}$ (Eqn. 9-12')
		→	**EXERCISE 9-5**
		→	**Problems** 9-21, 9-22, 9-23, 9-24, 9-25
17	What is the lowest energy level of an harmonic oscillator?	→	$E_v = h\nu_o[v + 1/2]$ (Eqn. 9-18) zero point energy $E_{v=0} = h\nu_o/2$ (Eqn. 9-20)
18	Sketch the energy levels and wavefunction for the harmonic oscillator.	→	**Fig. 9-21**
19	The effect to the fundamental frequency due to a change of mass (or reduced mass) and force constant from a give spectrum.	→	$\nu_o = (1/2\pi)\sqrt{k/\mu}$ (Eqn. 9-19)
		→	$\nu \propto \dfrac{1}{\lambda} \propto \sqrt{k/\mu}$
		→	**EXERCISE 9-6**
		→	**Problems** 9-26, 9-27, 9-28, 9-29, 9-30, 9-31

UNIT CHECK Chapter 9

Important Parameters of This Chapter	Popularly Used Unit	Important Unit Conversion
Energy of photon, E	J	
Planck's constant, h	J sec m² kg sec⁻¹	h =6.62606896(33)×10⁻³⁴ [J sec]
Frequency, ν	Hz sec⁻¹	
Momentum, p	kg·m·sec⁻¹	
de Broglie wavelength, λ	m	
position operator, x	m	
Momentum operator, $-i\hbar(d/dx)$	kg m sec⁻¹	
Planck constant/2π, ℏ	J·sec m² kg sec⁻¹	
Kinetic energy operator, $-\dfrac{\hbar^2}{2m}\dfrac{\partial^2}{\partial x^2}$	J	
Mass, m	kg	
Potential, V	J	
Wavefunction, Ψ	Same as the unit of an eigen value Location [m] momentum [kg m sec⁻¹] Kinetic energy [J]	
Probability, $|\Psi|^2$	Dimensionless	
Radius, r	m	
Bohr radius, a_o	m	a_o= 52.9177×10⁻¹² [m] =0.529 [Å]
Quantum number, n	dimension less	
Mass of electron, m_e	kg	m_e= 9.10938188×10⁻³¹ [kg]
Potential of harmonic oscillator, U	J	
Spring force constant, k	kg sec⁻²	
Reduced mass, μ	kg	
Vibrational quantum number, v	Dimension less	
Fundamental frequency, $ν_o$	Hz sec⁻¹	
Wavenumbers, 1/λ	m⁻¹ nm⁻¹	1[nm⁻¹]=10⁹[m⁻¹]

Chapter 9 A Taste of Quantum Mechanics

SUMMARY OF TRICKY TRAPS OF CHAPTER 9

☐	1	In Schrödinger's equation, don't treat wavefunction (Ψ) like a routine mathematical equation and cancel. An operator "works" on the wave function and extract eigen value and remain the same wave function back.
☐	2	**In Quantum mechanics, energy levels are discrete.**
☐	3	In a particle in a box, the particle treated in this text is an electron. The mass of a particle is , therefore, mass of an electron, (m_e).
☐	4	A common unit of the transition energy (ΔE in [J]) is "wavelength" ($1/\lambda$ in [1/cm]). $\Delta E = h\nu = hc/\lambda \rightarrow 1/\lambda = \Delta E/(ch)$

LAST MINUTE REVIEW OF MATH CHAPTER 9

(These are basic algebra which you have no excuse if you miss them.)

1. $i^2 = -1$
2. $\frac{d}{dx}\sin ax = a \cos ax$ $\frac{d}{dx}\cos ax = -a \sin ax$
3. $\frac{d}{dx}e^{ax} = ae^{ax}$

NOTE: Although there are many integrations involved in this chapter, I request you those to check the integration table rather than memorizing the results.

Nobel Prize and Your Knowledge From Chapter 9
(*: word appeared in Chapter 9)

The Nobel Prize in Chemistry 1999 was awarded to **Ahmed Zewail** for his studies of the transition states of chemical reactions using femtosecond spectroscopy. His experiments described formation and dissociation of chemical bonds with femtosecond spectroscopy, where laser pulse with the duration of femtosecond range was used to observe the reactions. In his experiment, the first pulse (pump pulse) initiates a chemical reaction by breaking chemical bonds, then the second pulse (probe pulse) excites the existent molecules at corresponding time stage and resulted light emission from these molecules are detected. The energy of these emissions corresponds to the reacting species or produced species and those energetic levels so that molecular structures of the species when the probe pulse arrived are identified. The femotosecond pulses are short enough can fully resolve chemical reaction. (No chemical reaction is considered to take place faster than femtosecond regime.) The chemical reactions which Zewail's group resolved those involve dissociations of chemical bond, bond formation (replacement of atomic position). (**Fig. 9-26**)In some reactions, bonds dissociation and bond formation takes place simultaneously in different location of a molecule, or bonds dissociates and form as an atom jumps from one molecule to another molecule. Zewail also probed the dissociation of a complex molecule where reaction goes through stages where bond dissociation occurs one at a time.

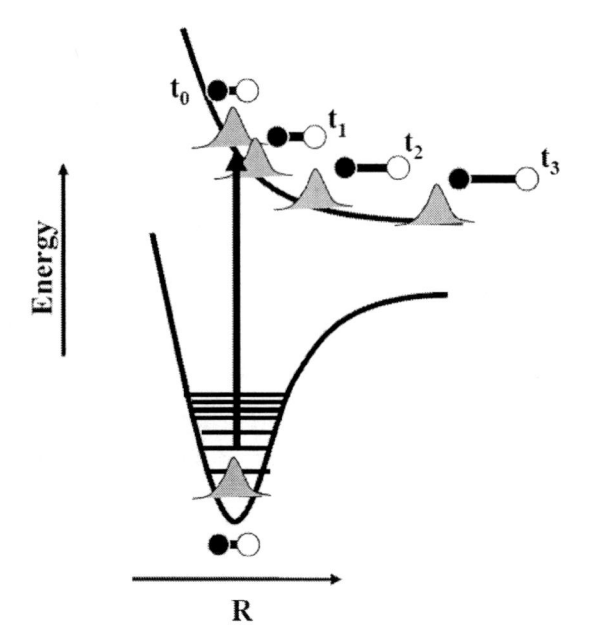

Fig. 9-26. The demonstration of excitation and dissociation of diatomic molecule (R: inter nuclear distance) and progression of the wave packet at time t_0, t_1, t_2, and t_3.

The observation of the femotchemistry is the observation of dynamics of quantum mechanical or chemical world in very short time. The state observed in short time should be inprinciple expressed by the wavefunction (or people call wave packet for the probablity finding the state). In **Chapter 9**, you learned the **Schrödinger's equation*** as shown in (**Eqn. 9-2**), where no time was involved. As an extension of **Schrödinger's equation*** equation learned in this chapter, time-dependent Schrodinger's equation is mentioned.

$$i\hbar \frac{\partial}{\partial t}\Psi(x,t) = \hat{H}\Psi(x,t)$$

Here, Ψ(x,t) is the wave function with location and time as parameters.

THE FOCUSED PHYSICAL CHEMISTRY EXPERIMENTAL APPROACH ASSOCIATED WITH CHAPTER 9
(*: word appeared in Chapter 9)

Laser

A **laser** (Light Amplification by Stimulated Emission of Radiation) produces electromagnetic radiation through optical amplification based on the stimulated emission of photons. The **stimulated emission** (which is theoretically explained by Einstein) is a **quantum mechanical phenomenon*** where an excited electron relaxes to the lower energy level under electromagnetic radiation is interacted. Since an atom can be regarded as a small electric dipole oscillator responding to an external electromagnetic radiation field, the rate of transitions between two states is more enhanced. While a transition to the higher state absorbs an energy, a transition from the higher to a lower state produces an extra photon (**stimulated emission**). (**Fig. 9-27**)As this transition takes place, the energy is transferred to that field. Under this process photon possesses the same phase, frequency, polarization, and traveling direction as those of the incident electromagnetic radiation.

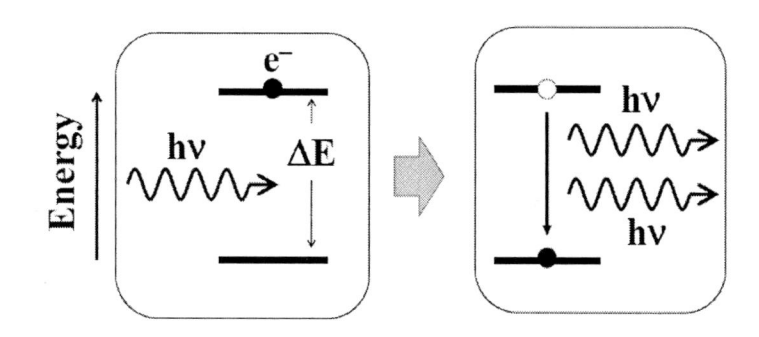

Fig. 9-27 Mechanism of stimulated emission.

An optical amplification can be achieved in a medium (or gain medium) as a population inversion makes the rate of stimulated emission exceeding the rate of absorption. The most remarkable feature of emitted laser light is that it possesses high degree of spatial and temporal coherence. Relating with the topics learned in **Chapter 9** (and **Chapter 10**), laser beam (or pulse) can prepare the particular quantum state (or ensemble of the states which last for very short amount of time see the work by Zewail described in "**Nobel Prize and Your Knowledge From Chapter 9**".

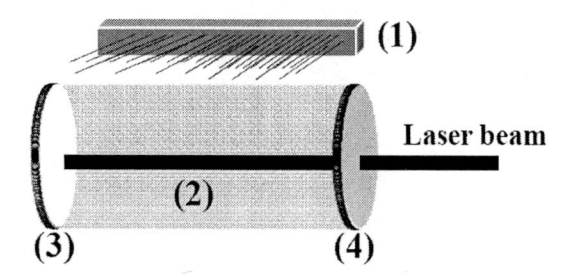

Fig. 9-28 A principle design of laser.
Principal components:(1). pumping energy, (2). Gain medium, (3). High reflector, and (4). Output coupler.

A laser (or laser cavity) consists of (1) pumping, (2) gain medium, (3) high reflection mirror, and (4) output coupler. (**Fig. 9-28**)

(1) pumping: This is the process of supplying the energy required for the amplification of stimulated emission. (e.g., flash lamp)
(2) gain medium: The gain medium is a material which amplifies light by stimulated emission.
(3) high reflection mirror (4) output coupler: The light bounces back and force between high reflection mirrors and output coupler in a cavity. Since output coupler, is partially transparent, laser beam is emitted through output coupler.

Chapter 9 Problems

9-1 [de Broglie wavelength] If the velocity of an electron beam of electron microscopy is 1.5×10^8 m/sec, what is the wavelength of an electron particle?

9-2 [de Broglie wavelength] The accelerated electrons are used in an electron microscopy. Calculate the velocity of an electron beam when the wavelength of an electron particle is 1 Å (10^{-10} m).

9-3 [de Broglie wavelength] The accelerated electrons are used in an electron microscopy. Calculate the velocity of an electron beam when the wavelength of an electron particle is 400 nm.

9-4 [probability of finding 1s electron] Calculate the radius of H 1s orbital which has 90% probability of finding electron.

9-5 [Schrödinger equation] Choose one Schrödinger equation which shows total energy of particle in x direction.

a) $-\dfrac{\hbar^2}{2m}\dfrac{d^2\psi}{dx^2} + U(x)\psi = E\psi$

b) $-im\hbar \dfrac{d\psi}{dx} = E\psi$

c) $U(x)\psi = E\psi$

9-6 [Hamiltonian] Find the eigen value, if the Hamiltonian of the particle in a square well is given as H = $-(m^2h/\pi)(d^2/dx^2)$, and the wave function is given by $\Psi = \alpha\cos[\alpha x/(nm)]$ (This is an imaginary situation.)

    a) $h^2n^2/(8m\alpha^2)$
    b) $-h\alpha^3/(n^2\pi)$
    c) $-h^2n^2/(m\alpha^2)$
    d) $h\alpha^2/(n^2\pi)$
    e) none of these

9-7 [Hamiltonian] Which function is an eigen function of the operator d/dx?

    a) $x^2 - 1$
    b) $e-ax$ where a is a constant
    c) $\sin kx$, where k is a constant
    d) $(-1 + \cos kx) - 1$, where k is a constant
    e) none of these

9-8 [particle in a box model] The particle in a box model can be used as an approximation to explain the trends in the UV spectra of conjugated polyenes because

    a) the π electrons move freely along the length of the molecule
    b) a conjugated polymer is a rigid molecule
    c) the energy is quantized
    d) all of the above (choices a, b, and c)
    e) none of choices a, b, and c.

9-9 [particle in a well- E_n] Calculate the lowest energy for an electron in a one dimensional box of length 10 [Å].

9-10 [particle in a well - E_n] An electron in a particle (of mass m) in a square well (well width of a) has an energy of $E_n = 1.56 \times 10^{-18}$ J at n = 3. We increased the particle mass by a factor of three and adjusted the well width to be $6a$. Calculate the energy, E_n, at n = 9.

9-11 [particle in a well - E_n] A particle (of mass m) in a square well (well width of a) has an energy of $E_n = 4.27 \times 10^{-18}$ J at n = 2. We decreased the particle mass by a factor of two and adjusted the well width to be $10a$. Calculate the energy, E_n, at n = 5 in J. [Choose the closest value.]

9-12 [particle in a well- sketch of ψ] The figure depicts the one-dimensional particle in a box wavefunction for n. Answer the quantum number, n.

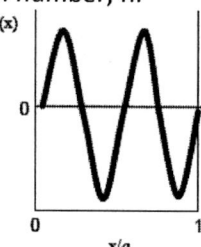

9-13 [particle in a well- sketch of |ψ²|] The figure depicts the square of the wavefunction for one-dimensional particle in a box. What is the quantum number for this wave function?:

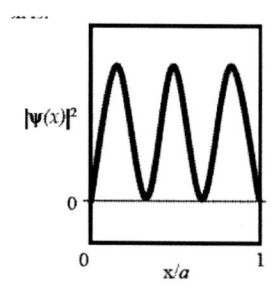

9-14 [particle in a well - ΔE→λ] For a box of length 1 [nm] (a = 1 [nm]), the longest wavelength transition is 200 [nm]. What is the wavelength if the mass of the particle is doubled?

9-15 [particle in a well -ΔE→λ] In "*a particle in a box*" model, the longest wavelength transition was 800 nm for a well of length 1 [nm]. What is the wavelength of the transition, if the mass of a particle is decreased by a factor of 4 (*i.e.*, the mass of a particle becomes 1/4 of the original mass.) ?

9-16 [length a in particle in a well] An organic sample has 5 conjugated double bonds. The long-wavelength maximum of this sample was 157.1 [nm]. By using particle in a square well model, calculate the effective length of this conjugated bond chain.

9-17 [β–Carotene - ΔE→λ (particle in a well)] β–Carotene has 11 conjugated double bonds (22 π electrons). The longest wavelength maximum of β-carotene is observed at 480 [nm]. Assign quantum numbers for this spectral transition.

9-18 [β-Carotene -length] β-Carotene has 11 conjugated double bonds (22 π electrons). By using particle in a square well model, calculate the length of chain. The long wavelength maximum of β-carotene is about 480 [nm].

9-19 [particle in a well, sketch of Ψ, probability, ΔE→λ] An electron is trapped in one dimensional well as shown below (V is potential and a =10 [Å]) :

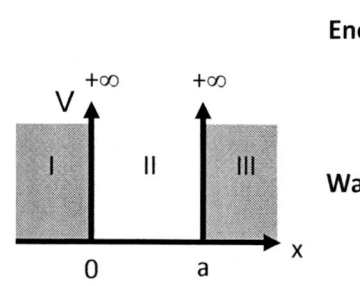

Energy levels $E = \dfrac{n^2 h^2}{8ma^2}$

n =1, 2, 3, ...(n : quantum number)

Wavefunctio $\psi = \left(\dfrac{2}{a}\right)^{1/2} \sin\left(\dfrac{n\pi x}{a}\right)$

for $0 \leq x \leq a$, where n =1, 2, 3, ...

a) Sketch the wave function of n =1 and n = 2 *as accurately as possible*. (Do not skip values in both x- and y axes.)
b) What is the probability that the electron is within 1 [Å] of the center of the box in the lowest energy state?
c) Calculate the energies of *the two states of lowest energy* for an electron in a one-dimensional box of length 10.0 [Å] (a = 10.0 [Å])
d) Calculate the longest-wavelength transition for an electron in this box.
Use $\Delta E = hc/\lambda$ (ΔE: transition energy in joules, h: Planck constant, c: speed of light, and λ: wavelength)

9-20 [particle in a well-Ψ, ΔE→λ] Based on the "particle in a box" wave-functions, four types of the MOs for the π bond ($\psi_1, \psi_2, \psi_3, \psi_4$) in terms of four equivalent p orbitals ($\psi_a, \psi_b, \psi_c, \psi_d$) are obtained as follows:

$\psi_1 = +0.372\psi_b + 0.602\psi_a - 0.602\psi_d - 0.372\psi_c$
$\psi_2 = -0.372\psi_d - 0.602\psi_b + 0.372\psi_a + 0.602\psi_c$
$\psi_3 = +0.602\psi_c + 0.372\psi_a + 0.602\psi_b + 0.372\psi_d$
$\psi_4 = 0.602\psi_a + 0.602\psi_d - 0.372\psi_b - 0.372\psi_c$

Rank these MOs in order of their energies.

9-21 [porphyrin -energy level] The π electrons of Fe-porphyrin ring can be modeled as electrons trapped in a two dimensional box model. Please assume that this particular Fe-porphyrin ring contains 16 π electrons. What is the next quantum level (n_x, n_y) to which an electron is excited?

9-22 [porphyrin -energy level] The π electrons of metal-porphyrin ring can be modeled as electrons trapped in a two dimensional box model. In this porphyrin, the length of x and y dimensions are x = a and y = 1.2a, respectively. Please assume that this particular porphyrin ring contains 10π electrons. What is the next quantum level (n_x, n_y) to which an electron is excited?

9-23 [porphyrin-ΔE→λ] The porphyrin structure measures about 1 [nm] on a side. Estimate the longest –wavelength absorption band of this molecule.

9-24 [porphyrin-ΔE→λ] The twenty six-π electrons of iron-porphyrin can be described using a simple model of free electrons in a two-dimensional box. The longest-wavelength transition of this iron porphyrin was observed at 430 [nm]. Calculate the second longest-wavelength transition of this porphyrin.

9-25 [3D-particle in a box] Nitrogenase contains an iron-sulfur cluster, Fe_4S_4, where the atoms of each type are arranged alternately at the corners of a cube. It can be modeled for an electron in a three-dimensional box whose edges have length a (See the Figure). The transition for excitation of an electron from the highest filled orbital to the lowest unfilled orbital is observed in the wavelength of 238 [nm]. Calculate the length of a in Å (Give three significant figures). Assume that the total number of valence electrons available is 20.

9-26 [oscillator -μ_{mass}] The fundamental vibration frequency of gaseous $^{14}N^{16}O$ is 1904 [cm^{-1}]. When $^{14}N^{16}O$ is bound to hemoglobin A, an absorption band at 1615 [cm^{-1}] was observed. Calculate the change in the force constant of $^{14}N^{16}O$ vibrator. Assume that the binding of $^{14}N^{16}O$ does not change the reduced mass.

9-27 [oscillator -μ_{mass}] The fundamental vibration frequency of gaseous molecule A is 2000 [cm^{-1}] and that of molecule B is 2500 [cm^{-1}]. If A and B has the same force constant, show the relationship of the reduced mass between A and B (μ_A and μ_B)

9-28 [oscillator -μ_{mass}] The fundamental vibration frequency of gaseous molecule A is 3600 [cm^{-1}] and that of molecule B is 2900 [cm^{-1}]. If A and B has the same force constant, show the relationship of the reduced mass between A and B (μ_A and μ_B).

9-29 [oscillator - sketch of ψ] The figure depicts the square of the harmonic oscillator wavefunction. What is the vibrational quantum number of this wavefunction?

Chapter 9 A Taste of Quantum Mechanics

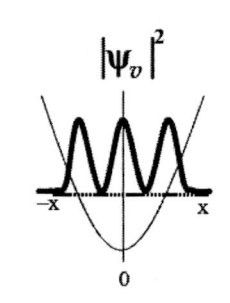

9-30 [ΔE-oscillator] The vibrational frequency for gaseous carbon monoxide is 2170 [cm^{-1}]. As CO chemisorbs on a metal porphyrin surface, the vibrational frequency is expected to
- a) remain unchanged
- b) increase because the C-O bond gets stronger when it attaches to a metal surface.
- c) decrease because of the decreased electron density between the carbon atom and the oxygen atom.
- d) increase because of the increased electron density between the carbon atom and the metal porphyrin surface.
- e) have two groups (one with decreased and the others increased frequency).

9-31 [ΔE-oscillator] Consider gaseous $^{12}C^{16}O$ as a harmonic oscillator with a force constant of 1902.5 [N/m]. By binding to the hemoglobin, the force constant of $^{12}C^{16}O$ is reduced to 72 % of force constant of gaseous $^{12}C^{16}O$. Calculate the difference of oscillator's wavenumbers between gaseous $^{12}C^{16}O$ and $^{12}C^{16}O$ bound to a hemoglobin. (This means that you need to calculate " $1/\lambda_1 - 1/\lambda_2$ ", where λ_1 is the wavelength of gaseous $^{12}C^{16}O$ and λ_2 is the wavelength of $^{12}C^{16}O$ bounded to a hemoglobin. The unit of wavenumbers is cm^{-1}). You may assume that the oxygen is so anchored that its effective mass becomes infinite when $^{12}C^{16}O$ binds to a hemoglobin. Mass of ^{12}C = 12.000 [amu] Mass of ^{16}O = 16.000 [amu].

Chapter 9 Answers. For Selected Problems

9-1	~5.0 [pm]
9-2	7.3×10^6 [m/s]
9-4	~1.4 [Å]
9-3	1.82×10^3 [m/s]
9-5	a
9-6	d
9-7	b
9-8	d
9-9	6.024×10^{-20} [J]
9-10	1.30×10^{-19} [J]
9-11	5.34×10^{-19}
9-12	$n = 4$
9-13	$n = 3$
9-14	~400 [nm]
9-15	200 [nm]
9-16	7.2×10^{-10} [m]
9-17	$n = 11$ and $n = 12$
9-18	18 [Å]
9-19	b) 0.10 c) 2.408×10^{-19} [J] d) 1099.9 [nm]
9-20	b) $\psi_3 < \psi_1 < \psi_4 < \psi_2$
9-21	$(n_x, n_y) = (4,1)$ or $(1,4)$
9-22	$(n_x, n_y) = (3,1)$
9-23	660 [nm]
9-25	$a = 2.69$ [Å]
9-27	$\mu_A = 1.56\ \mu_B$
9-28	$\mu_A = 0.65\ \mu_B$
9-29	$v = 2$
9-30	c
9-31	780 [cm^{-1}]

Chapter 10
Intermolecular Interaction and Essences of Spectroscopy

10-1 Charge Distribution and Dipole Moments
10-2 Dipole Moment and Transition
10-3 Quantum Yield
10-4 Intermolecular Forces
10-5 Absorption of the Light
10-6 Fluorescence Spectroscopy

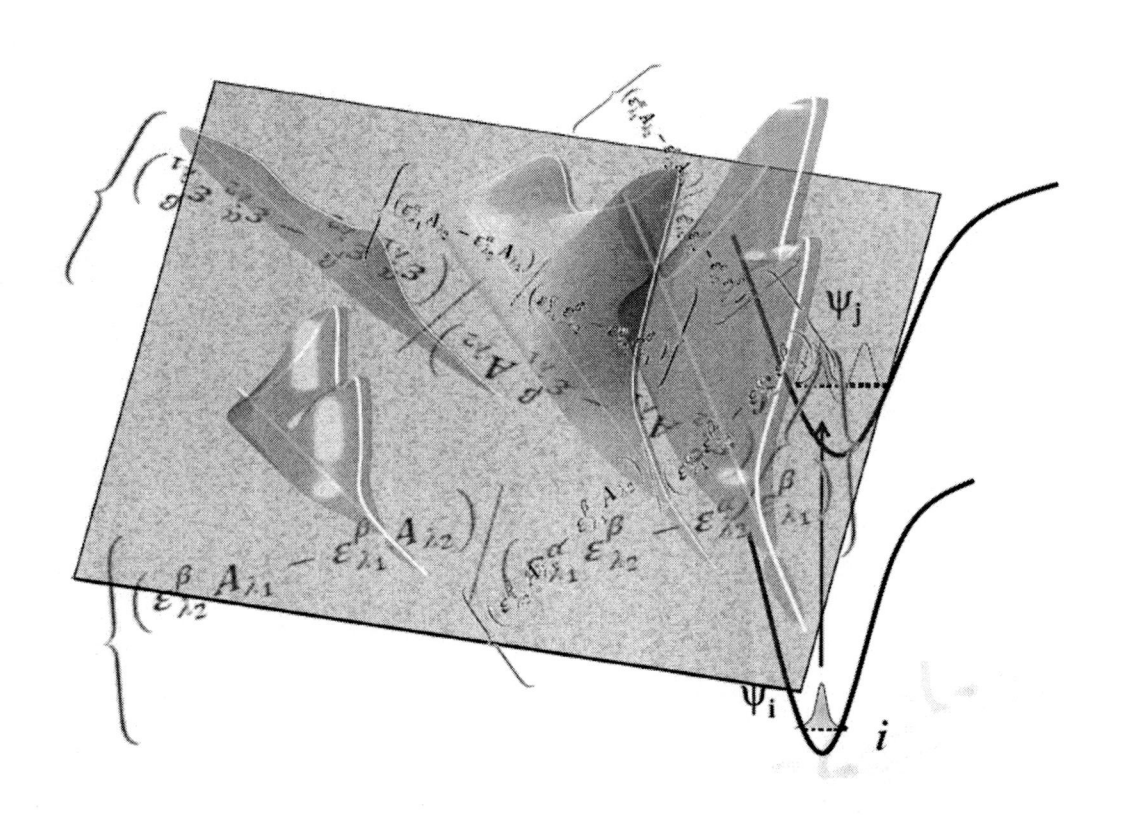

Chapter 10 Intermolecular Interaction and Essences of Spectroscopy

- **Why do I have to study this chapter?**

The dipole moment of the molecule is an origin of the intermolecular interaction. You will know how dipole moment is constructed. The types of molecular interaction will be organized. The interaction of molecules with light source is a critical method for extracting the structure or property of molecules. The spectroscopy is an experimental approach for extracting molecular structure and molecular interaction. In the previous chapter, the Quantum mechanics is introduced and many readers may be "suspicious" if it is true or not. Seeing is believing. The outcome of spectroscopy is the proof of Quantum mechanics.

- **Expected Hurdles Ahead in this Chapter**
  1. Calculating a net dipole moment.(See Section **10-1**)
  2. Calculating a net quantum yield.(See Section **10-3**)
  3. Extracting thermochemical information from absorption spectroscopy. (See Section **10-5**)

PREVIEW OF KEY-EQUATIONS

Dipole moment

$$\vec{\mu} = q\vec{r}$$

Magnitude of dipole moment

$$|\mu| = \sqrt{\mu_x^2 + \mu_y^2 + \mu_z^2}$$

Transition dipole moment

$$\mu_{ij} = \int \psi_j^* \hat{\mu} \psi_i d\tau$$

Quantum yield

$$\phi = n_\pi / n_p$$

Coulomb's Law

$$U(r) = q_1 q_2 / 4\pi\varepsilon_o r$$

Lambert –Beer's Law

$$I = I_0 10^{-\varepsilon l c} = I_0 10^{-A}$$

Absorbance

$$A = \varepsilon l c$$

Circular dichroism

$$\Delta A = A_L - A_R$$

Number of normal modes

$$3N - 5 \text{ (Linear molecule)}$$
$$3N - 6 \text{ (Non-linear molecule)}$$

Fluorescence intensity decay

$$I(t) = I_o e^{-t/\tau}$$
$$\frac{1}{\tau} = k$$

Quantum yield of fluorescence

$$\emptyset_f = \frac{k_o}{k_d}$$

PREVIEW OF KEY-TECHNICAL TERMS

Polarity, net dipole moment (μ), Cartesian coordinate, transition dipole moment, quantum yield (ϕ), photon, Beer-Lambert law, absorbance, molar extinction coefficient (ε), isosbestic point, circular dichroism, circularly polarized light, specific rotation, molar rotation, molar ellipticity, fluorescence, intermolecular force, Coulombic force, ion-ion interaction, ion-dipole interaction, dipole-dipole interaction, hydrogen bond, induced dipole interaction, dispersion force, London force, non-covalent interaction, van der Waals interaction, Debye force

10.1 Charge Distribution and Dipole Moments

The molecular structure is a main focus in chemistry and an important topic in physical chemistry where many physical chemistry approaches were proven to be assets for determining the molecular structure. Molecular structure determines if the molecule is polar or non-polar. The **polarity** of a molecule is an origin of how intermolecular force is described. A polar molecule possesses the (net) dipole moment, while a non-polar molecule does not. The intermolecular force defines the physical property such as boiling point or melting point, and others. The importance of the intermolecular force is seen in the coordination of the macromolecule, and such a macromolecule can be fully found in biological application. DNA, RNA, proteins are the perfect examples of the coordination of the molecules to cause a macromolecular structure. Since the examples of molecular structure can be limitless in biological application and can be overwhelming, we choose a typical and important portion of the peptide -(CO)-(NH)- bonding as an example of exploring the dipole moment. (**Fig. 10-1**)

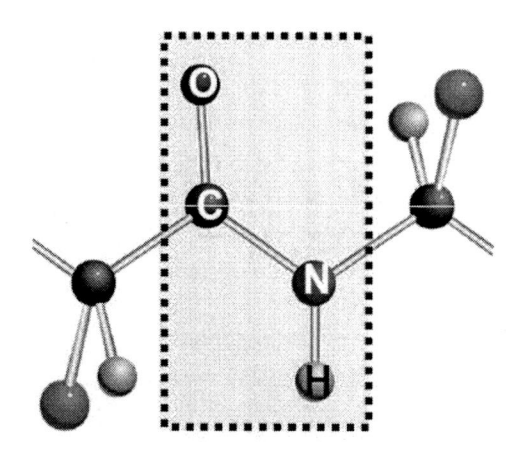

Fig. 10-1 Planar amide group

The net atomic charges and dipole moments, $\vec{\mu}$, is given by

$$\vec{\mu} = q\vec{r} \qquad \text{(Eqn. 10-1)}$$

Here, q is a charge and $\vec{r}$ is the location vector. (The dipole moment is also given by the vector as well). The component of dipole moment vector for each Cartesian coordinate is given by

$$\vec{\mu}_x = \Sigma_i q_i x_i \qquad \vec{\mu}_y = \Sigma_i q_i y_i \qquad \vec{\mu}_z = \Sigma_i q_i z_i \qquad \text{(Eqn.10-2)}$$

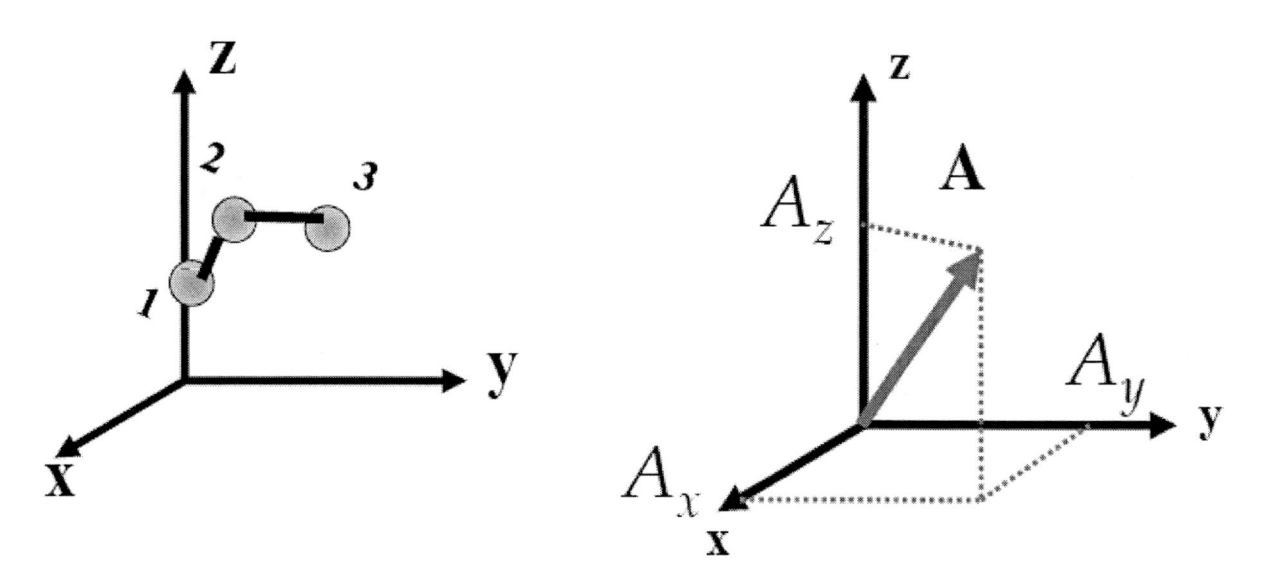

Fig. 10-2 Planar amide group

Fig. 10-3 Vector A in a Cartesian coordinate.

The component of each axis, x, y, and z is given by the summation of multiplication of charge and the coordinate of each axis. (**Fig. 10-2**) The magnitude of the vector $\vec{A}$ is given by,

$$|\vec{A}| = \sqrt{A_x^2 + A_y^2 + A_z^2} \qquad \text{(Eqn.10-3)}$$

For neutral molecules, the calculation of dipole moments is independent of where the origin is placed. (**Fig. 10.3**) Thus, the magnitude of the dipole moment of the dipole moment vector is given in a similar way as:

$$|\mu| = \sqrt{\mu_x^2 + \mu_y^2 + \mu_z^2} \qquad \text{(Eqn.10-4)}$$

Chapter 10 Intermolecular Interaction and Essences of Spectroscopy

> **EXERCISE 10-1**
> Adenine has the dipole moment of each component as:
> μ_x = 2.55 [D], μ_y = −2.03 [D], and μ_z = 0 [D]
> Calculate the entire magnitude of the dipole.
>
> **ANSWER**
>
> $$|\mu| = \sqrt{\mu_x^2 + \mu_y^2 + \mu_z^2} \qquad \text{(Eqn.10-4)}$$
>
> This molecule is planar from the fact that there is no z –component.
>
> $$|\mu| = \sqrt{(2.55)^2 + (-2.03)^2}$$
> = 3.26 [D]
>
> μ_z = 0 [D]
>
> Don't forget square each μ and root mean square of total sum. (For calculating a magnitude, take a positive side of root mean square.)

Since calculating net dipole is a bit tricky process, let's go through a guideline for calculation of a dipole moment on a part of a peptide bond. Then, you actually calculate the net dipole moment in **EXERCISE 10-2**.

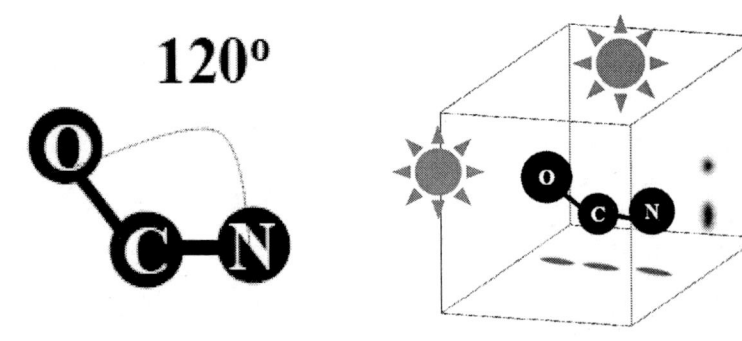

Fig. 10-4 A part of peptide bond.

Fig. 10-5 Projecting the component of the structure into each face of the surface

The peptide bonds can be shortened and simplified as the component consisted of O-C-N making an angle of 120°, as shown in (**Fig. 10-4**). Based on the problem setting each atom possesses the designated charges. By observing each component, you can enlighten the molecule from the other side of the surface and project it in either axis, x, y, and z or each plane. In some cases you may see the two atoms if the C and N are overlapped. Or you see three O, C, and N atoms if you project it from the top of the molecule. The dipole moment is an integration of the three components after all. So you need to make an easy way to decompose into three components. (**Fig. 10-5**) It is always true that the dipole moment can be easily obtained depending on the way of taking a coordinate or axis inside the molecule.

Chapter 10 Intermolecular Interaction and Essences of Spectroscopy

You may not agree with me, however, I think that by taking a closer look at the center of the origin in the N atom and the x axis along C-N bond, the molecule itself is planar so there will be no z component. (**Fig. 10-6**)

The approach for obtaining the dipole moment is as following.

1) Start collecting all components in x axis and add up the dipole moment for each segment. (μ_x) Each component of dipole (μ_x) is given by (**Eqn. 10-2**), so that make sure to multiply correct amount and direction (+ or − sign) to result a right direction of component. In this case, you have two components of μ (O − N)$_x$ and μ (C-N)$_x$.

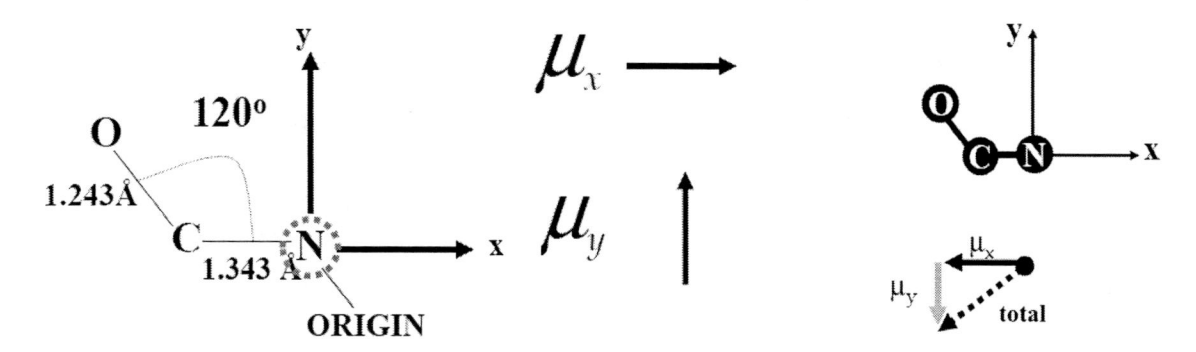

Fig. 10-6 Two components of dipole moment

Fig. 10-7 Total dipole moment.

2) Collect all for the y-component and add up the dipole moment for each segment (μ_y) as conducted in step 1). Based on (**Fig. 10-6**), you have only one components of μ (O-C)$_y$

3) Lastly, collect all of z-component to construct a net dipole moment on this axis.(μ_z) However, a molecule used in this example is a planar molecule and has no z-component. Thus, μ_z=0.

4) The net dipole (magnitude and the direction) can be simply confirmed by drawing on the diagram with use of vector concept. (See **Fig. 10-7**)

$$\vec{\mu} = \vec{\mu}_x + \vec{\mu}_y$$

(Please note that $\vec{\mu}_z$=0 in this case.)

5) The magnitude of the dipole moment will be calculated by (**Eqn. 10-4**), and here μ_z=0.

$$|\mu| = \sqrt{\mu_x^2 + \mu_y^2}$$

EXERCISE 10-2
An approximate MO (molecular orbital) calculation gives the following π-electron charges on an amide group: (See **Figs. 10-4 and 10-6**)
O: −0.33e   C: +0.18e   N: +0.15e
Calculate the magnitude of the π dipole moment

ANSWER
X-component
The charges of each atom is
O −0.33e   C +0.18e   N +0.15e   (1 e = 4.803 × 10⁻¹⁰ [esu])

The length of x component for O-N bond and C-N bond are,
$r(O-N)_x = r(O-C) \times \cos 60° + r(C-N)$
$\mu_x(O-N) = -0.33e \, (-1.243 \, [\text{Å}] \times \cos 60° - 1.343 \, [\text{Å}])$
$= +0.33e \, (1.243 \times 10^{-8} \, [\text{cm}] \times \cos 60° + 1.343 \times 10^{-8} \, [\text{cm}])$
$= +0.33 \times 4.803 \times 10^{-10} \, [\text{esu}] \times 1.965 \times 10^{-8} \, [\text{cm}]$
$= +3.11 \times 10^{-18} \, [\text{esu cm}]$
$= +3.11 \, [\text{D}]$

$r(C-N)_x = r(C-N) = 1.343 \, [\text{Å}] = 1.343 \times 10^{-8} \, [\text{cm}]$
$\mu_x(C-N) = +0.18e \times 1.343 \, [\text{Å}] = +0.18 \times 4.803 \times 10^{-10} \, [\text{esu}] \times 1.343 \times 10^{-8} \, [\text{cm}]$
$= -1.16 \times 10^{-18} \, [\text{esu cm}]$
$= -1.16 \, [\text{D}]$
Therefore, total sum of the x component is
$\mu_x = +3.11 \, [\text{D}] - 1.16 \, [\text{D}] = +1.95 \, [\text{D}]$

Y-component.
$r(O-C)_y = r(O-C) \times \sin 60°$
$\mu_y = -0.33e \times (1.243 \, [\text{Å}] \times \sin 60°)$
$= -0.33 \times 4.803 \times 10^{-10} \, [\text{esu}] \, (1.243 \times 10^{-8} \, [\text{cm}] \times \sin 60°)$
$= -0.33 \times 4.803 \times 10^{-10} \, [\text{esu}] \times 1.076 \times 10^{-8} \, [\text{cm}]$
$= -1.706 \times 10^{-18} \, [\text{esu cm}]$
$= -1.71 \, [\text{D}]$

$\mu_y = -1.71 \, [\text{D}]$

Therefore, the total dipole moment is the summation of the component x and y component as shown in (**Fig. 10-7**)
The magnitude of dipole moment is given by

$$|\mu| = \sqrt{\mu_x^2 + \mu_y^2 + \mu_z^2} \qquad (\text{Eqn.10-4})$$

$\mu_x = +1.95 \, [\text{D}], \mu_y = -1.71 \, [\text{D}]$

438

Chapter 10 Intermolecular Interaction and Essences of Spectroscopy

Thus,

$$|\mu| = \sqrt{(+1.95\,D)^2 + (-1.71\,D)^2} = 2.59\,[D]$$

① Don't forget there are two components (x and y) for planar molecule (no z-component).
② X-component has two terms. One from $(O - N)_x$ and one from $(C-N)_x$
③ 1 Debye [D] = 1 × 10^{-18} [esu cm]
④ Projection to the x-axis is given by cos function.
⑤ Y-component has only one term, $(O-C)_y$
⑥ Projection to the y-axis is given by sin function
⑦ $\mu_z = 0$
⑧ Don't worry about negative signs. It is showing a direction of a vector.
⑨ Don't forget square each μ and root mean square of total sum. (For calculating a magnitude, take a positive side of root mean square.)

Alternative Choice of Coordination

What if we change a choice of a coordinate as shown in below.

$\mu_x = \mu(C - N)_x + \mu(O - C)_x$
$= e_N r_2 - e_O r_1 \times \sin 60°$
$= (+0.15\,e) \times 1.343\,[\text{Å}] -$
$(-0.33\,e) \times 1.243\,[\text{Å}] \times \sin 30°$
$= +0.15 \times 4.803 \times 10^{-10}\,[\text{esu}] \times 1.343 \times 10^{-8}\,[\text{cm}]$
$\quad\quad + 0.33 \times 4.803 \times 10^{-10}\,[\text{esu}]$
$\times 1.243 \times 10^{-8}\,[\text{cm}] \times \sin 30°$
$= 9.6756 \times 10^{-19}\,[\text{esu cm}] + 9.8507 \times 10^{-19}\,[\text{esu cm}]$
$= 0.96756\,[D] + 0.98507\,[D]$
$= 1.952\,[D]$

This is the same value of that obtained under the previous choice of a coordinate.

Under this choice of a coordinate, the component μ_y is still the same of that obtained in the previous choice of a coordinate, $\mu_y = -1.71\,[D]$.

10-2 Dipole Moment and Transition

When a molecular system is excited by an external source, the ground energy state of an electron can be excited by electronically (or by other energetic states such as vibrational or rotational levels) making a transition of energy. Let's say that you want to excite from i-th state to the higher j-th state with energy amount of E_i and E_j, respectively. The difference of the energy amount or the amount required to make a transition form i-th to j-th is $\Delta E = E_j - E_i$ (>0). In quantum mechanics, however, the supply of the amount of energy (ΔE) does not necessary guarantee 100% to make a transition from i-th to j-th level. The probability and (selection rule) for the transition is determined by so called "**transition dipole moment**", which can be calculated by operating dipole moment operator to the wavefunction of a system. This is an important application of dipole moment learned in the above. As a matter of fact, the dipole moment operator ($\hat{\mu}$) has exactly the same format as a dipole moment given in (**Eqn. 10-1**).

$$\hat{\mu} = e\vec{r} \qquad \text{(Eqn. 10-5)}$$

By "sandwiching" a momentum operator between the wavefunction of i-th and j-th state, you can calculate the transition dipole moment between these two states by the following integration.

$$\mu_{ij} = \int \psi_j^* \hat{\mu} \psi_i d\tau \qquad \text{(Eqn. 10-6)}$$

The wavefunction of the ith (initial) state is given by ψ_i and that of the jth state which is given by ψ_j. The transition of ith state to the jth state can be pictured as a promotion of the wavefunction prepared at the ith state to the jth state, and examine the overlap between two wave functions. In (**Fig. 10-8**), you see that the wave function of the ith state (ψ_i) is projected on that of jth state wavefucntion (ψ_j), finding some overlaps between two wave functions. So that this transition has a probability to take place. Now, please recall "$|\Psi|^2$ **is the probability of finding an electron**" learned in Chapter 9. In a similar way, the probability of the transition is therefore proportional to a square of the μ_{ij} given in (Eqn. **10-6**).

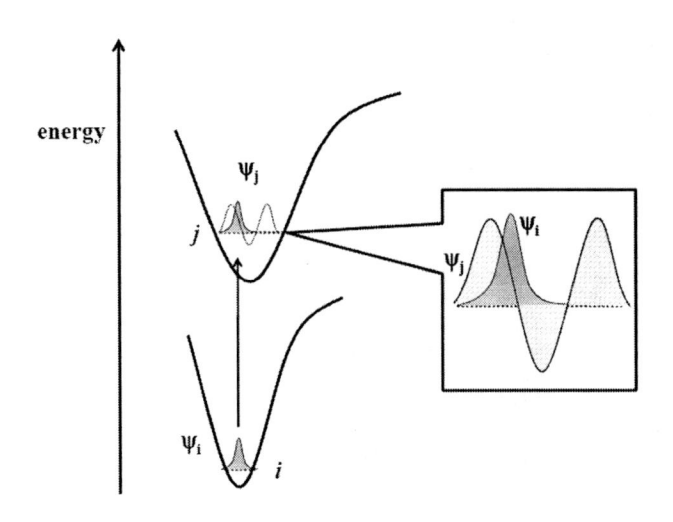

Fig. 10-8 Transition dipole moment.

$$|\mu_{ij}|^2 = \left| \int \psi_j^* \hat{\mu} \psi_i d\tau \right|^2 \qquad \text{(Eqn. 10-7)}$$

Thus, **$|\mu_{ij}|^2$ is probability of transition from i-th to j-th state**. The asterisk mark (*) on the wavefunction ψ_j implies a complex conjugate of this wave function. (Mathematically you take a conjugate of any imaginary number, e.g., $(i)^* = -i$) and $d\tau$ represents the integration over all spaces as shown in (**Eqn. 9-4**)'.

$$d\tau = 4\pi r^2 dr \qquad \text{(Eqn. 9-4)'}$$

Chapter 10 Intermolecular Interaction and Essences of Spectroscopy

But what is the value calculated by (**Eqn. 10-7**) good for? The transition probability is good for estimating or analyzing many spectral features including absorption spectrum. The dipole moment is proportional to dipole strength, and it will explain the intensity of the spectrum. Also, it will predict whether a particular transition is allowed or not allowed, therefore acting as a selection rule of the transition.

10-3 Quantum Yield

You may have seen that a super hero uses a light beam for attacking a bad beast in the comic books or movies. While all of these are described as fictional, I think some of these provide us with very good concepts about the photons as quanta (or particles). Especially when the beam pushes away the monster or break the wall carrying the idea that the photon beams are considered to be the particles. In Quantum world, it is possible to count how many photons and how much energy are involved. The Intensity of light (I) is defined as:

$$I = \frac{E_p}{(A \cdot t)} \qquad \text{(Eqn. 10-8)}$$

Here, E_p is the total amount of photon energy [J], A is a targeted area [m^2], and t is the amount of time [sec] of the light is emitted. (Commonly, the unit [J sec^{-1}] is replace by [W], thus, the unit of intensity I is given as [J sec^{-1} m^{-2}] =[W m^{-2}]. From **Chapter 9**, the energy of a photon with frequency (ν [Hz]) or wavelength (λ [m]) possesses an energy ν) of

$$\varepsilon = h\nu = \frac{hc}{\lambda} \qquad \text{(Eqn. 9-1)}$$

Here, h is Planck's constant (h = 6.62606896(33)×10^{-34} [J ·s]) and c is a speed of light in vacuum (c = 2.99792×10^8 [m ·sec^{-1}]). Therefore, a total photon energy E_p with number of photon of n_p is given as

$$E_p = n_p\varepsilon = n_p h\nu = n_p\left(\frac{hc}{\lambda}\right) \qquad \text{(Eqn. 10-9)}$$

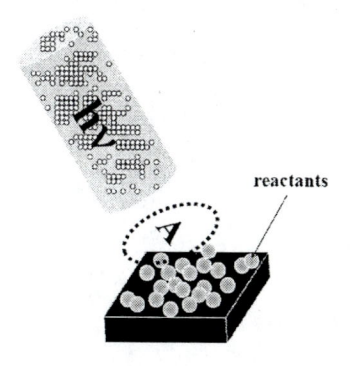

Fig. 10-9 Photons hitting to the reactants

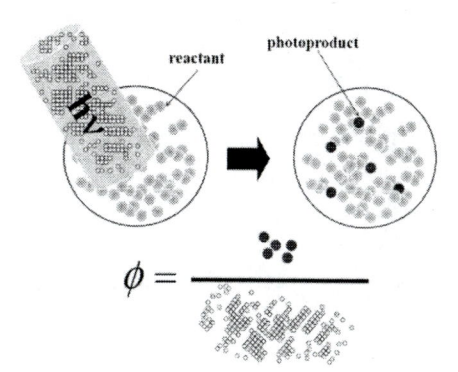

Fig. 10-10 A concept of "Quantum Yield"

Chapter 10 Intermolecular Interaction and Essences of Spectroscopy

Conventionally, we use "Einstein" as a unit indicating 1 mole of photon (i.e., 1 Einstein= 6.023×10^{23} photons). If we have a system where a reactant is changed into a product due to photo excitation (or absorbing the light), we can calculate the efficiency photons to change into how many of products (photoproducts). This is called **quantum yield** (ϕ) and defined as,

$$\phi = n_\pi / n_p \qquad \text{(Eqn. 10--10)}$$

Here, n_π is the number of photoproducts and n_p is the number of photons. The number of photons are always more (or equal) than the number of photoproducts. ($n_\pi \leq n_p$). Therefore, quantum yield is smaller than (or equal) 1. ($\phi \leq 1$)

EXERCISE 10-3
An average wavelength 550 [nm] of light 10 [W] was irradiated for 100 [sec] to a strain of algae and 5.75×10^{-4} [mol] of O_2 was produced. Calculate the quantum yield of O_2 formation.

ANSWER
Total energy of the photons absorbed (E_p) is

❶ (10[W]) × (100 [sec])
= 10^3 [J]

$$E_p = n_p \varepsilon = n_p h\nu = n_p (hc/\lambda) \qquad \text{(Eqn. 10-9)}$$

Thus,

$$n_p = E_p/\varepsilon = E_p(\lambda/hc)$$

Number of photons
$n_p = (10^3 \text{ [J]})(550 \times 10^{-9} \text{ [m]}) / \{6.62 \times 10^{-34} \text{ [J sec]} \times 3 \times 10^8 \text{[m/sec]}\}$
= 2.8×10^{21}

❷ Number of Einsteins = $(2.8 \times 10^{21} \text{ [J sec]}) / (6.0 \times 10^{23})$
= 4.6×10^{-3} [Einsteins (moles of photons)]
Number of products = 5.75×10^{-4} [mol]

❷ The quantum yield is

$$\phi = n_\pi / n_p \qquad \text{(Eqn. 10-10)}$$

❸ $$\phi = \frac{Number\ of\ molecules\ reacted}{Number\ of\ photons\ absorbed}$$

Quantum yield = $5.75 \times 10^{-4} / (4.6 \times 10^{-3})$
❹ = 0.125

---

❶ [W] = [J/sec]
❷ 1 [Einsteins] = 1 moles of photons
❸ Don't make this upside down.
❹ Make sure $\phi \leq 1$.

Chapter 10 Intermolecular Interaction and Essences of Spectroscopy

☹ MCM Most Common Mistake (42) -"Why I cannot count photons correctly?"

If you cannot obtain the correct number of photons, n_p, it can be due to the fact that the energy of one photon (ε) is not correctly calculated. Most mistakes found in the calculation of the one photon energy seem to come from the inconsistency of the unit. I recommend you to use the speed of light of c = 2.99792×10^8 [m sec^{-1}] instead of c = 2.99792×10^{10} [cm sec^{-1}]. This is because that the Planck constant uses the unit of [J] =[kg m^2 sec^{-2}] and the power of the light uses the unit of [W] = [J sec^{-1}]. The unit of the wavelength should be cautioned to use [m] unit but not others. (As is seen in **EXERCISE 10-3**, [nm] unit is commonly used. Make sure that you convert it to 10^{-9} [m].) If it helps you to know a ball park figure of energy of one photon (ε), it is around 10^{-19} J for the visible light.

☹ MCM Most Common Mistake (43) -"What's wrong with my quantum yield, it was perfect!"

You should always check if your calculated quantum yield (ϕ) is less than 1 ($\phi \leq 1$). By mistaking "quantum yield" as the amount of photon quanta, a very large quantum yield can be left untouched.

10-4 Intermolecular Forces

The force that dominates between the molecules are called **inter molecular forces**. (Fig. 10-11) Compared to the intra molecular force (bonding), the inter molecular forces are regarded as a weaker forces. The character of the intermolecular force determines many bulk property, since the bulk state is made out of the many molecules aggregated together. Thus, the forces between molecules will determine the character of the bulk. There are roughly five inter molecular forces, which I would like to focus in this section as shown in the **Table 10-1**.

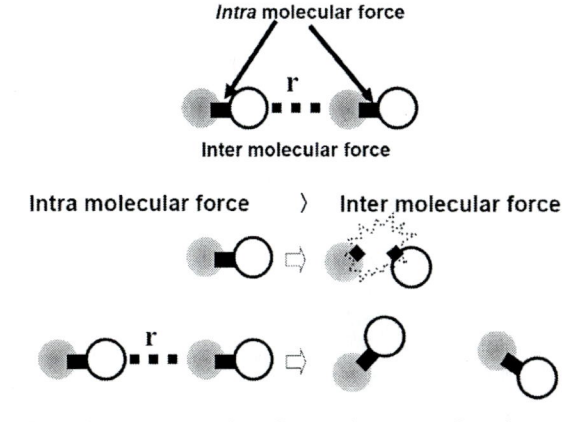

Fig. 10-11 Intramolecular and intermolecular forces.

Table 10-1 Summary of intermolecular forces.

Type	Distance (r) dependence	Typical value [kJ/mol]	Comment
Ion-ion	1/r	250	Only between ions
Ion-dipole	1/r^2	~15	
Dipole-dipole	1/r^3	~2	Between polar molecules
London (Dispersion)	1/r^6	~2	Between all types of molecules
Hydrogen bond		~20	

443

Chapter 10 Intermolecular Interaction and Essences of Spectroscopy

Fig. 10-12 Coulomb's law model.

The interactions which are not involved in the bonding can be categorized as **non-covalent Interactions**. The **Table 10-1** can be regarded as an important index to show the order of the interaction force (or magnitude). The ion-ion interaction is the highest due to an involvement of the **Coulombic interaction** (electrostatic interaction). The next strong interaction can be ion-dipole, where ion is also involved. Then **dipole-dipole interaction** or **London (dispersion) forces**. The extra category of the dipole-dipole interaction is **Hydrogen bonding** which has a different magnitude in dipole-dipole interaction.

The **Coulomb's Law** is an important principle which explains interaction between ions but also qualitatively explains the dipole-dipole interaction or any partial charges involved interactions. (**Fig. 10-12**)

$$U(r) = \frac{q_1 q_2}{4\pi\varepsilon_0 r} \quad \text{(Eqn. 10-11)}$$

Here, the unit of q_1 and q_2 are Coulombs and the unit of the r is given in [m]. The ε_0 is an electrostatic or permittivity constant (ε_0 =8.85418782×10^{-12} [F·m^{-1}] or [C^{2}N^{-1} m^{-2}]). The unit for the U(r) is in [J]. This formula can be expressed in different way as:

$$U(r) = 1389 \left(\frac{q_1 q_2}{r}\right) \quad \text{(Eqn. 10-12)}$$

Here, the unit of q_1 and q_2 are electron charges and the unit of the r is given in Å. The unit for the U(r) is in kJ/mol.

EXERCISE 10-4
Calculate the Coulombic potential for $q_1 = -1$ electronic charge and $q_2 = +1$ electronic charge R = 1.0 [Å].

ANSWER

$$U(r) = 1389(q_1 q_2/r) \quad \text{(Eqn. 10-12)}$$

$q_1 = -1$, $q_2 = +1$, and R=1.0 [Å]

$$U(r) = 1389 \frac{(-1)(+1)}{1.0}$$

= −1389 [kJ/mol]

When you use (**Eqn. 10-12**), the unit is [kJ/mol] and
1) you do **not** need to convert the unit of charge into [esu]
2) unit of the distance is [Å]
3) permittivity constant=8.854 × 10^{-12} [C^{2}N^{-1} m^{-2}] is not necessary when you use the above equation.
Negative sign shows that force is an attractive.

Chapter 10 Intermolecular Interaction and Essences of Spectroscopy

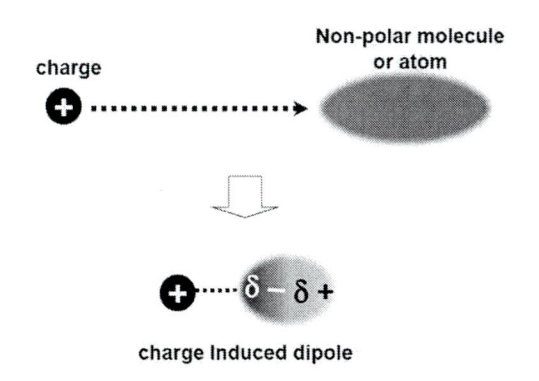

Fig. 10-13 A charge induced dipole interaction.

Generally, the Hydrogen bond is the dipole-dipole interaction between H atom in a polar bond and O, N, and F.(**Fig. 10-14**) In this Figure X is electronegative atom (e.g., O, N, and F), and the lone pairs of X interact with H atom by Coulombic force. The hydrogen bonding is quite important and crucial for the formation of the base pair in DNA or RNA. The structure can be controlled by the force dominated by hydrogen bonding, and this totally makes senses you see so many opportunities for the H and O atoms to meet in the structure. (**Fig. 10-15**)

The sum of the attractive or repulsive forces between molecules not originating from covalent and electrostatic interaction is categorized as **van der Waals interaction**. It is divided into the following three cases: i).dipole-dipole interaction, ii) dipole – induced dipole interaction (**Debye force**), and iii) induced dipole- induced dipole interaction (**London dispersion force**). When we describe these weak forces, polarizability is a key issue to characterize the degree of the interaction. The polarizability is like a measure of ease with which the electron density can be distorted. As the larger the number of electrons gets, the greater its polarizability.

The dipole-dipole interaction and dispersion forces (London force) are two major relatively weak forces. The dispersion Forces are the forces between non-polar molecule (atom) and ion or polar molecule. The dipole-dipole interaction is treated as "a kind of" Coulombic force, since the forces are originated from electrostatic interaction between partial charges. Since a dipole possesses a non-spherical shape, a degree of interaction can heavily depend upon the directionality of the mutual dipoles.

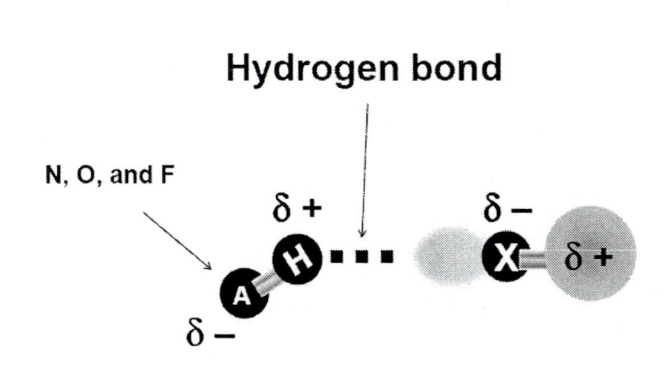

Fig. 10-14 Hydrogen bond.

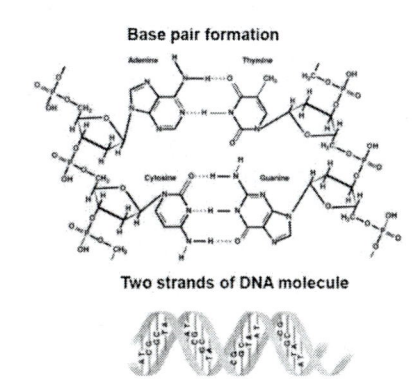

Fig. 10-15 Base pair formation

$$U(r) = [\vec{\mu_1} \cdot \vec{\mu_2} - 3(\vec{r} \cdot \vec{\mu_1})(\vec{r} \cdot \vec{\mu_2})]/r^3 \quad \text{(Eqn. 10-13)}$$

Here, the dipole 1 and 2 are indicated by a vectors ($\vec{\mu_1}$ and $\vec{\mu_2}$), and the distance between two dipoles are given by r. (When the distance is represented as a vector, it is noted as $\vec{r}$.) (**Fig. 10-16**)

Chapter 10 Intermolecular Interaction and Essences of Spectroscopy

When a dipole approaches to a non-polar molecule (or atom), the dipole is induced on this non-polar species. This interaction is called as dipole and –induced dipole interaction. (**Fig. 10-17**) The description of this force can be equally treated as the dipole-dipole interaction while the magnitude is smaller.

The London dispersion force arises from induced instantaneous dipoles in molecules. (**Fig. 10-18**) The London dispersion force is proportional to the 6th power of the distance between dipoles as,

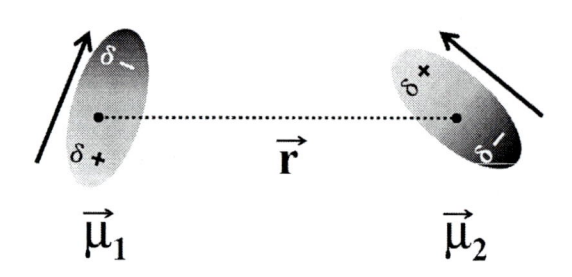

Fig. 10-16 A dipole-dipole interaction.

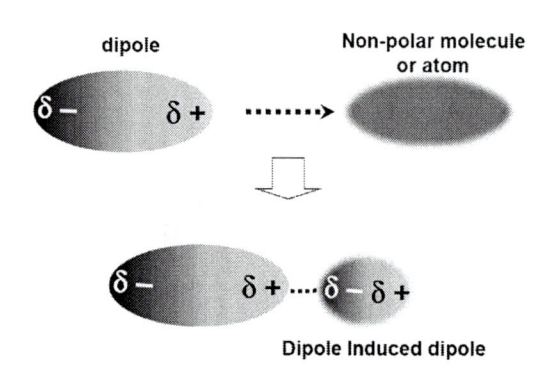

Fig. 10-17 A dipole induced dipole interaction

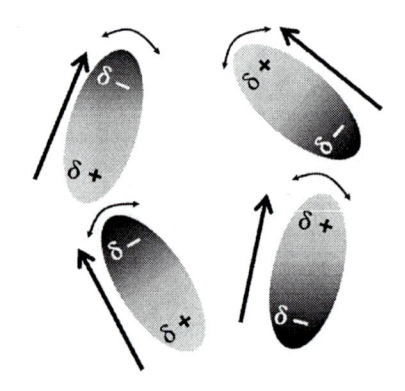

Fig. 10-18 An instantaneous induced-dipole interactions.

$$U(r) = -\alpha_{1,2}/r^6$$

Here, $\alpha_{1,2}$ is the constant between induced dipole 1 and 2, and the r is the distance between two dipoles.

10-5 Absorption of the Light

i. Beer-Lambert Law

One of the common spectroscopic investigation of the molecule is the absorption spectroscopy. The relationship between the intensity of the light emitted to the sample and that of passed a sample is described by **Beer-Lambert Law.**

$$I = I_0 10^{-\varepsilon l c} = I_0 10^{-A} \qquad \text{(Eqn. 10-14)}$$

Here, I_0 is intensity of incident light [einstein cm^{-2} sec^{-1}] and I is intensity of transmitting light. [einstein cm^{-2} sec^{-1}], and *l* is the path length [cm], c is the concentrtaion of sample [M], ε is molar absorptivity [M^{-1} cm^{-1}], and A is called as absorbance [optical density, OD].(**Fig. 10-19**) If the (**Eqn. 10-14**) is solved for A, the absorbance is expressed as

$$A = \log\left(I_0/I\right) = \varepsilon l c \qquad \textbf{(Eqn. 10-15)}$$

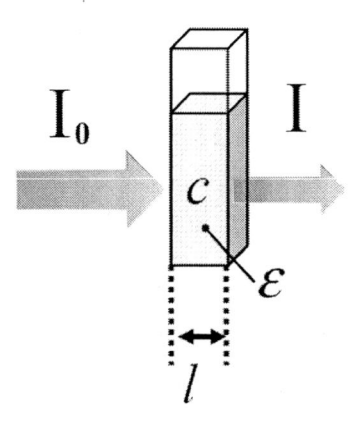

Fig. 10-19 Beer-Lambert Law

The another common index used in absorption spectroscopy is transmission (T)
$$T = I/I_0$$
and relationship between absorbance (A) and transmission (T) is, therefore,

$$T = 10^{-A}$$

(It is **not** T=1/A like many of my past students believed! So please be careful about this.)

Let's take an example of a photochemical reaction, and how Beer-Lambert law (and quantum yield) is applied. If the reactant A is changed into photoproduct B by the photochemical process (photon with energy hν),

$$A \xrightarrow{h\nu} B$$

Recalling what we learned in **Chapter 9**, the speed of the photoproduct formation, v [M sec^{-1}], is given by

$$v = -d[B]/dt = -2303\phi I_0 A/l \qquad (10\text{-}16)$$

The integrated expression for the concentration of the photoproduct, [B], is

$$[B] = [B]_0 e^{-2303\phi I_0 \varepsilon t} = [B]_0 e^{-kt} \qquad (10\text{-}17)$$

Please note that most of the photochemical reactions proceeds by the first order.

> **EXERCISE 10-5**
> Chloroplasts from spinach can photo-catalyze dye (D).
> $$2H_2O + 2D \xrightarrow{h\nu} (chloroplast) \to O_2 + 2DH_2$$
> The reaction speed of this reaction was, v = 6.5 ×10^{-12} [mol cm^{-3} sec^{-1}], when an incident light of I$_o$= 40 ×10^{-15} [Einstein cm^{-2} sec^{-1}] was emitted.
> The absorbance of the light at 625 [nm] is $A_{625}{}^{1cm}$ = 0.140, and path length of a sample cell is l = 1 [cm]. Calculate the quantum yield of this reaction.

ANSWER
I$_o$= 40 ×10^{-15} [Einstein cm^{-2} sec^{-1}]
v = 6.5 ×10^{-12} [mol cm^{-3} sec^{-1}]
l = [1 cm]
$A_{625}{}^{1cm}$ = 0.140

❶ $$v = -\frac{2303\phi I_0 A}{l} \qquad \text{(Eqn. 10-16)}$$

❷ $$\phi = \frac{vl}{(2.303)I_0 A 1000}$$

$$\frac{(6.5 \times 10^{-12}[mol\ cm^{-3}\ sec^{-1}])(1\ [cm])}{2.303(1000)(40 \times 10^{-15}[einstein\ cm^{-2}\ sec^{-1}])(0.140)}$$

❸ = 0.50

❶ When you use (**Eqn. 10-16**), the unit of v is [mol cm^{-3} sec^{-1}] but not [M sec^{-1}], and
1) unit of I$_o$ is [Einstein cm^{-2} sec^{-1}]
2) unit of the absorbance is [OD] (or you can think it as arbotraty unit or dimensionless for making it easy.)
3) unit of length *l* is [cm]

❷ The value "1000" is from
v : [mol cm^{-3} sec^{-1}]=1000 × [mol L^{-1} sec^{-1}],1 [L] =1000[cm^{-3}]

❸ Confirm that $\phi \leq 1$

When two different components are existent in a system, the absorbance is expressed as a linear sum of these components. When two component α and β are mixed in the solution, the absorbance at wavelength λ [nm], A$_\lambda$, is given as:

$$A_\lambda = A_\lambda^\alpha + A_\lambda^\beta$$

Here, A_λ^α is the absorbance of component α at wavelength λ [nm] and A_λ^β the absorbance of component β at wavelength λ [nm]. From Lambert-Beer's law, the absorbance at wavelength λ is given as shown in (**Eqn. 10-18**)

$$A_\lambda = \varepsilon_\lambda c l \qquad \text{(Eqn. 10-18)}$$

Chapter 10 Intermolecular Interaction and Essences of Spectroscopy

Thus, if the concentration of the component α and β are [α] and [β], respectively, and the path length of the sample is l [cm],

$$A_\lambda^\alpha = \varepsilon_\lambda^\alpha l[\alpha]$$
$$A_\lambda^\beta = \varepsilon_\lambda^\beta l[\beta]$$

Here, the extinction coefficient of α and β at wavelength λ is given as $\varepsilon_\lambda^\alpha$ and $\varepsilon_\lambda^\beta$, respectively. Therefore, by inserting A_λ^α and A_λ^β into the formula for A_λ,

$$A_\lambda = \varepsilon_\lambda^\alpha l[\alpha] + \varepsilon_\lambda^\beta l[\beta] = \left(\varepsilon_\lambda^M[\alpha] + \varepsilon_\lambda^N[\beta]\right)l \qquad \text{(Eqn. 10-19)}$$

If you take the measurement of the absorbance of this mixture at two wavelengths, λ_1 and λ_2 [nm] you are able to extract the concentration of the two mixtures as

$$[\alpha] = \left(1/l\right)\left\{\left(\varepsilon_{\lambda_2}^\beta A_{\lambda_1} - \varepsilon_{\lambda_1}^\beta A_{\lambda_2}\right) \Big/ \left(\varepsilon_{\lambda_1}^\alpha \varepsilon_{\lambda_2}^\beta - \varepsilon_{\lambda_2}^\alpha \varepsilon_{\lambda_1}^\beta\right)\right\} \qquad \text{(Eqn. 10-20)}$$

$$[\beta] = \left(1/l\right)\left\{\left(\varepsilon_{\lambda_1}^\alpha A_{\lambda_2} - \varepsilon_{\lambda_2}^\alpha A_{\lambda_1}\right) \Big/ \left(\varepsilon_{\lambda_1}^\alpha \varepsilon_{\lambda_2}^\beta - \varepsilon_{\lambda_2}^\alpha \varepsilon_{\lambda_1}^\beta\right)\right\} \qquad \text{(Eqn. 10-21)}$$

The molar extinction coefficient of α at wavelength λ_1 and λ_2 [nm] are given by $\varepsilon_{\lambda_1}^\alpha$ and $\varepsilon_{\lambda_2}^\alpha$, respectively. Also, and the molar extinction coefficient of β at wavelength λ_1 and λ_2 [nm] are given by $\varepsilon_{\lambda_1}^\beta$ and $\varepsilon_{\lambda_2}^\beta$, respectively.

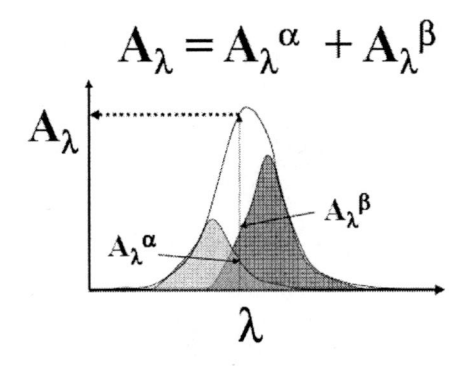

Fig. 10-20 Application of Beer's Law

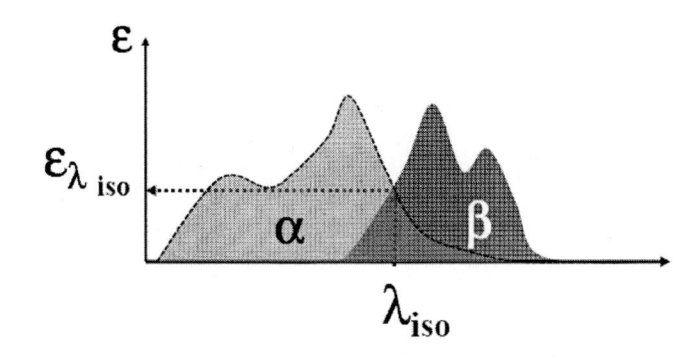

Fig. 10-21 The Isosbestic point is the point

When the absorbance of the two components is identical, that particular wavelength is called isosbestic point. At an isosbestic point, λ_{iso}, the molar extinction coefficient (ε_{iso}) of two components are equal.

$$\varepsilon^{\alpha}_{\lambda_{iso}} = \varepsilon^{\beta}_{\lambda_{iso}} = \varepsilon_{\lambda_{iso}}$$

Thus, the absorbance, $A_{\lambda_{iso}}$, is given as

$$A_{\lambda_{iso}} = \left(\varepsilon^{\alpha}_{\lambda_{iso}}[\alpha] + \varepsilon^{\beta}_{\lambda_{iso}}[\beta]\right) l = \varepsilon_{\lambda_{iso}} l ([\alpha] + [\beta]) \quad \text{(Eqn. 10-22)}$$

ii. Absorbance and Thermochemical Values

If the absorption spectrum is taken at various temperatures, the resulting information can be utilized for extracting reaction equilibrium constants and three thermochemical values (ΔH, ΔS, and ΔG). We will see how this is conducted in helix deformation reaction (**Fig. 10-22**). Let's assume that the double helix (D) can be formed or decomposed into single stranded monomer, (S and R), as

$$D \rightleftarrows S + R$$

For current situation, let's assume that only helix exist at T_1 [°C], whereas all helix decomposed into single strands S and R at the higher temperature T_2 [°C].

The equilibrium constant of this reaction is given as:

$$K = \frac{[S][R]}{[D]} \quad \text{(Eqn. 10-23)}$$

The double strand can be decomposed into single strand S and R by thermal decomposition. The amount of the D or S, R can depend on the temperature and the equilibrium constant can be also depending upon the temperature. (**Fig. 10-22**) The total concentration of the strands C_o is given by the summation of the [D] and [S], and [R]. However, there are two single strands in one double strand. Therefore,

$$C_o = 2[D] + [S] + [R]$$

Since [S] = [R],

$$C_o = 2[D] + 2[S]$$

Fig. 10-22 The formation of double stranded helix.

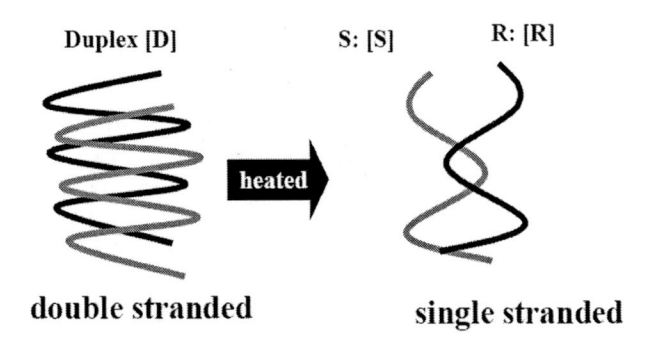

C_0 = total concentration of strands
= 2[D] + [S] + [R]

In order to reduce the numbers of the parameters, we adopt the concept of *f* as a fraction in single strands. This is defined as,

$$f = 2[S]/C_o$$

Therefore, the above formula gives an expression of [S] as,

$$[S] = C_o f / 2$$

If the fraction in single strands is given by f, the fraction of double strands is given as (1 – f), And this is defined as

$$1 - f = 2[D]/C_o$$

Thus, the concentration of [D] is

$$[D] = C_o(1-f)/2$$

By substituting [S], [R], and [D] into the equilibrium constant,

$$K = \frac{[S][R]}{[D]} = \frac{f^2 C_o^2}{4(C_o/2)(1-f)} = \frac{f^2 C_o}{2(1-f)}$$

If the absorbance of the strands is identified at the wavelength λ [nm], the absorbance at given temperature, T,

$$A_{\lambda,T} = \varepsilon_{\lambda,T}^D [D] + \varepsilon_{\lambda,T}^S [S] + \varepsilon_{\lambda,T}^R [R] = \varepsilon_{\lambda,T}^D [D] + (\varepsilon_{\lambda,T}^S + \varepsilon_{\lambda,T}^R)[S]$$

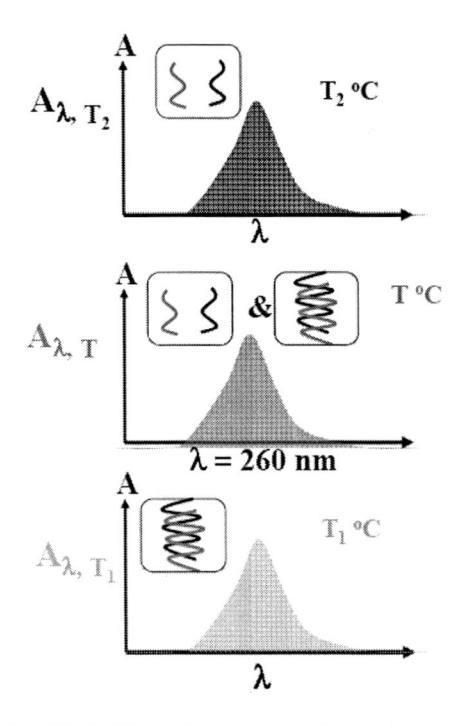

Fig. 10-23 The absorbance at various temperatures.

At the T_2 [°C], we know that no [D] is existent. Thus, absorbance at λ [nm] is given as

$$A_{\lambda,T_2} = \left(\varepsilon^S_{\lambda,T_2} + \varepsilon^R_{\lambda,T_2}\right)[S]$$
$$= \left(\varepsilon^S_{\lambda,T_2} + \varepsilon^R_{\lambda,T_2}\right)(C_o/2)$$

Here, we assume that $C_o \approx 2[S]$. On the other hand there will be no single strands at T_1 [°C].

$$A_{\lambda,T_1} = \varepsilon^D_{\lambda,T_1}[D] = \varepsilon^D_{\lambda,T_1}(C_o/2)$$

Here, $C_o \approx 2[D]$ was assumed.
The absorbance at the fraction of f is given as:

$$A_\lambda = A_{\lambda,T_1}(1-f) + A_{\lambda,T_2}f$$

And the fraction at any temperature ($A_{260,T}$) at λ [nm] can be given as,

$$f = \frac{A_{\lambda,T} - A_{\lambda,T_1}}{A_{\lambda,T_2} - A_{\lambda,T_1}}$$

The situation of the spectrum at T_1, T_2 [°C] and T in between are given in (**Fig. 10-23**) Here, we can connect temperature dependence of equilibrium constant s with absorbance at various temperature.
Let's recall van't Hoff equation (**Eqn. 2-13**)

$$\ln\frac{K_2}{K_1} = -\frac{\Delta H^o_{rxn}}{R}\left[\frac{1}{T_2} - \frac{1}{T_1}\right] \qquad \text{(Eqn. 2-13)}$$

The van't Hoff plot of ln K as a function of 1/T provides the line (if they follow) with a slope of $-\Delta H°/R$, so that you can get the value of the enthalpy change as well as the direction of heat (exothermic or endothermic). (**Fig. 2-6**) We can use this concept to estimate the enthalpy change first. This is an important first step for you to know to connect between chemical reaction (equilibrium constant) and the thermal property (enthalpy change in this case). Since this is a very good spot to review the thermochemical properties and its derivation from one after another, let me point out an important procedure we conducted in **Chapter 2**. Please view (**Fig. 2-6**) Starting from an equilibrium constant K, $\Delta G°$, $\Delta H°$, and $\Delta S°$ are obtained. [Please remember that the $\Delta G°$ is defined at a given temperature. I hope you recall "**Most Common Mistake(16)**".

Chapter 10 Intermolecular Interaction and Essences of Spectroscopy

EXERCISE 10-6

A double-stranded oligonucleotide whose concentration is 100 [μM] is melted in 1 [M] NaCl, pH 7. Below 10 [°C], the solution contains only duplex; above 60 [°C], the solution contains only single strands. From the temperature dependence of the equilibrium constant, calculate the ΔG°, ΔH°, and ΔS°, all at 25 [°C].

Assume that the molar extinction coefficients of the duplexes and its single strands are independent of temperature.

Temperature [°C]	A: absorbance
10	0.7900
15	0.800
20	0.813
25	0.822
35	0.852
30	0.890
40	0.940
45	0.971
50	0.990
55	1.003
60	1.114

ANSWER

K = [S][R]/[D]
C_0 = total concentration of strands = 200 [μm]
C_0 = 2[D] + [S] + [R]

Here, [S] = [R] and C_0 = 2[D] + 2[S]
The fraction in single strands, $f = 2[S]/C_0$
$1 - f$ = fraction in double strands = $2[D]/C_0$
The equilibrium constant the fraction, concentration,

$$K = \frac{f^2 C_0}{2(1-f)}$$

Thus,

$$K = \frac{f^2 C_0^2}{4(C_0/2)(1-f)} = \frac{f^2 C_0}{2(1-f)}$$

A = ε_D [D] + ε_S [S] + ε_R [R] = ε_D [D] + ($\varepsilon_S + \varepsilon_R$) [S]
A_{60} = A(60 [°C]) = ($\varepsilon_S + \varepsilon_R$) ($C_0 / 2$)
A_{10} = A(10 [°C]) = (ε_D) ($C_0 / 2$)
A = A_{10} (1 - f) + A_{60} f

By using the relationship of fraction, f, and the equilibrium constant, K,

$$f = \frac{A - A_{10}}{A_{60} - A_{10}}$$

Temperature [°C]	A: absorbance	f	K
10	0.7900	0.0000	0.000
15	0.800	0.0309	0.098
20	0.813	0.710	0.542
25	0.822	0.0988	1.082
35	0.852	0.1914	4.528
30	0.890	0.3086	13.78
40	0.940	0.4630	39.91
45	0.971	0.5586	70.71
50	0.990	0.6173	99.56
55	1.003	0.6574	126.15
60	1.114	1.000	

❻ Use the least square fit to ln K vs. (1/T) gives
$$\ln \frac{K_2}{K_1} = -\frac{\Delta H^o_{rxn}}{R}\left[\frac{1}{T_2} - \frac{1}{T_1}\right] \qquad \text{(Eqn. 2-13)}$$
ln K = 45.06 − 1.747× 10⁴ (1/T)

❼ ΔH° = 145.2 [kJ/mol]

The Gibbs energy at given temperature and the equilibrium constant is
$$\Delta G^o = -RT \ln K \qquad \text{(Eqn. 2-10)}$$

❽ At T = 25 [°C],
ΔG° = (− 8.314)(298.15) ln (1.082) =−195.37 [J/mol]

❾ At the end the entropy can be obtained from the

$$\Delta G = \Delta H - T\Delta S \qquad \text{(Eqn. 2-2)}$$

❿ ΔS° = 487 [J/ K mol]

---

❶ Don't forget that you have [S] and [R]

❷ [S] =[R] is a key condition.

❸ In two components' fraction, one side is a then the other side is 1 −a.

❹ T=10 [°C] (double strands only) and T= 60 [°C](single strands only) are two extreme cases.

❺ When f=0 K=0, and f=1, K= ∞. We cannot use the value when f=1 for plotting

❻ MS EXCEL- LINEST function

❼ Here, unit is [kJ/mol]

❽ Convert temperature in kelvins unit.

❾ Make absolutely sure that ΔG° is the value at T= 25 [°C]. (Please note that we are assuming that ΔG° is temperature independent)

❿ Here, unit is [J/K mol]

iii) Circular Dichroism

The amplitude of an electric field of electromagnetic wave can be prepared as linear polarized light or circularly polarized light as shown in (**Fig. 10-24**). The direction of circular motion can be divided into either "left circularly polarized light" and "right circularly polarized light".

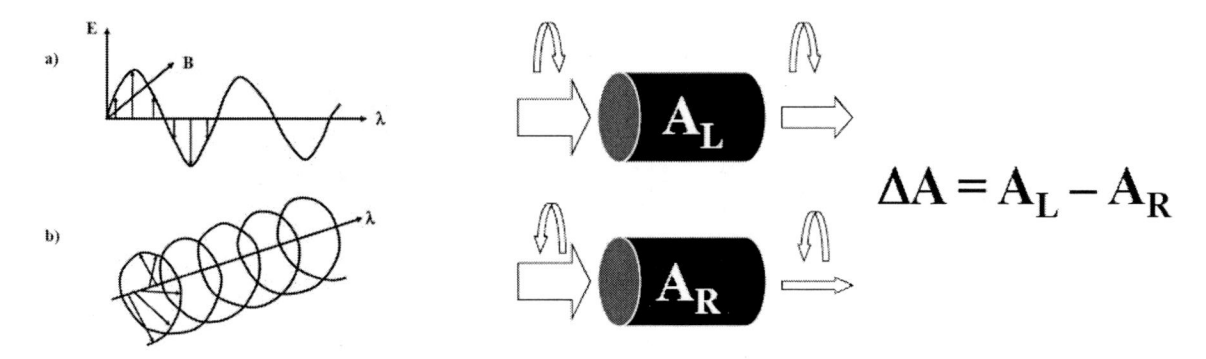

Fig. 10-24 a) Linear polarized light and b) circularly polarized light.

Fig. 10-25 The circular dichroism

The word "**dichroism**" represents the phenomena in which light with different polarizations are absorbed by different amounts. The **circular dichroism** is the difference of the absorbance between the light sources with two different circularly polarized light; A_L: absorbance from the left-circularly polarized light and A_R: absorption from right circularly polarized light. (See **Fig. 10-25**)

$$\Delta A = A_L - A_R \qquad \text{(Eqn. 10-24)}$$

This is the differential absorption of left- and right-circularly polarized light. (**Fig. 10-24**) there are some approaches to describe this physical property. The circular dichroism ($\Delta A \neq 0$) occurs at the absorption of many optically active biological molecules, (originating from their dextrorotary and levorotary components). The straightforward definition of circular dichroism is the difference of molar extinction coefficient of absorption for left circular polarized light (ε_L) and right circular polarized light (ε_R). Based on the definition of molar extinction coefficient in (**Eqn. 10-18**)

$$\varepsilon_\lambda = \frac{A_\lambda}{cl} \qquad \text{(Eqn. 10-18)}$$

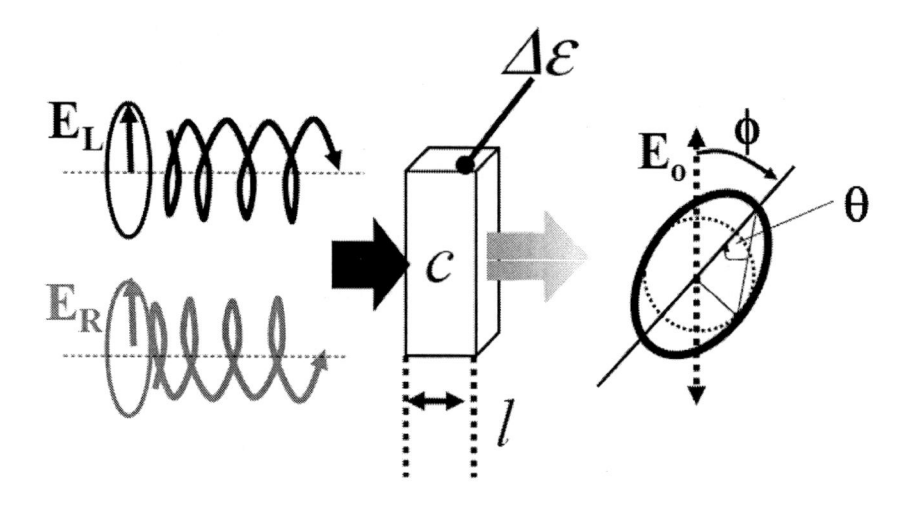

Chapter 10 Intermolecular Interaction and Essences of Spectroscopy

Fig. 10-26 The rotational angle and molar ellipticity.

Thus, **molar circular dichroism**, $\Delta\varepsilon$, is defined as:

$$\Delta\varepsilon = \varepsilon_L - \varepsilon_R = \frac{(A_L - A_R)}{lc} \quad \text{(Eqn. 10-25)}$$

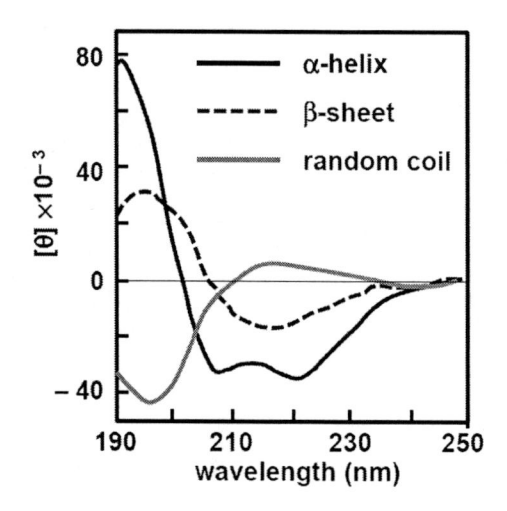

Fig. 10-27 The feature of circular dichroism.

Here, path length is l [cm]) and concentration of substance is c [M]. Thus, you can derive concentrtaion (c) of unknown sample by measuring $\Delta\varepsilon$ as:

$$c = \frac{(A_L - A_R)}{l\Delta\varepsilon} \quad \text{(Eqn. 10-25)}$$

Chapter 10 Intermolecular Interaction and Essences of Spectroscopy

While $\Delta\varepsilon$ is a directly measured value from circular dichroism spectrometer and I prefer to stick with this, molar ellipticity [θ] (unit is [degree cm² dmol⁻¹]) is the commonly reported value. (As far as I know, a customary usage of [θ] is just a simply historical reason.) The relationship is simple enough as:

$$[\theta] = 3298\Delta\varepsilon \quad \text{(Eqn. 10-26)}$$

Thus, let's not complain about converting between $\Delta\varepsilon$ and [θ]. Most importantly, the circular dichroism is commonly used for identifying the secondary structure of the protein (α-helix, β-sheet, and random coil). **(Fig. 10-27)**

MCM Most Common Mistake (44) "Ellipticity, θ" and "Molar Ellipticity, [θ]". Are they the same?

They are different but can easily be converted into each other. Because of the fact that the optical active molecule absorbs the two different circularly polarized differently, the net result of electric field appears as "elliptical" shape. As the difference of absorbance A_L and A_R increases, this ellipticity increases. The ellipticity is expressed by an angle defined in **(Fig. 10-28)** As a practice, ellipticity is usually reported in angles of mill degrees [mdeg or m°], whereas Molar ellipticity, [θ], is historically [deg cm²/dmol]. (Isn't this tedious!?) Regarding to how ellipticity, θ, is related with molar ellipticity [θ], I want you to take a look at the section of "**How did they get these formula?**" I just show the last outcome.

$$[\theta] = \frac{100\theta}{cl}$$

Here, c is the concentration [M] and l is a path length [cm]. Recall that conversion from $\Delta\varepsilon$ molar extinction coefficient to [θ] is

$$[\theta] = 3298\Delta\varepsilon \text{ (Eqn. 10-26)}$$

To calculate molar ellipticity, the sample concentration [g/L], cell path length [cm], and the molecular weight [g/mol] must be known. When you use CD machine, please take a good look at which value and unit are given to you.

EXERCISE 10-7

The circular dichroism was examined for the pure components 1.00×10^{-4} [M] concentrations of nucleotides per 1 [L] with a cell-length of 1 [cm]:

Wavelength [nm]	$A_L - A_R$ (DNA)	$A_L - A_R$ (RNA)
260	0.00	-6.0×10^{-4}
240	-2.20×10^{-4}	0.00

When RNA and DNA is mixed, its circular dichroism was obtained as $\Delta A(260 \text{ [nm]}) = 3.12 \times 10^{-4}$ and $\Delta A(240 \text{ [nm]}) = -0.24 \times 10^{-4}$. What are the concentrations of DNA and RNA in the mixture?

ANSWER

$$\Delta \varepsilon = \varepsilon_L - \varepsilon_R = \frac{(A_L - A_R)}{lc}$$

RNA :

$\varepsilon_L - \varepsilon_R$ (260 [nm])
$= (6.00 \times 10^{-4})/(1.00 \times 10^{-4})$
$= 6.00$ [M^{-1} cm^{-1}]
$c = (A_L - A_R) / l (\varepsilon_L - \varepsilon_R)$
$= (3.12 \times 10^{-4}) / (6.00)$
$= 0.52 \times 10^{-4}$ [M]

DNA :

$\varepsilon_L - \varepsilon_R$ (240 [nm])
$= (-2.20 \times 10^{-4})/(1.00 \times 10^{-4})$
$= -2.20$ [M^{-1} cm^{-1}]
$c = (A_L - A_R) / l (\varepsilon_L - \varepsilon_R)$
$= (-0.24 \times 10^{-4}) / (-2.20)$
$= 0.11 \times 10^{-4}$ [M]

We are obtaining molar circular dichroism

Careful with the unit.

The absorption of infrared (IR) radiation causes transitions between vibrational energy levels of a molecule (**infrared spectroscopy**). If molecule is made of N atoms, you can predict the number of vibration types (**normal modes of vibration**).

Linear molecule: Number of normal modes = 3N – 5
Non-linear molecule: Number of normal modes = 3N – 6

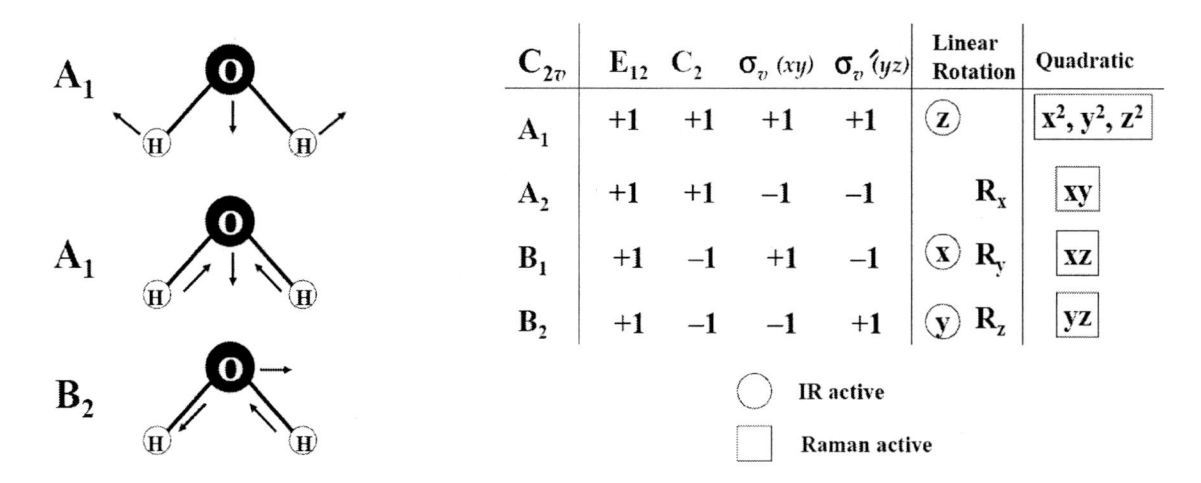

Chapter 10 Intermolecular Interaction and Essences of Spectroscopy

Fig. 10-27 Normal modes of water

Table 10-2 Character table for the C$_{2v}$ group

C$_{2v}$	E$_{12}$	C$_2$	σ_v (xy)	σ_v' (yz)	Linear Rotation	Quadratic
A$_1$	+1	+1	+1	+1	(z)	x², y², z²
A$_2$	+1	+1	−1	−1	R$_x$	xy
B$_1$	+1	−1	+1	−1	(x) R$_y$	xz
B$_2$	+1	−1	−1	+1	(y) R$_z$	yz

○ IR active
□ Raman active

Each normal mode of vibration has a fixed frequency. The formula on the previous page only lets you predict the "number" of normal modes but the symmetry of each mode needs to be categorized by group theory. Each normal mode possesses a specific frequency.

Here, let's examine water as an example. A molecular structure of water is categorized as a symmetrical group called C$_{2v}$ symmetry group. Since water is a non-linear molecule consisting of three atoms, number of normal modes =3×3− 6 =3. There are three normal modes of vibrations (A$_1$, A$_1$ and B$_2$ symmetry) in water. (See **Fig. 10-27**). However, there is a selection rule in vibrational modes, not all available normal modes may be observed by the IR absorption. By using a character table, one can predict if a normal mode has an allowed IR transition (**IR active**). Here, a character table of C$_{2v}$ symmetry group is shown in (**Table. 10-2**). Please take a look at the symmetry label provided at the right side of the table. If the symmetry label of a normal mode corresponds to x, y, or z, the fundamental transition for this normal mode will be IR active. For the case of water, there are two of A$_1$ symmetry modes and one B$_2$ symmetry mode. According to C$_{2v}$ Character Table A$_1$ symmetry has a symmetry label of "z" and B$_2$ symmetry has a symmetry label of y. Therefore both symmetry (or three normal modes shown in **Fig. 10-27**) is all IR active.

Routinely, IR absorption spectroscopy is conducted at room temperature. At room temperature major population of vibrational energy states of molecules are in their lowest levels (v = 0). Thus, the most probable vibrational transition occurs at the room temperature for each normal mode is from v=0 to the next highest level (v=1) with the transition energy ΔE given by (**Eqn. 9-21**).

$$\Delta E = h\nu_o \qquad \text{(Eqn. 9-21)}$$

The bands of spectrum originating from transition (v=0→ v=1) is called **fundamental bands**. Other transitions to higher excited states (e.g., v=0→ v=2) is called **overtone bands**. Generally, the absorbance of overtone bands is much weaker than fundamental bands.(**Fig. 10-29**).

While, I want you to wait this until next chapter (**Chapter 11**), there is another important vibrational spectroscopy originating from scattering not by absorption. It is **Raman spectroscopy.** If the symmetry label of a normal mode corresponds to products of x, y, or z (such as x^2 or yz) then the fundamental transition for this normal mode will be **Raman active**. For the case of water, A_1 possess x^2, y^2, and z^2 and B_2 possess yz. Thus, all modes (two A_1 and one B_2 symmetry) are all Raman active.

Fig. 10-29 Fundamental band and overtone band.

10-6 Fluorescence Spectroscopy

In fluorescence spectroscopy, emission of photon from vibrational states of the excited electronic state is observed. Since the energy of this emitted photon correspond to vibrational levels in the ground state, by analyzing the intensity and energy of fluorescence, the structure of the different vibrational levels are extracted. A mechanism of **fluorescence** is explained by the "**spontaneous emission**". Spontaneous emission is a decay of electronic energy levels under no external influence, and the direction and phase associated with the photon is random. If you happened to read the page of "**Nobel Prize and Your Knowledge in Chapter 9**", please compare spontaneous emission with **stimulated emission**, which possess specific traveling direction and the same phase.

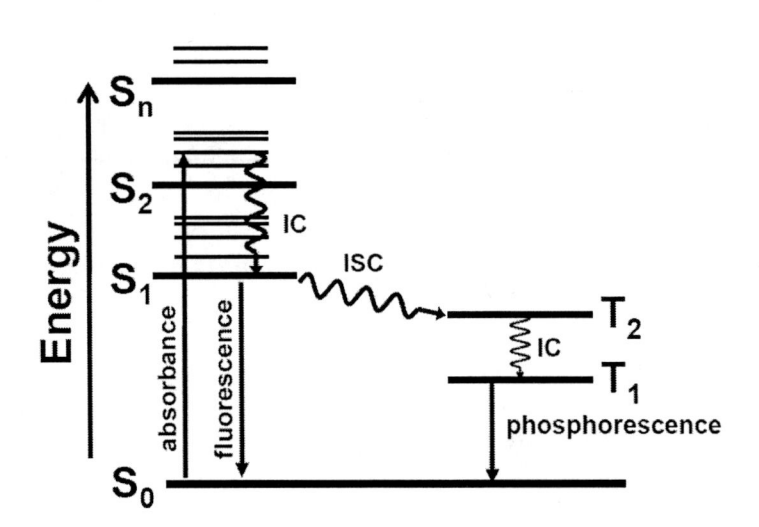

Fig. 10-30 Jablonski diagram. S_0, S_1, S_2, ...S_n : singlet electronic states.(S0: ground electronic state) T_1 and T_2: triplet electronic states. IC: internal conversion, ISC: intersystem crossing

In **Fig 10-30**, it shows the electronic states of a molecule and the transitions including fluorescence processes are shown. (**Jablonski diagram**) The states are arranged vertically by energy and grouped horizontally by spin multiplicity (S: singlet, T: triplet). The vibrational ground states of each electronic state are indicated with thick lines, the higher vibrational states with thinner lines. Here, straight arrows imply **radiative transitions** and squiggly arrows show **nonradiative transitions**. The internal conversions are the nonradiative process within the same spin multiplicity and intersystem crossing is nonradiative

Chapter 10 Intermolecular Interaction and Essences of Spectroscopy

process between different spin multiplicity states. The emission from the excited singlet state to the ground singlet state is fluorescence, whereas an emission from triplet state to the ground singlet state is called phosphorescence. Atypical lifetimes of fluorescence is 1 [μsec] to 1 [nsec] whereas and phosphorescence is longer and around 100 [μsec] to minutes or even hours. The relaxation of vibrational states is the common example of IC (internal conversion) with life time of ~1 [psec], and the typical life time of ISC (intersystem crossing) is 10 [nsec] to 1 [msec].

For Biochemistry or Biology students, the fluorescence from protein is an important tool to use as diagnostic of the conformational state of a protein. While the fluorescence of a folded protein is an ensemble from individual aromatic residues, most of the intrinsic fluorescence is originating from tryptophan (Trp) residues. Since many proteins contain only one or a few tryptophan residues, fluorescence of Trp is a good index to value conformational state of individual tryptophan residues. The absorption peak of λ_{abs} = 280 [nm] and an emission peak of λ_{flu} = 300~ 350 [nm]. Trp fluorescence spectrum is strongly influenced by the local environment of other residues. For example, *protonated* groups (Asp or Glu) are known to cause quenching of fluorescence of Trp by residing near Trp. Other good example is the a red-shift of Trp fluorescence when Trp is exposed to an hydrophilic environment from hydrophobic protein interior due to denaturization.

Fig. 10-30 Structure of L-tryptophan, tyrosine, and phenylalanine.

Other residues provide significant fluorescence is tyrosine and phenylalanine. (λ_{flu} = 295[nm].)

The fluorescence intensity decays exponentially and the intensity of the fluorescence at given time t, I(t) is given as

$$I(t) = I_o e^{-t/\tau} \quad \text{(Eqn. 10-27)}$$

Here, τ[sec] is fluorescence life time and decay rate k [1/sec] is an inverse of lifetime.

$$\frac{1}{\tau} = k \quad \text{(Eqn. 10-28)}$$

Let's define the rate of fluorescence intensity decays only with emission path is k_o. Also let's make the rate of fluorescence intensity decays with emission and other all decay paths is k_d.
Especially, an inverse of k_o is called as "natural life time", τ_o.

$$\tau_o = \frac{1}{k_o} \quad \text{(Eqn. 10-29)}$$

By using these two rates, **quantum yield of fluorescence** ϕf is defined as

$$\phi_f = \frac{k_o}{k_d} = \frac{number\ of\ photons\ fluoresced}{number\ of\ photons\ absorbed} \quad \text{(Eqn. 10-30)}$$

EXERCISE 10-8

An experiment observed that the fluorescence quantum yield of Chlorophyll *a* as 0.32. If natural life time of Chlorophyll *a* is 5 [nsec], what is the rate k_d?

ANSWER

① $\tau_o = \dfrac{1}{k_o}$ (Eqn. 10-29)

② $k_o = 1/(5 \times 10^{-9}\ [\text{sec}]) = 2 \times 10^{8}\ [\text{sec}^{-1}]$

$\varnothing_f = \dfrac{k_o}{k_d}$ (Eqn. 10-30)

③ $k_d = (k_o / \phi_f) = (2 \times 10^{8}\ [\text{sec}^{-1}] / 0.32)$

④ $= 6.25 \times 10^{8}\ [\text{sec}^{-1}]$

---

① τ is an inverse of k.

② 1 [nsec] = 10^{-9} [sec]

③ The unit of ϕ_f is dimensionless.

④ The unit of k is [sec^{-1}].

Chapter 10

How did you get these equations?
-The derivation of selected equations.

(Eqn. 10-16) $\quad v = -d[B]/dt = -2303\phi I_0 A/l$

(Eqn. 10-17) $\quad [B] = [B]_0 e^{-2303\phi I_0 \varepsilon t} = [B]_0 e^{-kt}$

$$v = -d[B]/dt = k[B]$$

$$v = -d[B]/dt = \phi I_{abs} 1000/l$$

Here, ϕ is quantum yield, I_{abs} is light absorbed by sample (, which is neither Io nor I) [Einsteins cm^{-2} sec^{-1}], and l is a path length [cm] of sample. The intensity of light absorbed (I_{abs}) is

$$I_{abs} = I_0 - I$$

and

$$I = I_0 10^{-A}$$

$$-d[B]/dt = \phi(I_0 - I)\, 1000/l = \phi I_0 (1 - 10^{-A})\, 1000/l$$

By using the relationship of

$$1 - 10^{-A} \cong 2.303 A$$

$$v = -d[B]/dt = -2303\phi I_0 A/l \quad\quad\text{(Eqn. 10-16)}$$

Since

$$A = \frac{\varepsilon [B]}{l}$$

$$-d[B]/dt = -2303\phi I_0 A/l = 2303\phi I_0 \varepsilon [B]$$

By arranging the above formula as

$$-d[B]/[B] = 2303\phi I_0 \varepsilon \, dt$$

The integration of both sides for [B] from $[B]_0$ to [B] and for t from t=0 to t gives,

$$-\int_{[B]_0}^{[B]} 1/[B] \, d[B] = 2303\phi I_0 \varepsilon \int_0^t dt$$

$$\ln\left([B]/[B]_0\right) = -2303\phi I_0 \varepsilon t = -kt$$

$$[B] = [B]_0 e^{-2303\phi I_0 \varepsilon t} = [B]_0 e^{-kt} \qquad \textbf{(Eqn. 10-17)}$$

(Eqn. 10-20)
$$[\alpha] = \left(1/l\right)\left\{\left(\varepsilon_{\lambda_2}^\beta A_{\lambda_1} - \varepsilon_{\lambda_1}^\beta A_{\lambda_2}\right) \Big/ \left(\varepsilon_{\lambda_1}^\alpha \varepsilon_{\lambda_2}^\beta - \varepsilon_{\lambda_2}^\alpha \varepsilon_{\lambda_1}^\beta\right)\right\}$$

(Eqn. 10-21)
$$[\beta] = \left(1/l\right)\left\{\left(\varepsilon_{\lambda_1}^\alpha A_{\lambda_2} - \varepsilon_{\lambda_2}^\alpha A_{\lambda_1}\right) \Big/ \left(\varepsilon_{\lambda_1}^\alpha \varepsilon_{\lambda_2}^\beta - \varepsilon_{\lambda_2}^\alpha \varepsilon_{\lambda_1}^\beta\right)\right\}$$

For wavelength λ [nm], the total absorbance is given by

$$A_\lambda = \varepsilon_\lambda^\alpha l[\alpha] + \varepsilon_\lambda^\beta l[\beta] = \left(\varepsilon_\lambda^M[\alpha] + \varepsilon_\lambda^N[\beta]\right)l \qquad \textbf{(Eqn. 10-19)}$$

For given two wavelengths λ_1 and λ_2 [nm], the molar extinction coefficient of α and β are given by $\varepsilon_{\lambda_1}^\alpha$ and $\varepsilon_{\lambda_2}^\alpha$ or $\varepsilon_{\lambda_1}^\beta$ and $\varepsilon_{\lambda_2}^\beta$, respectively. Therefore,

$$A_{\lambda_1} = \left(\varepsilon_{\lambda_1}^M[\alpha] + \varepsilon_{\lambda_1}^N[\beta]\right)l$$

$$A_{\lambda_2} = \left(\varepsilon_{\lambda_2}^M[\alpha] + \varepsilon_{\lambda_2}^N[\beta]\right)l$$

From the above two equations, we replace [β] in the above with an expression from below.

Chapter 10 Intermolecular Interaction and Essences of Spectroscopy

$$[\alpha] = \left(1/l\right) \left\{ \left(\varepsilon^{\beta}_{\lambda_2} A_{\lambda_1} - \varepsilon^{\beta}_{\lambda_1} A_{\lambda_2}\right) \Big/ \left(\varepsilon^{\alpha}_{\lambda_1} \varepsilon^{\beta}_{\lambda_2} - \varepsilon^{\alpha}_{\lambda_2} \varepsilon^{\beta}_{\lambda_1}\right) \right\} \quad \text{(Eqn. 10-20)}$$

$$[\beta] = \left(1/l\right) \left\{ \left(\varepsilon^{\alpha}_{\lambda_1} A_{\lambda_2} - \varepsilon^{\alpha}_{\lambda_2} A_{\lambda_1}\right) \Big/ \left(\varepsilon^{\alpha}_{\lambda_1} \varepsilon^{\beta}_{\lambda_2} - \varepsilon^{\alpha}_{\lambda_2} \varepsilon^{\beta}_{\lambda_1}\right) \right\} \quad \text{(Eqn. 10-21)}$$

(Eqn. 10-26) $[\theta] = 3298\Delta\varepsilon$

The definition of the ellipticity of the polarization is given as:

$$\tan\theta = \frac{E_R - E_L}{E_R + E_L}$$

Here, E_R and E_L are the magnitudes of the electric field vectors ($\vec{E}_R$ and $\vec{E}_L$) of the right-circularly and left-circularly polarized light, respectively.

$$E_R = |\vec{E}_R|$$

And

$$E_R = |\vec{E}_L|$$

When there is no difference in the absorbance of right- and left-circular polarized light, $E_R = E_L$ and $\theta = 0°$. This means that the light is linearly polarized. If there is complete absorbance of the circular polarized light in one direction ($E_R = 0$ or $E_L = 0$), $\theta = 45°$. This means that the light is circularly polarized. The circular dichroism effect is regarded as small effect and $\tan\theta$ becomes very small. In this case we can use an approximation of

$$\theta \approx \tan\theta$$

Here, θ is in the unit of [radian]. The intensity of light (I) is proportional to the square of the electric-field vector ($\vec{E}$),

$$E = |\vec{E}| = I^{\frac{1}{2}}$$

the ellipticity θ [radian] becomes:

$$\theta = \left(\frac{I_R^{\frac{1}{2}} - I_L^{\frac{1}{2}}}{I_R^{\frac{1}{2}} + I_L^{\frac{1}{2}}}\right)$$

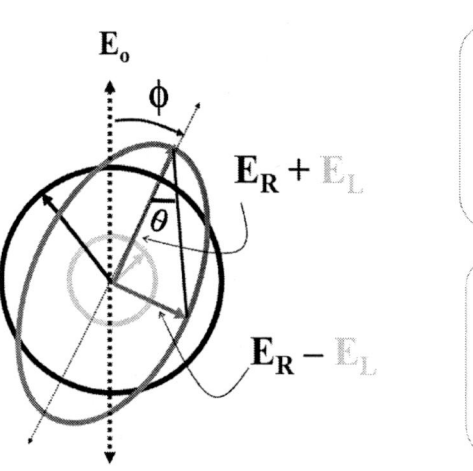

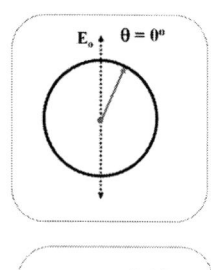

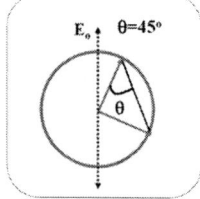

Fig. 10-31 Sketch of ellipticity, θ.
Elliptical polarized light (gray) is composed of unequal contributions of right (black) and left (right gray) circular polarized light. (Here, ϕ is optical rotation angle, which is chosen not to explained for details in this textbook.)

Let's replace I with an expression of Lambert-Beer law in natural logarithm form as:

$$I = I_0 e^{-A ln 10}$$

Then, ellipticity θ [radian] is written as:

$$\theta = \left(\frac{e^{-\frac{A_R}{2}ln10} - e^{-\frac{A_L}{2}ln10}}{e^{-\frac{A_R}{2}ln10} + e^{-\frac{A_L}{2}ln10}}\right) = \frac{e^{\Delta A \frac{ln10}{2}} - 1}{e^{\Delta A \frac{ln10}{2}} + 1}$$

This formula is approximated by expanding the exponentials in to a first-order of Taylor series, since ΔA<<1. By discarding terms of ΔA in comparison with unity and converting from [radian] to [degree],

$$\theta = \Delta A \left(\frac{ln10}{4}\right)\left(\frac{180}{\pi}\right)$$

The linear dependence of solute concentration and path length is removed by defining molar ellipticity as,

$$[\theta] = \frac{100\theta}{cl}$$

From (Eqn. 10-25) (Lambert-Berr law)

$$\Delta\varepsilon = \frac{(A_L - A_R)}{lc} = \frac{\Delta A}{lc} \text{ (Eqn. 10-25)}$$

Then combining the above three formulas,:

$$[\theta] = \frac{100\theta}{cl} = \frac{100}{cl}\left[\Delta A \left(\frac{ln10}{4}\right)\left(\frac{180}{\pi}\right)\right]$$

$$= \frac{100}{cl}\left[(lc\Delta\varepsilon)\left(\frac{ln10}{4}\right)\left(\frac{180}{\pi}\right)\right]$$

Thus,

$$[\theta] = 100\Delta\varepsilon \left(\frac{ln10}{4}\right)\left(\frac{180}{\pi}\right)$$

Thus
$$[\theta] = 3298\Delta\varepsilon \quad\quad\quad \text{(Eqn. 10-26)}$$

Chapter 10 Summary [Part 1]

(Use back page to cover the contents.)

1	dipole moment	$\vec{\mu} = q\vec{r}$ (Eqn. 10-1)
2	dipole moment of each x-, y-, and z-component	$\vec{\mu}_x = \sum_i q_i x_i \quad \vec{\mu}_y = \sum_i q_i y_i \quad \vec{\mu}_z = \sum_i q_i z_i$ (Eqn.12-2)
3	magnitude of the dipole $\|\mu\|$	$\|\mu\| = \sqrt{\mu_x^2 + \mu_y^2 + \mu_z^2}$ (Eqn.10-4)
4	transition probability($\|\mu_{ij}\|^2$) and transition dipole moment (μ_{ij})	$\|\mu_{ij}\|^2 = \|\int \psi_j^* \hat{\mu} \psi_i d\tau\|^2$ (Eqn. 10-7) $\mu_{ij} = \int \psi_j^* \hat{\mu} \psi_i d\tau$ (Eqn. 10-6) $\hat{\mu} = e\vec{r}$ (Eqn. 10-5)
5	Intensity of light (I) and number of photons (n_p)	$I = E_p / (A \cdot t)$ (Eqn. 10-8) E_p: the total amount of photon energy [J] A: targeted area [m^2], t: time [sec] of the light emitted $E_p = n_p \varepsilon$ (Eqn. 10-9) $\varepsilon = h\nu$ n_p: number of photons, ε: photon energy
6	quantum yield (ϕ)	$\phi = n_\pi / n_p$ (Eqn. 10-10) n_π: number of photoproducts n_p: number of supplied photons

[Fold the page at the double line and cover the right half.]

Chapter 10 Summary Check [Part 1]

(Use this page to cover and check the contents.)
Use ☐ as your check box. Write your comment at far right

#	Topic	Check	Comment
1	dipole moment	☐ ☐ ☐ ☐ ☐	
2	dipole moment of each x-, y, and z-component	☐ ☐ ☐ ☐ ☐	
3	magnitude of the dipole $|\mu|$	☐ ☐ ☐ ☐ ☐	
4	transition probability ($|\mu_{ij}|^2$) and transition dipole moment (μ_{ij})	☐ ☐ ☐ ☐ ☐	
5	Intensity of light (I) and number of photons (n_p)	☐ ☐ ☐ ☐ ☐	
6	quantum yield (ϕ)	☐ ☐ ☐ ☐ ☐	

Chapter 10 Summary [Part 2]

(Use back page to cover the contents.)

7	intermolecular force	**Table 10-1** Summary of intermolecular forces.		
		Type	Distance (r) dependence	Typical vale [kJ/mol]
		Ion-ion	$1/r$	250
		Ion-dipole	$1/r^2$	~15
		Hydrogen bond		~20
		Dipole-dipole	$1/r^3$	~2
		London (Dispersion)	$1/r^6$	~2

8	Coulomb's Law	$U(r) = {q_1 q_2}/{4\pi \varepsilon_o r}$ (Eqn. 10-11) U(r) [J]: electrostatic interaction between charged spices q_1 and q_2 separated by r[m] ε_o : electrostatic or permittivity constant (=8.85418782×10^{-12} [F·m^{-1}] or [C^{2}N^{-1} m^{-2}]).

9	Beer-Lambert Law	$I = I_0 10^{-\varepsilon l c} = I_0 10^{-A}$ (Eqn. 10-14) I$_0$: intensity of the light emitted I: intensity of the light passed through a sample $A = \varepsilon l c$ (Eqn. 10-15) A: absorbance, l : path length [cm], c : concentrtaion [M] ε: molar absorptivity [M^{-1} cm^{-1}] The observation of absorbance at various temperatures able to extract thermochemical properties. (ΔG, ΔH, and ΔS)

10	isosbestic point (λ_{iso})	molar extinction coefficient (ε_{iso}) of multi components are equal. $A_{\lambda_{iso}} = \varepsilon_{\lambda_{iso}} l([\alpha] + [\beta])$ (Eqn. 10-22)

[Fold the page at the double line and cover the right half.]

Chapter 10 Summary Check [Part 1]

(Use this page to cover and check the contents.)
Use ☐ as your check box. Write your comment at far right

7	intermolecular force	☐ ☐ ☐ ☐ ☐	
8	Coulomb's Law	☐ ☐ ☐ ☐ ☐	
9	Beer-Lambert Law	☐ ☐ ☐ ☐ ☐	
10	isosbestic point (λ_{iso})	☐ ☐ ☐ ☐ ☐	

Chapter 10 Summary [Part 3]

(Use back page to cover the contents.)

11	circular dichroism	$\Delta\varepsilon = \varepsilon_L - \varepsilon_R = \dfrac{\Delta A}{lc}$ (Eqn. 10-25) $\Delta A = A_L - A_R$ (Eqn. 10-24) $[\theta] = 3298\Delta\varepsilon$ (Eqn. 10-26) difference of the absorbance between the two different circularly polarized light. It is useful for identifying the secondary structure of the protein (α-helix, β sheet, and random coil).
12	The number normal modes of vibration of molecules with N atoms	**Linear molecule: Number of normal modes = 3N – 5** **Non-linear molecule: Number of normal modes = 3N – 6**
13	fluorescence intensity decay	$I(t) = I_o e^{-t/\tau}$ (Eqn. 10-33) τ: lifetime [sec]
14	quantum yield of fluorescence (ϕ_f)	$\phi_f = \dfrac{k_o}{k_d}$ (Eqn. 10-36) k_o: the rate of fluorescence intensity decays only with emission path k_d: the rate of fluorescence intensity decays with emission and other all decay paths **natural life time: τ_o** $\tau_o = \dfrac{1}{k_o}$ (Eqn. 10-35)

[Fold the page at the double line and cover the right half.]

Chapter 10 Summary Check [Part 1]

(Use this page to cover and check the contents.)
Use ☐ as your check box. Write your comment at far right

11	circular dichroism	☐ ☐ ☐ ☐ ☐	
12	The number normal modes of vibration of molecules with N atoms	☐ ☐ ☐ ☐ ☐	
13	fluorescence intensity decay	☐ ☐ ☐ ☐ ☐	
14	quantum yield of fluorescence (ϕ_f)	☐ ☐ ☐ ☐ ☐	

Chapter 10 - YOUR TEACHER MAY TEST YOU ON:

No.	What may be asked?		What you should know or do?
1	How can you calculate the net dipole moment of a polyatomic molecule?	→	set the "proper" coordinate to simplify the calculation
		→	Use $\vec{\mu}_x = \sum_i q_i x_i \quad \vec{\mu}_y = \sum_i q_i y_i \quad \vec{\mu}_z = \sum_i q_i z_i$ (Eqn.10-2) Calculate each component and conduct a vector sum for viewing the dipole moment in a coordinate.
		→	The amount of dipole moment is given by $\|\mu\| = \sqrt{\mu_x^2 + \mu_y^2 + \mu_z^2}$ (Eqn.10-4)
		→	**EXERCISES 10-1 and 10-2** (For 2-dimensional planary molecule)
		→	**Problems 10-1, 10-2**
2	What is a principle of predicting the transition probability (or transition selection rule)?	→	It is proportional to "$\|\mu_{ij}\|^2$" for i-th to j-th state
		→	$\|\mu_{ij}\|^2 = \|\int \psi_j^* \hat{\mu} \psi_i d\tau\|^2$ (Eqn. 10-7)
3	How do you calculate the number of photons?	→	Calculate the energy of one photon $\varepsilon = h\nu = hc/\lambda$ (Eqn. 9-1)
		→	Divide the total power by one photon energy. $n_p = E_p/\varepsilon$ (Eqn. 10-9)
4	How do you calculate the quantum yield of photochemical reaction?	→	Calculate the number of photons (n_p) and the number of products produced (n_π)
		→	Use $\emptyset = n_\pi/n_p$ (Eqn. 10-10)
		→	**EXERCISE 10-3**
		→	**Problems 10-3, 10-4**
5	What is the ball park figure for ion-ion, ion-dipole, dipole-dipole, dispersion, and hydrogen bond interaction?	→	**Table 10-1** Ion-ion (250 [kJ/mol])>ion-dipole (~15 [kJ/mol]) ≈ Hydrogen bond (~20 [kJ/mol]) > dipole-dipole ≈ Dispersion (~2 [kJ/mol])
6	How can you calculate the Coulobmic force, U(r) in [J]?	→	$U(r) = \dfrac{q_1 q_2}{4\pi\varepsilon_0 r} = 1389\left(\dfrac{q_1 q_2}{r}\right)$ (Eqn. 10-11) ε_0: electrostatic or permittivity constant =8.85418782×10^{-12} [F·m^{-1}] or [C^{2}N^{-1} m^{-2}]). q_1, q_2 : electron charges [C] r: distance between q_1 and q_2 [Å]
		→	**EXERCISE 10-4**
		→	**Problems 10-5, 10-6, 10-7, 10-8**
7	How do you calculate the intensity of the light passing from the sample with an absorbance A?	→	Use Beer-Lambert Law. $I = I_0 10^{-\varepsilon l c} = I_0 10^{-A}$ (Eqn. 10-14) $A = \varepsilon l c$ (Eqn. 10-15)
		→	**Problems 10-9, 10-10, 10-11**

8	How can you calculate the velocity of photochemical reaction (v) using absorbance and quantum yield?	→	$v = -d[B]/dt = -2303\phi I_0 A/l$ (Eqn. 10-16)
		→	**EXERCISE 10-5**
		→	**Problem 10-12**
9	How can you extract the concentration of two components mixed in a solution?	→	If they (α and β) have the absorbance at two different wavelengths λ_1 and λ_2 [nm], the concentration for each component can be given by (Eqn. 10-20) and (Eqn. 10-21)
		→	$[\alpha] = (1/l) \left\{ (\varepsilon^\beta_{\lambda_2} A_{\lambda_1} - \varepsilon^\beta_{\lambda_1} A_{\lambda_2}) / (\varepsilon^\alpha_{\lambda_1}\varepsilon^\beta_{\lambda_2} - \varepsilon^\alpha_{\lambda_2}\varepsilon^\beta_{\lambda_1}) \right\}$ (Eqn. 10-20)
			$[\beta] = (1/l) \left\{ (\varepsilon^\alpha_{\lambda_1} A_{\lambda_2} - \varepsilon^\alpha_{\lambda_2} A_{\lambda_1}) / (\varepsilon^\alpha_{\lambda_1}\varepsilon^\beta_{\lambda_2} - \varepsilon^\alpha_{\lambda_2}\varepsilon^\beta_{\lambda_1}) \right\}$ (Eqn. 10-21)
10	What is the relationship between absorbance and the concentration of two components at an **isosbestic point**?	→	$A_{\lambda_{iso}} = \varepsilon_{\lambda_{iso}} l ([\alpha] + [\beta])$ (Eqn. 10-22)
11	What is the procedure to extract the thermochemical properties of a reaction from absorbance?	→	Collect absorption spectrum at various temperatures, including temperatures where only mono component (reactant or product) exist.
		→	Relate the absorbance with concentration. Then express an equilibrium constant with absorbance at given temperature.
		→	The Gibbs energy change at given temperature is given from the equilibrium constant. $\Delta G^o = -RT \ln K$ (Eqn. 2-10)
		→	Using van't Hoff equation, the enthalpy change can be extracted. $\ln \frac{K_2}{K_1} = -\frac{\Delta H^o_{rxn}}{R}\left[\frac{1}{T_2} - \frac{1}{T_1}\right]$ (Eqn. 2-13)
		→	The entropy change for a given temperature is calculated by $\Delta G = \Delta H - T\Delta S$ (Eqn. 2-2)
		→	**EXERCISE 10-6**
		→	**Problems 10-13, 10-14**
12	How circular dichroism ($\Delta\varepsilon$ or $[\theta]$) is calculated?	→	$\Delta\varepsilon = \varepsilon_L - \varepsilon_R = \frac{\Delta A}{lc}$ (Eqn. 10-25) $\Delta A = A_L - A_R$ (Eqn. 10-24) $[\theta] = 3298\Delta\varepsilon$ (Eqn. 10-26)
		→	The absorbance by left- or right circular polarized

			light is given by A_L and A_R, respectively.
		→	**EXERCISE 10-7**
		→	**Problems 10-15, 10-16**
13	Predict The number **normal modes of vibration of** molecules with N atoms	→	**Linear molecule= 3N – 5** **Non-linear molecule=3N – 6**
		→	Example shown for the water (H_2O) N=3(non-linear) → 3× (3) – 6 =3
14	**Predict the mode with IR active**	→	Use character table and pick up the mode which has the symmetry label of x^2, y^2, or z^2
15	Calculate the fluorescence quantum yield (ϕ_f)	→	$\phi_f = \dfrac{k_o}{k_d}$ (Eqn. 10-30)
		→	**EXERCISE 10-8**
		→	**Problem 10-17**

Chapter 10 Intermolecular Interaction and Essences of Spectroscopy

UNIT CHECK Chapter 10

Important Parameters of This Chapter	Popularly Used Unit	Important Unit Conversion
Dipole moment, $\vec{\mu}$	C m D (scalar part)	1 Debye =1 [D]= 3.33564×10^{-30} [C·m] =1×10^{-18} [esu cm]
Charge, q	C esu	1 e = 4.803×10^{-10} [esu]
Location, r, x, y, z	m cm	
The magnitude of vector, $|\vec{A}|$	(same as the scalar part of each vector)	
Dipole moment operator, $\hat{\mu}$	C m D	1 Debye =1 [D] =3.33564×10^{-30} [C·m] =1×10^{-18} [esu cm]
Transition dipole moment, μ_{ij}	C m D	
Wavefunction, Ψ	Same as the unit of an eigen value Location [m] momentum [kg·m·sec^{-1}] Kinetic energy [J]	
Planck's constant, h	J sec m^2 kg sec^{-1}	h = $6.62606896(33) \times 10^{-34}$ [J sec]
Intensity of light, I	w·m^{-2} J sec^{-1}m^{-2}	[w]=[J/sec]
Area, A	m^2	
Time, t	Sec	
Wavelength, λ	M	
Energy of one photon, ε	J	
Frequency, ν	Hz sec^{-1}	
Speed of light, c	m/sec	c = 2.99792×10^8 [m/sec]
Number of photons, n_p	Dimension less, Einstein	1 Einstein is 1 mole = 6.0221415×10^{23}
Number of photo products, n_π	Dimensionless, mole	1 [mol] = 6.0221415×10^{23}
Quantum yield, ϕ	Dimension less	
Intensity of incident or passing light, I_0 or I	einstein cm^{-2} sec^{-1}	
Absorbance, A	optical density (OD)	
Molar absorptivity, ε	M^{-1} cm^{-1}	
Concentration of sample, c	M	
Path length of cell, l	cm	

Concentration reactant or photo product, [A] or [B]	M	
Concentration of components, [α] or [β]	M	
Fraction of double helix, f	Dimension less	
Temperature, T	°C	0 [°C] = 273.15 [K]
	K	
Gibbs Energy Change, ΔG	J/mol	
	kJ/mol	
Enthalpy change, ΔH	J/mol	
	kJ/mol	
Entropy change, ΔS	$J\,K^{-1}\,mol^{-1}$	
	$kJ\,K^{-1}\,mol^{-1}$	
Gas constant, R	$atm\,L\,K^{-1}\,mol^{-1}$	8.314472 $[J\,K^{-1}\,mol^{-1}]$
	$J\,K^{-1}\,mol^{-1}$	0.08205746 $[atm\cdot L\,K^{-1}\,mol^{-1}]$
Dichroism, ΔA	optical density	
	OD	
Specific rotation [α],	$deg\,cm^3\,dm^{-1}\,g^{-1}$	
Molar Rotation [ϕ],	$deg\,M^{-1}\,cm^{-1}$	
and Molar ellipticity [θ]	$rad\cdot cm^{-1}$	1 [degree] = 0.0175 [rad]
Circular dichroism, $\Delta\varepsilon$	$M^{-1}\,cm^{-1}$	
Rotational angle, α, ϕ	deg	
	rad	
Ellipticity, ψ	deg	
	rad	
Inter molecular force, U(r)	kJ/mol	
Electro permittivity constant, ε_o	$F\cdot m^{-1}$	ε_o =8.85418782×10^{-12} $[F\cdot m^{-1}]$ or $[C^2 N^{-1}\,m^{-2}]$
	$C^2 N^{-1}\,m^{-2}$	

Chapter 10 Intermolecular Interaction and Essences of Spectroscopy

SUMMARY OF TRICKY TRAPS OF CHAPTER 10

☐	1	Quantum yield $\phi \leq 1$ or $\phi_f \leq 1$
☐	2	The number of photons is (total power of light)/(energy of one photon)
☐	3	H-bond interaction is a strong dipole-dipole interaction
☐	4	Inter-molecular : between molecules, intra-molecular : within molecules

LAST MINUTE REVIEW OF MATH CHAPTER 10
(These are basic algebra which you have no excuse if you miss them.)

1. $\sin\theta = \dfrac{b}{a}$ $\cos\theta = \dfrac{c}{a}$
2. $\vec{c} = \vec{a} + \vec{b}$
3. $|\vec{a}| = \sqrt{a^2}$
4. $y = 10^{-x} \rightarrow x = -\log y$

Nobel Prize and Your Knowledge From Chapter 10
(*: word appeared in Chapter10)

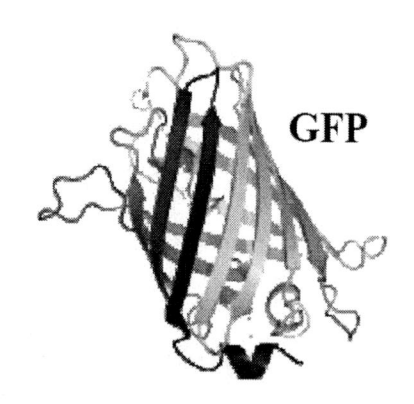

Fig. 10-32 Structure of GFP.

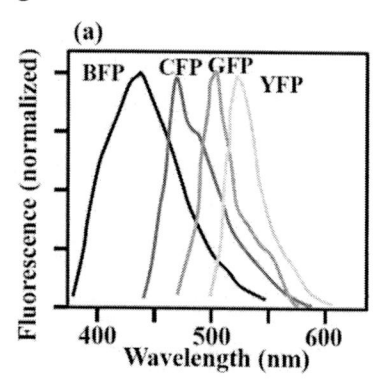

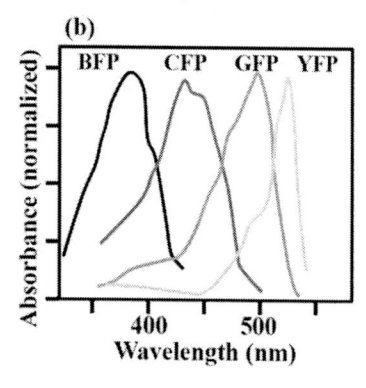

Fig. 10-33 a)Emission and b) Excitation spectrum of BFP, CFP, GFP, and YFP.

The Nobel Prize in Chemistry 2008 was awarded jointly to Osamu Shimomura, Martin Chalfie and Roger Y. Tsien *"for the discovery and development of the green fluorescent protein, GFP"*.

The **green fluorescent protein** (**GFP**) is a protein composed of 238 amino acid residues (26.9 [kDa]), which exhibits bright green fluorescence when exposed to blue light.(**Fig. 10-32**) Although many other marine organisms have similar green fluorescent proteins, GFP traditionally refers to the protein first isolated from the jellyfish *Aequorea victoria*. The GFP from *A. victoria* has a major **excitation peak*** at a wavelength of 395 [nm] and a minor one at 475 [nm]. Its **emission peak** *is at 509 [nm] which is in the lower green portion of the visible spectrum. The example of excitation spectrum and emission (fluorescence) spectrum of GFP (together with Blue FP, Cyan FP, and Yellow FP) are demonstrated in **Fig. 10-33**. Here, you may have no problem understanding emission spectrum (or fluorescence spectrum), the excitation spectrum needs to be briefly explained here. In emission (or fluorescence) spectrum the wavelength of the excitation is kept constant and the wavelength of emission (fluorescence) is varied (or scanned). On the other hand, an *excitation spectrum* is the opposite of the fluorescence (or emission) spectrum, where emission signal is detected as a function of the varying excitation light with the wavelength of emission light is remained constant. Thus, the excitation spectrum corresponds to absorption spectrum. Excitation spectrum can also create so called *emission map* (three dimensional contour map) by combining a series of excitation emission spectrum with different excitation wavelengths.

The GFP from the sea pansy (*Renilla reniformis*) has a single major excitation peak at 498 [nm]. In cell and molecular biology, the GFP gene is frequently used as a reporter of expression. In modified forms it has been used to make biosensors, and many animals have been created that express GFP as a proof-of-concept that a gene can be expressed throughout a given organism.

The GFP gene can be introduced into organisms and maintained in their genome through breeding, injection with a viral vector, or cell transformation. To date, the GFP gene has been introduced and expressed in many bacteria, yeast and other fungi, fish (such as zebrafish), plant, fly, and mammalian cells, including human.

THE FOCUSED PHYSICAL CHEMISTRY EXPERIMENTAL APPROACH ASSOCIATED WITH CHAPTER 10
(*: word appeared in Chapter 10)

Förster Resonance Energy Transfer (FRET)

Förster resonance energy transfer (abbreviated **FRET**) is a mechanism describing energy transfer between two chromophores. Energy transfer takes place from an electronically excited donor (D) to an acceptor (A) through **nonradiative dipole–dipole coupling*** (Energy is not transferred by fluorescence). A typical D-A distance is less than 1 nm. This energy transfer mechanism is called as "**Förster resonance energy transfer**". FRET is analogous to near field communication, in which the radius of interaction is much smaller compared to the wavelength of light emitted from the excited donor. The emission from donor is absorbed by an acceptor. The efficiency of energy transfer, ε, is the **quantum yield*** of the energy transfer transition, (number of energy transfer events per one donor excitation event), and is given by

$$\varepsilon = \frac{k_{ET}}{k_f + k_{ET} + \sum k_i} = \frac{1}{1+\left(\frac{r}{R_o}\right)^6}$$

[I am asking one simple question using the above question in Chapter 10 Problem. Try that if you are interested.] Here, the first term, k_{ET} is the rate of energy transfer, k_f the fluorescence or radiative decay rate and the k_i are the rate constants of any other decay pathway. In the second term, r is D-A distance and R_0 is the distance at which the energy transfer efficiency is 50%.(Förster distance)
The dipole-dipole coupling mechanism consider relative orientation of the emission dipole moment of D and the absorption dipole moment of A. The R_0 depends on the overlap integral of the emission spectrum of D with the absorption spectrum of A. Mutual molecular orientation between D and A is given by:

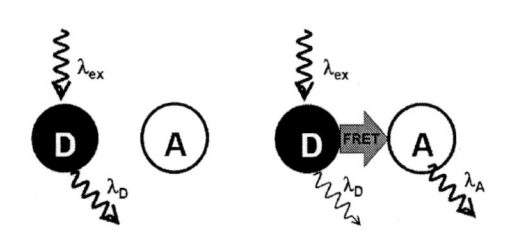

Fig. 10-34 FRET between A and D and resulting emission

$$R_o^6 = \frac{9000 \phi_f^D (ln10) \kappa^2 J}{128 \pi^5 n^4 N_A}$$

ϕ_f^D the fluorescence quantum yield of the donor, κ^2 is the dipole orientation factor (κ^2 =2/3 is often used for freely rotating and isotropically oriented D and A), n is the refractive index of the medium, N_A is Avogadro's number, and J is the spectral overlap integral.

$$J = \int f_D(\lambda) \epsilon_A(\lambda) \lambda^4 d\lambda$$

Here, f_D is emission spectrum of D, and ϵ_A is the molar extinction coefficient of A. The fluorescence lifetime of the D is related with ε as $\varepsilon = 1 - \tau'_D/\tau_D$ Here, τ'_D and τ_D are the fluorescence lifetimes of D in the presence and absence of A, respectively. $\varepsilon = 1 - I'_D/I_D$ where I'_D and I_D are the fluorescence intensities by D with and without A, respectively. FRET is a useful tool to quantify protein-protein (or DNA) interactions and protein conformational changes. FRET is popularly used in fluorescence confocal laser scanning microscopy. D or A fluorophore-labeled molecules are used for monitoring the complex formation between two molecules. As dissociation takes place, emission of D is probed upon the excitation of D. Whereas the emission of A is mainly observed at r=1-10 [nm] because of the intermolecular FRET from the D to A.(**Fig 10-34**) In order to monitor protein conformational changes, the target protein is labeled with D and A at two locations within proteins. As confirmation of protein change results in the change in r or orientation, change in FRET is probed.

Chapter 10 Problems.

10-1 [Calculation of Dipole moment - μ] An approximate MO calculation gives the following π-electron charges on an amide group:
O −33e   C +0.18e   N +0.15e
Calculate the magnitude of the π dipole moment.

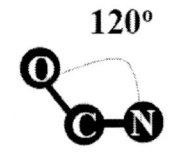

10-2 [Calculation of Dipole moment - μ] a) Show a mathematical expression for the y-component of the dipole moment of the molecule (B-A-C) shown below. [Charges: A −2.0e, B +1.8e, C +1.5e]
b) Obtain the magnitude of the dipole moment of molecule (B-A-C) and sketch a direction of dipole moment. r_1 = 1.43 [Å] and r_2 = 1.25 [Å]

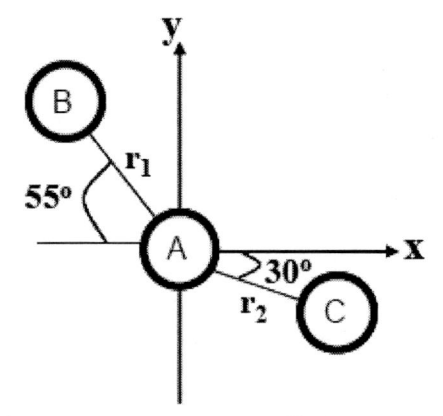

10-3a [E= hν, Quantum Yield, ϕ] a). The red color of hemoglobin (and therefore of blood) is a consequence of the strong absorption by this protein of yellow and green light in the wavelength range 500-600 [nm], and also of blue light in the wavelength range 400-450 [nm], leaving only red light transmitted. What is the energy of a quantum of yellow light absorbed by hemoglobin at 550 [nm]?
b) A wavelength 450 [nm] of pulse light 10 [mW] was irradiated for 1 [m] second to a strain of algae and 5.2×10^{14} molecules of O_2 was produced. Calculate the quantum yield of O_2 formation.

10-4 [Quantum Yield, ϕ] A pulse of light 10.0 [mW] with unknown wavelength x [nm] was irradiated for 1 m second to a reactant and 5.20×10^{11} of product was produced by this irradiation. Calculate the wavelength of this light, if the quantum yield of this photo-reaction is 0.020.

10-5 [Intermolecular force] A student found an inter-molecular force of about 1 [kJ/mol] between nonpolar molecules. This force can be identified as:
  a. H-bonding
  b. dipole-dipole interaction
  c. ion-dipole interaction
  d. dispersion force
  e. none of these

10-6 [Coulombic force] Calculate [O… H] hydrogen bond distance in [Å] when the interaction energy is 100 kcal/mol and the partial charge on O is −0.834 and on H is + 0.427 in units of electronic charges.

Chapter 10 Intermolecular Interaction and Essences of Spectroscopy

10-7 [Coulombic force] An ionic molecule AB has the charge of $q_A = 2e$ and $q_B = -e$ with inter nuclear distance of r_{AB}. The molecule CD has $q_C = (q_A)_{1/2}$ and $q_D = (2)^{-1/2} q_B$ with $rCD = 2^{1/2} r_{AB}$. (*Please treat "e" as a value.*) Show the relationship between electrostatic potential energy between molecule AB and CD (V_{AB} and V_{CD}).

10-8 [Coulombic force] A C-C-C bond angle is nearly 109.5° (tetrahedral). For a quadratic potential with a force constant of 0.0612 [kJ mol^{-1} degree^{-2}] how much energy would it take to distort the bond angle to a right angle (90°)?

10-9 [Beer Lambert Law] According to Beer-Lambert law, the absorbance increases by a factor of two if
    a. the length of the cell increases by *log* 4.
    b. the molar extinction coefficient is decreased to a half.
    c. the length of the cell decreases by a factor of two
    d. if the concentration is increased by 50% of the original.
    e. none of these

10-10 [Abs→ε] According to the data given below, derive expressions with numerical coefficients evaluated, that give the concentrations in μg/mL of chlorophyll, chlorophyll *b*, and total chlorophylls (*a* and *b*) for specific values of A_{645} and A_{663} measured using a 1 [cm] path length.

Wavelength [nm]	Specific absorptivity [L/ g cm]	
	Chl *a*	Chl *b*
645	16.75	45.60
663	82.04	9.27

10-11 [A→ Transmission] A double-stranded oligonucleotide whose concentration is 200.0 [μM] is melted in a solution. At 10.00 [°C], the solution contains only duplex; at 60.00 [°C], the solution contains only single strands. The table shown below is the transmission spectrum taken at various temperatures at 260.0 [nm].

Temperature [°C]	Transmission at 260.0 [nm], $T_{260\ nm}$
10.00	0.1622
20.00	0.1538
50.00	0.1023
60.00	0.0769

Calculate the $\Delta G°$ at 36.00 [°C]. (Assume that the molar extinction coefficients of the duplexes and its single strands are independent of temperature.) The relationship between transmission (T) and absorbance (A) is:

$$T = 10^{-A}$$

10-12 [Photochemistry, Abs (ε)→ ΔG→, concentration] A protein A is competitively inhibited by a dye B. A solution containing 1.00×10^{-4} [M] total protein A and 2.00×10^{-3} [M] total dye B has an absorbance in a 1 [cm] cell at 280 [nm] of A = 1.4:

Protein A + dye B ⇌ complex (protein A-dye B)

The molar absorptivities, ε, at 280 [nm] at 25 [°C] are:
ε(protein A) = 12,000 [M^{-1} cm^{-1}]; ε (dye B)= 0 [M^{-1} cm^{-1}]; ε (complex (protein A-dyeB)) =15,000 [M^{-1}cm^{-1}]
Calculate the concentration of complex (protein A-dye B) when absolute value of $\Delta G°_{rxn}$ decreases by 10%. (This means that you need to calculate the concentration of complex when $|\Delta G_{rxn}| = 0.9 \times |\Delta G°_{rxn}|$

Note that $\Delta G°_{rxn}$ is "Gibbs energy change of reaction at equilibrium and 25 [°C]" and ΔG_{rxn} is "Gibbs energy change of reaction at 25 [°C]).

10-13 [Abs, ε → K] The enzyme chymotrypsin is a protease that is competitively inhibited by a red dye. A solution containing 1.00×10^{-4} [M] total protein and 2.00×10^{-3} [M] total dye has an absorbance in a 1 [cm] cell at 280 [nm] of A=1.4.

$$\text{Protein + dye} \rightleftharpoons \text{complex}$$

The molar absorptivities at 280 [nm] are (units of M^{-1}): ε(protein) = 12,000; ε(dye)=0; ε(complex)=15,000. Calculate the equilibrium constant.

10-14 [Abs → ΔG, ΔH, ΔS] A double-stranded oligonucleotide whose concentration is 100 [μM] is melted in 1 [M] NaCl, pH 7. Below 10 [°C], the solution contains only duplex; above 60 [°C], the solution contains only single strands. From the temperature dependence of the equilibrium constant, calculate the $\Delta G°$, $\Delta H°$, and $\Delta S°$, all at 25 [°C].

Temperature [°C]	A: absorbance
10	0.7900
15	0.800
20	0.813
25	0.822
35	0.852
30	0.890
40	0.940
45	0.971
50	0.990
55	1.003
60	1.114

10-15 [CD] The pure components gave the following results for solutions containing 1.00×10^{-4} [M] concentrations of nucleotides per liter:

Wavelength [nm]	$A_L - A_R$ (DNA)	$A_L - A_R$ (RNA)
260	0.00	6.0×10^{-4}
240	-2.20×10^{-4}	0.00

When RNA and DNA is mixed, its circular dichroism was obtained as $\Delta A(260 \text{ [nm]}) = 1.86 \times 10^{-4}$ and $\Delta A(240 \text{ [nm]}) = -0.13 \times 10^{-4}$. What are the concentrations of DNA and RNA in the mixture?

10-16 [CD] The following optical parameters at 280 [nm] were obtained. (molecular weight = 323.2 [g/mol])

$\varepsilon = 8000 \text{ [M}^{-1}\text{]}$ and $\varepsilon_L - \varepsilon_R = 3 \text{[M}^{-1}\text{cm}^{-1}\text{]}$
$[\phi] = 7500 \text{ [deg M}^{-1}\text{cm}^{-1}\text{]}$
$[\alpha] = 2320 \text{ [deg cm}^3 \text{dm}^{-1}\text{g}^{-1}\text{]}$

10-17 [ϕ_f] An experiment observed that the fluorescence quantum yield of Trp as 0.13. If natural life time of Trp is 3.0 [nsec], what is the rate of k_d?

10-18 [τ → r, FRET] When the dansyl chromophore is 20 [Å] away from the 11-cis-retinal chromophore in rhodopsin, the efficiency of fluorescence energy transfer is 50 %. The observed fluorescence lifetime for the dansyl-rhodopsin complex is 6 [n sec]. If natural life time of dansyl is 25 [n sec], calculate the distance between the dansyl label and the retinal chromophore in rhodopsin.

Chapter 10 Answers. For Selected Problems

10-1 2.59 [D]

10-2 a) $1.8e\ r_1 \sin 35° - 1.5e\ r_2 \sin 30°$
b) $\mu_y = +5.64$ [D], $\mu_x = +0.703$ [D], $\mu = 5.68$ [D]

10-3 a) 3.62×10^{-12} [erg] = 218 [kJ/mol] ~200 [kJ/mol]

10-4 515.8 [nm]

10-5 d

10-6 r = 1.18 [Å]

10-7 $V_{AB} = (8\,e)^{1/2}\,V_{CD}$

10-8 23 [kJ/mol]

10-9 e

10-10 C_{a+b} [μg/mL] = 8.13 A_{663} + 20.30 A_{645}

10-11 $\Delta G° = 27.8$ [kJ/mol]

10-12 ~0.25 [M]

10-14 $\Delta H° = 145.2$ [kJ/mol], $\Delta S° = 374.6$ [J K^{-1} mol^{-1}], $\Delta G° = 33.6$ [kJ/mol]

10-16 $\alpha = 7.5 \times 10^{-3}$ [deg]

10-17 $k_d = 2.56 \times 10^9$ [sec^{-1}]

Chapter 11

Scattering

11-1 Scatterings
11-2 Rayleigh Scatterings
11-3 Mie Scatterings
11-4 Brillouin Scatterings
11-5 Raman Scatterings
11-6 Diffraction
11-7 X Ray Diffraction and Determination of Molecular Structure

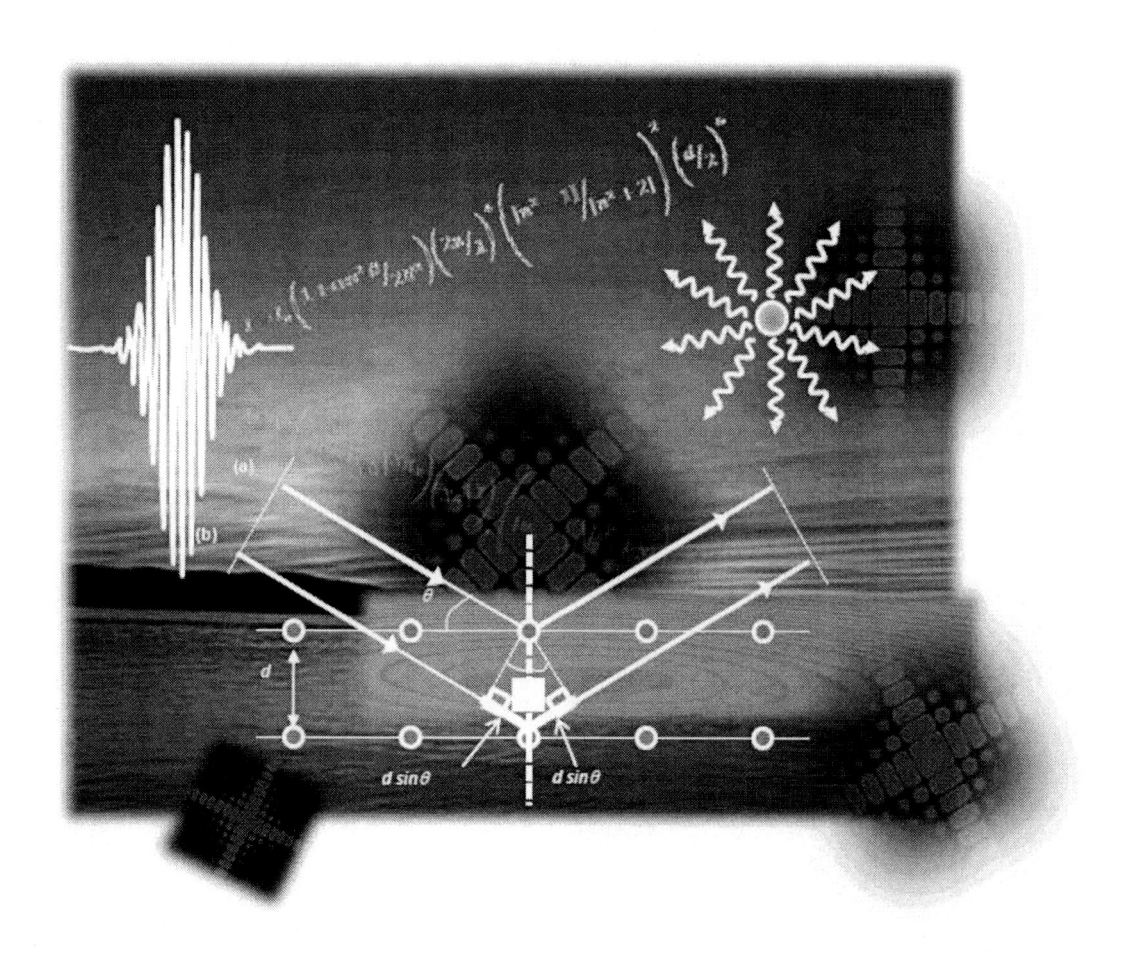

Chapter 11 Scattering

- ### *Why do I have to study this chapter?*

By starting with the idea of light (photons)as a substance with wave-like character, the feature of waves after they scatter or diffract can be established. If photons scatter to a substance, the constructive or destructive patters of the resultant wave follow a certain rules of physics. The light scattered from the substance has a fruitful information than you expected. The scattered radiation provides the information of the substance (scatterer), which are mostly crystals or molecules. While you are not expected to fully understand the entire process of constructing the structure of the crystal or molecule from the scattered radiation, you can be grasped the principle and essence.

- ### *Expected Hurdles Ahead in this Chapter*
1. Categorizing different types of scattering process (See Section **11-1**)
2. Mechanism and extracted information of Raman Spectroscopy (See Section **11-5**)
3. Interpretation of Miller indices (See Section **11-7**)
4. Processing X-ray scattering data (See Section **11-7**)

PREVIEW OF KEY-EQUATIONS

Parameter for categorizing the scattering situation

$$\alpha = \pi D_p / \lambda$$

Intensity of the light by Rayleigh scattering

$$I \propto \left(d^3 / \lambda^2 \right)^2$$

Selection rule for the Raman Scattering

$$\mu_{induced} = \alpha E$$
$$\partial \alpha / \partial Q \neq 0$$

Bragg's Diffraction Law

$$n\lambda = 2d \sin \theta$$

Chapter 11 Scattering

Laue conditions and Miller indices

$$\vec{a} \cdot \Delta\vec{\lambda} = 2\pi h$$
$$\vec{b} \cdot \Delta\vec{\lambda} = 2\pi k$$
$$\vec{c} \cdot \Delta\vec{\lambda} = 2\pi l$$

$$d_{hkl} = \left[\left(h^2/a^2\right) + \left(k^2/b^2\right) + \left(l^2/c^2\right)\right]^{-\frac{1}{2}}$$

$$n\lambda = 2d_{hkl} \sin\theta$$

Intensity of diffracted light

$$I = |F(h,k,l)|^2 = A^2 + B^2$$

$$F(h,k,l) = A + iB$$
$$A(h,k,l) = \sum_{j=1}^{n} f_j \cdot \cos[2\pi(hX_j + kY_j + lZ_j)]$$
$$B(h,k,l) = \sum_{j=1}^{n} f_j \cdot \sin[2\pi(hX_j + kY_j + lZ_j)]$$

Phase Factor

$$\alpha = \tan^{-1}\left[B/A\right]$$

PREVIEW OF KEY-TECHNICAL TERMS

Scattering, elastic scattering, inelastic scattering, Rayleigh scattering, Mie scattering, Brillouin scattering, Raman scattering, electric poolarizability (α), Stokes scattering, anti-stokes scattering, Boltzmann distribution, polarized Raman, depolarized Raman, character table, diffraction, Bragg diffraction, X-ray diffraction, neutron diffraction, Miller indices (h k l), specular reflection, scattering vector, Laue condition, Laue equation, reciprocal lattice vector, Fourier transformation, electron density, phase factor, neutron scattering

Chapter 11 Scattering

11-1 Scatterings

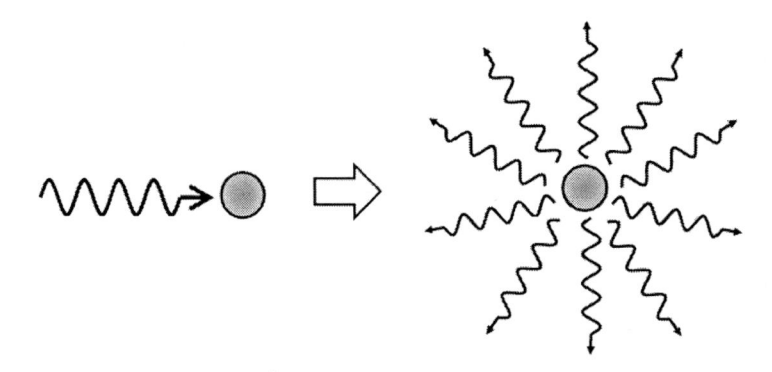

Fig. 11-1 Scattering phenomena

    Scattering is a process where radiation (such as light, sound, or moving particles) is deviated from its original straight trajectory. It also includes deviation of reflected radiation from the angle predicted by the law of reflection. (Reflections that undergo scattering are called *diffuse reflections* and unscattered reflections are called specular, mirror-like, reflections.) The non-uniformities that cause scattering are called as scatterers or scattering centers (e.g., fluids, bubbles, droplets, cells, and fibers). You should note that some areas of scattering theory provide a great benefit to a great amount of fields including radar sensing and medical ultrasound. There are two cases of scattering that you need to know. One is single scattering in which radiation is only scattered by one localized center. The other is called multiple scattering in which centers of scattering are grouped together and the radiation can scatter multiple times. The single scattering strongly depends on exact incoming trajectory and appears to be random, and thus, it is best described by probability distributions. On the other, the randomness of the interaction tends to be averaged out by the large number of scattering events in the multiple scattering, so that the final path of the radiation can be deterministic distribution of intensity. Since multiple scattering is very similar to diffusion, multiple scattering and diffusion are used interchangeably.

    Now, let's get into how we can deal with scattering phenomena on electromagnetic waves. Popular approach is to observe scattered radiation to determine properties of the radiation (or scatterer) before scattering event (inverse scattering problem). In this book, let's take a look at two elastic and two inelastic scatterings of electromagnetic waves. Two elastic light scattering under negligible energy transfer are **Rayleigh scattering** and **Mie scattering**, in which the energy (wavelength and frequency) of the light is almost conserved. Two inelastic scattering are **Brillouin scattering** and **Raman scattering**.

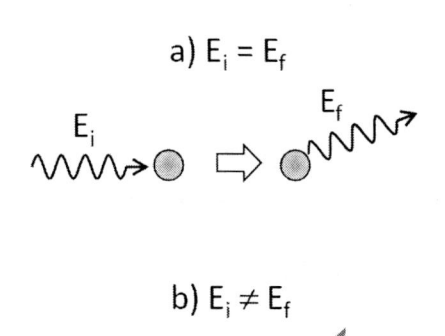

a) $E_i = E_f$

b) $E_i \neq E_f$

Fig. 11-2 Elastic scattering and inelastic scattering.

As for two elastic scatterings, they can be divided into two categories based on a size parameter, α, as:

$$\alpha = \pi D_p / \lambda \quad \text{[Eqn. 11-1]}$$

490

Here, πD_p is the circumference of a particle and λ is the wavelength of incident radiation.

If α<<1: **Rayleigh scattering** (small particle compared to wavelength of light)
If α≈1: **Mie scattering** (particle about the same size as wavelength of light)

If α>>1, it is categorized as geometric scattering and in this case particle size is much larger than wavelength of light.

The Brillouin and Raman scattering are categorized as inelastic scattering processes involving different correlation to the amount of energy lost. The Raman scattering processes involves the energy loss of the light corresponding to vibrational or rotational properties of molecules, while Brillouin scattering involves the scattering of photons from phonons. The Raman spectroscopy is used to determine molecular structure and Brillouin scattering measures properties on the elastic behavior of the material.

EXERCISE 11-1

If one intends to investigate the following particles by elastic scattering process with visible light 514.5 [nm] (of one of the lines from Ar⁺ ion laser), which scattering process does it correspond to?

a. A spherical protein with radius 6 [Å]
b. Gold nanoparticles with 200 [nm] diameter.

ANSWER
From (**Eqn. 11-1**), we can calculate the parameter α

$$\alpha = \pi D_p / \lambda \qquad \text{[Eqn. 11-1]}$$

The wavelength of the light is
❶ λ=514.5 [nm] = 5.145×10^{-7} [m]
For a) The diameter D_p is
❷ D_p = 2×6 [Å] = 12 Å = 1.2×10^{-9} [m]
$\alpha = (\pi \times 1.2 \times 10^{-9}$ [m])/ 5.145×10^{-7} [m] = 7.32×10^{-3}
The scattering from this particle is by Rayleigh scattering process.
For b) The diameter D_p is
❶ D_p = 200[nm] = 2.00×10^{-7} [m]
$\alpha = (\pi \times 2 \times 10^{-7}$ [m])/ 5.145×10^{-7} [m] = 1.220
The scattering from this particle is by Mie Scattering process.

❶ 1 [nm] = 10^{-9} [m]
❷ 1 [Å] = 10^{-10} [m] = 10^{-8} [cm]

11-2 Rayleigh Scatterings

Rayleigh scattering is a process in which electromagnetic radiation is scattered by a small spherical volume of variant refractive index (most prominently seen in gases), where diameter of a sphere is much smaller than the wavelength (λ) of the irradiating light. The Rayleigh scattering describes the elastic scattering of light by spherical particles with the diameter greatly smaller than the wavelength of light, λ. In Rayleigh scattering, the intensity of the scattered radiation, I, from the initial radiation (I_o) is described as

$$I = I_o \left(\frac{1+\cos^2\theta}{2R^2}\right)\left(\frac{2\pi}{\lambda}\right)^4 \left(\frac{[n^2-1]}{[n^2+2]}\right)^2 \left(\frac{d}{2}\right)^6 \quad \text{[Eqn. 11-2]}$$

Here, R is the distance between the particle (with diameter d) detecting point, ϑ is the scattering angle, and n is the refractive index of the scatterer. While the above equation contains many terms and may be saturating your mind, I would request you to focus on the dependence of the size of the particle (d) and the wavelengths (λ).

$$I \propto \lambda^{-4} \propto d^6 \propto \left(\frac{d^3}{\lambda^2}\right)^2 \quad \text{(Eqn. 11-3)}$$

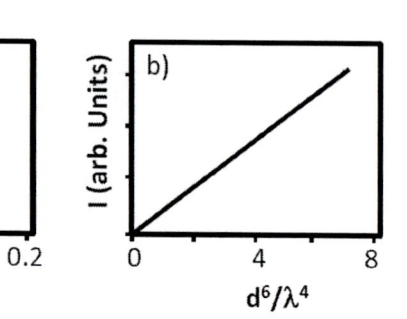

Fig. 11-3 Plots of I vs. d/λ for Rayleigh scattering a) I vs. (d/λ) and b) I vs. d^6/λ^4.

Rayleigh scattering is considered to be a function of the **electric polarizability** of the particles. Therefore, it makes sense that the intensity of the Rayleigh scattered radiation, I, drastically increases as the ratio of d/λ increases. Another important note for Rayleigh scattering is that the intensity is identical in the forward and reverse directions. (The Rayleigh scattering can become very popular scattering for you if you know this scattering mechanism how you see the blue color of the Earth's sky. Following Rayleigh's $1/\lambda^4$ relation, the shorter blue wavelengths of sunlight passing overhead are more strongly scattered than the longer red wavelengths).

EXERCISE 11-2

If one investigate a scattering nanomiscelle with diameter of 20 [nm] with visible light (for example He Ne laser light 632.8 [nm]). If you can increase the size of the membrane by 2.0 but requires to change the wavelength of the incident light in order to enhance the scattering signal by factor of 100, what should the wavelength of the incident light be?

ANSWER

From **[Eqn. 11-3]**, the intensity of the scattered light the Rayleigh scattering is

❶ $I \propto \left(d^3/\lambda^2\right)^2$ [Eqn. 11-3]

Thus, the intensity of two different conditions 1 and 2 are given as

$$I_1 \propto \left(d_1^3/\lambda_1^2\right)^2$$

$$I_2 \propto \left(d_2^3/\lambda_2^2\right)^2$$

Since we expect the factor of 100 enhancement at condition2,

❷ $I_2/I_1 = 100$

$$I_2/I_1 = 100 = \left(d_2^3/\lambda_2^2\right)^2 \left(d_1^3/\lambda_1^2\right)^{-2} = \left(\lambda_1^2 d_2^3 / d_1^3 \lambda_2^2\right)^2$$

❸ Here, $\lambda_1 = 632.8$ [nm] $= 6.328 \times 10^{-7}$ [m], $d_2 = 2 d_1$

$$100 = \left(\frac{(6.328 \times 10^{-7}[m])^2 (2d_2)^3}{d_1^3 \lambda_2^2}\right)^2$$

$$\sqrt{100} = \frac{8 \times (6.328 \times 10^{-7}[m])^2}{\lambda_2^2}$$

$$\lambda_2^2 = \frac{8 \times (6.328 \times 10^{-7}[m])^2}{10} = 3.203 \times 10^{-13} [m]$$

Thus,

$\lambda_2 = 565.9$ [nm]

---

❶ WE use only d and λ terms.
❷ (a/b)/(c/d) = (a/b) (d/c) = (ad)/(bc)
❸ You do not have to convert to the unit to [m], since the answer is requested in [nm]

11-3 Mie Scatterings

When the wavelength of the light is similar to or smaller than the size of the dielectric sphere, this scattering is handled by **Mie theory**. The Mie scattering is very sensitive to the shape of the scatterer. While Mie theory is best explained when the shape of the scatter is a sphere, this theory is applied to spheroids and ellipsoids with some modification. The intensity of Mie scattered radiation is the summation of an infinite series of terms, and it is roughly independent of wavelength. Another note for Mie scattering is that the scattering intensity is larger in the forward direction than in the reverse direction, and the more of the light is scattered in the forward direction as particle size becomes larger. Mie theory is applied for understanding the appearance of biological tissue. (A popular regard of the Mie theory can be found in the scattering of the water droplets in the cloud. Water droplets consisting of clouds possess a comparable size to the wavelengths in visible light. Thus, the scattering is described by Mie's model where all wavelengths of visible light are scattered approximately identically and the clouds therefore appear to be white or grey.) As an interesting application of Mie theory, the usage to the interferometry (FT-IR) and study of biological, biomedical samples (or cells) in a clinical setting is pointed out. Generally, samples consisting of isolated single biological cells are not best suited for analysis by absorption (including FTIR-Fourier Transformed Infra Red spectroscopy) since those cells generally scatter infrared radiation. Instead, this scattering signals corresponds to an absorption component that is distorted by scattering effects, and thus can compose the spectra of single cells using Mie scattering theory. By using the Mie theory, if scattered light from tissue corresponds to healthy or cancerous cell nuclei is determined through angle-resolved low-coherence interferometry.

Fig. 11-4 Mie scattering

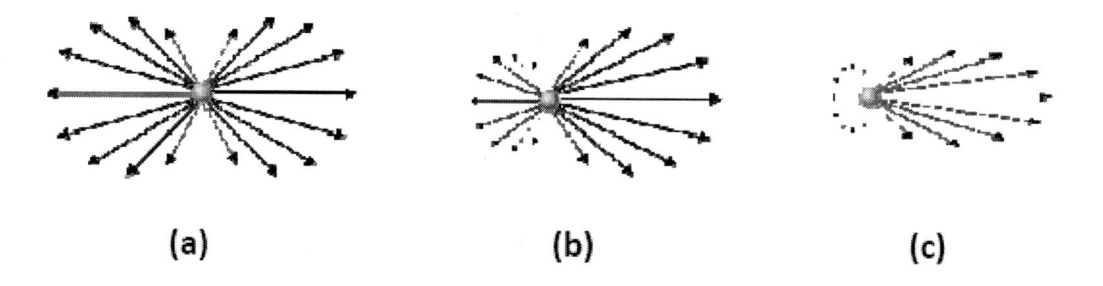

Fig. 11-5 (a) Rayleigh scattering, (b) Mie scattering with small particle (c) Mie scattering with large particle

11-4 Brillouin Scatterings

Brillouin scattering occurs when light in a medium interacts with time dependent optical density causing changes in energy and path. (The energy corresponds to frequency). The typical medium for this type of scattering is air, water or a crystal. The density variations are caused by acoustic modes or magnetic modes, or temperature gradients. The acoustic modes are caused by phonons (acoustic or vibrational quanta) and a magnetic modes are caused by magnons (magnetic spin waves). The sound waves in gas consist in travelling oscillations of pressure and density, whereas in condensed matter, the displacement atoms from their equilibrium positions create a set of vibrational waves which propagate within the lattice of crystal. The amplitude of the wave is associated with the displacements from their equilibrium positions of each atom. A minimum wavelength λ, is estimated to be twice of the equilibrium separation between atoms.

$$\lambda = 2\bar{d}_{eq} \qquad \text{(Eqn. 11-4)}$$

Fig. 11-6 Brillouin scattering and minimum scattering wavelength (λ)

A quantum mechanical explanation of Brillouin scattering is explained by an interaction of photons with phonons, magnons, or other low frequency quasi-particles. An important observation in the Brillouin scattering is that the energy of the scattered light is decreased for a Stokes process and increased for an anti-Stokes process. This energy change is called as the Brillouin shift, and this shift is equal to the energy of the interacting phonon or magnon. Thus, Brillouin scattering can be used to measure phonon or magnon energies. Both Rayleigh scattering and Brillouin scattering are caused by fluctuation in the density, composition and orientation of molecules. However, Brillouin scattering considers periodic fluctuations of phonons whereas Rayleigh scattering considers only random and incoherent thermal fluctuations. As laser light progresses into a material, the variations in the electric field of the beam itself cause acoustic vibrations in the medium via electrostriction. (For example, this can be observed as a laser beam travel through an optical fiber.) So that it produces Brillouin scattering from these vibrations mostly in the opposite direction to the incoming beam (**stimulated Brillouin scattering**). Typical frequency shifts are of the order of 1–10 GHz for liquids and gases.

> **EXERCISE 11-3**
> A crystalline sample was investigated by a scattering experiment. The minimum scattering wavelength by Brillouin scattering mechanism of a sample was identified as wave with frequency of 4×10^{15} [Hz]. Estimate the equilibrium separation of an atom of this sample.

ANSWER

❶ $\lambda = c/\nu$
   $= 2.99792458\times10^{10}$ [cm/sec] / 4×10^{15} [Hz]
   $= 7.49\times10^{-6}$ [cm]
   $= 7.49\times10^{-8}$ [m]

❷ $= 74.9$ [nm]
   $\lambda = 2\bar{d}_{eq}$ (Eqn. 11-4)
   $d_{eq} = 74.9$ [nm]/2

❸ $= 37.5$ [nm]

---

❶ Here, ν [Hz, or sec^{-1}] is given, and it needs to be converted into wavelength, λ.
   c = 2.99792458×10^{10} [cm/sec]

❷ 1 [μm] = 10^{-6} [m]

❸ d_{eq} is an estimated value.

11-5 Raman Scatterings

Raman scattering (Raman effect) is the inelastic scattering of a photon. Most of the scattered light from an atom or molecule is elastically scattered as you learned in Rayleigh scattering. However, a small fraction of the scattered light (~1 / 10^7 photons) is scattered having a frequency different from the frequency of the incident photons. This frequency change corresponds to vibrational, rotational or electronic energy of a molecule. There are two types of Raman scattering, one is **Stokes scattering** and the other is **anti-Stokes scattering**. The Stokes scattering takes place when molecule absorbs energy resulting scattering light's with the lower energy (longer wavelength) of the incident light. On the other hand, anti-stokes scattering occurs when molecule loses energy resulting blue shift of the incident light (i.e., the scattered light has the higher frequency than that of an incident light).The intensities of the Raman spectrum depended on the number of molecules occupying the vibrational (rotational or electronic) states when an incident light is introduced. Under thermal equilibrium, the relative numbers of

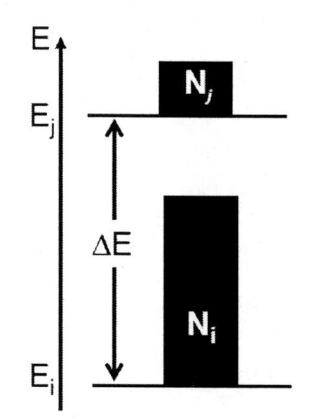

Fig. 11-7 Boltzmann distribution

Chapter 11 Scattering

molecules in states of different energy are described by the Boltzmann distribution as introduced in the supplemental section of **Chapter 6** (or **Chapter 11**). The **Boltzmann distribution** provides an important relationship between the number of distribution and energy of the system (**Fig. 11-7**).

$$N_j/N_i = (g_j/g_i) e^{-(E_j-E_i)/kT} = (g_j/g_i) e^{-\Delta E/k_B T} \qquad \text{(Eqn. 11-5)}$$

Here, N_i is the number of atoms in the lower i-th vibrational state, and N_j is the number of atoms in the higher j-th vibrational state. The g_i is degeneracy of the lower i-th vibrational state and g_j is the degeneracy of the higher j-th vibrational state. The ΔE_v corresponds to the energy difference between these two vibrational states. The k_B is Boltzmann constant and T is temperature. Since lower energy states will have more populations, the Stokes spectrum possesses higher intensity than anti-Stokes spectrum.

EXERCISE 11-4
The amide mode of the α-helix was identified as $\tilde{\nu}_o$=1345 [cm^{-1}]. What is the ratio of the population between the ground state and the 1st quanta (first excited state) of this mode at room temperature 25 [°C]. Please assume that these states have the same degeneracy.

ANSWER
The ratio of the population between two states is given by [**Eqn. 11-5**] as:

$$N_j/N_i = (g_j/g_i) e^{-(E_j-E_i)/kT} = (g_j/g_i) e^{-\Delta E/k_B T} \qquad \text{(Eqn. 11-5)}$$

The difference in energy between two vibrational states under the harmonic oscillator approximation is given by (**Eqn. 9-21**)

$\Delta E = h\nu_o$ (Eqn. 9-21)
h = 6.62606896(33)×10^{-34} [J sec]
$\tilde{\nu}_o$ = 1345 [cm^{-1}]
$\Delta E = h\nu_o = hc\tilde{\nu}_o$ (Eqn. 9-21)
k_B=1.3806503×10^{-23} [J/K]
T= 25+ 273.15 =298.15 [K]
ΔE=6.62606896(33)×10^{-34} [J s] × 2.99792458×10^{10} [cm/sec] × 1345 [cm^{-1}]
=2.6718×10^{-20} [J]
Since g_1/g_0=1,
N_1/N_0=exp{−2.6718×10^{-20} [J]/[(1.3806503×10^{-23} [J/K])(298.15 [K])]}
=exp{−2.6718×10^{-20} [J]/4.12×10^{-21}[J]}
=exp(− 6.49)
=1.518×10^{-3}

Here, there are no degeneracies. (g=1)
You may use "$E = h\nu_o$" often. It is also true for the transition energy, $\Delta E = h\nu_o$
ν_o is a fundamental vibrational frequency [Hz] of an oscillator.

❸	I am using the notification of v_o for the unit of [sec^{-1}] and $\tilde{v}_o$ for the unit of [cm^{-1}]. $$\tilde{v}_o = 1/\lambda = v/c$$ Here, $1/\lambda$ is given. c = 2.99792458×10^{10} [cm/sec] ($1/\lambda$ [cm^{-1}]. is the "**wavenumbers**" and it represents the numbers of waves existent in 1 [cm] of length.) Here, v is frequency [sec^{-1}], λ is the wavelength [cm], and c is the speed of light [c = 2.99792458×10^{10} [cm/sec]]
❹	Temperature is in Kelvins unit.
❺	Note that the calculation is exp (a/b) but not (exp a)/b
❻	You may think this value is too small. But it is supposed to be this small.

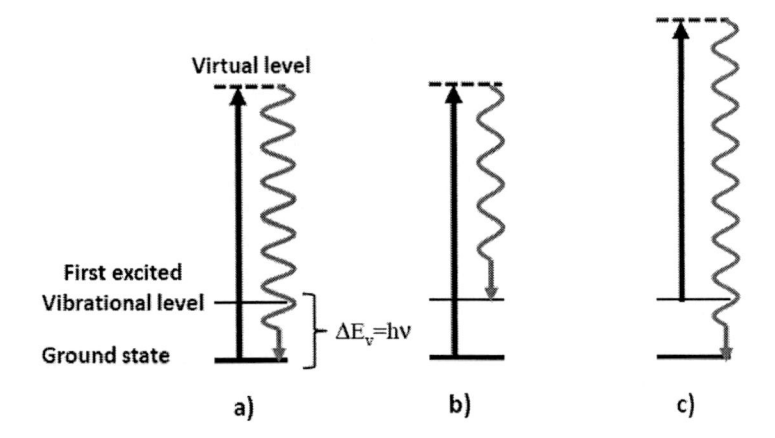

Fig. 11-8 The different light scattering: a) Rayleigh scattering (incident and emitted photons have an equal energy). b) Stokes scattering (the emitted photon has less energy than the absorbed photon). c) anti-Stokes scattering (the emitted photon has more energy than the absorbed photon)

You may be wondering how Raman effect happens. It is originating from the distortion of a molecule in an electric field (**polarizability**). The polarizability (α) is considered to be a measure of how easy it is to induce the dipole moment ($\mu_{induced}$) under an electric field (E, [esu-volt cm^{-1}]).

$$\mu_{induced} = \alpha E \qquad \text{[Eqn. 11-6]}$$

A Raman transition is caused only when polarizability (α [cm^3]) derivative with respect to the normal coordinate (Q) of vibration or rotation is non zero.

$$\partial\alpha/\partial Q \neq 0 \qquad \text{[Eqn. 11-7]}$$

Table 10-2 The character table for the C_{2v} group

C_{2v}	E_{12}	C_2	$\sigma_v (xy)$	$\sigma_v' (yz)$	Linear Rotation	Quadratic
A_1	+1	+1	+1	+1	z	x^2, y^2, z^2
A_2	+1	+1	−1	−1	R_x	xy
B_1	+1	−1	+1	−1	x R_y	xz
B_2	+1	−1	−1	+1	y R_z	yz

The meaning of **[Eqn 11-5]** can be rephrased as that there are certain rotational or vibrational mode which causes Raman effect (Raman active) or does not cause Raman effect (Raman inactive). These Raman active or inactive modes can be derived by using group theory. (You identify the symmetry by using the character table for each symmetry group.) While this textbook does not get too much detail into Group theory, let's recall how you can assign the Raman active mode (**Chapter 10**). Now, it is time to take a look at "**character table**" as was briefly introduced in **Chapter 10**. The way to identify the Raman active mode is easier than you think. If the symmetry label show the products of x, y, or z (including x^2, y^2, z^2, xy, yz, or zx), normal mode with these symmetries are Raman active. As for water case, there are three normal modes (symmetric stretch and bending with A_1, and anti symmetric stretch with B_2 symmetry) which are all Raman active. Now, another important assignment of the Raman modes is **polarized** or **depolarized Raman lines**. If the polarization of the scattered light is the same as that of the incident light (or it is intense only in the parallel direction of the injected light's polarization), then it is called polarized Raman line. Whereas the scattered light is equally intense in both the parallel and perpendicular direction of the polarization of the incident light, it is called as *depolarized* Raman line. A_1 normal mode with all characters = 1 in the **character table** produces polarized lines. This mode is also called as the totally symmetric vibrational mode. Let's take an example in water which was shown in **Chapter 10**. Two Raman active A_1 modes (totally symmetric mode) is the polarized one, and the other B_2 mode is depolarized Raman line.

EXERCISE 11-5

The ammonia has 6 normal modes with following symmetries.(C_{3v})

N–H symmetric stretching (A_1) 3534 [cm^{-1}]
Two N-H asymmetric stretching (E) 3464 [cm^{-1}]
Two H–N–N scissoring (E) 1765 [cm^{-1}]
N-H wagging (A_1) 1139 [cm^{-1}]

Use character table and predict the Raman active modes (polarized or depolarized Raman lines)

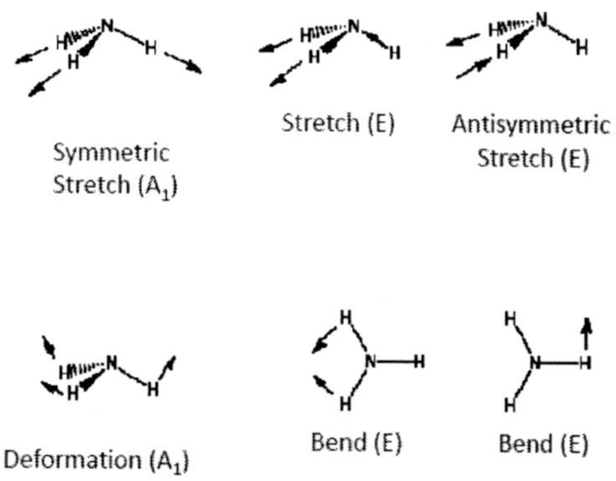

Table 11-1 C_{3v} point group character table.

C_{3v}	E_{12}	$2C_3(z)$	$3\sigma_v$ (xy)	Linear Rotation	Quadratic
A_1	+1	+1	+1	z	x^2+y^2, z^2
A_2	+1	+1	−1	R_z	
E	+2	−1	0	(x, y) (R_x, R_y)	(x^2-y^2, xy) (xz, yz)

Fig. 11-9 Six normal modes of ammonia.

(Symmetric Stretch (A_1), Stretch (E), Antisymmetric Stretch (E), Deformation (A_1), Bend (E), Bend (E))

ANSWER

❶ The modes with A_1 and E symmetries are Raman active.

❷ The mode with A_1 symmetry produces the polarized Raman line.

---

❶ The number of modes for NH3 is 3N-6 = 3(4) – 6 = 6. (See **Chapter 10**)

From the Table A_1 symmetry possesses $x^2 + y^2$, and z^2.
E symmetry possesses $x^2 - y^2$, xy, xz, and yz.

❷ A_1 mode is symmetric for all symmetric operations.

(By the way, C_{3v} point group has two 3- fold rotations and three reflection plane operations.)

11-6 Diffraction

From **Chapter 9**, Quantum mechanics showed that electrons and neutrons exhibits wave properties and can interfere and diffract. Please review the wavelength associated with a particle given by the **de Broglie wavelength (Eqn. 9-2)**

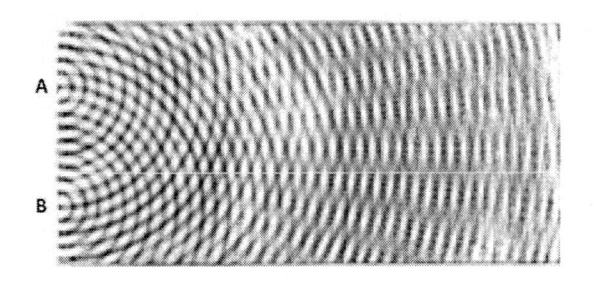

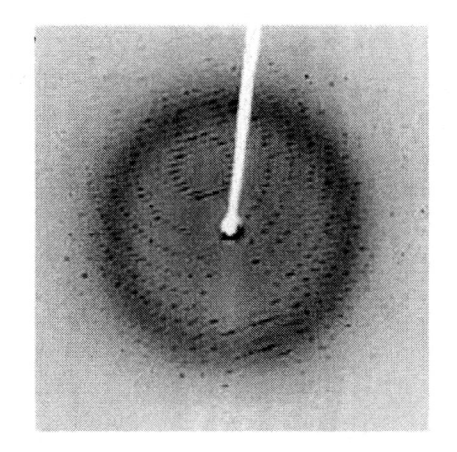

$$\lambda = h/p \qquad \text{(Eqn. 9-2)}$$

Fig. 11-10 a) Sketch of two-slit diffraction. b) A diffraction pattern formed from the constructive interference of X-rays passing through a crystal.

Here, h is Planck's constant and p is the momentum of the particle. While the *de* Brogile wavelength for macroscopic object is too short to be meaningless, diffraction of matter waves for the smaller particles (electrons, neutrons, and atoms) become visible. Thus, the short wavelength of these matter waves makes them ideally suited to study the atomic crystal structure of solids and proteins or buckyballs.

Diffraction is a phenomena where waves bend around small obstacles and spread out small openings. The diffraction is observed when light waves travel through a medium with a varying refractive index. It is most enhanced when wavelength is on the order

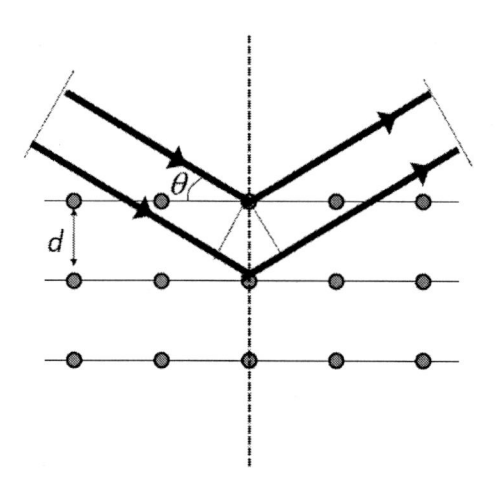

Fig. 11-11 With an incident angle θ, an incident beam injects into scatterers which are arranged symmetrically with a separation *d*.

of the size of the diffracting objects. Diffraction arises because waves propagation. Every point on a wave front is considered as a point source for a secondary radial wave, and the sequential propagation and addition of all these waves create the new wave front. When waves are summed up, they create wave interference pattern accordingly the relative phases as well as the amplitudes of the individual waves. (**diffraction patterns**). The simplest diffraction pattern can be reduced to a two-dimensional pattern. Some of the simpler cases of diffraction are considered below.

The description of diffraction through an interference between waves reflecting from a three dimensional periodic structure (e.g., crystal) is given by **Bragg diffraction**. This is very similar to what is discussed for the waves are scattered from a diffraction grating shown in the above. The condition of constructive interference is given as:

$$n\lambda = 2d \sin\theta \qquad \text{(Eqn. 11-8)}$$

Here, λ is the wavelength, *d* is the distance between crystal planes, θ is the angle of the diffracted wave, and *n* is the *order* of the diffracted beam (n= 1,2,3,…). Please note that Bragg diffraction are popularly carried out using very short wavelength of the EM wave such as x-rays or matter waves like neutrons (and electrons). Thus, the order of the wavelength is on the order of the atomic spacing.

EXERCISE 11-6

An X-ray beam of wavelength 2.15 [Å] injected to a crystal and scattered from the crystal. Calculate the possible path differences of the scattered lights if they are in phase.

ANSWER
From Bragg's law,
$n\lambda = 2d \sin\theta$ **[Eqn. 11-8]**

The path difference corresponds to $n\lambda$.
Therefore, path difference should be
0, 2.15 [Å], 4.30 [Å], 6.45 [Å], ...and so on.

n=0, 1, 2,...
Do not forget n=0 (when there is no difference in path length).

EXERCISE 11-7

When an X-ray beam of wavelength 4.55 Å injected into a crystal and reflected with an angle of 15° for the first order (n=1). Calculate the distance between the scattering planes in [Å].

ANSWER
The Bragg diffraction is given by **(Eqn. 11-8)** as
$n\lambda = 2d \sin\theta$ **(Eqn. 11-8)**
Here, n =1, θ= 15°.
λ=4.55 [Å]   4.55 [Å] =2d sin 15°
d=4.55 [Å]/ (2 sin 15°)
d= 8.79[Å]

Always check "n" value.

Check your calculator's mode for θ, if it is in degree or radian. 1 [degree] = 0.0175 [radian]

You do not have to convert [Å] into [m].

Most Common Mistake (45)-"I cannot calculate the Bragg diffraction. Why?"

The Bragg's diffraction given by **[Eqn. 11-8]** indicates very simple relationship between the scattering plane distance and the light reflected from the plane. However, there are a couple of cautions need to be taken for using this equation properly. First of all, you need to make sure that the unit for both d and wavelength, λ, should be the same. (Most commonly, we use Å). Secondly, the angle $\theta = 15°$ is given by degrees, but may need to be calculated by radians. If your calculator uses the radians unit, you need to convert your degrees into radians by using π radians=180°. For example, $\theta = 15°$ in **EXERCISE 11-6** becomes, $\theta = (15°)(\pi \text{ [radians]}/180°) = (15/180)(\pi \text{ [radians]}) = (0.08333)(3.14159265) = 0.2618$ [radians]. Lastly, you should confirm the order of the scattering (i.e. value of n). The first order corresponds to n=1, and the second order is n=2, and so on.

11-7 X Ray Diffraction and Determination of Molecular Structure

A practice and powerful use for the diffraction is the determination of the structure of a solid material through an irradiation of X-ray (neutron). The Bragg diffraction model learned in the above can be used intuitively to understand X-ray diffraction. Let's imagine a series of evenly spaced "sheets" running through a solid sample passing through the centers of the atoms of the material. The orientation of a particular set of "sheets" is described by spacing distance (d) and three indices (**Miller indices, h, k, l**). Then, an incoming X-rays are scattered "specularly" (i.e., mirror-like) from each imaginary plane. Each scattered spot is called as a *reflection*, since it is the reflection of the X-rays within the crystal. Now, the X-rays scattered from adjacent planes are combined constructively when a path-length difference, the angle θ between the plane, X-ray wavelength λ satisfies the relationship given in **(Eqn. 11-8)**

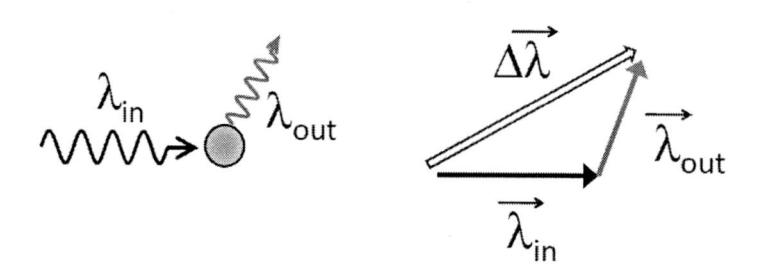

Fig. 11-12 Sketch of a scattering vector $\vec{\Delta\lambda}$

$$n\lambda = 2d \sin \theta \qquad \text{(Eqn. 11-8)}$$

Here, n is an integer (n = 1, 2, 3....). While Bragg's law provides a principle of understanding the alignment of atoms in a solid material, we have a serious problem solving for the arrangement of atoms since Bragg's law does not explain the relative intensities of the reflections.

Chapter 11 Scattering

Let's expand this Bragg's diffraction law to third dimension. In order to do so, I will introduce the wave vector (wave is given by a vector). Let's define the wave vector of incoming wave as $\vec{\lambda_{in}}$ and the wave vector of outgoing wave after scattering as $\vec{\lambda_{out}}$. Then, the difference of these two wave vectors are defined as the **scattering vector** as:

$$\Delta\vec{\lambda} = \vec{\lambda}_{out} - \vec{\lambda}_{in} \qquad \text{(Eqn. 11-9)}$$

This vector represents a diffracted beam due to a scattering. If we define the unit vector ($\vec{u}$) on a, b, and c, crystal primitive axes as

$$\vec{u} = \vec{a} + \vec{b} + \vec{c} \qquad \text{(Eqn. 11-10)}$$

The **Laue conditions (Laue's equation)** states that the scattering vector of each component should satisfy the following conditions,

$$\vec{a} \cdot \Delta\vec{\lambda} = 2\pi h$$
$$\vec{b} \cdot \Delta\vec{\lambda} = 2\pi k$$
$$\vec{c} \cdot \Delta\vec{\lambda} = 2\pi l \qquad \text{(Eqn. 11-11)}$$

Here, (h, k, l) are integers that also corresponds to reflection's reciprocal lattice indices. The meaning of the **[Eqn. 11-11]** is that the scattering vector must be oriented in a specific direction in relation to the primitive (unit) vectors of the crystal lattice ($\vec{a}, \vec{b}, \vec{c}$).

You may be wondering how important these integers (h, k, l) are. These are called **Miller indices**, and they are used as a notation n crystallography for planes and directions in crystal lattices. A family of lattice planes is determined by three integers h, k, and l, and commonly noted as (hkl). Each index denotes a plane orthogonal to a direction (h, k, l) in the basis of the "reciprocal lattice vectors". (You will see the meaning of this "reciprocal vector" later.)

The integers (hkl) are usually written in lowest terms, thus their greatest common divisor should be 1. Please go through the following example of to get hang with Miller indices and the meaning of "reciprocal vector". Let me use two-dimensional plane in order to make it simpler.

Chapter 11 Scattering

In a example figure, two-dimensional unit cell lattice and several group of parallel lines going through the lattice points. Each group of parallel lines can be indexed in the same Miller indices. In order to assign Miller indices (in this case it is (h,k)), you first pick any line (use the solid line for this example), then the intercepts that this line makes with a-axis and b-axis are 6*a* and 2*b* in this example, respectively (6, 2), Now, take the reciprocal of these (1/6, 1/2). Then, multiply by the least common multiple (LCM), which in this case it is 6. Then, this vector becomes (1,3). This is the final result of Miller indices (hk) =(13) for this case. While this example given here is for two dimensional plane, the same application is applied to the three dimensional case for a, b, and c crystal primitive axes. Using Miller indexes you can define three orthogonal planes to each axes. The Miller index 100 represents a plane orthogonal to a axis; index 010 represents a plane orthogonal to direction *b* axis, and index 001 represents a plane orthogonal to *c* axis. One more last thing, negative integers are written with a bar (e.g., $\bar{1}$ for –1) by convention.

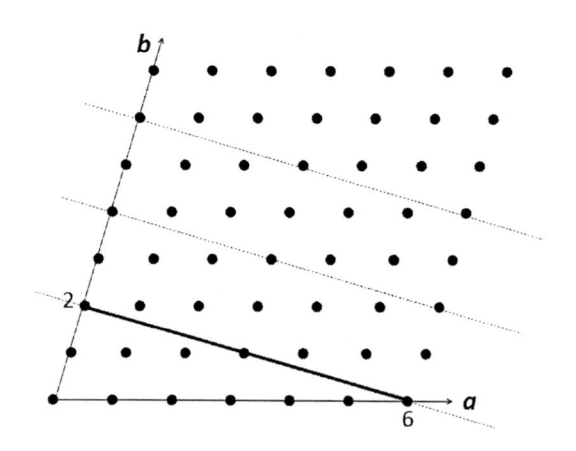

Fig. 11-13 Example of Miller indices

MCM Most Common Mistake (46)–"I thought this was Miller indices, but it is not!"

The Miller indices are noted by (hkl), and they are different from {hkl}, [hkl] nor ⟨hkl⟩.

1) The notation {hkl} denotes the set of all planes that are equivalent to (hkl) by the symmetry of the lattice.
2) The notation [ℓmn] with round brackets denotes a <u>direction</u> in the basis of the *direct* lattice vectors instead of the reciprocal lattice;
3) The notation ⟨hkl⟩ with brackets denotes the set of all <u>directions</u> that are equivalent to [hkl] by symmetry.
The second and the third one indicate the directions not planes.

Let's take a look at how distance between two (parallel) planes are calculated for the plane of Miller index (hkl) and the crystal lattice with the unit length of (a,b,c). For two dimensional case with Miller index (hk) and the lattice length (a, b), the distance d_{hk} between two adjacent parallel lines is given by

$$d_{hk} = 1 \Big/ \sqrt{\left(h^2/a^2\right) + \left(k^2/b^2\right)}$$

(Eqn. 11-12)

For three dimensional case, the Miller index is (hkl) and the length of each axis is (a,b,c). The distance d_{hkl} between two adjacent parallel planes is given by

Chapter 11 Scattering

$$d_{hkl} = 1 \Big/ \sqrt{\left(h^2/a^2\right) + \left(k^2/b^2\right) + \left(l^2/c^2\right)} \qquad \text{(Eqn. 11-13)}$$

When a light with wavelength λ is injected into the system which has parallel lines or parallel planes described by the Miller indices, you will satisfy the Bragg's diffraction similar to **[Eqn. 11-8]** as:

$$n\lambda = 2d_{hk} \sin \theta \qquad \text{[Eqn. 11-14]}$$

or

$$n\lambda = 2d_{hkl} \sin \theta \qquad \text{[Eqn. 11-15]}$$

In order to determine the formation of the atoms (or molecular structure) of a solid material, **Fourier transform method** is conducted. Since it involves an intense mathematical process, let me first show you a good example of Fourier transformation in (**Fig. 11-4**) **Fourier transformation** is the mathematical operation which decomposes a signal into its constituent frequencies. In **Fig. 11-4**, the data collected in time domain, $f(t)$, can be transformed into a function into frequency domain, $F(v)$. Conceptually, the Fourier transform transforms one complex-valued function of a real variable into another. This operation decomposes a function into oscillatory functions. With respect to what we are going to learn below, Fourier transform is considered to be an operation between the image in the spatial domain and Fourier transformed images in the spectral domain. (See **Fig. 11-15**)

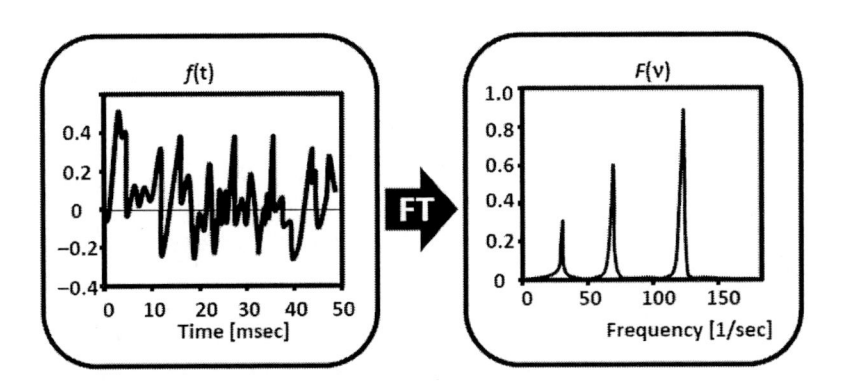

Fig. 11-14. Concept of Fourier transformation.

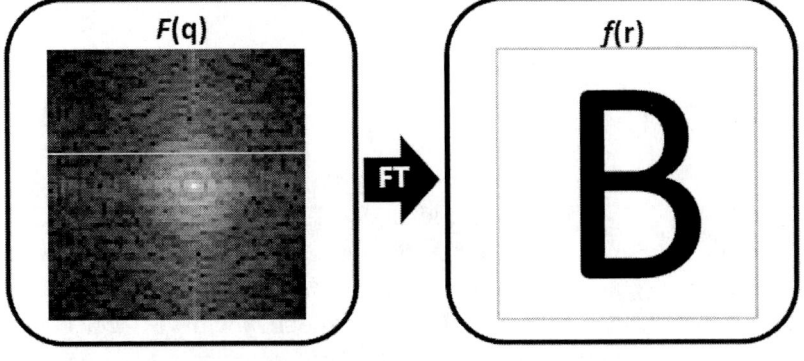

Fig. 11-15 Fourier transformation from F(X,Y,Z) to f(h,k,l).

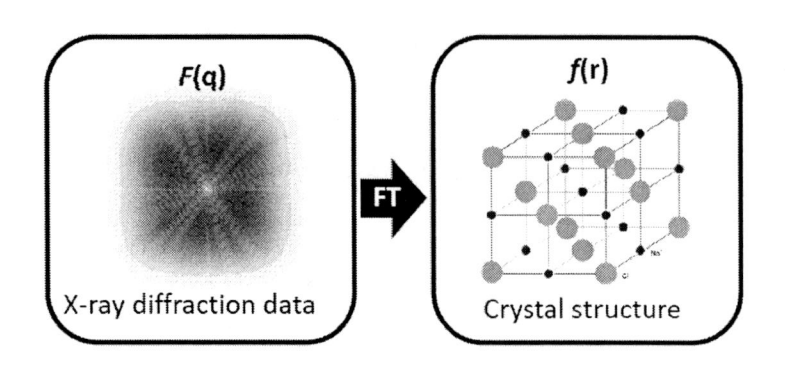

Fig. 11-16 Demonstration of the procedure obtained by Fourier transform in X-ray diffraction

The concept of Fourier transformation is applied to X-ray diffraction as follows. In this method, the final result (structure of molecule or alignment of the atoms) is expressed by the **density of electrons** $f(r)$ within the solid material (commonly a crystal) (Here, r is the three-dimensional position vector). The data collected by X-ray scattering, $F(q)$, is Fourier transformed to obtain the density, $f(r)$, in space as:

$$f(\vec{r}) = \int \left[F(\vec{q}) e^{i\vec{q}\cdot\vec{r}} \Big/ (2\pi)^3 \right] d\vec{q} \qquad \textbf{(Eqn. 11-16)}$$

Here, $\vec{q}$ is the three-dimensional real vector representing a point in reciprocal space. This means that it describes a particular oscillation in the electron density in the direction of vector $\vec{q}$. The scalar of this vector $|\vec{q}|$ is 2π divided by the wavelength of the oscillation. The corresponding formula for a Fourier transform of [Eqn. 14-15] is

$$F(\vec{q}) = \int f(\vec{r}) \, e^{-i\vec{q}\cdot\vec{r}} d\vec{r} \qquad \textbf{(Eqn. 11-17)}$$

Since $F(\vec{q})$ can be a complex number, it is useful to express this function as

$$F(\vec{q}) = |F(\vec{q})| e^{i\varphi(\vec{q})} \qquad \textbf{(Eqn. 11-18)}$$

Here, $|F(q)|$ is the magnitude and $\varphi(q)$ is the phase. The magnitudes $|F(q)|$ corresponds to the intensities in X-ray diffraction data. Since a combination of the magnitudes and phases produces the full Fourier transform function of $F(q)$ (and gives $f(r)$ by transformation). An example of $F(q)$ to $f(r)$ is shown in (**Fig. 11-15**). The phases needs to be obtained by collecting full sets of reflection with known alterations to the scattering, either by modulating the wavelength past a certain absorption edge or by adding strongly scattering metal atoms. In principle, an atomic structure can be determined by X-ray scattering to solid sample. Among any solid samples, crystals are considered to be a material possesses strongest signal because crystalline samples have periodicity which is composed of many repeating unit cells in three dimensions. When periodic patterns are Fourier transformed corresponding concentration of periodical repeating points in reciprocal space is observed and is called as **Bragg peaks**, which are the reflection spots observed in the diffraction image. The *intensity* of **Bragg peaks** are proportional to a square of number of scatterers, N^2. The X-ray diffraction determines the average chemical bond lengths and angles within a few thousandths of an Å and within a few tenths of a degree. What happens to the **Bragg peaks** for a liquid or amorphous materials? Since the orientation of the atoms in those are random, it will provide a uniform spread of points, and no orientational information is gained.

In order to provide mathematical accessible method for relating between $F(q)$ and $f(r)$, let's go through simpler methodology by using complex number notation. Let's represent the $F(q)$ and $f(r)$ **by Miller indices as** $F(q) = F(h,k,l)$ and $f(r) = f(h,k,l)$.

$$F(h, k, l) = FT[f(h, k, l)] = \sum_{j=1}^{n} \varphi_j e^{i\alpha_j(h,k,l)} \qquad \text{(Eqn. 11-19)}$$

(FT: indicates Fourier transformation)

Here, φ_j is **atomic scattering factor** of an atom, $\alpha_j(h,k,l)$ is the "**phase factor**" for scattering from the atom, and I is the complex number (i.e., $i = \sqrt{-1}$). The function $f(h,k,l)$ is based on the atomic coordinate (coordinate of scatterer, X, Y, Z), while the function $F(h,k,l)$ is based on the coordinate of observer. The phase factor α_j is expressed by the atomic coordinate and the Miller's indices as:

$$\alpha_j(h, k, l) = 2\pi(hX_j + kY_j + lZ_j) \qquad \text{(Eqn. 11-20)}$$

Please note that terms given in [**Eqn. 11-18**] have two parts and one is a real (A) and imaginary terms (B) since it has a complex number.

$$F(h, k, l) = A + iB \qquad \text{(Eqn. 11-21)}$$

Here,

$$A(h, k, l) = \sum_{j=1}^{n} \varphi_j \cdot \cos[2\pi(hX_j + kY_j + lZ_j)] \qquad \text{(Eqn. 11-22)}$$

$$B(h, k, l) = \sum_{j=1}^{n} \varphi_j \cdot \sin[2\pi(hX_j + kY_j + lZ_j)] \qquad \text{(Eqn. 11-23)}$$

The intensity of the scattered light is given by

$$I = |F(h, k, l)|^2 = A^2 + B^2 \qquad \text{(Eqn. 11-24)}$$

The phase factor can be calculated by

$$\alpha(h, k, l) = \tan^{-1}\left[B/A\right] \qquad \text{(Eqn. 11-25)}$$

Let's take a look at more realistic situation. When there is n scattering atoms in a crystal system, and i-th scattering coordinate scatterer is given as (x_i, y_i, z_i) along a, b, and c axes, respectively, then the (X_i, Y_i, Z_i) = (x_i/L, y_i/M, z_i/N), here L, M, N indicate the dimension of this crystal. (That is the length of this entire crystal is L along a –axis, M along b-axis, and N along c-axis.)

Chapter 11 Scattering

EXERCISE 11-8
A cubic unit cell contains an atom at the origin. Calculate the relative intensity of diffractions by (100), (200), and (110) planes, when the scattering factor of the atom at the origin (X, Y, Z) =(0,0,0) is *f*.

ANSWER
If the scattering factor of the atom is f,

$A(h, k, l) = \sum_{j=1}^{n} f_j \cdot \cos[2\pi(hX_j + kY_j + lZ_j)]$ (Eqn. 11-22)

$B(h, k, l) = \sum_{j=1}^{n} f_j \cdot \sin[2\pi(hX_j + kY_j + lZ_j)]$ (Eqn. 11-23)

The intensity of the scattered light

❶ $I = |F(h, k, l)|^2 = A^2 + B^2$ (Eqn. 11-24)

The coordinate of the scatterer is (X, Y, Z) = (0,0, 0) and (you can think j as 1 and n=1 in **(Eqn 11-22)** and **(Eqn. 11-23)**).

❷ A(h,k,l)= f cos[2π(h·0 + k·0+l·0)]=f
B(h,k,l)= f sin[2π(h·0 + k·0+l·0)]=0
I= $A^2 = f^2$

Thus, for any planes (h k l), the intensity of this case is the same amount of = f^2

❶ Intensity I, needs two components (real (A) and imaginary part (B)).
❷ cos θ ≠0 when θ=0.

MCM Most Common Mistake (47)-What is going on in this chapter?? There are (i) Fourier transform method and (ii) complex number notation method"

Both methods are trying to get the same coordinate of crystals (or molecules). The Fourier transform method (i) requires an intense computational work, whereas ii) complex number notation method is more accessible.

Chapter 11 Scattering

☹ **MCM Most Common Mistake (48)-Real part and imaginary part? How should I imagine an "imaginary part"?**

The original function given in (**Eqn. 11-19**) contains $e^{i\alpha}$ term

$$F(h,k,l) = \sum_{j=1}^{n} f_j e^{i\alpha_j}$$ [Eqn. 11-19]

The $e^{i\alpha}$ term this is mathematically expressed as
$$e^{ix} = \cos x + i\sin x$$

Therefore, a term given by cos function is a real term and the other term given by sin function is an imaginary part. [For the details, please see the "**How did you get these equations Chapter 10**".]
Common mistake is that an expression of I (intensity)
$$I = |F(h,k,l)|^2 = A^2 + B^2$$

[Eqn. 11-24]

The intensity I is often mistaken as

I = A² +2iAB–B²

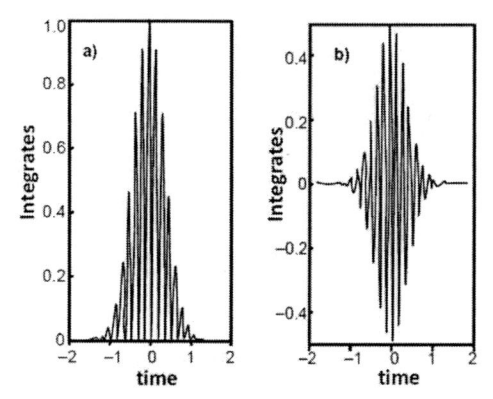

Fig. 11-17 Demonstration of real term and imaginary term. Here, a function is $f(t) = \cos(2\pi(3t))e^{-\pi t^2}$ and (a) real part: $Re\left(e^{-2\pi i(3t)}f(t)\right)$ and (b) imaginary part $Im\left(e^{-2\pi i(3t)}f(t)\right)$

It is probably because
$$F(h,k,l)^2 = (A+iB)^2$$
$$= A^2 + 2iAB + (iB)^2$$
$$= A^2 + 2iAB - B^2$$

However, ca correct procedure of calculation of I is
$$I = |F(h,k,l)|^2$$
$$= F^*(h,k,l)F(h,k,l)$$
$$= (A+iB)^*(A+iB)$$
$$= (A-iB)^*(A+iB)$$
$$= A^2 + B^2$$

The asterisk "*" indicates a complex conjugate. (i* =– i)
[For the details, please see the "**How did you get these equations Chapter 10**".

Chapter 11 Scattering

☹ **MCM Most Common Mistake (49)-You are showing X, Y, Z or x,y,z? Are these big deals?**

There is a discrete difference between x, y, z and X, Y, and Z. scattering
(x_i, y_i, z_i): the coordinates of a scatterer along a, b, and c axes.
(X, Y, Z): $(x_i/L, y_i/M, z_i/N)$ - L, M, N are length of this entire crystal along a-, b-, and c-axes, respectively. Thus, X, Y, Z indicate a relative position in each axis in an entire crystal dimension.

EXERCISE 11-9.
Consider the crystal of two dimensional protein with unit cell of 80 [Å] along a axis and 90 [Å] along b-axis. When gold is substituted in this crystal at the location of x=20 [Å] along *a*-axis and y=30 [Å] along b-axis. Determine the intensity of the diffraction spot for (0 1) reflection, phase. Use the scattering factor of the Au atom is 74.

ANSWER
If the scattering factor of the atom is *f*,

$A(h,k) = \sum_{j=1}^{n} f_j \cdot \cos[2\pi(hX_j + kY_j)]$ [Eqn. 11-23]

$B(h,k) = \sum_{j=1}^{n} f_j \cdot \sin[2\pi(hX_j + kY_j)]$ [Eqn. 11-24]

❶ ☞ $f = 74$, X= (20 [Å] /80 [Å]) and Y= (30 [Å] /90 [Å])

Thus,

❷ ☞ A(0,1)= 74cos[2π (30/90)]= 74cos(2π/3)= –37.00
B(0,1)= 74sin [2π(30/90))= 74sin(2π/3)=74 (0.866)=64.085

The intensity of the scattered light

❸ ☞ $I = A^2 + B^2$ (Eqn. 11-24)

Thus, I= (–37.00)² + (64.085)²= 5476

❹ ☞ $\alpha = \tan^{-1}[B/A]$ (Eqn. 11-25)

α=tan⁻¹[64.085/–37.00]

❹ ☞ = tan⁻¹ (–1.73)
= –60°

---

❶ ☞ (X, Y, Z) and (x, y, z) are related as (X, Y, Z) =(x/L, y/M. z/N)
❷ ☞ Separate A (real) and B (imaginary) part.
❸ ☞ Don't forget to add A² and B².
❹ ☞ tan⁻¹x =y is asking the angle y which gives the value x.

tan θ = b/a

Since **neutron diffraction** has so many concepts shared with X-ray diffraction and has been used as a powerful method to study biological system, let me explain about neutron diffraction briefly. In **Neutron diffraction,** neutrons are used to determine the atomic and/or magnetic structure of gasses, liquids or amorphous materials. Neutron diffraction is a form of elastic scattering, and the neutrons scattered from the sample materials have comparable energy to the incident neutrons. The technique used in neutron scattering is similar to that used in X-ray diffraction. However, neutron scattering has the different scattering properties than x-rays, thus complementary information can be gained. In a nuclear reactor, neutrons (whose wavelength of near one Ångström) can be released through nuclei decay as fission takes place. Now, how neutron scattering is different from X-ray scattering? Neutrons interact with matter differently than x-rays. While X-rays interact primarily with the electron around each atomic core and the intensity of the diffracted x-ray is proportional to atomic number (Z), neutrons interact directly with the *nucleus* of the atom and the intensity of diffraction patterns vary depending on isotope. The neutron scattering is originating from the nuclei, and the scattering power of an atom does not fall off with the scattering angle opposed to the case for X-rays. The scattering length also varies depending on isotope to isotope and has no dependence on the atomic number. For example, Vanadium scatters almost no neutrons but strong scatter X-rays. As the advantage of neutron scattering, it provides strong diffraction peaks even at high angles (i.e. high *resolution*) constructing precise atomic structure. Since neutrons (neutrals in charge) carry a spin, they interact with magnetic moments originating from the electron and reveal magnetic structure. Neutron diffraction is utilized to determine the structure of proteins and surfactants, since low atomic number materials (H, C, N, O,.. etc) possess higher neutron cross section. This can be regarded as a great advantage of neutron scattering since X-ray is very insensitive to H.

Chapter 11

How did you get these equations?
-The derivation of selected equations.

(Eqn. 11-8) $\quad n\lambda = 2d \sin \theta$

If the path length between a) and b) has exactly the difference of full wave length (λ), the phase of wave in these two paths should be the same and will interfere constructively. (If the difference in path length is a half of the wavelength (i.e., $\lambda/2$), they interfere destructively and the amplitude of wave will cancel each other.) In a given figure, the path (a) is shorter in length by path (b) with the amount of given by two grey lines. The length of one the grey line corresponds to d sin θ, using the triangle. Thus, the path difference between two lines are 2 d sin θ. In order to the two waves are constructively interfere, the path length should be equal to the integer (n) of the wavelength (λ). Thus,

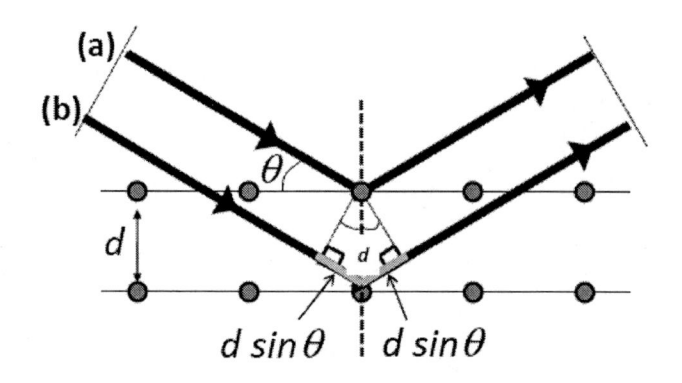

Fig. 11-18 Two different beam path scattered from a particle separated by distance d. The incoming and outgoing angle is θ.

$$n\lambda = 2d \sin \theta \quad \quad \textbf{(Eqn. 11-8)}$$

(Eqn. 11-16) $\quad f(\vec{r}) = \int \left[F(\vec{q}) e^{i\vec{q}\cdot\vec{r}} / (2\pi)^3 \right] d\vec{q}$

(Eqn. 11-17) $\quad F(\vec{q}) = \int f(\vec{r}) e^{-i\vec{q}\cdot\vec{r}} d\vec{r}$

The **Fourier transformation** is the mathematical operation which decomposes a *time domain* into its constituent frequencies (or frequency domain data). More precise definition, however, involves complex values. In the Fourier transformation, one complex-valued function of a

Chapter 11 Scattering

real variable is transformed into another function resulting in a decomposition of a function into oscillatory functions. It is possible to generalize the Fourier transformation into on discrete structures such as finite groups. Common convention for defining the Fourier transformation of an integral function $f: \mathbf{R} \to \mathbf{C}$ is :

$$\hat{f}(\xi) = \int_{-\infty}^{+\infty} f(x) e^{-2\pi i x \xi} dx$$

for every real number ξ. Here, x is the independent variable (in most cases it is time), and the transform variable ξ represents frequency for most cases..The function, f can be reconstructed from $\hat{f}$ by the **inverse transform** as:

$$f(x) = \int_{-\infty}^{+\infty} \hat{f}(\xi) e^{2\pi i x \xi} d\xi$$

for every real number x. Therefore, by replacing function $f(x)$ as $f(\vec{r})$ and $\hat{f}(\xi)$ as $F(\vec{q})$], the Fourier transformation between $f(\vec{r})$ and $F(\vec{q})$ are constructed.

$$f(\vec{r}) = \int \left[F(\vec{q}) e^{i\vec{q}\cdot\vec{r}} / (2\pi)^3 \right] d\vec{q} \qquad \text{(Eqn. 11-16]}$$

$$F(\vec{q}) = \int f(\vec{r}) e^{-i\vec{q}\cdot\vec{r}} d\vec{r} \qquad \text{(Eqn. 11-17)}$$

(Eqn. 11-24)

$$I = |F(h,k,l)|^2 = A^2 + B^2$$

$$F(h,k,l) = A + iB \qquad \text{(Eqn. 11-24)}$$

Since

$$e^{ix} = \cos x + i \sin x$$

These two terms can be expressed as

$$A(h,k,l) = \sum_{j=1}^{n} f_j \cdot Real[e^{i\alpha_j}]$$

$$= \sum_{j=1}^{n} f_j \cdot \cos[2\pi(hX_j + kY_j + lZ_j)] \qquad \text{(Eqn. 11-22)}$$

$$B(h,k,l) = \sum_{j=1}^{n} f_j \cdot imaginary[e^{i\alpha_j}]$$
$$= \sum_{j=1}^{n} f_j \cdot sin[2\pi(hX_j + kY_j + lZ_j)]$$

[Eqn. 11-23]

The intensity of the scattered light
$$I = |F(h,k,l)|^2 = F^*(h,k,l) \cdot F(h,k,l)$$

Here, * indicates a complex conjugate of the function. Since

$$F^*(h,k,l) = A - iB$$
$$I = |F(h,k,l)|^2 = A^2 + B^2$$

(Eqn. 11-24)

Chapter 11 Summary [Part 1]

(Use back page to cover the contents.)

1	Categorization of Rayleigh, Mie, Brillouin, Raman scatterings	**Rayleigh** and **Mie scattering**: elastic $$\alpha = \pi D_p / \lambda \qquad \text{[Eqn. 11-1]}$$ $\alpha \ll 1$: **Rayleigh scattering**, $\alpha \approx 1$: **Mie scattering** **Brillouin** and **Raman scattering**: inelastic
2	The intensity of the scattered light by Rayleigh scattering	$$I \propto d^6 / \lambda^4 \qquad \text{[Eqn. 11-2]}$$
3	minimum wavelength λ in Brillouin scattering	$\lambda = 2\bar{d}_{eq}$ (Eqn. 11-4) λ: a minimum wavelength, $\bar{d}_{eq}$: equilibrium separation between atoms.
4	Raman effect	It originates from the distortion of the polarizability due the electric field. $$\mu_{induced} = \alpha E \text{ (Eqn. 11-6)}$$ The Raman transition takes place when $$\partial \alpha / \partial Q \neq 0 \text{ (Eqn. 11-7)}$$ The scattered light possess energy difference from an incident light by vibrational, rotational or electronic energy of a molecule. **Stokes scattering** and **anti-Stokes scattering**. a) Rayleigh scattering, b) Stokes scattering, c) anti-Stokes scattering

[Fold the page at the double line and cover the right half.]

CHAPTER 11 SUMMARY CHECK [PART 1]

(Use this page to cover and check the contents.)
Use ☐ as your check box. Write your comment at far right

1	Categorization of Rayleigh, Mie, Brillouin, Raman scatterings	☐ ☐ ☐ ☐ ☐	
2	The intensity of the scattered light by Rayleigh scattering	☐ ☐ ☐ ☐ ☐	
3	minimum wavelength λ in Brillouin scattering	☐ ☐ ☐ ☐ ☐	
4	Raman effect	☐ ☐ ☐ ☐ ☐	

Chapter 11 Summary [Part 2]

(Use back page to cover the contents.)

5	Bragg's diffraction law	$n\lambda = 2d \sin\theta$ **(Eqn. 11-8)** λ: wavelength of an injected beam, d: distance between crystal planes, θ: angle of the diffracted wave, n: *order* of the diffracted beam (n= 1,2,3,...)
6	Laue conditions	$\vec{a} \cdot \Delta\vec{\lambda} = 2\pi h \quad \vec{b} \cdot \Delta\vec{\lambda} = 2\pi k \quad \vec{c} \cdot \Delta\vec{\lambda} = 2\pi l$ **(Eqn. 11-11)** (h, k, l): **Miller indices** integers which present planes and directions in crystal lattices. $(\vec{a}, \vec{b}, \vec{c})$: primitive (unit) vectors of the crystal lattice $d_{hkl} = 1 \Big/ \sqrt{(h^2/a^2) + (k^2/b^2) + (l^2/c^2)}$ **(Eqn. 11-13)** d_{hkl}: distance between two adjacent parallel planes $n\lambda = 2d_{hkl} \sin\theta$
7	Analysis of X-ray scattering by complex number notation method, intensity of the scattered light (I), phase factor (α).	$F(h,k,l) = \sum_{j=1}^{n} \varphi_j e^{i\alpha_j(h,k,l)} = A + iB$ **(Eqns. 11-19 & 11-21)** $F(h,k,l)$: collected data by X-ray scattering φ_j: atomic scattering factor of an atom j α_j: phase factor for scattering from the atom j $I = |F(h,k,l)|^2 = A^2 + B^2$ **(Eqn. 11-24)** $\alpha = \tan^{-1}[B/A]$ **(Eqn. 11-25)**

[Fold the page at the double line and cover the right half.]

CHAPTER 11 SUMMARY CHECK [PART 2]

(Use this page to cover and check the contents.)
Use ☐ as your check box. Write your comment at far right

5	Bragg's diffraction law	☐ ☐ ☐ ☐ ☐	
6	Laue conditions	☐ ☐ ☐ ☐ ☐	
7	Analysis of X-ray scattering by complex number notation method, intensity of the scattered light (I), phase factor (α).	☐ ☐ ☐ ☐ ☐	

Chapter 11 - YOUR TEACHER MAY TEST YOU ON:

No.	What may be asked?		What you should know or do?
1	What are the major scattering processes and index for categorizing each scattering process?	→	Elastic (Rayleigh and Mie scattering) and Inelastic (Brillouin and Raman scattering)
		→	$\alpha = \pi D_p / \lambda$ (Eqn. 11-1) $\alpha \ll 1$: Rayleigh scattering, $\alpha \approx 1$: Mie scattering
		→	EXERCISE 11-1
2	What is the wavelength of light (λ) or particle size dependence in the light intensity of the Rayleigh scattering?	→	$I \propto d^6/\lambda^4$ (Eqn. 11-3)
		→	EXERCISE 11-2
		→	Problem 11-2
3	How can you estimate the equilibrium separation of an atom from Brillouin scattering?	→	In Brillouin scattering, a minimum wavelength λ, is estimated to be twice of the equilibrium separation between atoms in a system
		→	EXERCISE 11-3
4	What is the ratio of the population of the states between ground and the first excited state of the typical normal mode (or Raman active mode)?	→	use the formula of Boltzmann distribution with $\Delta E = h\nu_e$, (ν_e is fundamental frequency) $N_j/N_i = (g_j/g_i) e^{-\Delta E/k_B T}$ (Eqn. 11-5)
		→	EXERCISE 11-4
5	How can you predict the Raman active mode (and polarized or depolarized Raman lines)?	→	Use the character table. Choose the mode with symmetry label showing the products of x, y, or z (including x^2, y^2 or z^2)
		→	Totally symmetric mode is polarized Raman lines.
		→	EXERCISE 11-5

Chapter 11 Scattering

6	How can you calculate the spacing between two parallel crystal planes from the scattering diffraction spots?	→	**Bragg's diffraction law** $n\lambda = 2d \sin\theta$ (Eqn. 11-8)
		→	**EXERCISES 11-6 and 11-7**
7	What is the definition of the Miller indices (hkl)?	→	The **Laue conditions (Laue's equation)** $\vec{a}\cdot\Delta\vec{\lambda} = 2\pi h, \vec{b}\cdot\Delta\vec{\lambda} = 2\pi k, \vec{c}\cdot\Delta\vec{\lambda} = 2\pi l$ (Eqn. 11-11)
		→	The (hkl) is a "reciprocal vector" Fig. 11-12
8	How can you calculate the separation of the planes of a given Miller index (hkl)?	→	$n\lambda = 2d_{hkl}\sin\theta$ (Eqn. 11-15)
9	How can you calculate the relative intensity (I) and phase (α) of diffractions by given (hkl) plane?	→	$I = |F(h,k,l)|^2 = A^2 + B^2$ (Eqn. 11-24) $F(h,k,l) = A + iB$ (Eqn. 11-21) $A(h,k,l) = \sum_{j=1}^{n} f_j \cdot \cos[2\pi(hX_j + kY_j + lZ_j)]$ (Eqn. 11-22) $B(h,k,l) = \sum_{j=1}^{n} f_j \cdot \sin[2\pi(hX_j + kY_j + lZ_j)]$ (Eqn. 11-23) $\alpha = \tan^{-1}[B/A]$ (Eqn. 11-25)
		→	$(X_i, Y_i, Z_i) = (x_i/L, y_i/M, z_i/N)$, here L, M, N indicate the dimension of this crystal. (That is the length of this entire crystal is L along a –axis, M along b-axis, and N along c-axis.)
		→	**EXERCISES 11-8 and 11-9**
		→	**Problems** 11-3, 11-5

UNIT CHECK CHAPTER 11

Important Parameters of This Chapter	Popularly Used Unit	Important Unit Conversion
Diameter of particle, D_p	M	
Wavelength of radiation, λ	M	
Size parameter, α	dimension less	
Intensity of the light, I or I_o	W m^{-2}	[W]=[J/sec]
Scattering angle, θ	° (degree) rad	180° = π [rad]
Diameter of particle, d	m	
Distance between particles, R	m	
Number of particles in the state, N_i or N_j	dimensionless	
Degeneracy, g_i or g_j	dimensionless	
Energy of the vibrational state, E_i or E_j	J cm^{-1} eV	1 eV = 1.6022×10^{-19} [J] 1 [cm^{-1}] = 1.98648×10^{-22} [J]
Boltzmann constant, k_B	J·K^{-1}	k_B = 1.3807 × 10^{-23} [J/K]
Induced dipole, $\mu_{induced}$	esu-volt cm^2	
Polarizability, α	cm^3	
Electric field, E	esu-volt cm^{-1}	
Normal coordinate, Q	m cm	
de Broglie wavelength, λ	m	
Planck's constant, h	J sec m^2 kg sec^{-1}	h = 6.62606896(33)×10^{-34} [J sec]
Momentum, p	kg m sec^{-1}	
Miller indices, (h k l)	dimensionless	
Phase, α	° (degree) rad	

Chapter 11 Scattering

SUMMARY OF TRICKY TRAPS OF CHAPTER 11

☐	1	Intensity of Rayleigh scattering is proportional to $1/\lambda^4$
☐	2	Raman active mode is predicted by a character table.
☐	3	E(Stokes scattering) < R (Rayleigh scattering) < E (anti-Stokes scattering)
☐	4	The Miller indices are "reciprocal" vector.
☐	5	The coordinate of scatterer is obtained from Fourier transformation of the collected X-ray data. However, this textbook uses complex number notation method. (It has real and imaginary parts)
☐	6	X, Y, Z = x/M, y/L, z/N

LAST MINUTE REVIEW OF MATH CHAPTER 11

(These are basic algebra which you have no excuse if you miss them.)

1. $\left(\frac{a^n}{b^m}\right)^x = \frac{a^{nx}}{b^{mx}}$

2.

$$\sin\theta = \frac{b}{c} \quad \cos\theta = \frac{a}{c} \quad \tan\theta = \frac{b}{a}$$

$$\sin^{-1}\frac{b}{c} = \theta \quad \cos^{-1}\frac{a}{c} = \theta \quad \tan^{-1}\frac{b}{a} = \theta$$

3. $i^2 = -1 \quad i^* = -i$

Nobel Prize and Your Knowledge From Chapter 11
(*: word appeared in Chapter 11)

I

Fig. 11-19 X-ray diffraction of hemoglobin. (inset: Structure of hemoglobin)

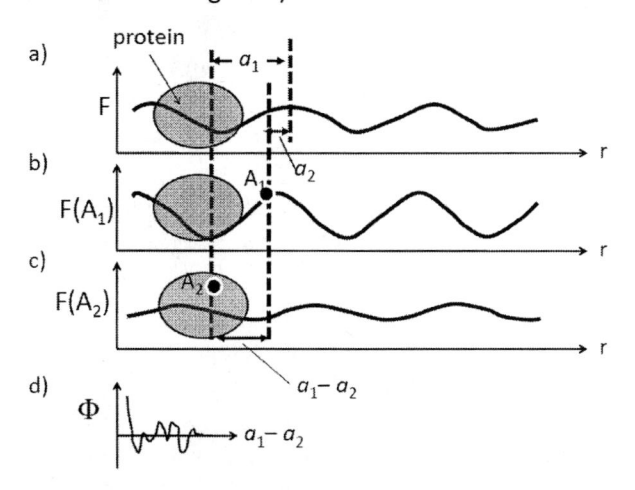

Fig. 11-20 a) F: scattering signal by protein alone, b) $F(A_1)$: scattering signal by protein and heavy atom H1, c) $F(A_2)$: scattering signal by protein and heavy atom A_2, d) vector function $\Phi: \sum_h (|F(A_1)| - |F(A_2)|)^2 \cos 2xhx$.

I.

The Nobel Prize in Chemistry 1962 was awarded jointly to **Max Ferdin** and **Perutzand John Cowdery Kendrew** *"for their studies of the structures of globular proteins"*. Kendrew and Perutz determined the first atomic structures of proteins using **X-ray crystallography***.(**Fig. 11-19**) Kendrew determined the structure of the protein myoglobin, which stores oxygen in muscle cells. The original studies were on the structure of sheep hemoglobin, but when this work had progressed as far as was possible using the resources then available, Kendrew embarked on the study of myoglobin, a molecule only a quarter the size of the hemoglobin molecule. His initial source of raw material was horse heart, but the crystals thus obtained were too small for X-ray analysis. Kendrew realized that the oxygen-conserving tissue of diving mammals could offer a better prospect, and a chance encounter led to his acquiring a large chunk of whale meat from Peru. Whale myoglobin did give large crystals with clean X-ray diffraction patterns. However, the problem still remained insurmountable, until in 1953 when Max Perutz discovered that the phase problem in analysis of the diffraction patterns could be solved by multiple isomorphous replacement, which is a comparison of patterns from several crystals; one from the native protein, and others that had been soaked in solutions of heavy metals and had metal ions introduced in different well-defined positions. An electron density map at 6 [Å] resolution was obtained by 1957, and by 1959 an atomic model could be built at 2 [Å] resolution.(**Fig. 11-19**)

Reference
M. F. Perutz, *Acta Cryst.*, 9 (1956) 867.

II.

The Nobel Prize in Chemistry 1982 was awarded to **Aaron Klug** for his development of crystallographic electron microscopy and structural elucidation of nucleic acid-protein complexes". Since1953, he started studying of viruses and later made discoveries in the structure of the tobacco mosaic virus. From 1962, he started using X-ray diffraction, microscopy and structural modeling to develop crystallographic electron microscopy. In his approach, he took a sequence of two-dimensional images of crystals from different angles and combined to produce three-dimensional images of the target. A heart of his approach is the Fourier method of the data, and it is the only one way solving the sets of the unknown three dimensional density distribution with known projections in different directions. The general method of reconstruction of three dimensional structural map is based on the projection theorem. The projection theorem explains that "the two-dimensional **Fourier Transform*** of a plane projection of a three-dimensional density distribution is identical to the corresponding central section of the three-dimensional transform normal to the direction of view." (Hey! Do you understand what it means? It is very complicated isn't it. It may be easier if you see the sketch shown in **Fig. 11-21**)

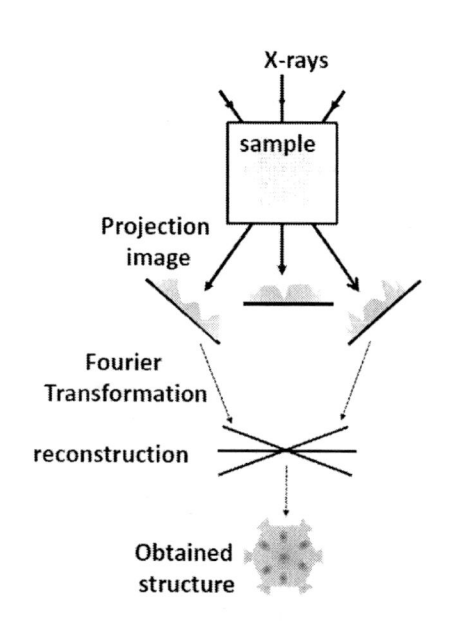

Fig. 11-21 Schematic view for processing 3D reconstruction of an object from different set of 2D projections.

By using transforms of different views (or angles) of the object, three-dimensional transform is constructed section by section. During this process, number of required different views for a required resolution and the way of recombination into a three-dimensional map are obtained without making any "guesses" of the structure. While the approach by Klug sounds very similar to conventional X-ray crystallography. Klug's method was able to calculate the phases of the X-ray diffraction pattern from a digitized image, whereas a conventional method cannot. The collection of set of data with different angle can be obtained from a single particle with tilting stage producing different angles in the microscope. However. data sets from many other particles with the identifiable orientations are commonly collected since imperfections of the crystal can be cancelled out by this way.

Reference
DeRosier, D. J., and Klug, A. Nature (London), 217, 130- 134 (1968).

THE FOCUSED PHYSICAL CHEMISTRY EXPERIMENTAL APPROACH ASSOCIATED WITH CHAPTER 11
(*: word appeared in Chapter 11)

Coherent Raman Imaging

Optical microscopy has been used as a powerful tool to visualize morphology of important biologically important molecules in tissue and cells with a resolution of tenth of μm or smaller. Typically, GFP and YFP (See Chapter 10 **Noble Prize and Your Knowledge in Chapter 10**) to are attached to targeted proteins as a fluoresce label and its signal is probed by microscopic approach. However, GFP or YFP can become significantly large and perturbing molecule for relatively small biologically important molecules and whose function can be altered due to an attachment of GFP or YFP. Thus, as a useful imaging approach for biological specimens and tissues with no use of labeling with GFP or YFP, Coherent Raman imaging technique is explained in here.

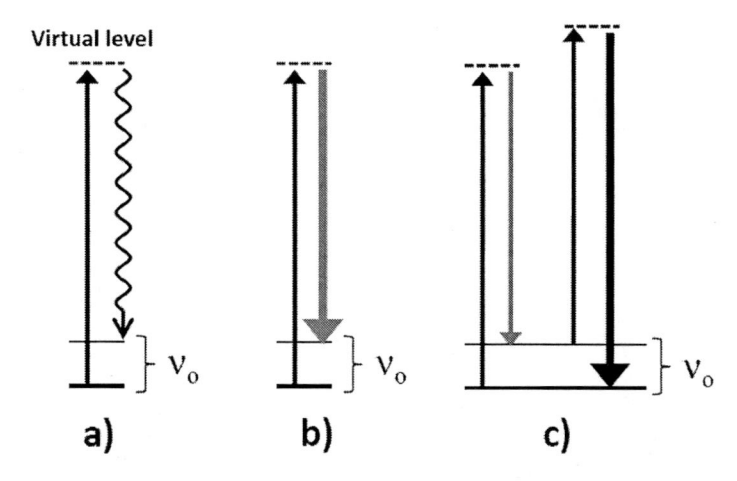

Fig. 11-22 a) Spontaneous Raman scattering microscopy, b) Stimulated Raman Scattering (SRS) microscopy, c) Coherent anti-Stokes Raman Scattering (CARS) microscopy

Let's review the mechanism of **Raman spectroscopy***, then view Stimulated Raman scattering (SRS) and Coherent Anti Stokes Raman scattering (CARS) using the energy diagram shown in **Fig. 11-22**. In spontaneous Raman scattering (**Fig. 11-22a**), excitation pulse (ν_{pump}) is scattered off molecular vibrations (ν_o) and Stokes line (ν_{Stokes}) is observed with frequencies

$$\nu_{Stokes} = \nu_{pump} - \nu_o$$

In Stimulated Raman Scattering (SRS), (**Fig. 11-22b**) two laser beams of excitation (ν_{pump}) and Stokes-frequencies (ν_{Stokes}) are injected to a sample. When difference of two beams ($\Delta\nu$) matches with molecular vibration,

$$\Delta\nu = \nu_{pump} - \nu_{Stokes} = \nu_o$$

stimulated excitation of vibration transitions takes place. As a result, field of the excitation beam is decreased while the field of Stokes line increases.

In Coherent anti-Stokes Raman Scattering (CARS), another laser beam with frequency corresponds to anti-Stokes transition ($\nu_{anti\text{-}Stokes}$) is added to the condition of Stimulated Raman Scattering. As you can see in **Fig. 11-22c**, the process is regarded as a "four-wave mixing process" having two components of ν_{pump}, ν_{Stokes}, and $\nu_{anti\text{-}Stokes}$. When energy difference of four waves ($\Delta\nu$) matches a molecular vibration (ν_o),

$$\Delta\nu = \nu_{pump} - \nu_{Stokes} = \nu_{anti-Stokes} - \nu_{pump} = \nu_o$$

the scattering process is resonantly enhanced generating a field at the anti-Stokes frequency ($\nu_{anti\text{-}Stokes}$), which is given as:

$$\nu_{anti-Stokes} = 2\nu_{pump} - \nu_{Stokes}$$

The great advantage of microscopic approach using SRS and CARS is that they enhances Raman signal with great penetration of beam inside of tissue or cell.

CHAPTER 11 PROBLEMS.

11-1 [Categorization of scattering] The elastic scattering process on the following particles are planned to be investigated with visible light 532 [nm] (second harmonics of Nd:YAG laser). Find α, and identify which scattering process does it corresponds to, respectively?
a). A spherical protein with radius 45 [Å]
b). Micelles with 0.2 [μm] diameter

11-2 [Rayleigh scattering] Rayleigh scattering of nanoparticle colloid with diameter of 20 [nm] was investigated with visible light (488 [nm]). Now, you need to investigate the nanoparticle with a 10% smaller size, however, you hope to gain a signal by a factor of 2 of enhancement. Calculate the wavelength of the incident light you need to use.

11-3 [Brillouin scattering] A crystal was found to produce scattering light by Brillouin scattering mechanism. The maximum wave numbers (i.e., minimum scattering wavelength) by Brillouin scattering mechanism of a sample was 7.25×10^6 [cm^{-1}]. Estimate the equilibrium separation of an atom of this sample.

11-4 [Population for Raman Scattering] The wavelength of one of the modes of a protein was identified as 525 [cm^{-1}]. What is the ratio of the population between the ground state and the 1st quanta (first excited state) at high temperature 55 [°C]. Please assume that these states have the same degeneracy.

11-5 [Raman active modes] How many normal modes are existent in SF$_6$ molecule (O$_h$ point group). Among available normal modes the following modes are identified. Are they Raman active or IR active?

$$\nu_1 (A_{1g}) = 845.3 \ [cm^{-1}]$$
$$\nu_2 (E_g) = 643.38 \ [cm^{-1}]$$
$$\nu_3 (^2T_{1u}) = 1100.2 \ [cm^{-1}]$$
$$\nu_4 (^1T_{1u}) = 737.4 \ [cm^{-1}]$$
$$\nu_5 (T_{2g}) = 547.2 \ [cm^{-1}]$$
$$\nu_6 (T_{2u}) = 369.9 \ [cm^{-1}]$$

Use character table for O$_h$ point group.

Character table for O$_h$ point group

	E	8C$_3$	6C$_2$	6C$_4$	3C$_2$ =(C$_4$)^2	i	6S$_4$	8S$_6$	3σ$_h$	6σ$_d$	linear, rotations	quadratic
A$_{1g}$	1	1	1	1	1	1	1	1	1	1		$x^2+y^2+z^2$
A$_{2g}$	1	1	-1	-1	1	1	-1	1	1	-1		
E$_g$	2	-1	0	0	2	2	0	-1	2	0		$(2z^2-x^2-y^2, x^2-y^2)$
T$_{1g}$	3	0	-1	1	-1	3	1	0	-1	-1	(R$_x$, R$_y$, R$_z$)	
T$_{2g}$	3	0	1	-1	-1	3	-1	0	-1	1		(xz, yz, xy)
A$_{1u}$	1	1	1	1	1	-1	-1	-1	-1	-1		
A$_{2u}$	1	1	-1	-1	1	-1	1	-1	-1	1		
E$_u$	2	-1	0	0	2	-2	0	1	-2	0		
T$_{1u}$	3	0	-1	1	-1	-3	-1	0	1	1	(x, y, z)	
T$_{2u}$	3	0	1	-1	-1	-3	1	0	1	-1		

Chapter 11 Scattering

11-6 [Bragg's law] An X-ray beam is injected to a crystal and scattered from the crystal. If the wavelength of this X-ray is of wavelength 3.75 [Å], what are the possible path differences of the scattered lights for the case a) when they are in phase and b) when they are out of phase.

11-7 [Bragg's law] When an X ray beam 5.00 [Å] is injected to a crystal sample, a Bragg reflection occurs in second order at 5.00°. What is the distance in Å between the scattering planes causing this reflection?

11-8 [Sketch of planes and Calculation of d_{hk}]

a) Sketch and label planes having the Miller indices (h,k) =(1, 0), (0,1), and (1,1) planes for two-dimensional rectangular lattice with unit cell dimensions 40 [Å] × 30 [Å] along the a- and b- axes, respectively. Calculate the distance between planes (d_{10}, d_{01}, d_{11}) and corresponding reflection angle θ when X-ray 2.25 [Å] is injected for the first order.

b). Sketch and label planes having the Miller indices (h,k) =(2,0), (1,2) and (2,1) planes for two-dimensional rectangular lattice with unit cell dimensions 40 [Å] × 30 [Å] along the a- and b- axes, respectively. Calculate the distance between planes (d_{20}, d_{12}, d_{21}) and corresponding reflection angle θ when X-ray 2.25 [Å] is injected for the first order.

11-9 [Calculation of diffraction Intensity two dimension] As explained in the "**Nobel Prize and Your Knowledge in Chapter 11**", heavy atom is used to label the protein. Suppose the unit cell contains (dimensions 55 [Å] × 35 [Å] along the a- and b- axes) one copy of a protein that has been labeled with two heavy atoms at (x,y) positions given by (10 [Å], 4 [Å]) and (20 [Å], 12 [Å]). The atomic scattering factor for this heavy atom is 78. Determine the intensity of the (h,k) = (1,0) and (2,0) reflections and the phase of the respective structure factors.

11-10 [Calculation of d_{hkl}] For a cubic lattice, (a=b=c = 5 Å) calculate d_{100}, d_{110}, and d_{111}

11-11 [Calculation of minimum d_{hkl}] From (**Eqn. 11-15**)

$$n\lambda = 2d_{hkl} \sin\theta \quad \text{(Eqn. 11-15)}$$

You can arrange this formula as

$$\frac{d_{hkl}}{n} = \frac{\lambda}{2\sin\theta} \quad \text{(Eqn. 11-15)}$$

For a fixed λ, the interplanar spacing (d_{hkl}/n) is proportional to (1/sinθ).

It implies that a scattering corresponding to the smallest spacing occurs at the maximum value of sinθ (i.e., sinθ= 90°). If λ = 2.55 [Å]-X rays are used, calculate the minimum spacing observable (n=1)? (This corresponds to theoretical limit of resolution.)

11-12 [Calculation of maximum and minimum d_{hkl}] A cubic crystal has a unit cell with side length of 6.5 [Å].

a) Estimate the largest distance (d_{hkl}) between two scattering planes that can occur in this crystal?

b) Estimate the shortest distance (d_{hkl}) between two scattering planes that can occur in this crystal?

11-13 [Calculation of Diffraction Intensity and phase] There is an imaginary one-dimensional crystal of atom X and its unit cell of atom X has a spacing of 5 [Å]. There are two atoms per unit cell at coordinates X=0 and X=1/3. The scattering intensities will depend on one Miller index, h. Calculate the intensity (I_h) for h=1. The atomic scattering factor for atom X is f_X =10.

11-14 [Calculation of d_{hkl} and θ] For λ=2.55 [Å], X rays, obtain the first order (n=1) Bragg angles for interplanar spacing of 2 [Å], 5 [Å], 20 [Å], 50 [Å], and 200 [Å].

11-15 [Calculation of Diffraction Intensity and phase] For three same atoms at the origin (X=Y=Z=0), at X=Y=Z= ½, and at X=Y=Z= 1/3 calculate the relative intensities of the diffractions by the 100, 200, and 110 planes of a cubic unit cell.

Chapter 11 Answers. For Selected Problems

11-1 1.180

11-2 a) $\alpha = 5.31 \times 10^{-2}$, Rayleigh scattering process, b) $\alpha = 1.180$, Mie scattering process

11-3 0.69 [nm]

11-4 0.1001

11-5 Raman Active Modes v_1 (A_{1g}), v_2 (E_g), v_5 (T_{2g}), IR Active- v_3 ($^2T_{1u}$), v_4 ($^1T_{1u}$)

11-6 a). 0, 3.75 [Å], 7.50 [Å], 11.25 [Å], and so on. b). 1.875 [Å], 4.125 [Å], 9.375 [Å], and so on.

11-8 a) (h,k) = (1,0) d_{hk} = 40.00 [Å], $\sin\theta$ = 0.0281, θ = 1.612°
(h,k) = (0,1) d_{hk} = 30.00 [Å], $\sin\theta$ = 0.0375, θ = 2.150°
(h,k) = (1,1) d_{hk} = 24.00 [Å], $\sin\theta$ = 0.0469, θ = 2.689°
b) (h,k) = (2,0) d_{hk} = 20.00 [Å], $\sin\theta$ = 0.0563, θ = 3.226°
(h,k) = (1,2) d_{hk} = 14.04 [Å], $\sin\theta$ = 0.0801, θ = 4.597°
(h,k) = (2,1) d_{hk} = 16.64 [Å], $\sin\theta$ = 0.0676, θ = 3.878°

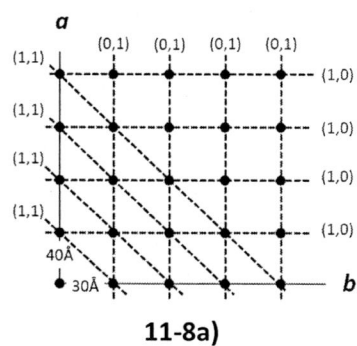

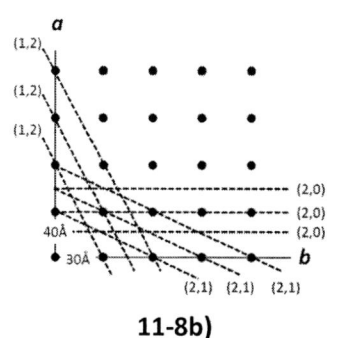

11-8a) **11-8b)**

11-9 A(1,0)=-18.57, B(1,0)=129.9
α = -81.91°, I(1,0) = 1.723 ×10^4, A(2,0) = -62.29, B(2,0) = -18.17, α = 16.27°, I(2,0) = 4.21×10^3

11-10 d_{100} = 5 [Å] d_{110} = 3.536 [Å] d_{111} = 2.887 [Å]

11-11 d_{hkl} = 1.275 [Å]

11-12 a) $d_{100} = d_{010} = d_{001} = a$ = 6.5 [Å] b) $d_{minimum}$ = 3.25 [Å]

11-13 I_1 = 99.99, α_1 = -0.7137 [radian]

11-14 If d_{hkl} = 2 [Å], θ = 39.62°, If d_{hkl} = 5 [Å], θ = 14.78°,
If d_{hkl} = 20 [Å], θ = 3.657°, If d_{hkl} = 50 [Å], θ = 1.462°, If d_{hkl} = 200 [Å], θ = 0.365°

11-15 For (h, k, l) = (1, 0,0) I=3f_1^2/4, For (h, k, l) = (2, 0,0) I=3f_1^2, For (h, k, l) = (1,1,0) I=3f_1^2

Chapter 12
Statistical Thermodynamics

12-1   Maxwell-Boltzmann Distribution
12-2   Partition Function
12-3   Canonical Ensemble and Partition Function
12-4   Helix-Coil Transition in Polypeptide
12-5   Random Walk

Chapter 12 Statistical Thermodynamics

- ## *Why do I have to study this chapter?*

You will learn the shocking (or may not be to you) fact that energy or speed of particles at given condition is not one value and are expressed as distribution of many other values. You will know how to handle large number of particles. When you deal with many particles, the statistics (probability) is the best way to predict the most probable situation. You may notice that quantum mechanical treatment is easier to deal with compared to the one handled by classically. There are many technical terms describing statistics. However, all you are doing in this chapter is to count the possible states and predict the most probable physical value. After all, you should know that two central quantities in statistical thermodynamics are the **Boltzmann** factor and the **partition function**.

- **Expected Hurdles Ahead in this Chapter**
1. Usage of Maxwell-Boltzmann distribution and expression of the speeds (See Section **12-1**)
2. Calculation of partition function (for harmonic oscillator). (See Section **12-2**)
3. Concept of ensembles (See Section **12-3**)
4. Description of Helix-Coil transition (See Section **12-4**)

PREVIEW OF KEY-EQUATIONS

Statistical Entropy

$$S = k_B \ln \Omega(E)$$

Boltzmann Distribution

$$P_i = e^{-\frac{E_i}{k_B T}} \Big/ \left\{ \sum_{i=1}^{all\ levels} e^{-\frac{E_i}{k_B T}} \right\}$$

Maxwell's distribution

$$f(u) = 4\pi \left[\frac{M}{2\pi RT}\right]^{3/2} u^2 e^{-Mu^2/2RT}$$

Most probable speed

$$u_{mp} = \sqrt{2k_B T / m}$$

Average speed

$$\langle u \rangle = \sqrt{8k_B T / \pi m}$$

The average translational kinetic energy at given temperature, T.

$$\bar{E}_{tr} = \frac{3}{2}RT$$

molecular partition function

$$z = \sum e^{-\beta \varepsilon_i} \quad \text{or} \quad z = \sum g_i e^{-\beta \varepsilon_i}$$

molecular partition function and probability

$$p_i = e^{-\frac{\varepsilon_i}{k_B T}} / z$$

molecular partition function of harmonic oscillator

$$z = \frac{1}{1 - e^{-\varepsilon_o \beta}}$$

Canonical partition function

$$Z = \sum e^{-E_i/k_B T}$$

Canonical partition function and probability

$$P_i = \left(1/Z\right) e^{-E_i/k_B T}$$

Canonical partition function and molecular partition function

$$Z = z^N$$

Internal energy and partition function

$$E - E_0 = -\frac{N}{Z}\left(\partial z/\partial \beta\right)_V$$

Entropy and partition function

$$S = \frac{E - E_0}{T} + N k_B \ln z$$

Variance of random walk and diffusion constant

$$\sigma^2 = \frac{t}{\Delta t}\varepsilon^2 = 6Dt$$

PREVIEW OF KEY-TECHNICAL TERMS
Statistical entropy (S), Maxwell-Boltzmann distribution, Kinetic theory, rms speed (u_{rms}), Maxwell-Boltzmann distribution, most probable speed (u_{mp}), average speed (u_{ave}), rms speed ($\bar{u}_{rms}$), mean square speed $<u^2>$, kinetic theory of gas, partition function (z), ensemble, canonical ensemble, micro canonical ensemble, grand canonical ensemble, canonical partition function (Z), random walk, Kronecker's delta (δ_{ij}), Gaussian distribution, variance (σ), Diffusion coefficient (D)

Chapter 12 Statistical Thermodynamics

12-1 Maxwell-Boltzmann Distribution

Statistical mechanics bridge the gap between the microscopic realm of atoms and molecules and the macroscopic realm of classical thermodynamics by handling a thermodynamic *system* as an assembly of *units*. The energies of these microscopic units are quantized, where the energies accessible to a macroscopic system form a virtual continuum of possibilities. Statistical mechanics, or statistical thermodynamics is the application of probability theory dealing with large populations to the study of the *thermodynamic* behavior of systems. It relates the microscopic properties of individual atoms and molecules to the macroscopic or bulk properties of materials. Thermodynamic quantities such as work, heat, free energy, and entropy are related to the spectroscopic data of individual molecules. Theories are originated from the second law of thermodynamics (entropy) as a function of the distribution of the system on its micro-states. The goal of statistical thermodynamics is to understand and to interpret the measurable macroscopic properties of materials in terms of the properties of their constituent particles and the interactions between them. The essential problem in statistical thermodynamics is to determine the distribution of a given amount of energy *E* over *N* identical systems by connecting thermodynamic functions to quantum-mechanic equations.

As a good start of realizing the existence of different states, let's see another definition for entropy of a thermodynamic system from a statistical perspective. (Not the one you saw in (**Eqn. 1-34**). It is called "**statistical entropy**" and it is defined as:

$$S = k_B \ln \Omega \qquad \qquad \text{(Eqn. 12-1)}$$

Here, k_B is Boltzmann's constant (k_B =1.38066×10^{-23} [J K^{-1}]) and Ω is the number of microstates corresponding to the observed thermodynamic macrostate. The (**Eqn. 12-1**) is valid only if each microstate is equally accessible, that is each microstate has an equal probability of occurrence).

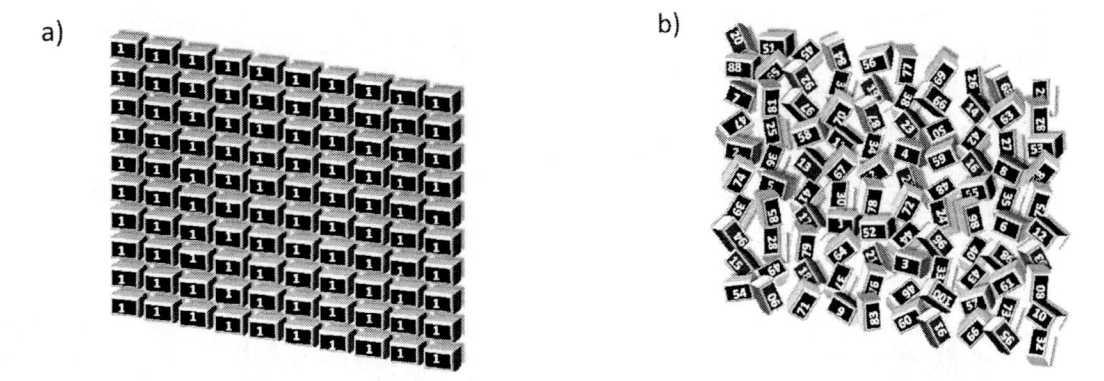

Fig. 12-1 The demonstration of number of different states and concept of entropy (randomness). a) All blocks are in the same sate. b) 100 blocks are all different states.

Here, using the number of the states, $\Omega(E)$, is very useful to understand 'entropy" - how it is related with disorder of a system. If the situation is more disordered, you need more states to express that condition.(The disordered situation contains the situations which are not present at the ordered situation.) From the above formula, the number of the state is expressed as

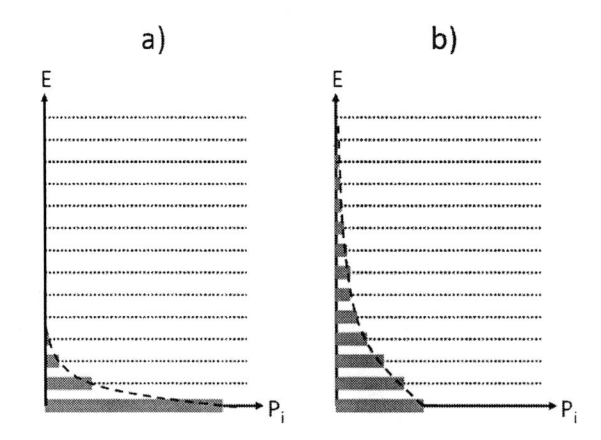

Fig.12-2 Demonstration of Boltzmann distribution at a) lower temperature and b) higher temperature.

$$\Omega(E) = e^{S/k_B} \quad \text{(Eqn. 12-1)'}$$

You immediately notice that the number of the states increases exponentially, if the entropy S increases. This matches very well with a picture that disorder or randomness of the system corresponds to an increase of the entropy. For example, if the number of states are increased by factor of 100, how do you express the magnitude of randomness? (**Fig. 12-1**)According to (**Eqn. 12-1**), S(N=100)/S(N=1)=ln (100)/ln(1)=+∞. The answer is "extremely a lot"!

If the system is large enough, the **Boltzmann distribution** can be used to approximate the distribution. If the total number of particles is N and the number of particles in the i-th (energy is E_i) is N_i, the Boltzmann distribution states:

$$P_i = \frac{n_i}{N} = \frac{e^{-\frac{E_i}{k_B T}}}{\left\{\sum_{i=1}^{\text{all levels}} e^{-\frac{E_i}{k_B T}}\right\}} \quad \text{(Eqn. 12-2)}$$

Here, P_i implies the probability of finding the particle in the -ith energy state. As temperature increases, the population (probability) of the higher state is increased as shown in **Fig. 12-2.** Since the total number of the states (N) may not be known for the most of the cases, it is more convenient to calculate the ratio of the populations between two different states I and j with corresponding energies E_i and E_j.

$$\frac{n_j}{n_i} = \frac{e^{-\frac{E_j}{k_B T}}}{e^{-\frac{E_j}{k_B T}}} = e^{-\frac{(E_j - E_i)}{k_B T}} \quad \text{(Eqn. 12-3)}$$

The **Maxwell–Boltzmann distribution** describes the distribution of the speeds of gaseous species forming the basis of **gaseous kinetic theory**. It describes the probability of a particle's speed as a function of speed, temperature, and mass. It also explains gaseous pressure and diffusion. The distribution of speed is represented by Maxwell-Boltzmann distribution, $f(u)$: **(Fig.12-1)**

$$f(u) = 4\pi \left[\frac{m}{2\pi k_B T}\right]^{3/2} u^2 e^{-mu^2/2k_B T} \quad \text{(Eqn. 12-4)}$$

or

$$f(u) = 4\pi \left[\frac{M}{2\pi RT}\right]^{3/2} u^2 e^{-Mu^2/2RT} \quad \text{(Eqn. 12-4)}$$

Here, m is a mass of a particle, and M is molar mass $M = N_A m$ (N_A: Avogadro's number), R is a gas constant, and k_B is Boltzmann's constant ($R = N_A k_B$). In order to avoid some trivial confusions, let me show another expression of the pre-exponential term which some people may prefer.

$$4\pi \left[\frac{M}{2\pi RT}\right]^{3/2} = \sqrt{\left(2/\pi\right)\left(M/RT\right)^3}$$

From Maxwell-Boltzmann distribution, important quantities on velocities are derived.

(1)**The most probable speed: u_{mp}**
The most probable speed (u_{mp}) is the speed most likely to be possessed by any molecule in the system. The most probable speed (u_{mp}) is defined as the speed at the maximum of the distribution $f(u)$, where

$$\frac{d}{du} f(u_{mp}) = 0 \quad \text{(Eqn. 12-5)}$$

and

$$u_{mp} = \sqrt{2RT/M} = \sqrt{2k_B T/m} \quad \text{(Eqn. 12-6)}$$

(2)**The average speed: <u>**
The average speed (mean speed), <u>, is the mathematical average of the distribution of the speed.

$$\langle u \rangle = \int_0^\infty u f(u) du = \sqrt{8RT/\pi M} = \sqrt{8k_B T/\pi m} \qquad \text{(Eqn. 12-7)}$$

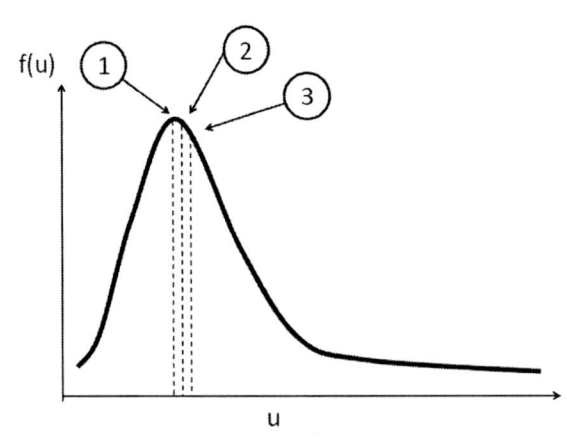

Fig.12-3 Maxwell distribution of speed (1) u_{mp}, (2) $\langle u \rangle$, and (3) $\bar{u}_{rms}$.

(3) Root mean-square (rms) speed: $\bar{u}_{rms}$,
First, the mean square speed $\langle u^2 \rangle$ ($= \bar{u}_{rms}^2$) is

$$\langle u^2 \rangle = \int_0^\infty u^2 f(u) du = 3RT/M \qquad \text{(Eqn. 12-8)}$$

Thus, rms speed is square root of the average squared speed, $\langle u^2 \rangle$.

$$\bar{u}_{rms} = \sqrt{\langle u^2 \rangle} = \sqrt{3RT/M} = \sqrt{3k_B T/m} \qquad \text{(Eqn. 12-9)}$$

It is a bit complicating to have three different expressions for the speed. They are also different in values as demonstrated in **Fig. 12-3**. Let's summarize three types of speed introduced above by viewing the order of magnitude.

$$u_{mp} = \sqrt{2RT/M} < \langle u \rangle = \left[8RT/\pi M\right]^{1/2} < \bar{u}_{rms} = \sqrt{3RT/M}$$

Chapter 12 Statistical Thermodynamics

$$u_{mp} = 0.886\langle u \rangle < \langle u \rangle < \bar{u}_{rms} = 1.085\langle u \rangle$$

The highest speed among three is **rms speed** ($\bar{u}_{rms}$) and the lowest one is the most probable speed (u_{mp}).

Let's view an important characteristic of the speed as a function of temperature (T) and molar mass (M) using the **(rms speed)**

$$\bar{u}_{rms} = \sqrt{3RT/M} \quad \text{(Eqn. 12-9)}$$

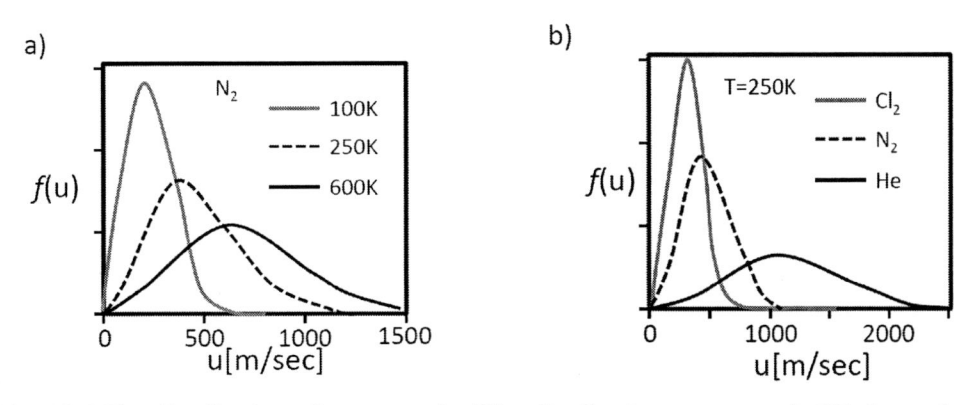

Fig. 12-4 The distribution of rms speed. a)The distribution rms speed of N_2 for various temperatures. b) The distribution of rms speeds for Cl_2, N_2, and He at 250 K.

The relationship shown in **(Eqn. 12-8)** describes two important characteristics of rms speed. The rms speed is proportional to square root of temperature and inversely proportional to square root of molar mass. These two features are demonstrated in **(Fig. 12-4)**. The distribution of the speed is maximized at the higher speed (rms speed becomes higher) as the temperature is increased **(Fig. 12-4a)**. On the other hand, the distribution of speed is shifted to the higher side (rms speed becomes higher) as molar mass is decreased. **(Fig. 12-4b)**

> **MCM Most Common Mistake (50)-Is this for one molecule (atom) or one mole?**
>
> It is critical to understand if the expression of rms speed ($\bar{u}_{rms}$) is using "for a particle" or "for one mole of particles". The expression in **(Eqn. 12-8)**
>
> $$\bar{u}_{rms} = \sqrt{3RT/M} \quad \text{(Eqn. 12-9)}$$
>
> is using an expression for one molecule, where gas constant R (R= 8.3145 [J K^{-1} mol^{-1}]) is used with molar mass (M [g/mol]). If rms speed is expressed for a particle,

$$\bar{u}_{rms} = \sqrt{3k_BT/m}$$

where m is the mass for a particle [kg] and k_B is Boltzmann constant (k_B = 1.3807 × 10^{-23} [J K^{-1}]). The gas constant, R, is given by the product of N_A (Avogadro's number) and k_B.

$$R = N_A k_B$$

Similarly, later you will see another example of this in the average kinetic energy for one particle (E_{tr}^o) and for entire particles (E_{tr}) are related as:

$$\bar{E}_{tr}^o = \frac{1}{2}m\langle u^2 \rangle \quad \text{(Eqn. 12-10)}$$

$$\bar{E}_{tr} = \frac{3}{2}RT \quad \text{(Eqn. 12-12)}$$

$$E_{tr}^o = \frac{E_{tr}}{N_A} = \frac{3}{2}\frac{RT}{N_A} = \frac{3}{2}k_BT$$

EXERCISE 12-1

If a person is holding a rose 10 [cm] away from the nose, how long does it take to realize the smell at 20 [°C]? Assume that geraniol (m.w. =154.2) is the main substance travels from a rose. Use the root-mean-square speed.

ANSWER
Calculating rms-speed

❶ $\bar{u}_{rms} = \sqrt{3RT/M}$ (Eqn. 12-9)*

❷ Here, R= 8.3145 [J K^{-1} mol^{-1}],

❸ T = 20 [°C] = 293.15 [K]

❹ M = 154.2 [g/mol].=0.1542 [kg/mol]

❺ $\langle u^2 \rangle^{1/2} = \left[\dfrac{3 \times 8.3145[J/K] \times 293[K]}{0.1542\ [kg/mol]} \right]^{1/2}$

=217.7 [m/sec]

❻ Time =0.1 [m]/217.7 [m/sec]
=4.59 ×10^{-4} [sec]
=0.459 [msec]

---

❶ Here, I am asking about rms speed. Don't mix with others (u_{mp} or $\langle u \rangle$)

❷ Use R= 8.3145 [J K^{-1} mol^{-1}] not R=0.082 [atm L K^{-1} mol^{-1}].

❸ Temperature is in Kelvins unit.

❹ If you will calculate the energy unit in [J], please be prepared to convert this value into [kg/mol] unit.

❺ [J] = [kg m^2 s^{-2}]

❻ Just in case, Time = distance ÷ velocity

Most Common Mistake (51)-"Why I can't I calculate the correct rms speed?"

When it comes to the calculation of rms speed, many call for help to calculate the correct values are made. As the first step to avoid making a mistake, it is useful is to know the ball park figures of rms speed as $\bar{u}_{rms}(H_2)$ =1920 [m/sec], $\bar{u}_{rms}(O_2)$ =482 [m/sec], $\bar{u}_{rms}(O_2)$ =515 [m/sec], and $\bar{u}_{rms}$ (macro molecule M= 500 [g/mol]) =122 [m/sec] at T= 25 [°C]. Thus, $\bar{u}_{rms}$ should range between a few hundreds to a few thousands of meters per second at 25 [°C]. In most cases, help is requested when the values are off by many orders of magnitude. Since a formula shown in (**Eqn. 12-8**) is simple enough, it is very frustrating if rms speed is not calculated right. The first spot to suspect is the point made in **Most Common Mistake (23)**, i.e., expression for one mole or for one particle. If you happen to use the formula expression for one particle

$$\bar{u}_{rms} = \sqrt{3k_BT/m}$$

m is the mass for a particle [kg] and k_B is Boltzmann constant (k_B = 1.3807 × 10^{-23} [J/ K]). For example mass of one molecule of oxygen gas (O_2) is 32.00 [g/mol] ÷ 6.0222× 10^{23} [molecules /mole] = 5.314 × 10^{-23} [g] = 5.314 × 10^{-26} [kg]). Be careful not to insert the molar mass into the above expression. Also, make sure that the unit of mass used in this formula is [kg] not [g]. If you are using an expression of rms speed for one mole of particles,

$$\bar{u}_{rms} = \sqrt{3RT/M} \qquad \text{(Eqn. 12-9)}$$

Another common misusage is on the gas constant R, as you have seen so many times in **Most Common Mistakes**. Use the value of R of 8.3145[J K^{-1} mol^{-1}] but not the one with 0.08205746 [atm L K^{-1} mol^{-1}]. Also the unit for the molar mass is recommended to use [kg/mol] but not [g/mol], if R = 8.3145 [J K^{-1} mol^{-1}] is used. [(Note that [J] = [kgm^2sec^{-2}])

As minor mistakes, you may be using u_{mp} (**Eqn.12-6**) or <u> (**Eqn. 12-7**) instead of the formula for $\bar{u}_{rms}$ (**Eqn. 12-9**). Or temperature in [°C] may be used instead of Kelvin unit. Do not forget to obtain square root of the value at the end.

Chapter 12 Statistical Thermodynamics

As the most simple case of investigating a motional property of molecules (or atoms), transportation of gaseous species is introduced first. The transportation of gaseous species is well characterized by **kinetic theory of gas.** The kinetic theory of gas utilizes very useful, but kind of "wrong" approximations. Major approximations are:

- Molecules (atoms) are considered to be points (very small spherical particle) with mass but large enough to be treated classically and statistically
- Neither attractive nor repulsive interaction forces in act between particles
- Particles are in random motion and constantly collide elastically with the walls
- The average kinetic energy of the particles depends only on the temperature
- The average distance between particles is large compared to their sizes.

Because of the above approximations, relatively simple and clear descriptions of kinetic energy on the gaseous substance are possible. So that important outline of kinetic energy and property of motion is understood. The average translational kinetic energy per one particle (molecule/atom), $\overline{E}_{tr}^{o}$, is given by

$$\overline{E}_{tr}^{o} = \frac{1}{2}m\langle u^2\rangle \qquad \text{(Eqn. 12-10)}$$

Here, m is a mass of a particle [kg], $\langle u^2 \rangle$ is mean square velocity [m/sec] (The bracket, < >, indicates the average of the values contained inside. The collisions of gaseous particles to the wall correspond to the pressure (P) of a system.

$$P \propto KI$$

Here, K is the rate of collision with the walls and I is an impulse per collision. If a pressure is observed in a system of N particles with mass m in volume V, pressure is given by

$$P = Nm\overline{u^2}/3V \qquad \text{(Eqn. 12-11)}$$

Here, $\overline{u^2}$ is called mean square speed. As pointed out in one of the assumptions listed above, a very useful characteristics in kinetic theory is that an average kinetic energy, $\overline{E}_{tr}$, depends on temperature.

$$\overline{E}_{tr} = \frac{3}{2}RT \qquad \text{(Eqn. 12-12)}$$

Here, $\overline{E}_{tr}^{o}$, is the average kinetic energy per particle, R is gas constant (R = 8.314472 [J mol^{-1}·K^{-1}]), and T is temperature [K].

Chapter 12 Statistical Thermodynamics

12-2 Partition Function

Now, I am going to introduce very important tool called "**partition function**" which is a critical index representing the ensemble and its essence is already introduced in the previous section. Let's consider how we can calculate a probability of finding macroscopic state i with energy of E_i as shown in (**Eqn. 12-2**) Since we learned that the Boltzmann distribution can describe the population of particles with energy E_i as:

$$p_i = \frac{n_i}{N} = \frac{e^{-\frac{E_i}{k_B T}}}{\left\{\sum_{i=1}^{all\ levels} e^{-\frac{E_i}{k_B T}}\right\}} \qquad \text{(Eqn. 12-2)}$$

Let's rephrase (**Eqn. 12-2**) as a probability p_i of a measurable macroscopic state i with energy of ε_i. In other words, it is a fractional particles in the state of I among total of N particles. In the above expression the part corresponds to the denominator is called the partition function. For non-degenerate systems,

$$z = \sum e^{-\beta \varepsilon_i} \qquad \text{(Eqn. 12-13)}$$

As for degenerate energy levels with the degeneracy factor g_j, the partition function is:

$$z = \sum g_i e^{-\beta \varepsilon_i} \qquad \text{(Eqn. 12-13)'}$$

Here, k_B is Boltzmann's constant and $\beta = 1 / (k_B T)$. The exponential term $e^{-\beta \cdot E_i}$ is known as the **Boltzmann factor**, where I (=1,2,3...) indicates an exact state with energy E_i. If you are not still realizing it, let me emphasize that partition function is one of the most important concepts in statistical mechanics. Why it is so important? It is because the partition function allows calculation of all the other thermodynamic properties of the system. In other words, the partition function counts the number of states which a system is able to occupy. If all states are equally probable to be occupied (i.e., all states have an equal energy).

> **The partition function is equivalent to the total number of possible states.**

The partition function shows how the probabilities are partitioned among the different microstates in the system with respect to individual energies, ε_i. By using the partition function, z, the probability of i-th state (when there is no degeneracies) is given by

$$p_i = \frac{e^{-\frac{\varepsilon_i}{k_B T}}}{z} \qquad \text{(Eqn. 12-14)}$$

Let's see an important confirmation on the partition function. What happens if we add all probabilities? Yes, the sum of an entire probability should become 1. (The case shown below is the for non-degenerate energy levels.)

$$\sum_i p_i = \left(1/z\right) \sum_i e^{-\beta \varepsilon_i} = \left(1/z\right) \cdot z = 1 \qquad \text{(Eqn. 12-15)}$$

😟 MCM Most Common Mistake (52) – "I thought that the partition function is the probability"

Because of the wording "partition", it is natural to think that "P" should be used as a symbol representing the "partition function" and is unfortunately misunderstood as "probability" which often abbreviated by "P". In this textbook, we use "P" for probability and "z" for the partition function. The partition function is not probability but related with probability as (Eqn. 12-14).

$$p_i = \left(1/z\right) e^{-\varepsilon_i / k_B T} \qquad \text{(Eqn. 12-14)}$$

The partition function shows how the probabilities are partitioned among the different microstates (i), and it is like a normalization factor. By the way, the letter Z originated from the Zustandssumme, "sum over states" in German. The partition function literally sum over the states available in the system.

While the concept of partition function is straight forward, the real calculation of the partition function may not be so simple. Let's take a look at a good example of calculating a partition function for the vibrational energy level of diatomic molecule introduced in **Chapter 9 (9-6)**. While it is not in reality, the energy spacing between adjacent vibrational energy level is assumed to be equal ($\Delta E = h\nu_o$) up to an infinite energy level for harmonic oscillator.(**Fig. 12-7**) Here, ν_o is the fundamental frequency of a harmonic oscillator in [sec^{-1}] (v=0,1,2,... and I = 1,2,3,...). Please note that we are assuming that $E_1=0$ opposing to the zero point energy explained in **Chapter 9 (Eqn. 9-20)**. Unofficially, it is "cheating" but officially it is said to be handling the problem "classically".

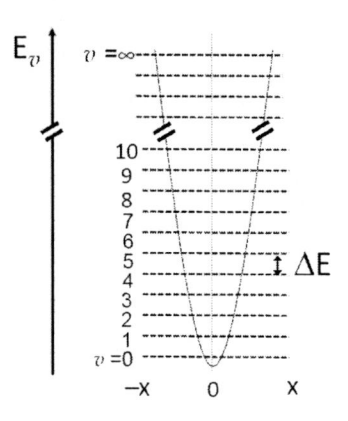

Thus, the molecular partition function z for this case is

$$z = \frac{1}{1-e^{-\varepsilon_0 \beta}} \qquad \text{(Eqn. 12-16)}$$

Fig. 12-5 The transition in harmonic oscillator.

Once again, $\varepsilon_0 = h\nu_0$, where ν_0 is a fundamental frequency of a harmonic oscillator. Using the (**Eqn. 12-16**), we can get more acquainted with the character of partition function. The molecular partition function z for harmonic oscillator varies as a function of temperature for fixed fundamental frequency ν_0 (**Fig. 12-5**) For a fixed fundamental frequency, ν_0, the partition function increases as the temperature increases or as β increases ($\beta = 1/K_B T$).

For those who have been very carefully studying this textbook, I should add one explanation about the way the partition function was extracted in the above. In **Chapter 9**, you learned that the difference between energy levels between classical mechanics and the quantum mechanics is that the energy level is continuous in classical mechanics and the energy levels are discrete in the quantum mechanics. The treatment of the energy level given above was quantum mechanical rather than classical since the partition function was expressed as a sum of discrete terms. In *classical* statistical mechanics, the position and momentum variables of a particle can vary continuously. Thus, a group of microstates is not countable as we did in the above. Then, what is the treatment for this case? The partition function must be treated by using an integral rather than a sum.

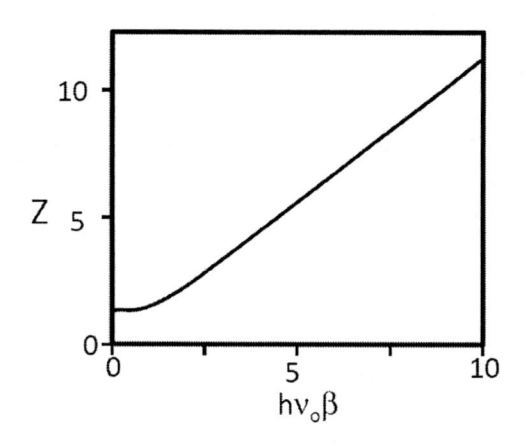

Fig. 12-6 Partition function of harmonic oscillator as a function of $h\nu_0\beta$.

The partition function of a gas of N identical classical particles is given by

$$z = \left(1/N!\right) \int e^{-\beta H} d\gamma d\varepsilon \qquad \text{(Eqn. 12-17)}$$

Chapter 12 Statistical Thermodynamics

$$dy = d^3p_1 \cdots d^3p_N \text{ and } d\varepsilon = d^3x_1 \cdots d^3x_N$$

Here, H is the classical Hamiltonian d the function of momentum vector $p_1, p_2, \ldots p_N$ and position vector $x_1, x_2, \ldots x_N$. Thus, $d^3\gamma$ and $d^3\varepsilon$ are indicating that vector and positions are integrated around three dimensional space.

EXERCISE 12-2

Assuming it is a simple harmonic oscillator, calculate the molecular partition function, z, of vibrational energy levels of a diatomic molecule at 25 [°C] with fundamental frequency of 150 [cm^{-1}].

ANSWER

❶ $z = \frac{1}{1-e^{-h\nu_o\beta}}$ (Eqn. 12-15)

Here, $\tilde{\nu}_o$ =150 [cm^{-1}]

$\nu_o = c\tilde{\nu}_o = 2.997 \times 10^{10}$ [cm/sec] × 150 [cm^{-1}] = 4.4969×10^{12} [sec^{-1}]

h= 6.626×10^{-34} [J/sec]

$h\nu_o$ = 6.626×10^{-34} [J/sec] × 4.4969×10^{12} [sec^{-1}]

= 2.9797×10^{-21} [J]

k_B = 1.38065 ×10^{-23} [J/K]

❷ T= 25 [°C]= 298.15 [K]

❸ 1/β= k_B T=1.38065 ×10^{-23} [J/K] ×298.15 [K]=4.12×10^{-21} [J]

$h\nu_o\beta$ = 2.9797×10^{-21} [J] /4.12×10^{-21} [J] = 0.724

$e^{-h\nu_o\beta}$

= 0.4849

❹ z=1/(1-0.4849)

=1.94

---

❶ Here, $\tilde{\nu}_o$ is wavelength in unit of [1/cm]. You need to convert this into [sec^{-1}] unit.

❷ Temperature in kelvins unit.

❸ Don't forget that β is an inverse of (k_B T).

❹ z=1/$\{1 - e^{-h\nu_o\beta}\}$

Chapter 12 Statistical Thermodynamics

😞 **Most Common Mistake (53)** –"I thought that the partition function is an integer number of the states."
Although the partition function is defined as the number of the states and sounded like it is an integer, z can be non integer. (See **EXERCISE 12-2**) Also many students expect the partition function to be a relatively large number such as 100 or 1000. For a harmonic oscillator with typical fundamental frequency, the partition function is routinely less than 5 or so for room temperature.

😞 **Most Common Mistake (54)** –"Yay! Now I am ready for calculating any partition function. What? Are you saying that I am not?"
An example for calculating partition function in this textbook is a harmonic oscillator only. In harmonic oscillator, the spacing of the adjacent energy level is equal and this let us handle the calculation easier. There are cases when the energy levels are equally spaced, and we have a good example of this case from a particle in a square well. In this case, the energy spacing increases proportional to quantum number n:

$$\Delta E(n \to n+1) = \left(h^2/8ma^2\right)(2n+1) \qquad \text{(Eqn. 9-13)}$$

And the energy between the lowest level (E_1) and the n-th level (E_n) is

$$E_n - E_1 = \frac{h^2}{8ma^2}(n^2 - 1)$$

By using the expression for calculating the partition function results

$$z = \left\{\frac{2\pi m}{\beta}\right\}^{\frac{1}{2}} \frac{a}{h} \qquad \text{(Eqn. 12-18)}$$

See this is completely different from the partition function used for harmonic oscillator given in (**Eqn. 12-16**).

$$z = \frac{1}{1 - e^{-\varepsilon_0 \beta}} \qquad \text{(Eqn. 12-16)}$$

Anyone who does not feel sick about viewing the derivation of the above formula may take a look at the section of "**How did they get this**". My conclusion here is that you cannot always use the partition function derived from the harmonic oscillator. In section **12-4**, you will see an example of helix-coil transition, and there you notice z has completely different form from the one shown in (**Eqn. 12-16**).

If you are not still sick and tired of exploring this issue, please try **Problem 12-17**. There, the partition function of translational energy in three dimensional case is introduced and asked. (Don't worry! I am asking a question of "plug and chug" not a derivation.) If this is your first time calculating the partition function of translational energy, you probably will not believe what you see first. The value is extremely big. Especially, if you are used to the value calculated for harmonic oscillator (which is 1 or 2), you must be shocked. But, yes you are right if you are getting z ~10^{29} (wow!!) for that problem.

12-3 Canonical Ensemble and Partition Function

As it is expected in statistical talking, we need to treat or deal with a collection of particles to view those parameter. Therefore, we will treat system of particles as "**ensemble**". A statistical ensemble represents a probability distribution of microscopic states of the system. There are three major types of ensembles, which are categorized depending on what parameters they share between particles.

> **i) Canonical Ensemble**: The system is allowed to exchange heat (not particle) with the environment under constant temperature (T), fixed volume (V), and number of particles (N). (The system which is in constant thermal contact with the environment, with a fixed temperature T).
>
> **ii) Micro Canonical Ensemble**: all the system has the same energy (E), fixed volume (V), number of particles (N), and each system is individually isolated. Since an isolated system maintains a constant energy, the total energy of the system does not fluctuate.
>
> **iii) Grand Canonical Ensemble**: Each system has the same volume (V) and temperature (T). However, they are open and allow to move matters (and heat) between systems maintaining the same chemical potential (μ). Thus, the composition of each system may change.

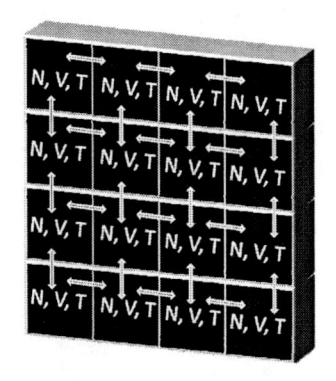

Fig. 12-7 Sketch of canonical ensemble. The double sided arrow indicate an exchange of heat.

Fig. 12-8 Sketch of microcanonical ensemble. (no contacts between each system)

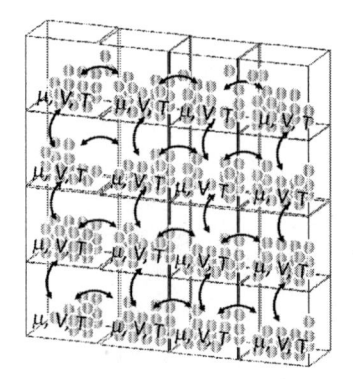

Fig. 12-9. Sketch of grand canonical ensemble. The double sided arrow indicate an exchange of particles.

In summary each ensemble is defined as possessing the following parameters.(It may help you to note that the meaning of "canon" is "according to a rule".)
> i).canonical ensemble: common N, V, T (thermal contact)
> ii).micro-canonical ensemble: common N, V, E (no contact)
> iii).grand-canonical ensemble: common μ, V, T (thermal and material contacts)

[N: number of particles, V: volume, T: temperature, E: total energy of system, μ: chemical potential]

Chapter 12 Statistical Thermodynamics

In canonical ensemble.

$$P_i = \left(1/Z\right) e^{-E_i/k_B T} \qquad \text{(Eqn. 12-19)}$$

Here, Z is **partition function** of the **canonical ensemble.** It is also called as **canonical partition function**, and it represents normalization factor in the denominator.

$$Z = \sum e^{-E_i/k_B T} = \sum e^{-\beta E_i} \qquad \text{(Eqn. 12-20)}$$

Here, k_B is Boltzmann's constant and $\beta = 1/(k_B T)$. The canonical partition function looks exactly the same as the molecular partition function z given in **(Eqn. 12-13)**. The relationship between z and Z is given as

$$Z = z^N \qquad \text{(Eqn. 12-21)}$$

The above formula is true only when N particles (atoms or molecules) are independent and distinguishable.

The canonical ensemble and its corresponding partition function are very popular tool and widely used in statistical mechanics to evaluate thermodynamic quantities, such as internal energy (E) and entropy (S). However, there is a string attached. For example, considering the internal energy (E) of the system, the value which you can obtain by using the partition function is $E - E_o$, where E_o is the internal energy value at T=0 [K].

$$E - E_0 = -\frac{N}{z}\left(\partial z / \partial \beta\right)_V \qquad \text{(Eqn. 12-22)}$$

In the above, z is molecular partition function. As for the entropy (S) is given by

$$S = \frac{E - E_0}{T} + N k_B \ln z \qquad \text{(Eqn. 12-23)}$$

EXERCISE 12-3
Calculate the entropy of a collection of N_A independent harmonic oscillator for an oscillator with $\tilde{v}_o$=150 [cm^{-1}] at 25 [°C]. (Here, N_A is Avogadro's number)

ANSWER
At 25 [°C], T=273.15 +25 =298.15 [K]

$1/\beta = k_B T$
$= 1.38065 \times 10^{-23}$ [J/K] $\times 298.15$ [K] $= 4.12 \times 10^{-21}$ [J]
$= 4.12 \times 10^{-21}$ [J] / 1.9864×10^{-23} [J/cm^{-1}]
$= 207.41$ [cm^{-1}]

By using [cm^{-1}] unit, you can calculate
$\varepsilon_o \beta = \tilde{v}_o \beta$
$= 150$ [cm^{-1}] / 207.41 [cm^{-1}] = 0.7232

The molecular partition function of an oscillator is given by (**Eqn. 12-16**)
$e^{-\varepsilon_o \beta} = e^{-0.7232}$
$= 0.4852$

$$Z = \frac{1}{1 - e^{-\varepsilon_o \beta}} \qquad \text{(Eqn. 12-16)}$$

$= 1/[1 - 0.4852] = 1.9425$

The internal energy is given by

$$E - E_0 = -\frac{N}{Z}\left(\frac{\partial z}{\partial \beta}\right)_V \qquad \text{(Eqn. 12-22)}$$

$$= -\frac{N}{\left\{\frac{1}{1-e^{-\varepsilon_o \beta}}\right\}} \frac{-\varepsilon_o e^{-\varepsilon_o \beta}}{(1-e^{-\varepsilon_o \beta})^2}$$

$$= +\frac{N\varepsilon_o e^{-\varepsilon_o \beta}}{1 - e^{-\varepsilon_o \beta}}$$

$$= +\frac{N\varepsilon_o}{e^{\varepsilon_o \beta} - 1}$$

$$= \frac{-N\varepsilon_o}{1 - e^{\varepsilon_o \beta}}$$

$= 1.69$ [kJ]

$$S = \frac{E - E_0}{T} + Nk_B \ln z \qquad \text{(Eqn. 12-23)}$$

$$= \left(-\frac{N\varepsilon_o}{1 - e^{\varepsilon_o \beta}}\right)\left(\frac{1}{T}\right) + Nk_B \ln\left(\frac{1}{1 - e^{-\varepsilon_o \beta}}\right)$$

$$= \left(-\frac{N\varepsilon_o}{1 - e^{\varepsilon_o \beta}}\right)(k_B)\left(\frac{1}{k_B T}\right) - Nk_B \ln(1 - e^{-\varepsilon_o \beta})$$

$$= \left(-\frac{Nk_B \varepsilon_o}{1 - e^{\varepsilon_o \beta}}\right)\beta - Nk_B \ln(1 - e^{-\varepsilon_o \beta})$$

$$= Nk_B\left[\left(-\frac{\varepsilon_o \beta}{1 - e^{\varepsilon_o \beta}}\right) - \ln(1 - e^{-\varepsilon_o \beta})\right]$$

$= 6.022 \times 10^{23}$ [oscillators/mol] $\times 1.38065 \times 10^{-23}$ [J/K]
$\times \{0.7232/(1-e^{0.7232}) - \ln(1-e^{-0.7232})\}$
$= 11.2$ [J K^{-1} mol^{-1}]

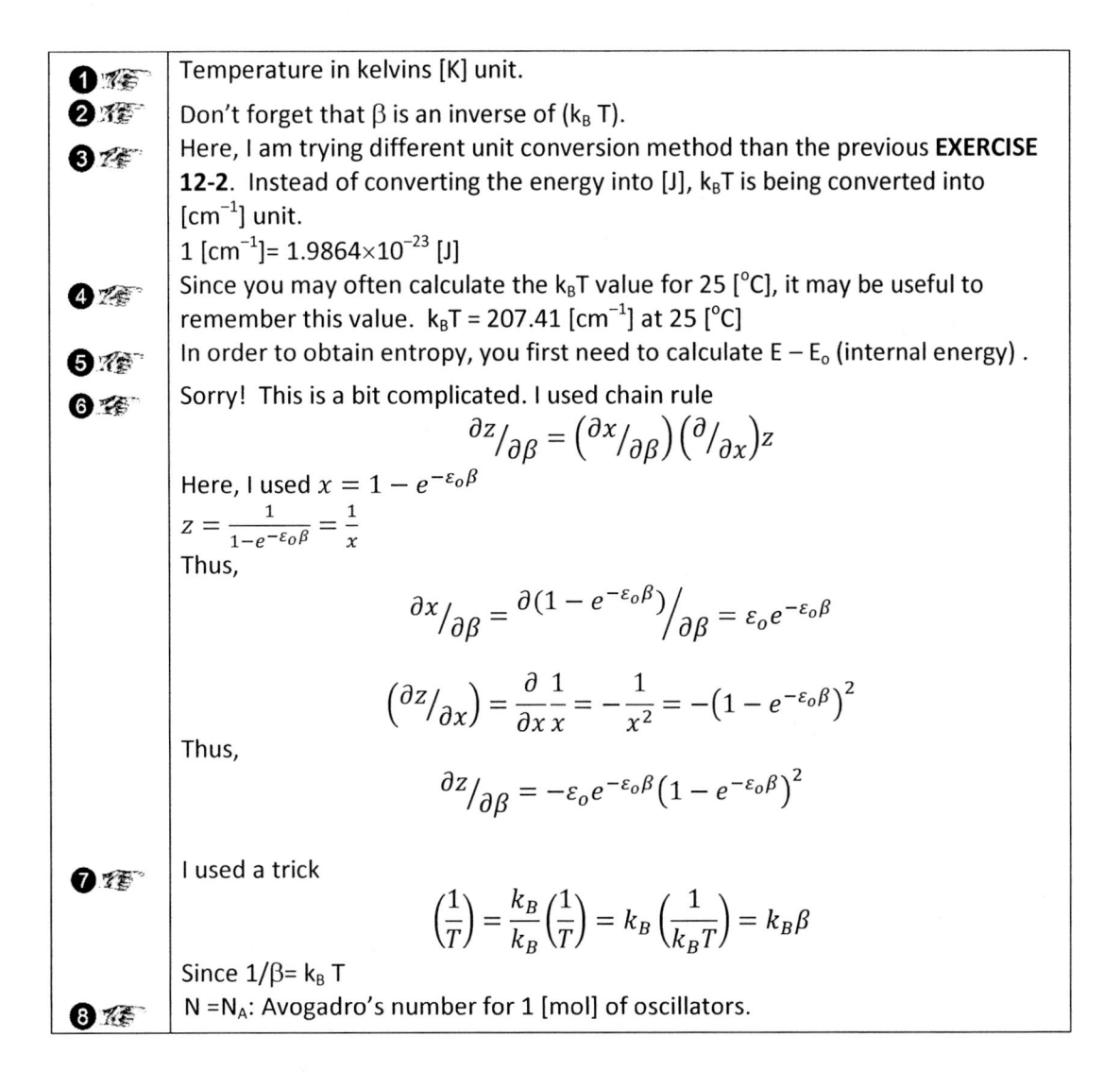

❶	Temperature in kelvins [K] unit.
❷	Don't forget that β is an inverse of (k_B T).
❸	Here, I am trying different unit conversion method than the previous **EXERCISE 12-2**. Instead of converting the energy into [J], k_BT is being converted into [cm^{-1}] unit. 1 [cm^{-1}] = 1.9864×10^{-23} [J]
❹	Since you may often calculate the k_BT value for 25 [°C], it may be useful to remember this value. k_BT = 207.41 [cm^{-1}] at 25 [°C]
❺	In order to obtain entropy, you first need to calculate $E - E_o$ (internal energy).
❻	Sorry! This is a bit complicated. I used chain rule $$\partial z/\partial \beta = (\partial x/\partial \beta)(\partial/\partial x)z$$ Here, I used $x = 1 - e^{-\varepsilon_o \beta}$ $$z = \frac{1}{1-e^{-\varepsilon_o \beta}} = \frac{1}{x}$$ Thus, $$\partial x/\partial \beta = \partial(1-e^{-\varepsilon_o \beta})/\partial \beta = \varepsilon_o e^{-\varepsilon_o \beta}$$ $$(\partial z/\partial x) = \frac{\partial}{\partial x}\frac{1}{x} = -\frac{1}{x^2} = -(1-e^{-\varepsilon_o \beta})^2$$ Thus, $$\partial z/\partial \beta = -\varepsilon_o e^{-\varepsilon_o \beta}(1-e^{-\varepsilon_o \beta})^2$$
❼	I used a trick $$\left(\frac{1}{T}\right) = \frac{k_B}{k_B}\left(\frac{1}{T}\right) = k_B\left(\frac{1}{k_BT}\right) = k_B\beta$$ Since $1/\beta = k_B$ T
❽	N = N_A: Avogadro's number for 1 [mol] of oscillators.

12-4 Helix-Coil Transition in Polypeptide

As you know very well, proteins are polymers that attain well-defined 3-dimensional structures both in solution and in biological cells. The proteins are basically poly peptides which are consisted of different amino acids together by peptide link –CONH-. Due to H-bonding between amino acids, a stable helical structure is constructed, and otherwise it is collapsed and turn into a random coil.(**Fig. 12-10**) In this transformation from helix to coil, polymer becomes more susceptible to structural changes once this transformation process starts. This type of transition is called "*cooperative transition*". The cooperativity of the helix-coil transition in polypeptide can be described by statistical thermodynamics.

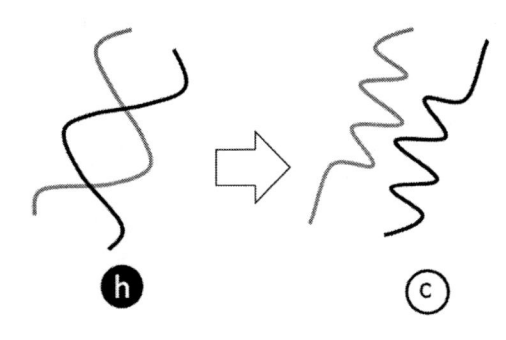

Fig. 12-10. Helix-coil transition

The fraction of polypeptide molecules existing in helix or coil can be calculated from the partition function for the various states of the molecule. In order to solve this system, we make some important assumptions. Each partition function differs from z_0 only by the energy of each conformation relative to the (...hhhh....) state (i.e., z_0). Another important assumption is that "conformational transformation is non-cooperative. The energy associated with changing one h amino acid into c amino acid has the same value regardless of how many h or c amino acid residues are in the reactant or product state.

$$\varepsilon_i - \varepsilon_0 = i\gamma \text{ or } \varepsilon - \varepsilon_0 = \gamma$$

By setting $\Gamma = N_A \gamma$ (N_A is Avogadro's number) and s as

$$s = e^{-\Gamma/RT}$$

The partition function, z, is given as

$$z = 1 + \sum_{i=1}^{n} C(n,i) s^i \qquad \text{(Eqn. 12-24)}$$

Here,

$$C(n,i) = \frac{n!}{(n-i)!\, i!}$$

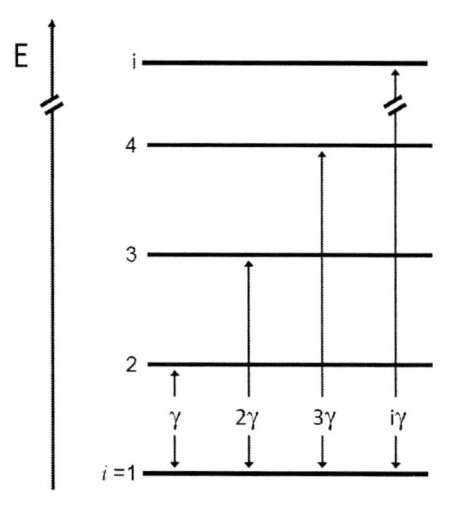

Fig. 12-11 Number of h→c transitions and energy level.

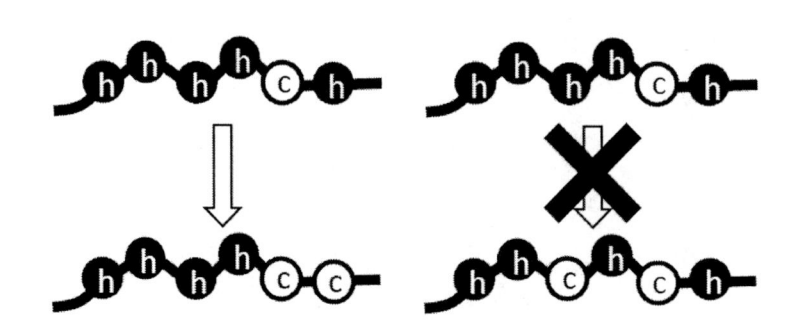

Fig. 12-12 Zipper model

In simple "**zipper model**" conversion from h to c is allowed only if a residue adjacent to the one undergoing the conversion is already a "c" residue. Thus, the zipper model allows a transition of the type

-hhhhch- -→ -hhhhcc-

However, the following transition is not allowed

-hhhhch- → -hhchch-

Chapter 12 Statistical Thermodynamics

However, you may claim that a conversion from h to c in a fully helical chain has to happen at very first step. This first conversion from h to c is called as a "nucleation step' and it has to be less favorable than the remaining conversions. Therefore, let's make a statistical weight (σ <<1) and replace s with σs. Each subsequent step is called as a "propagation step" and has a stability parameters (s). The partition function is given as

$$z = 1 + \sum_{i=1}^{n} N(n,i)\sigma s^i \quad \text{(Eqn. 12-25)}$$

with

$$N(n,i) = \frac{n!}{(n-i)!\,i!}$$

Here, C(n, i) is replaced by N(n,i) which is the number of ways in which a state with a number I of c amide acids can be formed under the zipper model. The fraction of molecules that has a number I of c amino acids is given as:

$$p_i = \frac{z_i}{z} \quad \text{(Eqn. 12-26)}^{\text{BONUS}}$$

Here, z_i is given from (**Eqn. 12-26**) as

$$z_i = \frac{n!}{(n-i)!\,i!} \sigma s^i$$

The simulation shown in **Fig. 12-13** indicates that most of polypeptide chains remain largely helical when s<1 and that the most of the chain exist largely as random coils when s>1. When s= 1, there is a more widespread distribution of length of random coil segments.

With a definition of p_i, a straightforward way of describing the index showing helix-coil conversion, the degree of conversion (θ), is

$$\theta = \frac{\langle i \rangle}{n} \quad \text{(Eqn. 12-27)}$$

Here, n is number of amino acids in a polypeptide with, the <i> is given by

$$\langle i \rangle = \sum_{i=1}^{n} i p_i$$

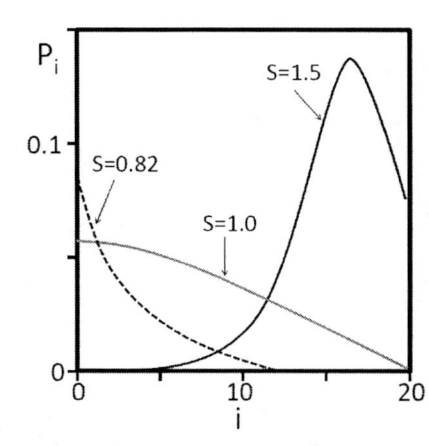

Fig. 12-13 P$_i$ vs. I (σ = 1x10^{-3})

However, it is more convenient and clear if the degree of conversion (θ) is expressed as a function of partition function. Since the partition function, z, is popularly expressed with s for general model of the helix-coil transition, a convenient form of θ is

$$\theta = \frac{s}{nz}\frac{dz}{ds} = \frac{1}{n}\frac{d}{d(\ln s)}\ln z \quad \text{(Eqn. 12-28)}$$

Here, n is the number of amino acids, s is stability parameter

$$s = e^{-\Gamma/RT}$$

The term in the exponent is replaced by $\Gamma = N_A \gamma$, where, N_A is Avogadro's number and γ is difference in energy between a one h→c transition.

Based on the model for the helix-coil transition must allow for helical segments to form in different regions of a long polypeptide chain, with the nascent helices being separated by shrinking coil segments, (Zimm-Bragg model)

$$\theta = \frac{1}{2}\left[1 + \frac{(s-1) + 2\sigma}{[(s-1)^2 + 4s\sigma]^{1/2}} \ln z\right]$$

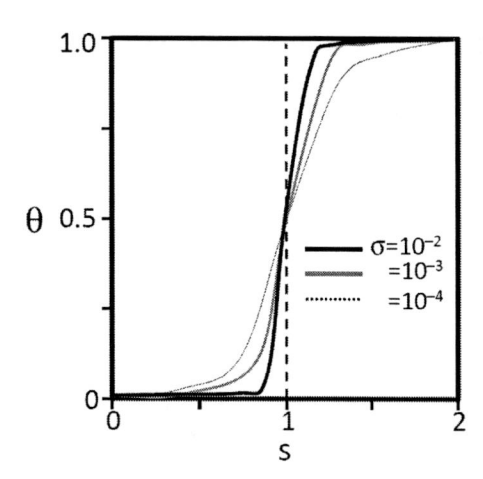

Fig. 12-14 θ vs. s (Zimm-Bragg model)

If you plot θ as a function of s, it exhibits a sigmoidal shape, which is characteristic of cooperative behavior. There is a sudden surge of transition to a random coil as s passes through 1 and, the smaller the parameter σ, the greater the sharpness and hence the greater the **cooperativity** of the transition. that is the harder it is to get coil formation started, the sharper the transition from helix to coil.

EXERCISE 12-4

For polypeptide with three amino acid (h: helical region and c; random coil region), express the partition function by using stability parameter (s).

ANSWER
There is one state of z_0, three states of z_1, three states of z_2 and one state of z_3.

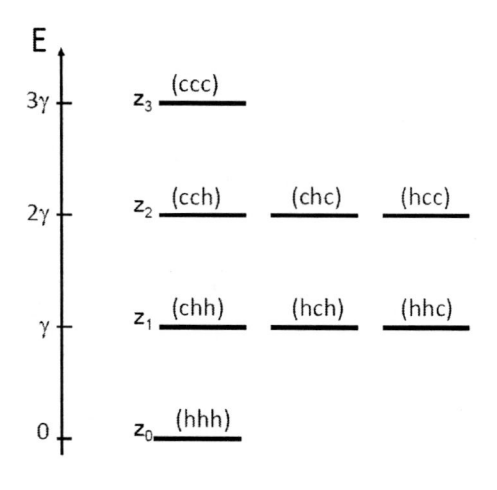

z_0 (hhh)
z_1 (chh), (hch), (hhc)
z_2 (cch), (chc), (hcc)
z_3 (ccc)

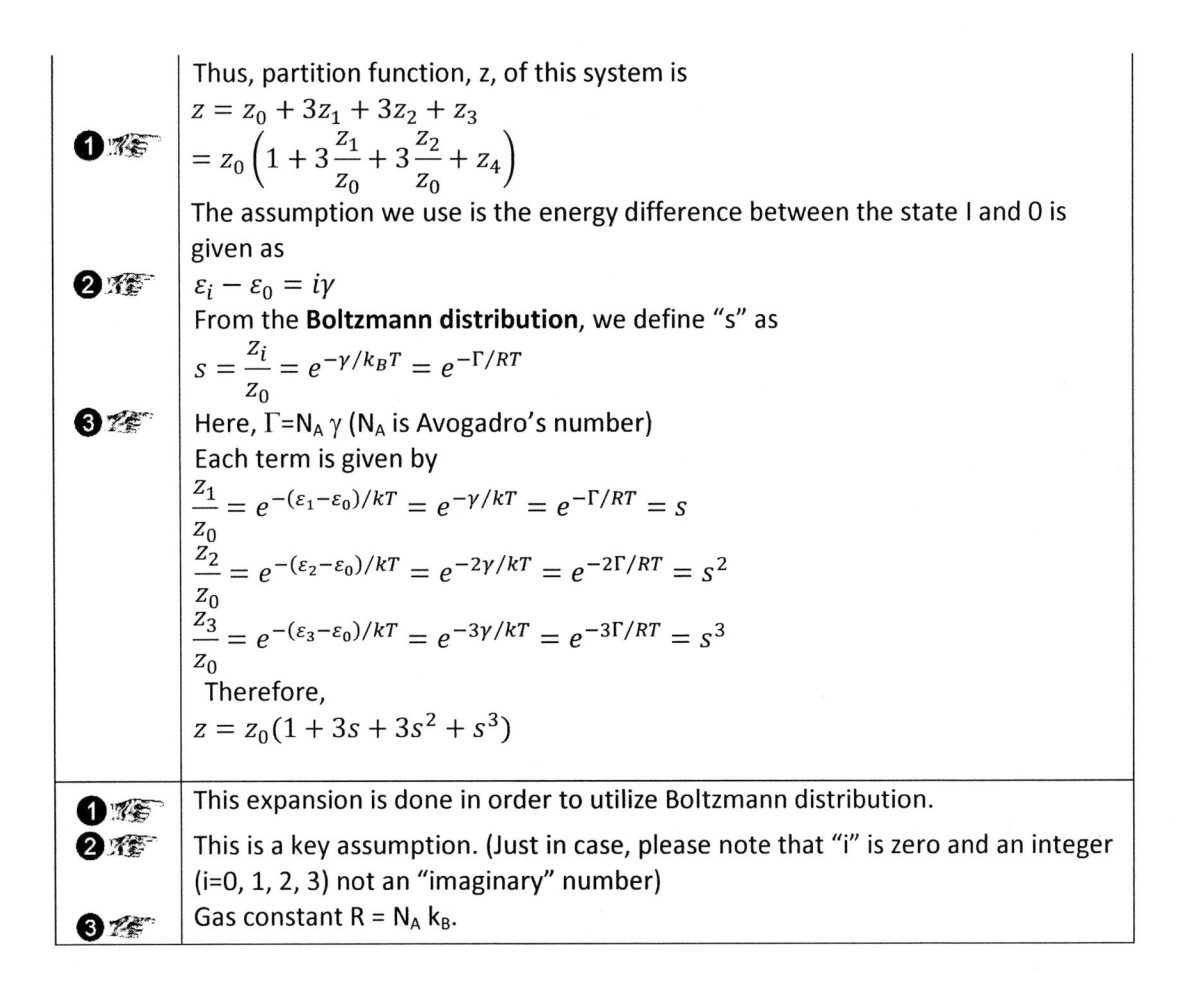

❶ ☞	Thus, partition function, z, of this system is $z = z_0 + 3z_1 + 3z_2 + z_3$ $= z_0 \left(1 + 3\dfrac{z_1}{z_0} + 3\dfrac{z_2}{z_0} + z_4\right)$
❷ ☞	The assumption we use is the energy difference between the state I and 0 is given as $\varepsilon_i - \varepsilon_0 = i\gamma$ From the **Boltzmann distribution**, we define "s" as $s = \dfrac{z_i}{z_0} = e^{-\gamma/k_B T} = e^{-\Gamma/RT}$
❸ ☞	Here, $\Gamma = N_A \gamma$ (N_A is Avogadro's number) Each term is given by $\dfrac{z_1}{z_0} = e^{-(\varepsilon_1-\varepsilon_0)/kT} = e^{-\gamma/kT} = e^{-\Gamma/RT} = s$ $\dfrac{z_2}{z_0} = e^{-(\varepsilon_2-\varepsilon_0)/kT} = e^{-2\gamma/kT} = e^{-2\Gamma/RT} = s^2$ $\dfrac{z_3}{z_0} = e^{-(\varepsilon_3-\varepsilon_0)/kT} = e^{-3\gamma/kT} = e^{-3\Gamma/RT} = s^3$ Therefore, $z = z_0(1 + 3s + 3s^2 + s^3)$
❶ ☞	This expansion is done in order to utilize Boltzmann distribution.
❷ ☞	This is a key assumption. (Just in case, please note that "i" is zero and an integer (i=0, 1, 2, 3) not an "imaginary" number)
❸ ☞	Gas constant $R = N_A k_B$.

12-5 Random Walk

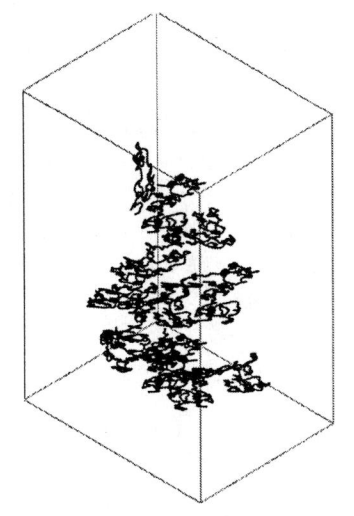

Fig. 12-15 Sketch of demonstrating the trajectory of random walk.

When a particle undergoes a random motion due to external forces in its surrounding, the trace of this particle's path is called as a **random walk**. Mathematically, a trajectory **random walk** is constructed by a series of successive random steps. Good examples of random walk are path taken by a molecule in a liquid or a gaseous media or Brownian motion for diffusion-limited aggregation. In biomedical field, random walk method is used to describe cascades of neuron firing in the brain and fixational eye movements. You may be surprised to hear this, but random walk model is used in psychology, to correlate the time it takes for an individual to make decision and the probability that a certain decision is made. Also, individual animal movements, processes of bio-diffusion, and population dynamics modeling can be described by random walk model.

If a particle moving in x-axis (one dimensional), a direction is either + or − under a fixed distance l. If d_i represents the position at i-th step.

Chapter 12 Statistical Thermodynamics

$$\langle d_i \rangle = 0$$

The average displacement of the train on the x-axis is 0, and it is because all position has an equal probability. Also,

$$\langle d_i d_j \rangle = l^2 \delta_{ij} \qquad \text{(Eqn. 12-29)}$$

The (**Eqn. 12-28**) is the correlation function, where delta (δ_{ij}) is called as the "**Kronecker's delta**" which becomes

$$\delta_{ij}=0 \text{ if } i \neq j$$
$$\delta_{ij}=1 \text{ if } i = j.$$

A travel distance, x, by a diffusion process can be regarded as a random walk process.

$$x = \sum_{i=1}^{N} d_i$$

$$\langle x \rangle = \langle \sum_{i=1}^{N} d_i \rangle = \sum_{i=1}^{N} \langle d_i \rangle$$

The root mean square value, x_{rms} is given as:

$$x_{rms} = \sqrt{\langle x^2 \rangle} = l\sqrt{N} \qquad \text{(Eqn. 12-30)}$$

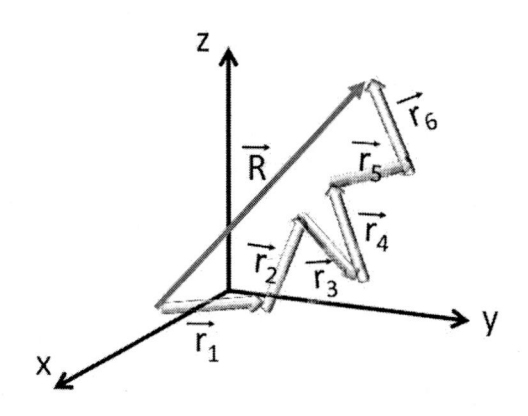

Fig. 12-16. A model of freely jointed chain vector for polymers.

In this section we focus on one important example of random walk to the spatial configuration of long chain polymers, which is like a series of snapshots of the path taken by a random walker in time. There are two types of random walk: self-avoiding random walks and pure random walks. The self-avoiding random walks are connected polymer chains with no overlapping. The pure random walks are connected polymer chains which can overlap but do not interact with each other. While the first case is applicable to physical systems, the solution is not easy to get. Let's focus on the latter case (pure random walk), where a series of connected chains can overlap without any interactions. By considering a freely jointed, non-interacting polymer chain, the end-to-end vector is

$$\vec{R} = \sum_{i=1}^{N} \vec{r_i} \qquad \text{(Eqn. 12-31)}$$

Here, $\vec{r_i}$ is the vector position of *i*-th link in the polymer chain. If N >> 1, it is known that a **Gaussian distribution** for the end-to-end vector is expected. For isotropic field, each vector $\vec{r_i}$ needs to satisfy

$$\langle \vec{r}_i \rangle = 0$$

Based on the idea introduced for one dimensional case, for three dimensional case

$$\langle \vec{r}_i \cdot \vec{r}_j \rangle = 3l^2 \delta_{ij} \qquad \text{(Eqn. 12-32)}$$

(It is assuming that each component of a chain is not interacting (or are uncorrelated) with one another).

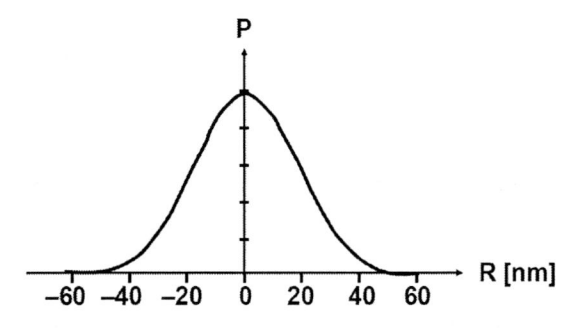

Fig. 12-17 Probability of distribution of identical polymer chains.

In a similar way,

$$\langle \vec{R} \rangle = 0$$

$$\langle \vec{R} \cdot \vec{R} \rangle = 3Nl^2$$

A probability (P) of distribution of a great amount of identical polymer chains is expected to be expressed by the **Gaussian function** as:

$$P = \left[2\pi Nl^2 / 3 \right]^{-3/2} e^{\left(-3\vec{R} \cdot \vec{R} / 2Nl^2 \right)} \qquad \text{(Eqn. 12-33)}$$

If a large number of independent steps are taken in the random walk, the final position is distributed according to a normal distribution of total variance (σ). As an important result derived for three dimensional random walk, the variance (σ) is **variance** associated to the position of the random walk is related with diffusion coefficient (D) as

$$\sigma^2 = \frac{t}{\Delta t} \varepsilon^2 = 6Dt \qquad \text{(Eqn. 12-34)}$$

Here, t is the time used for random walk, ε is a step size, and Δt is the time between successive two steps.

Chapter 12 Statistical Thermodynamics

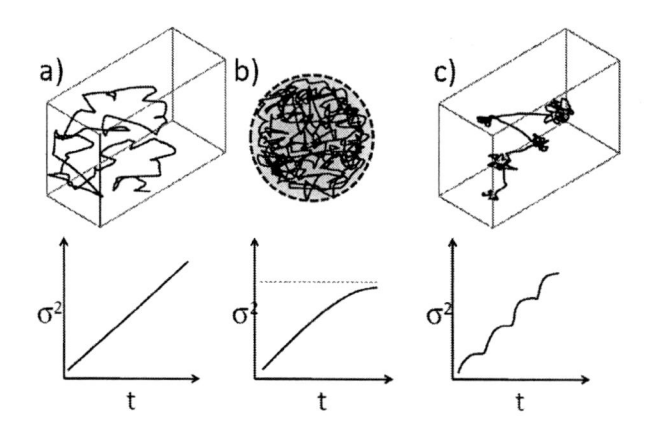

Fig. 12-18 Examples of types of random walk and expected feature observed in σ^2 vs. time (t) plot.

From (**Eqn. 12-34**) analysis of variance can be generally used, not only limited by the case for the polymer chain discussed here. If the plot σ^2 as a function of time (t), exhibit the linear correspondence, the diffusion coefficient D can be extracted as a slope of the line (**Fig. 12-16a**). However, if the diffusional motion is restricted in a certain spherical area (**Fig. 12-16b**) or if the diffusional motion takes a hopping motion (**Fig. 12-16c**), the (**Fig. 12-35**) is not simply applied.

EXERCISE 12-5

The diffusion coefficient of a bacterio phage T7 is estimated around 6×10^{-8} [cm^2 sec^{-1}] Calculate the step size (ε) and variance (σ), when trajectory of the bacterio phage T7 is studied for three hours with 2 [sec] per step.

ANSWER

$$\sigma^2 = \frac{t}{\Delta t}\varepsilon^2 = 6Dt \qquad \text{(Eqn. 12-29)}$$

D=6×10^{-8} [cm^2 sec^{-1}]

Δt=2 [sec]

❶
$$\frac{t}{\Delta t}\varepsilon^2 = 6Dt$$
$$\frac{\varepsilon^2}{\Delta t} = 6D$$
$$\varepsilon^2 = 6D\Delta t$$
$$\varepsilon = \sqrt{6D\Delta t}$$
=$(6\times 6\times10^{-8}$ [cm^2 sec^{-1}] $\times 2$ [sec])$^{\frac{1}{2}}$
=$(7.20\times10^{-7}$ [cm^2])$^{\frac{1}{2}}$
=8.49×10^{-4} [cm]

❷ t= 3 [hours] = 10800 [sec]
$$\sigma^2 = 6Dt$$

❸ $$\sigma = \sqrt{6Dt}$$

	={6× 6×10⁻⁸ [cm² sec⁻¹] ×1.08×10⁴ [sec]}^½ =(3.888 × 10⁻¹¹ [cm]²)^½ =6.23 × 10⁻⁶ [cm]
❶☞	Time (t) can be cancelled.
❷☞	Just in case 3 [hours] = 3[hours] × 60 [min/hour] × 60 [sec/min]
❸☞	Don't forget to take the root mean square.

Chapter 12

How did you get these equations?
-The derivation of selected equations.

(Eqn. 12-4) $$f(u) = 4\pi \left[\frac{m}{2\pi k_B T}\right]^{3/2} u^2 e^{-mu^2/2k_B T}$$

(Eqn. 12-4) $$f(u) = 4\pi \left[\frac{M}{2\pi RT}\right]^{3/2} u^2 e^{-Mu^2/2RT}$$

For the fraction of particle (atoms or molecules) of mass m with velocity vector $\vec{u} = (u_x, u_y, u_z)$, the kinetic energy is given by

$$E = \frac{1}{2}mu_x^2 + \frac{1}{2}mu_y^2 + \frac{1}{2}mu_z^2$$

From Boltzmann –distribution explained in this chapter, the fraction (f) of the particle with velocity u is given by

$$f = Ke^{-E/k_B T} = Ke^{-\left(\frac{1}{2}mu_x^2 + \frac{1}{2}mu_y^2 + \frac{1}{2}mu_z^2\right)/k_B T}$$

Since

$$x^{a+b+c} = x^a x^b x^c$$

$$f = Ke^{-E/k_B T} = Ke^{-mu_x^2/2k_B T} e^{-mu_y^2/2k_B T} e^{-mu_z^2/2k_B T}$$

Here, K is a constant.

Let's define the fraction of particle in each component x, y, z as $f(u_x)$, $f(u_y)$, and $f(u_z)$, respectively.

$$f(u) = f(u_x, u_y, u_z) = f(u_x)f(u_y)f(u_z)$$

Since each fraction contribute to the entire fraction equally,

$$f(u_x) = K^{\frac{1}{3}} e^{-mu_x^2/2k_B T}$$

Chapter 12 Statistical Thermodynamics

$$f(u_y) = K^{\frac{1}{3}} e^{-mu_y^2/2k_BT}$$

$$f(u_z) = K^{\frac{1}{3}} e^{-mu_z^2/2k_BT}$$

Next, we will try to determine the constant K,

$$\int_{-\infty}^{\infty} f(u_x) du_x = 1$$

$$\int_{-\infty}^{\infty} K^{\frac{1}{3}} e^{-mu_x^2/2k_BT} du_x = 1$$

$$\int_{-\infty}^{\infty} e^{-ax^2} dx = \frac{\pi}{a}$$

$$\int_{-\infty}^{\infty} K^{\frac{1}{3}} e^{-mu_x^2/2k_BT} du_x = K^{\frac{1}{3}} \left[\frac{2\pi k_B T}{m}\right]^{\frac{1}{2}}$$

Therefore,

$$K^{\frac{1}{3}} \left[\frac{2\pi k_B T}{m}\right]^{\frac{1}{2}} = 1$$

$$K = \left[\frac{m}{2\pi k_B T}\right]^{\frac{3}{2}}$$

Using this K,

$$f(u_x) = \left[\frac{m}{2\pi k_B T}\right]^{\frac{1}{2}} e^{-mu_x^2/2k_BT}$$

The probability that a molecule has a velocity in the range $u_x \rightarrow u_x + du_x$
Is given by

$$f(u_x) du_x = \left[\frac{m}{2\pi k_B T}\right]^{\frac{1}{2}} e^{-mu_x^2/2k_BT} du_x$$

Therefore, the probability that a molecule has a velocity in the range $u_x \rightarrow u_x + du_x$, $u_y \rightarrow u_y + du_y$, $U_z \rightarrow u_z + du_z$

563

Chapter 12 Statistical Thermodynamics

$$f(u_x)f(u_y)f(u_z)du_x du_y du_z$$
$$= \left[\frac{m}{2\pi k_B T}\right]^{\frac{1}{2}} e^{-mu_x^2/2k_B T} \left[\frac{m}{2\pi k_B T}\right]^{\frac{1}{2}} e^{-mu_y^2/2k_B T} \left[\frac{m}{2\pi k_B T}\right]^{\frac{1}{2}} e^{-mu_z^2/2k_B T} du_x du$$

$$= \left[\frac{m}{2\pi k_B T}\right]^{\frac{3}{2}} e^{-mu^2/2k_B T} du_x du_y du_z$$

The sum of the volume elements of $du_x\, du_y\, du_z$ is the volume of this shell, $4\pi u^2\, du$.

Thus,

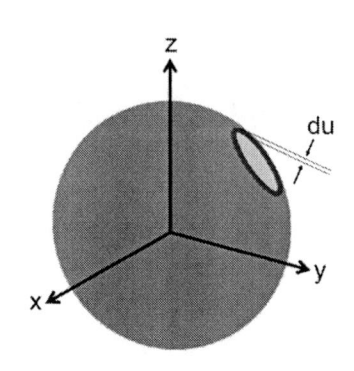

$$f(u) = 4\pi \left[\frac{m}{2\pi k_B T}\right]^{3/2} u^2 e^{-mu^2/2k_B T}$$

By using

$$M = mN_A$$

And

$$R = k_B N_A$$

$$f(u) = 4\pi \left[\frac{M}{2\pi RT}\right]^{3/2} u^2 e^{-Mu^2/2RT} \quad \text{(Eqn. 12-4)}$$

(Eqn. 12-12) $\quad \bar{E}_{tr} = \frac{3}{2}RT$

$$P = N m \overline{u^2} / 3V \quad \text{(Eqn. 12-10)}$$

$$PV = \frac{Nm\overline{u^2}}{3}$$

564

Chapter 12 Statistical Thermodynamics

From ideal gas law

$$PV = nRT$$

Thus,

$$\frac{Nm\overline{u^2}}{3} = nRT$$

From (**Eqn. 12-9**), the kinetic energy of translation is given as

$$\overline{E}_{tr}^{o} = \frac{1}{2}m\langle u^2 \rangle \qquad \text{(Eqn. 12-9)}$$

The kinetic energy, E_{tr}, is inserted into the above formula as:

$$\frac{N}{3} \cdot 2 \cdot \frac{1}{2}m\langle u^2 \rangle = nRT$$

$$\frac{N}{3} \cdot 2 \cdot \overline{E}_{tr}^{o} = nRT$$

By using the number of moles n is given as N/N_A, where N_A is Avogadro's number.

$$\frac{N}{3} \cdot 2 \cdot \left(\frac{N_A}{N_A}\right) \cdot \left(\overline{E}_{tr}^{o}\right) = nRT$$

$$\frac{2}{3} \cdot \left(\frac{N}{N_A}\right) \cdot N_A \left(\overline{E}_{tr}^{o}\right) = nRT$$

$$\frac{2}{3} \cdot n \cdot N_A \left(\overline{E}_{tr}^{o}\right) = nRT$$

$$\frac{2}{3} \cdot \overline{E}_{tr} = RT$$

$$\overline{E}_{tr} = (^3/_2)RT \qquad \text{(Eqn. 12-12)}$$

Here, please note that the following relationship is used.

$$\overline{E}_{tr} = N_A \times \overline{E}_{tr}^{o}$$

Chapter 12 Statistical Thermodynamics

(Eqn. 12-9) $$\bar{u}_{rms} = \sqrt{3RT/M}$$

Instead of using the $\langle u^2 \rangle$, let's try other approach.
From **(Eqn. 12-9)**, the kinetic energy of translation is given as

$$\bar{E}_{tr}^o = \frac{1}{2}m\langle u^2 \rangle \qquad \text{(Eqn. 12-10)}$$

The entire translational energy of a system is

$$\bar{E}_{tr} = N_A \times \bar{E}_{tr}^o = (3/2)RT \qquad \text{(Eqn. 12-12)}$$

Therefore,

$$N_A \times \frac{1}{2}m\langle u^2 \rangle = (3/2)RT$$
$$\frac{1}{2}M\langle u^2 \rangle = (3/2)RT$$

Here, N_A is Avogadro's number and M is molar mass [kg/mol]. We used the relationship shown as follows:

$$mN_A = M$$

Therefore,
$$\langle u^2 \rangle = 3RT/M$$

Taking the square root of both sides, rms speed ($\bar{u}_{rms}$) is given as

$$\bar{u}_{rms} = \sqrt{\langle u^2 \rangle} = \sqrt{3RT/M} \qquad \text{(Eqn. 12-9)}$$

(Eqn. 12-6) $$u_{mp} = \sqrt{2RT/M}$$

The Maxwell-Boltzmann distribution is

$$f(u) = 4\pi \left[\frac{M}{2\pi RT}\right]^{3/2} u^2 e^{-Mu^2/2RT} \qquad \text{(Eqn. 12-4)}$$

If we take the derivative of both sides against speed (u),

$$\frac{d}{du}f(u) = \frac{d}{du}\left[4\pi \left[\frac{M}{2\pi RT}\right]^{3/2} u^2 e^{-Mu^2/2RT}\right]$$

$$= 4\pi \left[\frac{M}{2\pi RT}\right]^{3/2} \frac{d}{du}[u^2 e^{-Mu^2/2RT}]$$

$$= 4\pi \left[\frac{M}{2\pi RT}\right]^{3/2} \frac{d}{du}[2u e^{-Mu^2/2RT} + (-2uM/2RT)u^2 e^{-Mu^2/2RT}]$$

Here, $\frac{d}{dx}[f(x)g(x)] = g(x) df(x)/dx + f(x) dg(x)/dx$ is used.

Thus,

$$\frac{d}{du}f(u) = \frac{d}{du}[2u e^{-Mu^2/2RT} - (uM/RT)u^2 e^{-Mu^2/2RT}]$$

Chapter 12 Statistical Thermodynamics

At the $u=u_{mp}$, the distribution is at the maximum. That is

$$\frac{d}{du}f(u_{mp}) = 0 \qquad \text{(Eqn. 12-5)}$$

$$\frac{d}{du}\left[2u_{mp}e^{-Mu_{mp}^2/2RT} - \left(u_{mp}M/RT\right)u_{mp}^2 e^{-Mu_{mp}^2/2RT}\right] = 0$$

$$2u_{mp}e^{-Mu_{mp}^2/2RT} = \left(u_{mp}M/RT\right)u_{mp}^2 e^{-Mu_{mp}^2/2RT}$$

$$2u_{mp} = \left(u_{mp}M/RT\right)u_{mp}^2$$

$$2(RT/M) = u_{mp}^2$$

Thus,

$$u_{mp} = \sqrt{2RT/M} \qquad \text{(Eqn. 12-6)}$$

(Eqn. 12-7) $\quad \langle u \rangle = \int_0^\infty uf(u)du = \sqrt{8RT/\pi M}$

The Maxwell-Boltzmann distribution is

$$f(u) = 4\pi\left[\frac{M}{2\pi RT}\right]^{3/2} u^2 e^{-Mu^2/2RT} \qquad \text{(Eqn. 12-4)}$$

$$\langle u \rangle = \int_0^\infty u 4\pi\left[\frac{M}{2\pi RT}\right]^{3/2} u^2 e^{-Mu^2/2RT} du$$

From the integration table,

$$\int_0^\infty x^{2n+1}e^{-ax^2}dx = n!/2a^{n+1} \qquad (a>0, n = 0, 1, 2\ldots\ldots)$$

For the present case, n=1 and a=M/2RT. Therefore, the mean velocity city <u> is

$$\langle u \rangle = \int_0^\infty u 4\pi\left[\frac{M}{2\pi RT}\right]^{3/2} u^2 e^{-Mu^2/2RT} du$$

$$= 4\pi\left[\frac{M}{2\pi RT}\right]^{3/2} \int_0^\infty u^3 e^{-Mu^2/2RT} du$$

$$= 4\pi\left[\frac{M}{2\pi RT}\right]^{3/2} \left[1/2(M/2RT)^2\right]$$

$$= 4\pi\left[\frac{M}{2\pi RT}\right]^{3/2} \left[2(RT/M)^2\right]$$

Chapter 12 Statistical Thermodynamics

$$= [8RT/\pi M]^{1/2} \quad \text{(Eqn. 12-7)}$$

(Eqn. 12-8) $\quad \langle u^2 \rangle = \int_0^\infty u^2 f(u) du = 3RT/M$

(Eqn. 12-9) $\quad \bar{u}_{rms} = \sqrt{\langle u^2 \rangle} = \sqrt{3RT/M}$

The Maxwell-Boltzmann distribution is

$$f(u) = 4\pi \left[\frac{M}{2\pi RT}\right]^{3/2} u^2 e^{-Mu^2/2RT} \quad \text{(Eqn. 12-4)}$$

$$\langle u^2 \rangle = \int_0^\infty u^2 f(u) du$$

$$= \int_0^\infty u^2 4\pi \left[\frac{M}{2\pi RT}\right]^{3/2} u^2 e^{-Mu^2/2RT} du$$

From the integration table,

$$\int_0^\infty x^{2n} e^{-ax^2} dx = \left[\frac{(2n)!}{n! \, 2^{2n+1}}\right] \sqrt{\pi/a^{2n+1}}$$

(a>0, n = 0, 1, 2.......)

For the present case, n=2 and a=M/2RT.

$$\int_0^\infty x^2 e^{-ax^2} dx = \left(\frac{4!}{2! \, 2^5}\right) \sqrt{\pi/a^5}$$

Therefore, the mean square velocity <u²> is

$$\langle u^2 \rangle = \int_0^\infty u^2 4\pi \left[\frac{M}{2\pi RT}\right]^{3/2} u^2 e^{-Mu^2/2RT} du$$

$$= 4\pi \left[\frac{M}{2\pi RT}\right]^{3/2} \int_0^\infty u^4 e^{-Mu^2/2RT} du$$

$$= 4\pi \left[\frac{M}{2\pi RT}\right]^{3/2} [3/2^3] \sqrt{\pi/(M/2RT)^5}$$

$$= 4\pi \left[\frac{M}{2\pi RT}\right]^{3/2} [3/2^3] \pi^{1/2} \left[\frac{RT}{M}\right]^{5/2}$$

$$= 3RT/M$$

Thus, rms speed is

$$\bar{u}_{rms} = \sqrt{\langle u^2 \rangle} = \sqrt{3RT/M} \quad \text{(Eqn. 12-9)}$$

Chapter 12 Statistical Thermodynamics

(Eqn. 12-16) $$z = \frac{1}{1-e^{-\varepsilon_0\beta}}$$

The partition function is given as

$$z = \sum g_i e^{-\beta E_i} \quad \text{(Eqn. 12-13)}$$

For the harmonic oscillator with no degeneracies in energy levels,
$z = \sum_{i=1}^{\infty} e^{-\beta E_i}$
The energy of i-th vibrational level (i=0, 1, 2,...) of harmonic oscillator is given as

$$E_i = (i-1)(h\nu_o)$$

Thus, partition function for harmonic oscillator is given as

$$z = \sum_{i=1}^{\infty} e^{-\beta\varepsilon_i} = 1 + e^{-\varepsilon_0\beta} + e^{-2\varepsilon_0\beta} + e^{-3\varepsilon_0\beta} + \cdots + e^{-n\varepsilon_0\beta} + \cdots$$

The **Maclaurin series expansions** states (for $|x| < 1$)

$$\sum_{n=0}^{\infty} x^n = 1 + x + x^2 + \cdots + x^n + \cdots = \frac{1}{1-x}$$

In the present case, $x = e^{-\beta\varepsilon_0}$. Thus, the molecular partition function z for this case is

$$z = \frac{1}{1-e^{-\varepsilon_0\beta}} \quad \text{(Eqn. 12-16)}$$

(Eqn. 12-18) $$z = \left\{\frac{2\pi m}{\beta}\right\}^{\frac{1}{2}} \frac{a}{h}$$

For a particle in a square well, the energy level with quantum number n is given by

$$E_n = n^2 h^2 / 8ma^2 \quad \text{(Eqn. 9-8)}$$
(n=1,2,3,...)

Thus, the energy between the lowest level (E_1) and the n-th level (E_n) is

$$E_n - E_1 = \frac{h^2}{8ma^2}(n^2 - 1)$$

The partition function z is
$$z = \sum e^{-\beta\varepsilon_i} \quad \text{(Eqn. 12-13)'}$$

For particle in a square well, the partition function z is

$$z = \sum_{i=1}^{\infty} e^{-(n^2-1)\beta\frac{h^2}{8ma^2}}$$

$$= \int_1^{\infty} e^{-(n^2-1)\beta\frac{h^2}{8ma^2}} dn$$

569

Chapter 12 Statistical Thermodynamics

$$= \int_0^\infty e^{-n^2\beta\frac{h^2}{8ma^2}} dn$$

At the last term $n^2 - 1$ is replaced by n^2. Thus, the lower limit became 0 instead of 1.

Let's try one more replacement, $x^2 = n^2\beta\frac{h^2}{8ma}$ in order to make calculation accessible.

Then,

$$x = \sqrt{n^2\beta\frac{h^2}{8ma^2}} = \sqrt{\beta\frac{h^2}{8ma^2}}\, n$$

It leads to

$$dx = \sqrt{\beta\frac{h^2}{8ma^2}}\, dn$$

$$dn = \sqrt{\frac{8ma^2}{\beta h^2}}\, dx$$

$$z = \int_0^\infty e^{-n^2\beta\frac{h^2}{8ma^2}} dn$$

$$= \sqrt{\frac{8ma^2}{\beta h^2}} \int_0^\infty e^{-x^2} dx$$

From the integration table, $\int_0^\infty e^{-x^2} dx = \frac{\sqrt{\pi}}{2}$

$$z = \sqrt{\frac{8ma^2}{\beta h^2}} \left(\frac{\sqrt{\pi}}{2}\right)$$

$$= \sqrt{\frac{8ma^2\pi}{4\beta h^2}}$$

$$= \sqrt{\frac{2m\pi}{\beta}}\frac{a}{h} \qquad \text{(Eqn. 12-18)}$$

Here, we transformed summation into integral by assuming the energy levels are very close each other.

[Bonus]
If you get this far, you may want to see what happens to the case of three dimension problem, since it is a few steps of calculations.

Since the total energy for a particle in a cube is

Chapter 12 Statistical Thermodynamics

Since
$$\varepsilon_{n_x,n_y,n_z} = \varepsilon_{n_x} + \varepsilon_{n_y} + \varepsilon_{n_z}$$

$$e^{a+b+c} = e^a e^b e^c$$

$$z = \sum_{n_x,n_y,n_z}^{\infty} e^{-\beta \varepsilon_{n_x,n_y,n_z}} = \sum_{n_x,n_y,n_z}^{\infty} e^{-\beta \varepsilon_{n_x}} e^{-\beta \varepsilon_{n_y}} e^{-\beta \varepsilon_{n_z}}$$

$$= \left(\sum_{n_x}^{\infty} e^{-\beta \varepsilon_{n_x}}\right)\left(\sum_{n_y}^{\infty} e^{-\beta \varepsilon_{n_y}}\right)\left(\sum_{n_z}^{\infty} e^{-\beta \varepsilon_{n_z}}\right)$$

$$= z_x z_y z_z$$

Here, zx, zy, zz indicate the partition function for x, y, and z- axes..
Using the result of partition function for the one dimensional case,

$$z_x = \sqrt{\frac{2m\pi}{\beta}} \frac{a}{h}$$

$$z_y = \sqrt{\frac{2m\pi}{\beta}} \frac{b}{h}$$

$$z_z = \sqrt{\frac{2m\pi}{\beta}} \frac{c}{h}$$

Here, a, b, c are the length of the box in x, y, and z axes, respectively

$$z = \left(\sqrt{\frac{2m\pi}{\beta}} h\right)^3 abc$$

By replacing abc = V (volume) of a box,

$$z = \left(\sqrt{\frac{2m\pi}{\beta}} h\right)^3 V$$

or
$$z = \frac{V}{\Lambda^3}$$

where
$$\Lambda = \frac{h}{(2\pi m k_B T)^{\frac{1}{2}}}$$

You will see this expression in **Problem 12-17**.

(Eqn. 12-24)
$$z = 1 + \sum_{i=1}^{n} C(n,i) s^i$$

The fraction of polypeptide molecules existing in helix or coil can be calculated from the partition function for the various states of the molecule. Let's take an example of polypeptide with four amino acid (h: helical region and c; random coil region). Let's take the number of

Chapter 12 Statistical Thermodynamics

random coil as m and the state z_m implies the corresponding state with the number of random coil. For example z_0 implies helix only (hhhh) and z_4 corresponds to the state with random coil only (cccc) for the case of four amino acids chain. Then, you will notice there are four ways of q_1, 6 ways (state s) of q_2 and four states of z_3 In addition to one q_4 and one z_4 state.

z_0 (hhhh)
z_1 (chhh), (hchh), (hhch), (hhhc)
z_2 (cchh), (chch), (chhc), (hcch), (hchc), (hhcc)
z_3 (ccch), (cchc), (chcc), (hccc)
z_4 (cccc),

Therefore, partition function z of this system is

$$z = z_0 + 4z_1 + 6z_2 + 4z_3 + z_4$$

This formula can be also expanded as

$$z = z_0\left(1 + 4\frac{z_1}{z_0} + 6\frac{z_2}{z_0} + 4\frac{z_3}{z_0} + \frac{z_4}{z_0}\right)$$

Here, there is an important assumption in order to solve this system. We assume that each partition function differs from z_0 only by the energy of each conformation relative to (hhhh) state (i.e., z_0)

$$\frac{z_i}{z_0} = e^{-(\varepsilon_i - \varepsilon_0)/kT}$$

Another important assumption is that "conformational transformation" is non-cooperative. The energy associated with changing one h amino acid into c amino acid has the same value regardless of how many h or c amino acid residues are in the reactant or product state. Thus, here we assume that difference in energy between $c^i h^{4-i}$ and $c^{i+1} h^{3-i}$ has the same value γ for all i:

$$\varepsilon_i - \varepsilon_0 = i\gamma$$

By setting $\Gamma = N_A \gamma$ (N_A is Avogadro's number), s (stability parameter) is given as

$$s = e^{-\Gamma/RT}$$

Thus,
$$\frac{z_1}{z_0} = e^{-(\varepsilon_1-\varepsilon_0)/kT} = e^{-\gamma/kT} = e^{-\Gamma/RT} = s$$
$$\frac{z_2}{z_0} = e^{-(\varepsilon_2-\varepsilon_0)/kT} = e^{-2\gamma/kT} = e^{-2\Gamma/RT} = s^2$$

Chapter 12 Statistical Thermodynamics

$$\frac{Z_3}{Z_0} = e^{-(\varepsilon_3-\varepsilon_0)/kT} = e^{-3\gamma/kT} = e^{-3\Gamma/RT} = s^3$$

$$\frac{Z_4}{Z_0} = e^{-(\varepsilon_4-\varepsilon_0)/kT} = e^{-4\gamma/kT} = e^{-4\Gamma/RT} = s^4$$

Therefore,

$$z = z_0(1 + 4s + 6s^2 + 4s^3 + s^4)$$

Please take a close look at the term in parenthesis. It is equal to $(1+s)^4$.
(This is generally called as binomial expansion")

$$1 + 4s + 6s^2 + 4s^3 + s^4 = (1+s)^4$$

Here, we used the expression of binomial expansion as

$$(1+x)^n = \sum_{i=0}^{n} C(n,i) x^i$$

$$C(n,i) = \frac{n!}{(n-i)!\,i!}$$

(I : the number of ways in which a state with I c amino acids can be formed.)

Therefore,

$$\frac{z}{z_0} = \sum_{i=0}^{4} C(4,i) s^i$$

$$C(4,i) = \frac{4!}{(4-i)!\,i!}$$

Let's extend this formula into the general case of n amino acids chain

$$\frac{z}{z_0} = \sum_{i=0}^{n} C(n,i) s^i = C(n,0) s^0 + \sum_{i=1}^{n} C(n,i) s^i = 1 + \sum_{i=1}^{n} C(n,i) s^i$$

Since $q_0 = 1$, it is rephrased as

$$z = 1 + \sum_{i=1}^{n} C(n,i) s^i \qquad \text{(Eqn. 12-24)}$$

(Eqn. 12-26) $p_i = \frac{z_i}{z}$

[Bonus Feature]
As a bonus feature, here I explain how you can express the partition function with expanded form. Here, $N(n,i) = n-I+1$

$$z = 1 + \sigma(n+1) \sum_{i=1}^{n} s^i - \sigma \sum_{i=1}^{n} i s^i$$

After evaluating both geometric series by using the two relations

Chapter 12 Statistical Thermodynamics

$$\sum_{i=1}^{n} x^i = \frac{x^{n+1} - x}{x - 1}$$

$$\sum_{i=1}^{n} ix^i = \frac{x}{(x-1)^2}\{nx^{n+1} - (n+1)x^n + 1\}$$

Thus,

$$z = 1 + \frac{\sigma s[s^{n+1} - (n+1)s^n + 1]}{(s-1)^2}$$

$$z_i = \sigma(n+1)s^i - \sigma i s^i$$

(Eqn. 12-28)
$$\theta = \frac{1}{n}\frac{d}{d(\ln s)}\ln z$$

The partition function is given as

$$z = 1 + \sum_{i=1}^{n} N(n,i)\sigma s^i$$

Here, C(n, i) is replaced by N(n,i) which is the number of ways in which a state with a number I of c amide acids can be formed under the zipper model.

$$z = 1 + \sum_{i=1}^{n} N_i \sigma s^i$$

Ni is the number of ways in which a state with a number I of c amide acids can be formed under the zipper model (N(n,i) = N_i).

$$\frac{dz}{ds} = \sum_{i=1}^{n} N_i \sigma s^{i-1} = s^{-1} \sum_{i=1}^{n} i N_i \sigma s^i$$

and

$$\sum_{i=1}^{n} i N_i \sigma s^i = \frac{dz}{ds}$$

$$\theta = \left(\frac{1}{nz}\right)\sum_{i=1}^{n} i N_i \sigma s^i = \frac{s}{nz}\frac{ds}{dz}$$

Since

574

Chapter 12 Statistical Thermodynamics

and

$$\frac{dz}{z} = d(\ln z)$$

$$\frac{ds}{s} = d(\ln z)$$

Thus,

$$\theta = \frac{1}{n}\frac{d}{d(\ln s)} \ln x$$

$$\theta = \frac{1}{n}\frac{d}{d(\ln s)} \ln z \qquad \text{(Eqn. 12-28)}$$

[Bonus] How θ is expressed by using (Eqn. 12-28)

$$z = 1 + \frac{\sigma s[s^{n+1} - (n+1)s^n + 1]}{(s-1)^2}$$

and

$$\theta = \frac{s}{nz}\frac{dz}{ds} \qquad \text{(Eqn. 12-27)}$$

Although It is tedious to go through the differentiation by using

$$\frac{d}{dx}\frac{f(x)}{g(x)} = \frac{f'(x)g(x) - f(x)g'(x)}{(g(x))^2}$$

$$\frac{dz}{ds} = \frac{\sigma}{(s-1)^4}\left\{\begin{matrix}ns^{n+3} - (n+2)(n+1)s^{n+2} + (2n+1)(n+1)s^{n+1} \\ -(n+1)^2 s^n - s^2 + 1\end{matrix}\right\}$$

Thus,

$$\theta = \frac{s}{nz}\frac{\sigma}{(s-1)^4}\left\{\begin{matrix}ns^{n+3} - (n+2)(n+1)s^{n+2} + (2n+1)(n+1)s^{n+1} \\ -(n+1)^2 s^n - s^2 + 1\end{matrix}\right\}$$

Chapter 12 Summary [Part 1]

(Use back page to cover the contents.)

1	statistical entropy	$S = k_B \ln \Omega$ (Eqn. 12-1) k_B is Boltzmann's constant, Ω: number of microstates
2	Boltzmann distribution	$P_i = \dfrac{n_i}{N} = \dfrac{e^{-\frac{E_i}{k_B T}}}{\left\{\sum_{i=1}^{\text{all levels}} e^{-\frac{E_i}{k_B T}}\right\}}$ (Eqn. 12-2) $\dfrac{n_j}{n_i} = \dfrac{e^{-\frac{E_j}{k_B T}}}{e^{-\frac{E_i}{k_B T}}} = e^{-\frac{(E_j - E_i)}{k_B T}}$ (Eqn. 12-3)
3	equal a priori probability postulate	Given an isolated system in equilibrium, it is found with equal probability in each of its accessible microstates (P= 1/N)
4	Maxwell–Boltzmann distribution	$f(u) = 4\pi \left[\dfrac{M}{2\pi RT}\right]^{3/2} u^2 e^{-mu^2/2k_B T}$ (Eqn. 12-4) M: molar mass $M = N_A m$, (m: mass of a particle, N_A: Avogadro's number), R: gas constant, k_B is Boltzmann's constant
5	most probable speed (u_{mp}), average speed (<u>), and Root mean-square (rms) speed: ($\bar{u}_{rms}$)	$u_{mp} = \sqrt{2RT/M}$ (Eqn. 12-6) $\langle u \rangle = \sqrt{8RT/\pi M}$ (Eqn. 12-7) $\bar{u}_{rms} = \sqrt{3RT/M}$ (Eqn. 12-9) $u_{mp} = 0.886 \langle u \rangle < \langle u \rangle < \bar{u}_{rms} = 1.085 \langle u \rangle$ Generally speaking $u \propto \sqrt{T/M}$
6	kinetic theory of gas	It assumes gas species: as points with mass, with no interaction forces, being in random motion, with the average kinetic energy depends only on the temperature, and with the average distance which is large than particles' sizes. $\bar{E}_{tr} = \dfrac{3}{2} RT$ (Eqn. 12-12)

[Fold the page at the double line and cover the right half.]

CHAPTER 12 SUMMARY CHECK [PART 1]

(Use this page to cover and check the contents.)

Use ☐ as your check box. Write your comment at far right

1	statistical entropy	☐ ☐ ☐ ☐ ☐	
2	Boltzmann distribution	☐ ☐ ☐ ☐ ☐	
3	equal a priori probability postulate	☐ ☐ ☐ ☐ ☐	
4	Maxwell–Boltzmann distribution	☐ ☐ ☐ ☐ ☐	
5	most probable speed (u_{mp}), average speed ($<u>$), and Root mean-square (rms) speed: ($\bar{u}_{rms}$)	☐ ☐ ☐ ☐ ☐	
6	kinetic theory of gas	☐ ☐ ☐ ☐ ☐	

Chapter 12 Summary [Part 2]

(Use back page to cover the contents.)

7	partition function (z)	It is equivalent to the total number of possible states $$z = \sum g_i e^{-\beta \varepsilon_i} \quad \text{(Eqn. 12-13)}'$$ (g=1 if there are no degeneracies.)
8	Partition function of harmonic oscillator	$$z = \frac{1}{1 - e^{-\varepsilon_0 \beta}} \quad \text{(Eqn. 12-16)}$$
9	Canonical, micro canonical, grand canonical ensemble	i). canonical ensemble: common N, V, T (thermal contact) ii). micro-canonical ensemble: common N, V, E (no contact) iii). grand-canonical ensemble: common μ, V, T (thermal and material contacts) [N: number of particles, V: volume, T: temperature, E: total energy of system, μ: chemical potential]
10	Canonical partition function	$$Z = \sum e^{-E_i/k_B T} = \sum e^{-\beta E_i} \quad \text{(Eqn. 12-20)}$$ For independent and distinguishable N particles, $$Z = z^N \quad \text{(Eqn. 12-21)}$$
11	internal energy (E) and Partition function	$$E - E_0 = -\frac{N}{z}\left(\frac{\partial z}{\partial \beta}\right)_V \quad \text{(Eqn. 12-22)}$$ z: molecular partition function
12	Entropy (S) and Partition function	$$S = \frac{E - E_0}{T} + N k_B \ln z \quad \text{(Eqn. 12-23)}$$ z: molecular partition function
13	Helix –Coil transition and partition function	$z = 1 + \sum_{i=1}^{n} N(n,i)\sigma s^i$ **(Eqn. 12-25)** $N(n,i) = \dfrac{n!}{(n-i)!\, i!}$ $s = e^{-\Gamma/RT}$, $\Gamma = N_A \gamma$, and $\varepsilon - \varepsilon_0 = \gamma$ $\theta = \dfrac{\langle i \rangle}{n} = \dfrac{s}{nz}\dfrac{dz}{ds} = \dfrac{1}{n}\dfrac{d}{d(\ln s)} \ln z$ **(Eqn. 12-28)** $\langle i \rangle = \sum_{i=1}^{n} i p_i$ and $p_i = \dfrac{z_i}{z}$ **(Eqn. 12-26)**
14	variance (σ) of random walk	$\sigma^2 = 6Dt$ **(Eqn. 12-34)** D: diffusion coefficient

[Fold the page at the double line and cover the right half.]

Chapter 12 Summary Check [Part 2]

(Use this page to cover and check the contents.)
Use ☐ as your check box. Write your comment at far right

7	partition function (z)	☐ ☐ ☐ ☐ ☐	
8	Partition function of harmonic oscillator	☐ ☐ ☐ ☐ ☐	
9	Canonical, micro canonical, grand canonical ensemble	☐ ☐ ☐ ☐ ☐	
10	Canonical partition function	☐ ☐ ☐ ☐ ☐	
11	internal energy (E) and Partition function	☐ ☐ ☐ ☐ ☐	
12	Entropy (S) and Partition function	☐ ☐ ☐ ☐ ☐	
13	Helix –Coil transition and partition function	☐ ☐ ☐ ☐ ☐	
14	variance (σ) of random walk	☐ ☐ ☐ ☐ ☐	

Chapter 12 - YOUR TEACHER MAY TEST YOU ON:

No.	What may be asked?		What you should know or do?
1	How do you calculate statistical entropy? How do you calculate the number of the states from known statistical entropy?	→	$S = k_B \ln \Omega$ (Eqn. 12-1) $\Omega(E) = e^{S/k_B}$ (Eqn. 12-1)'
		→	Problems 12-1, 12-2
2	How do you calculate the population of the particles with E_i by using Boltzmann distribution?	→	$P_i = \dfrac{n_i}{N} = \dfrac{e^{-\frac{E_i}{k_B T}}}{\left\{\sum_{i=1}^{\text{all levels}} e^{-\frac{E_j}{k_B T}}\right\}}$ (Eqn. 12-2) $\dfrac{n_j}{n_i} = \dfrac{e^{-\frac{E_j}{k_B T}}}{e^{-\frac{E_i}{k_B T}}} = e^{-\frac{(E_j - E_i)}{k_B T}}$ (Eqn. 12-3)
		→	Problems 12-3, 12-4
3	How do you explain the most probable speed (ump), average speed (<u>), and rms speed by using the Maxwell-Boltzmann distribution?	→	Maxwell-Boltzmann distribution $f(u) = 4\pi \left[\dfrac{M}{2\pi RT}\right]^{3/2} u^2 e^{-Mu^2/2RT}$ (Eqn. 12-4) $\dfrac{d}{du} f(u_{mp}) = 0$ (Eqn. 12-5) $u_{mp} = \sqrt{2RT/M}$ (Eqn. 12-6) $\langle u \rangle = \int_0^\infty u f(u) du = \sqrt{8RT/\pi M}$ (Eqn. 12-7) $u_{rms} = \sqrt{\int_0^\infty u^2 f(u) du} = \sqrt{3RT/M}$ (Eqn. 12-9)
		→	$u_{mp} = \langle u \rangle < \bar{u}_{rms}$
		→	$u \propto \sqrt{T/M}$
		→	EXERCISE 12-1
		→	Problems 12-5, 12-6, 12-7, 12-8, 12-12
4	How do you calculate the average kinetic energy at temperature T based on the kinetic theory of gas?	→	$\bar{E}_{tr} = \dfrac{3}{2} RT$ (Eqn. 12-12)
		→	Problems 12-10, 12-11, 12-12
5	How do you calculate the partition function of harmonic oscillator?	→	$z = \sum e^{-\beta \varepsilon_i}$ (Eqn. 12-13) $z = \dfrac{1}{1 - e^{-\varepsilon_0 \beta}}$ (Eqn. 12-16)
		→	EXERCISE 12-2
		→	Problems 12-13, 12-14, 12-15, 12-16, 12-17
6	How do you calculate the canonical	→	$Z = \sum e^{-\beta E_i}$ (Eqn. 12-19)

	partition function? How canonical partition function is related with molecular partition function, if particles are independent and distinguishable?		$Z = z^N$	(Eqn. 12-20)
7	How do you calculate the internal energy and entropy of canonical ensemble by using the partition function?	→	$E - E_0 = -\frac{N}{z}\left(\partial z/\partial \beta\right)_V$ $S = \frac{E-E_0}{T} + Nk_B \ln z$	(Eqn. 12-22) (Eqn. 12-23)
		→	EXERCISE 12-3	
		→	Problems 12-18, 12-19	
8	Calculate the degree of the conversion from helix to random coil by using the results of zipper model.	→	$\theta = \frac{s}{nz}\frac{dz}{ds} = \frac{1}{n}\frac{d}{d(\ln s)}\ln z$ $z = 1 + \sum_{i=1}^{n} N(n,i)\sigma s^i$ $s = e^{-\Gamma/RT}$ $\Gamma = N_A \gamma$ $\varepsilon - \varepsilon_0 = \gamma$	(Eqn. 12-28) (Eqn. 12-25)
		→	EXERCISE 12-4	
		→	Problems 12-20, 12-21	
9	How do you calculate the diffusion coefficient from the variance (σ) of random walk model?	→	$\sigma^2 = \frac{t}{\Delta t}\varepsilon^2 = 6Dt$	(Eqn. 12-34)
		→	EXERCISE 12-5	
		→	Problems 12-22, 12-23	

UNIT CHECK CHAPTER 12

Important Parameters of This Chapter	Popularly Used Unit	Important Unit Conversion
Entropy, S	J K^{-1} mol^{-1}	
	kJ K^{-1} mol^{-1}	
Number of microstates, Ω	dimension less	
Boltzmann constant, k	J/K	1.380 6504(24)×10^{-23}[J/K]
Probability (P$_i$)	dimension less	
Temperature, T	°C	0 [°C] = 273.15 K
	K	
Maxwell–Boltzmann distribution, $f(u)$	sec/m	
Most probable speed (u$_{mp}$), Average speed (<u>), RMS speed ($\bar{u}_{rms}$)	m/sec	
Avogadro's number, N$_A$	particles/mol	N$_A$ =6.0221415×10^{23}[particles/mol]
Molar mass, M	g/mol	
	kg/mol	
Gas constant, R	atm L K^{-1} mol^{-1}	8.314472[J K^{-1} mol^{-1}]
	J K^{-1} mol^{-1}	0.08205746 [atm L K^{-1} mol^{-1}],
Mass of a particle, m	Kg	
Average translational kinetic energy per one particle, $\bar{E}_{tr}^{o}$,	J	
Pressure, P	atm	1 [atm] =101.325 [Pa]=760 [torr]
Volume, V	m^3	
Average kinetic energy, $\bar{E}_{tr}$	J/mol	
Molecular partition function, z	dimensionless	
Degeneracy, g	dimensionless	
Probability, p$_i$	dimensionless	
Boltzmann factor, β	J^{-1}	$\beta = 1/(k_BT)$
Energy spacing of oscillator, ΔE or ε_o	J	
Planck constant, h	J sec	h=6.6260689(33) ×10^{-34}[J sec]
Fundamental frequency, ν_o	sec^{-1}	
Wavelength, $\tilde{\nu}_o$ or $1/\lambda$	cm^{-1}	
Number of particles, N	dimensionless	
Chemical potential, μ	J/mol	
Internal Energy, E	J/mol	Note: [J] =[kg m^{2}sec^{-2}]
	kJ/mol	
Canonical partition	dimension less	

function, Z	
Statistical weight, σ	dimensionless
Degree of conversion from helix to random coil, θ	dimensionless
Position of ith step of random walk, d_i	m cm
Kronecker's delta, δ_{ij}	dimensionless
Travel distance by Random walk, x	m cm
Position vector, $\vec{R}$ or $\vec{r_i}$	(x, y, z) =(cm, cm, cm)
Variance of random walk, σ	cm
Duration time of random walk, t	sec
Step time of random walk, Δt	sec
Step size of random walk, ε	cm
Diffusion coefficient, D	$cm^2 \, sec^{-1}$

LAST MINUTE REVIEW OF MATH CHAPTER 12
(The followings listing only basic algebra which you have no excuse if you miss them.)

1. $y = \ln x \rightarrow x = e^y$

2. $[x]^{m/2} = \sqrt{x^m}$

3. $\frac{d}{dx} f(x)g(x) = \frac{df(x)}{dx} g(x) + \frac{dg(x)}{dx} f(x)$

4. $\frac{d}{dx} e^{ax} = ae^{ax}$

SUMMARY OF TRICKY TRAPS OF CHAPTER 12

☐	1	Kinetic theory provides three types of speed for gas u_{rms}, u_{mp}, u_{ave}. The rms speed (u_{rms}) is root-mean-square speed, so it is not a squared speed. Thus, for completing a calculation of u_{rms}, it needs to conduct a root mean square.
☐	2	For any speed of an particle, k_B [J/K] and m (mass of a particle [kg]) is used, whereas, for one mole of particle, gas constant R [J/mol·K] and M (molar mass, [kg/mol]). The unit for a mass is recommended to use it in [kg], and the unit for length is in [m]. for m → k_B for M → R
☐	3	Kinetic theory of gas contains many unrealistic assumptions.
☐	4	Partition function indicates the total number of possible states, and it can be any positive numbers (can be non integers),
☐	5.	The final form of partition function can be different depending on how energy level is expressed. (In this textbook, harmonic oscillator case is focused .)

Chapter 12 Statistical Thermodynamics

Nobel Prize and Your Knowledge From Chapter 12
(*: word appeared in Chapter 12)

The Nobel Prize in Chemistry 1974 was awarded to Paul J. Flory "for his fundamental achievements, both theoretical and experimental, in the physical chemistry of the macromolecules.

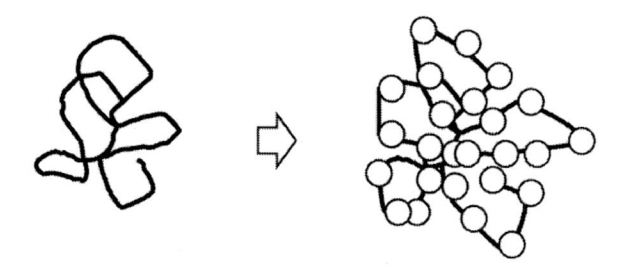

Fig. 12-19 The sketch showing the effect caused by excluded volume. (a) Random coil in the absence of exclusion volume (chain is given by line) (b) each unit of chain is represented by a certain volume (sphere) causing the increase in average size of the configuration.

In 1938, Flory started conducting a theoretical work for mainly the polymerization, and developed a **statistical mechanical theory** for polymer mixtures in 1940. A breakthrough brought by Flory for treating polymer molecules was the concept of "excluded volume" which explains that portions of long chain molecule does not occupy already occupied by another portion of the chain. As a result of this, the ends of a polymer chain becomes further apart, and this excluding volume explained physical properties of long-chain molecules in solutions. (**Fig. 12-19**).

In Flory convention of the coordinate, the bond lengths (L_i), bond angles (θ_i) and the dihedral angles (ϕ_i) are given for each bond i. (**Fig. 12-20**) For a randomly moving chain consisting of n bonds with each of length L, the **mean square of the distance r*** between the ends of the chain, $\langle r^2 \rangle$, was shown as

$$\langle r^2 \rangle = CnL^2$$

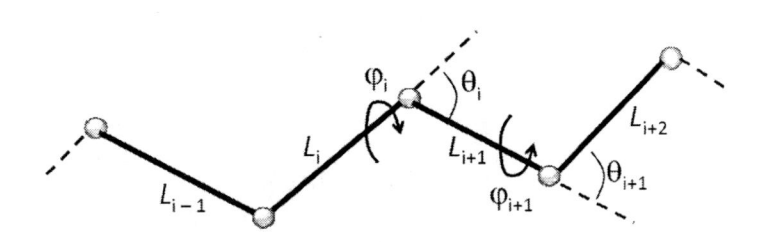

Fig. 12-20 Flory convention of representing the skeletal bonds.

Here, C is a constant for a given polymer. The $\langle r^2 \rangle$ is averaged over configurations caused by the effect of excluded volume interactions. Thus, the volume (V) is expressed as

$$V = A\langle r^2 \rangle^{3/2}$$

With the above basic idea and usage of distribution (and **partition function***) of r, it indicated that the expansion of the configuration due to volume exclusion increases with chain length and the degree of increase was also predicted. The increase of exclusion volume indicates the enhancement of interactions between segments that are remote in sequence along the chain. Thus, the excluded volume effect is considered to correspond to a long-range interaction. The set of experimental conditions neutralize the excluded volume effect is called as a theta point, where the long-range interactions originating from excluded volume are removed. So that, at theta point, only short-range features including structural geometry, bond rotation potentials, and steric interactions between near-neighboring groups are extracted. It enables to accurately characterize chain dimension in polymer. One good example of this which you may recall from **Chapter 6** Is an intrinsic viscosity [η], which is known to proportionally to M if the excluded volume effect is ignored. However, the exclusion volume increases as M increases and at this region intrinsic viscosity is explained as

$$[\eta] = KM^a$$

Where K is constant and $0.5 \leq a \leq 8$. As another accomplishment, Flory contributed to characterize the movement of polymers in solution.

THE FOCUSED PHYSICAL CHEMISTRY EXPERIMENTAL APPROACH ASSOCIATED WITH CHAPTER 12
(*: word appeared in Chapter 12)

Single Molecule Imaging

The "single molecule" is a detection of "single-fluorophore" or a single molecule (such as protein) or aggregates which is attached with a single fluorophore. Investigation of single molecule exhibits a characteristics of individual molecules and the average values of ensembles of molecules. Single-molecule detection techniques is utilized in many microscopic /spectroscopic approaches including single-molecule fluorescence imaging, fluorescence correlation spectroscopy, and atomic force microscopy. The typical resolution is tens of nanometers. For single-molecule fluorescence detection, concentration of the sample needs to be diluted enough so that an individual molecule is distinguishable. Also the Highest possible magnification and pixel resolution of the CCD camera determine the maximal concentration of particles

A schematic of setup for imaging is shown in **Fig. 12-21**. In order to obtain the maximal count rate of fluorescence signals, lasers are popularly used for the excitation light source. Commonly laser beam is blocked by an acuosto-optical transmission filter (AOTF) and duration of the excitation is reduced in order to avoid the bleaching of sample. The detection of fluorescence is commonly conducted by CCD-cameras.

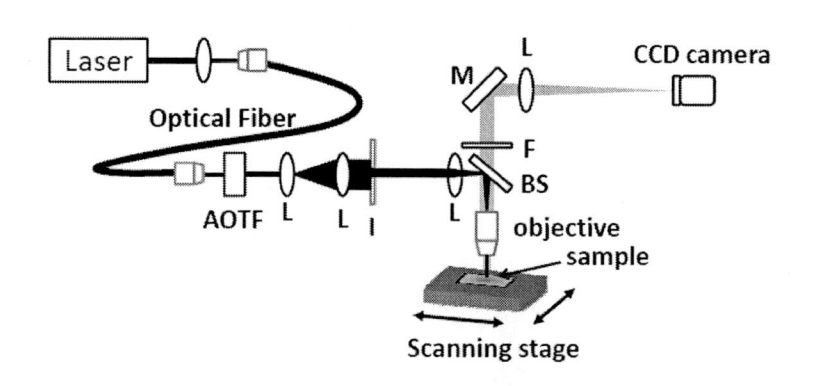

Fig. 12-21 A set up for single molecule imaging fluorescence microscopy using laser for excitation. BS: dichroic beam splitter, L:lense, I : iris, F: filter, M: mirror

In order to achieve good detection of single molecule, a magnification of the microscope and resolution (pixel) of the CCD camera should make differentiation of single fluorophore possible. It is known that the maximum resolution (d) of an optical microscopy is limited by the diffraction of the light (diffraction limit), and it is given by

$$d = \frac{\lambda}{2n \sin \alpha}$$

While most fluorophores and labeled bio-molecules have dimensions of a few nanometers, the diffraction limit reaches to over tens or a few hundred nanometers.
In single molecule fluorescence imaging, single molecules is captured as fluorescent spots with an intensity distributed in several pixels of CCD camera. This distribution function is called " point spread function (PSF)". By fitting the theoretical PSF to the measured two-dimensional intensity distribution it is possible to determine the position of the particle with an accuracy breaking the diffraction limit.

By tracing the trajectory of fluorescence signal of single molecule, the Brownian motion can be observed. Brownian motion is stochastic movements of small particles suspended in a solution, and the movements are explained by the results of **random walk*** introduced in **Chapter 12**.

$$\sigma^2 = 6Dt \qquad \text{(Eqn. 12-34)*}$$

While the movement observed in microscopy is on x-y plane (two dimensional), the squared variance (σ^2) is still expected to be proportional to Dt. If the plotting of σ^2 vs. time show linear correlation, the diffusion coefficient, D, is extracted from slope of the line.(**Fig. 12-18**)

CHAPTER 12 PROBLEMS.

12-1 [statistical entropy] Calculate the effect of entropy increase when the number of micro states increased from N=5 to 10^5. (Calculate $S_{final}/S_{initial}$)

12-2 [statistical entropy] A system consisted of the number of states N=10 experienced the increase of the entropy purely due the increase of number of the states. If the entropy increase is a factor 5, what is the resulting number of the states, N?

12-3 [Boltzmann distribution] Use the Boltzmann distribution, estimate the ratio of population of between the lowest energy state ($E_1=0$ [J]) and the n-th level with $E_n = 1.25 \times 10^{-21}$ [J] (N_n/N_1) at 25 [°C]

12-4 [Boltzmann distribution] The i-th level has the energy has $E_i = 8.43 \times 10^{-22}$ [J] at 25 [°C] is increased and want to increase the population ratio increase a factor of 5% (1.05). If so, what is the temperature has to be?

12-5 [Maxwell distribution] Which statement is correct for *Maxwell distribution* of the speed, $f(u)$.

$$f(u) = 4\pi \left[\frac{m}{2\pi k_B T}\right]^{3/2} u^2 e^{-mu^2/2k_B T}$$

    a. It provides that the most probable speed as $(2RT/M)^{1/2}$
    b. Each $f(u)$ is always not greater than 1 for a given speed u.
    c. The first derivative of the $f(u)$ shows the average speed, $(8RT/\pi M)^{1/2}$
    d. The $f(u)$ does not depend on 1/T.
    e. If you integrate $uf(u)$ over an entire u (from 0 to infinite), it will provide rms (root-mean-square) speed.

12-6 [u_{rms}] It took *t* seconds for a gaseous substance (molar mass of M [g/mol]) to travel distance L [cm] at temperature T. Calculate new temperature, if you want to make this gaseous substance to achieve the traveling time to be t/2 [sec] for a traveling distance of 2L [cm].

12-7 [u_{rms}] The geraniol (molecular weight = 4.18×10^2 [g/mol]) is a gaseous substance travels from a rose. If a person is holding a rose 10.5 [cm] away from the nose, how many seconds does it take to realize the smell at 22 [°C]? Assume that geraniol is the main substance travels from a rose.

12-8 [<v>] Calculate the average speed <v> of an O_2 gas molecule at 1 [bar] and 25 [°C].

12-9 [kinetic theory] True or false: In "Kinetic Theory of Gas", each particle is considered to be a point with electrostatic interaction potential.

12-10 [E_{ave}] Calculate the difference of average kinetic energy between oxygen and hydrogen molecule at 20 [°C].

12-11 [E_{ave}] For N_2 gas at 0 [°C] and 1 [atm], calculate the average translational kinetic energy of **one** N_2 molecules (mass of nitrogen atom = 14.01 [amu])

12-12 [u_{rms} & E_{ave}] Under a certain condition, a chamber was filled up with hydrogen atoms at 0 [°C] and 1 [atm]. Answer the following questions for the hydrogen atom.
    a) Calculate the root-mean-square velocity of hydrogen atom at 0 [°C] and 1 [atm].
    b) Calculate the average translational kinetic energy, E_1, of a hydrogen atom at 0 [°C] and 1 [atm].

12-13 [molecular partition function, z] Using the definition of molecular partition function, derive the partition function for the case of two levels with $\varepsilon_1 = 0$ and $\varepsilon_2 = \varepsilon$.

12-14 [molecular partition function, z] For the case of two energy level systems $\varepsilon_1=0$ and $\varepsilon_2=2.500\times10^{-20}$ [J], calculate the partition function at T= 25 [°C] and T= 500 [°C].

12-15 [molecular partition function, z] For the case of two energy level systems $\varepsilon_1 = 0$ and $\varepsilon_2 = 2.500\times10^{-20}$ [J], calculate the probability of level of ε_1 and ε_2 at T= 25[°C] and T= 500 [°C].

Chapter 12 Statistical Thermodynamics

12-16 [partition function of harmonic oscillator]. Calculate the molecular partition function a simple harmonic oscillator (fundamental frequency of 2500 [cm^{-1}]) at 25[°C] and 500 [°C]

12-17 [partition function of translational energy]. The partition function of translational energy is given by

$$z = \frac{V}{\Lambda^3}$$

where

$$\Lambda = \frac{h}{(2\pi m k_B T)^{\frac{1}{2}}}$$

Using the above expression, calculate the partition function of O_2 molecule confined in V= 500 [cm^3] container at 25 [°C]

12-18 [Statistical internal energy] Calculate the internal energy ($E - E_o$) of a mole of an independent harmonic oscillators with $\tilde{v}_o$=2500 [cm^{-1}] at 25 [°C] and at 500 [°C]

12-19 [Statistical entropy] Calculate the entropy (S) of a collection of N independent harmonic oscillator for an oscillator with $\tilde{v}_o$=150 [cm^{-1}] at 25 [°C]

12-20 [Helix-coil transition] For polypeptide with ten amino acids calculate the Z and Z_i (I = 5) by using

$$z = 1 + \frac{\sigma s[s^{n+1} - (n+1)s^n + 1]}{(s-1)^2}$$

$$z_i = \sigma(n+1)s^i - \sigma i s^i$$

Here, use σ= 1x10^{-3} and s=0.5.

12-21 [Helix-coil transition] For polypeptide with ten amino acids calculate the degree of conversion from helix to random coil (θ) by using

$$\theta = \frac{s}{nz}\frac{dz}{ds} \quad \text{(Eqn. 12-27)}$$

Here, use σ= 1x10^{-3} and s=1.0. Please use the following expression for θ (This is explained in the section of **"How did they get these".**)

$$\theta = \frac{s}{nz}\frac{\sigma}{(s-1)^4}\{ns^{n+3} - (n+2)(n+1)s^{n+2} + (2n+1)(n+1)s^{n+1} - (n+1)^2 s^n - s^2 + 1\}$$

Use the following expression for z.

$$z = 1 + \frac{\sigma s[s^{n+1} - (n+1)s^n + 1]}{(s-1)^2}$$

12-22 [Random walk] The diffusion coefficient of a bacteria is estimated around 1.58×10^{-6} [cm^2 sec^{-1}] Calculate the variance (σ), when trajectory of this bacteria is studied for one hour.

12-23 [Random walk] The Brownian motion of a colloidal droplet was studied by random walk model for an hour every 5 [sec]. Then, the step size (ε) was found to be 2 [mm] Calculate the diffusion coefficient of this droplet.

Chapter 12 Answers. For Selected Problems

12-1 factor of 7.15 increase
12-2 N(final) = 10^5
12-3 0.0267
12-4 T_{final} = 118.3 [$^{\circ}$C]
12-5 a
12-7 u_{rms} = 132.7 [m/sec], t = 7.91×10^{-4} [sec]
12-8 440 [m/sec]
12-9 False
12-10 No difference
12-11 5.65×10^{-21} [J]
12-12 a) 2.598×10^3 [m/sec], b) 5.67×10^{-21} [J]
12-13 $Z = 1 + e^{-\varepsilon\beta}$
12-14 For T= 25 [$^{\circ}$C] z=1.0023, For T= 500 [$^{\circ}$C] z=1.096
12-15 For T= 25 [$^{\circ}$C] z=1.0023, p_1=0.9977, p_2=0.0023, For T= 500 [$^{\circ}$C], z=1.096, p_1=0.9123, p_2=0.0877
12-16 z=1.00
12-17 $\Lambda = 1.7878 \times 10^{-11}$ [m], $Z = 8.750 \times 10^{28}$
12-18 $E - E_o$ (at 25 [$^{\circ}$C])= −0.172 [J], $E - E_o$ (at 500 [$^{\circ}$C])= −288 [J]
12-19 S= -5.30×10^{-4} [J/K mol] at 25 [$^{\circ}$C], S= −0.293 [J/K mol] at 500 [$^{\circ}$C]
12-20 Z=1.00198, Z (i=5) = 2.25×10^{-3}
12-21 θ=0.00157
12-22 $\sigma = 1.07 \times 10^{-1}$ [cm]
12-23 D = 1.3×10^{-3} [cm]